BETWEEN LIGHT AND SHADOW:
THE WORLD BANK, THE INTERNATIONAL MONETARY FUND, AND INTERNATIONAL HUMAN RIGHTS LAW

Much has been written on the human rights relevance and impacts of the policies and activities of the World Bank and IMF—or International Financial Institutions (IFIs). However while many of the human rights-based critiques of the Bank and Fund purport to link broadly defined reforms with obligations under international human rights law, rarely has this been carried out through a rigorous and in-depth application of international legal rules governing the proper interpretation of the institutions' mandates, and rarely have the policy consequences and practical possibilities for human rights integration been explored in any detail. These are the principal gaps that the present book attempts to contribute towards filling, by reference to a sample of the IFIs' most important and controversial contemporary activities.

Volume 1 in the series, Studies in International Law

Studies in International Law

Volume 1: Between Light and Shadow: The World Bank, the International Monetary Fund and International Human Rights Law   *Mac Darrow*

Between Light and Shadow: The World Bank, the International Monetary Fund and International Human Rights Law

MAC DARROW

·HART·
PUBLISHING
OXFORD – PORTLAND OREGON
2003

Published in North America (US and Canada) by
Hart Publishing
c/o International Specialized Book Services
5804 NE Hassalo Street
Portland, Oregon
97213-3644
USA

Hart Publishing is a specialist legal publisher based in Oxford, England. To
order further copies of this book or to request a list of other publications
please write to:

Hart Publishing, Salters Boatyard, Folly Bridge,
Abingdon Rd, Oxford, OX1 4LB
Telephone: +44 (0)1865 245533 Fax: +44 (0) 1865 794882
email: mail@hartpub.co.uk
WEBSITE: http//:www.hartpub.co.uk

British Library Cataloguing in Publication Data
Data Available

ISBN 1–84113–390–6 (hardback)

Typeset by Hope Services (Abingdon Ltd)
Printed and bound in Great Britain by
Biddles Ltd, _www.biddles.co.uk_

To the Darrow clan

Acknowledgements

This book is based upon my PhD thesis at the University of Utrecht, submitted in October 2001. I would not initially have thought of undertaking a PhD on a part-time and external basis had Philip Alston not suggested it, in early 1997. I am very grateful to him for having done so, and also to Fried van Hoof and former and present directors of the Netherlands Institute for Human Rights (SIM)—Professors Peter Baehr and Cees Flinterman—for having accepted my thesis proposal on such generous and flexible terms from my point of view. The task of balancing part-time research and book writing with the demands of 'real' jobs has not always been easy. An enormous measure of gratitude goes to Philip for his support and guidance along the way and for helping me to balance these various demands. Thanks also to Fried for his guidance and impressive reserves of patience in the face of my frequent lulls in progress.

I would also like to thank Marcella Kiel, Sanne Hirs and Maeyken Hoeneveld at the SIM Secretariat for their help and practical guidance as the original manuscript was finalised, and likewise to Kitty Arambulo and Ineke Boerefijn for their encouraging words of experience (and Kitty for mercifully offering to translate my thesis summary into Dutch). I should add that the original scope of the PhD research was current only to December 2000. The task of updating the research, analysis and current events across such a wide range of issues in a fast moving field would have been impossible without the guidance and regular feedback of a group of anonymous referees, further to those listed in the Annex. Many thanks to all who spared the time for these discussions and feedback sessions along the way. Needless to say responsibility for the views expressed herein, along with any errors, is purely my own and should not be attributed to the Office of the High Commissioner for Human Rights or the United Nations.

Gratitude most of all to family and friends, to Sakuntala, to the Florentine Sunday runners' club for making weekend work seem far more palatable, and to James, Mara and Simon for their bravery in agreeing to find out what acting as my *paranimfen* at my thesis defence might entail.

Mac Darrow
August 2002

Contents

List of Abbreviations

ADB	Asian Development Bank
BWIs	Bretton Woods Institutions
CAO	Compliance Advisor Ombudsman, IFC
CCA	Common Country Assessment, within UNDAF Framework (CCA/UNDAF)
CRC	Convention on the Rights of the Child
CEDAW	International Convention on the Elimination of All Forms of Discrimination Against Women
CERD	International Convention on the Elimination of All Forms of Racial Discrimination
CFF	Compensatory Financing Facility
CCL	Contingent Credit Line
CDF	Comprehensive Development Framework (of the World Bank)
CHR	Commission on Human Rights, United Nations
DAC	Development Assistance Committee of the Organisation for Economic Cooperation and Development (OECD)
DFID	Department for International Development, UK
EA	Environmental Assessment
EBRD	European Bank for Reconstruction and Development
EFF	Extended Fund Facility
ESAF	Enhanced Structural Adjustment Facility
ESW	Economic and Sector Work (of the World Bank)
G–7	Group of 7 industrialised countries: United States, Japan, Germany, United Kingdom, France, Italy and Canada
GA	General Assembly of the United Nations
G.A. Res.	General Assembly Resolution
GDP	Gross Domestic Product
HDI	Human Development Index
HDR	Human Development Report
HIPC	Highly Indebted Poor Country
IADB	Inter-American Development Bank
IBRD	International Bank for Reconstruction and Development
ICCPR	International Covenant on Civil and Political Rights
ICESCR	International Covenant on Economic, Social and Cultural Rights
ICJ	International Court of Justice
IDA	International Development Association

IEO	Independent Evaluation Office, IMF
IFC	International Financial Corporation
IFIs	International Financial Institutions
ILO	International Labour Organisation
IMF	International Monetary Fund
IMFC	International Monetary and Financial Committee, IMF (formerly known as 'Interim Committee')
IMS	International Monetary System
Interim Committee	See IMFC
JSA	Joint Staff Assessment (of PRSPs)
MIGA	Multilateral Investment Guarantee Agency
NGO	Non-government Organisation
NHRI	National Human Rights Institutions
OD	Operational Directive (of the World Bank)
OECD	Organisation for Economic Cooperation and Development
OED	Operations Evaluation Development, World Bank
OHCHR	Office of the High Commissioner for Human Rights
OP	Operational Policy (of the World Bank)
PFP	Policy Framework Paper (for EFF and ESAF arrangements)
PIN	Press Information Notice (of the IMF)
PRGF	Poverty Reduction and Growth Facility
PRSP	Poverty Reduction Strategy Paper
SAL	Structural Adjustment Loan
SAP	Structural Adjustment Programme
SECAL	Sectoral Adjustment Loan
SBA	Stand-by Arrangement
SDR	Special Drawing Rights
SRF	Supplemental Reserve Facility
SSN	Social Safety Net
STF	Systemic Transformation Facility
Sub-Commission	Sub-Commission on the Promotion and Protection of Human Rights, United Nations (formerly: Sub-Commission for the Prevention of Discrimination and Protection of Minorities)
TNC	Trans-National Corporation
UDHR	Universal Declaration of Human Rights
UN	United Nations
UNDAF	United Nations Development Assistance Framework
UNDP	United Nations Development Programme
UNICEF	United Nations Children's Fund
UNIFEM	United Nations Development Fund for Women
UNO	United Nations Organisation

UNTS	United Nations Treaty Series
Vienna Convention	Vienna Convention on the Law of Treaties 1969
WDR	World Development Report
WHO	World Health Organisation
WTO	World Trade Organisation

I

Introduction

———⊶∘⊷———

THE WORLD Bank[1] and International Monetary Fund (IMF)[2] have rarely stood far from controversy. Established in 1944,[3] the 'Bretton Woods twins,' as they are sometimes known in honour of their birthplace, began life vested with specific and—it was assumed—mutually exclusive sets of economic and monetary functions, within the emerging overall post-war international order. In contrast to the blueprint for the United Nations (UN) drawn up one year later, the Charters of the Bank and Fund were rooted unabashedly in political realism, rather than on the assumption of the equality of all nation states.[4] The fact that primary ownership and control was reserved to a small number of economically dominant states fuelled considerable controversy at the outset,[5]

[1] References to the World Bank, or 'Bank,' in this book are intended to refer to the International Development Association (IDA) and International Bank for Reconstruction and Development (IBRD), described shortly. This is consistent with the Bank's own terminology; both the IBRD and IDA have the same staff and follow the same policy guidelines and similar, if not identical, procedures concerning project implementation and appraisal. C Payer, *The World Bank: A Critical Analysis* (1982) at 28.

[2] The terms IMF and 'the Fund' are used here interchangeably. The terms 'International Financial Institutions' (IFIs) and 'Bretton Woods Institutions' (BWIs) are likewise interchangeable, and are intended to refer to the Bank (including the IDA) and Fund collectively.

[3] In fact, in terms of the institutions which are the focus of the present study, it was only the IBRD and IMF which take their origins from the Bretton Woods conference of 1944. The Bank's concessional transfers—that is, the IDA credits—did not begin until 1960.

[4] D Kapur, J Lewis, J. and R Webb (eds), *The World Bank: Its First Half Century (Vol 1: History)* (1997) [hereinafter, D Kapur *et al* (eds) (1997) (Vol. 1)] at 2: 'The founders vested predominant ownership and control in the economically more powerful countries, which, it appeared, would have been unwilling to delegate as much voice and as many resources to the Bretton Woods institutions had the case been otherwise.' Not all of the six principal organs of the UN Organisation (UNO) are founded upon the principal of equality of nation states, however. As with the BWIs' founding rationale, the institutionalised dominance of the UN Security Council by only five (present and erstwhile) major powers was designed precisely to secure at least a formal commitment of those major powers to multilateralism. For a discussion see M Darrow, 'Directions in Security Council Reform' (1995) 16 *Australian Year Book of International Law* 285–310, 286–87.

[5] Mason and Asher have remarked that the IBRD was, 'at least in its initial stages, far from being a bona fide international institution, since the United States supplied most of its loanable funds and was by far the predominant market for Bank securities,' and was headquartered in the United States. . . . Certainly the institution, as it emerged from Bretton Woods, was an Anglo Saxon creation, with the United States very much the senior partner.' E Mason and R Asher, *The World Bank Since Bretton Woods* (1973) at 28. Furthermore, although representatives of the former Soviet Union participated in the Bretton Woods conference, the USSR failed to ratify the Articles of Association of either the Bank or Fund. Although several factors explain this failure, at a meeting of the UN General Assembly in 1947 the Soviet representative charged that the BWIs were merely 'branches of

burgeoning in line with the expansion of the IFIs' mandates and their growing and disproportionate influence in the affairs of the less powerful states. The case for reform has undoubtedly assumed added urgency in the polarised world of post-'September 11,' with a complex web of geopolitical tensions and a seemingly isolationist US administration undermining aspirations for even-handed multilateral approaches to multi-facted development problems.

Whether grounded in objections concerning legitimacy, accountability, transparency, neoliberal imperialism, or in more specific allegations regarding adverse impacts of IFI-supported policies and activities, human rights have been either the stated or unstated basis for much of the controversy in which the IFIs currently find themselves embroiled.[6] Accordingly it may seem surprising that human rights, and in particular international human rights law, have been so marginal an influence on the research, policy and operational activities of both the Bank and Fund in their relatively short lives to date. All the more so, in light of their status as specialised agencies of the UN system and subjects of international law, and the fact that human rights are at the very core of the UN system's purposes.[7]

While many of the human rights-based critiques of the Bank and Fund purport to link broadly defined reforms with obligations under international human rights law,[8] rarely has this been carried out through a rigorous and in-depth application of international legal rules governing the proper interpretation of the institutions' mandates, and rarely have the policy consequences and practical possibilities for human rights integration been explored in any detail. These are the principal gaps that the present book attempts to contribute towards filling, by reference to a sample of the IFIs' most important contemporary activities.

The starting point of this book is that both the Bank and the Fund have responsibilities under international human rights law, and are under intense pressure to contribute more directly to the fulfilment of human rights standards.

Wall St,' and that the Bank was 'subordinated to political purposes which make it the instrument of one great power.' K Knorr, 'The Bretton Woods Institutions in Transition' (1940) 2 *International Organisation* 35–6, cited in E Mason and R Asher (1973) at 29, n 46.

[6] For some notable critiques see R Culpeper, A Berry and F Stewart (eds), *Global Development Fifty Years after Bretton Woods* (1997); C Caufield, *Masters of Illusion: The World Bank and the Poverty of Nations* (1996); B Rich, *Mortgaging the Earth: The World Bank, Environmental Impoverishment and the Crisis of Development* (1994); D Bandow and I Vásquez, *Perpetuating Poverty: The World Bank, the IMF, and the Developing World* (1994); S George, and F Sabelli, *Faith and Credit: The World Bank's Secular Empire* (1994).

[7] See Articles 1, 55 and 56 of the UN Charter.

[8] For a sampling see S Skogly, *The Human Rights Obligations of the World Bank and International Monetary Fund* (2001); D Bradlow, 'The World Bank, the IMF and Human Rights' (1996) 6(1) *Transnational Law and Contemporary Problems* 47; D Bradlow and C Grossman, 'Limited Mandates and Intertwined Problems: A New Challenge for the World Bank and the IMF' (1995) 17 *Human Rights Quarterly* 411–42; B Rajagopal, 'Crossing the Rubicon: Synthesising the Soft International Law of the IMF and Human Rights' (1993) 11 *Boston University International Law Journal* 81; S Skogly, 'The Position of the World Bank and International Monetary Fund in the Field of Human Rights' in R Hanski, and M Suksi, *An Introduction to the International Protection of Human Rights* 193–205 (1997); and E/CN.4/Sub.2/1999/11, Working paper submitted by J Oloka-Onyango and Deepika Udagama in accordance with Sub-Commission resolution 1998/12.

The principal legal arguments for the IFIs' more direct responsibility for human rights as a matter of international law are dealt with at length elsewhere.[9] It is beyond the scope of this book to revisit that framework in any depth, although a short summary of the principal sources of international human rights law binding upon the IFIs is provided at the beginning of chapter IV. Rather, the principal objectives of this book are the following: (1) to document the IFIs' neglect of, and impacts upon, human rights, as important parts of the case for more explicit recognition and engagement by the IFIs with their responsibilities under international human rights law; (2) in light of the IFIs' contemporary roles and activities—and against frequently-heard disclaimers of responsibility for human rights within the Bank and Fund—to identify and apply relevant international legal rules of interpretation to these institutions' mandates as a basis for assessing their legal capacities to take human rights into account; and (3) to consider a range of policy proposals consistent with the legal position as to mandate width, including suggestions as to appropriate limits of engagement. The study is based upon a broad overview of relevant legal and economic literature, journal and newspaper databases, and upon interview programs carried out in: (a) Washington DC and New York in March/April 1999; (b) Indonesia in October 1999; and (c) Washington DC and New York in February 2000. A list of interviewees is provided in the Annex.

For the purposes of this book, the choice to treat the Bank and Fund together—which is the case for most of the specific issues selected here for examination—was by no means natural or inevitable. At least in terms of their historical origins and the black letter of their own constitutions, they are very different kinds of institutions, with different responsibilities, comparative advantages, and legitimate fields of specialisation. While these waters have been muddied considerably since 1944, and while—as will be seen—the legal merits of the case for compartmentalisation along 'functionalist' lines are at best doubtful, it by no means follows that the Bank and Fund are anything like the same kind of beast.

To the contrary, the material differences abound, on a range of levels. Perhaps most notably, the 'core' mandates and responsibilities of these 'international cooperatives'[10] remain quite different. The Bank behaves very much as a 'bank', albeit one in the poverty reduction, structural reform, and social development businesses.[11] The Fund's core concerns, on the other hand, are the promotion of sound macro-economic and financial policies and international financial stability, chiefly through its technical advisory, balance of payments financing and monetary surveillance activities.[12] On an institutional level, the

---

[9] For the most comprehensive recent overview see S Skogly (2001).

[10] This is the term used by D Kapur *et al* (eds) (1997) (Vol. 1) at 2.

[11] See eg DFID, *Eliminating World Poverty: Making Globalisation Work for the Poor—White Paper on International Development* (2000) 52.

[12] Of course this is no more than a thumbnail sketch. A fuller account of their responsibilities and activities is provided in chapter II below.

Bank has been described as a 'travelling seminar,' a massive organisation with increasing decentralisation at country level, accommodating a wide range of perspectives within its vast inchoate bureaucratic 'matrix.'[13] By contrast the Fund clings tenaciously to its disciplinary homogeneity and purity, crafting and dispensing its macroeconomic prescriptions from the relative isolation of its Washington DC headquarters, within a considerably smaller 'command and control' management hierarchy. Or to extend the military analogy, if the Fund is the Prussian army, the Bank may perhaps be characterised as the Mexican army![14]

Nevertheless the common origins of the Bank and Fund, their shared international legal personality and common institutional inheritances,[15] and the growing areas of convergence and overlap between their 'development' and 'monetarist' mandates, especially in the context of their joint mission against poverty (as will be seen), do justify the joint analysis here of numerous specific issues of mutual concern, aggregated within the overall scope of this book.[16]

The book first examines the origins and contemporary functions of the Bank and Fund and considers the extent to which their existing policies, procedures and activities incorporate, take cognisance of, or are consistent with, internationally accepted human rights standards. The succeeding chapters of this book describe the kinds of impacts that the IFIs' activities have been claimed to have on the enjoyment of human rights, and examine the extent to which the Bank and Fund as a matter of international law may (and to a lesser extent, must) take explicit account of human rights within their activities and policies. The book then canvasses some of the main practical and theoretical barriers to the explicit incorporation of human rights, and concludes with a series of recommendations on the case for the adoption by the Bank and Fund of formal human rights policies, with suggestions as to appropriate content.

References to the term 'human rights' or international human rights law in this book should, unless a contrary intention appears, be taken to refer to the

---

[13] The Bank itself has used the term 'matrix' in describing its organisational structure. See eg 'Country Focus and Safeguard Policies: Institutional Issues' (12 June 2000), Annexed to World Bank, 'Management Report and Recommendation in Response to the Inspection Panel Investigation Report, China: Western Poverty Reduction Project, Qinghai Component (Credit No. 3255-CHA; Loan No. 4501-CHA) (2000) ['Qinghai: Bank Management Response to Panel Report (2000)'] at 6. For an excellent account of the Bank's evolution from the point of view of organisational theory see M Miller-Adams, *The World Bank: New Agendas in a Changing World* (1999) 4–8.

[14] E Crooks, 'The Odd Couple of Global Finance,' *Financial Times*, 6 July 2002, quoting Charles Wyplosz of the Centre for Economic Policy Research, a former visiting scholar at the IMF.

[15] One cross-cutting institutional theme which has already been mentioned, but will be covered more fully shortly, is the dominance of both Bank and Fund by the major industrialised powers—especially the USA—and the various consequences that this has had for the legitimacy and effectiveness of each.

[16] Indeed this is the approach reflected taken by some of the leading writers on human rights and the Bank and Fund. See eg D Bradlow,(1996); and D Bradlow and C Grossman (1995). Collective analyses have been considered appropriate in the poverty reduction context as well. See eg OECD, *DAC Scoping Study of Donor Poverty Reduction Policies and Practices* (1999) ['OECD/DAC Poverty Study (1999)'], at chapter 2, comparing and contrasting the various aspects of the Bank's and Fund's efforts to 'mainstream' poverty reduction into their activities.

corpus of international law binding upon states by reason of the ratification of one or more of the six 'core' human rights treaties—the International Covenant on Economic, Social and Cultural Rights (ICESCR),[17] the International Covenant on Civil and Political Rights (ICCPR)[18] (together with the ICESCR known as 'the Covenants'), the Convention on the Rights of the Child (CRC),[19] the International Convention on the Elimination of All Forms of Discrimination Against Women (CEDAW),[20] the International Convention on the Elimination of All Forms of Racial Discrimination (CERD),[21] and the Convention Against Torture and Other Cruel, Inhuman or Degrading Treatment or Punishment.[22] The principal reason for this is an unabashedly practical one: the fact that all UN member states have ratified at least one of these conventions, giving tangible legal expression to the universality of the norms embodied therein, and that as at August 2002 approximately 80 per cent of states had ratified four or more.[23] The Universal Declaration of Human Rights (UDHR),[24] which with the Covenants comprise what has become known as the 'International Bill of Rights,' is also of relevance in particular respects. As will be seen in chapter IV, this body of treaty law also has a very important bearing upon the sources and content of international human rights law binding upon the Bank and Fund, although as already stated it is not this book's main purpose to revisit that basic international legal framework in any depth.

The practical relevance of the present study's inquiries arises from certain key characteristics of a 'human rights approach to development,' as this or equivalent terms have evolved in the last several years. A human rights approach is said to bring a range of comparative advantages to development programming and policy making, such as:

1. a solid normative basis for values and policy choices which otherwise are more readily negotiable;[25]

---

[17] GA Res 2200 A (XXI), 16 December 1966. There were 145 states parties in August 2002.

[18] GA Res 2200 A (XXI), 16 December 1966. There were 148 states parties in August 2002.

[19] GA Res 44/25, 20 November 1989. There were 191 states parties in August 2002.

[20] GA Res 34/180, 18 December 1979. There were 170 states parties in August 2002.

[21] GA Res 2106 A (XX), 21 December 1965. There were 162 states parties in August 2002.

[22] GA Res 39/46, 10 December 1984. There were 130 states parties in August 2002.

[23] See the human rights treaty database of the Office of the United Nations High Commissioner for Human Rights at http://www.unhchr.ch. The six treaties chosen above are included within the UN's 'Core Group of Multilateral Treaties Deposited with the Secretary-General Representative of the Organisation's Key Objectives,' in advance of the Millennium Summit in September 2000. See http://untreaty.un.org/English/millennium/law/contents.htm. Reliance is not placed here on the International Convention on the Protection of the Rights of All Migrant Workers and Members of Their Families (GA Res 45/158, 18 December 1990) given that, as at August 2002, it had not yet entered into force.

[24] GA Res 217 A (III), 10 December 1948.

[25] A concrete (albeit anecdotal) illustration of the potential value of the CRC in this regard was cited by an anonymous referee from UNICEF, in relation to negotiations on principles for cost sharing in education and health care under the United Nations Economic Commission for Africa (UNECA) auspices. According to this commentator there was at least some measure of progress at the turn of the century towards the elimination of compulsory fees for primary education, and progress also towards consensus on the need to eliminate health fees for the poorest. Consensus was

2. a predictable framework for action, with the advantage of objectivity, determinacy, and the definition of appropriate legal limits;
3. a quintessentially *empowering* strategy for the achievement of human-centred development goals;
4. a ready legal means to secure redress for violations; and
5. a secure basis for accountability, not only for the State Party concerned, but a significantly wider range of actors in international development cooperation.[26]

Rights also lend 'moral legitimacy and the principle of social justice' to development objectives, and help shift the focus of analysis to the most deprived and excluded, especially to deprivations caused by discrimination.[27] A human rights approach also demands that attention be directed to 'the need for information and political voice for all people as a development issue—and to civil and political rights as integral parts of the development process.'[28] A number of these factors are revisited in chapter VI, as part of the framework for policy recommendations.

The most significant caveats to be identified at the outset are that a human rights approach in a given situation: (1) will frequently provide little more than an analytical and procedural framework for the consideration of the complex issues involved in the development equation, rather than (necessarily) definitive

reached in 1998 between UNECA, the Bank, UNICEF and others on 15 principles within a framework dubbed the 'Addis Ababa Consensus on Principles of Cost Sharing in Education and Health.' See *Implementing the 20/20 Initiative: Achieving Universal Access to Basic Social Services*, A joint publication of UNDP, UNESCO, UNFPA, UNICEF, WHO and the World Bank (September 1998) at 22–25. According to the UNICEF commentator, the 'fact of ratification of the CRC was persuasive with the African Finance Ministers,' facilitating the consensus reached. In this context the CRC 'added a powerful additional argument,' putting over the point that the issues in question were 'not optional.' Interviews in New York in February 2000.

[26] See P Alston, 'What's in a Name: Does it Really Matter if Development Policies Refer to Goals, Ideals or Human Rights?' in H Helmich and E Borghese (eds), *Human Rights in Development Cooperation* 95–106, 105–6 (1998); United Nations Office of the High Commissioner for Human Rights (OHCHR), 'Development and Human Rights: the Undeniable Nexus,' speech of Mary Robinson, United Nations High Commissioner for Human Rights (UNHCHR), Geneva, 26 June 2000. The UNHCHR sets out a similar list of the comparative advantages of a 'rights-based approach,' but includes: (a) 'higher levels of . . . ownership and free, meaningful and active participation; (b) easier consensus and increased transparency in national development processes; (c) integrated safeguards against unintentional harm by development projects; (d) more effective and complete analysis; and (e) a more authoritative basis for advocacy.' The UNHCHR declares the need for 'a more critical approach to the integration of human rights into the work of development—one that asks the hard questions about obligations, duties and action.' In that context she argues that 'all partners in the development process—local, national, regional and international—must accept higher levels of accountability[,]' and that '[a]ccountable aid is the responsibility of every donor, aid agency and international financial institution.' For similar formulae see F MacKay, 'Universal Rights or a Universe Unto Itself? Indigenous Peoples' Human Rights and the World Bank's Draft Operational Policy 4.10 on Indigenous Peoples' (2002) 17 *American University International Law Review* 527–624, 534, and the Report of the Independent Expert of the Commission on Human Rights on the Right to Development, E/CN.4/2000/WG.18/CRP.1 (2000).

[27] UNDP, *Human Development Report 2000: Human Rights and Development* (2000) [hereinafter 'Human Development Report 2000'] at 2.

[28] Human Development Report 2000 at 2.

answers; (2) while contributing greatly to a framework for policy prioritisation, should not necessarily be expected to shed light on the optimal policy mix; and (3) should not rely upon unrealistic assumptions concerning the practical value of formal redress through legal processes and institutions. As vital and instrumental as formal legal mechanisms might be in a given situation, human rights need to be seen as open-textured and flexible, and capable of application in diverse situations in ways not limited to adjudication in courts and tribunals.[29] Accountability can be realised through many other avenues and mechanisms, including monitoring, reporting, public debate and greater popular participation in public service delivery.

Finally, a cautionary note is warranted on the broad scope and interdisciplinary relevance of this study, as a consequence of which has not been possible to treat a number of empirically based arguments below in other than a cursory fashion. In particular, it must be emphasised that numerous factual propositions in this book—especially those relating to human rights impacts of IFIs' activities—are based to some degree either upon anecdotal accounts, or findings in the empirical literature that are largely beyond the competence of the present author to evaluate. It has not been possible to conduct thorough independent research to verify claims on all issues, some of which are admittedly quite contentious. Rather, the more modest and pragmatic approach here has been to attempt to raise all relevant issues in their appropriate context, drawing attention to areas of particular ambiguity or controversy where necessary. While the validity of the principal legal conclusions drawn in this book is unaffected by such evidential controversies, it is conceded at the outset that the practical impacts of those conclusions at a policy level might be.

---

[29] See eg DFID, 'Strategies for Achieving the International Development Targets: Human Rights for Poor People,' Consultation paper, February 2000 ['*DFID Human Rights Paper* 2000'], at 11: '[T]he supply of legal services [in developing countries] by both lawyers and judges tends to reflect the preferences and needs of their most common users—mainly propertied and salaried classes. Poor people are rarely able to use formal legal systems to pursue their claims. The actual costs of engaging a lawyer, the opportunity cost of time spent in court, and the general level of skill and education required to litigate effectively, all serve as deterrents.' However, reliance on alternative structures and mechanisms may likewise have its limitations: '[P]oor people may prefer or have no choice but to use traditional and customary systems. While such informal systems are often closer to the lives and concerns of poor people, they may be based on authority structures, practices and values which do not comply with human rights norms. Traditional and customary systems of law do not necessarily provide justice and protection for the poor or vulnerable.' For a fuller discussion of the possibilities and preconditions for the formal legal vindication of human rights claims see below chapter V at n 31 and accompanying text.

II

The IFIs' Origins and Contemporary Functions

⟶•⟵

THE IBRD

THE World Bank has been described as 'the world's foremost international development agency. Some call it the best, some call it the worst; but no one escapes its influence.'[1] The World Bank Group consists of the IBRD; the IDA; the International Finance Corporation (IFC); and the Multilateral Investment Guarantee Agency (MIGA); and the International Centre for the Settlement of Investment Disputes (ICSID).[2] The IBRD and IDA are both specialised agencies of the United Nations,[3] and both loan or grant funds for development directly to developing nations.[4]

The IBRD, founded at the Bretton Woods conference in 1944, was designed to provide relatively long-term funds for investment in productive endeavours. The IBRD's Articles of Agreement state that its purposes include 'assist[ing] in the reconstruction and development of territories of members,' and 'promot[ing] the long range balanced growth of international trade and the maintenance of equilibrium in balance of payments . . . thereby assisting in raising productivity, the standard of living and conditions of labour in [members'] countries.'[5] As at 2000 the IBRD was owned by the governments of 181

---

[1] C Payer *The World Bank: A Critical Analysis* (1982) at 15.

[2] World Bank Annual Report 2000.

[3] See 'Agreement Between the United Nations and the International Bank for Reconstruction and Development,' Article IV(2), 16 UNTS 346 at 348 (1948), reprinted in (1948) 2 *International Organisations* (hereafter referred to as the Relationship Agreement); and 'Agreement Between the United Nations and the International Development Association,' GA Res 1594, UN GAOR, 15th Sess., Supp. No. 16A, at 17, republished UN GAOR, 15th Sess., Annex 2, Agenda item 91 (1960).

[4] The IFC is also a lending institution, however it works more closely with private investors and invests in commercial enterprises in developing countries—World Bank Annual Report 2000. The IFC was created in 1956 in recognition of the reluctance of private corporations to borrow directly from the IBRD, given that the government guarantee required by the IBRD usually brought with it a higher degree of scrutiny of the corporations' books than they desired—C Payer (1982) at 25.

[5] Articles of Agreement of the International Bank for Reconstruction and Development, 27 December 1945, 60 Stat 1440, TIAS No 1502, 2 UNTS 134, amended, 17 December 1965, 16 UST 1942 (hereafter called 'IBRD Articles), at Article I. Its other purposes are: 'to promote private foreign capital by means of guarantees or participation in loans and other investments made by private investors, . . . to arrange the loans made or guaranteed by [the IBRD, and] . . . to conduct its

countries.[6] Membership in the IBRD is conditional on membership in the IMF, the intention being to oblige countries to agree to standards in the monetary field as a condition for receiving the benefits of Bank membership.[7]

Under the Bank's Articles of Agreement, of its twenty-four executive directors, five are appointed by the five members having the largest number of shares of capital stock (in the year 2000 these were the US, Japan, Germany, France and the United Kingdom[8]), while the remainder are elected by governors representing the rest of the member countries.[9] As the only major power to have escaped devastation in World War II, and hence the only feasible source of loanable funds, the United States' role was dominant from the outset, initially holding over 37 per cent of the IBRD's voting power.[10] As at 2000 it was still the largest shareholder, although its voting power had fallen to 16.50 per cent.[11] Significantly, the choice of Washington as the site for the IBRD's headquarters, rather than New York,[12] reflected the 'victory of the US view that the World Bank [and the IMF] should be subject to rather close control by national governments over Keynes's hope that they could be operated as autonomous, technocratic institutions divorced from the vicissitudes of national politics.'[13]

The IBRD makes loans on relatively conventional terms, but for the fact that the loans generally have a grace period of five years, and are repayable over fifteen to twenty years.[14] According to the Bank, the IBRD lends 'only to credit

operations with due regard to the effect of international investment on business conditions in the territories of members' [Article I, (ii) (iv) and (v)]. See also D Bradlow (1996) at 53–55.

[6] World Bank Annual Report 2000. The IBRD is 'owned' by its shareholders—the member countries—who hold voting rights proportional to their shareholdings. But only part of the share capital is paid in. The remainder is callable and can be used only as guarantee funds for the Bank's creditors. The bulk of the IBRD's funds for development are borrowed on capital markets, and from central banks and national governments. The existence of the guarantee of the uncalled portion of the Bank's capital means that the Bank is able to borrow on very favourable terms, close to or identical with the rates obtained on the securities of governments of the countries in which it sells its bonds. The Bank borrows mainly from countries running balance of payment surpluses, since this is nominally easier and less costly, and is able to lend money at rates that are significantly more favourable for most borrowers than what they could otherwise obtain on the open market—C Payer (1982) at 28–32.

[7] C Payer (1982) at 22.

[8] World Bank Annual Report 2000 at 119.

[9] Under the Bank's Articles of Agreement, the Bank's powers are vested in a Board of Governors, one from each member country governor (usually that country's Minister of Finance, or equivalent, acting *ex officio*). The Board meets only once per year, dealing only with a limited range of particularly significant matters. Day to day operations of the Bank are carried out by the Board of Executive Directors, chaired by the President. See C Payer (1982) at 39; World Bank Annual Report 2000 at 36–37.

[10] C Payer (1982) at 22.

[11] World Bank Annual Report 2000 at 119. For a discussion of US dominance in the Bank, see C Payer (1982) at 39–44; B Brown, *The United State and the Politicization of the World Bank. Issues of International Law and Policy* (1992).

[12] The IBRD's charter provide that its headquarters should be located in the territory of the member holding the greatest number of shares.

[13] C Payer (1982) at 23.

[14] Lawyers Committee for Human Rights, *The World Bank: Governance and Human Rights* (2nd ed) (1995) at 5.

worthy borrowers and only for projects that promise high real rates of economic return to the country.'[15] The majority of Bank funds are lent for projects; the remainder involves structural adjustment loans.[16] The project cycle is lengthy, often taking several years to complete. It comprises a number of stages: identification, preparation, appraisal, negotiations and Board approval, implementation and supervision, and evaluation.[17] The implementation phase itself takes an average of seven years.[18] Although primary responsibility for implementation rests with the client countries, the Bank has come to play an increasingly central and active role.[19] Importantly, in order to receive Executive Board approval, Bank-financed projects need to have an economic rate of return of at least ten percent 'in real terms,' or its 'qualitative equivalent' when such an assessment is difficult.[20]

The IBRD's cumulative lending to member countries from the 1990 to 2000 fiscal years was US$162,789 million.[21] The majority of this lending was focused in the East Asian and Pacific, Europe and Central Asia, and Latin American and Caribbean regions.[22] The sectors attracting proportionally greatest attention between 1990 and 2000 were agriculture, 'economic policy,' 'electric power and other energy,' finance and transportation.[23]

THE IDA

The IDA was created in 1960 in response to demands from a growing group of under-developed countries for a more liberal type of development fund.[24] The IBRD, after initially opposing the creation of such a fund, decided it would be wiser to 'co-opt' this demand by incorporating this new institution into its own structure, rather than continue its opposition. The Bank's perception was that its own powers of leverage would be enhanced if it were able to control the

---

[15] World Bank Annual Report 1997 at x.

[16] 'Structural adjustment' is defined below at nn 53–58 and accompanying text, discussed in more detail from a human rights perspective in chapter III.

[17] A Kolk, *Forests in International Environmental Politics: International Organisations, NGOs and the Brazilian Amazon* (1996) at 193.

[18] A Kolk (1996) at 193.

[19] See eg P Mosley *et al*, *Aid and Power: The World Bank and Policy-Based Lending* (1991) at 65–67; J Cahn 'Challenging the New Imperial Authority: The World Bank and the Democratisation of Development' (1993) 6 *Harvard Human Rights Journal* 159 at 171–80; D Bradlow and C Grossman (1995) at 422.

[20] A Kolk (1996) at 193. Environmental and poverty alleviation projects, for example, are not suited to quantitative assessment alone.

[21] World Bank Annual Report 2000 at 143.

[22] World Bank Annual Report 2000 at 143.

[23] US$15,700, $20,026, $17,153, $19,057 and $21,396 million, respectively. Education sector lending also rated quite highly with US$10,792 million, although environmental lending was relatively low, at US$4,774 million. Cumulative lending in other social sectors was as follows: 'health, nutrition and population' (US$6,042 million); 'social protection' (US$7,712 million); and 'water supply and sanitation' ($US6,739 million)—World Bank Annual Report 2000 at 143.

[24] C Payer (1982) at 25.

disbursal of concessionary aid funds.[25] The mission of the IDA is to provide assistance for the same purposes as the IBRD, but primarily to poorer developing countries and on terms that, relative to IBRD loans, weigh less heavily on their balance of payments situations.[26] Only those countries with an annual per capita gross national product of $885 or less (in 1999 US dollars) and lack the financial ability to borrow from the IBRD are eligible for IDA credits.[27]

All members of the IBRD are eligible to join the IDA, and 161 had done so as at 2000.[28] Unlike the IBRD, the majority of the IDA's funds are contributed by its wealthier members, although some developing countries contribute as well. Furthermore, the IDA receives transfers from the net earnings of the IBRD, and repayments on its credits.[29] IDA credits are made only to governments, over a thirty-five to forty year repayment period with a ten-year grace period on repayment of principal. There is no interest charge, however credits carry a small service charge, which as at 2002 was 0.75 per cent on disbursed balances.[30] The grace period and maturity of the credits are so long that it is virtually grant aid.[31] Since 1980, IDA lending has amounted to 12–18 per cent of total official development assistance to eligible borrower countries.[32]

Although the IDA's constitution declares it to be 'an entity separate and distinct from the [IBRD]' [Article 6, section 6(a)], it is simply a separate account managed by IBRD officers and staff, financing the same types of projects (or in certain cases the same projects) as the IBRD, in accordance with common standards and procedures.[33] But unlike the IBRD, the IDA requires regular infusions of new appropriations. Accordingly, the IDA is particularly exposed to shifts in the political climate for aid. A number of important political ramifications flow from this, as Payer explains: 'Budgets are made, and financial replenishments are required, at three-year intervals, which means that in practice the lobbying activity on behalf of the IDA must be virtually constant. The United States is the key contributor, and replenishments cannot come into force without the US contribution, but [as at 1982] the United States [had] been late five out of five times with its share.'[34] As

---

[25] C Payer (1982) at 25.

[26] Lawyers Committee for Human Rights (1995) at 6. The IDA's Articles of Agreement state that its purposes are to 'promote economic development, increase productivity and thus raise standards of living in the less developed areas of the world . . . thereby furthering the developmental objectives of the [IBRD]'—Articles of Agreement of the International Development Association, 26 January 1960, 11 UST 2284, TIAS No. 4607, 439 UNTS 249 [hereafter called IDA Articles], at Article I.

[27] Operations Evaluation Department, *IDA's Partnership for Poverty Reduction: An Independent Evaluation of Fiscal Years 1994–2000* (2002) [hereafter OED (2002)] at 75, on which basis 78 countries—representing 2.3 billion of the world's people—were eligible for IDA assistance as at 2002.

[28] World Bank Annual Report 2000.

[29] OED (2002) at 75.

[30] OED (2002) at 75.

[31] C Payer (1982) at 33.

[32] OED (2002) at 75.

[33] C Payer (1982) at 33.

[34] By the year 2002 there had been thirteen replenishments of IDA, almost every one of which had run into trouble with the US Congress. See eg C Caufield (1996) at 198–202.

amendments to the Bank's constitution, the Articles of Agreement, require three-fifths of the members holding four-fifths of the voting power, the United States with approximately one-sixth of the votes on the Executive Board had (as at 2000) a near-veto over amendments.[35]

The US Congressional stranglehold in these respects is obviously inherently objectionable to the extent that unaccountable power is wielded by US legislators over the affairs of IDA client countries. While the IDA, as with the IBRD, is at least in formal terms prohibited from accepting earmarked contributions,[36] the US Congress (through threats to reduce or cut off IDA funding) is uniquely placed to force the Bank to accept conditions upon US contributions that impact significantly upon the lives of those in IDA client countries. The impacts need not necessarily be negative, in human rights terms, of course. Congressional leverage in this regard has been a major factor in the adoption by the Bank of several key reforms, including a wider use of environmental impact assessments of Bank loans,[37] improvements to the Bank's information policy,[38] and the establishment in 1993 of the Inspection Panel, a mechanism established to review complaints regarding compliance with Bank operational policies.[39] But the problem of Congressional power without accountability to those most directly affected by its demands, and the difficult task of assessing the impacts of structural adjustment and wholesale transplantation of a neoliberal economic template, render the overall human rights equation a very complex one indeed.

Between the 1990 and 2000 fiscal years the IDA committed an overall total of US$62,020 million in credits.[40] The majority of this activity was centred in the African and South Asian regions.[41] The sectors earmarked for the greatest degree of assistance in dollar terms over that period were agriculture, 'economic

---

[35] C Payer (1982) at 34. As at 2000 the United States had 14.86% of the votes on the IDA Board, slightly less than the one-fifth requirement—World Bank Annual Report 2000 at 119. However the practical significance of the US's gradual diminution below the one-fifth level should probably not be overstated. The various ways in which that country's influence is manifested are explored more fully later.

[36] This prohibition hasn't always prevented 'earmarking by the side door,' however. Caufield relates the interesting example in 1978 of former Bank President McNamara circumventing purported Congressional earmarking (by means of an amendment to the foreign appropriations bill banning US funds from being used for loans to Vietnam and five other 'unfriendly' countries, the effect of which would have been to force the Bank to refuse the entire US IDA contribution) by sending a letter to the House of Representatives Subcommittee on Foreign Operations, stating that the Bank would make no more loans to Vietnam on account of that country's putative lack of a 'rational development policy.' C Caufield (1996) at 199–200.

[37] For a discussion see R Wade, 'Greening the Bank: The Struggle Over the Environment, 1970–1995' in Kapur *et al* (eds) (1997) (Vol. 2), 611–734 at 658–59, 662–67 and 681–87; and N Bridgeman, 'World Bank Reform in the "Post Policy" Era,' 13 *Georgetown International Environmental Law Review* 1013–46, 1020–21 (2001).

[38] See chapter VI below, at nn 29–30 and accompanying text.

[39] C Caufield (1996) at 202.

[40] World Bank Annual Report 2000 at 144.

[41] These two regions received US$24,984 million and US$17,996 million respectively: World Bank Annual Report 2000 at 144.

policy,' education, 'health, nutrition and population,' and transportation.[42]
A small group of Asian countries—mainly India, Pakistan, Bangladesh and
Indonesia—has consistently consumed a very large proportion of IDA credits.
In fact the focus upon the first country in the above list led the IDA at one time
to be nicknamed the 'India Development Association.'[43] India continued as the
IDA's most significant client in the fiscal year 2000, with new commitments
totalling US$867 million.[44]

THE EVOLUTION OF DEVELOPMENT THINKING AT THE BANK

*In the old story, the peasant goes to the priest for advice on saving his dying chickens.
The priest recommends prayer, but the chickens continue to die. The priest then recommends music for the chicken coop, but the deaths continue unabated. Pondering
again, the priest recommends repainting the chicken coop in bright colours. Finally,
all the chickens die. 'What a shame,' the priest tells the peasant. 'I had so many more
good ideas.'[45]*

Development thinking has advanced markedly since the founding of the United
Nations system. At that time, a particular vision prevailed, a conception of
development as a purely 'economic' phenomenon.[46] In the 1960s the 'fad' at the
World Bank and among many donor States moved to 'development planning.'[47]
The widespread belief was that 'economic growth was the most important element in a country's development equation and that growth was both necessary
and sufficient to settle a host of other problems, including such social questions
as employment and poverty.'[48]

The flawed assumptions of 'trickle-down' economics, and in particular the
realisation that 'the pursuit of growth without a reasonable concern for equity
is socially destabilising,'[49] led to the emergence in the 1970's of the 'basic needs'
approach. While the Bank itself did not originate this shift, it does claim some
credit for intellectual leadership in terms of how the contours of the debate
unfolded.[50] As important as 'basic needs' was in elevating poverty reduction to

---

[42] Credits approved for these sectors totalled US$11,303, $6,915, $6,899, $6,749 and $6,626 mil-
lion, respectively, over the 10-year period. World Bank Annual Report 2000 at 144.

[43] C Payer (1982) at 34–35.

[44] World Bank Annual Report 2000.

[45] J Sachs 'Growth in Africa: It can be done,' *The Economist*, 29 June 1996, at 23.

[46] See eg N Moller, 'The World Bank: Human Rights, Democracy and Governance' (1997) 15(1)
Netherlands Quarterly of Human Rights 21–45 at 24.

[47] J Sachs (1996) at 23.

[48] L Emmerij, 'Development Thinking and Practice: Introductory Essay and Policy Conclusions'
in L Emmerij, (ed) *Economic and Social Development into the XXI Century* (1997) at 5. One of the
more influential studies calling for a fundamental re-think of the 'growth as development' thesis was
H Chenery, M Ahluwalia, C Bell, J Duloy and R Jolly, *Redistribution with Growth* (1974).

[49] N Stern with F Ferreira, 'The World Bank as an "Intellectual Actor,"' in D Kapur *et al* (1997)
(Vol. 2), 523–609, 549.

[50] N Stern with F Ferreira (1997) at 549–50 and 600.

the top of the Bank's agenda, surprisingly by the turn of the century debates continued to rage over the relevance of distribution and equity to economic performance. In mid-2000, a full five years after the IMF's former Managing Director declared his organisation's commitment to 'high quality growth' and 'equity through equality of opportunity,' commentators from different quarters—including influential researchers at the Bank—were still fiercely arguing the relative importance of 'economic growth' and 'distribution', in a manner viewed by many as reflecting the long-discredited premises of trickle-down economics.[51] In any case, the 'basic needs' approach generated a decidedly mixed set of results in practice, partly because of their failure to include stakeholder participation and related civil and political rights in anything other than a symbolic and technocratic fashion.[52]

A re-emphasis on the market ensued in the 1980s, the decade of the international debt crisis, and 'structural adjustment' came into vogue. The term 'structural adjustment' refers to fast-disbursing policy-based loans provided primarily by multilateral development banks such as the World Bank, intended to help developing countries achieve any agreed objective, typically 'growth' accompanied by improvements in the level of human development.[53]

---

[51] See eg D Dollar and A Kraay, 'Growth is Good for the Poor,' *Working Paper Series* No 2587 (2000). While denying that their findings reflect 'trickle down' economics, the general finding that economic growth is as good for the poor as everyone else, and that the poor participate in full from the benefits of economic globalisation (essentially, that the rising tide lifts all boats) attracted considerable controversy internationally, leading to the authors to publish the clarification that their research did not intend to bear out the proposition that economic growth was sufficient in and of itself for poverty reduction. See *World Bank Development News* (www.worldbank.org) 25 May 2000, and 9 June 2000, conveying OXFAM's criticism that the rate at which growth is converted into poverty reduction—a function of income distribution and opportunity—also matters. In this sense it has been argued that the authors of the report ignored the Bank's research on the redistributive policies required to redress inequities and produce sustainable 'high quality' growth. Dollar and Kraay subsequently defended their research against such allegations, emphasising that 'growth-enhancing policies are just one part of a poverty-reduction strategy which must also include targeted redistributive measures.' *World Bank Development News*, 20 June 2000.

[52] Had the 'basic needs' philosophy been accompanied by modern conceptions of 'governance,' and civil and political rights dimensions suited to unleashing the full energies of participation, a much more appropriate set of prescriptions may have resulted. See eg P Alston, 'Human Rights and the Basic Needs Strategy for Development,' *Human Rights and Development Working Papers, No 2, Anti-Slavery Society* 1 (1979); cf J Sachs (1996) at 23. And on the relationship between the 'basic needs' philosophy and the functionalist origins of the UN system see J Gatthi, 'Good Governance as a Counter Insurgency Agenda to Oppositional and Transformative Social Projects in International Law' (1999) 5 *Buffalo Human Rights Law Review* 107, 133–41.

[53] G Ranis, 'Successes and Failures of Development Experience Since the 1980s' in L Emmerij (ed) (1997) at 89. See also D Bradlow and C Grossman (1995) at 421: '[T]he Bank, in addition to its project lending operations, has begun to fund both general and sector-specific adjustment programs. The loans for these programs provide borrowers with quick disbursing general purpose support conditioned upon adoption of certain policy reforms. The conditions, which are contractually binding, relate to the adoption of certain institutional or legislative measures intended to "adjust" the structures within which economic activity occurs, or social and economic policy is made, so that these structures are more likely to produce economic growth.' The share of policy-based lending has been limited in recent years to around 25% of the Bank's total portfolio: Bretton Woods Project, 'Bretton Woods Update' (July/August 2002) at 3 (available at http://www.brettonwoodsproject.org).

'Adjustment' programs initially cut heavily into public investments, both physical and human, and have been claimed in many cases to have brought economic
growth to a 'grinding halt.'[54] At the turn of the century structural adjustment
programmes remained deeply controversial. While some gains, such as a rise in
global per capita GDP,[55] have been claimed, criticism has been levelled on a
range of grounds including adverse human rights and environmental impacts,
lack of distributional equity, poor cost-effectiveness, the failure of 'conditionality' and its objectionable political and ideological biases, and difficulties with
evaluation of outcomes.[56] At least in the case of the World Bank, to these criticisms could be added the failure adequately to prioritise interventions,[57] and
failure to remedy institutional cultural problems within the organisation itself,
reducing the structural adjustment loan approval process into a 'rather time-
consuming and expensive ritual dance.'[58]

The end of the 1980s also represented the height of the dominance of the market over the State in development thinking, embodied in what became known as
the 'Washington consensus.' As Louis Emmerij puts it, this doctrine advocated
the 'development of a market economy that would create confidence among private entrepreneurs and enterprises, leading them to increase their productivity
and exports. Liberalisation of imports, deregulation, privatisation of most state-
owned enterprises, and radical reform of the government sector would stabilise
and improve macro-economic conditions, strengthen market forces, and bring
about achievement-oriented competition and . . . specialisation of the economies
through pursuit of optimal participation in the global marketplace.'[59] Or, as
Joseph Stiglitz puts it, 'to promote sound money and free trade, to free up
domestic markets, and to encourage policy-makers to go home early and stop
interfering with markets.'[60]

The East Asian 'miracle boom'—riding to a significant degree on interven-
tionist and protectionist policies administered by a robust state—and subsequent crash laid bare the inadequacies of the simplistic 'Washington consensus'

---

[54] L Emmerij (1997) at 7. However as the decade progressed a move towards 'adjustment with
growth and equity' ensued, thanks to factors such as the exceptional efforts made by UNICEF—see
L Emmerij (1997) at 8, and UNICEF, *Adjustment with a Human Face* (1987).

[55] However on the limitations of GDP measures, Joseph Stiglitz observes that '[a] mine in a
remote corner of a country might lead to increased GDP, but is likely to have little impact on the
development transformation.' J Stiglitz, 'Introduction' in C Gilbert and D Vines (eds), *The World
Bank: Structure and Policies* 1–9, 2 (2000).

[56] See eg G Ranis (1997) at 89–92; and D Bradlow and C Grossman (1995) at 421: 'Many countries that have undergone Bank and IMF-funded adjustment programs have experienced, in addition
to macroeconomic stability and increased growth rates, widening income disparities, declining standards of human welfare, and deteriorating environments.' For further discussion see below chapter
III at nn 61–80 and accompanying text.

[57] J Sachs (1996) at 23; G Ranis (1997) at 83.

[58] G Ranis (1997) at 91. See chapter V below for a fuller account of 'approval culture' problems
within the Bank.

[59] L Emmerij (1997) at 8.

[60] J Stiglitz (2000) at 1.

as a framework for thinking about development policy.[61] In the ensuing frustration, it was realised that certain forms of poverty reduction are, in fact, necessary for sustained growth.[62] Redressing the historic neglect of the public sector and institutional dimensions of development, the focus in the mid-1990s also shifted more strongly towards 'governance.'[63] A bewildering array of complex interventions were implemented in the name of 'good governance' during the late 1990s, as will be seen shortly. It is partly the complexity and range of interventions made under various governance labels, along with the lessons of market failure and the East Asian boom and bust, that led the 1990s away from the traditional development confrontation between the market and the State, towards a more balanced and nuanced approach capable of embracing the comparative advantages of each.[64] However the term 'governance' is inherently elastic and susceptible to manipulation. Governance-related adjustment conditions have been accused of serving the interests of global capital and the IFIs' major shareholders, rather than the people in developing countries, and of being applied in a mechanistic template fashion without proper regard for local cultural, legal, political and social institutions and conditions.[65] As at the year 2002 the prospects for consensus on an objectively-founded and clearly articulated concept of governance, the acceptable means to measure its implementation, and on the proper role for human rights within it, looked as remote as ever.[66]

The 1990s also ushered human beings onto centre stage of development discourse; that is to say, human beings as the ends themselves of development, rather than or in addition to the means. Participating States at the 1995 World

---

[61] J Stiglitz (2000) at 1.

[62] C Gilbert and D Vines, 'The World Bank: An Overview of Some Major Issues' in C Gilbert and D Vines (eds), *The World Bank: Structure and Policies* 10–38, 19 (2000), and more generally, R Kanbur and D Vines, 'The World Bank and Poverty Reduction: Past, Present and Future' in C Gilbert and D Vines (eds) (2000), 87–107.

[63] See J Sachs (1996) at 23; World Bank, *Sub-Saharan Africa: From Crisis to Sustainable Growth* (1989) esp at 60–61; World Bank, 'Ah yes: Governance!' *Development Brief,* Number 40, August 1994; World Bank, *Governance and Development* (1992); J Stiglitz (2000) at 2, emphasising also social and political organisational aspects, and culture change.

[64] G Ranis (1997) at 84 and 93; A Sen, 'Development Thinking at the Beginning of the XXI Century' in L Emmerij (ed) (1997) at 532–33; J Stiglitz, 'An Agenda for Development in the Twentieth Century: Keynote Address to the Ninth Annual Bank Conference on Development Economics,' Washington DC, 30 April 1997; J Williamson, 'The Washington Consensus Revisited' in L Emmerij (ed) (1997) at 48–61; F Stewart, 'John Williamson and the Washington Consensus Revisited' in L Emmerij (ed) (1997) at 62–68, esp at 65–68.

[65] D Kapur and R Webb, 'Governance-related Conditionalities of the International Financial Institutions,' *G-24 Discussion Paper Series (UNCTAD),* No. 6 (August 2000). Indeed the 'transplantation' problem can perhaps be viewed as but one manifestation of more foundational shortcomings of the global capitalist system itself. See H De Soto, *The Mystery of Capital: Why Capitalism Triumphs in the West and Fails Everywhere Else* (2001), with particular emphasis upon the alleged failure of capitalism and its institutional champions to take adequate account of Third World assets falling outside the world of enforceable legal representations.

[66] UNDP, *Governance for Sustainable Human Development: A UNDP Policy Document* (1997) at 2; cf Lawyers Committee for Human Rights (1995) at 43–102. On the question of measurement see D Kaufman, A Kraay and P Zoido-Lobatón, 'Governance Matters: From Measurement to Action' (2000) 37(2) *Finance and Development* 10–13.

Summit for Social Development emphasised that sustainable and equitable development must embrace democracy; social justice; economic development; environmental protection; transparent and accountable governance; and universal respect for and observance of all human rights.[67] A record 147 Heads of State and government (and 191 nations in total) at the September 2000 Millennium Summit gave unprecedented political weight to human-centred development goals, embodied in the terms of the Millennium Declaration[68] and subsequent distillation of an agreed set of 'Millennium Development Goals' (or MDGs).[69]

The UNDP's Human Development Report (HDR) for the year 2000 was dedicated entirely to explaining the normative and functional rationales and linkages between human rights and development.[70] Speeches, publications and other policy statements within the World Bank reflect acceptance of these linkages,[71] as does the Bank's new Comprehensive Development Framework (CDF),[72] albeit rarely in explicit human rights terms. And while it did not quite

---

[67] Copenhagen Declaration on Social Development in Report of the UN World Summit for Social Development, A/CONF.166/9 (1995) ('Copenhagen Declaration') at para 26. See also D Bradlow (1996) at 48.

[68] A/RES/55/2 of 8 September 2000. The Declaration set forth a catalogue of shared principles, along with time-bound development goals. Section V of the Declaration (entitled 'Human rights, democracy and good governance') includes a series of undertakings to respect, promote and uphold all internationally recognised human rights.

[69] The eight MDGs are (1) eradicate extreme poverty and hunger; (2) achieve universal primary education; (3) promote gender equality and empower women; (4) reduce child mortality; (5) improve maternal health; (6) combat HIV/AIDS, malaria and other diseases; (7) ensure environmental sustainability; and (8) develop a global partnership for development. In the terms of the Millennium Declaration, all 189 UN member states have undertaken to achieve these goals and their (18) associated targets by the year 2015. See http://www.un.org/millenniumgoals/index.html. In September 2001 the UN Secretary-General promulgated a 'Road map towards implementation of the UN Millennium Declaration' (UN Doc. A/56/326, September 2001) containing a set of 48 indicators for measurement of progress towards the 8 MDGs and 18 associated targets, with some observable overlap with human rights-based monitoring methodology, and a fairly extensive set of suggested strategies for implementing Section V of the Declaration. Specific human rights elements are reflected in other parts of the Road Map as well; for example, Section VI ('Protecting the vulnerable') includes among its goals the 'ratification and full implementation' of the CRC and its two Optional Protocols.

[70] UNDP, *Human Development Report: Development and Human Rights* (2000) [hereafter HDR 2000].

[71] J Wolfensohn, 'The Challenge of Inclusion,' Annual Meetings Address, Hong Kong SAR, China, 23 September 1997; J Wolfensohn, 'The World Bank and the Evolving Challenges of Development,' Speech at the Overseas Development Council Congressional Staff Forum, Washington DC, 16 May 1997; J Stiglitz, 'Redefining the Role of the State: *What* should it do? *How* should it do it? And *how* should these decisions be made?' Speech Presented on the Tenth Anniversary of MITI Research Institute, Tokyo, 17 March 1988; S Sandstrom, 'The East Asia Crisis and the Role of the World Bank: Statement to the Bretton Woods Committee,' Washington DC, 13 February 1998; I Shihata, 'Human Rights, Development and International Financial Institutions' (1992) 8 *American University Journal of International Law and Policy* 27; I Shihata, 'The World Bank and Human Rights: An Analysis of the Legal Issues and the Record of Achievements' (1988) 17 *Denver Journal of International Law and Policy* 39.

[72] See World Bank, 'Comprehensive Development Framework: questions and answers,' available at http://www.worldbank.org/cdf/cdf-faq.htm. The CDF approach to development—while not recognised by all within the Bank as especially 'new'—attempts to be comprehensive in two

go as far as proclaiming human beings as the ends of development, the World Development Report (2000/2001)[73]—devoted to the theme of poverty—provided an important benchmark of the extent of the Bank's own conceptual shift, focusing upon 'opportunity, empowerment and security' as legitimate facets of development. While these and other premises of the WDR 2000 have not been embraced universally within the field of development economics, and while consensus on the appropriate ends of development remains elusive, the centrality of human beings within the overall development equation as a matter of general principle is no longer seriously disputed.

WHAT ROLE FOR HUMAN RIGHTS?

Human rights issues arise in a potentially wide range of the Bank's activities. Apart from well documented human rights consequences of major infrastructure projects[74] and other kinds of Bank-supported activities, to be discussed further in chapter III, many of the Banks more recent concerns such as gender in development, HIV/AIDS, child labour and corruption and governance issues, have particularly obvious and potentially dramatic human rights implications.

The general policy position of the Bank on human rights issues is that explicit engagement with human rights is beyond its mandate as a development agency, but that in indirect terms human rights (with a focus on economic, social and cultural rights) are indirectly enhanced by the Bank's work.[75] The boundaries of the development/human rights relationship—with a notable emphasis on civil and political rights—have nonetheless been pushed somewhat further than this within the Bank's research program, traceable most notably back to the landmark study of Landell-Mills and Serageldin in 1991 on 'Governance and the External Factor',[76] invoking the UDHR as a relevant measure of adequate governance, through to a series of related empirical studies in the 1990s revealing a causal relationship between civil liberties and the economic rate of return of

---

respects—across different aspects of development, and across participants in the development process. However the challenges of how to prioritise interventions within the Bank's vast menu, and how to coordinate the and synthesise the energies of a wide range of new participants, are still to be meaningfully addressed. Stiglitz, J (2000) at 6. For a more far-reaching critique from a 'micro-development' perspective see R Blake, 'The World Bank's Draft Comprehensive Development Framework and the Micro-Paradigm of Law and Development' (2000) 3 *Yale Human Rights and Development Law Journal* 159–89, with a focus on inadequate measure to ensure civil society participation, claimed in 'CDF pilot' countries to have resulted in prioritisation of relations between CDF governments and international donors, rather than with the poorest of the poor in their own countries.

[73] Hereinafter WDR 2000.

[74] B Morse and T Berger, *Sardar Sarovar: The Report of the Independent Review* (1992) ['the Morse report (1992)'], discussed further in chapters III–V.

[75] World Bank, *Development and Human Rights: the Role of the World Bank* (1998).

[76] P Landell-Mills and I Serageldin, *Governance and the External Factor* (1991), proposing international human rights standards as embodied in the UDHR as a measure of good governance.

Bank-supported projects.[77] By way of illustration, one such study used a cross-national data set on the performance of government investment projects financed by the World Bank, set against four alternative measures of 'civil liberties.'[78] All of the civil liberties measures embraced internationally recognised civil and political rights, and in three of the four cases, certain economic and social rights.[79] The authors concluded that the measure of respect and protection of 'civil liberties' as defined in the study had a 'substantial impact on the successful implementation of government investment projects financed by the World Bank.'[80] The strong effect of civil liberties protection was found to hold true even when controlling for the level of democracy.[81] Moreover, the effects of civil liberties on project returns were empirically large compared with the more celebrated impacts of macro-economic policy and economic distortions.[82]

---

[77] J Isham, D Kaufman and L Pritchett, 'Civil Liberties, Democracy, and the Performance of Government Projects' (1997) 11(2) *The World Bank Economic Review* 219. Exploring the interrelationships among civil liberties, civil strife, and project performance, the study suggests that the possible flow of causation is from more civil liberties to increased citizen voice to better projects. Also relevant are R Barro, 'Economic Growth in a Cross-Section of Countries' (1991) 106 *Quarterly Journal of Economics* 407; S Ozler and D Rodrik, 'External Shocks, Politics, and Private Investment: Some Theory and Empirical Evidence' (1992) *Journal of Development Economics* 141; A Banerji and H Ghanem, 'Does the Type of Political Regime Matter for Trade and Labour Market Policies?' (1997) 11(1) *World Bank Economic Review* 171, 188; and D Kaufman, A Kraay, and P Zoido-Lobatón, *Governance Matters* (1999). However on the limitations of the reliability of composite indices for comparative purposes see D Kaufman, A Kraa and P Zoido-Lobatón, *Aggregating Governance Indicators* (1999), and for a critique of the ideological bias of the Freedom House and Humana indices see P Alston, 'Towards a Human Rights Accountability Index,' *Background Papers: Human Development Report 2000* (2000).

[78] J Isham, D, Kaufman and L Pritchett (1997).

[79] J Isham, D, Kaufman and L Pritchett (1997). The authors (at 228) found high correlations among all four measures of civil liberties, hence the choice of measure was not significant for the purposes of their study. The Freedom House (1994) measure is the most comprehensive, ranking civil liberties on a scale of 1 to 7 for 165 countries from 1972 to 1994 based upon a checklist which includes 'media free of censorship, open public discussion, freedom of assembly and demonstration, freedom of political organisation, non-discriminatory rule of law in politically relevant cases, freedom from unjustified political terror, free trade unions, . . . free businesses and co-operatives, free professional and private organisations, free religious institutions, personal social rights (for example, the right to own property and to travel internally and externally), socio-economic rights, freedom from gross socio-economic inequality, and freedom from gross government indifference or corruption.' By way of contrast, the Humana (1986) index ranks human rights achievements in 89 countries for 1985 on a scale of zero to one hundred based upon the human rights contained in the ICCPR, which include the right of peaceful assembly, freedom of opinion and expression, the right and opportunity to take part in the conduct of public affairs, and the right to form trade unions.

[80] J Isham, D, Kaufman and L Pritchett (1997) at 237.

[81] J Isham, D, Kaufman and L Pritchett (1997) at 219 and 233–35.

[82] J Isham, D, Kaufman and L Pritchett (1997) at 230 and 237. This result adds to the evidence for the view that increasing citizen voice and public accountability—through both participation and better governance—can lead to greater efficacy in government action. But importantly, the authors recognise (at 237) that '[t]he most important aspects of civil liberties and political regimes go beyond whether they promote or discourage economic outcomes.' Although the authors focused upon civil liberties' instrumental value, they emphasised that 'government respect for civil liberties is valuable regardless of its instrumental economic value.'

The Bank's research on the linkages between development and the human rights of women has been similarly striking.[83]

The case for civil and political rights in development has not been put more famously than by Amartya Sen: '[N]o substantial famine has ever occurred in a country that is independent, that has systematic multiparty elections, that has opposition parties to voice criticisms, and that permits newspapers to report freely and to question without extensive censorship the wisdom of current government policies. This generalisation applies not only to the affluent countries of Europe and America but also to countries that happen to be very poor, such as India, Botswana, or Zimbabwe.'[84] Further, '(t)he basic issue is not only the existence of political and civil rights in the official legal system but also their active use. Much depends, therefore, on the determination and dedication of opposition groups.' On this basis, '(t)he need to take note of the actions of opposition groups as well as of the government in office can be quite critical in the political economy of development.'[85]

Commenting on the centrality and inter-relatedness of human rights vis-à-vis related development issues, Bradlow and Grossman observe: '[The World Bank] cannot consider the problem of poverty . . . of developing countries without considering the issues of refugees, environmental degradation, the capacity of the state to effectively and equitably manage its resources, population policy, and human rights, including the status of women, indigenous people, and minorities. Environmentalists cannot seek resolution of environmental

[83] In a World Bank Policy Research study entitled *Engendering Development—Through Gender Equality in Rights, Resources, and Voice,* released on 1 June 2000, Bank researchers found that countries that adopt specific measures to protect women's rights and increase their access to resources and schooling have less corruption and achieve faster economic growth than countries that do not. *World Bank Development News,* 2 June and 5 June 2000. 'Much of the recent debate about gender and development has pitted growth-oriented approaches against rights-oriented approaches,' said Elizabeth King, one of the authors who compiled the report. 'But the evidence we examined suggests that economic development and institutional change are complimentary—and that both are necessary.' Bank President James Wolfensohn welcomed the report, saying 'There is absolutely no doubt in my mind that the single most important issue in most of the countries we are dealing with is the enfranchisement of women.' *World Bank Development News,* 2 June 2000. The report is available at http://www.worldbank.org/gender/prr/index.htm, visited May 2002.

[84] A Sen, 'Development Thinking at the Beginning of the XXI Century' in L Emmerij (ed) *Economic and Social Development into the XXI Century* 532–33, 539 (1997). See generally A Sen, *Development as Freedom* (1999), and A Sen, 'Why Half the Planet is Hungry,' *The Observer,* 16 June 2002.

[85] A Sen (1997) at 539; J Dreze and A Sen, *Hunger and Public Action* (1989). Sen has remarked that: 'A remarkable thing about the Chinese famine is that the disastrous economic policies that had led to it were not revised through three years of intense suffering and mortality during which the government lost none of its power and control—a situation that would be impossible in a multiparty democracy'—A Sen (1997) at 539; A Sen, *Resources, Values and Development* (1984), Essay 19. Of course none of this should be taken to imply the sufficiency of any particular model of democracy from a human rights perspective, nor to question the undoubted capacity of democratic regimes to commit or contribute directly or indirectly to development disasters and patterns of human rights violations in their own or third countries. For a discussion of some of the key preconditions for effective democratic governance see UNDP, *Human Development Report 2002: Deepening Democracy in a Fragmented World* (2002) (hereinafter HDR 2002).

problems without addressing issues of poverty, refugees, information flows, population, and even security concerns. Trade organisations can no longer effectively regulate trade without seeking agreement on environmental issues, labour policy, investment matters, the regulation of intellectual property (which in itself raises important cultural rights issues), and the regulation of trade in services (which also raises important monetary, financial, and immigration policy questions).'[86] Further, '[h]uman rights organisations cannot seek effective protection of human rights without considering the impact of poverty, foreign investment, trade, and environmental degradation.'[87]

The Bank's influential former General Counsel acknowledged a relatively expansive view of development, and the central place of human rights within it, stating that: 'While the Bank is prohibited from being influenced by political considerations, its staff increasingly realise that human needs are not limited to the material "basic needs" often emphasised in the 1970s. Civil rights are also basic to human development and happiness . . . [N]o balanced development can be achieved without the realisation of a minimum degree of all human rights, material or otherwise, in an environment that allows each people to preserve their culture while continuously improving their living standards.'[88]

The extent and pattern of recognition of human rights in the work of the Bank, however, belies the superficiality of official rhetoric and appears to take only selective account of its own research. An increasing number of functional units and thematic teams within the Networks (the advisory parts of the Bank) and Regions (the operational side) seem cautiously to be fluttering around the flame of human rights—or at least the 'St Elmo's fire' of development euphemisms—in circles of ever diminishing radius.[89] In cases such as the HIV/AIDS program, human rights are very clearly at the core of current diagnoses of the problem, and at the heart of needed solutions, eg regarding rights to confidentiality, rights in the work place, public services, discrimination, stigmatisation, and women's rights.[90] The relevance of children's rights has been recognised too, for example concerning reproductive rights, sexual exploita-

---

[86]   D Bradlow and C Grossman (1995) at 415.

[87]   D Bradlow and C Grossman (1995) at 416 and the references at n 11, esp P Alston, 'International Trade as an Instrument of Positive Human Rights Policy' (1982) 4 *Human Rights Quarterly* 155; W Shutkin, 'International Human Rights Law and the Earth: The Protection of Indigenous Peoples and the Environment' (1991)31 *Virginia Journal of International Law* 479.

[88]   I Shihata, *The World Bank in a Changing World* (1991) at 133, cited in H Moller (1997) at 25. See also I Shihata, 'Human Rights, Development, and International Financial Institutions' (1992) 8 *American University Journal of International Law and Policy* 27 at 28: '. . . [A] guarantee of human rights protection is central to the development process.'

[89]   For a sampling see below nn 95–100 and accompanying text, and chapter IV below, at nn 202–8 and 246–52 and accompanying text.

[90]   As to women's rights in particular, elements are: (1) inheritance problems on the death of husbands (in certain cases the brother of the deceased even inherits the deceased's wife); (2) women's economic rights and disempowerment; (3) reproductive rights; and (4) rights to negotiate terms within a marriage. See J Mann and D Tarantola (eds), *AIDS in the World II* (1996); HDR 2000 at 42.

tion, access to condoms,[91] and education. The linkages have been summarised in the following way:

> Protection and fulfilment of human rights is essential for an effective response to HIV/AIDS. Respect for human rights helps to reduce vulnerability to HIV/AIDS, to ensure that those living with or affected by HIV/AIDS live a life of dignity without discrimination and to alleviate the personal and societal impact of HIV infection. Conversely, violations of human rights are primary forces in the spread of HIV/AIDS. Disrespect for civil and political rights makes society-wide mobilisation against HIV/AIDS and open dialogue about prevention impossible. And poverty and deprivation contribute to the spread of HIV/AIDS. Where people lack access to information about the risks of HIV/AIDS and are denied adequate education, prevention efforts are bound to fail and the epidemic will spread more quickly. HIV/AIDS is also likely to be spread more quickly in countries where the right to health is neglected. Marginalisation and disempowerment of women make them more vulnerable to infection and exacerbate the effects of the epidemic. Discrimination against people affected by HIV/AIDS leads to shame, silence and denial, fuelling the epidemic.[92]

Unfortunately, in regions of the world worst hit by HIV/AIDS, national and international responses have frequently been too little, arriving too late. The scale of the pandemic has been out of all proportion to the resources and political will mustered to combat it,[93] and all too often the remedial and preventive strategies implemented have not directly targeted the pandemic's complex human rights causes and manifestations. The Bank's HIV/AIDS advocacy and programming accelerated from the year 2000, commensurate with the mounting global death toll and increasing degree of political support for serious action.[94]

[91] According to Bank sources as at February 2000 approximately one half of girls in Africa were likely to be pregnant by 20 years old, however most African countries at that time prohibited the distribution of condoms.

[92] HDR 2000 at 42. For more detailed discussion of the functional linkages see J Mann and D Tarantola (eds) (1996); the International Guidelines on HIV/AIDS and Human Rights, E/CN.4/1997/37, annex I; S Gruskin, K Tomasevski and A Hendriks, 'Human Rights and Responses to HIV/AIDS' in J Mann and D Tarantola (eds), *AIDS in the World II* 326–40 (1996); and S Gruskin and D Tarantola, 'Health and Human Rights,' *François-Xavier Bagnoud Centre for Health and Human Rights Working Paper No 10* (2000), available in full text at: http://www.hsph.harvard. edu/fxbcenter/FXBC_WP10—Gruskin_and_Tarantola.pdf.

[93] Interestingly Jeffrey Sachs attributes the late and inadequate international response to US domestic politics: 'Twenty-two years into the AIDS pandemic the Bush Administration insists that it won't let emotion push it into action. We need a plan, says the US; we cannot throw money at the problem. As in the late 19th century, we have the spectacle of the world's superpower treating indifference as a sign of seriousness! The truth is simpler. Africans barely count in American politics. Africans don't vote; they don't buy US products; they don't threaten violence. They are simply poor, hungry, and disease-ridden.' J Sachs, 'Deaths of the Poor and Responsibilities of the Rich,' *Project Syndicate*, June 2002, http://www.project-syndicate.cz/series/series_text.php4?id=885. See also E Lederer, 'UN chief says world leaders aren't moving fast enough to cut poverty, improve education and fight AIDS,' *Associated Press*, 29 August 2002; J Lamont, 'UN to focus on corporate help to fight AIDS,' *Financial Times*, 29 August 2002, reporting that the UN 'has abandoned its policy of relying on governments to tackle the HIV/AIDS crisis,' acknowledging that 'companies have the resources to tackle health problems where governments and NGOs are overstretched or failing.'

[94] A 'Multi-Country HIV/AIDS Program' (MAP) for Africa was approved in September 2000, the first phase of a long-term effort in Africa, involving inter alia US$1 billion to scale up ongoing activities.

The Bank's programmes in a number of countries have begun to incorporate explicit human rights components, particularly insofar as prevention strategies are concerned,[95] with strongly principled stands evident in particular cases on the requirement for appropriate legislative measures.[96] However as at 2002 these elements seemed to be very far from mainstreamed.

The same thing might be said of the CRC—the most universally ratified of the six core human rights conventions—in relation to the Bank's approaches on issues such as child labour, health, and education. The CRC is occasionally acknowledged explicitly as being part of the overarching international legal framework within which the Bank's responses are situated,[97] and more frequently as a source of 'inspiration' for the Bank's approaches, or benchmarks of international community concern or consensus on issues within the Bank's mandate. In exceptional cases the Bank has explicitly—albeit without reliance upon specific jurisprudential grounds—alleged that a client country had violated its obligations under the CRC, for example in connection with the Bank's criticisms of orphanages in Bulgaria in April 2001.[98] There is also some evidence that the CRC has assisted the Bank in defining certain legal issues: for example, the IFC and MIGA have child labour policies that have borrowed the CRC definition of child labour.[99]

Finally there are anecdotal claims that international human rights conventions, even where the country concerned has not ratified them, sometimes serve as 'reference points' for Bank appraisals of national laws and international obligations in the social and environmental assessment processes. Indeed quite a striking example is to be found in the work of the Bank's Gender and Law Thematic Group, posting a ratification chart of major international human rights instruments (ICCPR, ICESCR, CEDAW, the CRC, and ILO Conventions) bearing on equality of access to the labour market in the Middle East and Northern Africa Region.[100] However on the basis of publicly available

[95] Human rights elements of selected Bank HIV/AIDS projects are considered in chapter IV.

[96] See eg 'Zambia to provide free AIDS drugs in pilot project,' South African Broadcasting Commission, 22 August 2002 (http://www.sabcnews.com), reporting that the Bank withheld a $42 million loan until Zambia enacted legislation criminalising the deliberate infection of HIV.

[97] See eg World Bank, *Child Labour: Issues and Directions for the World Bank* (1998). As at the year 2000 this was not a formal policy document, although it had by then been considered by the Board on an informal basis, and in the view of some Bank officials was likely eventually to become Bank policy.

[98] *World Bank Development News*, 2 April 2001.

[99] Interviews in Washington DC in February 2000. Indeed the IFC's work on child labour is significantly more advanced in its recognition of relevant international standards than is the comparable work of the IDA/IBRD. See chapter IV below at nn 226–45, and chapter VI below at nn 269–76 and accompanying text.

[100] See 'Gender—Work in Progress' links at http://lnweb18.worldbank.org/mna/mena.nsf/, last updated February 2002. As stated there, 'in order to comprehensively address the gender gap in the [Middle East and North Africa, or MNA] region, the World Bank commissioned a study to better understand the possible impact of MNA countries' legal frameworks on women's economic participation in the region. In this context, many analysts have recognised that legal frameworks are, on their own, not a sufficient indicator of progress or otherwise regarding women's status in a country. On the one hand, the law may discriminate, but in practice the discriminatory texts may not be

resources this would appear to be an isolated case. Certainly, as of the year 2002, written internal guidance or policy material encouraging more systematic exploration of such normative and functional linkages—in the gender, HIV/AIDS, child labour, judicial reform or other areas—did not appear to exist.

On the basis of overall research and interviews, it seems safe to conclude that international human rights standards and instruments, while known to many officials within the Bank, normally those working directly in areas such as education, gender issues, HIV/AIDS issues, child labour, and to some extent judicial reform, have:

(i) arisen only very selectively—and usually marginally—in a practical pro-grammatic context;[101]

(ii) been of little practical relevance in the discharge of the Bank's social safe-guard functions and assessment procedures; and

(iii) been of at best marginal or 'inspirational' relevance to the Bank's research agenda and substantive policy development.

THE IMF

The IMF, like the World Bank, is a specialised agency of the United Nations.[102] It was established during the 1944 Bretton Woods Conference in order to help regulate the international monetary system, encourage international co-operation to counter prevailing recession and protectionism, and to 'discourage individual countries from pursuing policies that would beggar their neighbours and eventually themselves.'[103] Against the international chaos of the 1930s, it was envisaged that the IMF 'would generate benefits for international trade in the form of stable (though not necessarily fixed) exchange rates, whilst, at the same time, avoiding the deflationary rigidities of the gold standard mecha-nism.'[104] Thus the essential characteristic of the Bretton Woods order was that

applied. In other instances, the law may be progressive, but can be ignored, misinterpreted, misap-plied or simply unknown to those who could make the most use of it, whether affected parties or those in the legal profession.'

[101] This is not to say, of course, that the Bank has ignored important human rights issues like child labour in practice. The Bank reportedly has withdrawn its support from projects in the past where child labour has been reported. However the Bank's policies and selective programmatic responses appear to be linked more strongly to ILO Convention No. 182 on Extreme Forms of Child Labour, a Convention of relatively limited scope dealing only with extreme forms of exploitation rather than 'child labour' in the more holistic sense dealt with in the CRC. No doubt ILO 182—the terms of which the Bank appears to have influenced to some degree at the outset—presents a rela-tively easy and (in political terms) uncontroversial set of operational parameters as far as the Bank is concerned, posited against the added normative and functional inter-linkages and cultural com-plexities implicit in article 32 of the CRC. For more detailed discussion see chapter IV below at nn 226–45, and chapter VI below at nn 269–76 and accompanying text.

[102] Agreement Between the United Nations and the International Monetary Fund, Article IV(2), 16 UNTS 328, 332 (1948) [hereinafter called the IMF/UN Relationship Agreement].

[103] G Bird, *IMF Lending to Developing Countries: Issues and Evidence* (1995) at 1.

[104] G Bird (1995) at 1.

exchange rate relationships, rather than being within the domain of domestic economic policy, were to be governed by a set of internationally agreed rules, based essentially on the defence of established 'par values.'[105] The overall ambition of the system's architects was to ensure a world of full employment and economic growth.[106]

Membership in the Fund is open to all countries that subscribe to the principles contained in the Articles of Agreement.[107] IMF membership also entitles States to join the World Bank, where lower income members can obtaining financing for development projects.[108] As for the Bank, the highest governing authority in the IMF resides in its Board of Governors, consisting of one Governor and one Alternative Governor appointed by each member country, usually drawn from member States' Ministers of Finance or heads of central banks.[109] Day-to-day management of the affairs of the Fund is carried out by the Executive Board, to whom the Board of Governors has delegated many of its powers.[110] Selected by the Executive Board, the IMF's Managing Director chairs Executive Board meetings, and serves as head of the organisation's staff. The International Monetary and Financial Committee (which until September 1999 was known as the 'Interim Committee,' notwithstanding that it had been in existence since the 1970s)[111]—a body composed of 24 IMF Governors, ministers or other 'officials of comparable rank'—meets twice per year and provides ministerial guidance to the Executive Board, and also reports to the Board of Governors on the management and functioning of the international monetary system and on proposals to amend the Articles of Agreement.[112] Finally, a body known as the Development Committee—composed of 24 Governors of the World Bank or the IMF (or ministers or others of comparable rank)—advises and reports to the Boards of Governors of both the Bank and the Fund on development issues.[113]

---

[105] M Guitián, 'The Unique Nature of the Responsibilities of the International Monetary Fund,' *IMF Pamphlet Series* No.46 (1992) at 7; G Bird (1995) at 2. See further discussion below nn 124–27 and accompanying text.

[106] G Bird (1995) at 1.

[107] See Article II, Sections 1 and 2: 'The original members of the Fund shall be those of the countries represented at the United Nations Monetary and Financial Conference whose governments accept membership before December 31, 1945. Membership shall be open to other countries at such times and in accordance with such terms as may be prescribed by the Board of Governors. The terms, including the terms for subscriptions, shall be based on principles consistent with those applied to other countries that are already members.'

[108] D Bradlow and C Grossman (1995) at 419.

[109] See Article XII, Sections 1 and 2 of the Articles of Association; and 'Organisation: IMF Structure Shaped by Articles of Agreement' (1997) 26 *IMF Survey* 3.

[110] See Article XII, Section 3 of the Articles of Agreement.

[111] Its full name was the 'Interim Committee of the Board of Governors on the International Monetary System': 'Organisation: IMF Structure Shaped by Articles of Agreement' (1997) 26 *IMF Survey* 3. See IMF Factsheet at http://www.imf.org.

[112] 'Organisation: IMF Structure Shaped by Articles of Agreement,' 26 *IMF Survey* 3 (1997); IMF Factsheet http://www.imf.org.

[113] 'Organisation: IMF Structure Shaped by Articles of Agreement,' 26 *IMF Survey* 3, 4 (1997); IMF Factsheet http://www.imf.org.

As for the Bank, of the Fund's 24 Executive Directors nineteen are elected by the other members, and five are appointed by the five members having the largest quotas.[114] At the turn of the century the five members with the largest quota holdings and voting power, respectively, in percentage terms were: the United States (17.49 per cent and 17.16 per cent); Germany (6.12 per cent and 6.02 per cent); Japan (6.27 per cent and 6.16 per cent); France (5.06 per cent and 4.97 per cent); and the United Kingdom (5.06 per cent and 4.97 per cent).[115] As with the World Bank, the weighted voting system in the Fund is one of its most controversial features. The combined voting power of the five appointed Executive Directors, alone, is almost forty percent of total, proportionately far in excess of the voting power of developing country Executive Directors, who represent the needs of the members most critically in need of IMF assistance. The G–7 countries together account for a majority of voting shares, and therefore are in a position to determine Fund policy. Further, any IMF program needs an eighty-five percent majority vote in order to pass,[116] which gives the United States an effective veto. Not only does the United States representative wield enormous influence, but the United States Secretary of the Treasury has 'complete authority' in directing the Executive Director's position on particular issues.[117] The practice of consensus decision-making on the IFIs' Executive

[114] Each member of the Fund has a 'quota,' expressed in terms of 'Special Drawing Rights' [hereinafter 'SDRs'], that is equal to its subscription in the IMF. The SDR is an international reserve asset created by the Fund in 1969, allocated to members in order to supplant existing reserve assets. It functions as the Fund's basic unit of account, and occasionally that of other international and regional organisations and international conventions.' See 'SDR: An International Reserve Asset' (1997) 26 *IMF Survey* 20. The SDR's value is determined daily on the basis of a basket of four currencies: the US dollar, the euro, the Japanese yen, and the pound sterling. As at August 2002 the SDR was worth approximately US$1.33. Member States' quotas, broadly designed to reflect size of economy, are fundamental determinants of their financial and organisational relations with the Fund. Quota subscriptions provide the Fund with financial resources and thereby enable it to fulfil its obligations to members in need of balance of payments assistance. Quotas also determine members' voting power, and entitlement to IMF resources and SDR allocations: 'Quotas: Quotas Determine Members' Voting Power, Financial Access' (1997) 26 *IMF Survey* 4, 4–5, and Articles III, XII (Section 5) and XIX of the Articles of Association. IMF, 'IMF Financial Activities: Update August 30, 2002,' http://www.imf.org/external/np/tre/activity/2002/083002.htm.

[115] About the IMF, http://www.imf.org.

[116] J Gold, 'Natural Disasters and Other Emergencies Beyond Control: Assistance by the IMF' (1990) 24(3) *The International Lawyer* 621, 627.

[117] Former Treasury Secretary Blumenthal emphasised his influential role in directing US policies in the multilateral banks to the US Congress: 'I would not and I would like the record to show that, exaggerate [sic] the degree of authority I have in this matter. I have complete authority . . . to direct how our executive directors vote. I can only be overruled by the [United States] President himself'— *Foreign Assistance and Related Agencies Appropriations for 1979: Hearings Before the Subcommittee on Foreign Operations and Related Agencies of the House Committee on Appropriations*, 95th Cong., 2d Sess. Pt. 1, 429 (1978), cited in M Elahi, 'The Impact of Financial Institutions on the Realisation of Human Rights: Case Study of the International Monetary Fund in Chile' (1986) 6 *Boston College Third World Law Journal* 143, 145. See also J Gold, 'Weighted Voting Power: Some Limits and Some Problems' (1974) 68 *American Journal of International Law* 687–89; and a discussion of relevant US legislation (including the *Foreign Assistance Act 1961*) in M Elahi (1986) at 158–59; A Chayes and A Chayes, *The New Sovereignty: Compliance with International Regulatory Agreements* (1995) at 91 and 335; F Smith, Jr, 'The Politics of IMF Lending' (1984) 4(1) *Cato Journal* 211–41, 213–14; and E Spiro (1979) at 136–38.

Boards does little more than mask these underlying power imbalances.[118] With these factors in mind, along with the 'informal influence' exercised by the US government in Washington DC, the IMF's power structure has been criticised as providing the US with the ability to pursue its own foreign policy objectives through the Fund, cloaked in the 'illusion of multi-lateralism.'[119]

This asymmetry in decision-making power makes a mockery of the contention, still heard with surprising frequency today, that the Fund is an apolitical body. But as has been clear for a long time, 'decisions to provide loans and credits to other nations are *inherently political* and cannot be separated from the larger policy framework of international relations'[120] [emphasis added]. The IMF is 'intensely, and unavoidably,' a 'political institution whose policies are determined solely by the majority vote of shareholders—meaning in nearly all cases the consensus of the developed nations.'[121] Further, it is increasingly obvious that at very least a thorough understanding of political and social circumstances at the national level, whether or not such issues form an element of direct conditionality, is required in order to increase the prospects for success of financial interventions.[122] Finally, as is the case under the World Bank's Charter, traditional distinctions between economic and political or social or other non-'economic' factors have become difficult if not impossible to sustain in practice, as a review of the Fund's current policies and activities will shortly confirm.

---

[118] HDR 2002, 'Deepening Democracy at the Global Level' (chapter 5), at 113: 'Although many organisations work by "consensus" and say that this diminishes the importance of formal voting power and seats, consensus decisions are always underpinned by the realities of power and a knowledge of which actors can veto or push final decisions. In reality, consensus decision-making seldom gives voice to marginalised actors.'

[119] C Payer (1974) at 31. This (im)balance of power explains why decisions are possible in the Fund which would be unthinkable in other parts of the UN system. For example in 1982 the Fund approved a loan of 1.1 billion US dollars to South Africa, notwithstanding that the UN General Assembly during the same year had rejected a proposal for financial assistance for the apartheid regime by 121 votes to 10, with 14 abstentions (see GA Res. 37/39 of 3 December 1982). Developing member state demands that the loan be subject to conditionality, in particular a departure from apartheid, were not heeded. With the backing of Canada and a number of industrialised Western European members, the US secured approval for a loan with low conditionality by a 53% majority of votes on the Executive Board. See W Berg and G Thole, 'IMF Policies and Their Adverse Consequences for Human Rights' (1986) 3 *GDR Committee for Human Rights Bulletin* 164–74, 165; E Brett, 'The World's View of the IMF' in *Latin America Bureau, The Poverty Brokers: The IMF and Latin America* 30–48, 41–42 (1983); and 'US Treasury Denies Bias on IMF Loans,' *The Guardian*, 19 May 1983, referring to a report prepared for the House Foreign Affairs Sub-Committee by the Congressional Research Service, containing allegations of US influence in the multi-lateral financial institutions for political purposes.

[120] A Hirschman, *National Power and the Structure of the State* (1980), cited without page reference in N Ball, J, Friedman and C Rossiter, 'The Role of International Financial Institutions in Preventing and Resolving Conflict' in D Cortright (ed), *The Price of Peace: Incentives and International Conflict Prevention* 243–64, 245 (1997). As those authors observe (at 245): '[T]his diplomatic fiction has long been dispensed with in loan negotiations.'

[121] N Ball, J Friedman and C Rossiter (1997) at 245–46.

[122] See eg E Solingen, 'The New Multilateralism and Nonproliferation: Bringing in Domestic Politics' (1995) 1(2) *Global Governance* 220–21; N Ball, J Friedman and C Rossiter (1997) at 250.

The Role, Policies and Facilities of the Fund Today

As amended in 1978 and unchanged to date,[123] the specific purposes of the Fund are set out in Article I of its Articles of Agreement.[124] That Article provides:

The purposes of the International Monetary Fund are:

(i) To promote international monetary co-operation through a permanent institution which provides the machinery for consultation and collaboration on international monetary problems.

(ii) To facilitate the expansion and balanced growth of international trade, and to contribute thereby to the promotion and maintenance of high levels of employment and real income and to the development of the productive resources of all members as primary objectives of economic policy.

(iii) To promote exchange stability, to maintain orderly exchange arrangements among members, and to avoid competitive exchange depreciation.

(iv) To assist in the establishment of a multilateral system of payments in respect of current transactions between members and in the elimination of foreign exchange restrictions which hamper the growth of world trade.

(v) To give confidence to members by making the general resources of the Fund temporarily available to them under adequate safeguards, thus providing them with the opportunity to correct maladjustments in their balance of payments without resorting to measures destructive of national or international prosperity.

(vi) In accordance with the above, to shorten the duration and lessen the degree of disequilibrium in the international balances of payments of members.

The Fund shall be guided in all its policies and decisions by the purposes set forth in this Article.

---

[123] During the late 1990s the Fund campaigned actively for an amendment to include the liberalisation of capital accounts within its authorised purposes. However as at July 2000 momentum for changes of this kind appeared to diminish, chiefly as a result of the following factors: (a) criticism over the Fund's policies during the East Asian crisis, including the very pointed criticisms by the outspoken former Bank Chief Economist Joseph Stiglitz directed at the Fund's erstwhile missionary zeal against capital controls of any kind; (b) the relatively successful use of capital controls by Malaysia during the East Asian crisis; and (c) the reality revealed in East Asia, Russia, and elsewhere that (if it should not already have been apparent) sound (economic) institutions are prerequisites to successful liberalisation strategies. See the record of interview with Bank Chief Economist Nicholas Stern in *World Bank Development News*, 27 July 2000. As the Fund's Deputy Managing Director put it in June 2000: 'The Asian crisis . . . aroused a spirited debate over capital account liberalisation. The IMF has emphasised an orderly and well-sequenced liberalisation process, supported by an adequate institutional setup to strengthen the ability of financial intermediaries and other market participants to manage risk. Introducing or tightening capital controls is not an effective means to deal with fundamental economic imbalances. Any temporary breathing space such measures provide has to be used wisely and needs to be weighed against the long-term damage to investor confidence and the distorting effects on resource allocation.' IMF, 'Vienna address: Sugisaki reviews issues and reforms that have absorbed the IMF over past 15 years' (2000) 29(13) *IMF Survey* 215–16, 216.

[124] Articles of Agreement of the International Monetary Fund, 27 December 1945, 60 Stat. 1401, 2 UNTS 39, amended, 28 July 1969, 20 UST 2775, amended 1 April 1978, 29 UST 2203 [hereinafter IMF Articles].

As indicated earlier this scheme of international monetary cooperation was based upon a fixed linkage between currencies in the international system, established by assigning each currency a 'par value' against gold. Once this value was fixed, the currency would only be permitted to fluctuate within narrow limits.[125] Moreover the convertibility of currencies within this system was guaranteed, with the value of the currencies not only fixed to gold but redeemable at gold value.[126] The final element within this system was the establishment of a pool of currencies and gold for short-term purchase by members experiencing temporary balance of payments difficulties,[127] to be considered in more depth shortly.

The breakdown of the 'par value' system the early 1970s[128] for the first time brought critical evaluation of the IMF's role in the international monetary system. Few questions had been asked throughout most of the 1950s and 1960s, given that by most measures the world economy had been performing satisfactorily. In these circumstances, 'the question of the extent to which success was due to the [IMF] simply did not arise.'[129] But the breakdown of the Bretton Woods system and its replacement with a much looser set of international monetary arrangements left the IMF disoriented, with little or no obvious systemic role.[130] The IMF's marginalisation was exacerbated in the 1970s and 1980s by a number of factors, most importantly:

(a) the substantial privatisation of balance of payments financing;[131]
(b) the evolution of international financial arrangements towards generalised flexible exchange rates, over which the Fund appeared unable to exercise effective control;[132]

---

[125] A Orford, 'Globalisation and the Right to Development' in P Alston (ed), *People's Rights* 127–84, 147–48 (2001).

[126] As Orford explains: 'The US dollar operated as the reserve currency of global commerce. Any dealer could trade any currency linked to the IMF system for US dollars, which were "as good as gold." The quotation of prices for goods and services in international trade could be denominated in US dollars. It was thought that the growth of international trade would therefore be possible, due to the freely convertible nature of currencies.' A Orford (2001) at 148.

[127] See A Orford (2001) at 148.

[128] For a discussion on the reasons for this see M de Vries, *The IMF in a Changing World 1945–85* (1986) at 40–41 and 94–95; M Malloy, 'Shifting Paradigms: Institutional Roles in a Changing World' (1994) 62 *Fordham Law Review* 1911, 1922; R Edwards *International Monetary Collaboration* (1985) at 497–98; J Gold, 'Strengthening the Soft International Law of Exchange Arrangements' in J Gold (ed), Vol. II *Legal and Institutional Aspects of the International Monetary System: Selected Essays* 515, 518–27 (1984). As Orford relates: 'The system of monetary cooperation and exchange controls failed from the 1960s. As early as 1962, countries ceased adhering to fixed exchange rates in order to manage domestic economic needs. The episode that officially brought to an end the system envisaged at Bretton Woods was the withdrawal of the US dollar from convertibility on 15 August 1971. In that year, the US showed its first trade deficit, and with foreign holdings of US$80 billion outstanding, only US$10 billion in reserves and a run on the US dollar by speculators imminent, President Richard Nixon withdrew convertibility to protect the dollar. That withdrawal fractured the basis for the IMF.' A Orford (2001) at 148.

[129] G Bird (1995) at 2–3.

[130] G Bird (1995) at 3; A Orford (2001) at 147–49.

[131] G Bird (1995) at 4–5.

[132] M de Vries (1986) at 95; G Bird (1995) at 3–4.

(c) the diminishing importance of the Fund as a source of official reserve creation;[133] and

(d) the trend away from international monetary arrangements towards regional ones, most clearly illustrated in 1979 with the establishment of the European Monetary System,[134] and echoed more recently in the Asian region in the aftermath of the East Asian crisis.

The 'retreat from policy co-ordination' continued through the 1980s, and such co-ordination as existed was managed largely outside the IMF by the G–7 (now G–8) or G–3 countries.[135] The downgrading of the Fund's systemic role, as industrial countries and some of the more creditworthy developing countries turned elsewhere for finance, left the Fund to deal with the low income countries that had nowhere else to go.[136] This remained the case throughout the 1990s, with increasing reliance on concessional and other new and relatively long-term financing facilities (particularly the Enhanced Structural Adjustment Facility—ESAF—and its successor the Poverty Reduction and Growth Facility—PRGF—to be discussed shortly), contributing to unease both within and outside the Fund as to the extent to which the Fund was seen to be (or was in fact) taking on 'development agency' responsibilities.[137] The often harsh conditions

---

[133] 'Ironically, [the 1970s] had begun with the introduction of the [SDR]; and even as late as 1976, . . . the Fund was setting the objective of establishing the SDR as the principal reserve asset in the international financial system. The reality, however, was that, with flexible exchange rates and the private financing of payments deficits, the quantity of official reserves became viewed as an unimportant issue. The "system" moved over to the wider use of certain national currencies as international reserve assets, thereby becoming a multiple currency system; SDR creation was not maintained, and attempts to introduce a substitution account failed; . . . Some critics observed gleefully that, rather than just being marginalised, the SDR had been almost obliterated. Certainly no effective role seemed to be left for the Fund in influencing global reserve adequacy—a role that had appeared central in the 1960s'—G Bird (1995) at 4–5.

[134] G Bird (1995) at 5; M Malloy (1994) at 1923.

[135] 'The late 1980s illustrated the degree of overlap between the former systemic role of the IMF in terms of exchange rate management, balance of payments adjustment, and the avoidance of world-wide inflation or deflation, and the actual role being contemporaneously played by a small sub-group of powerful industrial countries outside the auspices of the Fund'—G Bird (1995) at 4. Needless to say this kind of 'forum shopping' by the major industrialised powers, wresting responsibility for global economic issues properly within the mandates of more (but far from perfectly) accountable and representative forums, continues to be highly controversial. See eg G Monbiot, 'They don't owe us, we owe them,' *The Guardian*, 20 July 2000.

[136] See generally G Bird. (1995) at 5–47 and 50–51; and A Orford (2001) at 148–49: 'The role and function of the IMF has . . . changed dramatically from that imagined for it in 1945. . . . Par values have been eliminated and currency values are established largely through currency markets. The IMF no longer directly influences the monetary policies of the world's developed economies. Developed countries no longer use the IMF's pool of extended resources which expose them to IMF conditions and advice. The IMF has a significant impact, however, on the policies of governments of developing countries. It has changed its focus from promoting exchange stability and international monetary cooperation amongst the richest countries to managing and monitoring the economies of the poorest.'

[137] See eg D Carreau, 'Why Not Merge the International Monetary Fund (IMF) with the International Bank for Reconstruction and Development (World Bank)?' (1990) 62 *Fordham Law Review* 1989, 1998: 'The IMF thus became involved in managing the long-term economic policies of its developing and "transforming" members. Its assistance, originally limited to financing

attaching to IMF assistance and the contested ideological assumptions under-pinning them have also generated widespread criticism, given that low income countries, alone, are exposed to IMF 'medicine' as a lender of last resort.[138]

Surveillance

The Fund does retain systemic responsibilities under the Articles of Agreement, although not nearly to the extent envisaged by their drafters. Article IV, Section 3(a) provides that '[t]he Fund shall oversee the international monetary system in order to ensure its effective operation, and shall oversee the compliance of each member with its obligations under Section 1 of this Article.' Elements of the international monetary system [IMS] and members' obligations are elaborated in Article IV, Section 1 as follows, although naturally these must be read in light of the evolution of the Fund's role in practice:

> Recognising that the essential purpose of the international monetary system is to pro-vide a framework that facilitates the exchange of goods, services, and capital among countries, *and that sustains sound economic growth*, and that *a principal objective is the continuing development of the orderly underlying conditions that are necessary for financial and economic stability*, each member undertakes to collaborate with the Fund and other members to assure orderly exchange arrangements and to promote a stable system of exchange rates. In particular, each member shall:
>
> (i) endeavour to direct its economic and financial policies toward the objective of *fostering orderly economic growth* with reasonable price stability, with due regard to its circumstances;
> (ii) seek to promote stability by fostering orderly underlying economic and financial conditions and a monetary system that does not tend to produce erratic disruptions;
> (iii) avoid manipulating exchange rates or the international monetary system in order to prevent effective balance of payments adjustment or to gain an unfair competitive advantage over other members; and
> (iv) follow exchange policies compatible with the undertakings under this Section [emphasis added].

In practice, the enforcement of international monetary rules as set out in the Articles varies in accordance with how the member's deviation manifests itself. In cases where the member's monetary policies produce balance of payments problems serious enough to lead it to seek IMF financial assistance, the IMF uses its conditionality policies to enforce its rules. In other cases, the IMF seeks to promote compliance only through 'peer pressure.'[139]

---

short-term difficulties, has been completely modified to address long-term, structural imbalances. And this is precisely the World Bank's mission.'

[138] See eg D Carreau (1990) at 1998.

[139] See D Bradlow and C Grossman (1995) at 419; J Gold (ed) (1984) at 527–30; R Edwards (1985) at 638–42; N Ball, J Friedman and C Rossiter (1997) at 246–47.

The Fund's surveillance functions are spelled out in detail in Article IV, Section 3(b):

In order to fulfil its functions under [Article IV, Section 3(a)], the Fund shall exercise firm surveillance over the exchange rate policies of members, and shall adopt specific principles for the guidance of all members with respect to those policies.[140] *Each member shall provide the Fund with the information necessary for such surveillance,* and, when requested by the Fund, shall consult with it on the member's exchange rate policies. The principles adopted by the Fund shall be consistent with co-operative arrangements by which members maintain the value of their currencies in relation to the value of the currency or currencies of other members, as well as with other exchange arrangements of a member's choice consistent with the purposes of the Fund and Section 1 of this Article. *These principles shall respect the domestic social and political policies of members,* and in applying these principles *the Fund shall pay due regard to the circumstances of members.*' [emphasis added]

The IMF fulfils its surveillance responsibilities principally through annual bilateral 'Article IV' consultations with individual countries, and multilateral surveillance twice per year in the context of its World Economic Outlook exercise.[141] The italicised extracts in Article IV, Section 1 above have been cited in support of the proposition that an exploration by the Fund of member States' underlying social and political conditions—which under contemporary development thinking are inseparable from what once were considered purely 'economic' factors[142]—is within power, contrary to the Fund's official interpretation of that provision.[143] These and other arguments concerning the limits of the Fund's regulatory and supervisory jurisdiction will be explored more fully

---

[140] The Fund, acting under Article IV, has announced three principles for the guidance of all members with respect to their exchange rate policies. These are: '(A) A member shall avoid manipulating exchange rates or the international monetary system in order to prevent effective balance of payments adjustment or to gain an unfair competitive advantage over other members. (B) A member should intervene in the exchange market if necessary to counter disorderly conditions which may be characterised *inter alia* by disruptive short-term movements in the exchange value of its currency. (C) Members should take into account in their intervention policies the interests of other members, including those of the countries in whose currencies they intervene': Decision No. 5392-(77/63), *Selected Decisions of the International Monetary Fund and Selected Documents* [hereinafter *Selected Decisions*], 9th (1981), pp. 11–12, cited in J Gold (ed) (1984) at 546.

[141] See eg IMF, *World Economic Outlook May 1998: A Survey by the Staff of the International Monetary Fund* (1998). Other means of monitoring in the absence of IMF resources are 'precautionary arrangements, enhanced surveillance, and program monitoring'—'The IMF at a Glance,' April 1998 http://www.imf.org/external/np/exr/facts/glance.htm.

[142] See below chapter III at nn 179–80 and accompanying text.

[143] B Rajagopal, 'Crossing the Rubicon: Synthesising the Soft International Law of the IMF and Human Rights' (1993) 11 *Boston University International Law Journal* 81 at 102–3. See also R Edwards (1985) at 508: According to former influential IMF figure Jacques Polak, 'French and US negotiators reached the view that exchange rate stability should be pursued not primarily by intervention or exchange control but by aiming at a stable domestic system. This is the message conveyed by [Article IV, Section 1] . . . The most fundamental layer would be something like social and political conditions—if they are stable, then one is more likely to have stable economic conditions[.]' These arguments suggest that the boundaries of the IMS over which the Fund must exercise supervisory jurisdiction extend well beyond the traditional realms of international monetary law.

shortly, after considering the extent of the IMF's human rights impacts and responsibilities.

For present purposes it is sufficient to note that the Fund has gone some way towards recognising the need to address certain politically sensitive issues—such as domestic military expenditures[144]—during the course of its Article IV consultations, but clearly there is some way further to go. On a technical level the collapse of the 'par value' system was probably the factor which contributed most significantly to the expansion in the range of issues considered by the Fund to be within its mandate under Article IV. As Bradlow explains, in a floating exchange rate system, 'the exchange rate becomes only one of the many economic variables that can influence the country's balance of payments. Floating exchange rates allow a country to correct a balance of payments problem by making adjustments either in the value of its currency or in its domestic economy.'[145] This dramatically expanded the range of issues that needed to be included in Article IV consultations. Any issues that might directly affect the value of a member's currency and its ability to adjust to changes in its balance of payments—including issues such as labour, agricultural policies and health—need to be included.[146] The IMF has expanded this list over time, with the result that, apart from military expenditures, during the course of its Article IV consultations the IMF regularly canvasses such matters as environmental issues, governance issues and corruption, education, housing, welfare and unemploy-

---

[144] See eg A Chayes and A Chayes (1995) at 236: 'Traditionally, discussion of members' military expenditures was taboo in [Article IV] consultations, on national security and sovereignty grounds. In 1989, IMF managing director Michel Camdessus began speaking out publicly about the impact of military expenditures on developing country economic development and stability. The campaign intensified through 1991, culminating in Camdessus's closing address at the IMF annual meeting in October of that year, where he said: "As regards military spending, I was impressed by the broad support for our aim to study more carefully the problem. An immediate priority must be to collect full and accurate information, and analyse the economic implications." In the carefully modulated language of the IMF, this was clear notice that the existing norms of monetary conduct were changing. The Executive Directors instructed the staff to include the subject of military expenditures in Article IV consultations. *Thenceforth military spending would be viewed as an economic as well as a strategic/political issue.* Military spending decisions would be dealt with on the same footing as other fiscal decisions. *Trade-offs would be examined more systematically so as to achieve a sounder balance among military, monetary, and development priorities'* [emphasis added]. For an assessment of the Fund's effectiveness in this regard, see N Ball, J Friedman and C Rossiter (1997) at 246–47. And for a discussion on the incompatibility of military spending and 'militarism' with both human rights and economic growth, see W Felice, 'Militarism and Human Rights' (1998) 74(1) *International Affairs* 25–40. By way of illustration, the IMF reportedly led the international donor community in suspending aid to the government of Zimbabwe, due at least partly to excessive military spending arising from Zimbabwe's military adventurism in the DRC. In September 2000 the Fund stated that 'no support would be given to Zimbabwe until President Robert Mugabe solves such issues as illegal seizures of white-owned farms, political violence and uncontrolled spending.' See *World Bank Development News*, 15 June 2000, and UN Wire (www.unfoundation.org), 14 September 2000.

[145] D Bradlow (1996) at 69. See generally J Sachs and F Larrain, *Macroeconomics in the Global Economy* (1993).

[146] D Bradlow (1996) at 69–70.

ment related matters (the latter three coming within the term 'social safety net', SSN).[147]

On a superficial level there is little 'enforcement' atmosphere evident in the dialogues carried out under Article IV. Rather, the emphasis is said to be on obtaining a clear picture of developments in members' monetary and overall economic situations, and identifying potential or emerging problems in a timely fashion. The methodology has been described elsewhere as 'professional analysis, argument, and persuasion about what are treated as technical issues of economic policy.'[148] One needs to be cautious about accepting the myth of technicality and neutrality, however, a concern addressed in more depth shortly.

As for the specific provisions in Article IV, the obligations on member States are of a 'soft law' character. While there are obvious advantages in this in promoting policy flexibility for governments, the (imprecisely drafted) obligations themselves limit the possibilities for firm enforcement measures.[149] This wide latitude is reflected in the non-judgemental character of Executive Board 'conclusions' taken under Article IV, in contrast to the more legally authoritative 'decisions' on other items of Fund business.[150]

The final point to be made here, to be explored in greater detail later, is that the extent of the Fund's policy influence or leverage under Article IV varies significantly according to the country and circumstances concerned. A crisis-stricken nation in sub-Saharan Africa—irrespective of their actual technical capacity to implement the Fund's wide-ranging reform menu—will nonetheless have an obvious incentive to win the Fund's stamp of approval as a necessary precondition to development aid programs,[151] foreign direct investment and other capital in-flows. Benign and technocratic characterisations of the 'advisory' or 'soft law' nature of Article IV consultations need to be taken with a pinch of salt in such circumstances, posited against the (at best) glancing impact of external advice upon the Teflon hides of the major shareholder states.

---

[147] D Bradlow (1996) at 70; H Morais, 'A Festschrift Honoring Professor Louis B Sohn (April 8, 2000): The Globalisation of Human Rights Law and the Role of International Financial Institutions in Promoting Human Rights' (2000) 33 *George Washington International Law Review* 71–96, 86; IMF, 'Good Governance: The IMF's Role' (1997), http://www.imf.org/external/pubs/ft/exrp/govern/govindex.htm; IMF, 'Social Dimensions of the IMF's Policy Dialogue,' *IMF Pamphlet Series* No. 47 (1995).

[148] A Chayes and A Chayes (1995) at 236.

[149] 'The intervention policy of the United States demonstrates that members adopt their own understanding of [the term "disorderly conditions" in Principle B of the Fund's principles under Article IV, Section 3(b)] and that the concept is sufficiently imprecise to permit sharp changes in policy': J Gold (ed) (1984) at 550.

[150] J Gold (ed) (1984) at 567. And at 543: 'The word "conclusions" was chosen because it sounded less like an assertion of authority than "decisions." Furthermore, the Executive Board does not adopt conclusions that it purports to have formulated itself. It implicitly endorses as the conclusions of its debate the summing up by the Managing Director as Chairman of the Executive Board.'

[151] Under the practice known as 'cross-conditionality' the Bank will ordinarily not enter into a program with a country in which an IMF 'stabilisation' program is not in place. As at July 2000 there were some signs within the IMF Executive Board to relax this requirement, however. See *World Bank Development News*, 18 July 2000. See chapter III, n 36 and accompanying text.

Financial Assistance

Apart from surveillance, the other principal activities of the Fund relate to financial assistance.[152] Although the legal mandate for IMF financing is separate and distinct from the mandate for surveillance, financing is said to interact in a 'symbiotic' fashion with the purposes of, and needs for, surveillance.[153] Except in the case of the ESAF and PRGF, members avail themselves of the IMF's financial resources by purchasing other members' currencies or SDRs with an equivalent amount of their own currencies.[154] Under Article V, Section 3(b) of the Articles, a member's entitlement to the use of the Fund's general resources is subject to the following conditions:

(i)   the member's use of the general resources would be in accordance with the provisions of the Articles and the policies adopted under them;

(ii) the member is able to demonstrate that it has a need to make the purchase because of its balance of payments or its reserve position or developments in its reserves;

(iii) the proposed purchase would be a reserve tranche purchase (see below), or would not cause the Fund's holdings of the purchasing member's currency to exceed two hundred percent of its quota; and

(iv) the Fund has not previously made a declaration under any of Articles V (Section 5), VI (Section 1) or XXVI [Section 2(a)], that the member wishing to purchase is ineligible to use the general resources of the Fund.[155]

(1) Financial Policies

The IMF's financial policies represent the modalities for use of its financial resources under existing financial facilities. The most important policies for present purposes are the following:

---

[152] 'The IMF at a Glance,' April 1998 http://www.imf.org/external/np/exr/facts/glance.htm. The Fund also maintains significant technical assistance capacities and functions in a range of areas, including the design and implementation of monetary policy, institution-building (such as the development of central banks or treasuries), handling and accounting for transactions with the Fund, and the collection and refinement of statistical data. It is beyond the scope of this chapter to include any detailed survey of these and other technical assistance measures, although their broad parameters and limitations emerge from the general discussion below concerning the Fund's financial assistance activities, and conditionality in particular.

[153] IMF, 'The Role of the IMF: Financing and Its Interactions with Adjustment and Surveillance,' *IMF Pamphlet Series* (1995) at 3–4.

[154] Article V, Section 2(a). See J Gold, 'Use of the International Monetary Fund's Resources: "Conditionality" and "Unconditionality" as Legal Categories' (1971) 6 *Journal of International Law and Economics* 1, 7.

[155] Article V, Section 5 deals with members (in the opinion of the Fund) using the general resources in a manner contrary to the Fund's purposes. Article VI, Section 1 is directed against members using the Fund's general resources to meet 'a large or sustained outflow of capital,' except from the reserve tranche. Article XXVI, Section 2(a)—without intending to limit the operation of the first two mentioned Articles—concerns the failure by a member to fulfil any of its obligations under the Articles.

(a) Reserve Tranche policies: A member may withdraw up to twenty-five percent of its quota at any time, subject only to balance of payments needs. This drawing does not constitute a use of IMF credit and is not subject to an obligation to repay.[156]

(b) Credit Tranche policies: Credits under regular IMF facilities—Stand-by Arrangements (SBAs) and the Extended Fund Facility (EFF)—are made available to members in tranches, or segments, of 25 percent of quota. Once a member has submitted a request to purchase from the credit tranches, it is then obliged to abide by IMF recommendations concerning its fiscal policy, payment plan, exchange rates, and adjustment program.[157] According to the Fund, for first credit tranche drawings (ie for the first 25 percent of quota), members are required to do no more than demonstrate reasonable efforts to overcome their balance of payments imbalance. The Fund sets no specific demands concerning particular macro-economic indicators that affect the balance of payments, nor any specific date for repurchase.[158] It is only upper credit tranche drawings (over 25 percent of quota) that are normally 'phased,'[159] depending upon the satisfaction by the member of the Fund's 'performance criteria.'[160]

Other financial policies include the Policy on Emergency Assistance, allowing members to make drawings to meet balance of payments needs arising from 'sudden and unforeseeable natural disasters and in post-conflict situations.' Such assistance is normally available to a limit of 25 percent of quota, 'providing that the member is co-operating with the IMF[,]' and does not entail performance criteria or a phasing of disbursements. A basic rate of charge applies, and loans must be repaid within 3 and a quarter to five years. Of further interest are the Debt and Debt-Service Reduction Policies. According to the Fund, '[p]art of a credit extended to a member by the IMF under regular facilities can be set aside to finance operations involving debt principal and debt service reduction.

---

[156] See Article V, Section 3(b)(iii), (c), and Article XXX(c).

[157] M Elahi (1986) at 146.

[158] Decision No. 6056-(79/38), 2 March 1979, reprinted in *Selected Decisions* 10th (1983) at 20, cited in B Trubitt, 'International Monetary Fund Conditionality and Options for Aggrieved Members' (1987) 20(4) *Vanderbilt Journal of Transnational Law* 665, 673.

[159] Although the IMF prefers benign and clinical expressions such as 'phasing' of drawings, subject to satisfaction of Fund conditions, alternative descriptions abound, for example: C Lichtenstein, 'Aiding the Transformation of Economies: Is the Fund's Conditionality Appropriate to the Task?' (1994) 62 *Fordham Law Review* 1943, 1947–48: 'The Fund is an exemplar of the theory of familial relations called "tough love" . . . [T]he Fund has sought to enforce an applicant's adherence to the agreed-upon economic policies by dribbling out its loans. A country initially gets to take only part of its [SBA] . . . If the applicant country adheres to the agreed-upon macro-economic policies, then it gets to take out more. The Fund is so conditioned to set conditions that it is no longer capable of imagining making a transfer of funds that, say, simply makes up a budget deficit while the country drawing upon the Fund's resources decides itself upon the economic policies that might best aid it in its particular circumstances to grow, to transform, to achieve whatever *are* the goals of the lending.'

[160] 'The IMF at a Glance,' April 1998 http://www.imf.org/external/np/exr/facts/glance.htm.

The exact amount of the set-aside is determined on a case-by-case basis and its availability is generally phased in line with program performance.'[161]

(2) Financial Facilities

The Fund's general resources are made available through a variety of financial facilities. As indicated earlier the regular IMF facilities consist of SBAs and the EFF. SBAs are designed to provide short-term (typically 12–18 months' duration) balance of payments assistance for deficits of a temporary or cyclical nature. Drawings are 'phased' on a quarterly basis, subject to periodic program reviews and the satisfaction of Fund conditionality. Repurchases are made between 3¼ and five years after purchase.[162]

In upper-tranche drawings, SBAs are the rule rather than the exception. The SBA is the result of consultations and negotiations between representatives of the Fund and of the member, following the member's initial request for use of resources in the credit tranches and a visit to the member country by a team of IMF economists. After meeting with senior banking officials and government figures (often the finance minister, but occasionally the head of government) in the requesting country, the IMF recommends a specific fiscal policy as a prerequisite to approval of further funding for the member country.[163] 'This "seal of approval" by the IMF indicates to other investors that the country is "safe" for capital investment.'[164] A Letter of Intent, reflecting the outcome of the consultations and negotiations, sets out the policies for the member government to follow, including the IMF-approved performance criteria. The Fund conditions continued drawings under the SBA on the member's success in meeting those criteria.[165]

The EFF, on the other hand, is designed to support medium-term programs that generally run for three years. Created in 1974, the EFF allows a member encountering balance of payments difficulties to obtain financial assistance beyond the measure that the quota in the credit tranches would allow. Under this facility Fund holdings of a member's currency are permitted to rise as high

---

[161] 'The IMF at a Glance,' April 1998 http://www.imf.org/external/np/exr/facts/glance.htm; IMF, 'IMF Financial Activities: Update August 30, 2002,' http://www.imf.org/external/np/tre/activity/2002/083002.htm.

[162] The following definition of a stand-by arrangement appears in Article XXX(b): 'Stand-by arrangement means a decision of the Fund by which a member is assured that it will be able to make purchases from the General Resources Account in accordance with the terms of the decision during a specified period and up to a specified amount.' See also 'The IMF at a Glance,' April 1998 http://www.imf.org/external/np/exr/facts/glance.htm.

[163] In fact, '[t]he negotiations may be protracted and involve several staff missions, trips to the IMF in Washington, DC, by country technicians and representatives,' in addition to direct negotiations with the finance minister or head of government: R Eckaus, 'How the IMF Lives with Its Conditionality' (1986) 19 *Policy Sciences* 237, 243.

[164] See M Elahi (1986) at 147; C Payer (1974); B Trubitt (1987) at 673; and A Orford (2001) at 151–52.

[165] B Trubitt (1987) at 673–74; J Gold, *Financial Assistance by the International Monetary Fund: Law and Practice* 2 (IMF Pamphlet Series No. 27, 2nd ed. 1980) at 20–21.

as 265 percent of quota.[166] The goal of the EFF is a long-term adjustment in a structural balance of payments deficit. Accordingly, conditionality is high.[167] Repurchases are made in 4½ to ten years.[168] The Fund and the member negotiate performance criteria and policy changes in the same manner as they do for credit tranche purchases, although the unequal bargaining power between the Fund and member and the overall uniformity of resulting policy prescriptions call into question the value of those negotiations.[169] Although EFF programs were little different in practice from normal stand-by programs, and in spite of the general lack of enthusiasm among Fund staff for the EFF, its introduction 'clouded the distinction' between the traditional short-term temporary balance of payments financing activities of the Fund, and the longer term development work of the World Bank.[170] While on no sensible construction of its Articles of Association could the Fund be characterised purely as a 'development institution,' the EFF signalled how far the Fund had come from its original core purpose of promoting international monetary cooperation and exchange stability, towards remedying conditions that are virtually synonymous with underdevelopment.[171]

The distinction between the Bank and Fund was further blurred throughout the 1980s, 'first by the Bank's initiation of a programme of structural adjustment lending through structural adjustment loans (SALs) and sectoral adjustment loans (SECALs), which incorporated conditionality linked to the structural causation of balance of payments deficits, and second by the Fund's introduction of the Structural Adjustment Facility and then the [ESAF]. As practiced by the Fund, in conjunction with the World Bank, 'structural adjustment involves liberalisation of prices, trade, and exchange followed by "public enterprise reform" (read privatisation) and "financial and banking sector reform,"[172]

---

[166] Cf Article V, Section 3(b)(iii).

[167] B Trubitt (1987) at 676; J Gold (1980) at 21: 'The inevitable determinant of the severity of a [conditionality] program . . . is the intensity of a member's problem.'

[168] M Elahi (1986) at 146; and generally, 'The IMF at a Glance,' April 1998 http://www.imf.org/external/np/exr/facts/glance.htm.

[169] This is no more than a generalisation. A more nuanced account of how conditionality works (or does not work) in practice is provided below at chapter V, nn 45–54 and accompanying text.

[170] G Bird (1995) at 49.

[171] S Haggard 'The Politics of Adjustment: Lessons from the IMF's Extended Fund Facility' (1985) 39(3) *International Organization* 505, 506; B Eichengreen and P Kenen, 'Managing the World Economy Under the Bretton Woods System: An Overview' in P Kenen, *Managing the World Economy; Fifty Years After Bretton Woods* 46–47 (1994); and D Bradlow and C Grossman (1995) at 420–21. Cf J Gold, ' "[T]o Contribute Thereby to Development": Aspects of the Relations of the International Monetary Fund with its Development Members' (1991) 10 *Colombia Journal of Transnational Law* 267, 271; and E Carrasco and M Kose, 'Income Distribution and the Bretton Woods Institutions: Promoting an Enabling Environment for Social Development' (1996) 6(1) *Transnational Law and Contemporary Problems* 1, 8.

[172] C Lichtenstein (1994) at 1949. But (at 1949–50): 'Underlying the formal description [of SAP measures] seems to be the conviction that *only* market economies can grow and that financial assistance, at least in the case of the Fund's special facilities, is to help the countries receiving the facilities deal with the disruptions caused by the move from state ownership to private ownership of means of production, the removal of tariffs, and the freeing of prices . . . Of course, it will be recalled

along with requirements that borrowers adopt policies of foreign investment deregulation, cuts to government spending on health and education, labour market deregulation, lowering of the minimum wage, and a focus on the production of good for export rather than local production.[173] In terminology as well as in areas of involvement, structural adjustment had served to create an important area of overlap between the Fund and Bank.'[174]

The overlap with development was entrenched with the introduction of the ESAF, established in 1987, enlarged and extended in 1994, and replaced in 1999 by the PRGF, to be discussed shortly. The ESAF was a concessional facility designed for low-income countries with protracted balance of payments problems. In contrast to the regular IMF facilities referred to earlier, ESAF drawings were loans, not purchases of other members' currencies, made available in support of three-year programs in terms set out in 'Policy Framework Papers' (PFPs), sometimes claimed to be country-owned but in fact historically designed almost exclusively in Washington at IMF headquarters. ESAF drawings carried an interest rate of 0.5 percent, with a 5-year grace period and a 10-year maturity. ESAF programs were subject to 'quarterly benchmarks and semi-annual performance criteria.' As at September 1999, eighty low-income countries were entitled to use this facility, and fifty-six had done so.[175] Although the ESAF was intended to give prominence to the objective of fostering economic growth, in contrast to the more exclusive concentration in SBAs on balance of payments viability, the extent to which ESAF programs actually fulfilled that objective is open to doubt.[176]

---

that, under the Fund's charter, what the Fund is supposed to be doing is aiding members with balance of payments problems. But what *if* those problems are caused by the Fund's own medicine prescribed *to create* growth?'

[173] A Orford (2001) at 151.

[174] G Bird (1995) at 49. As at August 2002 the Bank was considering renaming adjustment lending to 'development policy support lending,' although whether any substantive changes were likely was then still an open question: Bretton Woods Project, 'Bretton Woods Update' (July/August 2002) at 3 (available at http://www.brettonwoodsproject.org).

[175] IMF, 'IMF Concessional Financing Through ESAF: A Factsheet,' http://www.imf.org.

[176] See IMF, *External Evaluation of the ESAF: Report by a Group of Independent Experts* (1998); and also T Killick (1995) at 612–13. In a critique of a review by the Fund in 1993 of experiences of 51 ESAF programs in 19 countries, Killick remarks (at 612–13) that 'ESAF programmes depress growth rather than accelerating [sic] it . . . The standard Fund response would be to appeal to the full wording of the ESAF guidelines, which talk of '*creating the conditions* to achieve sustained economic growth' [emphasis added] and to urge that ESAF programmes are indeed creating those conditions. The difficulty with this defence, however, is that it is identical with the one the Fund has always used with respect to its conventional stand-by programmes (with distressingly little statistical evidence in support), which only goes to underline the lack of difference between ESAF and stand-by programmes in this regard.' On this point Killick concludes (at 615) that 'the ESAF's stated growth objective is more presentational than operational, although by addressing deficit countries' structural weaknesses the ESAF *should* have a positive longer-term growth effect.' For a reply see S Schadler, 'Can the IMF Help Low-Income Countries: A Reply' (1995) 18(4) *The World Economy* 617–25, 623–24, emphasising *inter alia* the need to evaluate growth objectives over a longer time horizon than that reflected in the IMF evaluation.

In November 1999, the PRGF was introduced to replace the ESAF.[177] The essential purpose of the PRGF is to bring poverty reduction within the key objectives of IMF concessional lending to low-income countries. The major factors precipitating its introduction have been said to be: (i) the critical findings of an external evaluation of the ESAF in 1998;[178] (ii) the need to address criticisms over the Fund's handling of the East Asia crisis; and (iii) the demands of debt relief and associated pressures from the Jubilee 2000 debt relief campaign.[179] Credit under the PRGF is provided at an interest rate of 0.5 to 1 per cent to eligible low-income members. The loans are repayable in ten equal semi-annual instalments five and a half to ten years after drawdown. There were thirty-eight PRGF arrangements in place as at August 2002, with agreed commitments totalling 4,757 million SDRs, and total outstanding credit of 5,486 million SDRs.[180]

Under the PRGF the countries themselves are intended to devise their own 'medium term budgetary frameworks' containing 'explicit and specific poverty-reducing policies.'[181] To the extent that this system works as intended, the IMF would rely extensively upon the judgements of the World Bank and other multilateral regional development banks for an assessment of those budgetary priorities and their costing.[182] At least in theory the PRGF reflects the realisations that: (a) distributional equity, gender and other disparities and explicitly 'pro-poor' measures need to be factored in by the Fund, in order to promote what it calls 'high quality growth' and relieve the adverse impacts of structural adjustment programs;[183] (b) the participation of the poor themselves in the development process, along with the ideals of 'country ownership' of development strategies and accountability for outcomes, are instrumental values for the Fund's purposes;[184] and (c) strict conditionality has not been effective. The PRGF, and its predecessor the ESAF, assume critical importance in context of

---

[177] IMF, *Social Policy Issues in IMF-Supported Programs: Follow-up on the 1995 World Summit for Social Development* (2000) at 2.

[178] IMF, *External Evaluation of the ESAF: Report by a Group of Independent Experts* (1998); IMF, *Social Policy Issues in IMF-Supported Programs: Follow-up on the 1995 World Summit for Social Development* (2000) at 4.

[179] Interviews in Washington DC in February 2000.

[180] IMF, 'IMF Financial Activities: Update August 30, 2002,' http://www.imf.org/external/np/tre/activity/2002/083002.htm.

[181] IMF, 'Remarks by Aninat: International community collaborates on design of policies to promote poverty reduction' (2000) 29(13) *IMF Survey* 211–12, 211.

[182] As put by the Fund's Deputy Managing Director Eduardo Aninat in June 2000, the Fund's role is 'to help ensure that these [budgetary] outlays are consistent with the available financing and with macroeconomic stability and faster, sustainable growth. If available financing is insufficient to meet priority spending needs in countries where additional resources could be used effectively, we will actively support countries in seeking additional resources from the donor community.' IMF, 'Remarks by Aninat: International community collaborates on design of policies to promote poverty reduction' (2000) 29(13) *IMF Survey* 211–12, 211.

[183] IMF, *Social Policy Issues in IMF-Supported Programs: Follow-up on the 1995 World Summit for Social Development* (2000) at 2–3.

[184] IMF, *Social Policy Issues in IMF-Supported Programs: Follow-up on the 1995 World Summit for Social Development* (2000) at 3.

the Highly Indebted Poor Country (HIPC) debt relief initiative, under which the satisfaction of successive ESAF/PRGF programs is a formal prerequisite for eligibility.[185]

The PRGF is designed to make poverty reduction a more explicit element of growth-oriented strategies at country level, through the preparation of comprehensive Poverty Reduction Strategy Papers (PRSPs) by the client countries themselves, on the basis of extensive consultation processes with 'domestic stakeholders, regional development banks, the UN, bilateral donors as well as the World Bank and the IMF.'[186] The PRSP is also the basis for the World Banks' Poverty Reduction and Support Credits (PRSC), introduced in 2001 to support low-income countries implementing poverty reduction strategies. A related document is the 'interim PRSP' (or iPRSP), a shorter and less detailed document than the PRSP, which has also functioned as a condition for highly endebted countries to reach 'decision point' (the point at which debt relief begins) within the 'enhanced HIPC initiative.'[187]

PRSPs are intended to contain three core elements: (a) poverty diagnosis; (b) targets, indicators and monitoring systems; and (c) priority public actions over a three year period.[188] Under a set of 'core principles' adopted by the Bank and Fund, PRSPs should be: (1) country-driven, involving broad-based participation by civil society and the private sector in all operational steps; (2) results-oriented, and focused on outcomes beneficial to the poor; (3) comprehensive in recognising the multi-dimensional character of poverty, but also prioritised so that implementation is feasible in both fiscal and institutional terms; (4) partnership-oriented, involving coordinated participation of bilateral, multilateral and non-government development partners; and (5) based on a long-term perspective for poverty reduction.[189]

---

[185] See IMF, *HIPC Initiative—Strengthening the Link Between Debt Relief and Poverty Reduction*, 12 August 1999, http://www.imf.org/external/np/esafhipc/1999/index.htm. For a disussion and critique see DFID, *Department Report 2001: Making Globalisation Work for the Poor* 37 (2001). As at August 2002 thirty-three HIPC countries had reached what is known as 'decision point' under the 'enhanced HIPC' framework, the milestone at which debt relief starts to flow. However out of these only twelve had reached 'completion point' under the HIPC process, entitling them to final, irrevocable debt relief. IMF, 'IMF Financial Activities: Update August 30, 2002,' http://www.imf.org/external/np/tre/activity/2002/083002.htm.

[186] IMF, *Social Policy Issues in IMF-Supported Programs: Follow-up on the 1995 World Summit for Social Development* (2000) at 3 and 14–15.

[187] UNCTAD, *The Least Developed Countries Report 2002: Escaping the Poverty Trap* 169 (2002). As that report relates (at 169), as at 2002 thirty-four countries were engaged in producing or implementing full or interim PRSPs. The six full PRSPs were in Burkina Faso, Mauritania, Mozambique, Niger, Uganda and the United Republic of Tanzania. As at March 2002 it was expected that by mid-2002 17 of the countries that had produced iPRSP's would have completed full PRSPs, and a further seven lesser developed countries would have produced iPRSP's. Of the countries engaged in the process, all but six were HIPC countries.

[188] UNCTAD (2002) at 169.

[189] World Bank, 'Poverty Reduction Strategy Papers: A Renewed Approach for Attacking Poverty, http://www.worldbank.org at 2. For a critique of these assumptions however see Canadian International Development Agency (CIDA), 'The Canadian International Development Agency's Experience with the PRSP Process in Bolivia: A Report Prepared by CIDA's Bolivia Country Programme and Policy Branch, 11 December 2001 (at 9–12).

On a procedural level the intention is that PRSPs—by dint of public participation and 'ownership' at the national level—should better reflect national level
policy priorities and have better prospects for sustained and effective implementation. On the substantive policy level the intention is that macroeconomic
policies should be 'better integrated with the social and sectoral policies and
goals, to ensure that they are mutually supportive and consistent with the
broader objective[s]' of sustainable economic growth and poverty reduction.[190]
The so-called 'international development goals'—a set of OECD-inspired
undertakings distilled from a number of global summits on development related
issues in the 1990s[191]—were adopted initially by the IFIs as benchmarks for this
purpose, re-affirmed and broadened subsequently in the Millennium
Declaration of September 2000 and its associated 'Millennium Development
Goals', or MDGs.[192]

In the respects just outlined, the PRSP is designed to overcome some of the
most obvious defects of the PFP. This logically brings the Fund into closer cooperative relations not only with the Bank, but with a very wide range of actors
from whom its operations and processes have historically been hermetically
sealed. The ability and early efforts of the Fund to meet these demands are
critically reviewed in chapter III below.

---

[190] IMF, *Social Policy Issues in IMF-Supported Programs: Follow-up on the 1995 World Summit
for Social Development* (2000) at 14. For a more extensive list of the key differences brought by the
PRGF see IMF, 'Remarks by Aninat: International community collaborates on design of policies to
promote poverty reduction' (2000) 29(13) *IMF Survey* 211–12.

[191] The international development goals—more a guide to donor commitment rather than a
framework for accountability in human rights terms—set out a list of desirable development outcomes such as halving world poverty by the year 2015, reducing infant mortality, improving primary
school attendance rates, maternal well-being, and so forth, based upon governments' undertakings
at Copenhagen (1995), Beijing (1995), and other world conferences. But significantly, goals from the
World Conference on Human Rights in Vienna (1993) are not included. See OECD/DAC, *DAC
Guidelines on Poverty Reduction* (1999); OECD, OECD, *In the Face of Poverty: Meeting the Global
Challenge Through Partnerships* (2001).

[192] See above nn 68–69 and accompanying text. For an example of how the MDGs are being integrated within PRSPs as a central frame of reference for indicator setting, see IMF/IDA, 'Joint Staff
Assessment: Malawi,' 23 August 2002 at para 14. See also IMF, 'IMF Supports UN's Millennium
Development Goals,' *News Brief* No. 01/90, 19 September 2001. Human rights goals are not explicit
included within the MDGs, which instead are directed towards global numerical targets based on
average figures, hardly consonant with human rights precepts such as reaching the excluded, monitoring both conduct and outcome, disaggregating data, strengthening process factors such as participation, strengthening empowerment and accountability, and so forth. The Secretary-General's
Road Map for implementing the Millennium Declaration (including Section V thereof and other
human rights-specific elements) along with his suggested indicator set for the MDGs and their sub-
targets are somewhat more helpful in that regard. For PRSP purposes the IFIs have explicitly
embraced the MDGs and their 18 sub-targets, rather than the Millennium Declaration (and the
Secretary-General's Road Map) in their entirety. However the IDA Executive Directors have
emphasised the importance of the IDA 'reporting on progress toward the MDGs and other priorities . . . in conjunction with other partners,' with particular reference to the more extensive indicator set presented in the Secretary-Generals Road Map. IDA, 'Additions to IDA Resources:
Thirteenth Replenishment—Supporting Poverty Reduction Strategies,' Report from the Executive
Directors of the IDA to the Board of Governors, 25 July 2002 at 31.

Finally, the Fund operates a number of 'special' facilities, namely the Systemic Transformation Facility (STF), the Compensatory Financing Facility (CFF), the Supplemental Reserve Facility (SRF), and the Contingent Credit Line (CCL) facility.[193] The STF, a temporary facility,[194] was designed specifically for the purpose of lending to Russia 'and the other states of the former Soviet Union as well as other economies in transition.'[195] Under the CFF members can draw on the IMF to compensate for temporary export shortfalls, and compensatory financing for excesses in cereal import costs, when, due to an unpredictable event beyond the member's direct control, there is a sudden drop in the member's export-commodity revenues.[196] The SRF, introduced in 1997 in the face of upredecented capital flight in emerging market economies, provides financial assistance for exceptional balance of payments difficulties due to a large short-term financing needs resulting from 'sudden and disruptive loss of market confidence.'[197] The CCL differs from other IMF facilities in that is aims to help members prevent crises. Established in 1999, the CCL aims to provide members with strong economic policies a precautionary line of defence which would be readily available against balance of payments problems that might arise from international financial contagion. The repayment period for CCL financing is the same as for the SRF,[198] however the CCL has proved to be something of a dead letter in practice.[199] And finally, 'Emergency Assistance' is also provided

[193] 'About the IMF,' http://www.imf.org.

[194] The term 'temporary facility' has been described as 'Fund jargon for the specialised forms of lending that the Fund has created in recent years': C Lichtenstein (1994) at 1944, n 6 and accompanying text.

[195] For a critique of the STF, including arguments that the Fund (and STF in particular) were merely used as instruments of the G–7 in order to promote its own foreign policy goal of Russia's hoped-for democratic transformation, and the inappropriateness of the Fund's policy conditions in that regard, see generally C Lichtenstein (1994); and also J Sachs, 'The Reformers' Tragedy,' *New York Times*, 23 January 1994, at 17: 'The US and its allies had turned over the task of bailing out Russia to the [IMF] and World Bank, principally because these institutions could make loans that did not require Congressional or parliamentary authorisation . . . The IMF's relentless advice was to cut the deficit, not to find acceptable and non-inflationary ways to finance part of it.' For other criticisms, particularly the fact that the lengthy period of time required to 'shake off the Soviet legacy' in Russia is 'not a time scale that appeals to Western investors,' see A Philps, 'Economic "Absurdistan" Baffles Badly Needed Investors,' *Sydney Morning Herald*, 26 August 1998. See also T Heritage, 'Russia: Resistance to IMF Austerity Plan Grows,' *Sydney Morning Herald*, 25 July 1998; and P Blustein, 'Tense Times at IMF: A World of Worries with Limited Rescue Funds,' *International Herald Tribune*, 30 July 1998 at 6; 'Russia Devalued,' *The Economist*, 22 August 1998 at 13–14 and 55–57.

[196] M Elahi (1986) at 146; 'The IMF at a Glance,' April 1998 http://www.imf.org/external/np/exr/facts/glance.htm.

[197] 'The IMF at a Glance,' April 1998 http://www.imf.org/external/np/exr/facts/glance.htm; IMF, 'IMF Financial Activities: Update August 30, 2002,' http://www.imf.org/external/np/tre/activity/2002/083002.htm. For a description of other Fund facilities over time, see B Trubit (1987) at 674–78.

[198] IMF, 'IMF Financial Activities: Update August 30, 2002,' http://www.imf.org/external/np/tre/activity/2002/083002.htm.

[199] See IMF Public Information Notice (PIN) No. 00/79, 18 September 2000, 'IMF Board Agrees on Changes to Fund Financial Facilities.'

by the Fund to help members finance their recovery efforts and support economic adjustment following a natural disaster or conflict.[200]

Conditionality

In basic terms, '[c]onditionality is a *portmanteau* word that encompasses all the policies that the Fund wishes a member to follow so that it can resolve its problem consistently with the Articles.'[201] Certain of its features and underlying assumptions have already been referred to in passing. While a subject of equal practical relevance to the financial assistance activities of both the Bank and Fund, the legal doctrine purporting to regulate the exercise of conditionality at the Fund is quite specific and relatively well developed, and accordingly warrants separate analysis here. Other practical questions relating to conditionality's effectiveness, of equal application to both the Bank and Fund, are dealt with later.

From the earliest days of the IMF, conditionality, the key determinant of members' access to financial assistance, has been a controversial issue and, as such, has attracted close scrutiny both inside and outside the Fund.[202] A few of the most important caveats will be mentioned shortly, following a brief examination of the legal basis and content of conditionality. The human rights effects of IMF conditionality will be dealt with separately thereafter. Apart from 'performance criteria' referred to earlier, the other technical elements of conditionality embrace 'prior actions' or 'preconditions' (ie things that a program country needs to agree to do in order to qualify for financial assistance),[203] 'benchmarks', and 'conditions for completing a review.'[204] However in the following discussion, unless the contrary intention appears, the term 'conditionality' is intended to be understood in a less technical sense, embracing both the direct and express terms upon which IMF financial services are offered, as well as

---

[200] IMF, 'IMF Emergency Assistance Related to Natural Disasters and Post-Conflict Situations: A Factsheet,' http://www.imf.org.

[201] M Guitián, 'Fund Conditionality: Evolution of Principles and Practices,' IMF Pamphlet Series, No. 38 (1981); J Gold, 'Conditionality,' *IMF Pamphlet Series*, No. 31 (1979), esp at pp 2, 30–31 and 34. Conditionality is officially defined as 'the link between the approval or continuation of the Fund's financing and the implementation of specified elements of economic policy by the country receiving this financing.' See IMF, 'Conditionality in Fund-Supported Programs—Overview', http://www.imf.org.

[202] M Guitián (1981) at 2.

[203] Paragraph 7 of the Fund's guidelines on conditionality [Decision No. 6056-(79/38), *Selected Decisions* 10th (1983)] provides in part: 'The Managing Director will recommend that the Executive Board approve a member's request for the use of the Fund's general resources in the credit tranches when it is his judgement that *the program is consistent with the Fund's provisions and policies and that it will be carried out.* A member may be expected to adopt some corrective measures before a stand-by arrangement is approved by the Fund, but only if necessary to enable the member to adopt and carry out a program consistent with the Fund's provisions and policies.' For further discussion of preconditions see Gold, J (1979) at 28.

[204] IMF, 'Conditionality in Fund-Supported Programs—Overview', http://www.imf.org.

other (often no less compelling) forms of pressure and policy influence exerted by the Fund through Article IV consultations or other means.[205]

(1) Legal Basis for Conditionality

At the Bretton Woods conference, the delegations from Great Britain and the United States differed markedly on the question of whether members 'would be entitled to draw at will on the pools of currencies in the Fund.'[206] Great Britain, led by Lord John Maynard Keynes, favoured a relatively liberal regime for access to the Fund's general resources, which was not surprising given the task of reconstruction faced by that nation at the end of the Second World War. The United States, led by Harry Dexter White, preferred the position that drawings could be permitted 'if the Fund's resources were to be conserved for the purposes for which the Fund was established and if the Fund were to be influential in promoting what it considered to be appropriate financial policies.'[207] This position, likewise, was hardly surprising, in view of the relative economic strength of the US in the post-War years.

The term 'conditionality' was not expressly included in the original Articles, however, nor in subsequent amendments. Neither did the original Articles contain any explicit statement that the Fund had to adopt policies on the use of its resources.[208] However a series of early Executive Board decisions and Annual Report references[209] put the matter beyond doubt. The view that the Fund could prevent any proposed uses of Fund resources that it considered improper prevailed in a decision of 10 March 1948,[210] a decision representing 'a thoroughgoing adoption of the United States view that drawing rights were to be

---

[205] For a discussion of the phenomenon of 'indirect conditionality,' see A Chayes and A Chayes (1995) at 236–37; and D Cortright (ed) (1997) at 248–49: 'Placing pressure on a recipient government is often referred to as "conditionality," meaning the policy change is a precondition for the provision of assistance. International financial institutions may apply pressure both indirectly and directly. Indirect pressure, which is applied without explicit conditions on the policies in question, can have the same goals as explicit, direct pressure.' For example, '[t]he IMF can . . . indirectly affect the military sector by setting targets for cutting fiscal deficits that make it difficult for recipient countries to avoid reductions in military expenditures.'

[206] A Lowenfeld, *The International Monetary System* (1984) at 28.

[207] R Gardner, *Sterling-Dollar Diplomacy in Current Perspective* (1980) at 113, cited in Lichtenstein, C. (1994) at 1947.

[208] J Gold (1979) at 3.

[209] J Gold (1979) at 2: 'Something in the nature of a definition appeared in the Annual Report of the Fund for 1964: "Drawings beyond [a measure of contribution known as the 'gold tranche,' since replaced by the reserve tranche policy] . . . are conditional, in greater or lesser degree, on the adoption by the drawing countries of policies designed to ensure the temporary character of their payments problem, and designed also to eliminate or reduce the member's reliance on exchange restrictions or certain other exchange practices." The Annual Report for 1965 contained the following statement about what it called conditional liquidity: ". . . the credit tranches . . . , which are made available on condition that the drawing country maintains or adopts policies calculated to correct in due time the payments deficit in question, constitute 'conditional' liquidity." '

[210] Decision No 284-4, 10 March 1948, *Selected Decisions*, 8th (1976) at 35–36, cited in Gold, J (1979) at 3, 49.

conditional.'[211] Further decisions of a similar character followed, but fell short of explaining what uses of resources the Fund would regard as 'proper.'[212] This was gradually clarified through subsequent Executive Board decisions,[213] Annual Report statements and practice, until the First Amendment in 1968 included for the first time clear language requiring the Fund to have policies on the use of its resources.[214] An Executive Board decision on 20 September 1968 set forth the results of a review of the Fund's policy on the use of its resources under SBAs, in the light of experience. The preamble to those conclusions 'drew attention to the necessity for adequate safeguards and the need for flexibility while ensuring uniform and equitable treatment for all members.'[215] This decision was revised and extended by the decision of 2 March 1979 [hereinafter 'the Guidelines'],[216] which will be discussed in greater detail shortly, when looking at the content of IMF conditionality.

Following the Second Amendment in 1976,[217] the legal basis for conditionality is found primarily in Article I(v), the purpose of giving 'confidence to members by making the general resources of the Fund *temporarily available to them under adequate safeguards*' [emphasis added], and Article V, Section 3(a) which provides:

> The Fund shall adopt policies on the use of its general resources, *including policies on stand-by or similar arrangements*,[218] and may adopt special policies for special balance of payments problems, that will assist members to solve their balance of payments problems in a manner consistent with the provisions of this Agreement and that

[211] A Lowenfeld (1984) at 29.

[212] See J Gold (1979) at 3–4.

[213] In particular, the decision of 13 February 1952, designed to 'assure members that they would be able to use the Fund's resources at least to the extent that they had made a demonstrable contribution to the Fund's activities and were in a creditor or net creditor position . [.]'—J Gold (1979) at 3–4.

[214] See generally J Gold (1979) at 3–10.

[215] J Gold (1979) at 7–8.

[216] Decision No. 6056-(79/38), *Selected Decisions* 10th (1983) at 20. See the discussion of the Guidelines in J Gold (1979) at 14–36. In its most recent review in July 1994 of the experience with conditionality in IMF-supported adjustment programs, the Executive Board concluded that the guidelines on conditionality adopted in 1979 continued in general to provide an appropriate basis for IMF policies on the use of its resources. See IMF, 'Financial Organisation and Operations of the IMF,' *IMF Pamphlet Series* No. 45 (1998).

[217] Accounts have been established to administer resources for support for the low-income and heavily indebted members (HIPC and ESAF, subsequently PRGF). There are several other Administered Accounts established for different purposes, including a Framework Administered Account to administer resources to finance technical assistance activities. The Special Disbursement Account (SDA) is the vehicle for (1) receiving and investing profits from the sale of the IMF's gold (that is, the net proceeds in excess of the book value of SDR 35 per fine ounce); and (2) making transfers for special purposes authorized in the Articles. The SDA was activated in 1981 initially to receive transfers from the Trust Fund, which had been funded from gold sales, upon its termination. For fuller discussion see IMF, 'Financial Organisation and Operations of the IMF,' *IMF Pamphlet Series* No. 45 (1998).

[218] The expression 'similar arrangements' was introduced into the Articles as part of the Second Amendment in 1979 'mainly in recognition of extended arrangements but also to make room for further categories of arrangements if they should be found necessary'—J Gold (1979) at 11.

will establish *adequate safeguards for the temporary use of the general resources of the Fund* [emphasis added].

Of further relevance is Article V, Section 3(b)(i), stipulating that a member's use of the Fund's general resources 'be in accordance with the provisions of this Agreement and the policies adopted under them,' such as the Guidelines concerning access to the credit tranches, and Article V, Section 3(c), compelling the IMF to examine requests for purchases (except in relation to the reserve tranche) to determine their consistency with Fund purposes and policies. Finally, Article V, Section 2(b), which applies to the administered accounts (trust fund monies for the ESAF and PRGF), and Article V, Section 12(f) which applies to funds in the 'Special Disbursement Account,' stipulate only that the use of these resources be 'consistent with the purposes of the Fund.'[219]

(2) Content of Conditionality Policies

The official policy of the Fund concerning conditionality remains quite vague, permitting the Fund a high degree of flexibility in its policy prescriptions. A reasonable measure of latitude is certainly desirable from the perspective of meeting the wide variety of circumstances in which requests for financial assistance arise. Officially, the Fund's policy is to achieve a balance between the need for flexibility and the need for even-handed treatment. As far as access to general resources is concerned, paragraph 8 of the Guidelines provides: 'The Managing Director will ensure adequate co-ordination in the application of policies relating to the use of the Fund's general resources with a view to maintaining the *non-discriminatory treatment of members*' [emphasis added].[220]

On a systemic level, the Fund's conditionality practice has evolved markedly over time. However this has less to do with any conscious application of the Guidelines' concern for flexibility, than with a need to adapt to the demands of a new clientele in a rapidly, and to some degree independently, evolving external environment. Although the original purpose of the Fund was to provide for short term drawings against a pool of currencies to relieve temporary balances of payments crises, following the debt crisis in the 1970s and early 1980s the question became 'how a country could start earning enough hard currency to repay the debt it had borrowed from the banks and official lenders and be able

---

[219] See IMF, 'Financial Organisation and Operations of the IMF,' *IMF Pamphlet Series* No. 45 (1998).

[220] Decision No 6056-(79/38), *Selected Decisions* 10th (1983) at 20, paragraph 8. See also M Guitián (1981) at 3–4: 'It is ... necessary to strike a delicate balance between uniformity and flexibility of treatment; the principle of uniformity cannot be applied rigidly—that is, regardless of individual country circumstances—nor can individual circumstances be given such weight that uniform treatment loses all meaning. A common feature of the situations that involve programs supported by Fund resources is the existence of an adjustment need, and conditionality ensures that an appropriate adjustment effort is undertaken to meet this need. In general terms, *uniformity* of treatment requires that for any given degree of need, the *effort of economic adjustment sought by the Fund in programs be broadly equivalent among its members*' [emphasis added].

to return to the capital markets for additional funding.'[221] Accordingly, '[t]he concept of Fund aid changed from balance of payments funding to aiding indebted countries to "grow" their way out of their extreme debt burden.'[222]

Further guidance on the content of performance criteria is provided in paragraph 9 of the Guidelines:

> The number and content of performance criteria may vary because of the diversity of problems and institutional arrangements of members. Performance criteria will be limited to those that are necessary to evaluate implementation of the program with a view to ensuring the achievement of its objectives. Performance criteria will normally be confined to (i) *macroeconomic* variables, and (ii) those *necessary to implement specific provisions of the Articles or policies adopted under them. Performance criteria may relate to other variables only in exceptional cases when they are essential for the effectiveness of the member's program because of their macroeconomic impact* [emphasis added].

Paragraph 9 of the Guidelines, appropriately, is framed reasonably broadly, setting the general benchmark of 'macroeconomic impact'[223] as a basis for determining the sorts of performance criteria to be included. In particular, considerable discretion is left on the determination of what (non-macroeconomic) criteria might be 'necessary' for the observance of the Articles or Fund policies, and for determining the range of 'exceptional' cases under which (non-macroeconomic) factors might be 'essential' for the effectiveness of a program due to their macroeconomic impacts.

It is interesting to witness the manner in which these criteria been interpreted in practice. Naturally, economic prescriptions appropriate for the Fund's

---

[221] C Lichtenstein (1994) at 1948–49.

[222] C Lichtenstein (1994) at 1949.

[223] According to Sir Joseph Gold, '[t]he concept of "macroeconomic" variables involves the idea of aggregation, but the definition and scope of the concept may be less clear. It undoubtedly includes the broadest possible aggregate in an economic category. Variables dealing with the total expansion of credit or the volume of external borrowing are examples. The intentions to which this principle gives effect are that the Fund should not become involved in the detailed decisions by which general policies are put into operation, and that members should have maximum room for economic management without risking their access to the Fund's resources . . . Specific prices of commodities or services, specific taxes, or other detailed measures to increase revenues or to reduce expenditures would not be considered macroeconomic variables. The Fund may wish to know, however, what a member's intentions are on matters of this kind in order to have a view on whether there is a reasonable prospect that the member will be able to meet performance criteria'—J Gold (1979) at 33. Although paragraph 9 of the Guidelines recognises that there is no fixed list of acceptable performance criteria, Gold (at 33–34) suggests that imposition of a ceiling on credit expansion is 'always employed' due to the effect of excessive demand in the economy on the balance of payments, as are terms directed against multiple currency practices, restrictions on payments and transfers for current international transactions, and restrictions on trade. Other usual criteria regulate the amount and maturity of certain forms of new foreign debt, and the maintenance of a certain minimum level of net foreign exchange reserves. In view of the highly prescriptive and standardised nature of the Fund's conditions in recent times, the original intention behind paragraph 9 as stated above by Joseph Gold (ie 'that the Fund should not become involved in the detailed decisions by which general policies are put into operation, and that members should have maximum room for economic management without risking their access to the Fund's resources') appears to have been lost. See eg D Kapur and R Webb (2000).

expanding developing country clientele are not identical with those of industrialised countries, and measures suitable for the resolution of temporary balance of payments imbalances[224] are quite different to those required for growth. As Bradlow explains: '[t]he balance of payments problems of developing countries, in part, are attributable to their level of development. Consequently, their balance of payments problems have structural dimensions which cannot easily be resolved within the parameters of the IMF's standard short-term arrangement.'[225] Accordingly the IMF's 'therapy' for its new clientele evolved into principally two strands: 'stabilisation programs' and 'structural adjustment programs' (SAPs), briefly introduced earlier.[226]

In the course of its traditional twelve to eighteen month SBAs, the Fund's normal assumption is that the member State has limited potential to increase the amount and range of goods and services it produces. Consequently, conditionalities within such a time-frame have tended to focus on *demand reduction* as the main strategy for resolving its balance of payments imbalance.[227] With the introduction of the longer term facilities such as the ESAF and PRGF 'the IMF was able to change its assumptions about which factors should be treated as fixed and which as variable in the design of its stabilisation and adjustment programs.'[228] The most significant of these was the relaxation by the Fund of its assumption about the fixed nature of the 'supply' side of members' economics, facilitating the introduction of measures designed to produce changes in members' production profiles.[229] As a consequence the Fund, when considering how to incorporate supply-side issues into its policies and programs, is not able to avoid focusing on social and cultural (as well as economic) factors in a member State which might impede the speed at which and extent to which people in the country concerned can actually make changes in the production side of the econ-

---

[224] For a discussion of the range of potential sources of balance of payments difficulties, see eg G Bird (1995) at 12–14.

[225] D Bradlow (1996) at 71. As Bradlow observes (at 72) even in its longer term facilities the Fund operates on a shorter time horizon than the World Bank, with the precise performance criteria being established approximately on a twelve-monthly basis.

[226] See above nn 53–58 and 172–74 and accompanying text, and also M Lucas, 'The International Monetary Fund's Conditionality and the International Covenant on Economic, Social and Cultural Rights: An Attempt to Define the Relation,' 1 *Revue Belge de Droit International* 104, 107–8 (1992): '[Stabilisation programs] contain budgetary and monetary measures aimed at resolving balance of payments problems in the short term; [SAPs] contain measures relating to production, distribution and exchange of goods with a view to resolving structural deficits in the long term . . . [B]ut it would be wrong to think that those two categories are exclusive, since the SAPs also involve monetary and budgetary measures.' See also C Payer (1974) at 33.

[227] D Bradlow (1996) at 71. However according to Guitián, as early as 1981: 'Strictly speaking, interest in supply is not a new development in the Fund. While the achievement of a sustainable level of aggregate demand and the consequent achievement of financial stability may have been the *proximate* objectives of Fund policies, the attainment of supply potential has always been the ultimate aim'—M Guitián (1981) at 26.

[228] D Bradlow (1996) at 71.

[229] D Bradlow (1996) at 71. However for suggested limitations on the Fund's influence over supply-side variables, see T Killick with M Malik (1992) at 630.

omy.[230] It has therefore become quite typical for Fund conditionality in SBAs and ESAF and PRGF arrangements to include such matters as social safety nets (SSNs, incorporating housing, welfare and unemployment issues), the need for transparent and accountable government, market-oriented reforms, and the rule of law.

What Role for Human Rights?

The Fund's official premise is that 'social issues' (and human rights) are best addressed by the Fund indirectly, through presumptive improvements flowing from a stabilised, privatised and liberalised economic base, deemed appropriate for ensuring growth.[231] The systematic characterisation of human rights as 'social' concerns is itself alarming, ignoring human rights' very obvious 'economic' aspects, and consigning them by this definition to macro-economic irrelevance.

The division of labour between the Bank (in charge of longer-term development and 'social' issues) and Fund (in charge of macro-economic design) is one of the principal reasons why human rights have not made it onto the Fund's radar. The suggested compartmentalisation is far from completely watertight, however, in the respects just discussed. Moreover since 1988 a set of confidential standard instructions from the Managing Director's office has reportedly been in place, suggesting that IMF country missions should take into consideration the possible socioeconomic consequences of adjustment programmes.[232]

---

[230] D Bradlow (1996) at 71. An examination of these underlying factors would be broadly consistent with Paragraph 4 of the IMF conditionality Guidelines: 'In helping members to devise adjustment programs, the Fund will pay due regard to the domestic social and political objectives, the economic priorities, and the circumstances of members, including the causes of their balance of payments problems.' According to Sir Joseph Gold, paragraph 4 was intended to meet developing member concerns relating to exogenous causes of balance of payments imbalances, and the routine imposition of standardised developed country models for stabilisation programs. In this regard, '[p]aragraph 4 goes some way in recognising the special character of difficulties that have resulted from circumstances over which a member has had no control in its reference to "the causes of their balance of payments problems[,]" . . . but there is no implication that adjustment and conditionality will be unnecessary if a member's difficulty arises from circumstances beyond its control'— J Gold (1979) at 24–25. In its terms, paragraph 4 would also seem to require the Fund to pay due regard to the system of government in the member state concerned, and to whether that system is compatible with the usual IMF prescriptions [eg concerning privatisation and public service reform—C Lichtenstein (1994)]. Finally, to the extent that paragraph 4 of the Guidelines implies that the Fund does no more than 'help' borrowing States to devise their own tailored and specific adjustment programs, it is misleading, as the discussion in chapter V below on the practical problems of conditionality indicates.

[231] See eg G Capdevila 'IMF Not Taking into Account Human Rights Issues,' Dawn, 13 August 2001, http://www.globalpolicy.org/socecon/bwi-wto/imf/2001/0813hr.htm, summarising a meeting between the assistant director of the IMF's office in Geneva and members of the Sub-Commission on Promotion and Protection of Human Rights.

[232] E Denters *Law and Policy of IMF Conditionality* 135–36 (1996). Denters intimated (at n. 38) that three members of IMF staff had confirmed this to him in interviews, but would not disclose copies of the written instructions themselves.

According to insiders' accounts '[t]hese instructions stipulate that missions must inform governments—if such is the case—that the adjustment programme may have negative consequences for certain sections of the population. This statement should be followed by the question whether the authorities are interested in arranging exceptional measures in order to limit the damage. The government may say yes or no. If the answer is affirmative, the IMF, in concert with the member country, may seek a solution within the framework of the programme. If the answer is negative, the Fund shall not insist, and no exceptional measures will be taken.'[233]

However at least formally the Fund continues to regard all 'social issues' and the design of SSNs as being squarely within the province of the Bank. The historical lack of harmonious working relations between Bank and Fund, and the fact that at times the Bank was only given periods of 48 hours or so in which to 'bolt on'[234] an SSN to the Fund's PFP, are matters of great concern. There is little evident sign within the Fund that it plans to assume a significant degree of direct responsibility in the social areas,[235] although two Social Development Specialists were recruited late in 1999 to the Fund's African Department in order to help the Fund discharge its responsibilities within the PRSP framework. But as at 2002 the prospects for international human rights standards intruding onto the Fund's radar—to the extent necessary or desirable—seemed as distant as ever.

---

[233] E Denters (1996) at 136. As Denters observes, the putatively 'passive role of the IMF' in the context just described 'may lead to a situation where the organisation resigns itself to being or to making itself an "accomplice" to serious shortfalls in the maintenance of socioeconomic standards when governments show a lack of interest.'

[234] The term 'bolt on' appears to have been coined by OXFAM's Kevin Watkins.

[235] This is of course not to say that the Fund—as presently structured—is as a matter of principle an appropriate body to be given substantial and direct programmatic responsibilities in the human rights or social areas. See further the discussion in chapter VI.

III

The Importance of the Question: Comments on the Human Rights Impacts of the IFIs' Policies and Activities

---

PRELIMINARY REMARKS

Subject to the methodological constraints to be canvassed shortly, a discussion of the relevance of international human rights law to the IFIs would be incomplete without at least a brief analysis of the ways in which their policies and activities can impact—positively and negatively, and directly or indirectly—upon the realisation of human rights.

Apart from underscoring the importance of the general question under consideration, the following analysis serves the valuable secondary functions of: (a) signalling the chief conceptual and operational limitations provoking demands for reform, and (b) establishing relevant institutional parameters within which reform proposals—the subject of chapter VI—should be situated.

Causation in Context

It is not the purpose of this study to rehearse or evaluate the empirical literature concerning whether or the extent to which:

(a) Fund or Bank programmes have definitively and demonstrably caused human rights violations; or

(b) subject to (a), and to an evaluation of the legal parameters of the Bank's and Fund's constitutive documents, an explicit human rights approach would demonstrably have ameliorated the situation.

As to question (a), the empirical literature is vast, and cannot feasibly be synthesised here. For present purposes is will suffice to rely upon a select number of the more influential internal and external studies and evaluations.

The technical barriers to evaluation of pre- and post-economic 'crisis' situations are well known,[1] as are the more generic limitations of quantitative analysis of structural adjustment programs.[2] Data availability, consistency and comparability problems are dealt with at some length in the Human Development Report 2000.[3] The data availability constraints on crisis assessment naturally also hinder evaluations of responsibility, including that of the IFIs. As with the former task, it must openly be admitted that calibrating the degree of IFI responsibility for violations of human rights consequent upon economic crises or more generally is not an exact science. In certain cases assumptions must plainly be made, and to quite a significant extent those conclusions that can be drawn must necessarily rely upon qualitative rather than (or in addition to) quantitative information, including anecdotal accounts, and insights and opinions of informed observers.[4]

Furthermore, as to both (a) and (b), the promise of empirical certainty should not too readily be assumed. Considerable scope for good faith disagreement exists even with empirically-based methods, which in any event have been of

---

[1] See eg United Nations Support Facility for Indonesian Recovery (UNSFIR), *The Social Implications of the Indonesian Economic Crisis: Perceptions and Policy* (1999) at 6–7, and 11–26 on the limitations of small-scale assessments. The authors conclude (at 25): 'Given the weaknesses of the data currently [as at April 1999] available, the difficulty of comparing surveys' results, and the technically inaccurate exercise of generalising at the national level, care should be taken in using available data for programmatic purposes, in particular targeting.' See also: Speech by Jean-Michel Severino, Vice President, East Asia and Pacific Region, World Bank, at the Third Asia-Pacific Economic Cooperation Human Resources Development Ministerial Meeting, Washington DC, 28 July 1999, on the information gaps and unheard 'voices of the silent poor' during the East Asian crisis.

[2] On methodological limitations in evaluating the effects of structural adjustment, with a focus on the problem of data reliability and adequacy, see P Lundy, 'Limitations of Quantative [sic] Research in the Study of Structural Adjustment' (1996) 42 *Soc Sci Med* 313, 324, cited in E Curtis 'Child Health and the International Monetary Fund' (1998) 352, Issue 9140 *Lancet* 1622–24, 1624.

[3] HDR 2000 at 90–96, 106 and 141–43.

[4] One such observer, OXFAM, has summarised the Fund's culpability for the human consequences of the East Asian crisis in the following way: 'The IMF was not responsible for East Asia's crisis, but it was responsible for deepening and prolonging the recession. The economic costs have been enormous. Less visible, and less easy to estimate, are the human welfare costs. Poverty and vulnerability have increased across the region; some of the consequences may be irreversible.' OXFAM (1999) at 31. And see also OXFAM, *Education Now: Break the Cycle of Poverty* (1999) at 190–92; and OXFAM, October 1998 report on human cost of IMF programs: 'IMF policies based on the imposition of high interest rates, supposedly to "restore investor confidence," have exacerbated the situation and contributed to poverty. The most dramatic effects have been in Indonesia where gross domestic product is expected to contract by 20 percent.' By way of comparison, assessing IFI responsibility for the famine in Malawi, Action Aid Malawi has labelled as a 'fallacy' allegations that the IMF caused the famine by ordering the government to sell its grain reserves. However that NGO does allege that both the Bank and Fund 'had a hand in the growing indebtedness of the agency responsible for the reserve, and recommendations to reduce the reserve which were based on inaccurate information on crop yields.' See Bretton Woods Project, 'Bretton Woods Update' (July/August 2002; available at http://www.brettonwoods.org) at 7; Action Aid Malawi, *State of Disaster: Causes, Consequences and Policy Lessons from Malawi* (www.actionaid.org/newsandmedia/the_malawi_famine_of_2002.pdf); and cf IMF Country Report No. 02/181, August 2002, 'Malawi: Article IV Consultation and Economic Program for 2002—Staff Report; Staff Supplement; and Public Information Notice on the Executive Board Discussion.

only selective importance in justifying the expansion of the World Bank's and IMF's increasingly complex agendas.[5]

One of the most notorious difficulties—colouring the reliability of (frequently external) critiques and (frequently internal) claims, alike—is the requirement to compare hypothetical alternative situations. The threshold question itself is a difficult one: 'success in terms of what?'[6] An answer to this question in any given set of circumstances not only presupposes agreement as to the criteria for economic success, about which there is a considerable divergence of views,[7] but also as to the appropriate standards for measuring policy results and economic performance as a result of the Bank' and Fund's involvement.[8] In the latter respect, it is no doubt correct to say that practical standards purporting to measure member country performance simply by comparing their economic results (however defined) to the situation prevailing in the economy *prior* to the IFIs' involvement, are conceptually unsuited to the task.[9] The methodology of certain of the Fund's SAF and ESAF evaluations has been criticised on this basis.[10] Rather, the required comparison must be between the actual economic outcome (however defined), and the best outcome that was potentially achievable in the circumstances.[11] These conclusions will naturally be attended by a significant element of subjectivity, 'both because they involve

---

[5] It is often remarked that authoritative—even if empirically unsubstantiated—opinions of Nobel Prize-winning economists such as Amartya Sen and Joseph Stiglitz and others of similar stature are legitimate influences on policy development. For a criticism in the context of health policy see K Abbasi, 'The World Bank and World Health: Under Fire' (1999) 318, Issue 7189 *British Medical Journal* 1003–1006, 1006. And see R Wade (1997) for a discussion of the influence of NGOs and other (non-empirically based) factors in driving the Bank's 'green' agenda.

[6] J Williamson, 'On Judging the Success of IMF Policy Advice' in J Williamson (ed), *IMF Conditionality* 129–43 (1983) at 129.

[7] For a general discussion see J Williamson (1983) at 132–40.

[8] See M Guitián, *Fund Conditionality: Evolution of Principles and Practices* (1981) at 37; and J Williamson, 'On Judging the Success of IMF Policy Advice' in J Williamson (ed) (1983) at 130–32.

[9] S Dell, 'Stabilisation: The Political Economy of Overkill' in J Williamson, (ed) 17–45 (1983) at 39; J Williamson, 'On Judging the Success of IMF Policy Advice' in J Williamson (ed) (1983) at 131; T Killick, M Moazzam and M Manuel, 'What Can We Know About the Effects of IMF Programmes?' (1992) 15 *World Economy* 575–97; and for a fuller evaluation, see M Goldstein and P Montiel, 'Evaluating Fund Stabilisation Programs with Multicountry Data: Some Methodological Pitfalls' (1986) 33 *IMF Staff Papers* 2. Although these references deal principally with Fund conditionality in a formal sense, the principles discussed are also relevant to other aspects of the Fund's influence, and those of the Bank.

[10] T Killick, 'Can the IMF Help Low-Income Countries? Experiences with its Structural Adjustment Facilities' (1995) 18(4) *The World Economy* 603–16, 606–11.

[11] Still on the IMF example, it has been suggested that the Fund's performance should be considered against 'the improvement (one hopes) in economic performance in the actual outcome . . . , as opposed to the situation that would have occurred without Fund involvement . . . , as a proportion of the potential improvement from [that state] to the best potentially feasible outcome.' In this respect, '[a] finding that Fund involvement led to an improvement in performance would not suffice to justify endorsement of the role of the Fund: one also needs to consider whether the improvement came close to that potentially possible in the circumstances.' But conversely, 'it would not be enough to show that the outcome fell short of potential to condemn the Fund; one would also need to show that Fund involvement led to a deterioration in performance compared with what would otherwise have occurred'—J Williamson, 'On Judging the Success of IMF Policy Advice' in J Williamson (ed) (1983) at 132.

value judgements about trade-offs among competing objectives and because they require comparisons involving hypothetical alternative situations.'[12]

Empirically viable conclusions would require analysis with the benefit of scientific methods and resources beyond those contemplated by this study, and to a large extent beyond the author's expertise. As stated at the outset, the value and validity of this study do not rest upon empirically verifiable conclusions as to causation. While further research on those questions with the benefit of appropriate expertise and methodology is clearly warranted, the legal validity of the conclusions reached in chapter VI are unaffected thereby. The practical impact of those conclusions, however, will to some extent vary with the evolving contours of the causation debates.

The final and perhaps most important caveat to be made on causation is that to limit the expression of values such as human rights purely to quantitative and instrumental analysis, is to risk ignoring their essential character and importance. Irrespective of whether education, food, or free speech helps or hinders growth, project performance or prevailing development ideals on the empirical evidence, one of the basic premises of this study is that questions of fundamental 'human right' as a matter of principle cannot simply be laid upon the table and bargained away on the same basis as any other factor in development.

The Question of Bank and Fund Influence

The second preliminary issue is that none of this discussion would be relevant in a practical sense if it were the case, as is often claimed by officials at both the Bank and Fund, that the policy influence of the Bank and Fund in client countries is grossly inflated by popular imagination. As a practical matter, the impact of the conclusions reached in this (and like) studies vary in direct proportion with the actual extent of IFI influence in a particular set of circumstances.

To begin with, an assessment of the direct influence of the IFIs' chief decision-making organs—as bodies constituted by national government representatives—is complicated and clouded to some degree by boardroom protocol and the language of consensus and diplomatic compromise. The limitations (as Joseph Gold sees them) for the Fund in this respect have been summarised in the following way:

---

[12] J Williamson, 'On Judging the Success of IMF Policy Advice' in J Williamson (ed) (1983) at 142. As is noted there (at 142): 'it is surely better to make relevant but subjective comparisons rather than objective but fundamentally irrelevant comparisons.' See also S Dell (1983) at 39. However according to Mikesell, 'a feasible approach to evaluating the Fund's conditionality programs may be to look at the current policies of the developing countries that have been receiving IMF assistance under stand-by and extended facility arrangements in relation to the policies that have proved to be most effective in achieving balance of payments adjustment with successful growth'—R Mikesell, 'Appraising IMF Conditionality: Too Loose, Too Tight, Or Just Right?', in J Williamson (ed) 47–62 (1983) at 53.

It is difficult to assess the influence of statements by organs or other bodies within the Fund or within other international entities that urge policies on governments. The statements are often formulated in the language of compromise that is typical of committee prose. The statements may have a sharper focus in the first draft prepared by international civil servants, but the text is then blurred by the ministers or officials who compose the body issuing the statement. The motive for this blurring may be the absence of a true accord or the wish by governments to avoid firm commitments. Even when a clear text does survive in the drafting of a communiqué, an instrument of that character has no binding legal force. Governments are not subject to reproach that they are neglecting obligations if they give decisive effect to national, rather than to international, interests.[13]

Secondly, in trying to evaluate IFI policy leverage, the very obvious point needs to be made that generalisations can only take us so far. The extent of the IFIs' influence varies significantly according to the particular situation and country, and type of program or activity concerned. As a general proposition, it seems reasonably clear that the strength of the IFIs' influence and policy voice is linked to the 'relative indispensability' of their financial assistance.[14] The Bank's Economic and Sector Work (ESW), for example, like other precursors to policy-based lending in the 1970's, was not by itself very influential.[15] And the effectiveness of the Fund's Article IV consultations varies markedly according to the country concerned, and whether a Fund program is in place.[16] As a matter of perception both within and outside the Bank, the capacity to induce policy reforms in client countries has always been seen to be linked to 'having money on the table.'[17]

But the general proposition is in need of substantial qualification. In assessing the effectiveness of the international monetary regime, for example, Chayes and Chayes have downplayed the importance of the incentive and coercive measures at the Fund's disposal, suggesting instead that dialogue and persuasion have in fact been its most effective weapons even as against some of the poorer client states.[18] It would be simplistic and misleading to suggest that the Fund's

---

[13] J Gold (ed) (1984) at 558–59.

[14] D Kapur *et al* (eds) (1997) (Vol. 1) at 488.

[15] D Kapur *et al* (eds) (1997) (Vol. 1) at 488.

[16] See the discussion on Fund surveillance above chapter II, and also IMF, *External Evaluation of IMF Surveillance: Report by a Group of Independent Experts* (September 1999).

[17] D Kapur *et al* (eds) (1997) (Vol. 1) at 488. This is a double-edged sword however, to the extent that tying IMF-prompted policy reforms to lending diminishes the credibility of those reforms in the eyes of external investors. On this issue see J Sewell, N Birdsall and K Morrison, (Overseas Development Council), 'The Right Role for the IMF in Development,' *Global Policy Forum*, May 2000, http://www.globalpolicy.org/socecon/bwi-wto/imf/odc.htm.

[18] A Chayes and A Chayes (1995) argue from a regime theoretical perspective (at 234): 'Much of the commentary among regime theorists on the effectiveness of the international monetary regime emphasises the incentive/coercive measures at the Fund's disposal. It is of course true that in these activities the IMF carries a big stick. But in actual practice, the sanctions are much less real than they would seem. Like all ultimate weapons, the IMF's power to cut off funds is not easy to use. What is perhaps surprising is how closely, in the concrete setting of standby decisions, the Fund is confined to the instruments of dialogue and persuasion and how much freedom the most destitute of borrowers are able to maintain. The conception of the Fund's activities that emerges from its history

influence is anything close to absolute, notwithstanding the extent of industrialised country dominance of decision-making at Board level.[19] Negotiations
with the Fund over conditionality are frequently very genuine, protracted and
intense.[20] Borrowing countries often renege on 'agreed' conditions, leading to
nothing more than temporary suspensions of assistance followed by subsequent
re-negotiations on terms which better accommodate the borrower's concerns.[21]
This phenomenon has been portrayed in various ways, from Trubitt's account
of debtor nations 'stringing the Fund along' in order to minimise austerity and
maximise policy stability,[22] to Helleiner's description of the 'borrowers' famil-
iar account . . . of Washington's arrogance, and messianic zeal, with periodic
changes of religion, generating cynicism and eventually resorting to complex
"con games" to get at the desired resources.'[23]

Negotiations over the Jamaican and Argentine SBAs during the 1970s and
1980s are good illustrations of this complex dynamic,[24] as was the Fund's relationship with Indonesia in the 1990s. There are a range of explanations for this
from the Fund's perspective of course, including pressure for policy flexibility in
the face of public backlashes to prescribed austerity measures (including large
scale riots in numerous cases),[25] and the desire—motivated by variable combi-
nations of strategic, economic, political and humanitarian impulses—to stay
engaged with a defaulting country even at the risk of throwing 'good money
after bad.'[26] There may be more subtle reasons in other cases, such as what has

and practice is rather different from the conventional picture of the IMF as an effective wielder of
carrots and sticks.'

[19] See eg B Trubitt (1987) at 685–87, on dimensions of the 'compromise' between the Fund and
debtor nations.

[20] See eg C Payer, *The Debt Trap: The IMF and the Third World* (1974) at 33: '[SBA] negotiations are often hard-fought and bitter—a far cry from the image which the IMF would like to project of its highly competent staff dispensing impartial expert advice to grateful country officials.'

[21] See eg M Conklin and D Davidson, 'The IMF and Economic and Social Human Rights: A Case
Study of Argentina, 1958–1985' (1986) 8(1) *Human Rights Quarterly* 227–69; and G Helleiner,
'Panel Discussion' in J Williamson (ed) (1983) 581–88 at 585.

[22] B Trubitt (1987) at 685–87 and 692–93.

[23] G Helleiner, 'Panel Discussion' in J Williamson (ed) (1983) 581–88 at 585.

[24] B Trubitt (1987) at 692–93.

[25] For specific examples see L Williams, 'Indonesia food crisis: $4bn plea,' *Sydney Morning
Herald,* 26 June 1998: 'Sharp rises in fuel prices in May [1998], due to the scaling back of subsidies
under the original conditions of the IMF bailout, sparked rioting in the port city of Medan, which
then spread to Jakarta, toppling the former Soeharto Government, killing more than 1000 people
and causing massive damage to commercial districts.' See also M Barlow, 'Desperate Bolivians
Fought Street Battles to Half a Water-for-Profit Scheme: World Bank Must Realise Water is a Basic
Human Right,' *Toronto Globe and Mail,* 9 May 2000; and for an especially strident critique,
R Borosage, 'The IMF, peddling misery,' *International Herald Tribune,* 23–24 September 2000, at
4, asserting bluntly that: 'So the next time there are riots in Nigeria against IMF-mandated hikes in
fuel prices, demonstrations in Bolivia against privatisation of the water works, upheavals in
Tanzania against spreading hunger and desperation, don't be surprised. The IMF will have been
there, peddling misery, leaving devastation in its wake.'

[26] Indeed some degree of pragmatism in some circumstances is almost inevitable, especially
where capital flight might on reasonable grounds be expected to follow suspension of IMF support.
See eg F Smith, Jr, 'The Politics of IMF Lending' (1984) 4(1) *Cato Journal* 211–41 at 220 n 7.
However the manner of the Fund's dealings in Argentina's crisis in 2002 might constitute an

been called the 'rigour problem,' a reference to pressure from major shareholders or management for program conditions that only *appear* to be harsh and
far-reaching.[27] As Tony Killick has observed, these pressures 'strain the limited
policy implementation capabilities of borrowing governments, causing "non-
compliance" and suspicions of bad faith.'[28]

None of this is to question the generally superior bargaining position and policy leverage enjoyed by both the Bank and Fund vis a vis the lowest per capita
GDP client countries.[29] While the glare of public criticism has been focused as
never before upon both institutions following the East Asia crisis, HIPC countries and most others eligible for concessional assistance come to the Bank
and Fund on bended knee, seeking not only the IFIs' support and financing but
the 'seal of approval' that a Fund or Bank program will give to leverage other
critical external resource flows.[30]

exception to this rule. See eg Bretton Woods Project, 'Bretton Woods Update' (July/August 2002;
available at http://www.brettonwoods.org) 'IMF Fiddles While Argentina Burns' (at 8): 'Despite
repealing the financial crimes law on 30 May, an essential precondition to further loan negotiations,
progress with the Fund remains exasperatingly slow. . . . The real pressure on the IMF to ink a deal
in Argentina is now coming from the threat of financial contagion. In a 1 July [2002] editorial, the
New York Times chided the Bush Administration for being "far too passive, making little effort to
exhort the IMF to reach a deal with Buenos Aires." Fear of financial instability spreading first to
Brazil and then throughout the region, combined with a broader backlash against the liberalisation
agenda is fuelling the calls for action.'

[27] T Killick, 'Adjustment and Economic Growth' in J Broughton and K Lateef (eds), *Fifty Years
After Bretton Woods: The Future of the IMF and the World Bank* (1995) 139–59, 154.

[28] T Killick, 'Adjustment and Economic Growth' in J Broughton and K Lateef (eds), (1995) at
154: 'Alternatively, when combined with continuing pressures on staff to maintain the levels of
adjustment lending, these pressures give rise to "paper programs"—the penning of ambitious-seem-
ing commitments to reforms that both parties tacitly understand but which cannot or will not be
implemented . . . There is a good deal of pretence in conditionality: paper agreements that the staffs
of the Bretton Woods institutions know cannot stick but that are intended to impress managements
and boards and to "keep the money moving," or just to give the appearance that borrowing governments are being treated equally.' A pertinent illustration might be found in the Bank's announce-
ment in July 2000 that Cameroon—ranked 134 out of 174 on UNDP's Human Development Index
(HDI) for the year 2000 (see Human Development Report 2000 at 159) and last place on
Transparency International's corruption rankings for the year 1999—had 'broadly hit the targets set
under its recently concluded structural adjustment program.' For details of the program see World
Bank, 'Cameroon: Third Structural Adjustment Credit Project (Vol 1), 29 April 1998, Project
Information Document No. 6517, involving such challenging components as regulatory and institutional reform, privatisation and financial sector reform. One wonders about the extent to which
pressure for timely debt relief without compromise to HIPC terms weighs upon official program
assessments in such cases. See *World Bank Development News* (www.worldbank.org), 19 July 2000.

[29] See eg D Bradlow (1996) at 50, n 15; J Hippler, *The Democratisation of Disempowerment: The
Problem of Democracy in the Third World* (1995); and A Orford, 'Globalisation and the Right to
Development' in P Alston (ed), *People's Rights* (2001) 127–84, 151–52.

[30] On the Bank's leverage see N Bridgeman, 'World Bank Reform in the "Post-Policy" Era' (2001)
13 *Georgetown International Environmental Law Review* 1013–46, 1019. In the IMF's case see eg A
Orford, 'Locating the International: Military and Monetary Interventions after the Cold War'
(1997) 38 *Harvard International Law Journal* 443: 'Since 1982, the IMF has played a central role in
arranging for private banks to take part in concerted or co-ordinated lending packages. The involvement of the IMF is seen as desirable, not only because it provides extra liquidity, but more importantly because private banks assume that a lending package that includes the imposition of IMF
conditionality will guarantee better and more stable economic policies in the debtor country.' See
also W Cline, *International Debt Re-examined* (1995) at 206, and A Orford (2001) at 151–52. This

Furthermore the lowest per capita GDP countries almost invariably lack technical capacity to design (let alone implement) their own macro-economic policy framework, and consequently are especially vulnerable to the 'magic' of the Washington economists' expertise. It is no secret that PFP's—giving a lie to the rhetoric of 'country ownership'—have in the general run of cases been IMF creations, drafted in Washington and flown out to the borrowing country with the IMF country mission as a *fait accompli*.[31] One cannot help but notice the striking similarity in the basic elements of PFPs across the board, defying the great diversity of member states' political systems, development priorities, and social, economic and cultural characteristics. While it is still too early to judge the question definitively, as at 2002 there were reasons to doubt the potential of the PRSP process to rectify these sorts of deficiencies.[32]

While it is impossible here to calibrate even a generalised scale of IFI influence applicable in all countries in all situations, the case of Indonesia in the mid/late 1990s provides a prominent and useful illustration. Notwithstanding official disclaimers by both the Bank and Fund to the contrary, a summary appraisal of the events throughout the East Asian crisis shows readily that the IFIs' policy influence was at all material times considerable, even if something short of omnipotent.[33] For example, in the case of the Fund, one senior Indonesian government official interviewed in October 1999 stated that it was the IMF that determined the percentage allocation in the budget for education and health, albeit 'in conjunction with the government.' However the Fund has its own preconceived 'international (macroeconomic) formula,' and needs to be 'convinced why the standard model is inapplicable in a given situation, or needs to be varied,'[34] which is not an easy onus to discharge.

In further support of this general position reliance is placed principally upon:

type of leverage was acknowledged expressly by the Bank's Chief Economist in July 2000 in the case of Russia, remarking that among the prerequisites for that country's economic recovery was 'an IMF program so that discussions in other international fora can move more easily.' See *World Bank Development News*, 27 July 2000.

[31] Interviews in Washington DC, February 2000.

[32] This is an especially difficult question to judge, in view of the limited administrative and technical capacities in most HIPC and IDA countries. But for early criticisms see the discussion below at nn 132–51 and accompanying text.

[33] For manifestations of the Fund's influence over the pace and content of Indonesia's economic reform program, and indirectly, the composition of its Cabinet, see eg 'News Update: Wahid Sacks Two Ministers,' *Sydney Morning Herald On-Line*, 25 April 2000, http://www.smh.com.au. However the fact of successive program failures are re-negotiations reminds us of the need for critical rigour and balance in appraising the power relations between the Fund and this particular client.

[34] Interviews in Jakarta, October 1999. Furthermore according to this official a major problem lies in the fact that when the need to vary the standard model arises from social or cultural or anthropological or other non-economic factors, these reasons are 'difficult to communicate' to the IMF, because of their macro-economic disciplinary purity. And as at October 1999 a director of one of Indonesia's most prominent development NGOs remarked that the IFIs still 'dictate to the government of Indonesia' to a great extent.

—a survey of media reports and evaluations from 1997 until mid-2000;[35]

—a proper appreciation of the significance of the phenomenon of cross-conditionality[36] and the Fund's role (in particular) as 'gatekeeper' for international and bilateral aid and private capital flows;[37] and

—an objective appraisal of the timing and degree of correspondence between the IFIs' and the government of Indonesia's publicly stated policy priorities, including on such matters as institutional and structural reform, the pursuit of high level corruption prosecutions, and perhaps most tellingly of all, the handling of the 1999 East Timor referendum's aftermath.[38]

One important consequence that flows from this, at least on moral grounds, is that with a greater degree of influence ought to flow a greater degree of responsibility.

[35] For a recent example see D O'Sullivan, 'IMF spurs Indonesian reform,' *Financial Times*, 9 April 2000. The extract which follows illustrates some of the complexities in the 'leverage' equation in Indonesia, in particular (apart from continuing confirmation of the Fund's extensive policy influence) the kinds of domestic political agendas that the IFIs' role can serve: 'The IMF warned that lack of real structural reform could undermine the current growth spurt. . . . Galvanised into action, ministers rushed through some key measures and promised to implement others by April 21. . . . The IMF has said the loan could now be paid out in May. "What the IMF has done is issue a wake-up call," said Emil Salim, a senior economic adviser to President Abdurrahman Wahid. Indonesia will also go ahead with plans to ask Paris Club official creditors for a rescheduling of $2.1bn in sovereign debt. A Paris Club meeting will start as planned on Wednesday, though diplomats expect any agreement to be conditional on Jakarta winning back the IMF's approval. . . . Analysts said the last few days had shown Jakarta could push through reforms if it wanted to. "People have worked very hard and in good faith in the last 10 days," said a source at a multilateral institution. But critics are asking why so little was done until the IMF threatened to hold up its loans. Much of the blame is being directed at the team of ministers in charge of the economy. . . . None [of the Ministers] has been in government before and some are said to resent what they see as meddling by the IMF and the World Bank. . . . Rumours have resurfaced in Jakarta that Mr Wahid, who has long wanted to purge his cabinet, may now be planning to get rid of some of the economic team. "This hue and cry by the IMF has presented him with a golden opportunity to do so," said HS Dillon, another presidential adviser.'

[36] The general practice of the Bank has been not to lend to a country in which a Fund program is not in place. For an excellent discussion of this phenomenon see OXFAM (1999) at 12–14. Interestingly however as at July 2000 there were emerging signs that as the cross-conditionality phenomenon might be weakening, with the Fund's Executive Directors reported to be open-minded about the Bank (in conjunction with political pressure on the Fund to retreat into narrowly defined and presumptively firewalled 'macroeconomic' areas) engaging in non-IMF 'client' countries. See *World Bank Development News*, 18 July and 19 July 2000.

[37] As one insider put it, the London and Paris Club donors 'won't move without a Fund program at the country level.' Interviews in Washington DC in February 2000. This type of leverage was acknowledged expressly by the Bank's Chief Economist in July 2000 in the case of Russia, remarking that among the prerequisites for that country's economic recovery was 'an IMF program so that discussions in other international fora can move more easily.' See *World Bank Development News*, 27 July 2000. By way of an aside, evidence (including insiders' admissions) of this kind of leverage is of great interest in view of the increasing putative reliance by the Fund lately on the need to defer to donors in cases such as East Timor, Pakistan and Russia, in a way that appears to abrogate responsibility for independent and principled action. This disclaimer seems particularly unconvincing when the reciprocal aspect of the dynamic—the power the Fund wields in particular cases as 'gatekeeper' for international donor support and financial flows—is omitted.

[38] Relevant aspects of the IFIs' roles in East Timor are discussed in more detail in chapter IV.

Models of Human Rights Influence

As a final preliminary matter, in order to illustrate the kinds of presumptive effects on human rights of IFI economic (and other) policies, it may be helpful to adapt de Vylder's 'concentric circles' model.[39] While that model is expressed to be limited to children's rights and macroeconomics, there is no reason (for limited expository purposes) why it should not apply to all human rights and disadvantaged groups more broadly, and to the (non-'macroeconomic') policies of the Bank as well as the Fund. At the hub of de Vylder's circle are said to be those policies and legislation which explicitly target children, 'such as provision of primary health and education, and regulations against exploitative child labour.'[40] According to de Vylder, 'most of the Articles in the [CRC] are to be found in this inner circle.'[41] In the 'middle circle' are said to be 'policies and institutions which have a strong, but more indirect, impact,' such as 'redistributive tax and public expenditure policies, traditional social security and welfare policies and, in general, policies directly affecting the situation of the family.'[42] Finally, in the outermost circle are 'general policies where the impact may still be strong but even more indirect, such as trade and exchange rate policies, WTO rules, monetary policies or environmental policies.'[43]

In conceptual terms de Vylder's explicitly rights-based model is very similar to the three-tiered classification system of anti-poverty aims and operational objectives shared by the World Bank and the international development agencies of Germany, Sweden, and the UK.[44] The latter system—while in its terms best suited to providing a basis for evaluation of *positive* impacts, alone, on any given set of indicators—classifies interventions into three groups:

1. 'Direct or focused actions,' defined as those actions that 'aim directly and predominantly to focus on the rights, interests and needs of poor people;'
2. 'Indirect or inclusive actions,' defined as 'actions which aim to benefit broad population groups including poor people,' but which also address human rights related issues such as distributional equity, and barriers to the participation or access of poor people; and
3. 'Enabling actions,' defined as 'structural measures aimed at underpinning pro-poor economic growth or other policies leading to social, environmental or economic benefits for poor people.'[45]

---

[39] See S de Vylder, *Development Strategies, Macro-economic Policies and the Rights of the Child*, Discussion Paper for Radda Barnen (1996) at 9.

[40] S de Vylder, (1996) at 9.

[41] S de Vylder, (1996) at 9.

[42] S de Vylder, (1996) at 9.

[43] S de Vylder, (1996) at 10. For an illustration of ways in which these 'third circle' policies affected poverty in the East Asian crisis see T Atinc and M Walton, *Social Consequences of the East Asian Financial Crisis* (1998) at 26–27.

[44] OECD/DAC Poverty Study (1999) at 3.

[45] OECD/DAC Poverty Study (1999) at 3.

While there is no special magic or science to either of these models, they do provide a useful and basic conceptual delineation of the principal levels at which an appraisal of the human rights impacts—both positive and negative—of IFI interventions could be undertaken.

The IMF

On a purely abstract level, describing the nature of the IMF's positive human rights impacts is relatively straightforward. As will be canvassed in more detail later, the official position of the Fund is that explicit engagement with human rights, and even poverty 'as an overarching goal,'[46] is beyond its lawful mandate, and most definitely beyond its expertise, which all but rules out any impacts on level (1) in the immediately preceding classification.[47] Nevertheless, the Fund's policies and activities are capable of impacting in a positive sense on levels (2) and (3).

In terms of its 'enabling actions' (category 3), and without critically evaluating the case made, the Fund's basic case is that 'macroeconomic stability, market-friendly structural reforms, and good governance are crucial ingredients for rapid sustainable economic growth,' which is said to be a 'prerequisite for enduring poverty reduction.'[48] In other words, stable macroeconomic foundations provide the necessary enabling environment for the realisation of all human rights.

'Indirect or inclusive' human rights benefits (category 2) could in theory flow through efficiencies generated by health and education sector reforms in Fund-sponsored structural adjustment programs, furthering the progressive

---

[46] See eg OECD/DAC Poverty Report (1999) at 2. Nevertheless, as has been discussed, the replacement of the ESAF with the PRGF in November 1999 has placed poverty reduction as a 'key objective for IMF concessional lending to low-income countries.' IMF, *Social Policy Issues in IMF-Supported Programs: Follow-up on the 1995 World Summit for Social Development* (2000) at 2.

[47] The Fund has on occasion taken a direct role in support of human rights in the form of labour standards, as will be discussed shortly. And it has claimed to 'support the Core Labour Standards for which the [ILO] is the responsible institution,' including freedom of association and the right to collective bargaining, and freedom from discrimination, forced labour, and exploitative child labour.' IMF, 'Women 2000: IMF support aims to enhance participation by women in social and economic development' (2000) 29(12) *IMF Survey* 202. However these are in terms of ILO Conventions rather than the core universal human rights norms which are the focus of the present study, and in any case it is not clear how the Fund's stated 'support' of the labour standards—which through the eyes of many serve to protect the commercial interests of major shareholder manufacturers and exporters as much as exploited workers in developing countries—actually translates to tangible impacts in human rights terms.

[48] IMF, *Social Policy Issues in IMF-Supported Programs: Follow-up on the 1995 World Summit for Social Development* (2000) at 2. To similar effect see H Morais, 'A Festschrift Honoring Professor Louis B Sohn (April 8, 2000): The Globalisation of Human Rights Law and the Role of International Financial Institutions in Promoting Human Rights' (2000) 33 *George Washington International Law Review* 71–96, 87.

realisation of the rights to health and education under the CRC and ICESCR.[49] The rights of women and children—who often suffer first and most severely in times of economic duress[50]—may indirectly be promoted through the Fund's poverty reduction and crisis prevention efforts.[51] Another example might be indirect enhancement of independence of the judiciary and quality of administration of justice through 'governance' and rule of law conditionality, with potential human rights benefits (positive externalities) reaching well beyond the financial and 'commercial' concerns of the IMF's mandate strictly construed. A particularly topical example of a category 2 human rights benefit could be the indirect enhancement of the rights to freedom of expression and freedom of association under the ICCPR, participatory rights of the child,[52] and other human rights benefits relating to freedom of information, participation in public affairs, and transparency and accountability in government, to the extent that the PRSP process (in conjunction with the Bank, international agencies, donors and other relevant actors) is implemented faithfully to its original design and premises.

Finally, no assessment of 'category 2' impacts would be complete without reference to the evolution of the Fund's social policy advice and design (with the Bank and regional development banks taking the lead) of SSNs in the 1990s, and its concerns to target expenditures in education and health on the poorest and most vulnerable members of society during a crisis, and agreement to subsidies on essential items within the constraints of client countries' negotiating capacities. Through targeted—albeit not explicitly 'human rights'—measures of this kind, the rights to health, education, adequate standard of living, and the right to life, itself, can no doubt indirectly be safeguarded and, ideally, enhanced.

The Bank

Again on an abstract level, most if not all of the World Bank's activities might be hoped to result in positive human rights outcomes on de Vylder's or the OECD's three-tiered classification, consistent with its explicit anti-poverty

---

[49] The Fund's ideological zeal for privatisation of education and health services does not always, of course, result in a net benefit in human rights terms. However the purpose of the present discussion is simply to illustrate—in human rights terms—the kinds of potentially positive entries on the overall ledger that do exist, without purporting to evaluate overall outcomes.

[50] Women have sometimes been described as the 'shock absorbers' of shock therapy and structural adjustment. See below n 69 and accompanying text.

[51] For this example see IMF, 'Women 2000: IMF support aims to enhance participation by women in social and economic development' (2000) 29(12) *IMF Survey* 202. The 'indirect'—rather than direct—effects are made clear in the statement that '[t]he IMF's primary contribution to sustainable economic and human development, including gender equality, is through its work to promote macroeconomic stability and high-quality growth. High-quality growth encompasses policies that reduce poverty and improve equality of opportunity for all of society's members, in particular its most vulnerable segments, which frequently consist of women and children.' It is made clear that direct responsibility for these 'social' issues lies with others, notably the Bank, the UN, and regional development banks.

[52] Article 12 of the CRC.

mission.[53] As with the IMF, categories two and three are paramount, by reason of the Bank's formal insistence that while human rights are relevant to the Bank's work, direct responsibility for human rights implementation as such falls beyond its mandate.[54] But notwithstanding this, to a degree exceeding the undisclosed direct human rights work of the IMF, the 'category one' activities undertaken by the Bank in recent years have not been without significance. Examples include human rights components of Bank-supported judicial reform projects and HIV/AIDS strategies, instances of advocacy expressly based upon relevant international human rights instruments, human rights conditionality (express or implicit) in connection with lending activities, human rights components of the Bank's Operational Directive (OD) 4.20 on Indigenous Peoples,[55] and policy developments concerning exploitative child labour. These are discussed in more detail in chapter IV.

Examples of potentially positive 'category two' impacts would include the Bank's efforts through lending and technical assistance activities to build effective legal institutions and accountable political institutions at the national level,[56]

[53] One must of course be wary of accepting the anti-poverty mission at face value. See eg J Gatthi, 'Good Governance as a Counter Insurgency Agenda to Oppositional and Transformative Social Projects in International Law' (1999) 5 *Buffalo Human Rights Law Review* 107, 146: 'The Bank boasts that its efforts in alleviating poverty constitute an important human rights role, since "no other human rights could be fully enjoyed" if freedom from poverty was not addressed. However, there is a simple response to this very opportunistic claim. Poverty alleviation not only features tangentially in its (the Bank's) lending programs, but it is also based on a weak approach to basic needs insofar as it takes for granted and fails to challenge the existing disparities of wealth and power within borrowing countries as well as within the international order.'

[54] World Bank, *Development and Human Rights: The Role of the World Bank* (1998). Interestingly in mid-2002 Bank President Wolfensohn directed his staff to prepare an explicit strategy for the Bank on human rights: Bretton Woods Project, 'Bretton Woods Update' (July/August 2002; available at http://www.brettonwoods.org) 'Bank Declaration of Human Rights' at 1 (see chapter VI below at n 66 and accompanying text). However based upon statements on the matter by the Bank's General Counsel Ko-Yung Tung, it was not clear whether the terms of reference for this exercise would countenance express recognition of legal accountability for human rights observance (let alone promotion or fulfillment). The General Counsel's remarks (Bretton Woods Project July/August 2002, p 1) seemed to strongly echo the basic position in the Bank's 1998 *Development and Human Rights* publication, to the effect that the Bank's poverty-reduction work indirectly helped client countries realise the human rights entitlements of their peoples, but that the Bank itself had no direct responsibility in that regard.

[55] Although for a strong critique see F MacKay, 'Universal Rights or a Universe Unto Itself? Indigenous Peoples' Human Rights and the World Bank's Draft Operational Policy 4.10 on Indigenous Peoples' (2002) 17 *American University International Law Review* 527–624.

[56] However for a foundational human rights critique of the capacity of the Bank's 'good governance' agenda to co-opt and defuse more fundamental resistance to the neo-liberal agenda, see J Gatthi (1999) at 141–47, 155 and 162. At 155: '[O]ne may read [former Bank General Counsel Ibrahim Shihata's] more subtle definition of the role of rights in the World Bank's work as part and parcel of a strategy of defusing and appropriating human rights opposition to World Bank policies.' And at 162: '[T]he good governance proposals are part of a conservative agenda for human rights in that it is based on establishing a connection between human rights and the World Bank's development policies which may themselves be inimical to the protection of human rights, and social and economic rights. By emphasising the supposedly reinforcing character of human rights and economic policy, as if they were always mutually supportive, human rights activists have established a foothold to negotiate with the Bank. In my view, this has only served to legitimise the economically disastrous programs of neo-liberal economic reform embraced by the World Bank and IMF.'

which in conjunction with provision of supporting educational guarantees and basic social services might improve citizen's political participation and access to justice—important development goods as well as prerequisites for the fulfilment of human rights obligations under the ICCPR and ICESCR. The same might be said of the potential human rights relevance of the PRSP process—to the extent that it's implementation in a given situation promotes genuine country ownership of economic policies, and increases the scope for meaningful participation and for political and legal accountability at the national level. The protection afforded under the Bank's social safeguard policies is another good example. Properly implemented, the putatively binding provisions of OD 4.30 on Involuntary Resettlement, Operational Policy (OP) 4.20 on the Gender Dimension of Development, and OD 4.01 on Environmental Assessment, while containing little explicit human rights content, have an important bearing on the implementation by States parties of their obligations under the ICESCR, CRC, CEDAW and a potentially wide range of other such instruments.

Finally, at the highest level of abstraction, examples of potentially positive 'category three' enabling actions would include the human rights flow-on effects from the Bank's Economic and Sector Work—for example the policy influence of its flagship 'WDRs' and associated research on the factors vital for development—and technical assistance in connection with structural issues such as trade and fiscal policy, and environmental policy. One could also include as an 'enabling action' the leveraging of the Bank's policy influence at Consultative Group (donor) meetings and other international forums, with potential for resource mobilisation in directions conducive to human rights promotion. Also relevant in this category are the Bank's own information disclosure policies and the establishment of internal accountability mechanisms—in particular the Operations Evaluation Department and (in 1993) the Inspection Panel[57]—the effective functioning of which would encourage the exercise of the Bank's policy influence in directions consistent with shareholder members' obligations under applicable human rights treaties.

THE NEGATIVE SIDE OF THE LEDGER

The first point to be made as far as macro-economic design is concerned is that the Fund in general appears to remain convinced of the appropriateness of the

---

[57] The three-member Inspection Panel was established by the Bank in 1993: The World Bank Inspection Panel, IBRD Resolution No. 93–10, 22 September 1993; IDA Resolution No. 93–6. Under paragraph 1–2 of the Resolution, the Panel is designed to be independent of Bank staff, reporting directly to the Executive Directors. Its mandate is to review complaints from any group of private persons alleging that they are suffering or expect to suffer material adverse effects from the failure of the Bank to follow its operational policies and procedures (paragraph 12 of the Resolution). For a general discussion see D Bradlow, 'International Organisations and Private Complaints: The Case of the World Bank Inspection Panel' (1994) 34 *Virginia Journal of International Law* 553. The Panel's central role is to promote compliance by Bank staff and Management with the binding terms of Operational Policies.

basic ingredients of its neo-liberal economic prescriptions, in East Asia, Russia, and anywhere else.[58] If anything, Fund officials will often say, the problem is that client countries have failed to implement its prescriptions sufficiently. To the extent that culpability for erroneous program design is admitted, the concessions generally go to issues of timing and sequencing, rather than content, although admissions of general failure to predict the severity of the East Asian crisis are fairly self-evident and proffered freely.[59] However for reasons stated

[58] See eg *World Bank Development News*, 7 April 2000: 'Acting IMF Managing Director Stanley Fischer yesterday delivered a robust defense of the so-called "Washington consensus", saying that macroeconomic stabilization and structural reforms were essential for achieving sustained and equitable growth in Russia, the Financial Times (p 2) reports. "After 10 years of experience in over 25 transition economies, the evidence is clear that the basic economic reform and growth strategy recommended by mainstream economists works," Fischer said at an economic conference in Moscow.'

[59] See eg 'IMF admits it "badly" miscalculated Asian crisis,' *Asia Pulse: Philippine Newspaper Highlights*, 21 January 1999: 'The IMF admitted that it "badly misguaged" the severity of the East Asian economic collapse and inadequately financed the programmes it engineered to rescue Thailand, Indonesia and South Korea.'). Admissions of the error of unwarranted fiscal contraction early in the crisis have also been made. The IMF has also admitted its error in East Asia in imposing unwarranted and unduly strict fiscal discipline at the outset, thereby worsening the crisis. In the circumstances of pre-crisis Indonesia, it is now widely recognised that a slight fiscal expansion, rather than a contraction, would have been a more appropriate response. The Banks' former chief economist Joseph Stiglitz was making this point frequently in public addresses in 1999. See also T Atinc and M Walton, *Social Consequences of the East Asia Financial Crisis* (1998) at 26: 'To help reduce poverty there is a strong case to err on the side of [macro-economic policy] expansion,' although investor confidence and inflationary and economic growth risks need to be weighed. 'Moderating economic contraction is important for the poor, and may be distributionally favourable. How the fiscal expansion is financed is equally important.' As OXFAM put it in 1999: 'The flawed prescription follows a misdiagnosis of the disease: Fund staff have discovered budget deficit problems where no such problems existed.' OXFAM, *The IMF: Wrong Diagnosis, Wrong Medicine* (1999) at 29. In sharp contrast to Latin America in the 1980s each of the East Asian countries in the mid- to late-1990s had high levels of savings and a sustainable budget position, and accordingly were 'emphatically not basket cases of fiscal profligacy.' OXFAM International Briefing, 'The Real Crisis in Asia' (April 1998). OXFAM added that: 'Monetary and fiscal policy has been tightened to the point of strangulation, threatening to kill or disable the patient during the first phase of treatment.' It was argued that coupled with high interest rates, amounting to over 100 per cent in Indonesia, 'domestic firms were faced with a near exclusion from trade credit markets, undermining their capacity to generate output and exports. Import demand collapsed in the face of the credit squeeze and currency devaluations . . . This in turn undermined prospects for recovery. In Indonesia, financing problems contributed to a 35 per cent drop in export earnings for the textile sector due to shortages of raw materials.' OXFAM International Policy Paper, *East Asian 'Recovery' Leaves the Poor Sinking* (October 1998). This was said to illustrate how 'misplaced financial stringency and inadequate attention to investment conditions undermined the potential for recovery and deepened the recession.' OXFAM International Policy Paper, *East Asian 'Recovery' Leaves the Poor Sinking* (October 1998). For similar criticisms by Robert Wade and Martin Khor, see M Khor, 'The Economic Crisis in East Asia: Causes, Effects, Lessons' in *Oslo Symposium Report 1998* at 151–54, focusing upon the Fund's anti-inflationary 'Asian water torture' measures of high interest rates, and the fallacious assumption (due to high indebtedness of Asian companies and the adverse presentational effects of high rates and fiscal austerity) that such measures would stabilise currency markets, dampen pressure for competitive devaluations and make it easier for East Asian governments to repay foreign creditors. To the contrary, according to Financial Times reports at that time, such measures in the East Asian context seemed destined to 'condemn [East Asian countries] to a never-ending spiral of recession and bankruptcy.' OXFAM has concluded that '[t]he resulting austerity measures have increased poverty and undermined human welfare. Some of the effects will be felt by the next generation as public health deteriorates and large numbers of children are withdrawn from school.' OXFAM (1999) at 29. For criticisms of the IMF's anti-inflationary

earlier, namely the difficulties of arguing convincingly either way without adequately addressing the range of possible counterfactual situations, issues of technical program design will not be canvassed here in any great detail. Rather, an attempt has been made to focus upon issues of more systemic importance.[60]

Structural Adjustment Generally

The performance record of the Bank and Fund's structural adjustment programs in economic terms, as with those programs' human rights impacts, has been a matter of fierce debate since the 1980s. According to some reviewers, including some internal IMF studies, 'countries that have followed the IMF's structural adjustment programme have lagged in terms of per capita income compared to those that have not.'[61] While some improvements were claimed in the late 1990s, at the turn of the century the Bank's Operations Evaluation Department and an independent expert review at the IMF still found considerable cause for criticism,[62] and the controversial 'Meltzer Commission Report' by the US Congress International Financial Institutions Advisory Committee claimed that fifty-five to sixty percent of World Bank-financed operations were failures.[63] By this time

---

zeal in Argentina's crisis see J Stiglitz, 'Argentina's Lessons', *Project Syndicate* (January 2002), http://www.project-syndicate.cz/series/series_text.php4?id=760.

[60] One systemic issue which it is not possible to discuss here in any detail is the Fund's role in the 1980s debt crisis. For a number of criticisms however see eg P Körner, G Maass, T Siebold and T Rainer, *The IMF and the Debt Crisis: A Guide to the Third World's Dilemmas* (1986); E Altvater, K Hübner, J Lorentzen and R Rojas (eds), *The Poverty of Nations: A Guide to the Debt Crisis from Argentina to Zaire* (1991); and D Ghai (ed), *The IMF and the South: The Social Impact of Crisis and Adjustment* (1991).

[61] S Ambrose, 'Challenging the IMF, intellectually and politically,' *International Herald Tribune*, 29 April 1998, cited in Standing (1999) at 14. See also J Sachs (1989) at 269–85. In particular (at 279): 'The post-war history of stabilisation, liberalisation, and conditionality can make a pessimist of the most tenacious optimist. Few stabilisation and liberalisation plans meet their initial objectives, and many fail miserably.' See also S Haggard (1985); E Carrasco and M Kose (1996) at 31–34; T Killick, 'Adjustment and Economic Growth' in J Broughton and K Lateef (eds) (1995) at 153.

[62] IMF, *External Evaluation of the ESAF: Report by a Group of Independent Experts* (1998); World Bank Operations Evaluation Department, *1999 Annual Review of Development Effectiveness: Toward a Comprehensive Development Strategy* (1999). In 2000 the OED concluded that only seventy-two percent of the Bank's projects achieved a 'satisfactory or better outcome.' World Bank Operations Evaluation Department, 'Development Effectiveness at the Bank: What is the Score?' 24 *OED Reach* 1 (Spring 2000). Bank Management appears to distinguish between an unsatisfactory record of performance in the 1980s, and an improving record in the 1990s 'as the lessons from experience and research evaluations were built into [adjustment] operations.' Bretton Woods Project, 'Bretton Woods Update' (July/August 2002) at 3 (available at http://www.bretton woods.org). However many independent studies suggest that adjustment has resulted in far less satisfactory outcomes—including during the 1990s—in human development terms (Bretton Woods Project (July/August 2002) at 3). See also nn 9–11 above, and also chapter II at nn 53–58 and accompanying text.

[63] Meltzer Commission Report, International Financial Institutions Advisory Commission: Hearing Before the Senate Committee on Foreign Relations, 106th Congress (2000). For a critique of this report however see chapter IV below at n 280 and accompanying text.

'conditionality' as a vehicle for policy reform had likewise roundly been discredited.[64]

But beyond the question of economic efficiency, an independent expert of the Commission on Human Rights has claimed that structural adjustment programs have had 'distinct (and generally adverse) impacts' on human rights at the economic and political levels.[65] Such criticisms can be traced back to seminal studies in 1991 and 1992 by the Sub-Commission's Special Rapporteur for the realisation of economic, social and cultural rights. In his report in 1991 the Special Rapporteur catalogued in some detail the ways in which austerity measures and other aspects of adjustment programs could impair (and in the opinion of the Special Rapporteur, had impaired) the fulfilment of numerous rights guaranteed in the ICESCR at the national level, with particular focus upon the rights to education, health, food, adequate housing, and employment.[66] The criticisms in his final report in 1992 were expanded to take account of lack of symmetry in the burdens of adjustment, a bias towards the trade interests and constituencies of developed countries, the erosion of economic self-determination, reliance on a contested and widely inapplicable economic template and failure to explore alternatives, the ineffectual nature of conditionality and program supervision, and negative human rights impacts of privatisation and liberalisation.[67]

Criticisms of this kind continue to resonate at the turn of the century, even in Uganda, often cited as one of the few 'blue eyed boys' of structural adjustment.[68] The economically and socially disadvantaged people in society, it has been remarked, continue to serve as the 'mine shaft canaries' of the global

---

[64] See eg J Stiglitz, 'The World Bank at the Millennium' (1999) 109 *Economic Journal* 577–97, 591; C Gilbert, A Powell and D Vines, 'Positioning the World Bank' (1999) 109 *Economic Journal* 598–633, 617–19.

[65] See E/CN.4/2000/6 at para 32, and the report of the open-ended working group on structural adjustment programmes and economic, social and cultural rights on its second session, 1–3 March 1999, E/CN.4/1999/51, at para 11(a).

[66] 'The Realisation of Economic, Social and Cultural Rights,' second progress report by Danilo Türk, Special Rapporteur, Subcommission for the Prevention of Discrimination and Protection of Minorities, 43rd Session, UN Doc. E/CN.4/Sub.2/1991/17 (1991) at 36–51. See also W Berg and G Thole (1986) at 168–69, on violations of economic, social and cultural rights; B Trubitt (1987) at 684, 686–87; and B Rajagopal, 'Crossing the Rubicon: Synthesising the Soft International Law of the IMF and Human Rights' (1993) 11 *Boston University International Law Journal* 81 at 93, n 62 and the numerous references referred to there.

[67] See 'The Realisation of Economic, Social and Cultural Rights,' Final Report submitted by Danilo Türk, Special Rapporteur, Subcommission for the Prevention of Discrimination and Protection of Minorities, 49th Session, UN Doc. E/CN.4/Sub.2/1992/16 (1992) at 11–18. For further arguments that adjustment policies 'massively violate' the rights contained in the UDHR and ICESCR and widen the gap between rich and poor, see B Trubitt (1987). To similar effect, see M Conklin and D Davidson (1986) at 254–57; and M Elahi, 'The Impact of Financial Institutions on the Realisation of Human Rights: Case Study of the International Monetary Fund in Chile' (1986) 6 *Boston College Third World Law Journal* 143, 145 at 155–57.

[68] J Oloka-Onyango, 'Poverty, Human Rights and the Quest for Sustainable Human Development in Structurally-Adjusted Uganda' (2000) 18(1) *Netherlands Quarterly of Human Rights* 23–44.

economy.[69] Spending cuts, as directed by SAPs, are usually focused on 'politically easy targets—health, education and support for small farmers—while the interests of the powerful and the wealthy are protected by the states.'[70] Currency devaluation, privatisation, public sector layoffs and other measures associated with adjustment programs have been linked to violations of the right to health in Nicaragua and Peru, especially insofar as efforts to control malaria and HIV/AIDS are concerned,[71] and to the creation of a climate in which abuses of human rights such as the right to freedom from torture or the right to life might be more likely to occur.[72] Evidence has mounted that adjustment programs even contributed to the conditions which sparked ethnic conflict and genocide in Rwanda and the former Yugoslavia,[73] as is discussed in more detail shortly. OXFAM raises further grounds for concern, relating to the Fund's role in particular, on grounds including:

1. departure by the Fund from its core mandate (defined as 'responding to balance of payments problems by expanding demand') by introducing loan conditions which 'cut demand through lower public spending and high interest rates;'
2. 'rigorous' protection by the Fund of creditor claims, transferring the burden of adjustment to debtors;[74]

---

[69] P Farmer and D Bertrand, 'Hypocrisies of Development and the Health of the Haitian Poor' in JY Kim *et al* (eds), *Dying for Growth: Global Inequality and the Health of the Poor* 87 (2000). Women have sometimes been described as the 'shock absorbers' of shock therapy and structural adjustment programmes. Women are 'often the first to face the loss of employment security when the IMF or the World Bank require the public sector to reduce the number of employees, or when the workforce is casualised. Women are likely to be required to pick up the burden of caring for the sick, homeless or mentally ill family or community members when the state divests itself of those responsibilities.' A Orford (2001) at 155.

[70] H Krugmann, 'Overcoming Africa's Crisis: Adjusting Structural Adjustment Towards Sustainable Development in Africa' in K Mengisteab and B Loban (eds), *Beyond Economic Liberalisation in Africa: Structural Adjustment and the Alternatives* 129, 147 (1995). For a general critique of the social costs of adjustment see M Monshipouri, 'State Prerogatives, Civil Society, and Liberalisation: The Paradoxes of the Late Twentieth Century in the Third World' (1997) 11 *Ethics and International Affairs* 240–42.

[71] M Monshipouri, 'Promoting Universal Human Rights: Dilemmas of Integrating Developing Countries' (2001) 4 *Yale Human Rights and Development Law Journal* 25–61, 41–42 and 57.

[72] Structural adjustment and shock therapy programmes 'have led to increased levels of insecurity and political destabilisation in target states. The effect of IMF and World Bank policies is to strip the state of most of its functions, except maintaining law and order and facilitating private investment. At the same time, the interests of investors are protected and secured. In situations where the state appears to address only the interests of international economic institutions and corporate investors, the insecurity, vulnerability and frustration of people increases. Violent protests, political destabilisation, attempted succession and populist nationalism emerge as responses to governments that appear to be accountable only to foreign investors.' A Orford (2001) at 154.

[73] See eg A Storey, 'Economics and Ethnic Conflict: Structural Adjustment in Rwanda' (1999) 17 *Development Policy Review* 43–63; R Andersen, 'How Multilateral Development Assistance Triggered the Conflict in Rwanda' (2000) 21(3) *Third World Quarterly* 441–56; S Woodward, *Balkan Tragedy: Chaos and Dissolution After the Cold War* (1995), and further discussion below nn 216–36 and accompanying text.

[74] See eg E Denters, *Law and Policy of IMF Conditionality* 130–31 (1996). The G-24 is reported to regard 'unilateral' or asymmetrical adjustment—where the burdens and performance conditions

3. programmatic bias in favour of neo-liberal orthodoxy and major share-holder strategic and economic interests; and

4. the problem of weak implementation and frequent interruption of structural adjustment programmes, their failure to generate a sense of national 'ownership,' and their unenviable record as a vehicle for economic growth, equity of distribution, and poverty alleviation.[75] Indeed, the launch of the PRSP initiative in late 1999 was at least partly driven by a need to react to critical findings of the above kind in the Independent Evaluation of the ESAF.

It is also the case that client States almost invariably come to the Fund on bended knee, accepting the prospect of IMF 'medicine' as a final resort, having explored and exhausted all alternative avenues for financial assistance. In these circumstances, the harshness of Fund conditionality is actually self-defeating. To the extent that the bitterness of the IMF 'pill' delays remedial action, the prospects for constructive assistance are diminished. In Feldstein's vivid metaphor:

[T]he tough [IMF] program conditions make it difficult to get a country to work with the IMF until it is absolutely necessary. The IMF appears like the painful dentist of the old days: just as patients postponed visits until their teeth had to be pulled, the countries with problems wait too long to seek technical advice and modest amounts of financial help.[76]

This kind of dynamic is obviously inimical to the Fund's desired role in crisis prevention, through such vehicles as Article IV surveillance and its ill-fated CCL facility.

Finally, it is worth recalling that: 'From a purely economic viewpoint, structural adjustment policies and economic reform policies are viewed as short-term austerities that lead to long-term growth and development. These inter-temporal trade-offs, however, are not always acceptable in health.'[77] As Curtis has argued, '[t]he quantitative data available on the impact of structural adjustment programs provides a restricted view of the situation. In many developing countries, there are no reliable data, and available data do not assess the

---

of adjustment are borne solely by developing countries—as 'the most important single shortcoming of the IMF under present conditions.'

[75] OXFAM (1999) at 12–18.

[76] M Feldstein (1998) at 30. See also M Elahi (1986) at 147; G Bird (1995) at 75; T Killick, 'Adjustment and Economic Growth' in J Broughton and K Lateef (eds) (1995) at 154; and W Cline, 'Economic Stabilisation in Developing Countries: Theory and Stylized Facts' in J Williamson (1983) 175–208 at 203. Such a process also seems to be difficult to reconcile with paragraph 1 of the IMF conditionality Guidelines, which provide in part: 'Members should be encouraged to adopt corrective measures, which could be supported by use of the Fund's general resources in accordance with the Fund's policies, *at an early stage of their balance of payments difficulties or as a precaution against the emergence of such difficulties*' [emphasis added]. But it does not automatically follow that conditionality will necessarily be less harsh in circumstances where a member state requests IMF assistance in the relatively early stages of a crisis: T Killick, 'Kenya, the IMF, and the Unsuccessful Quest for Stabilisation' in J Williamson (ed) (1983) 381–413 at 409.

[77] J Peabody, 'Economic Reform and Health Sector Policy: Lessons from Structural Adjustment Programs' (1996) 43 *Soc Sci Med* 823, 835, cited in E Curtis (1998) at 1624.

impact on people's lives or the despair that the programs bring with them.'[78] The Bank's own 'Voices of the Poor' research purports to demonstrate the many profound and enduring ways in which poverty is manifest and felt by poor people themselves, including on a psychological level, exacerbating their disempowerment.[79] The potentially irretrievable losses accruing through denial of the right to education are likewise a source of alarm. Early in the crisis in Indonesia Carol Bellamy warned of a 'lost generation' of Indonesian children, forced out of education and into a vicious cycle of lost opportunity and potentially hazardous and exploitative labour, with increased vulnerability to a wide range of human rights abuses, an assessment with which many commentators have agreed.[80]

The World Bank and Major Infrastructure Projects

While the level of the Bank's lending for major infrastructure projects fell significantly during the 1990s in proportion to other sectors within its overall portfolio, the human rights impacts of the Bank's work in the infrastructure sector have been—and to some extent continues to be—the source of considerable controversy.[81] These issues came into sharp and public focus following the

[78] P Lundy, 'Limitations of Quantative [sic] Research in the Study of Structural Adjustment' (1996) 42 *Soc Sci Med* 313, 324, cited in E Curtis (1998) at 1624.

[79] See *World Bank Development News* 15 March, and 30 March 2000: '[P]overty is multidimensional: being poor means not only being hungry but also difficulties in finding shelter, getting health care, and providing education for one's children. It is often linked with injustice and a lack of protection of any kind. The psychological effects are important, says the story: in their relationship with the state and other sources of power, the poor often experience dependency, shame, and humiliation. Their alienation is first and foremost economic, and the state, seen by the poor, is often absent or inefficient. Nor have NGOs managed to step into the state's role. The World Bank urges the international community to adapt its approaches to poverty reduction and put in place "innovative strategies" that empower the poor.' See D Narayan and P Petesch (eds), *Voices of the Poor: From Many Lands* (2002); D Narayan, R Chambers, M Shah and P Petesch (eds) *Voices of the Poor: Crying Out for Change* (2002); and R Patel, K Schafft, A Rademacher and S Koch-Schulte (eds), *Voices of the Poor: Can Anyone Hear Us?* (2002).

[80] See eg OXFAM, *The IMF: Wrong Diagnosis, Wrong Medicine* (1999) at 31: 'Many of the children [in East Asia] who have been removed from school will lose out permanently on opportunities for education, increasing the risk of poverty. Increased malnutrition will have long-term consequences.'

[81] See eg World Bank Inspection Panel, Report No. 23998, 'Uganda: Third Power Project—Credit 2268-UG; Fourth Power Project—Credit 3345-UG and the Bujagali Hydropower Project—PRG No. B 003-UG, IPN Request RQ01/3 of 7 August 2001,' 23 May 2002. The Panel's report raises a range of deficiencies in Bank Management's compliance with its social safeguard policies (including OP 4.01 on Environmental Assessment and OD 4.30 on Involuntary Resettlement). For a general discussion of the human rights challenges arising from the construction of large dams, see B Rajagopal, 'Human Rights and Development,' Contributing Paper Prepared for Thematic Review No. 4, World Commission on Dams (Regulation, Compliance and Implementation Options) (1999) at 9–11, focusing on potential breaches of the right to self-determination, the right to development, rights relating to autonomy, land and culture, the right to participation, the right to life, the rights of particular vulnerable groups, and the legal and policy implications of the right to a remedy for violations. See also E MacDonald, 'Playing by the Rules: The World Bank's Failure to Adhere to Policy in the Funding of Large-Scale Hydropower Projects' (2001) 31 *Environmental Law* 1101–1049.

resettlement and environmental disasters associated with the Sardar Sarovar dam project in the Narmada Valley in Madhya Pradesh, India, in the mid- to late-1980s.[82] The need to acknowledge and adhere to international human rights standards featured strongly in an Independent Review's recommendations: '. . . India, in conformity with the development of international standards of human rights, has subscribed to certain minimum conditions that must be observed even when the national interest is involved. They reflect the inalienable human rights of the [displaced persons]. We believe that these norms must be adhered to.'[83]

Yet the lure of major infrastructure project involvement remains strong. Against years of international protest, in mid-2002 the Bank was still strongly considering giving its support to the controversial 'Nam Theun 2' hydropower project[84] in Lao Peoples Democratic Republic (Lao PDR), notwithstanding the high human rights and environmental risks involved, the relative lack of freedom of expression to permit legitimate public debate on such major policy issues in Lao PDR, and compelling evidence of contravention of the 'World Commission on Dams' guidelines for big dams.[85]

[82] See eg B Morse and T Berger, *Sardar Sarovar: The Report of the Independent Review* (1992) ['the Morse report (1992)']. However many aspects of the Narmada dam plans which were condemned in the Morse report are still being implemented, albeit without the Bank's support: K Sharma, 'Out, out dam spotlight,' *Crosslines Global Report*, May/June 1997 at 54–57.

[83] The Morse report (1992) at 356–57. Further (at 357): 'The fragile assumptions that have supported this project can be found elsewhere. Failure to consider the human rights of the displaced and failure to consider environmental impacts occur in the development of megaprojects in both developed and developing countries. If the human rights obligations identified by [ILO Convention 107] and in Bank policy are acknowledged and respected, if the commitment to the environment is real, and if these are properly integrated into project design at the outset, more effective and equitable development will ensue. Some believe that these requirements make it more difficult, often more costly, to build megaprojects like Sardar Sarovar. This implies that human and environmental costs are to be heavily discounted in project planning and execution. But hard lessons from the past have taught us that this is unacceptable.' See also the Morse Report (1992) at pp 17–38 and 50–59.

[84] For history and a brief overview of the project, including status of the Bank's involvement, see Bank Information Centre Factsheet No. 18, 'The proposed World Bank-funded Nam Theun 2 Hydropower Project, Lao PDR,' 6 February 2002; World Bank, 'Lao PDR: World Bank Mission— Aide Memoire,' 1 April 2002, at pp. 1 and 6. Key messages from the Bank's August 2001 mission included the following: 'The World Bank is prepared to consider its support to the proposed Nam Theun 2 project only if it is strongly embedded in a development framework, characterised by concrete performance, that aims at poverty reduction and environmental protection.' Following the April 2002 mission: '[T]he Bank is prepared to gear up activities related to due diligence on the project . . . and the review of compliance with Bank safeguard policies.' Strangely, the subject of the Nam Theun 2 project arises only once, and only peripherally, in the Bank's and IMF's Joint Staff Assessment of Lao PDR's PRSP Preparation Status Report (12 July 2002), with the staffs recommending that the National Poverty Eradication Plan 'clarifies how the hydropower projects (ie, Nam Theun 2 and other projects) would contribute to reducing poverty through the use of additional revenues generated.'

[85] World Commission on Dams, *Dams and Development: A New Framework for Decision-Making* (2000), discussed in chapter VI below, at nn 257–60 and accompanying text. For a sampling of the critiques see E MacDonald (2001) at 1038–39; A Imhof, 'An Analysis of Nam Theun 2 Compliance with World Commission on Dams Guidelines,' May 2001; International Rivers Network, 'The Nam Theun 2 Hydropower Project in Laos: Another World Bank Disaster in the Making,' *Briefing Paper* (May 2002); Centre for Public Policy and Analysis, 'Opposition to Nam Theun II Dam Financing,' 26 December 2001; and Congressional Briefings on Nam Theun 2,

The lure of support for such projects is strong and likely to remain so, by reason of the leveraging effects in such circumstances of the Bank's 'moral guarantor' role,[86] the sheer 'bang for the buck' in loan approval terms from Bank Management's perspective,[87] and the probability that hazardous projects will proceed in many cases with or without the Bank's involvement (and attendant social risk insurance).[88] However Lao PDR, as with India in Narmada's case, is party to a host of international human rights treaties with direct implications and entitlements for indigenous peoples and others threatened with forcible displacement. The human rights and environmental risks in the present case are both high and readily foreseeable. It would be a grim irony indeed if the experience of Sardar Sarovar was now to be replayed in slow motion before the eyes of the world, flouting the lessons so painfully learned.

The Legitimacy Deficit

In his seminal work 'Legitimacy in the International System,' Thomas Franck posited that the legitimacy of an international rule and hence its ability to 'exert pull to compliance and to command voluntary obedience' essentially comes down to a question of perception: whether the norm in question was brought

---

'Statement by Bruce Shoemaker, Independent Researcher, to the Congressional Human Rights Caucus briefing on "Environmental Impacts and Human Rights in Laos—The Name Theun 2 Hydropower Project,' 22 May 2002: 'Given the worldwide criticism of many large dam projects on economic, social, environmental and human rights grounds it is time for much caution in proceeding with such projects. Even tho ugh it has been in the works for more than 12 years, Nam Theun 2 project proponents have now been trying to repackage it as a new model, compliant with recently issued World Commission on Dams guidelines, that will focus on poverty alleviation. Believing this requires much faith and little regard for the experiences to date with hydropower and other large infrastructure projects in Laos . . . [T]he World Bank's Panel of Experts (which instead of providing neutral advice and analysis have become unabashed promoters of the project) are proposing an untested model. Such a model would be a risk even in an open society with the presence of an independent media, independent judiciary, and strong civil society groups that could provide accountability mechanisms. All that is lacking in Laos and the World Bank certainly has no demonstrated enforcement capacity to ensure that [official] promises are kept.' As to the seriousness of the political constraints the International Herald Tribune reported that '[s]ince the end of the Vietnam war in 1975, Laos has been ruled by a Communist regime that in the view of some analysts is as secretive, corrupt and resistant to real economic and political reform as the military junta in Burma.' M Richardson, 'In its water, Laos sees power to cut poverty,' *International Herald Tribune*, 11 March 2002.

[86] As in Lao PDR's case, '[c]ompanies often consider World Bank involvement vital to securing investor confidence in poor or politically unstable countries.' Richardson, M. (2002). This phenomenon is discussed in more depth in the context of the controversial Bank-supported Chad/Cameroon pipeline project, chapter V below at nn 75–76 and accompanying text.

[87] The so-called 'approval culture' and related incentive problems are discussed in chapter V below at nn 4–23 and accompanying text.

[88] Indeed this has been the case with the Narmada dam project, and also with respect to another of the more controversial fiascos of recent times, the China Western Poverty Reduction project of 1999, discussed in chapter V below at nn 14–16, 40 and accompanying text.

into being 'in accordance with right process.'[89] While perhaps open to criticism from those with a more Machiavellian slant on international relations, to the extent of its validity Franck's 'legitimacy—effectiveness' relationship is a dynamic of fairly obvious and direct application here, although with a particular focus on the institutional rather than normative plane.

A useful point of departure for this comparative analysis arises from Joseph Gold's study of the preconditions for the effectiveness of the Fund's surveillance activities under Article IV. While expressed to be limited to Article IV, the conclusions drawn are of wider application. At least in part, Gold postulated that the extent to which Article IV consultations can be expected to influence the adjustment of individual balances of payments or the international co-ordination of policies is determined by members' perceptions as to the degree of 'uniformity' and 'symmetry' exercised by the Fund in the administration of Article IV.[90] As Joseph Gold explains:

> Members will not support policies or procedures unless they perceive a net advantage notwithstanding the international constraints they are called on to observe. Uniformity and symmetry in the application of the safeguards would contribute to this perception not simply because of the aesthetic appeal of even-handedness but also because the surrender of some degree of freedom by each member is a concession of authority to other members.[91]

Any number of factors might be capable of eroding perceptions of 'uniformity' and 'symmetry' in the application by the Fund of monetary safeguards, and the

---

[89] T Franck, 'Legitimacy in the International System,' 82 *American Journal of International Law* 705, 725 (1988). For a wider treatment of the subject beyond the scope of the present discussion see T Franck, *The Power of Legitimacy Among Nations* (1990), defining the components of legitimacy as consisting of determinacy, symbolic validation, coherence and adherence. On legitimacy as a prerequisite to effective and credible multilateralism in the context of the World Bank's operations, and on the tensions to which this gives rise vis-à-vis its dominant shareholder, see N Woods, 'The Challenges of Multilateralism and Governance' in C Gilbert and D Vines (eds), *The World Bank: Structure and Policies* 132–56, 135–37 (2000).

[90] 'Uniformity is a characteristic of the treatment of the members that are deemed to constitute a class; symmetry is a characteristic of the treatment of classes. Uniform treatment can be said to be the same treatment; symmetrical treatment can be said to be comparable treatment': J Gold (ed) (1984) at 563; J Gold, 'Symmetry as a Legal Objective of the International Monetary System' (1980) 12 *New York University Journal of International Law and Politics* 423–77. But this is probably only part of the picture. Most regime theorists concerned with the effectiveness of the international monetary regime emphasise the 'coercive,' as well as incentive, measures at the Fund's disposal: see eg B Cohen, 'Balance of Payments Financing: Evolution of a Regime' in S Krasner (ed), *International Regimes* (1983) at 315, 332. Although the 'coercive' possibilities for Fund action are at least indirectly relevant to an assessment of the influence that the Fund is likely to exert over a low income member country during the course of Article IV consultations, those aspects are left for consideration later in this chapter as one element of an broader exploration of the Fund's conditionality policies.

[91] J Gold (ed) (1984) at 563. Further, at 559: 'The treatment accepted by the United States is almost always a major influence on the perceptions of members.' But given the luke-warm signals emanating from the United States government concerning the value of Article IV consultations as a policy co-ordination tool—in contrast to mere dissemination of information and the cultivation of international understanding [J Gold (ed) (1984) at 559–60]—there is little reason to expect other members to encourage the Fund in the pursuit of its systemic purposes under Article IV either.

legitimacy (according to Franck's criteria) of the IFIs' activities in a broader sense, including:

(a) the industrialised countries' dominance of voting power and IFI policy;

(b) perceptions of ulterior purposes and contested ideological assumptions behind IFI policy prescriptions and loan conditions;

(c) lack of symmetry in allocation of the burdens of structural adjustment;[92]

(d) criticisms of the content, flexibility and severity of the IFIs' conditionalities;[93] and

(e) the fact that the IFIs' influence is disproportionately felt in developing countries.[94]

Other relevant problems include the failure of the IFIs' standardised economic prescriptions, forged by 'Washington Consensus,' to take sufficient account of local circumstances. The standard prescriptions ignore legitimate contesting theories concerning optimal growth strategies,[95] and assume 'marketisation' and economic liberalisation as 'natural and inevitable.'[96] The formula for

[92] S Dell, 'Stabilisation: The Political Economy of Overkill' in J Williamson (ed) 17–45 (1993) at 21–26. In particular (at 21–22): 'The IMF continues to insist that the origin of a balance of payments deficit, whether internal or external, has no bearing on the adjustment measures required . . . In taking this position, the Fund appears to shrug off its responsibility for ensuring that the burden of adjustment is distributed equitably and efficiently among countries[,]' contrary to positions previously taken not only by the Interim Committee, but even the United States government: cf *Economic Report of the President* (January 1973) cited in S Dell (1983) at 22, and *IMF Annual Report* (1980) at 153. In the view of the Interim Committee [as it was then known] (at 153): '[i]t was particularly important . . . that the industrial countries, in the design of their economic policies, pay particular attention to the economic needs of developing countries. In this connection, a wide range of policies was seen to be relevant, including the reduction of protectionist measures; the opening of import markets to exports of manufactures and commodities from developing countries and of capital markets to outflows of funds to such countries; and measures to give new impetus to the flow of official development assistance, which [as at October 1979] had stagnated in recent years.' Dell concludes (at 44) that '[t]he concept of unilateral adjustment—with one group of countries at best neutral toward, and at worst frustrating, the adjustment process of the other group—is not an acceptable basis for IMF supervision of the international monetary system. There is a pressing need for the Fund to reconsider its position on this basic issue.' To similar effect see S Edwards, 'Structural Adjustment in Highly Indebted Countries' in J Sachs (ed), *Developing Country Debt and Economic Performance* (Volume 1, The International Financial System) (1989) 159–207, 202.

[93] See above nn 61–80, and chapter V below at nn 45–54 and accompanying text.

[94] See chapter V below at nn 39–41, and chapter VI below at nn 26–27 and accompanying text. See also J Gold (ed) (1984) at 566, and T Killick, 'Adjustment and Economic Growth' in J Broughton and K Lateef (eds) (1995) at 155.

[95] See eg M Feldstein, 'Refocusing the IMF' (1998) 77(2) *Foreign Affairs* 20, 29–30: 'There is nothing like unanimity about the appropriate policies for Korea or Southeast Asia. Korea's outstanding performance combining persistently high growth, low inflation, and low unemployment suggests that the current structure of the Korean economy may now be well suited to Korea's stage of economic and political development and to Korean cultural values stressing thrift, self-sacrifice, patriotism, and worker solidarity. Even if it were desirable for Korea to shift toward labour, goods, and capital markets more like those of the United States, it may be best to evolve in that direction more gradually and with fewer shocks to existing business.' See also E Shin, 'The International Monetary Fund: Is it the Right or Wrong Prescription for Korea?' (1999) 22(3) *Hastings International and Comparative Law Review* 597–615.

[96] For a critique of the role of dramatic liberalisation in assisting to resolve debt or stabilisation crises, with particular regard to adverse employment effects (at least in the short run), see

privatisation, 'external viability,' and opening up the local economy to foreign investment is the focus of considerable resentment and legitimate concern, particularly from the point of view of lower income countries critical of industrialised member dominance in IFI policy-making,[97] and resentful of the inequitable terms of trade. The IMF's role in Korea, for example, has provoked a significant degree of criticism on the grounds that the Fund's reform program apparently serves the interests of certain major industrialised powers and transnational corporations, rather than Korea's need to revive access to international funds. As Feldstein has remarked:

> Several features of the IMF plan [for Korea] are replays of the policies that Japan and the United States have long been trying to get Korea to adopt. These included accelerating the previously agreed upon reductions of trade barriers to specific Japanese products and opening capital markets so that foreign investors can have majority ownership of Korean firms, engage in hostile take-overs opposed by local management, and expand direct participation in banking and other financial services. Although greater competition from manufactured imports and more foreign ownership could in principle help the Korean economy, Koreans and others saw this aspect of the plan as an abuse of IMF power to force Korea at a time of weakness to accept trade and investment policies it had previously rejected.
>
> The IMF would be more effective in its actions and more legitimate in the eyes of emerging-market countries if it pursued the less ambitious goal of maintaining countries' access to global capital markets and international bank lending . . . [The Fund] should strongly resist the pressure from the United States, Japan and other major countries to make their trade and investment agenda part of the IMF funding conditions.[98]

S Edwards, 'Structural Adjustment Policies in Highly Indebted Countries' in J Sachs (ed) (1989) 159–207. See also A Orford (1997) at 478–83. Orford observes (at 478) that the structure and practice of international law is partly to blame for the acceptance of the inevitability of marketisation and liberalisation: '[T]he focus on the role of international institutions and international law in intervening for human rights and democracy obscures the role played by international institutions and laws in contributing to economic liberalisation. By focusing only on norms of international law that relate to public issues, international lawyers fail to make visible the norms and institutions that facilitate the making of a global market. That failure contributes to the sense that economic liberalisation is natural and inevitable. Global economic restructuring becomes a given[.] Accordingly, the conduct of business as usual appears both natural and politically neutral. While international lawyers have successfully politicised the making of international government, we now have to politicise the norms and institutions that facilitate the market.'

[97] See eg C Payer (1974) at 38: 'The Fund's enthusiasm for private capital as an aid to the balance of payments follows naturally from its position as a defender of international trade and payments and the fact that it is under the control of capital-investing countries. It is less easy to square with the Fund's assumed posture as adviser on balance of payments problems to poor countries, since present investments will represent balance of payments burdens, in the form of profit repatriation, in the future.'

[98] M Feldstein (1998) at 32. For a reaction to these criticisms on the Fund's behalf, couched in general terms of defending its role in Asia rather than meeting some of Feldstein's more specific concerns relating to formularisation and *mala fides*, see S Fischer, 'Response: In Defense of the IMF—Specialised Tools for a Specialised Task' (1998) 77(4) *Foreign Affairs* 103–6; S Fischer, 'The IMF and the Asian Crisis,' Forum Funds Lecture at the University of California Los Angeles, 20 March 1998, http://www.imf.org/external/np/speeches/1998/032098.HTM. For further arguments concerning the pursuit by the Fund of interests of particular industrialised members and trans-national

On the general issue of 'politicisation' OXFAM, noting the disproportionate influence (especially through the phenomenon of cross-conditionality) wielded by the Fund, has remarked that '[p]olitically, IMF loan conditions provide its major shareholders with far more influence than they would enjoy separately, enabling them to challenge the policy sovereignty of governments in low-income countries.'[99] The

> recent loan conditions for East Asia have included the liberalisation of import markets for cars, the extension of foreign ownership in financial sectors, and sweeping reforms in areas such as agricultural marketing. All too often, these conditions owe more to the strategic trade and financial interests of major shareholders, notably the USA.[100] For their part, European governments enthusiastically support loan conditions which they would never implement at home, requiring the liberalisation of agricultural trade and sweeping labour market reforms.[101]

Congressional records from the Oversight Hearings on the IMF in early 1999 are especially revealing in this respect. Undoubtedly driven at least in part by a need to preserve Congressional support for the Fund, senior US bureaucrats and Chamber of Commerce officials have spared little expense to illustrate to the Senate Banking, Housing and Urban Affairs Committee (Subcommittee on International Trade and Finance) the ways in which the Fund serves, and should be further encouraged to serve, the US's economic interests. The prepared testimony of the Under Secretary for International Finance in the Treasury Department, for instance, recounted at length various 'improvements' in the design of IMF policies and programs which directly serve US interests, in areas

corporations, see W Berg and G Thole (1986) at 165–67, 173; L Taylor, 'Editorial: The Revival of the Liberal Creed—The IMF and the World Bank in a Globalised Economy' (1997) 25(2) *World Development* 145–52, 146 and 150. Taylor remarks (at 147): 'Disguising a multi-million dollar ideological marketing operation as research has not been a heartening trend over the past dozen years for the World Bank.' Other literature warns of the 'threat . . . posed by the political lobbying of major shareholders in favour of (or against) particular borrowing countries, in promotion of their own foreign policy objectives[,]' an activity 'both common and subversive of what the IMF [is] trying to do'—T Killick with M Malik, 'Country Experiences with IMF Programmes in the 1980s' (1992) 5 *World Economy* 599–632, 629–30. That study concludes (at 630) that '[t]he frequency with which [such political lobbying] occurs, and also the reluctance of major shareholders to expand the Fund's resources in line with developing countries' needs, raise questions about the seriousness of industrial-country commitment to the IMF's stabilisation mandate.'

[99] OXFAM (1999) at 13.

[100] For an interesting historical account of the convergence between World Bank and US ideology and strategic interests see M Berger and M Beeson, 'Lineages of Liberalism and Miracles of Modernisation: The World Bank, the East Asian Trajectory and the International Development Debate' (1998) 19(3) *Third World Quarterly* 487–504. And on related aspects of opportunism, see OXFAM International Policy Paper, *East Asian 'Recovery' Leaves the Poor Sinking* (October 1998): 'Trade credits have been provided as part of the rescue effort. Unfortunately, these have often been directed towards the pursuit of commercial advantage on the part of the supplier, rather than economic need. The US, for instance, has linked its $460m allocation to Indonesia to the purchase of American cotton, soybeans, flour, wheat and corn. Australia has provided financing in some of the same areas, as much to protect its market share as to meet the real needs of the Indonesian economy.'

[101] OXFAM (1999) at 13.

such as trade liberalisation,[102] privatisation of state-owned enterprises,[103] and behind the scenes lobbying for ratification of ILO Conventions and enforcement of labour standards.[104] Key benefits to US interests from trade and financial liberalisation and privatisation initiatives were further spelled out in testimony from the Assistant Secretary for Market Access and Compliance in the Commerce Department.[105] Furthermore the testimony of the Vice President of the US Chamber of Commerce, following a discussion of IMF reforms implemented in Brazil and East Asia, concluded as follows: 'The important task now is to make sure that reforms recommended by the IMF continue to be consistent with American interests. The US Chamber of Commerce looks forward to working together with the US Congress to monitor IMF programs and policies to ensure that they are not at odds with American prosperity.'[106] As to the relative effectiveness of the US government's various avenues of influence, principally the Federal Treasury and Congress, the testimony of Gerald O'Driscoll of the Heritage Foundation reveals the following:

> The US Treasury Department exercises influence over IMF policy far in excess of the explicit percentage vote possessed by the United States. IMF policy does not and will not deviate in any important or fundamental way from the policy of the US Treasury. If Congress is displeased with IMF policy, it should address its concerns to Secretary Rubin and Deputy Secretary Summers. That is where IMF policy originates and can be effectively altered. . . . Congress can influence IMF policy in the same way it influences policy in any Executive Branch agency: through oversight hearings, like this one, and through the power of the purse. Any other route, such as requiring the US Executive Director to use her 'voice and vote' in IMF deliberations, diminishes congressional influence and is unlikely to have a significant impact on IMF policy. In a real sense the long delay in effecting US funding for the IMF and the vigorous congressional debate that took place in 1997 and 1998 had more impact within the IMF than 'voice and vote' instructions can ever have.[107]

[102] For a strong critique of inequities in the global trading regime and its damaging effects on human development see OXFAM, *Rigged Rules and Double Standards: Trade, Globalisation and the Fight Against Poverty* (2002), with strong echoes in HDR 2002 and the Bank's own *World Development Report 2002: Sustainable Development in a Dynamic World* (2002).

[103] In one instance it was specified that a 'majority stake in Korea First Bank [would] be sold to an investor group led by two US firms.' Senate Banking, Housing and Urban Affairs Committee, Subcommittee on International Trade and Finance, Oversight Hearing on the IMF, Prepared Testimony of the Honourable Timothy Geithner, Under Secretary for International Finance, United States Treasury, 10.30 am, Tuesday 9 March 1999.

[104] The labour standards issue is discussed further later, in the context of an analysis of the breadth of non-officially-mandated issues over which the Fund has assumed varying degrees of responsibility in practice.

[105] Senate Banking, Housing and Urban Affairs Committee, Subcommittee on International Trade and Finance, Oversight Hearing on the IMF, Prepared Testimony of the Honourable Patrick A Molloy, Assistant Secretary for Market Access and Compliance, United States Commerce Department, 10.30 am, Tuesday 9 March 1999.

[106] Senate Banking, Housing and Urban Affairs Committee, Subcommittee on International Trade and Finance, Oversight Hearing on the IMF, Prepared Testimony of Mr Williard Workman, Vice President, International US Chamber of Commerce, 10.30 am, Tuesday 9 March 1999.

[107] Senate Banking, Housing and Urban Affairs Committee, Subcommittee on International Trade and Finance, Oversight Hearing on the IMF, Prepared Testimony of Mr Gerald O'Driscoll,

This is not only a problem of perceptions, but a fundamental legal problem as well, affecting the Fund's compliance with its Conditionality Guidelines and Articles, and its ability to fulfil its (evolving) mandated objectives. In particular, it is difficult to see how blanket insistence on a standard Washington-produced macro-economic template could be reconciled with legal requirements in the Fund's Conditionality Guidelines concerning flexibility and the need to pay due regard to political and social circumstances.[108] Further it must be seriously questioned whether uniform application of such prescriptions are compatible with the 'primary objectives' of national prosperity contained in Articles I(ii) and (v).

These problems are compounded by the lack of adequate accountability mechanisms, evident in the Bank to a considerable degree, albeit to a lesser extent than at the Fund. Focusing upon 'vertical' accountability at the IMF in particular, Fund staff have a high degree of autonomy in the negotiation process since it is only after terms of agreement have been reached between staff and the government authorities, with the endorsement of the Managing Director, that the Managing Director takes the agreement to the Executive Board for its approval.[109]

Senior Fellow, The Heritage Foundation, 10.30 am, Tuesday 9 March 1999. The reasons stated for the ineffectiveness of 'voice and vote' legislation were: (1) the fact that the IMF operates by consensus rather than formal votes; and (2) more importantly, the significant influence of the US Treasury over IMF policy, said to be 'far in excess of the explicit percentage vote possessed by the United States.' And to illustrate the extent of US Treasury influence over Fund policies, O'Driscoll recounted that '[a] visiting delegation of legislators from an Asian country recently observed that, in separate visits to the US Treasury Department and the IMF, not only are the same policies recommended, but in the very same words. For foreigners, there is no doubt that the script for the IMF is written in the US Treasury.'

[108] For an interesting argument along these lines in the context of the Fund's 'single-minded' attack on inflation, see S Dell, 'Stabilisation: The Political Economy of Overkill' in J Williamson (ed) (1983) 17–45 at 18. This is as much a practical objection, as a legal one, as Haggard and Kaufman have observed—'In the end . . . there is no substitute for a nuanced understanding of the particular political setting into which economic programs are introduced': S Haggard and R Kaufman, 'The Politics of Stabilisation and Structural Adjustment' in J Sachs (ed) (1989) 209–54 at 249. And for a more strident criticism see J Stiglitz, 'The Insider: What I Learned at the World Economic Crisis,' posted at http://www.socwatch.org.uy/2000/eng/updates/financing/ngohear_background_theinsider.htm. When the IMF decides to assist a country, it dispatches a "mission" of economists. These economists frequently lack extensive experience in the country; they are more likely to have firsthand knowledge of its five-star hotels than of the villages that dot its countryside. They work hard, poring over numbers deep into the night. But their task is impossible. In a period of days or, at most, weeks, they are charged with developing a coherent program sensitive to the needs of the country. Needless to say, a little number-crunching rarely provides adequate insights into the development strategy for an entire nation. Even worse, the number-crunching isn't always that good. The mathematical models the IMF uses are frequently flawed or out-of-date. Critics accuse the institution of taking a cookie-cutter approach to economics, and they're right. Country teams have been known to compose draft reports before visiting. I heard stories of one unfortunate incident when team members copied large parts of the text for one country's report and transferred them wholesale to another. They might have gotten away with it, except the "search and replace" function on the word processor didn't work properly, leaving the original country's name in a few places. Oops.'

[109] R Eckaus (1986) at 237, 234. See also A Chayes and A Chayes (1995) at 237 n 32 and accompanying text. Staff autonomy and power is particularly obvious in relation to the determination of 'preconditions'—relating, for example, to currency controls and associated tax, expenditure, or interest rate policy changes—over which the Executive Board has little or no *ex ante* control: J Williamson, 'The Lending Policies of the International Monetary Fund' in J Williamson (ed) (1983) 605–60 at 633.

According to Eckaus, at least as at 1986, 'the Executive Board [had] never rejected an agreement proposed by the Managing Director and no member [had] ever appealed to the Executive Board against a negative decision by the Managing Director.'[110] And as to criteria for evaluation of staff performance, it has been remarked that 'the IMF rewards staff for their technical proficiency rather than for taking the time to engage in the wide-ranging consultations and exchanges of information necessary to ensure that the IMF's operations are transparent and sensitive to the interests of those who will be affected by them.'[111]

A key element of the comparative advantage of IMF staff is that negotiations are cloaked in the presumed objectivity and neutrality of technocratic jargon.[112] In many cases government representatives of lower income countries seeking IMF assistance will not speak this language at all, much less the representatives of affected people or NGOs and other interested parties who (in the ordinary course) have little or no prospect for meaningful participation.[113] In other cases the government representatives and finance ministry officials will in fact be willing accomplices, supported by the interests of private sector elites who stand to benefit most—through means fair or foul—from privatisation and trade liberalisation measures.[114] This helps to obfuscate important underlying questions regarding the supposed inevitability of the dominant model of economic globalisation, and the legitimacy of international governance exercised by or through elitist and undemocratic[115] international financial institutions. As Anne Orford explains:

---

[110] R Eckaus (1986) at 237, 234 and 251 n 16. To similar effect see C Payer (1974) at 32.

[111] D Bradlow (1996) at 75. For discussion of retrograde incentives operating on Bank staff see N Bridgeman (2001) at 1027–41 and chapter V below.

[112] By analogy, in relation to development work at the Bank, it has been remarked that: 'Decisions in the World Bank have been influenced by political factors since its inception, but bank leadership has always sought to call political factors by other names and to tie them firmly to economic goals. The pretence that development lending is a purely economic activity is considered indispensable. Eugene Black, the third president of the World Bank (1949–1962), once said: "We ask a lot of questions, and attach a lot of conditions to our loans. I need hardly say that *we would never get away with this if we did not bend every effort to render the language of economics as morally antiseptic as the language the weather forecaster uses* in giving tomorrow's prediction. We look on ourselves as technicians or artisans"' [emphasis added]: E Spiro, 'Front Door or Back Stairs: US Human Rights Policy in the International Financial Institutions' in B Rubin and E Spiro (eds), *Human Rights and US Foreign Policy* (1979) 133, 147.

[113] See eg D Bradlow (1996) at 77, n 126 and accompanying text. The fact that the IMF generally tends to focus its attention on the Finance Ministries and Central Banks in its member states means that it is able to make policies without even consulting all interested line ministries in the relevant country's government, let alone NGOs and people likely to be directly or indirectly affected. See also J Sachs (1989) at 264.

[114] See eg A Orford (1997) at 476: 'Governments make use of an "internationalist discourse" about the need to adjust to a changing world economy in order to ensure that citizens endorse "the modernising actions taken by the state on [their] behalf."' And from a slightly different angle, the IMF may provide a convenient scapegoat for local governing and private sector elites in instituting free market reforms with painful consequences: F Smith, Jr (1984) at 230.

[115] See eg HDR 2002, chapter 5, 'Deepening Democracy at the Global Level.' But as Orford notes, '[t]he role of international activity and institutions in contributing to the erosion of substantive democracy, popular sovereignty, and protection of human rights is somewhat more complicated where citizens elect economically rationalist governments which then proceed to restructure the state'—A Orford (1997) at 475.

The idea of a globalised economy legitimises the development of a culture in which political decisions that would once have been at least theoretically within the realm of parliamentary decision-making, popular sovereignty, or democratic government, are now made by experts in economics. Internationalism serves to reinforce this political culture based on 'continual assertion of the magic of expertise' and the authority generated by an 'exquisite mastery of [economic] data.' Governments [not uncommonly] make use of a sense of national crisis in the face of global economic changes in order to de-legitimise popular participation in decision-making about vital political issues, which are now re-characterised as purely economic and technical.

The inability of most people to contest and challenge decisions about many issues that shape their lives is presented as inevitable and natural, as a consequence of the disciplines and requirements of international competitiveness and globalisation. The result is the ascendancy of a technocratic vision of 'democracy-as-management,' in which governments and experts are engaged in management of the economy and 'politics is treated as having somehow already happened elsewhere . . .'[116]

Adverse perceptions of the Fund in particular are fuelled through its continuing lack of transparency, and the secrecy under which Article IV consultations are conducted.[117] The Fund's practice since the late 1990s of issuing Press Information Notices (PIN's) at the conclusion of Article IV consultations, at the request of the member concerned, making the IMF's views publicly available, represents a step forward in promoting the transparency of the Fund's policy assessments.[118] As at 2002 the Fund was also pressing governments to permit greater disclosure and publication of policies and agreements with the IMF.[119] Enhanced transparency might well be expected to promote uniformity and symmetry, thereby enhancing perceptions of 'net advantage' (in Gold's terms) and support for Fund policies. Moreover transparency in policy making may in some circumstances be supported and vindicated as a matter of human right, as witnessed in the landmark decision of the South African Constitutional Court

---

[116] A Orford (1997) at 476, citing from M Morris, 'Ecstasy and Economics (A Portrait of Paul Keating)' in *Ecstasy and Economics* (1992) 17, 76. But as Orford notes (at 476, n 147), the responsiveness of governments to the dictates of globalisation is highly selective: 'While many governments of industrialised states have been quick to reshape domestic law and institutions according to international economic law and the dictates of international financial institutions, they have been reluctant to incorporate into the domestic realm those aspects of international law that might subvert the aims of economic rationalists.'

[117] Decision No. 5392-(77/63), *Selected Decisions*, 9th (1981) pp 11–12, cited in J Gold (ed) (1984) at 567. As recently as 1994 Jeffrey Sachs claimed that it was harder to get information from the IMF than from the CIA! See 'Oversight of the IMF and World Bank, Meeting of a Multinational Group of Parliamentarians Involved in Oversight of the IMF and World Bank Before the Subcommittee on International Development, Finance, and Monetary Policy Trade of the House Committee on Banking, Finance and Urban Affairs,' 103rd Cong., 2nd Sess,. 26–28, 47–48 (1994) (statement of Jeffrey Sachs, Professor of Economics), cited in D Bradlow (1996) at 75, n 116.

[118] See eg Press Information Notice (PIN) No. 98/45, 26 June 1998, 'IMF Concludes Article IV Consultation with Tunisia' http://www.imf.org/external/np/sec/pn/1998/PN9845.HTM; Press Information Notice (PIN) No. 98/44, 25 June 1998, 'IMF Concludes Article IV Consultation with Thailand' http://www.imf.org/external/np/sec/pn/1998/PN9844.HTM.

[119] HDR 2002 at 115.

in *Minister for Health and Others v Treatment Action Campaign and Others*,[120] to be considered in more depth in chapter VI.

However despite these advances, serious gaps in transparency remain. As at the year 2002 the publication of agreements was still far from comprehensive, with borrowing government concerns for commercial confidentiality outweighing the demand for disclosure. As far as Article IV is concerned, the PINs purport to reflect only the 'main features' of the Board's discussion of particular country situations, clouding the prospects for an accurate assessment of uniformity and symmetry, and therefore, legitimacy and effectiveness. But perhaps most seriously of all, decisions by the Fund's and Bank's Executive Boards remain shrouded in secrecy. Minutes of Board meetings are not published. Votes are rarely taken, and so cannot be recorded or publicised. The result is that citizens of shareholder countries have no means of holding Executive Directors or their governments accountable for their policies in the Fund or Bank,[121] policies with frequently major human rights dimensions and consequences.

A Bias Towards Authoritarian Regimes?

A number of commentators allege that the harshness of Fund conditionality, with particular regard to now discredited 'shock therapy'[122] measures, is

---

[120] *Minister for Health and Others v Treatment Action Campaign and Others*, Case CCT 8/02 (5 July 2002). The Constitutional Court in this case upheld an entitlement of the public to 'transparency' in public policy development as a matter of constitutional right, independent of any assessment of mutually reinforcing or constitutive rights of political participation or representation, freedom of information and so forth. Paragraph 123 (pp 68–69) of the judgement stated: 'The magnitude of the HIV/AIDS challenge facing the country calls for a concerted, co-operative and co-ordinated national effort in which government in each of its three spheres and the panoply of resources and skills of civil society are marshalled, inspired and led. This can be achieved only if there is proper communication, especially by government. In order for it to be implemented optimally, a public health programme must be made known effectively to all concerned, down to the district nurse and patients. Indeed, for a public programme such as this to meet the constitutional requirement of "reasonableness," its contents must be made known appropriately.' While the 'reasonableness' criterion may or may not translate directly to a great many other constitutional orders, this rationale would appear to offer much to those seeking to ground human rights-based approaches within locally-specific normative frameworks, helping further to elevate 'transparency' beyond a mere instrumental 'good governance' value or principle, to a matter of non-discretionary legal entitlement not to be bartered away within the overall development equation. See chapter VI for further discussion of this case.

[121] HDR 2002 at 115. Experience elsewhere affirms that secrecy of this kind is unsustainable as a matter of principle, as the UNDP Human Development Report office notes (at 115): 'The secrecy of board deliberations and members' positions is often defended on the grounds that it reinforces the collegiality of the Executive Board, the frankness of discussion and its capacity to make decisions by consensus. Interestingly, the Monetary Policy Committee of the Bank of England once made a similar argument—debunked by the subsequent experience of that agency, whose minutes and votes have been recorded and published shortly after meetings since 1998.'

[122] The 'shock therapy' model was developed by Jeffrey Sachs in a famous 1990 article, as a means for dealing with states in transitions from communism to capitalism: J Sachs, 'What is to Be Done?', *The Economist*, 13 January 1990 at 19. For critiques of 'shock therapy' and its

responsible to some degree for the emergence or survival of authoritarian regimes in certain parts of the world.

The rationale underlying this concern is that the standard austerity, stabilisation, adjustment and 'shock therapy' recipe is one that inevitably generates a high degree of social upheaval and political unrest. In a functioning representative democracy where the freedom of expression, press freedoms and associated civil and political rights are safeguarded, public dissatisfaction with the harsh effects of IMF prescriptions naturally flows through to the ballot box, or otherwise swells into a tide of opposition, thereby increasing political instability and (in many cases) leading to a change of government. According to this rationale, it is only when political freedoms are curtailed and opposition effectively stymied, that regimes can successfully overcome popular resistance to harsh measures and successfully implement IMF programs.[123]

Furthermore according to this model, irrespective of whether economic prosperity results, local governing and business elites are able to consolidate their positions and advantages and profit from popular disempowerment, cloaked in the presumed legitimacy afforded by the perceived imperatives of economic globalisation. The IMF assistance granted to Chile in 1973 under General Pinochet's rule, arguably, is a case in point:

> The IMF's austerity program in conjunction with the 'Chicago free-market Model' could only be imposed and maintained in Chile because the authoritarian regime had created an artificially 'acquiescent' environment for the enforcement of these policies. In the Chilean case, the symbiotic nexus between the free-market economic system and the authoritarian political system is evident. In order to implement the stringent economic policies, the Junta provided the repression that was allegedly necessary to stifle any democratic objections and dissent to the pressures caused by the IMF's austerity program. Thus the IMF had a direct and powerful impact in directing the politico-economic policies and was an influential actor in the undermining of legally required respect for human rights in Chile.[124]

Quite a startling example is to be found in the implementation of conditions contained in the Fund's 1976 and 1977 SBA's with Argentina. In the context of an examination of breaches of workers' rights, Conklin and Davidson have argued that:

---

consequences, see P Gowan, 'Neo-Liberal Theory and Practice for Eastern Europe,' *New Left Review*, Sept/Oct 1995 at 3, cited in A Orford (1997) at 454, n 40; R Rothstein, 'Less Shock, More Help Needed for Russia,' *San Francisco Chronicle*, 12 January 1994; and I Belot, 'The Role of the IMF and the World Bank in Rebuilding the CIS' (1995) 9 *Temple International and Comparative Law Journal* 83–113, 89 and 101–2.

[123] See eg C Aké, 'The Democratisation of Disempowerment in Africa' in J Hippler (1995) 70 at 75: '[T]he development literature has tended to regard a political "strong hand" as an asset rather than an obstacle to economic development, ensuring the political stability seen as a prerequisite to development, maintaining discipline among workers and curbing demands for redistribution.'

[124] M Elahi (1986) at 157. See M Elahi (1986) at 155–57 generally for the catalogue of human rights abuses (civil, political, economic, social and cultural) allegedly committed in ostensible pursuit of the IMF program.

[T]he most egregious violations of workers' rights occurred as a result of the implementation of the conditions contained [in the 1976 and 1977 SBAs]. Not only did the
conditions of these standbys outlaw collective bargaining and require all wages to be
controlled by government decree, but the government of Videla in carrying out these
measures placed all unions under military control and banned all strikes. According to
a New York Times analyst: '[i]t is not likely that workers would have accepted such a
drastic reduction in income however necessary to balance the budget, if the military
had not outlawed strikes, arrested union delegates regarded as subversive and placed
military officers in charge of most major unions.' Moreover, widespread violence was
used to suppress labour unrest during this period . . .

   In contrast to [various Argentine regimes] which were forced to violate workers'
rights in order to implement the IMF standby conditions, those governments which
have attempted to institute pro-labour policies contrary to IMF advice or conditions
have been cut off from further international loans and eventually overthrown . . . This
correlation between the repression of labour and continued access to standby credits
under the IMF stabilisation programs in Argentina has led Frenkel and O'Donnell to
conclude that '[the]se programs . . . cannot be implemented without a state that is
sufficiently authoritarian to suppress the opposition rising against their huge social
cost.'[125]

As striking as this alleged symbiosis seems, one must be wary of inflating it to
the status of a general rule. Proponents of this relationship used to point with
pride to the alleged success stories in Chile and Argentina. However one sees far
less of this in Chile's case in the aftermath of the Pinochet prosecution, and likewise in Argentina's case with the economic (and social and political) crisis there
escalating as at mid-2002. Indeed in a study entitled 'Argentina and the Fund:
From Triumph to Tragedy,' the former IMF Chief Economist Michael Mussa
has argued that the Fund itself bears heavy responsibility for Argentina's economic collapse.[126] According to Mussa Argentina is an especially important
case study for evaluating the performance and role of the Fund, given that unlike
most of its other prominent clients Argentina did not request Fund support
immediately prior to or during a crisis, but rather was under the sustained IMF
scrutiny throughout an extended period. Accordingly 'although the key decisions in the vital areas of fiscal, monetary, and exchange rate policy were

[125] M Conklin and D Davidson (1986) at 256–57. Along similar lines see R Frenkel and
G O'Donnell, 'The "Stabilisation Programs" of the IMF and Their International Impacts' in
R Fagan (ed), *Capitalism and the State in US-Latin American Relations* (1979) 171, 212; D Pion-
Berlin, 'Political Repression and Economic Doctrines: the Case of Argentina' (1983) 16 *Comparative
Law Studies* 37, 198–216; and by analogy with the World Bank, E Spiro (1979) at 158: 'If human
rights ever became a significant factor in lending decisions there might well be a more rapid change
in governments and more democratic governments as clients of the development agencies. Generally
the worst dictators remain in office for the longest periods of time. The criticism [of those who
would reject the incorporation of a "short-list" of human rights issues in lending criteria on the
grounds that to do so would deny "due process" to the government concerned], then, reveals much
about the preferences of the critics for regimes with which stable institutional relationships and
influence can be maintained.'
[126] M Mussa, 'Argentina and the Fund: From Triumph to Tragedy' (2002) 67 *Policy Analyses in
International Economics*, Institute for International Economics.

undoubtedly those of the Argentine authorities and generally enjoyed broad popular support, the IMF supported and praised these policies and thus must bear significant responsibility for their final tragic failure.'[127]

Advocates of the authoritarian regime/development relationship have also sought to draw authority (at least until the beginning of the Asian currency crisis in 1997) from the experiences of the so-called 'tiger economies' of Southeast Asia and Northern Asia.[128] However Stephen Haggard argues that 'the conventional wisdom that an "elective affinity" exists between authoritarianism and IMF stabilisation programs is oversimplified. Authoritarian polities, both those dominated by narrow, clientelistic [sic] elites and those depending on broader systems of state patronage for their legitimacy, present daunting barriers to economic adjustment.'[129] This suggestion appears particularly persuasive in view

---

[127] M Mussa (2002), reported in Institute of International Economics News Release, 'Former IMF Official Blames Fund in Argentina's Economic Collapse,' 16 July 2002 (http://www.iie.com/press/argentina.htm). In light of this experience Mussa recommends a range of institutional reforms aimed at strengthening the Fund's accountability incentives and mechanisms, broadly reflected in the reform proposals in chapter VI below. As to the Fund's ongoing involvement, see J Sachs, 'The IMF is Bleeding Argentina to Death,' *Project Syndicate* (April 2002), available at http://www.project-syndicate.cz/series/series_text.php4?id=850: 'The IMF lacks a clear idea about what to do in Argentina. It continues to pound on one theme alone: that Argentina's economic crisis is the result of fiscal profligacy, the result of a government living beyond its means. So it emphasises the need for Argentina to cut budget expenditures. . . . This is something like the 18th century medical practice in which doctors "treated" feverish patients by drawing blood from them, weakening the patients further and frequently hastening their deaths. . . . [T]he IMF recommends antiquated and phony solutions. By focusing on the budget deficit, it is chasing symptoms, not causes. It is putting forward economically and politically impossible recommendations, telling Argentina to cut public services to the extreme, when schools and hospitals are already on the verge of collapse. For centuries, doctors weakened or killed their patients in large numbers through bleeding, until medicine became a science. It is high time that the IMF approach its mission scientifically and recognise that it is on the wrong track in Argentina. As a result, the IMF must increasingly share responsibility and blame for Argentina's havoc.' To similar effect see J Stiglitz, 'Argentina's Lessons', *Project Syndicate* (January 2002), http://www.project-syndicate.cz/series/series_text.ph p4?id=760. Interestingly among the first two subjects for investigation by the Fund's new Independent Evaluation Office is the theme of fiscal adjustment in IMF-supported programmes. See chapter VI below, nn 42–43 and accompanying text.

[128] For example, Japan, South Korea, Thailand, Singapore, Taiwan, Hong Kong, Malaysia and China have all been cited by proponents of the political 'strong hand' so-called 'orthodoxy': C Aké, 'The Democratisation of Disempowerment in Africa' in J Hippler (1995) 70 at 75. Indonesia is an especially compelling case study. See nn 152–71 below and accompanying text. By way of further background see eg L Williams, 'Sorry for Abuses, Habibie Tells the Nation,' *Sydney Morning Herald*, 17 August 1998; A Marshall, 'General Under Spotlight: Army Star Accused Over Kidnap of Dissidents,' *Sydney Morning Herald*, 10 August 1998; L Williams, 'Indonesian Riots: Junior Police Jailed for Killings,' *Sydney Morning Herald*, 13 August 1998; and 'Report Tallies 780 Killings in Aceh,' *Sydney Morning Herald*, 26 August 1998, outlining a catalogue of human rights abuses perpetrated by the police and military over a number of years, including the killing, abduction and torture of activists during the final months of the Soeharto regime, and the link between student killings and widespread rioting in Jakarta, with killings and other human rights violations on a large scale. Cf IMF, 'International Monetary Fund Press Briefing on First Review of Indonesia's Economic Program by Stanley Fischer and Hubert Ness,' 4 May 1998, Washington DC, where it is implied that IMF officials may have raised concerns such as human rights violations by the Indonesian military during the course of ESAF negotiations.

[129] S Haggard (1985) at 529. Haggard suggests (at 530–32) that three other political factors are important in explaining a regime's capacity to make economic adjustments, namely: 'availability of

of the emerging emphasis by the World Bank and Fund on combating corruption, as part of their good governance strategies, to the extent of corruption's negative effects on sustainable growth. Further, according to Aké, simplistic comparisons concerning the social and political correlates of development in different regions of the world frequently fail to differentiate political authoritarianism according to historical, social and cultural context. There are a great many more influential factors governing a country's prospects for development than the mere presence or absence of authoritarian rule.[130]

On balance, therefore, it is probably not valid to characterise the relationship between conditionality and authoritarianism as 'symbiotic,' at least in a general sense. But to the extent that IMF strategies in governance and other areas (in tandem with the Bank's, particularly in the PRSP context) continue to fail to take sufficient account of human rights issues,[131] then the possibilities for IMF assistance strengthening the hand of authoritarian regimes (inadvertently or otherwise), to the detriment of the overall human rights situation and prospects for sustainable growth, will persist.

The PRSP: 'Old Wine in a New Bottle'?

There are some worrying early signs that the PRSP's promises of participation and country ownership, at least in some cases, may prove to be little more than paper ones. A number of Jubilee 2000 campaigners have alleged that 'one of the . . . great breakthroughs proclaimed [in 1999]—full consultation with civil

non-conditional resources' and, 'perhaps more importantly, the ideological orientation of bureaucratic elites and the strength of administrative structures.' See further M Monshipouri, *Democratisation, Liberalisation and Human Rights in the Third World* (1995) at 56–57.

[130] The timing of electoral cycles is one such factor, along with the prevailing national administrative capacity and character of bureaucratic politics, and the requirement to understand local social and political conditions and build coalitions of support: S Haggard and R Kaufman (1989) at 220–49. See also C Aké, 'The Democratisation of Disempowerment in Africa' in J Hippler (1995) 70 at 75: 'We need to know a lot more than the simple fact than an African country is authoritarian to understand its prospects for development or the lack of them. The particular ways in which African countries are authoritarian and the social and cultural context of their authoritarianism are determinant.' In Africa, according to Aké (at 75–76), this factors include: 'a dynamic of political competition which prevents the crystallisation of the political class and makes it all but impossible to devise, let alone implement, a national development project; [t]he colonial legacy of a national leadership which is a salariat rather than a bourgeoisie;' and '[t]he use of state power by those to have access to it for the accumulation of wealth, with the result that energies that might otherwise have gone into capitalist accumulation are diverted into the struggle for control of state power.' The result is vividly described by Aké (at 76) as 'a deformed capitalism which encourages parasitism rather than profit-driven productivity and an alienation of states and leaders from their people, who are consequently not available to be mobilised for development.'

[131] It is worth recalling Amartya Sen's reminder of the instrumentally vital role of a free press and dedicated opposition groups insofar as good governance is concerned. See chapter II above at nn 84–85 and accompanying text. However for this or any comparable list of civil and political rights guarantees to be meaningful, mutually supporting core minimum economic and social rights guarantees are also required.

society over poverty reduction strategy papers—has proved to be a bit of a joke.'[132] It was reported that '[t]he IMF told Mozambique and Mauritania that they could obtain rapid approval for debt relief under HIPC only if they did not put the PRSP out for public consultation.'[133] More recent feedback in 2002 from PRSP processes in various regions of the world suggested that (with the possible exception of Bolivia[134]) civil society participation rarely reflected much more than 'hasty, ad hoc and perfunctory' consultations.[135] The Institute for Development Studies reported 'a broad consensus among [its] civil society sources in Ghana, Malawi, Mozambique, Tanzania, Zambia and Bolivia that their coalitions have been totally unable to influence macro-economic policy or even engage governments in dialogue about it.'[136] Even where some degree of meaningful participation has taken place, rarely is there ever any strong or systematic link between poor peoples' diagnoses of their situation and the

---

[132] L Elliott, 'Poor Nations' Rights are Wronged,' *The Guardian*, 3 April 2000, p 25. Furthermore one insider interviewed in February 2000 remarked that Jubilee 2000 'won the HIPC battle, but may be losing the war.' PRSP is supposed to embrace 'flexibility, participation and partnerships,' but its guidelines 'go back to enforcing strict deadlines and conditionality,' which are inconsistent with those purposes. This commentator queried whether the PRSP will be 'just another way of doing business as usual,' with 'the same stuff sneaking in through the back door.' The comment was made that the 'criteria for debt relief are the same (although the benchmarks have been lowered to some extent), the gatekeeper (the IMF) is the same, and resources are still uncertain, to put it mildly.' Countries are required to 'frontload' efforts regarding the formulation of a poverty strategy, into a 'questionable process' and uncertain future. This commentator questioned whether this was all a 'substitute for concrete action for the poor,' and referred to the fact that the CDF was already a dead letter in practical terms.

[133] L Elliott, 'Poor Nations' Rights are Wronged,' *The Guardian*, 3 April 2000, p 25. For a critique of the scheme for debt relief under HIPC see C Denny, 'West's fine words leave debts piled high,' *The Guardian*, 21 July 2000: 'Most [highly indebted poor countries] already have to meet strict economic rules to qualify for assistance from the IMF and the World Bank. Now, in addition, to qualify for full debt relief, these countries have to produce a detailed [PRSP] explaining to the West how the money will be spent. Although a draft plan [interim PRSP] is sufficient to get the process started, the drafts are proving to be large and complex documents which take a long time to prepare. The requirement to consult widely before producing [PRSPs], and the need for speedy debt relief, are mutually exclusive. Most poor countries already have their macroeconomic policies dictated by the IMF, and many have been tempted to ask staff from the Washington financial institutions to write [a PRSP] which they know will satisfy the boards of the IMF and the Bank. The IMF is slowing down debt relief in several countries to force them to implement unpopular aspects of the Fund's macro-economic reform programmes.' See also Editorial comment: 'Debt relief's lost momentum,' *Financial Times*, 21 July 2000, and OXFAM International Policy Paper, *Outcome of the IMF/World Bank September 1999 Annual Meetings: Implications for Poverty Reduction and Debt Relief* (October 1999) at 8, commenting that the 'enhanced HIPC' initiative 'only goes half way to achieving debt sustainability' for many of the eligible countries.

[134] See eg Canadian International Development Agency (CIDA), 'The Canadian International Development Agency's Experience with the PRSP Process in Bolivia: A Report Prepared by CIDA's Bolivia Country Programme and Policy Branch, 11 December 2001 (at 4 and 8–9), indicating that the national dialogues and consultations undertaken there had not translated into the degree of political and popular support hoped for. For a stronger criticism see ActionAid, 'Inclusive Circles Lost in Exclusive Cycles: An Action Aid contribution to the first Global Poverty Reduction Strategies Comprehensive Review,' 25 January 2002.

[135] UNDP, 'UNDP Review of the Poverty Reduction Strategy Paper (PRSP), December 2001. See also ActionAid (2002).

[136] Institute for Development Studies, 'Assessing Participation in Poverty Reduction Strategy Papers: A Desk-based Synthesis of Experience in Sub-Saharan African (2002).

government's own perceptions and strategies.[137] In the general run of cases it would appear that PRSPs are prepared without parliamentary endorsement, under the leadership of the Finance Ministry.[138] Among the barriers to effective participation identified so far have been the counter-incentives for speedy debt relief under the 'interim PRSP' framework,[139] variable capacities at national level to contribute to macro-economic debates, unwillingness of the IMF to compromise on its core macro-economic assumptions, and weak development of civil society organisations in certain countries.[140]

Process deficiencies have led to substantive shortcomings. PRSPs have generally recognised that poverty is multi-dimensional and multi-causal, but they have tended not to pay attention to sustainable livelihood strategies or to social dimensions of anti-poverty strategies.[141] Neither the PRSP documents nor their corresponding Joint Staff Assessments (by the Bank and Fund) pay significant attention to sustainability, vulnerability, security, inequality, social integration, empowerment, ethnicity or other human rights-related themes,[142] an incongruous state of affairs if the Bank's 'Voices of the Poor' survey constitutes anything close to a valid representation of poor peoples' experiences for PRSP

---

[137] N Thin, M Underwood and J Gilling, 'Sub-Saharan Africa's Poverty Reduction Strategy Papers from Social Policy and Sustainable Livelihoods Perspectives: A Report for the Department of International Development (March 2001) at 11.

[138] UNDP (2001) at 7. Presidential endorsement has nonetheless been obtained in certain cases, and sectoral ministries have been involved through participation in thematic groups, and in the development of sector-specific strategies.

[139] UNCTAD, *The Least Developed Countries Report 2002: Escaping the Poverty Trap* (2002) 193.

[140] UNDP (2001); CIDA (2001). CIDA (at 10–12) regards some of these difficulties, especially the constraints posed by limited national capacities, to be inherent in the PRSP framework's design, and warranting a slower and 'less comprehensive and holistic' process than that envisaged when the PRSP framework was first developed. And for an argument for 'development oriented poverty reduction strategies', rather than the integration of pro-poor public expenditure patterns with deeper structural reforms and 1990s-style macro-economic policies, see UNCTAD (2002) at 173–77 and 179.

[141] N Thin, M Underwood and J Gilling (2001). DFID has recommended urgent introduction of Poverty and Social Impacts Analysis (PSIA) methodology: DFID, 'DFID Views on the PRSP Process,' December 2001 (at 6–7).

[142] N Thin, M Underwood and J Gilling (2001). Reviewing sixteen iPRSPs and three PRSPs and associated JSAs, the authors noted (at 14) that: 'Most documents have some mention of rights, but this does not get beyond affirmation of the importance of women's and occasionally children's rights plus sporadic references to land rights or generalised references to "needs and rights". As with empowerment, there is an absence of strategies on rights, although there are exceptions including promises to revise legal frameworks and institutions.' See also UNFPA (Population and Development Branch Technical Support Division), 'Coverage of Population and Development Themes in Poverty Reduction Strategy Papers (PRSPs): Challenges and Opportunities for UNFPA,' 11 March 2002 at 7–8, and ActionAid (2002) noting (at 3–4) noting the inclusion within PRSPs of affirmative action policies for people with disabilities (Kenya), people living with HIV/AIDs (Malawi) and women (Malawi, Kenya and Uganda), following public pressure for such measures. See also S Pereira Leite, 'Human Rights and the IMF,' 38(4) *Finance and Development*, http://www.imf.org/external/pubs/ft/fandd/2001/12/leite.htm, suggesting (based albeit on quite a generic conception of human rights) that countries where the poverty reduction strategies 'deal with human rights' include Burkina Faso, Cambodia, Cameroon, Nicaragua, Rwanda, Tanzania and Vietnam.

purposes.[143] Bolivia's PRSP has attracted pointed criticism in this regard, as failing to explore the implications of the long-standing exclusion of Bolivia's indigenous peoples, who account for over sixty percent of the total population.[144] Rwanda's PRSP would appear to be one of the notable exceptions that proves the rule, and perhaps to some degree that of Nicaragua. The 'good governance' section of Rwanda's PRSP contains a section dedicated to human rights, declaring the government's commitment to integrating human rights into all its programmes and exploring the linkages between poverty reduction and human rights, and emphasising the role to be played by the National Human Rights Commission (NHRC) in that regard.[145] The Nicaragua PRSP provides for the reinforcement of the offices for the defence of human rights and the public defenders for the protection of children, women and indigenous populations.[146]

Clearly many countries, and by no coincidence many of those within the ambit of the HIPC program and PRSP process, have very poor traditions of public accountability and popular involvement in policy-making activities. Those states with some measure of genuine commitment to the PRSP framework will usually be working from the ground upwards in order to build the requisite technical and institutional capacities to meet the 'participation' demands. Other states will no doubt be looking for ways to window-dress less bona fide 'consultation,' rather than genuine participatory, mechanisms. Defining a stance on these issues is one of the biggest challenges faced by the Bank and Fund Boards. With the staff of the IFIs limited to 'describing'[147] the consultation process, the

---

[143] See above n 79 and accompanying text. Contrary to development orthodoxy, the perceptions of the 60,000 or so 'Voices of the Poor' interviewees world-wide was that poverty is not merely the *absence of commodities and services* to meet basic needs, but rather a question of *disempowerment*. When asked what was needed most to increase their freedom of choice and improve their lives, the answers read much like a synopsis of the UDHR, with the key 'assets and capabilities' (or in human rights terms, constitutive and legally enforceable characteristics of human dignity and freedom) included such things as employment, freedom from hunger and disease, freedom from violence and abuse, freedom from fear (including from agencies of the State), self-respect, respect from others and the community, education, ability to organise and mobilise, and ability to influence those in power and enhance the accountability of those in power.

[144] CIDA (2001) at 6–7. CIDA concede (at 7) that the PRSP 'does propose some specific measures to address ethnically-based exclusion and its effects,' including strengthening of the capacity of the Ombudsman's office to protect the rights of indigenous peoples. 'However, these proposals seem relatively minor given the evident magnitude of this sensitive problem.'

[145] The Government of Rwanda, *Poverty Reduction Strategy Paper: National Poverty Reduction Programme*, Ministry of Finance and Economic Planning, June 2002, at pp 57–64, especially p 60. Specifically the NHRC is enjoined to assist in promoting and protecting human rights in Rwanda and monitor the human rights aspects of decentralisation and other relevant government policies relevant to good governance and poverty reduction. National reconciliation was likewise identified as a prerequisite in Rwanda for sustainable poverty reduction. Admittedly human rights within this structure are to a significant extent quarantined in the 'good governance' area, rather than mainstreamed throughout the PRSP. However especially in light of Rwanda's deeply troubled recent past, the treatment of human rights within this document does constitute the most striking example of human rights integration into PRSPs as at mid-2002.

[146] Government of Nicaragua, *A Strengthened Growth and Poverty Reduction Strategy*, July 2001, paragraph 147.

[147] Guidelines for Joint Staff Assessment of a Poverty Reduction Strategy Paper, 18 April 2001; available at http://www.worldbank.org/participation/jsaguidelines.htm.

scope for the Boards' case-by-case decision-making to be influenced by the extraneous political and geo-strategic interests of the dominant shareholder states remains troubling.

Related to the power relations calculus and the 'magic of expertise' critique discussed earlier, there is a real issue of 'dependence' upon the Fund at the technical level, witnessed in the Fund's work in Africa, and in particular in the HIPC and ESAF/PRGF contexts.[148] Many within the Fund appear to view this as entirely appropriate and even inevitable, seeing little if any difference between the Fund's role in the PRSP process and the way that PFP preparation was carried out, ie 'the work should be done largely by the IMF in Washington prior to the country mission.' The prevailing view within the Fund appears to be that 'governments must rely on the technicians' at the IMF.[149] On this view the value of the 'ownership' idea within the PRSP is more to be seen in helping countries better 'understand' macro-economic issues and what it is that the Fund does. While the PRSP framework has to some degree reduced the potential for 'off the peg [poverty reduction] plans from Washington,'[150] the record of implementation to date lays bare the challenges ahead at both national and international levels, before rhetoric can be matched with reality.[151]

Pragmatism v Principle? Lessons from the Indonesian Experience

A series of strong critiques of the Bank's policy approaches in Indonesia were revealed in the Operation Evaluation Department's Country Assistance Note, in

---

[148] For a developing country perspective on this, a Finance Minister of a PRSP client country was reported (anonomously) to have said: 'We don't need to second guess the Fund. We prefer to give them what they want before they start lecturing us about this and that. By doing so, we send a clear message that we know what we are doing—ie, we believe in structural adjustment.' F Cheru, 'Human Rights Assessment of the Poverty Reduction Strategy Papers (PRSP),' UN Commission on Human Rights (2001), quoted in ActionAid (2002). To similar effect see UNCTAD (2002) at 193: 'Some country-level studies . . . indicate that there has been a degree of "self-censorship" by national authorities, whereby they have held back certain policy ideas which they believed to be heterodox in the IMF and World Bank terms, in order to ensure the acceptability of the PRSPs.'

[149] Interviews in Washington DC and New York in February 2000. By contrast a modest degree of flexibility—within the apparent limitation of the 'pace and sequencing' of reforms rather than the need for the reforms themselves—appears in the remarks of the Fund's Deputy Managing Director Eduardo Aninat in June 2000, outlining some of the practical consequences of the Fund's new anti-poverty mission under the PRGF: 'There will be greater variation across countries in the pace and sequencing of reforms. But here, a word of caution: donors—and the international financial institutions—have a responsibility to be explicit about the sorts of reforms they will continue to favour. They must also give countries greater discretion to experiment and, even, to fail: more room for ownership!' IMF, 'Remarks by Aninat: International community collaborates on design of policies to promote poverty reduction'(2000) 29(13) *IMF Survey* 211–12, 211 .

[150] C Denny, 'West's fine words leave debts piled high,' *The Guardian*, 21 July 2000.

[151] For an especially sober prognosis of future prospects see Jubilee South, Focus on the Global South, AWEPON, and the Centro de Estudios Internacionales with the support of the World Council of Churches, 'The World Bank and the PRSP: Flawed Thinking and Failing Experiences,' 16 November 2001.

February 1999.[152] The Evaluation illustrates the general political parameters of, and constraints upon, the Bank's dealings with government in Indonesia before and at the beginning of the crisis, and reaction to such systemic issues as corruption. While expressly limited of course to Indonesia, it does shed light on some of the central challenges with which the Bank (and to a significant extent the Fund) is faced, in balancing the desires for a productive business relationship and harmonious relations at country level, with the need to avoiding compromising its principles. The word 'principles' here is intended to be used in a broad sense, not necessarily limited to principles embodied in operating policies, but also others of instrumental value to development effectiveness (for example in the anti-corruption context) or applicable as a matter of international law, including human rights principles.

As the Evaluation indicated, the Bank has had an unusually close and long-standing relationship with the government in Indonesia,[153] and 'willingly and for many years on a large scale funded projects linked to Soeharto.'[154] The Bank's relationship blossomed immediately after Soeharto's political ascendancy in March 1966. In the view of many, the Bank's leverage and capacity for independent and principled (according to its own policies regarding corruption, in particular) action was diminished as a consequence of the relationship with the government.[155] As Ngaire Woods notes, '[t]he very substantial levels of corruption, the failure to meet World Bank conditions regarding the state oil company Pertamina, not to mention the regime's human rights record, were all overlooked. Rather more important in explaining the Bank's relationship with Indonesia was the backdrop of US strategic concerns about South East Asia and communist insurgency. The right kind of government in Indonesia, in the context of the Cold War, simply had to be assisted.'[156]

---

[152] Indonesia—OED (World Bank) Country Assistance Note, 4 February 1999 (hereafter 'OED Note').

[153] For a more comprehensive account of that relationship see Kapur, D. *et al* (eds) (1997) (Vol. 1) at 467–71 and 488–95; and also paras 3.8–3.10 at 15–16 of the OED Note.

[154] Page 3, para 1.14 of the OED Note refers to the corruption problem. See also G Standing, (ILO), EUI European Forum conference paper, Global Trajectories: Ideas, Transnational Policy Transfer and 'Models' of Welfare Reform, Florence, 25–26 March 1999, 'New Development Paradigm or Third Wayism? A Critique of the World Bank Rethink,' at 12; and OED Country Assistance Note (February 1999) at para 3.10, reporting former Bank President MacNamara's warnings on corruption even during the 1970s. As for the early–mid 1990s, one insider interviewed in October 1999 speculated that the former Bank Director in Jakarta, in the face of the challenges of dealing with the Soeharto government, possibly 'just stopped trying' at some point along the way!

[155] See eg G Standing (1999) at 12: The Bank's VP for East Asia in late 1997 said that the Bank knew 'exactly where our money is going' in Indonesia (WSJ, 19 August 1998). However the Bank's memorandum in September 1998 and subsequent early 1999 evaluation estimated that 20% of the funds allocated to Bank projects in Indonesia had been 'diverted' to politicians and bureaucrats.' Independent anecdotal accounts in Indonesia in late 1999 generally put the figure at somewhere like 30%.

[156] N Woods, 'The Challenges of Multilateralism and Governance' in C Gilbert and D Vines (eds), *The World Bank: Structure and Policies* (2000) 132–56, 146. For a more detailed account of the political history see M Green, *Indonesia: Crisis and Transformation, 1965–1968* (1990). As Woods notes (at 146) 'the Bank's closeness to Indonesia (and other countries) also developed out of

The account in the OED country note suggests that senior Bank management were severely compromised in their dealings with the government of Indonesia, playing down Board concerns about the Bank's strategy, ignoring staff warnings in deference to the preservation of the Bank/government relationship, and bending unduly to prevailing indicators of Indonesia's economic performance.[157] Staffing changes within the Bank appear to have affected institutional memory and in other respects further impaired the Bank's capacity to respond.[158] The OED particularly questioned the decision of the Bank to avoid financial sector conditionality that would have accompanied a structural adjustment loan, instead (in July 1998) implementing a fast-disbursing 'PRSL' to address Indonesia's systemic problems.[159] Consequences of choosing this quick-disbursing instrument were said to include an inability to track disbursements and seriously attempt to remedy systemic reforms.[160]

Several of the criticisms within the OED Note are especially blunt, alleging that quite clear evidence of financial sector strategy failure (essentially involving the liberalisation of interest rates and financial sector deregulation without adequate legal or accounting structures or the capacity to supervise) was overlooked or at least played down and postponed in deference to the need to preserve the Bank/government relationship, and that 'unjustified penalties' were visited upon the 'career prospects of some Bank staff who had brought the issues to light.'[161]

Anecdotally, some within the Bank take issue with the OED's views and assumptions on certain points, including on the latter point regarding disciplinary action being visited upon whistle-blowing staff. The counter-arguments include the contentions that the OED:

(i)   is somewhat removed from the action;
(ii)   overstated their allegations of Bank officials ignoring corruption;[162]

relations between Bank staff and a particular set of interlocutors: in Indonesia a group of young US trained economists (or "technocrats" as they came to be called) who were brought into government by General Suharto. From the Bank's side, the most senior staff member in Jakarta was given unprecedented powers to make loans and report directly to the World Bank President. Significantly, once the Bank's technocratic interlocutors lost some of their influence and power so, too, Indonesia's relationship with the Bank became a more distant one.'

[157] OED Note at paras 2.11–2.20 and 3.8–3.10 and 3.29 and p 26. One respected independent Indonesian commentator interviewed in October 1999 affirmed that the Bank was unduly concerned with preserving good relations between the US and the Indonesian government, in the (US) interests of preserving 'democracy' and combating communism.

[158] OED Note at para 2.17.

[159] See OED Note, paras 9–10.

[160] OED Note, para 2.20. There appears to have been a belated formal acknowledgement of the deficiencies of this approach. See *World Bank Development News*, 18 April 2000: '. . . Le Figaro (p V) notes that Wolfensohn acknowledged that in 1999, the major part of Bank lending was in fast-disbursing structural adjustment credits for the countries hit by the Asian crisis. This would change in future, he promised, adding that there would be a better division of labour with the IMF.'

[161] OED Note at paras 3.27–3.29.

[162] Indeed by some accounts the Bank's concerns regarding corruption were raised from time to time with the government of Indonesia, although almost always behind closed doors.

(iii) discounted the difficulties associated with the government being the sole interlocutor at country level;

(iv) overstated the degree of the Bank's influence in Indonesia; and

(v) is not in a position to weigh the difficult political balance upon which the Bank's continued presence and ability to operate in Indonesia at all material times rested.

A further anecdotal criticism of the OED report was that it failed to recognise that increased use of conditionality to the point of public confrontation or suspension of lending may have pushed the government over the precipice by dint of private sector reaction and capital flight, following the World Bank's lead. However this explanation seems difficult to reconcile with broadly drawn disclaimers concerning the limits of the Bank's policy influence in Indonesia at material times.

While it is not the purpose of this book to resolve these disputed accounts beyond all reasonable doubt, it is important to bear such objections to the OED evaluation in mind when weighing the criticisms and recommendations (many of which resonate for the broader purposes of this book) contained therein. And to keep criticisms in context, it is clear that the Bank's approach on corruption and the political parameters of its (and the Fund's) engagement at country level have taken a relatively principled,[163] and generally more constructive, turn in light of subsequent events in Indonesia, as witnessed in:

(i) the relatively principled responses of both the Bank and Fund to the 'Bank Bali' corruption scandal and prosecution of other high-level corruption cases;[164]

(ii) pressure for improvement of human rights in October 1999 in East Timor, and in September 2000 in West Timor;[165] and

(iii) increasing dealings and cooperation with non-governmental partners.[166]

---

[163] Although some, including certain NGOs and independent observers in Indonesia, would characterise the post-crisis approach as overly-interventionist.

[164] The 'Bali Gate' scandal began in July 1999, when investigators discovered that one of Indonesia's leading private banks, Bank Bali, had diverted about US$70 million in public funds to a top Golkar (ruling party) official, apparently in order to help gain support for a plan to keep Bank Bali afloat. See *New York Times*, 8 September 1999.

[165] See eg 'World Bank backs US warning for Timor militia control,' *The Straits Times Interactive*, 19 September 2000; G Kitney, 'Wahid warned aid may stop,' *Sydney Morning Herald*, 19 September 2000; S Mufson, 'Curb militias, World Bank warns Wahid,' *Sydney Morning Herald*, 13 September 2000.

[166] The seachange in this respect was evident soon after President Habibie was elected in 1998. In 5 Oct 1999 *World Bank Development News* reported, per Reuters and AFP: 'The IMF said yesterday it plans technical talks with Indonesia, but reiterated that no new lending would take place until "significant progress" was made on the Bank Bali investigation, Reuters reports. The Fund said in a statement it would talk with the government, major political parties, universities, and other economic institutions with a view to reaching a consensus on a suitable macroeconomic policy for the country. The Fund said the consultations would be held in response to requests from government and non-government sources in Indonesia, and that it would undertake technical discussions aimed at forging a consensus "on the macroeconomic framework that should guide policy in the period ahead," quotes AFP. It said the talks should help the resumption of IMF lending once a new

Certain programmatic improvements have also been ushered in, involving participatory and empowering community-driven implementation strategies, strengthened local level accountability, and strengthened linkages between governance and poverty reduction,[167] and a general 'civil society outreach' initiative by both Bank and Fund, driven by a combination of public pressure, standard instrumentalist developmental rationales, and the practical necessity to explore new partnerships and modes of cooperation in the post-Soeharto political void. Moreover opinion is almost unanimous on the positive changes in direction brought by a change of country office directorship in 1999.[168]

But notwithstanding these factors, and irrespective of whether or how the different perspectives of the Bank's Task Managers and OED are to be resolved, it is quite clear from all accounts (official as well as anecdotal) that the Bank's performance in Indonesia fell well below desirable standards throughout the 1980s and 1990s. Many of the OED criticisms had strong echoes in the Bank's relationships with other countries presently or formerly allied to the West, such as Turkey, Mexico, Iran (in particular in the late 1970s) and the Philippines,[169] with continuing relevance in the year 2002 in certain cases, such as Papua and New Guinea.[170] The consequences of compromise are potentially extremely

government has been established.' Obviously the falling from grace of the once omnipotent Soeharto government and associated social, political and economic upheaval bear prime responsibility for this expansion of political space, in effect drawing in a whole new range of interlocutors almost by default, to fill the vacuum.

[167] 'Village Infrastructure Projects' and the Kecamatan Development Project are said to be examples of this. For an outline of these and other elements of the revised Country Assistance Strategy for Indonesia see D Narayan (ed), *Empowerment and Poverty Reduction: A Sourcebook* (2002) at 125–35 ('Empowerment and the World Bank's Country Assistance Strategy for Indonesia').

[168] This goes for most independent critics of the Bank in Indonesia (even if disagreement over more systemic issues remains), as well as Bank personnel. One insider observed that new director Mark Baird 'had to pretty well start from scratch,' but was 'doing some good things' and was an advocate of trying to bring a broader perspective and genuine poverty focus to the Bank's in-country work.

[169] N Woods (2000) at 146: 'In all of these cases the issues of corruption, human rights abuses and failure to meet conditions of loans were overlooked in favour of close and generous treatment from the World Bank, closely supported by the US Treasury and State Departments. Equally importantly, close relations in each case were formed between Bank officials and "technocrats" (often US-economics trained) in the borrowing government and suffered when technocrats lost their positions or influence.'

[170] The Bank's chequered recent history in Papau and New Guinea reveals quite clearly the difficulties in sustaining principled positions on such delicate but vital matters as corruption, against the tide of local and international political imperatives and vested interests. A Fowle, 'The Insider,' *4 Corners* (ABC Australia: http://www.abc.net.au/4Corners, 24 June 2002, reporting the futile attempts of the World Bank Representative to effectively monitor governance and anti-corruption elements of the country programme against resistance from the ruling political party, diplomatic pressure from the Australian government not to portray Papua New Guinea in a bad light, and ultimately, loss of support from Bank headquarters in Washington DC. See also P Brown, 'Forest Corruption Report Covered Up: Governments, Big Business, World Bank and IMF Named in Investigation,' The Guardian, 29 May 2000, http://www.guardian.co.uk/Archive/Article/0,4273, 4023274,00.html; M Pitts, 'Crime and Corruption: Does Papua New Guinea Have the Capacity to Control It?' (2001) 16(2) *Pacific Economic Bulletin* 127–34 http://peb.anu.edu.au/pdf/ PEB 16-2pitts.pdf; ABC Transcripts, 'World Bank Denies PNG Claim over Future Relationship,'

serious in human rights terms: international lending snowballs into unsustainable debt burdens in circumstances where disbursed funds are permitted to be diverted by non-reforming regimes towards unproductive ends. To the extent of the Bank's (as well as the Fund's) complicity, it is unconscionable for these institutions to insist on the repayment of 'bad' loans,[171] posited against urgent, legitimate and competing demands for fulfillment of human rights entitlements.

Fractured Situation Analysis: The Compartmentalisation Problem

In the face of persistent accusations of failure, the IMF still has not made much progress towards the development of a coherent strategy for promoting sustainable growth while minimising adverse impacts. The introduction of social safety nets was a positive step in this regard, however. The IMF's growing interest in social policy issues is said to have emerged from 'social concerns' (such as 'rising unemployment, malnutrition, and social marginalisation') arising in the context of macroeconomic stabilisation and SAPs, and 'an explicit recognition that more importance must be attached to equity and the full development of human resources if reform programs are to be viable in the long run.'[172] Or as the Fund phrased it in one particular ESAF (in a rather desiccated technocratic euphemism): 'Since a deterioration of the stock of human capital would have detrimental effects on [a client country's] prospects for growth,' budgetary outlays on education are justified.[173]

In terms of squaring an active concern with these issues with its mandate, it has already been seen that the IMF's 'economic growth' mission has broadened considerably in recent years. As has been expressed on behalf of the Fund's staff: 'In the last few years, a broader concept of high-quality growth has emerged, namely, economic growth that brings lasting employment gains and poverty

16 February 2001, http://www.abc.net.au/ra/asiapac/archive/2001/feb/raap-19feb2001-4.htm; Eco-Forestry Forum, Press Release (19 February 2001), 'Papua New Guinea: World Bank Ready to Abandon Forestry Reform?', available at http://forests.org/recent/2001/bankabrd.htm. For details of the Bank's 'Governance Promotion Adjustment Loan' see World Bank News Release No: 2002/170/S, 21 December 2001.

[171] The Indonesian Parliament put the case for debt cancellation in blunt terms to the Bank and Fund in a letter dated 5 July 2002: 'It was principally due to the obsequious support of the IMF to an extremely corrupt and incompetent economic regime which made that regime viable and powerful. The IMF has been fully cognisant and therefore condoning the extensive plundering of the loans provided under [IMF] auspices.' Bretton Woods Project, 'Bretton Woods Update' (July/August 2002; available at http://www.brettonwoods.org) 'Indonesian MPs: Write-off IMF Loans' (at 8). The Bank's former Representative in Papua and New Guinea (1997–2001) expresses similar concerns in the circumstances of that case: A Fowle, 'The Insider,' *4 Corners* (ABC Australia: http://www.abc.net.au/4Corners), 24 June 2002.

[172] IMF, 'Social Dimensions of the IMF's Policy Dialogue,' April 1998, http://www.imf.org/external/np/exr/facts/social.htm.

[173] Georgia—ESAF Policy Framework Paper, 1997–1999, 24 February 1997 at paragraph 43. Or as the IMF Interim Committee put it: '[T]he sustainability of economic growth depends on development of human resources'—Interim Committee Declaration: 'Partnership for Sustainable Growth,' 29 September 1996, Washington, DC.

reduction, provides greater equality of income through greater equality of opportunity, including for women, and respects human freedom and protects the environment.'[174] And the widespread emergence of more open and participatory forms of governance has been claimed to provoke recognition by the Fund that popular support for traditional adjustment programs is an 'essential precondition for their ultimate success.'[175]

But as potentially significant as such developments are on their face, in the general run of cases 'social' provisions have occupied a tiny proportion of overall ESAF policy framework, tacked on to the end of the lengthy list of fiscal and macroeconomic prescriptions, without seeking to explore their interrelationships in a focused and balanced fashion.[176] Further, the Fund's conditions in the area of social policy have frequently seemed to be quite general in nature, setting broad parameters and flexible goals, to the neglect of targets, strategies and indicators that might more clearly reveal progress in the elimination of adverse human impacts and improvement of the overall human rights situation, supporting the demand for sustainable growth.[177]

More seriously still, the Fund's 'social' benchmarks in the health and education sectors under ESAF/PFP arrangements have frequently privileged the blinkered quest for privatisation over competing demands for balanced and contextualised situation assessment.[178] Moreover the scope for inclusion of any effective empowering strategies has been limited all too often by the exclusion within standard SBA and extended facility negotiation arrangements of any real scope for meaningful and effective participation. Based upon the content of the general run of publicly available PFPs, it is doubtful that many 'policy matrixes' have been informed by thorough and appropriately nuanced assessments of the social and political conditions in the countries concerned. The PRSP/PRGF

---

[174] IMF, 'Social Dimensions of the IMF's Policy Dialogue,' *IMF Pamphlet Series* No. 47 (1995) at 11–12.

[175] IMF, 'Social Dimensions of the IMF's Policy Dialogue,' April 1998, http://www.imf.org/external/np/exr/facts/social.htm.

[176] See eg Kyrgyz Republic—ESAF Policy Framework Paper, 1998–2000 at paragraphs 35–38; Azerbaijan Republic—ESAF and EFF Policy Framework Paper, 1997–2000 at paragraphs 46–50. One of the exceptions to this general picture is the Letter of Intent and Memorandum on Economic Policies of the Royal Thai Government, 26 May 1998, covering a relatively broad range of issues such as employment, health, education, poverty reduction, community participation, training and rural development.

[177] Provisions in the Indonesian Supplementary Memorandum of Economic and Financial Policies, 10 April 1998, is illustrative of this point. Among other things, Annex 1 ('Social Safety Net') provides that the government will 'ensure sufficient quantities of essential foodstuffs,' 'substantially expand' certain employment programs, and 'increase budgetary allocations for the existing social programs targeted to the children of poor households.'

[178] A good example is the case of Georgia—ESAF Policy Framework Paper, 1997–1999, 24 February 1997, at paragraphs 23–24, although many other could be cited. See K Tomasevski, 'Economic Costs of Human Rights' in P Baehr, C Flinterman and M Senders (eds), *Innovation and Inspiration: Fifty Years of the Universal Declaration of Human Rights* (1999) 49–60 at 59, on potential human rights implications of privatisation. For further discussion of the problem of ideological bias in this respect see chapter VI below at nn 265–68 and accompanying text.

framework is intended to remedy precisely these kinds of shortcomings,[179] although as was seen earlier in this chapter the jury as at mid-2002 was still well and truly out.[180]

As a matter of logic, as Gunnar Myrdal has observed, 'the isolation of one part of social reality by demarcating it as "economic"' is not feasible. 'In reality, there are not "economic," "sociological" or "psychological" problems, but just problems, and they are complex.'[181] Early in the Indonesian crisis the World Bank's Katherine Marshall warned that '[a] common danger is to over-segregate macroeconomic and sector policy. The debates around IMF Letters of Intent, rescue packages, World Bank financial sector and structural adjustment loans tend to be led by macroeconomic teams.' After citing the relatively positive case of Korea, where social policy issues (relating especially to labour policy, the labour movement having been relatively strong at all material times) were

---

[179] See eg IMF, 'The IMF's Poverty Reduction and Growth Facility (PRGF): A Factsheet,' March 2001, http://www.imf.org/external/np/exr/facts/prgf.htm: 'It is expected that PRGF-supported programs will cover only areas within the primary responsibility of the IMF unless a particular structural measure is judged to have a direct, critical macro-economic impact.' However no clarification is offered on the meaning of the term 'direct, critical macro-economic impact.' Experience of the Bank's Legal Department in interpreting Article IV, section 10 of the Bank's articles (see chapter IV below) bear eloquent testimony to the difficulties of elaborating and applying such tests in an objective, convincing and even-handed fashion.

[180] This is most certainly the case from the point of view of national authorities in PRGF countries, as revealed through survey responses to IMF questionnaires: IMF, 'Review of the Poverty Reduction and Growth Facility: Issues and Options,' Prepared by the Policy Development and Review and Fiscal Affairs Departments, 14 February 2002, at Appendix I, reflecting ambivalence at the extent of change ushered in so far (eg only slightly over half of the respondents agreeing that the PRGF streamlined conditionality and allowed increased opportunity to influence program design, and only 1 in 20 respondents 'strongly agreeing,' which in any event was based on a comparison with the relatively clear shortcomings in these respects under the ESAF/PFP arrangements). Moreover as at March 2002 the IMF Executive Board, in reviewing progress to date under the PRGF, 'urged continued improvements in coordination and definition of roles between the IMF and World Bank.' And while welcoming the progress made in incorporating poverty and social impact analyses (PSIA) into PRGF-supported programs and staff documents, the Board 'indicated that there was scope for a more systematic treatment of this issue in PRGF documents.' IMF, PIN No. 02/30, 15 March 2002, 'IMF Executive Board Reviews the Poverty Reduction and Growth Facility (PRGF),' http://www.imf.org/external/np/sec/pn/2002/pn0230.htm.

[181] G Myrdal, *Against the Stream: Critical Essays on Economics* (1975) at 142. Recent research by Jeffrey Sachs and others into the cumulative economic costs of the malaria epidemic in Africa graphically exposes the compartmentalisation fallacy: B Barber, 'Malaria Cripples African Economy,' *The Washington Times*, 25 April 2000; 'Africa Confronts Malaria,' *BBC News Online*, 25 April 2000. See also H Morais, 'A Festschrift Honoring Professor Louis B Sohn (April 8, 2000): The Globalisation of Human Rights Law and the Role of International Financial Institutions in Promoting Human Rights' (2000) 33 *George Washington International Law Review* 71–96, 89–90: '[T]here is growing recognition among scholars that it is difficult to draw a clear distinction between "politics" and "economics." The concept of the "political economy" suggests that although the state as the embodiment of politics and the market as the embodiment of economics are distinctive features of the modern world, they obviously cannot be totally separated. . . . The state profoundly influences the outcome of market activities by determining the nature and distribution of property rights as well as the rules governing economic behaviour. Thus, decisions of governments, run by politicians and responsible for the management of a country's resources, directly influence the economic, financial and social outcomes for their people. Recent history teaches us that repressive political regimes that trampled on human rights failed dismally in their pursuit of economic growth and prosperity.'

squarely on the table at the outset, she lamented: 'Still, policy debates have tended once again to take place largely in separate domains. The paramount importance of macroeconomic outcomes and policies for social welfare [and surely, vice versa] is much more starkly appreciated in the Asian case than it was before[.]'[182]

Other commentators such as Kevin Watkins from OXFAM have long criticised the 'bolt-on' approach of the IFIs, attaching (frequently hastily conceived) SSN's onto a pre-conceived IMF macro-economic template.[183] The incongruousness of this division of labour has been portrayed in the following way in the East Asian context:

> The IMF itself has pointed to the introduction of social-welfare mechanisms aimed at mitigating the effects of the crisis on poor households as evidence of institutional concern with poverty. In fact, the World Bank assumed responsibility for mobilising donor support in this area, much as the IMF has assumed responsibility for managing support for macroeconomic management. As a result, social policy considerations were conspicuous by their absence from the initial stabilisation plans. They were subsequently introduced as an appendage to these plans in a policy environment which, because of the impact of deflation on household poverty, was not conducive to an effective social-welfare response. In effect, the World Bank was used to fight a forest fire, the flames of which were being fanned by the IMF.[184]

OXFAM's and like criticisms appear to have resonated at the IFIs, adding to momentum for reforms along the lines that have been seen flowing from the ESAF External Review and PRSP initiative. The inherently flawed 'compartmentalisation' assumption has been laid bare by the apparently new premises of conceptual coherence and functional symbiosis between macro-economic and social issues within the PRSP framework.[185]

---

[182] K Marshall, 'Social Dimensions of the East Asia Crisis: Some Reflections Based on Experience from the Adjustment Eras in Africa and Latin America,' Paper for IDS East Asia Crisis Meeting, 13–14 July 1998.

[183] See eg OXFAM International Policy Paper, *East Asian 'Recovery' Leaves the Poor Sinking* (October 1998): 'Treating poverty reduction as an appendage to economic reform is inconsistent with the policy commitment of both [the Bank and Fund], as well as being inimical to the interests of the poor in East Asia. And more recently, OXFAM International Policy Paper, *Outcome of the IMF/World Bank September 1999 Annual Meetings: Implications for Poverty Reduction and Debt Relief* (October 1999) at 5: 'For too long the approach [to programme design] has actually been backwards, with poverty reduction coming as an afterthought to harsh structural adjustment programming by the IMF and World Bank. The Bank has often attached "social funds" to adjustment programs, claiming that these often politicised and disconnected programs are successfully addressing poverty even while the overall adjustment policies do not. Senior staff of both institutions now acknowledge the failures of this approach, and the pressure is now on them to get this right.'

[184] OXFAM, *Education Now: Break the Cycle of Poverty* (1999) at 190. Or as the same organisation has put the matter more simply: SSN's are 'ineffective in an environment where poorly designed economic reforms are destroying livelihoods.' *Jakarta Post*, 27 September 1999.

[185] Malawi is a striking case, where the Article IV consultations covered a very wide range of issues including a lengthy and focused discussion on food security policy, as well as discussions on governance and anti-corruption institutions and legal frameworks, special measures for the vulnerable, freedom of the press, legislative constraints on freedom of expression and other legislative initiatives entrenching the political control of the ruling party, and the participatory process behind the

SSNs: Targeting and Other Problems

Apart from the compartmentalisation problem, one of the most fundamental critiques of SSNs arises from perceived lack of coherence with other components of country programs.[186] Firstly, focusing again upon the Indonesian crisis, the IFIs have been accused of making little apparent distinction between programs with shorter and longer-term objectives. Secondly, a number of SSN elements in Indonesia were simply 'piggybacked' onto existing programs. As UNSFIR remarked, '[t]hese [latter] programs were designed before the crisis and in some areas have functioned fairly well. However, it cannot be assumed that these programs will be able to operate just as effectively under current [crisis] circumstances.'[187]

Targeting under the SSN has proven to be a serious problem as well, and has done little to promote equity.[188] One of the apparent justifications of the Fund in allocating sole responsibility to the Bank for design and implementation of the SSN is that 'welfare payments can be targeted at those households most at risk.'[189] However as OXFAM has stated:

> [e]xperience has shown that targeting during periods of economic crisis is a hazardous affair. In Indonesia, World Bank efforts to provide educational assistance to poor households have been hampered by corruption and weak administrative systems. Scholarship schemes intended to protect vulnerable households have frequently missed their target, including children who have dropped out of the school system.[190]

PRSP. IMF Country Report No. 02/181, August 2002, 'Malawi: Article IV Consultation and Economic Program for 2002—Staff Report; Staff Supplement; and Public Information Notice on the Executive Board Discussion.

[186] United Nations Support Facility for Indonesian Recovery (UNSFIR), *The Social Implications of the Indonesian Economic Crisis: Perceptions and Policy* (1999) at 98.

[187] UNSFIR (1999) at 98. See 98–101 for a discussion of a range of SSN implementation issues, including other aspects of program design, targeting of beneficiaries, delivery mechanisms, capacity of local authorities, and sustainability.

[188] As one senior independent economist interviewed in October 1999 saw it, the question is how to identify where the targets are, and how to design and execute the program in a sustainable way. In that commentator's view SSN's are needed, but the focus must be on 'identification, targeting, and design.' Indonesia is characterised by great diversity in social arrangements, economic activity, and basic service delivery (eg farmers within and outside of Java are different, and fisherman within Java will be different). A 'cushion' is needed, but what sort? In this respect there is a very real tension from the Bank's point of view between 'recognition of diversity' v. 'efficient management of programs,' the latter factor tending towards homogeneity in approaches.

[189] OXFAM (1999) at 35.

[190] OXFAM (1999) at 35. See also above n 1 and accompanying text, and J Knowles, E Pernia and M Racelis, 'Social Consequences of the Financial Crisis in Asia: the Deeper Crisis,' paper prepared for Manila Social Forum: New Social Agenda for East and South-east Asia, 8–12 November 1999 at 10: 'Targeting is more difficult during a crisis because there is much "churning" into and out of the ranks of the poor. A lot of experimentation and careful evaluation are therefore required to develop effective targeting mechanisms for social safety nets.' And the findings of the Social Monitoring and Early Response Unit (SMERU) see A Suryahadi, Y Suharso and S Sumarto, 'Coverage and Targeting in the Indonesian Social Safety Net Programs,' paper prepared for Manila Social Forum: New Social Agenda for East and South-east Asia, 8–12 November 1999 at 19–20: While discounting for some regional variation, the authors conclude: 'The findings of this study, unfortunately, point out that

Anecdotal accounts in Jakarta and Yogjakarta in October 1999 very much supported these observations,[191] as did the OED evaluation, whose criticisms included: (a) alleged failure to target the 'near poor;' (b) the need for the Bank to deepen its understanding of how well-targeted and effective the government's poverty programs were; and (c) the need to institute 'subjective' poverty lines based upon people's own assessments of the adequacy of their consumption, rather than adhering solely to 'traditional survey methods.'[192]

Among the other major flaws in the SSN scheme as a whole, in the opinion of one respected Indonesian social scientist, is the systemic problem that it tends to create or exacerbate dependencies. This can be viewed as one particular variant, or component, of the 'social capital erosion' critique, to be addressed shortly. Other problems include: (a) the fact that '[i]n comparison with the income losses sustained by poor households and the overall decline in social-sector provision, the resources available [under the Bank and ADB sponsored 'Stay in School' programme] are grossly inadequate;' (b) an inherent regional inequity and bias towards Java in the national welfare system through which donors work; (c) failure to capture children who weren't formally enrolled in the school system; and (d) the scale of the loss of SSN funds through corruption.[193]

Social Capital Depreciation and the Commodification of Social Relationships

'Social capital' is a difficult concept to define. In its simplest sense it can probably be characterised as voluntary forms of social regulation, with the following attributes and parameters:

in many cases the target groups have been largely missed by the programs—both in terms of low coverage and being only loosely targeted in practice. . . . The general picture . . . points to the need for a large improvement in program implementations, in particular in targeting the beneficiaries of a particular program and raising coverage within the target groups.' However see United Nations Support Facility for Indonesian Recovery (UNSFIR), *The Social Implications of the Indonesian Economic Crisis: Perceptions and Policy* (1999) at 6–7, and 11–26 on the methodological limitations of small-scale assessments, including the above '100 villages study.'

[191] However for a more upbeat assessment from the Bank's perspective see the speech of Jean-Michel Severino, 'Is Asia Rising? An Update: Report Prepared for a Presentation to the World Bank Board of Executive Directors,' Washington DC, 13 July 1999.

[192] OED Note (1999) at paras 3.30, 3.32 and 3.35.

[193] OXFAM, *Education Now: Break the Cycle of Poverty* (1999) at 187–88. On a more general level, against the growing political unrest and social tension in Indonesia in 1998, one observer has claimed that that Bank then 'had no choice but to shore up the dwindling legitimacy of the Indonesian state with ample loans.' See J Breman, 'Politics of Poverty and a Leaking Safety Net' (1999) 34(20) *Economic and Political Weekly* 1177–78, 1177. However Breman (at 1177–78) criticised the lack of effectiveness of the SSN on the following grounds: (i) failure of distribution systems for subsidised rice; (ii) failure of public works programs, and lack of any apparent 'serious attempt' (in Breman's view) to combat unemployment; and (iii) inadequacies in the system of granting small-scale credit. Corruption was obviously a major factor in these failures. In Breman's view (at 1178) as important as 'charitable' acts to relieve the suffering of the poorest are (through SSN's or otherwise) in Indonesia, on the whole they 'remain far from any structural combating of poverty[,]' which 'requires a redistribution of economic and political power.' According to Breman (at 1178) as at 1999 '[t]he fight for social equality [had] hardly begun.'

Unlike physical capital that is wholly tangible and human capital that is embodied in the skills and knowledge of an individual, social capital exists in relations among persons. . . . It places not just the human being at the centre but above all the relation among human beings. They are important because they constitute the basis on which moral communities are built. Human capital seeks to improve the ability of an individual to make decisions; social capital seeks to improve the ability of a collectivity to make decisions. Naturally, however, the two are not mutually exclusive; a more skilled individual will also enrich collectivities, while more harmonious collectivities will make individual skills more meaningful and effective.[194]

If we broaden the definition of social capital somewhat, we may also include formal and informal processes and structures, that is, how different institutions relate to each other, power structures, norms and networks within and between different organisations, issues related to accountability and transparency, the degree of democratic participation and control, and other issues. The cultural setting, including the family and gender structure, extent of ethnic diversity, the role of customary law and traditions, define the broader context in which social capital is being accumulated (or depreciated).[195]

With reference to the Bank's research, some independent commentators have averred to the danger in seeing 'social capital' as a convenient answer to objections concerning the reduced role of the state within the neoliberal paradigm, and queried the motives for the Bank's enthusiasm about social capital. The alternative view is that there should be a role for the state in helping to nurture the conditions for the development of 'social capital,' seeing social capital as a complement, rather than alternative, to an active governmental role.

Erosion of social capital was identified as one of the key impacts of the crisis for Indonesia.[196] Various commentators have alleged that the Bank can destroy 'social capital' (and indeed in Indonesia did do so) with too much social lending, in contrast to the possibility of acting as a catalyst or stimulant for families and communities, empowering them to do the work themselves.[197] According to one critic, as at October 1998 the Bank had failed to accord sufficient recog-

---

[194] T Banuri, G Hyden, C Juma and M Rivera, *Sustainable Human Development from Concept to Operation: A Guide for the Practitioner*, A UNDP Discussion Paper (1994) at 18–19, cited in de S Vylder, *Sustainable Human Development and Macroeconomics: Strategic Links and Implications*, A UNDP Discussion Paper (1996) at 12–13.

[195] S de Vylder (1996) at 13. The term 'trust, reciprocity and networks of support' has also be used as a definition: C Robb, 'Social Aspects of the East Asian Financial Crisis: Perceptions of Poor Communities,' Paper prepared for DFID's seminar on Implications of the East Asian Crisis for Poverty Elimination, 15 July 1998.

[196] J Knowles, E Pernia and M Racelis, 'Social Consequences of the Financial Crisis in Asia: the Deeper Crisis,' paper prepared for Manila Social Forum: New Social Agenda for East and Southeast Asia, 8–12 November 1999 at 6: 'In Indonesia, traditional practices to help the poorest members of the community prospered in the early part of the crisis, but faltered, along with religious gatherings, as the crisis deepened.' See also C Robb (1998), dealing with the issue in terms of 'conflict' and 'vulnerability and insecurity.'

[197] Indeed one UNICEF official remarked that the Bank's money effectively 'puts UNICEF out of business', destroying local capacities and social capital. Social Safety Net (SSN, or JPS as it is known in Indonesia) funds are 'given away free.'

nition to three sources of strength in Indonesian society: family, religious organisations, and community self-help.[198]

> Promises of large amounts of money for Indonesia's [SSN] to be provided with no quid
> pro quo may damage the willingness of poor people to reciprocate the support they
> traditionally receive. . . . [T]op-down giving of free goods will not promote a sustain-
> able answer to Indonesia's crisis. The rapidly escalating problems of maternal and
> infant malnutrition, reduced access to quality health care on the part of poor families
> and school drop-out levels can best be solved by strengthening Indonesia's existing
> social capital, not by imposing an alien social safety net.[199]

A different commentator complained of the 'seriously flawed assumption' at the
'macro' level of evaluation (by the Bank and government) that 'local coping
capacity is zero.'[200] A senior UNICEF economist concurred,[201] describing social
capital as 'community based,' and that 'you can't throw around large amounts
of financial resources in all situations,' and effectively 'co-opt indigenous organisations.' This commentator pointed out that UNICEF was at fault here too, to
some degree, for the simple reason that 'the whole international system needs

---

[198] S Woodhouse, 'Tradition of Mutual Help Damping the Crisis,' *The Jakarta Post*, 26 October
1998. The strengths as elaborated are: 'First, there is the power of the extended family to look after
the interests of all members, with a particular focus on protecting the poorest, most-vulnerable
members first. Extended family gatherings are commonplace and often involve specific plans for
helping family members in the short and long term. However, reciprocity is also important . . . The
second strength is the power of religious leaders. All the major religions here share a common commitment to help the poor . . . The third strength is *gotong royong* (community self-help) with its
numerous manifestations that vary from area to area . . . Indonesia's excellent system of community
health and nutrition posts (Posyandu) is also rooted in *gotong royong*. There are about 250,000 such
posts throughout the country . . . In most parts of Indonesia, community work such as clearing
drains, maintaining public thoroughfares and independence day celebrations is done based on the
spirit of mutual self-help. As with everywhere, there is no such thing as a free lunch, and everyone
contributes what they can.'
[199] S Woodhouse, 'Tradition of Mutual Help Damping the Crisis,' *The Jakarta Post*, 26 October
1998. In his article Woodhouse spelled out a number of specific means how that could be done. It is
worth recalling (above n 167 and accompanying text) that some of these lessons would appear to
have been incorporated by the Bank into the *Country Assistance Strategy Fiscal Year 2001–2003* for
Indonesia.
[200] One commentator gave an example from the 'IDT' poverty reduction program commenced
by government of Indonesia in 1993 (IDT being said to be the bahasa Indonesia acronym for 'aid for
backward villages!'). One of the indicators used in that program to calibrate the seriousness of the
effects of the drought at that time, and hence influencing the targeting of assistance, was whether the
home in question had dirt—or alternatively cement—floors. Funding was directed more to the former. However in reality the families residing in houses with dirt floors were more often those who
practised 'traditional' livelihoods, and hence could revert to those traditional coping mechanisms
when required. Owners of cement-floored homes were comparatively vulnerable, yet paradoxically
were targeted for proportionately less assistance.
[201] One commentator has referred to this phenomenon as the 'commoditisation [sic] of social
relationships.' See J Breman, 'Politics of Poverty and a Leaking Safety Net' (1999) 34(20) *Economic
and Political Weekly* 1177–78, 1177. Yash Ghai uses the term 'commodification' in Y Ghai, 'Rights,
Markets and Globalisation: East Asian Experience' in *Oslo Symposium Report 1998* 126–32, 128:
'Commodification thus sets in motion a process in which, instead of social relationships subsuming
economic ones, economic relationships and considerations become dominant over social relationships, even close kinship relations. In the end we see the dependence on the markets of individuals,
families and communities.'

to be based upon indigenous systems.' It is simply impossible to 'go out and "create" social capital, under the "capacity-building" rubric or otherwise.'[202]

Privatisation, Internationalisation, and the 'Empty Shell of Democracy'

The removal of political power from national decision-making structures significantly undermines the rights of people to self-determination, in other words, to 'freely determine their political status and freely pursue their economic, social and cultural development.'[203] The functional link between the right to self-determination and development, in particular the notion of popular participation in development, was noted by the UN Special Rapporteur on the right to self-determination as far back as 1981.[204] More recently, Jochen Hippler has illustrated the link in the following way: '[t]he IMF [and the World Bank], for ideological reasons, are dismantling the state and removing from it some of its most important classical functions.'[205] Large scale privatisation removes services in a range of economic areas (as well as education and health) and bequeaths them to private actors within the country concerned or to international corporations. The possibilities for the enjoyment of popular sovereignty and substantive democratic rights diminish accordingly. The result is vividly captured in the following passage from Hippler:

> Other functions, particularly in the fields of economic and fiscal policy, that have such a big influence on politics and social policies, are being internationalised, in other words, are being exercised, directly or indirectly, in Washington or London. The central economic variables in the impoverished and indebted states of the Third World are often being negotiated today directly between their finance ministers and the World Bank/IMF, the latter with their centre in Washington, and it is always the Third World Finance Minister who has the least clout. Third World parliaments, and even prime ministers, are often excluded from the decision-making process and quite often don't even have the necessary information. Even domestic states budgets are often

---

[202] Interviews in Washington DC and New York, February 2000.

[203] See common Article 1 of the ICCPR and ICESCR. As Feldstein has remarked: 'The legitimate political institutions of the country should determine the nation's economic structure and the nature of its institutions. A nation's desperate need for short-term financial help does not give the IMF the moral right to substitute its technical judgements for the outcomes of the nation's political processes'—M Feldstein (1998) at 27. For a broader range of human rights criticisms including erosion of self-determination see 'The Realisation of Economic, Social and Cultural Rights,' Final Report submitted by Danilo Türk, Special Rapporteur, Subcommission for the Prevention of Discrimination and Protection of Minorities, 49th Session, UN Doc. E/CN.4/Sub.2/1992/16 (1992) at 11–18.

[204] '[D]evelopment can neither be exported nor imported . . . It presupposes the participation of the entire people inspired by a common ideal, and individual and collective creativity in devising the most adequate solutions to problems arising from local conditions, needs and aspirations.' UN Doc.E/CN.4/Sub.2/404/Rev.1 (1981), cited in N Udombana, 'The Third World and the Right to Development: Agenda for the Next Millennium' (2000) 22 *Human Rights Quarterly* 753–87, 786.

[205] J Hippler, 'Democratisation of the Third World After the End of the Cold War' in J Hippler (ed) (1995) 1 at 23.

decided by bureaucrats of the IMF and World Bank who have never been directly elected and are not responsible to anyone.[206] In many regions of the Third World, the state is gutted. A country that doesn't have sovereignty over its own national budget has no chance of determining its own destiny. In addition, international financial institutions intervene directly in these countries, determining interest rates, deciding on the value, especially the devaluation, of the national currency and dictating food and energy prices through cutbacks in state subsidies. Weak and poorly functioning state apparatuses are not made more efficient but are in fact made devoid of any function whatsoever. In these poorer countries, the privatisation and internationalisation of so many state functions leaves just an empty hull of a state, something no Northern state would tolerate in spite of all their enthusiasm for the ideology of privatisation and free markets. What the state is left with in so many Third World countries are the police, the army and the secret service: the instruments of repression. By their nature, these can't be privatised or transferred to the North.[207]

While Hippler himself draws no express linkage with the legal content of the self-determination norm as embodied in Covenants,[208] nonetheless the consequences of state restructuring can include erosion of democracy and restriction of the scope for exercising self-determination. With government being left with effective jurisdiction over only a fraction of its original domain, in extreme cases, the possibilities for the newly liberalised market economies being unravelled through democratically exercised expressions of popular will are significantly reduced. Beyond their residual mandates, government exists only (or substantially) to foster conditions necessary for the implementation of the broad-ranging and far-reaching internationally mandated 'reform' agenda. What was once local, within the sphere of popular participation and public accountability, has now become international, far removed from the influence of the governed.[209]

---

[206] A further obvious problem, apart from the lack of accountability, is that bureaucrats from international financial institutions cannot be expected to have as detailed an understanding of local political, social and economic conditions as do the local decision-makers and their constituencies.

[207] J Hippler, 'Democratisation of the Third World After the End of the Cold War' in J Hippler (ed) (1995) 1 at 24.

[208] For a discussion of the legal relationship between the right to self-determination and the right to development see N Udombana (2000) at 769–70. On the particular question of economic self-determination see 'The Realisation of Economic, Social and Cultural Rights,' Final Report submitted by Danilo Türk, Special Rapporteur, Subcommission for the Prevention of Discrimination and Protection of Minorities, 49th Session, UN Doc. E/CN.4/Sub.2/1992/16 (1992). And on the relevance of article 25 of the ICCPR in this context, dealing with the right to participate in the conduct of public affairs, see M Scheinin, 'The Right to Enjoy a Distinct Culture: Indigenous and Competing Uses of Land' in T Orlin, A Rosas and M Scheinin (eds), *The Jurisprudence of Human Rights Law: A Comparative Interpretive Approach* 163–64 (2000); cf M Turpel, 'Indigenous People's Rights of Participation and Self-Determination: Recent International Legal Developments and the Continuing Struggle for Recognition' (1992) 25(3) *Cornell International Law Journal* 579–602, 596.

[209] As Hippler puts it: '[S]tate structures are created with an undeniable "market orientation." A "democratisation" of these structures is then purely a matter of form, with no risks [to the liberalisation reform agenda] involved. Having taken away their most important functions, the North then "democratises" the empty hull that remains. Elections can be organised, possibly even ones that are free and fair. But they are largely irrelevant since the elected representatives no longer have the power to organise and structure their own country's policies. Claude Aké has aptly described this as

Naturally these impacts are highly discriminatory, targeted overwhelmingly at lower income countries desperate for financial assistance and vulnerable to IFI influence and conditionality. Equally obviously, the extent of this is more dramatic in some of those member states than others, depending among other things on the pre-existing degree of central planning, public funding of essential services and utilities, robustness and responsiveness of political institutions, and traditions of public accountability.[210] But removing choices in these fundamental areas from the public domain, in the absence of corresponding mechanisms for vertical accountability and without consensus on optimal political and macro-economic policies or the prerequisites for economic growth, represents one of the most systemic and significant ongoing human rights abuses for which the IFIs stand accused.[211]

International Peace and Security—the Cases of the Former Yugoslavia and Rwanda

While it is not possible to say that any one factor was responsible for the outbreak of hostilities in the Balkans in the early 1990s, it has nonetheless been claimed that IMF-sponsored restructuring was a significant contributing factor.

a "democratisation of disempowerment." Democracy is reduced to the administration of a situation that essentially cannot be improved: democracy becomes meaningless. This also answers the question why the North needs to have no fear of democratisation in the South: in the context of structural adjustment, it is only the *empty shell of democracy*' [emphasis added]—J Hippler, 'Democratisation of the Third World After the End of the Cold War' in J Hippler (ed) (1995) 1 at 24. For a discussion of the 'democratic deficit' at the international level see R Keohane, 'International Institutions: Can Interdependence Work?' *Foreign Policy* 82–96, 91–92 (Spring 1998).

[210] See, for example, the case of Jamaica, discussed in S Haggard (1985) at 520–22; and W James, 'The IMF and Democratic Socialism in Jamaica' in Latin American Bureau, *The Poverty Brokers: The IMF and Latin America* (1983) 85–108. Critiqueing the Bank's *World Development Report 1997: The State in a Changing World*, Anne Orford canvasses a range of policy issues impliedly foreclosed by the Washington Consensus and removed from the domestic political arena. 'There is no suggestion in [the WDR 1997], for example, of the possibility that the people of states targeted by World Bank policies have a right to reject the World Bank's model of development entirely, to decide that particular development projects or policies should not be implemented at all, to choose to participate in the development process by deciding to nationalise all private investment, or to decide that the state should guarantee full public funding for food, health, education or social security. At best, the [WDR 1997] envisages processes by which people are consulted about the way particular projects and policies which have been controlled and decided upon by the World Bank should be implemented. The World Bank thus continues to recommend a model of development in which communities and individuals have no real capacity to participate in or control the development process, as required by the right to development. Of course, very often the regimes governing such states may in any case seek to deny such rights to the people. The World Bank, however, despite the fact that it is controlled by states who present themselves as liberal and democratic, is no less repressive than many authoritarian regimes in that respect.' A Orford (2001) at 157.

[211] See eg W Berg and G Thole (1986) at 173: 'The policy of the IMF demonstrates that the institution's main concern is to ensure the profits of the trans-national corporations, including the big banks, and to safeguard the capitalist system. This policy represents a direct onslaught on the right of peoples to self-determination. Its repercussions hit the poor in the developing countries, exacerbate poverty, increase unemployment and lead to a curtailment of civil and political rights.'

The IMF had been heavily involved in re-structuring in the former Yugoslavia for years, prior to its disintegration in late 1992. In fact, at that time, Yugoslavia had become the sixth largest user of IMF funds.[212]

As Anne Orford argues, there are at least four ways in which IMF structural adjustment, stabilisation, and later 'shock therapy' programs contributed to the conditions which led to the political destabilisation of the former Yugoslavia.[213] Firstly, the programs contributed to a sense of insecurity and resulting social instability for the people of former Yugoslavia. Destabilising elements of early IMF austerity programs included many of the standard ingredients that have already been discussed, notably the abandonment of food subsidies, unemployment or threat of unemployment, falling real incomes, inflation, and rising prices for certain essential commodities such as gasoline and heating fuel, due to import restriction measures and the push for exports.[214]

Secondly, economically motivated political and constitutional reforms destroyed minority rights protections within the socialist system.[215] As Susan Woodward explains:

> The primary protection of minority rights in the socialist system—the proportional distribution of government jobs and the budgetary outlays for cultural rights—could not be sustained economically in the face of deep fiscal cuts or politically in the face of confrontation between rich and poor over taxation and federally mandated redistribution that economic crisis brought . . . Absent were institutionalised and professional restraints on the media, political organisations based on economic interests that cut across national identities and can moderate debate, and accepted procedural safeguards for those whose rights were being abused. The primary mechanism of holding governments accountable for protecting of [sic] rights and freedoms during the liberalising period of the 1980s was the country's extensive political decentralisation. It created multiple political arenas in the various republics: journalists who could not publish in one republic could get an audience in another; people facing discrimination

---

[212] W Reinecke, 'Can International Financial Institutions Prevent Internal Violence? The Sources of Ethno-National Conflict in Transitional Societies' in A Chayes and A Chayes (eds), *Preventing Conflict in the Post-Communist World: Mobilising International and Regional Organisations* (1996) 281–338, 282.

[213] See generally A Orford (1997) at 456–59. More generally, 'IMF economic intervention, ethnic dominance and a low level of economic development are conceived as sources of group discontent. This discontent is deemed likely to result in violence if the environment is conducive to the mobilisation of resources for collective action'—D Carment and P James, 'Escalation of Ethnic Conflict' (1998) 35(1) *International Politics* 65–82, 69.

[214] A Orford (1997) at 456. See also W Reinicke (1996) on sources of conflict in Eastern and Central Europe, and the former Soviet Union (at 305): 'Political disintegration is accompanied by considerable socio-economic disintegration. The centrally planned economic system has been discredited, and its failure is seen as one of the principal sources of systemic collapse. In addition, the economic and social hardships caused by the transformation process toward a market economy, heightened by overly optimistic initial expectations, further contribute to declining confidence in the economic outlook of individuals, fuelling the forces of disintegration as economic corruption and crime take on an increasing significance. With the collapse of the political power structure and the economic system that was used to rationalise and legitimise its existence, acculturation and cultural assimilation have also lost their integrative attributes, further stimulating societal disintegration.'

[215] A Orford (1997) at 456–57.

in one republic could emigrate temporarily to another; and social movements repressed in one republic might hope for publicity and outside pressure in another.[216]

The Fund's programs contributed to the destruction of these mechanisms through their prescriptions for political re-centralisation, fiscal cuts, and 'an end to nationality-based distribution of voting and positions.'[217]

The third factor flows directly from the first two, and the preceding discussion concerning privatisation and internationalisation of governance, and creation of the 'empty shell of democracy.' That is to say, the cumulative impacts of social polarisation, the erosion of minority rights protection mechanisms, and IMF constitutional and institutional 'reforms,' ushering the emergence in the late 1980s of a republican nationalistic dynamic.[218] With the 'empty shell' of the state being left virtually powerless and discredited, the people of Yugoslavia began to look for other more important sources of identity and community, and ways through which they could recapture a sense of control over their own destiny. [219] In these circumstances, with the 're-centralised' Yugoslav government being perceived to have lost its legitimacy, ethnic or ethnic-religious identity became more important.[220] A number of other factors contributed to the 'anti-federal' republican focus of the nationalist dynamic, such as the attack on established systems of welfare, and the emerging gulf between richer and poorer republics, the former being driven to abandon the latter in the interests of prompt 'insertion into capitalist Europe.'[221]

This analysis is consistent with research elsewhere regarding the causes for the escalation of 'ethno-national'[222] conflict in recent times, within the context

[216] S Woodward, *Balkan Tragedy: Chaos and Dissolution After the Cold War* (1995) at 381. Woodward adds (at 381) that '[w]hile far from satisfactory as a means of protection, this form of competition ended when Slovenia and Croatia chose to leave the federation and those outsiders negotiating the country's dissolution failed to insist on conditions that would foster alternative protections in the new states.' See also D Carment and P James (1998) at 77–78.

[217] A Orford (1997) at 457.

[218] A Orford (1997) at 457.

[219] See eg J Hippler, 'Democratisation of the Third World After the End of the Cold War' in J Hippler (ed) (1995) 1 at 25; D Carment and P James (1998) at 77–78; S Haggard and R Kaufman, 'Economic Adjustment and the Prospects for Democracy' in S Haggard and R Kaufman (eds) (1992) 319–50, 349–50. And see D Rodrik, 'Globalisation, Social Conflict and Economic Growth' (1998) 21(2) *The World Economy* 143–58, 156–58 on the importance *inter alia* of civil liberties, education, a credible state apparatus, robust and viable political parties and avenues for popular participation, and workable 'social insurance' mechanisms, for ensuring the legitimacy and effectiveness of macro-economic stabilisation measures.

[220] See also S Woodward (1995) at 17: The sense of community on ethnic or ethnic-religious or nationalistic grounds is highly prized, in these circumstances, 'not because of the historical persistence and power of ethnic identities and cultural attachments, as the ethnic conflict school insists, but because the bases of existing communities have collapsed and governments are radically narrowing what they will or can provide in terms of previously guaranteed rights to subsistence, land, public employment, and even citizenship.'

[221] A Orford (1997) at 458 especially at nn 67–69 and the references referred to there.

[222] The term 'ethno-nationalism,' as opposed to its 'territorial, civic version embodied in the concept of the nation-state, envisions the nation as a "genealogical and vernacular cultural community." While territorial and civic nationalist definitions of a "nation" centre on a community of shared culture, common laws, and citizenship, ethnic nationalists define a nation *solely* on the basis

of the liberalisation and marketisation policy imperatives. As Reinicke remarks, following political and social disintegration and the elimination or restructuring of state institutions in Eastern and Central Europe and the former Soviet Union:

> From the perspectives of the different ethnic group(s), with the likely exception of the one group that was in control of the system, the political and economic structures as well as the dominant culture are now openly recognised as unjust and illegitimate instruments of ethnic subordination. At the same time, new system-wide structures and institutions, if existing at all, are still in their formative stages and viewed with suspicion. They lack integrative power not the least because competing ethnic elites find it easy to discredit any emerging system-wide political or economic structure as yet another form of forced integration.
>
> Indeed it is this forced nature of societal integration across ethnic lines under vertical hierarchy and its sudden de-legitimisation in the wake of system collapse that leads to a strong resurgence of ethnic identity[.] . . In the absence of fully developed political and economic structures and institutions[,] . . . ethnicity is becoming the principal basis of societal integration, subordinating the political, economic, and cultural components of an ethnic collective. This dynamic—the system-wide political, economic, and cultural disintegration and subsequent attempts at reintegration along ethnic lines—is the principal source for the emergence of ethno-national conflict.[223]

The final, and intrinsically related, causal factor in the former Yugoslavia case was the speed with which restructuring and 'shock therapy' was required to be carried out.[224] Although time was necessary in order to do the political work required in order to reverse the disintegration,[225] the economic logic of shock

---

of the genealogy of its members'—W Reinicke (1996) at 299. Reinicke distinguishes five related types of ethno-nationalism as found in Eastern and Central Europe and the former Soviet Union: 'cultural revivalism, political autonomism, self-determinism, separatism, and irredentisim' (see ibid at 299–301 for a discussion).

[223] W Reinicke. (1996) at 305–6. That de-legitimatisation of central government and retreat into alternative sources of community (on ethno-national grounds) provide a recipe for violent conflict, including interstate conflict, is clear: 'In the political realm, when state institutions have or are perceived as having lost their autonomy, they themselves become the target of competition and a "prize to be occupied and exploited by contending ethnic groups." In many instances, however, competition over political power also implies competition over space, that is, the appropriation of territory. Competition is particularly intense over those territories that are populated by more than one ethnic group. Spatial competition may also occur, when a territory populated by a single ethnic group is contested by another one. The basis for such a claim is often historical, such as an externally imposed decision that had or has lost legitimacy for the competing group. This second type of competition over space does not necessarily have to occur within a single state, but could also be the subject of interstate competition, adding a further dimension to the dynamics of ethno-nationalism and providing a source for potential interstate ethnic conflict' (Reinicke, at 306–7). See also J Rothschild, *Ethnopolitics: A Conceptual Framework* (1981) at 118; Carment, D. and James, P. (1998) at 68–79.

[224] A Orford (1997) at 458–59. See also K Halverson, 'Privatisation in the Yugoslav Republics' (1991) 25(6) *Journal of World Trade* 66.

[225] Such as build 'cross-republican, society-wide political organisations', to 'bargain compromises, to develop alternatives to the previous order, to create procedures for resolving systemic conflicts peacefully, to build new governmental capacity, and to await adjustment and membership in Western organisations for which they were redesigning their domestic order'—S Woodward (1995) at 17 and 384. But for doubts regarding the ability of *any* central authority, benign or otherwise, to

therapy dictated that 'speed was of the essence.'[226] Accordingly, the federal government in Yugoslavia proceeded with the implementation of 'far-reaching political and constitutional reforms to enable a rapid transition from a socialist economic structure to a purely market-based regime, even after the nationalist climate and violent resistance to those radical reforms became apparent.'[227]

Naturally the Fund's involvement was not the sole cause of the break up of the former Yugoslavia and the genocide.[228] The heinous human rights violations that occurred during the course of bitter ethnic, ethno-religious and nationalist conflict were obviously perpetrated directly by local actors. And equally obviously, shock therapy and structural adjustment programs have been implemented elsewhere without leading to genocide.[229] But account must be taken of the extent to which the economic austerity program and Fund-sponsored political and constitutional transformations contributed to political and ethnic polarisation and the escalation of the crisis. In this sense, responsibility for the violence in former Yugoslavia belongs *both* to international actors (notably the Fund) *and* local actors, not the local actors alone.[230]

Turning to the case of Rwanda, structural adjustment has been claimed to have impacted adversely in a number of ways prior to the 1994 genocide,[231] including:

oversee systematic transitions under IMF prescriptions with their frequently complex and far-reaching political and social consequences, see A Orford (1997) at 456, n 55. Rather than looking upon the (IMF-influenced) erosion of the state's capacity to manage transition as a further cause of the crisis in Yugoslavia, Orford suggests 'that the Yugoslav crisis, *inter alia*, demonstrates the need to rethink the logic of late capitalism. Slovenian intellectual Slavoj Zizek, for example, argues that such cycles of racist viciousness are in part a product of capitalism's economy of enjoyment. The answer for [Orford] lies with contesting the New Right's logic of efficiency and culture of control, rather than attempting to "moderate" extremes of poverty and wealth maintained by this global system.' See S Zizek, *Tarrying with the Negative: Kant, Hegel and the Critique of Ideology* (1993).

[226] A Orford (1997) at 459. See also J Sachs (1990) at 19.

[227] A Orford (1997) at 459. See also K Halverson (1991) at 66: 'Advocates of shock therapy . . . discount the fact that the political impact of economic reform may disrupt the fragile political consensus behind it, thus rendering economic efficiency goals irrelevant. The Yugoslav case is a perfect illustration of how rapid change can derail economic reform by exacerbating political instability.' See further *Wall Street Journal*, Section A, at 11, col 1 (18 March 1991): 'The rising unemployment and uncompetitiveness of Yugoslav exports that results from [IMF shock therapy prescriptions] were factors that contributed to [then] Prime Minister Markovic's failure to win a substantial vote in any of the Yugoslav Republic's democratic elections. Instead, the vote went to nationalist extremists who criticised the Prime Minister's economic policies.'

[228] D Carment and P James (1998) at 77; D Orentlicher, 'Separation Anxiety: International Responses to Ethno-Separatist Claims,' 23(1) *Yale Journal of International Law* 1–78, 71, n 409 and the various references referred to there.

[229] A Orford (1997) at 459.

[230] To this effect see R Väyrynen, 'Economic Incentives and the Bosnian Peace Process' in D Cortright (ed) (1997) 155–79 at 157; S Woodward (1995) at 47–81; A Orford (1997) at 459. As Orford remarks (at 459): 'Experts acting on behalf of international economic institutions appear to assume that there are no limits to the ways in which local peoples can be required to conform to new economic models and priorities. The disastrous outcome of economic restructuring in the former Yugoslavia is just one example of the impact of the belief held by economic experts that human beings are infinitely and rapidly re-codeable, and that cultures and political systems are infinitely malleable.'

[231] For a detailed account of the genocide see the very comprehensive account by P Uvin, *Aiding Violence: The Development Enterprise in Rwanda* (1998).

1. A devaluation-led rise in inflation, although food prices did not rise significantly, and a large proportion of the poor were outside the cash economy;
2. The abolition of long-established subsidies for coffee-producers, resulting in a fall in coffee exports;
3. Added burdens on the poor through introduction of user fees for health and education;
4. Commercialisation of agriculture and creation of a private market in scarce land resources, exacerbating community tensions and the climate of competition; and
5. Recruitment freezes and job losses in state and parastatal concerns, the impact of which was especially 'ethnicised,' falling disproportionately upon the ruling Hutu.[232]

Furthermore, from a political perspective, it has been suggested that a linking of support from the IMF and other international donors to a 'narrow concept of democratisation based on a Western-style multiparty system' posed significant threats to the vested interests of ruling elites, and hence constituted a major contributory factor to the political dynamics underlying the 1994 genocide.[233]

Again, this is not to say that adjustment measures were the sole or dominant cause of the outbreak of mass violence.[234] However there does appear to be ample evidence to conclude, at a minimum, that the adjustment program took inadequate account of the political effects that it was likely to generate.[235] Woodward concludes that '[e]ven if the adjustment programme did not contribute directly to the tragic events of 1994, such a reckless disregard for social and political sensitivities in such a conspicuously sensitive situation would unquestionably have increased the risk of creating or compounding a potentially explosive situation.'[236]

SUMMARY—THE IFIS' HUMAN RIGHTS IMPACTS AND INFLUENCE

The influence wielded by the IFIs—whether as a direct or indirect consequence of credit decisions, lending policies and associated conditionalities, or through

---

[232] A Storey (1999) at 47–55.

[233] D Woodward, *The IMF, the World Bank and Economic Policy in Rwanda: Economic, Social and Political Implications* (1996) at 24.

[234] See the range of qualifications in A Storey (1999) at 49–51, including the fact that the Rwandan economy had already begun to be liberalised prior to the beginning of the IFI-sponsored adjustment program, the lack of comprehensive implementation of the IFIs' prescriptions, and the fundamental fact that—with or without the adjustment program—the economy would have been in crisis, with state services being under enormous strain at material times.

[235] A Storey (1999) at 57. However for stronger conclusions on causation see R Andersen (2000) at 452.

[236] D Woodward (1996) at 25. See also A Storey (1999) at 57. On conflict prevention Reinicke (1996) remarks (at 311): '[G]iven their deep involvement and interest in system transformation, [international financial institutions] cannot divorce themselves from the phenomenon of ethno-national mobilisation and the possibility that it might turn violent.'

technical advisory services or less direct means[237]—over the human rights situations in many of their member states is considerable. This pattern of influence is markedly asymmetrical, with the IFIs' human rights impacts being experienced most strongly in developing country shareholder states. Within these countries, the broadened and extended scope of the IFIs' activities means that they not infrequently determine, or at least significantly influence, national policy in areas with obvious human rights dimensions and consequences, such as: health; education; the right to food and adequate standard of living; women's human rights; environmental protection; employment and labour rights; social security; and (through conditions promoting 'good governance' and the rule of law) the framework within which civil and political rights are exercised.[238]

Given the large scale human rights impacts of the IFIs' policies and activities—in the areas described above and in relation to the design and implementation of programs in the general run of cases—the Bank and Fund have a clear responsibility to take better account of human rights factors in the spheres affected by their increasingly broad and complex mandates. The grounds for obligations to this effect under international human rights law are canvassed briefly in the next chapter.

It is not claimed here that the implementation of a 'human rights approach' by any particular definition would magically remove all of the shortcomings just catalogued. Far from it. But at a minimum the preceding discussion should serve to illustrate some of the main reasons why the international human rights framework and the activities and policies of the IFIs need to be understood in more direct relation to each other. But the question is: to what extent do the IFIs' mandates permit, or oblige, them to consider human rights issues?

---

[237] As Chayes and Chayes observe, in terms of the Fund's capacity to influence policy, the distinction between the formal *means* of influence—Article IV consultations, or conditionality—should not be overstated: 'The impact of Article IV surveillance on national policy is illustrated by the recent efforts of the IMF (in co-ordination with the World Bank) to bring military expenditures into the economic and fiscal review . . . The IMF has insisted that this is a "policy dialogue" confined to Article IV surveillance, and that it will not apply military-related conditions to drawings against the Fund's resources. Even if this distinction is maintained, however, the dialogue can influence policy in a variety of ways. The first is in capacity building: educating government officials about the desirability of better military budgeting practices and the benefits of greater transparency with respect to military expenditures. In countries where the military plays a strong role in internal politics, "merely discussing the importance of treating the military budget in the same fashion as other portions of the budget is a significant event. Reviewing military spending, even if available only in aggregate terms, will not only provide lenders with data but will also be a first step toward making military-related data available to other departments of the government and, ultimately, the public." Second, governments are not monolithic. There are almost always elements supporting compliance, in this case, perhaps, civilians interested in reducing military expenditures in favour of other priorities or simply competing for power. Review and assessment gives them a basis for raising the issue with their armed forces, and the necessity of defending the level of military expenditures in an outside forum strengthens their hand in internal debates. Finally, without addressing military expenditures directly, the IMF can set targets in other sectors so as to squeeze the military.': A Chayes and A Chayes (1995) at 236–37.

[238] Although for reasons explained elsewhere this influence is far greater in lower income countries dependent upon IMF assistance.

IV

To What Extent Can the World Bank and IMF Deal with Human Rights? A Brief Exploration of their Legal Mandates

To help in the development of a coherent and progressive body of interpretation notwithstanding the difficulties is a primary function of the legal staff of the organisation. In the turbulent waters of changes in conditions and in the personnel of the organisation responding to them, the legal staff must steer clear of entrapment by the Scylla of an exaggerated belief in the pellucidity of language and the Charybdis of pragmatism.[1]

THE central question for this book is the extent to which the IFIs *can*—within their mandated powers and functions—lawfully consider human rights factors. The reason for such a focused inquiry is to meet the oft-heard disclaimer that 'yes, human rights are clearly vital for development, however the Bank and Fund are prohibited from dealing directly with them.' Brief consideration will also be given to the extent to which the IFIs *must*—under ordinary principles of international law—engage with human rights. However the difficulties of defining appropriate limits of engagement as matter of international legal obligation require separate treatment of that subject.[2] Half-hearted efforts in the latter regard may achieve little more than disclosing the policy preferences of the reviewer.

The international legal literature is replete with analyses at varying levels of sophistication on the legal parameters of IFI engagement with human

---

[1] J Gold, *Interpretation: The IMF and International Law* (1996) 20.

[2] See eg S Skogly, *The Human Rights Obligations of the World Bank and International Monetary Fund* (2001). Cf M Darrow, 'Human Rights Accountability of the World Bank and IMF: Possibilities and Limits of Legal Analysis' 12(1) *Social and Legal Studies* (forthcoming 2003) 133–44. In any case the division between these two levels of analysis is not watertight, as will be seen, in light of the requirement under Article 31(3)(c) of the 1969 Vienna Convention on the Law of Treaties to interpret treaties (such as the Bank's and Fund's Articles of Association) in context, in light of any relevant rules of international law applicable in the relations between Bank and Fund members.

rights.[3] Recalling the essential elements of that legal analysis is a necessary first step here. However, guided by the requirement to consider the IFIs' Articles in a purposive fashion, in light of actual practical requirements and challenges incumbent upon them, the broader ambition in the subsequent sections is to give interpretative flesh to the legal bones, illustrating selectively the ways in which their mandates have been implemented in practice as a guide to an assessment of their flexibility and scope.

While the legal principles discussed below are (unless otherwise expressly indicated) of equal application to the Bank and Fund, a slightly different emphasis is warranted in their application. The locus of contention in terms of the Bank's mandate is one particular provision of its Articles of Association, the so-called 'political prohibition' in Article IV, Section 10 of the IBRD Articles and its IDA equivalent, as will shortly be seen. Perhaps paradoxically in light of its comparatively limited express purposes, there is no single equivalent provision within the Fund's Articles purporting to provide a basis for disclaiming human rights responsibility. Rather, such disclaimers have usually relied on more foundational assertions of mandate specificity and technical specialisation. Accordingly legal argumentation in the latter case focuses principally on the application of the doctrine of 'implied powers,' focusing on the scope of inherent authority within the Fund's charter, rather than a contextual application of the rules of treaty interpretation.[4] However this differentiated application should not be mistaken for mutual exclusivity: the 'implied powers' doctrine bears just as directly on the Bank's mandate as the (Vienna Convention[5]) prin-

---

[3] Among the more authoritative and useful analyses are: S Skogly (2001); D Bradlow, 'The World Bank, the IMF and Human Rights' (1996) 6(1) *Transnational Law and Contemporary Problems* 47–90; and D Bradlow and C Grossman, 'Limited Mandates and Intertwined Problems: A New Challenge for the World Bank and the IMF' (1995) 17 *Human Rights Quarterly* 411–42; I Shihata, 'Issues of "Governance" in Borrowing Members: The Extent of Their Relevance Under the Bank's Articles of Agreement,' Legal Memorandum of the General Counsel, 21 December 1990; I Shihata, 'Prohibition of Political Activities in the Bank's Work: Legal Opinion by the Senior Vice President and General Counsel,' 12 July 1995; F Gianviti, 'Economic, Social and Cultural Rights and the International Monetary Fund (30 May 2001; unpublished paper on file with author); G Brodnig, 'The World Bank and Human Rights: Mission Impossible?', *Carr Centre for Human Rights Policy Working Paper* T-01-05 (2001); and J Ciorciari, 'The Lawful Scope of Human Rights Criteria in World Bank Credit Decisions: An Interpretive Analysis of the IBRD and IDA Articles of Agreement' (2000) 33 *Cornell International Law Journal* 331. See also M Lucas, 'The International Monetary Fund's Conditionality and the International Covenant on Economic, Social and Cultural Rights: An Attempt to Define the Relation' (1992) 1 *Revue Belge de Droit International* 104, 107–8 at 114–22; M Elahi, 'The Impact of Financial Institutions on the Realisation of Human Rights: Case Study of the International Monetary Fund in Chile' (1986) 6 *Boston College Third World Law Journal* 143, 145 at 148–51.

[4] J Alvarez, 'Constitutional Interpretation in International Organisations' in J-M Coicaud and V Heiskanen (eds), *The Legitimacy of International Organisations* (2001) 104–54, 121–23. For support for differentiated analysis along these lines see J Gold (1996) at 45: 'The IMF has made frequent use of implied powers, inspired in part by a teleological approach to interpretation, but it is necessary to distinguish between interpretation and implied powers. Interpretation can be described loosely as the search for meaning of the text and implied powers as the discovery of authority not expressed in the text.'

[5] See n 11 below and accompanying text.

ciples do on the interpretation of any particular provision of the Fund's Articles of Association. As will shortly be seen, the lines are blurred further by the fact that both levels of inquiry are underpinned by the doctrine of 'institutional effectiveness' as a unifying principle.[6]

LEGAL INTERPRETATION OF THE IFIS' MANDATES

'An Art, Not a Science'

The point of departure for the task at hand is to acknowledge that the application of rules and principles is not necessarily a value-neutral exercise. As Jennings famously remarked, legal interpretation is 'an art, not a science,' although it is a characteristic or part of the art to disguise it as science.[7] However even if objectivity and determinacy are elusive, we need not abandon that quest to arbitrariness. Implicit in legal argumentation and constitutional discourse is a structure of self-imposed constraints, and an appeal—and even accountability—to an 'interpretative community.'[8] While aspirations for 'ineluctably correct' and compelling legal answers must certainly be kept in check, the value of legal analysis should not be underestimated.[9] As Ian Johnstone put it, 'law is not infinitely manipulable' but is 'constrained by the need to remain faithful to its accepted processes and sources of authority: that is, to maintain its credibility before its intended addresses.'[10] Applied to the task at hand, there is a significant area of legal common ground between the IFIs' (especially the Bank's) supporters and human rights critics, as will shortly be seen, upon which the relevant 'interpretative community' can engage and debate outstanding issues of controversy. Moreover, the precepts and content of international human rights law have developed in recent years to a level of determinacy permitting the ready exposure of shallow or self-serving argumentation. This of course does not mean that there is no longer scope for good faith disagreement. However these factors do reassure us that the quest for objectivity through legal analysis is one most definitely worth undertaking in the present context, providing that reasoning is transparent and policy preferences are thereby exposed.

---

[6] See eg J Gold (1996) at 45; J Alvarez (2001) at 117–23.

[7] Jennings, 'General Course on Principles of International Law' (1967-II) *Recueil des cours*, 121, 323 at 544.

[8] I Johnstone, 'Treaty Interpretation: The Authority of Interpretative Communities' (1991) 12 *Michegan Journal of International Law* 418; M Koskenneimi, 'The Place of Law in Collective Security' (1996) 17 *Michegan Journal of International Law* 455, 478.

[9] J Gold (1996) at 20: '[T]here is no need to be troubled by the conclusion of many jurists and other philosophers that interpretation does not reveal one ineluctably correct version, with the consequence that, in adjudication for example, a choice must be made among correct versions on the basis of considerations unrelated to the text.'

[10] I Johnstone (1991) at 418, and see the discussion in J Alvarez (2001) at 134–35.

Guiding Principles and Interpretative Methodology

Given that the IBRD, IDA and IMF Articles predate the 1969 Vienna Convention on the Law of Treaties[11] (hereafter 'Vienna Convention'), the relevant international rules governing interpretation in the present circumstances are those comprising the corpus of customary international law as it existed at the time that the IFIs' constitutive agreements were concluded.[12] The result of a project initiated by the International Law Commission in 1949, it is generally accepted that the Vienna Convention largely represents a codification of pre-existing norms of customary international law.[13] Articles 31 and 32 of the Vienna Convention reflect the fundamental rules of interpretation for present purposes. Each of these provisions was adopted without a dissenting vote, and are considered in particular to be declaratory of pre-existing customary international law.[14]

Article 31 sets down the general rule of interpretation as follows:

1. A treaty shall be interpreted in good faith in accordance with the ordinary meaning to be given to the terms of the treaty in their context and in the light of its object and purpose.
2. The context for the purpose of the interpretation of a treaty shall comprise, in addition to the text, including its preamble and annexes: (a) Any agreement relating to the treaty which was made between all the parties in connection with the conclusion of the treaty; (b) Any instrument which was made by one or more parties in connection with the conclusion of the treaty and accepted by the other parties as an instrument related to the treaty.
3. There shall be taken into account, together with the context: (a) Any subsequent agreement between the parties regarding the interpretation of the treaty or the application of its provisions; (b) Any *subsequent practice in the application of the treaty which establishes the agreement of the parties regarding its interpretation*; (c) Any *relevant rules of international law applicable in the relations between the parties* [emphasis added].

---

[11] Convention on the Law of Treaties, 23 May 1969, 1155 *United Nations Treaty Series* 331. Also relevant is the 1986 Vienna Convention on the Law of Treaties between States and International Organisations or between International Organisations (UN Doc. A/CONF.129/15)—hereinafter 'Vienna II Convention'—although as at the year 2002 it had not yet entered into force.

[12] Article 4 of the Vienna Convention stipulates that the Convention does not have retrospective application, but that its provisions apply 'without prejudice to the application of any rules set forth in the present Convention to which treaties would be subject under international law independently of the Convention.'

[13] M Akehurst, *A Modern Introduction to International Law* (5th ed) (1984) 121; I Brownlie, *Principles of Public International Law* (5th ed) (1998) 632; J Ciorciari (2000) at n 49 and accompanying text.

[14] J Ciorciari (2000) at n 49 and accompanying text; E de Arechaga, 'International Law in the Past Third of a Century' (1978) 159 *Recueil de Cours* 35–49, 39, 42.

4. A special meaning shall be given to a term if it is established that the parties so intended.

Furthermore under Article 32, '[r]ecourse may be had to supplementary means of interpretation, including the preparatory work of the treaty [hereinafter *travaux preparatoires*] and circumstances of its conclusion, in order to confirm the meaning resulting from the application of article 31, or to determine the meaning when the interpretation according to article 31: (a) Leaves the meaning ambiguous or obscure; or (b) Leads to a result which is manifestly absurd or unreasonable.'

As Ciorciari observes, Articles 31 and 32 'neither establish "two distinct and successive phases in the process of interpretation" nor require that *travaux preparatoires* only be examined after first exhausting all intrinsic sources. Rather, the process of interpretation may proceed with *travaux preparatoires* playing an ongoing and important, though secondary, role in the interpretation of the text.'[15]

Even if the applicability of 'constitutional' analogies remains open for debate,[16] it is now widely accepted that the Articles of Agreement of the Bank and Fund constitute living documents, required (both through the mechanism of formal amendments and through interpretation) to be sufficiently flexible to respond to evolving operational circumstances.[17] In both treaty and constitutional law, the 20th century saw the advance of what Fassbender called the 'dynamic-evolutionary' method of interpretation, over the 'once undisputed static or textual approach.'[18] Indeed this is the approach that the Executive

---

[15] J Ciorciari (2000) at 342, citing E de Arechaga (1978) at 47.

[16] F Mann, 'The "Interpretation" of the Constitutions of International Financial Institutions' (1968/9) 43 *British Yearbook of International Law* 1, 18, and J Alvarez (2001) at 110: '[A]ll international organisations are mechanisms to achieve limited horizontal interstate goals with limited access given to non-governmental actors (much less individuals).' Nonetheless, '[c]onstitutional rhetoric, along with a commitment to the rule of law and the primacy of "constitutional" principles over subordinate rules, is evident in, for example, the decisions issued by the legal secretariats of international organisations, a growing number of specialised as well as more general international courts, international bodies charged with the implementation of human rights, and WTO panels. . . . [T]he presence and persistence of constitutional analogies remains a firm part of real world legal practice.'

[17] For parallel arguments relating to the status of the UN Charter, see B Fassbender, 'The United Nations Charter As Constitution of the International Community' (1998) 36 *Columbia Journal of Transnational Law* 529–619, 594–95; J Brierly, 'The Covenant and the Charter' (1946) 23 *British Yearbook of International Law* 83. See also C Tomuschat, 'Obligations Arising for States Without or Against Their Will' (1993-IV) 241 *Hague Recueil Des Cours* 195, 251–52, referring to the UN as 'an entire system which is in constant movement, not unlike a national constitution whose original texture will be unavoidably modified by thick layers of political practice and jurisprudence.' The diminution of the originally conceived boundaries of state sovereignty, the invention of peacekeeping operations, and the expansion of the UN's human rights functions and procedures are notable manifestations of this 'modification.'

[18] B Fassbender (1998) at 597. Cf F Mann (1968/9) at 18, and I Brownlie (5th ed) (1998) at 634–38. Yet Brownlie (at 637–38) does concede that 'in a small specialised organisation, with supranational elements and efficient procedures for amendment of constituent treaties and rules regulations, the teleological approach, with its aspect of judicial legislation, may be thought to have a constructive role to play.'

Board of the Bank has applied to the IBRD Articles in practice, pursuant to a principle of 'institutional effectiveness' and in recognition of constitutions as 'developing instruments.'[19] Even interpreters who would ostensibly limit their inquires to the 'plain meaning' (or textual interpretation) of a text are nonetheless authorised by Article 31(3) of the Vienna Convention to rely on a range of sources including 'subsequent practice' and (frequently imprecise) 'relevant rules of international law,' including those coming into force after the treaty's conclusion.[20] The measure of discretion accorded the interpreter is potentially quite generous, although this is also the case to a large degree for apparently circumscribed 'plain meaning' approaches.[21]

As to the question of 'who interprets' the drafting history of the UN Charter suggests that authoritative interpretation does not require any particular procedure.[22] The Articles of Association of both the Bank and Fund do establish a particular process for resolution of questions of interpretation, with the Executive Board—and ultimately Board of Governors—having authority to decide.[23] In recognition of the pitfalls of weighted voting the IMF also established a 'Committee on Interpretation,'[24] although in practice formal interpre-

---

[19] C Amerasinghe, 'Interpretation of Texts in Open International Organisations' (1995) *British Yearbook of International Law* 175–209, 203: 'The natural and ordinary meaning may in certain circumstances be modified in the light of the principle of effectiveness, as happened in the case of the interpretation by the Executive Directors of Article II, section 2, of the IBRD's Articles of Agreement. International organs would be cautious in doing this as the contextual natural and ordinary meaning enjoys some sanctity, but it is not inconceivable that such organs may take that course of action *ut res magis valeat quam pereat*. In the case of constitutions which, so to speak, have a life of their own, this is not to be discouraged, provided an attempt is made to respect the ordinary and natural meaning and not vandalise a text, where this is possible. In the case of constitutions there is more reason than in other cases to give effect to the principle of effectiveness, even where there is no ambiguity or possibility of an unreasonable result, because positive considerations of policy may require such an approach to be taken. There is every reason to treat constitutions as developing instruments.' Cf J Alvarez (2001) at 104–10.

[20] J Alvarez (2001) at 115.

[21] B Sloan, 'The United Nations Charter as a Constitution' (1961) 1 *Pace Year Book of International Law* 61; O Schachter, 'Interpretation of the Charter in the Political Organs of the United Nations' in S Engel (ed), *Law, State and the International Legal Order* (1964) 274; and J Alvarez (2001) at 116–17: 'Determining "ordinary meaning" is often a matter of applying "canons of interpretation" that are open to considerable discretion as applied.' Canons of interpretation, even when they do not conflict, are also commonly interpreted in light of the 'architecture' of the institutions defined by the text. Moreover the provisions of international organisation charters are often deliberately open-textured, with room for disagreement not only on the scope of more precisely drawn rules, but on the specific content and application of general principles and standards.

[22] J Alvarez (2001) at 113.

[23] See Article IX (a)–(b) (IBRD Articles), Article X (a)–(b) (IDA Articles) and Article XVIII (a)–(b) (IMF Articles). These provisions purport to address the specific situation of a dispute on a question of interpretation as between members or between the Bank and a member, however it is arguable that they could be read broadly to cover any question of interpretation, whether arising on a specific issue or one of general concern to the IFIs and their members, and whether raised by the Managing Director or by a member or in general debate in the Executive Board. See J Fawcett, 'The Place of Law in an International Organisation' (1960) 36 *British Yearbook of International Law* 321, 326.

[24] J Gold, *Membership and Non-Membership in the International Monetary Fund* (1974) 388–90; and H Schermers and N Blokker (1995) at 843, n 68: 'The IMF *travaux préparatoires* show that France and other European states proposed to charge an independent tribunal with matters of

tations have almost always been issued by the Executive Board and Board of Governors, the latter having the power to overrule the Committee on Interpretation by an 85 per cent majority of the total voting power.[25] However the express provisions in the IFIs' Articles do not cover the entire field.[26] The de facto modus operandi for most international organisations is that all elements of the organisation—members, organs and adjudicating and governing bodies—are potential participants.[27] Most interpretations carried out by the IFIs are of an informal rather than 'authoritative' (formally in accordance with specific provisions in the Articles) kind, a pattern not likely to change in future.[28] Interpretations issued or made through the day-to-day practice of international organisations, and which are not disputed by their members, are presumptively legal and are generally accepted as constituting 'precedents' for interpretative purposes.[29]

The principal criterion governing the interpretative relevance of institutional 'practice' under Article 31(3)(b) of the Vienna Convention appears to be the reasonably self-evident requirement that the practice be within the (frequently broad) purposes of the organisation.[30] On consent-based or 'agency'-based

interpretation. The arbitrators of this tribunal would not decide by weighted voting. This would however limit US influence within the IMF. As a compromise, the Committee on Interpretation was created.'

[25] According to H Schermers and N Blokker (1995) at 843.

[26] J Gold. (1996) at 16 and 31–40; F Mann (1968/9), and J Alvarez (2001) at 112: 'Even [international organisations, or IO's] whose charters provide for a precise or more formal mechanism for authoritative interpretations have relied on [an informal and less structured] approach in practice: ordinarily, interpretative disputes are initially resolved by institutional organs, as IO officials must decide whether or not to pursue a course of action. Most of the time their decisions are not challenged, and there is no resort to any more formal methods of interpretation even where these are available.' See also J Fawcett (1960) at 323–25, discussing the potential for conflict of interest in the application of Article XVIII (IMF Articles) in the case of elected Executive Directors representing the interests of several Board members, and F Mann (1968/9) at 2–3 for the limited number of cases where Article XVIII (as at 1969) had been invoked.

[27] J Alvarez (2001) at 113. See also J Gold, *Interpretation by the Fund* (IMF Pamphlet Series No. 11, 1968) at 14, and E Hexner 'Interpretation by Public International Organisations of their Basic Documents' (1959) *American Journal of International Law* 341, 350.

[28] J Gold (1996) at 3: 'Few [Article XVIII] decisions have been adopted, and . . . it is doubtful that there will be may more, or any at all, in the future.' See also J Gold (1996) at 16, 39–40, and at 30–41 for a discussion of practical limitations in relying upon the so-called 'authoritative' (Article XVIII) interpretation mechanism, including procedural inefficiencies and prejudice to the overriding principle of institutional effectiveness.

[29] J Alvarez (2001) at 112, citing a foundational interpretative decision of the UN Charter drafters. See also B Fassbender (1998) at 597–58, nn 240–45 and the various references referred to there, reflecting a relatively expansive view on the capacity of UN organs—and the 'international legal community' as a whole—to interpret relevant provisions of the UN Charter. However for a cautionary note on the scope of this competence in light of recent ICJ jurisprudence see D Akande, 'The Competence of International Organisations and the Advisory Jurisdiction of the International Court of Justice' (1998) 9(3) *European Journal of International Law* 437–67.

[30] See eg S Engel, ' "Living" International Constitutions and the World Court (The Subsequent Practice of International Organs Under Their Constituent Instruments)' (1967) 16 *International and Comparative Law Quarterly* 865; Advisory Opinion of the ICJ in 'Competence of the General Assembly,' *ICJ Reports* (1950), 9; J Fawcett, 'Détournement de Pouvoir by International Organisations' (1957) 33 *British Yearbook of International Law* 311, 316; and I Brownlie (5th ed) (1998) at 635.

justifications for institutional practice in this context, there need not be unanimous support for particular organisational practices in order for these to have probative value.[31] While it is sometimes said that the use of subsequent practice should be limited to constitutional 'gap-filling,' ambiguities in determining the existence of such 'gaps'—along with infrequent application of this limitation in practice—seem to undermine the relevance of this caveat for present purposes.[32]

However despite widespread reliance on institutional practice, questions about the relative weight to be accorded to practice—as opposed to text, negotiating history, teleological purposes or other factors—remain unresolved.[33] Whether focusing upon the statements and practices of Management, the General Counsel's office or the Executive Board, the interpretative value of the IFIs' 'practice' within the meaning of Article 31(3)(b) can probably be taken to vary in accordance with the directness of an imputation of consent of the institutions' respective governing bodies.[34] The extent and persistence of objections to a certain practice will bear upon, but rarely dispose of, the question of consent.[35] In principle an imputation of Executive Board consent will more clearly drawn where the focus of discussion is upon a lending or credit decision or the terms of Operational Policies or Operational Directives or other matters requiring express Board endorsement, rather than upon matters of day-to-day policy development or legal pronouncement at Management level.[36] However there is certainly no basis for excluding 'practice' in the latter categories, whether for the immediate purposes of Article 31(3)(b) or as an indication of future directions in which the IFIs' mandates might be expected to evolve. This is a question of relative weight, rather than relevance.

These basic principles are broadly reflected within legal doctrine at the Bank. Former General Counsel Ibrahim Shihata affirmed the relevance to the Bank of customary rules embodied in Articles 31 and 32 of the Vienna Convention[37] and

---

[31] See F Mann (1968/9) at 18 on the possibility of consensual or customary practices of members to displace strictly 'legal' interpretations undertaken under Article XVIII (Fund Articles). See also J Alvarez (2001) at 119, but also at 120–21 for an indication of some of the potential objections to consent-based theories.

[32] J Alvarez (2001) at 120, citing the 'extreme teleological' approach advocated by former World Bank General Counsel Aron Broches, to the effect that 'the Bank's authority extends to any matter not prohibited in or positively inconsistent with its basic instrument if the matter achieves the Bank's purposes.' A Broches, 'International Legal Aspects of the Operations of the World Bank' (1959) 98 *Receuil des Cours* 304.

[33] J Alvarez (2001) at 119.

[34] As reflected in Article IX (a)–(b) (IBRD Articles), Article X (a)–(b) (IDA Articles) and Article XVIII (a)–(b) (IMF Articles), read puposively [per J Fawcett (1960) at 326].

[35] J Alvarez (2001) at 120–21.

[36] Even in latter categories there will be variations as to degree, depending upon the extent to which the Executive Board has viewed—and therefore effectively vetted—particular policy developments (for example in relation to child labour, to be discussed below), and the extent of influence of the opinions from the General Counsel's office.

[37] The Bank's former General Counsel Ibrahim Shihata recognised that 'the legal interpretation of treaty provisions such as the Bank's Articles is subject to general rules of international law developed through centuries of state practice, judicial precedents and scholarly works. Such "customary"

the importance of a purposive or teleological interpretation for charters of inter-national organisations in general, the rationale being that 'by nature of their respective mandates, [they] must be able to respond to the world's changing needs.'[38] In so doing, consistent with the Vienna Convention on the Law of Treaties, care must be taken not to 'conflict with the ordinary meaning of the words as used in their context (unless it is clear that a special meaning was intended or that the ordinary meaning leads to absurd or contradictory results).'[39] However Shihata quite properly cautions that '[f]lexibility in the interpretation process cannot . . . reasonably substitute this process for the amendment of the Articles, which goes beyond the powers of the [Executive Directors] or, for that matter, the Board of Governors.'[40]

Taking these principles of interpretation as well established, the central inquiry in this chapter concerns the manner in which the IFIs themselves have interpreted their mandates in practice through word and deed, sufficient to estab-lish current agreement of the member states as to the scope of application of their constitutive documents. As indicated earlier this exercise will be undertaken by specific reference to Article IV, Section 10 of the IBRD Articles and its IDA equiv-alent (the so-called 'political prohibition'), with argumentation in the Fund's case focusing upon an application of the 'implied powers' doctrine (exploring the scope of inherent authority under the Fund's charter). It will be shown below that the flexibility with which the mandates of each of the Bank and Fund have been interpreted in practice, along with the imperative for inter-institutional cooperation in the context of inter alia the HIPC and PRSP processes[41] and other complex challenges such as reconstruction in the wake of the East Asian crisis, afford ample scope for the incorporation of human rights dimensions to their policies and operations to the extent that this is necessary or desirable.[42] Brief

---

rules have been codified in two articles of the 1969 Vienna Convention on the Law of Treaties.' I Shihata (1990) at 21.

[38] I Shihata (1999) at 1049.

[39] This is intended to capture the cumulative effect of Articles 31 and 32 of the Vienna Convention.

[40] I Shihata (1999) at 1049. However see J Fawcett (1960) at 332 for caveats on the practical util-ity of formal amendment mechanisms, including political and constitutional difficulties, and hesi-tancy of members to re-open discussion on provisions embodying hard-won compromises at Bretton Woods.

[41] For a strong critique of HIPC see OXFAM, *From Unsustainable Debt to Poverty Reduction: Reforming the Heavily Indebted Poor Countries Initiative*, prepared by OXFAM GB Policy Department for UNICEF, (August 1999). Interestingly, the reform initiatives set in train by the IFIs following the September 1999 Executive Board meetings ('enhanced HIPC' and the PRSP) mirror closely the recommendations set out in the OXFAM publication (at 23–29).

[42] As indicated earlier it is beyond the scope of this book to deal at length with foundational ques-tions going to the extent to which human rights mainstreaming in the IFIs might be considered desir-able. For a suggestion of some of the more fundamental objections from a critical legal point of view, with particular emphasis on the need to go behind and expose vehicles for further dissemina-tion and reinforcement of the dominant neo-liberal orthodoxy (even if the Trojan horse wears a human rights cloak), see J Gatthi, 'Good Governance as a Counter Insurgency Agenda to Oppositional and Transformative Social Projects in International Law' (1999) 5 *Buffalo Human Rights Law Review* 107.

consideration will also be given to the scope of the applicable international human rights law 'in the relations between the parties' (within the meaning of Article 31(3) of the Vienna Convention), and in the Bank's case, the relevance and import of the *travaux preparatoires* on the width of that institution's 'political affairs' prohibition. Some suggestions as to the actual content of the IFIs' human rights obligations are left for discussion in chapter VI.

HOW VITAL AN ISSUE IS THE 'LEGAL MANDATE' QUESTION IN
A PRACTICAL SENSE?

The World Bank

The World Bank's legal department has an important role to play within the institution's operational and internal accountability structures, and as part of the policy development process.[43] The opinions from the General Counsel's office on the lawful limits of the Bank's mandate, particularly in connection with that institution's foray into the 'governance' domain, have generally been regarded as highly authoritative even if not legally binding. However opinions differ on the actual extent of the legal department's and General Counsel's influence. The Bank's overall record in practice tends to show incremental and opportunistic mandate expansion, belying internal logic or anything close to systematic legal regulation. Anecdotal accounts suggest that key officials in the legal area have not infrequently been taken by surprise on major policy developments, such as selective forays by the Bank into areas such as criminal law reform, and prior to that, Bank President Wolfensohn's declared intention to tackle corruption. Such developments have on occasion been followed up by ex-post-facto, and occasionally slightly tortured, 'economic effects' justifications.

By contrast in the case of the East Timor crisis in mid-1999, to be discussed in more detail later in this chapter, according to some independent commentators genuine efforts were made to obtain legal department approval prior to a letter being sent from Bank President Wolfensohn to then Indonesian President Habibie, effectively threatening human rights-based conditionality. Against the human rights-aversion and traditional conservatism of the Bank's legal department, something in the nature of an accommodation was said to have been reached, with the terms of the letter referring to the need for Indonesia to honour its agreements relating to the 1999 East Timor referendum outcome[44] rather than invoking 'human rights conditionality' in bald terms. However it is not

---

[43] See generally I Shihata, 'The Creative Role of the Lawyer—Example: The Office of the World Bank's General Counsel' (1999) 48(4) *Catholic University Law Review* 1041–53, 1048–49.

[44] Interviews in Washington DC in February 2000. To similar effect see World Bank News Release No. 99/035/EAP, 'World Bank Statement on East Timor,' 7 September 1999. The letter from Bank President Wolfensohn to the President of Indonesia is reprinted in H Steiner and P Alston, *International Human Rights in Context: Law, Politics, Morals* (2nd ed) (2000) 1340. See the discussion below n 350 and accompanying text.

clear whether formal express consent of the legal department was received (or even required), or alternatively whether the UN agreements merely provided the legal department with a face-saving 'out'.[45]

In other respects there is reasonably clear evidence of well developed legal institutions and culture at the Bank, and an established system of internal law, albeit one skewed more towards contractual rather than international law in terms of the Bank's day to day operations. However one would expect that the Bank's complex and vast institutional structure and increasing decentralisation to country level will present ever increasing challenges to those charged with keeping operations and policies within a centrally defined and coherent legal framework. On balance, the role of legal adviser at the Bank appears to be important, but very far from all-pervasive, or necessarily dispositive of all issues carrying international legal dimensions.

The IMF

The Fund quite clearly has an active regard for a well developed conception of the 'rule of law,' and over time has paid disciplined heed to carefully articulated and actively promoted legal constraints on the width of its mandate.[46] And to a greater degree than the Bank, evidence suggests that the Fund's lawyers play something close to a systematic role in policy development.[47] This is not to say however that all official pronouncements on the nature and limits of the Fund's mission—say in relation to issues concerning 'equity' and 'quality of growth' arising from its longer-term financial facilities—necessarily bear legal department imprimata. And as will be seen further below, in some respects the fixed official legal interpretation of the breadth of the Fund's Articles of Association rests uneasily with the increasingly wide and complex range of issues for which staff are assuming responsibility, especially within the PRSP framework.[48] But the basic point here, these qualifications aside, is that while it is difficult to quantify, the role of the legal advisor within the Fund does appear to be somewhat stronger than that at the Bank.

---

[45] Interviews in Washington DC and New York in February 2000.

[46] See eg J Fawcett (1960); J Gold, 'Certain Aspects of the Law and Practice of the International Monetary Fund', in S Schwebel (ed), *The Effectiveness of International Decisions* (1971) 71–99; J Gold, *Legal and Institutional Aspects of the International Monetary System: Selected Essays* (1979).

[47] See eg H Schermers and N Blokker, *International Institutional Law: Unity within Diversity* (1995) 844, suggesting that legal interpretations issued by former IMF General Counsel Sir Joseph Gold (even in his personal capacity) have been extremely influential in practice.

[48] Although this is not to say that the expansion began with the PRSP. See eg D Bradlow (1996) at 69–72.

ISSUES COMMON TO THE BANK AND FUND

Relationship Agreements with the United Nations

As indicated in chapter II, the Bank and Fund are specialised agencies of the United Nations, by agreement entered into with the Economic and Social Council (ECOSOC) in accordance with Articles 63 and 57 of the UN Charter.[49] Article 1(2) of the Bank's Relationship Agreement states:

> The Bank is a specialised agency established by agreement among its member governments and having wide international responsibilities, as defined in its Articles of Agreement, in economic and related fields within the meaning of Article 57 of the Charter of the United Nations. By reason of the nature of its international responsibilities, the Bank is, and is required to function as, in independent organisation.[50]

The Fund's Relationship Agreement has an equivalent provision, establishing its independent operation within the UN system.

There are degrees of 'independence' among specialised agencies in the UN family,[51] with the Bank and Fund among the more distant members. Nevertheless their Relationship Agreements (identical in structure) do descend to some detail in describing the scope for cooperation with the UN, including on such matters as an entitlement to reciprocal representation (Article 2), the possibility to propose items of business for consideration by the other (Article 3), consultation on matters of mutual concern (Article 4) and exchange of information (Article 5).[52]

---

[49] For references to the WB/UN and IMF/UN Relationship Agreements in chapter II above, nn 3 and 102. These Relationship Agreements are subject to the ordinary rules of interpretation in international law: B Simma, *The Charter of the United Nations: A Commentary* (1994) 805. Article 57 of the UN Charter provides: '(1) The various specialised agencies, established by inter-governmental agreement and having wide international responsibilities, as defined in their basic instruments, in economic, social, cultural, educational, health, and related fields, shall be brought into relationship with the United Nations in accordance with the provisions of Article 63. (2) Such agencies thus brought into relationship with the United Nations are hereinafter referred to as specialised agencies.' Article 63(2) of the Charter provides that ECOSOC 'may co-ordinate the activities of the specialised agencies through consultation with and recommendations to such agencies and through recommendations to the General Assembly and to the members of the UN.'

[50] See chapter II above, n 3.

[51] See eg S Skogly (2001) at 103–4, describing the comparatively close relationship between the UN and the WHO.

[52] The IFIs' Articles of Agreement elaborate further in certain respects. Article V, Section 8 of the IBRD Articles states: '(a) The Bank, within the terms of this Agreement, shall co-operate with any international organisation and with public international organisations having specialised responsibilities in related fields. Any arrangements for such co-operation which would involve a modification of any provision of this Agreement may be effected only after amendment to this Agreement under Article VIII. (b) In making decisions on applications for loans or guarantees relating to matters directly within the competence of any international organisation of the types specified in the preceding paragraph and participated in primarily by members of the Bank, the Bank shall give consideration to the views and recommendations of such organisations.'

The Bank is also expressly bound to acknowledge the primacy of decisions of the Security Council in international law. Article 6(1) of the IBRD Articles obliges it to conduct its activities with 'due regard for decisions of the Security Council under Articles 41 and 42 of the United Nations Charter.' Further, according to the Bank's legal advice, Article 48 of the UN Charter obliges UN member States to carry out Security Council decisions 'directly and through their action in the appropriate international agencies of which they are members.'[53] To a significant extent of course the application of such provisions is governed at least as much by *realpolitique* as the black letter of the law. The Bank's General Counsel has observed that: '[A]s a matter of fact, the Bank would not be in a position to extend lending at a normal scale to a country where pervasive [human rights] violations and/or Security Council decisions create conditions where it becomes unrealistic for such lending to receive support by the required majority in the Bank's Board of Executive Directors.'[54] Given that three of the five permanent members of the Security Council (the US, France and the United Kingdom) have reserved seats on the Board of Executive Directors, exercising roughly a quarter of the Bank's voting power,[55] this would go a long way towards curtailing Bank loans to any country against which Security Council sanctions have been directed, in response to large-scale human rights violations.[56]

Hence the outward 'independence' of the Bank and Fund sits at odds with the scheme of cooperation envisaged by the drafters of the UN Charter. While the aim and precise parameters of cooperation don't emerge with clarity from the Charter or the IFIs' Relationship Agreements with the UN, it is reasonable to assume that the motive was to marshall all of the UN system's resources for the promotion and fulfilment of the Charter's objectives.[57] The independent status of the IFIs under their Relationship Agreements cannot be construed to frustrate this objective, nor to undermine their obligations to respect the human rights purposes and principles of the Charter, to be discussed shortly.

---

[53] Shihata (1990) at 32.

[54] I Shihata, 'Human Rights, Development and International Financial Institutions' (paper prepared for Conference on Human Rights, Public Finance, and the Development Process, 24 January 1992, Washington DC) cited in Lawyers Committee for Human Rights (1995) at 27 [hereafter cited as I Shihata, 'Human Rights' (1992)].

[55] See World Bank Annual Report 2000 at 119–21.

[56] In particular the Bank's former General Counsel observed that: '(V)iolations of political rights may . . . reach such proportions as to become a Bank concern . . . if it results in international obligations relevant to the Bank such as those mandated by binding decisions of the UN Security Council.' I Shihata, 'Human Rights' (1992), cited in Lawyers Committee for Human Rights (1995) at 27–28. Naturally, the economic power of the United States represents a more powerful constraint on World Bank action than its percentage of voting power (16.5% for the IBRD and 14.86% for the IDA in 2000) suggests. As Payer observes, 'if the US executive were ever seriously displeased by a decision of the Bank, it could withdraw from the organisation, or simply refuse to contribute to IDA, which would leave the Bank financially impotent'—C Payer (1982) at 40.

[57] S Skogly (2001) at 105.

The IFIs as Subjects of International Law

The activities of the IFIs are governed primarily by their respective Articles of Agreement, however the applicability of other international agreements, general international law, the general principles of law and municipal law have all to be considered.[58]

The starting point for an inquiry into the international legal obligations of the Bank and Fund is whether these institutions can be said to possess international legal personality.[59] For an organisation to be a subject of international law (ie to possess international legal personality) implies an entitlement to rely upon legal rights, an obligation to respect legal duties, and a privilege to utilise legal processes, independent of the rights and obligations of its members.[60]

International legal personality was not specifically conferred upon the IFIs within their Articles of Agreement. Hence the resolution of this question is a matter of construction, having regard to the powers and functions specifically conferred in their constituent documents, along with other evidence of a capacity to create international rights and obligations and have international claims brought or asserted against them.[61] In the case of both the Bank and the Fund, the nature of the specific powers granted under their Articles (notably the power to conclude agreements governed by international law, and the provisions establishing their relationship with other international organisations), their entitlement to specified privileges and immunities, and the fact that that they operate extensively within the international sphere, indicate international legal personality separate from their members.[62] As a consequence of this, the Bank and Fund are bound by any obligations incumbent upon them under their constitutions, international agreements to which they are party, and general rules of international law (including international human rights law).[63]

---

[58] J Fawcett (1960) at 336.

[59] A Broches, *Selected Essays: World Bank, ICSID and Other Subjects of Public and Private International Law* (1995) 22.

[60] M Janis, *An Introduction to International Law* (2nd ed) (1993) 176. See the discussion in S Skogly (2001) at 63–71.

[61] ICJ advisory opinion in *Reparations for Injuries Suffered in the Service of the United Nations*, 1949 ICJ 174 (11 April) (hereafter 'Reparations case'), dealing with the capacity of the UN Organisation to bring an international claim in respect of injury to its personal and consequent injury to the Organisation itself. See also the *International Tin Council* case (House of Lords, 26 October 1989), reprinted in (1990) 29 *International Legal Materials* 670.

[62] S Skogly (2001) at 63–71; A Broches (1959) at 19; *Interpretation of the Agreement of 25 March 1951 between the WHO and Egypt*, ICJ, Reports of Judgments, Advisory Opinions and Orders, 1980 at 89–90.

[63] *Interpretation of the Agreement of 25 March 1951 between the WHO and Egypt*, ICJ, Reports of Judgments, Advisory Opinions and Orders, 1980 at 89–90. For an early illustration of the application of public international law to the Fund in connection with the regulatory schemes for SBA's and membership issues see Fawcett, J. (1960) at 339–40. A more contemporary acknowledgement of international law's relevance and impacts on the Bank appears in the Environment Department's March 1996 update to its Environmental Assessment Sourcebook, 'Public international law governs conduct among states and international public organisations. The World Bank, an organisation

Obligations Arising from the UN Charter

At a very basic level, human rights are at the centre of the purposes of the United Nations system.[64] Article 55 of the UN Charter is central to this discussion, and is worth setting out in full:

> 55. With a view to the creation of conditions of stability and well-being which are necessary for peaceful and friendly relations among nations based on respect for the principle of equal rights and self-determination of peoples, the United Nations shall promote:
>
> (a) higher standards of living, full employment, and conditions of economic and social progress and development;
>
> (b) solutions of international economic, social, health, and related problems; and international cultural and educational co-operation; and
>
> (c) universal respect for, and observance of, human rights and fundamental freedoms for all without distinction as to race, sex, language, or religion.'

Further, Article 56 of the Charter provides that: '[a]ll Members pledge themselves to take joint and separate action in co-operation with the [United Nations] Organisation for the achievement of the purposes set forth in Article 55.'[65] Despite the generality of these provisions, the ICJ has held that they do generate a binding obligation on members States to respect human rights.[66] The Universal Declaration on Human Rights [UDHR][67] states the 'common understanding of the peoples of the world concerning the inalienable and inviolable rights of all members of the human family and constitutes an obligation for the members of the international community.'[68] Along with the body of international human rights law built upon it, the UDHR 'is viewed by many as a further elaboration of the brief references to human rights in the Charter,'[69]

created and governed by public international law, undertakes its operations in compliance with applicable public international law principles and rules. These principles and rules are set forth in instruments such as treaties, conventions, or other multilateral, regional or bilateral agreements [as well as certain "legally significant non-binding instruments"].' World Bank, 'International Agreements on Environment and Natural Resources: Relevance and Application in Environmental Assessment,' *Environmental Assessment Sourcebook (Vol. 1): Policies, Procedures and Cross-sectoral Issues* (World Bank Technical Paper No. 139, Environment Department, 1996), at 63.

[64] Article 1 of the UN Charter provides, in part: 'The Purposes of the United Nations are: . . . 3. To achieve international co-operation in solving international problems of an economic, social, cultural, or humanitarian character, and in promoting and encouraging respect for human rights and for fundamental freedoms for all.'

[65] Certain commentators [eg see M Elahi (1986) at 148] have suggested that Article 57, along with Article 56, binds all UN member states and specialised agencies to act within a co-operative framework with the UN in order to enhance the goals stated in Article 55.

[66] *The Legal Consequences for States of the Continued Presence of South Africa in Namibia, notwithstanding Security Council Resolution 260 (1970),* ICJ Report 58, 1971, para 129.

[67] GA Res. 217A, UN Doc. A/810, at 71 (1948).

[68] International Conference on Human Rights in Teheran, UN Doc. A/Conf. At 32/41; UN Publ. E. 68.XIV.2 (1968).

[69] H Steiner and O Alston, *International Human Rights in Context: Law, Politics, Morals* (1996) 121; K Drzewicki, 'The United Nations Charter and the Universal Declaration of Human Rights' in

or more specifically, an 'authoritative interpretation' of the nature of those Charter-based obligations.[70] Moreover while the IFIs' constituent documents recognise their members retain sovereign power and exclusive authority over matters untouched by their obligations of membership in the Bank and Fund, the decisions of the ICJ in the *Barcelona Traction*[71] and *Legal Consequences for States of the Continued Presence of South Africa in Namibia (South West Africa)*[72] cases have made clear that fundamental UN Charter-based human rights obligations, as elaborated in the UDHR, do not fall within the exclusive sovereign preserve.[73]

Looking at Articles 55–57 as a whole, in conjunction with the IMF/UN and Bank/UN Relationship Agreements,[74] it is strongly arguable that co-operation between the IFIs and the UN in the economic and social fields[75] should be based, at least in part, on the principles animating Chapter IX of the Charter.[76] These principles include, at a minimum, the human rights purposes as stated in Article 55, as elaborated in the UDHR and the body of international human rights law built upon it. This interpretation appears to be reinforced by Article 59 of the

R Hanski and M Suksi (eds), *An Introduction to the International Protection of Human Rights* (1997) 65–78, 68–69 and 75; M Nowak, *UN Covenant on Civil and Political Rights: CCPR Commentary* (1993) at XVII. See further I Brownlie, *Principles of Public International Law* (5th ed) (1998) 574–75.

[70] P Alston and B Simma, 'The Sources of Human Rights Law: Custom, *Jus Cogens*, and General Principles, (1992) 12 *Australian Year Book of International Law* 82–108, 100–1, discussed there in the context of a broader inquiry into the status of the UDHR under customary international law. For similar views on the interpretative value and legitimacy of the UDHR viz Articles 55 and 56 see L Sohn, 'The New International Law: Protection of the Rights of Individuals Rather Than States' (1982) 32 *American University Law Review* 1, 17; I Brownlie (5th ed) (1998) at 575; T Buergenthal, 'International Human Rights Law and Institutions: Accomplishments and Prospects' (1988) 63 *Washington Law Review* 1, although the latter purports to exclude economic, social and cultural rights from the UDHR's scope in this regard; and H Hannum, 'The Status of the Universal Declaration of Human Rights in National and International Law' (1995/96) 25 *Georgia Journal of International and Comparative Law* 287–397, 323–25 and the various references referred to there. Sohn at least is of the view that the two Covenants 'partake of the creative force found in the [UDHR] and constitute in a similar fashion an authoritative interpretation' of Charter-based human rights rules: L Sohn, 'The Human Rights Law of the Charter' (1977) 12 *Texas International Law Journal* 129, 135–36. It has also been suggested that the ICERD falls into this category: F MacKay, 'Universal Rights or Universe Unto Itself? Indigenous Peoples' Human Rights and the World Bank's Draft Operational Policy 4.10 on Indigenous Peoples' (2002) 17 *American University International Law Review* 527, 572. Whether the nearly universally ratified CRC—even if lacking the Covenants' 'creative' (as Sohn argues) nexus with the UDHR—could now be taken to embody contemporary expectations and values connected with fundamental Charter purposes is similarly worthy of serious consideration. The ICESCR, ICCPR and CRC all recall the UN Charter and UDHR in their preambles.

[71] *Barcelona Traction, Light and Power Co., Ltd. (Belgium v Spain)*, 1970 ICJ 3.

[72] *Legal Consequences for States of the Continued Presence of South Africa in Namibia (South West Africa) Notwithstanding Security Council Resolution 276*, 1971 ICJ 16.

[73] For a discussion see G Brodnig (2001) at 18–19.

[74] See discussion above nn 49–57 and accompanying text, and S Skogly (2001) at 103–5.

[75] Chapter IX of the Charter, in which Articles 55–57 fall, deals with international economic *and social* co-operation.

[76] See also B Rajagopal, 'Crossing the Rubicon: Synthesising the Soft International Law of the IMF and Human Rights' (1993) 11 *Boston University International Law Journal* 81 at 94–95.

Charter, pursuant to which 'the creation of any new specialised agencies require[s] accomplishment of the purposes set forth in article 55.'[77] Moreover Article 103 of the UN Charter elevates UN member States' Charter-based obligations over other treaty-based obligations in international law. As specialised agencies within the terms of their respective Relationship Agreements with the UN, and as subjects of international law, the IFIs are at a minimum required to respect the (human rights and other) purposes and principles reflected in the UN Charter, and their members' Charter-based human rights obligations.[78]

Experts in the Sub-Commission for the Promotion and Protection of Human Rights attempted to encapsulate the relevant inquiry in a slightly different way, arguing that an unduly restrictive or blinkered 'honouring of the Bank's (or Fund's) charter' has the effect of placing small 'c' charter obligations above any international obligations which the IFIs may have by virtue of membership in the United Nations family, in particular, big 'C' Charter obligations. As was pointed out in their report to the Sub-Commission in 1999: 'Such an approach could imply that any action permitted by the Bank's charter may appropriately be pursued regardless of the adverse human rights or other consequences that may result or the fact that it may offend the Charter of the United Nations or the Universal Declaration of Human Rights.'[79] The main problem with the 'honouring the charter' or 'privileging the Articles' approach is that it 'subordinates the international human rights instruments to the charters of the agencies in question when, as a matter of law, the reverse should be the case.'[80] While not every international lawyer would agree that the IFIs' charters must necessarily be 'subordinated' to relevant international human rights instruments, clearly the latter have a more relevant and robust role to play in the interpretation of the former than the IFIs themselves have been willing to countenance.

Scope of Human Rights Obligations

The sources of international human rights obligation for present purposes can be referenced to those articulated within Article 38 of the Statute of the International Court of Justice, ie treaty law, customary international law, and general principles of law, along with *jus cogens*.[81] Beyond providing a framework of obligation in a broad sense, this analysis is of direct relevance to the manner in which the IFIs' Articles ought to be interpreted, having regard to Article 31(3)(c) of the Vienna Convention.

[77] See also B Rajagopal (1993) at 94–95.
[78] See eg S Skogly (2001) at 99–106.
[79] E/CN.4/Sub.2/1999/11, Working paper submitted by J Oloka-Onyango and Deepika Udagama in accordance with Sub-Commission resolution 1998/12, at para 30.
[80] E/CN.4/Sub.2/1999/11 at para 33.
[81] S Skogly (2001) at 80–91. '*Jus cogens*' refers to a peremptory norm from which no derogation is permitted, and which can be modified only by subsequent norms of general international law having the same character (per Article 53 of the Vienna Convention).

Treaty law is less directly relevant for present purposes, save as an interpretative guide to Charter-based obligations binding upon the IFIs. Nonetheless, subject to 'functional necessity' of so doing, the possibility of the IFIs acceding to human rights treaties should not be discounted.[82] Treaty provisions might nonetheless be indirectly relevant to the extent that they embody customary law rules or general principles of international law binding on the IFIs as subjects of international law.[83]

The extent to which the UDHR is binding as a matter of customary international law is a matter of ongoing dispute. The requirements of a generalisation of State practice accompanied by *opinio juris*[84] are difficult to demonstrate convincingly for many human rights standards without doing violence to the 'State practice' requirement.[85] Most authoritative lists of rights that have achieved 'customary' status are limited to a small number of freedoms (seldom if ever including economic, social or cultural rights) such as prohibition on slavery, genocide, arbitrary killing, prolonged arbitrary imprisonment, systematic racial discrimination or indeed any consistent pattern of gross violations of internationally recognised human rights,[86] most of which would in any case qualify as *jus cogens*[87] or obligations *erga omnes*.[88] Obligations arising under

---

[82] On capacity to conclude treaties and the functional necessity test see H Schermers and N Blokker (1995) at 1096–103. There is nothing in the core human rights treaties that expressly excludes specialised agency adherence, and no express prohibition in the IFIs' Articles. The advantages of clarifying the content of applicable obligations incumbent upon them, and strengthening associated procedural obligations, may well be of relevance to a 'functional necessity' analysis, reading the IFIs' constitutions in light of the UN Charter. By analogy, the European Commission has taken the view that it could adhere to the European Convention on Human Rights, and that this would promote the protection of human rights in Europe. H Schermers and N Blokker (1995) at 1118. However by way of further analogy, it is worth noting that the Office of Legal Affairs of the UN has taken the view that the UN cannot adhere to the 1949 Geneva Conventions by reason of the fact that many of its obligations can only be discharged by the exercise of juridical and administrative powers that the UN does not possess, such as authority to exercise criminal jurisdiction over members of armed Forces, and administrative competence relating to territorial authority (Schermers and Blokker at 1118).

[83] H Schermers and N Blokker (1995) at 982–89. See in particular pp 984–88 for a discussion of the conditions and rationales under which international organisations may be bound by general principles of law deriving from provisions of treaties to which the organisations themselves are not party. The number of ratifications to the treaty in question is regard by Schermers and Blokker (at 987) as a relevant matter.

[84] *Military and Paramilitary Activities in and against Nicaragua (Nicaragua v USA), Merits*, ICJ Rep 1986, p 14 at 97–98.

[85] See B Simma and P Alston, 'The Sources of Human Rights Law: Custom, *Jus Cogens* and General Principles' (1992) 12 *Australian Year Book of International Law* 82.

[86] A consensus position remains elusive however. See eg O Schachter, 'International Law in Theory and Practice: General Course in Public International Law' (1982-V) 178 *Recueil des cours* 21, 333–42, and T Meron, *Human Rights and Humanitarian Norms as Customary Law* (1989).

[87] According to Simma and Alston, 'we are safe in concluding that the threshold requirement for the emergence of *jus cogens*, namely the generality, or universality, of acceptance and recognition, is set at least as high as that necessary for the development of general (or universal) customary law.' B Simma and P Alston. (1992) at 103. However (at 103): 'Settled practices of States as regards *jus cogens* are elusive to grasp, mainly because most, if not all, rules of *jus cogens* are prohibitive in substance; they are rules of abstention. How does one marshall conclusive evidence of abstentions?'

[88] See Vienna Convention, Article 53, and *Barcelona Traction, Light and Power Co., Ltd. (Belg.*

'general principles'[89] of international law assume particular importance, to the extent of custom's limited reach. The sources of general principles can derive either from legal principles developed in domestic jurisdictions, or from acceptance or recognition affected on the international plane.[90] This source of law corresponds more closely than custom to a situation where 'a norm invented with strong inherent authority is widely accepted even though widely violated.'[91] 'General principles' of law derived from domestic legal systems have been resorted to in practice in a number of circumstances, including in elucidating the general terms of the Fund's Articles of Agreement and establishing 'equity' in the administration of staff relations.[92]

The content of the resultant human rights-based obligations is of course a separate matter, requiring a much more detailed and fundamental set of normative inquiries than is possible within the scope of this book. In general terms human rights obligations can be classified in accordance with requirements to 'respect, protect and fulfil' applicable normative standards.[93] In general terms the obligation to 'respect' requires the duty holder to refrain from interfering directly or indirectly with the right in question (a 'negative' duty). In some contexts an obligation to 'respect' has also been interpreted to give rise to positive duties.[94] The obligation to 'protect' requires the duty holder to take measures to prevent third parties from interfering with enjoyment of the right. And the obligation to 'fulfil' (sometimes broken down into 'facilitate' and 'provide') requires the adoption of positive measures directed towards the full realisation of the right in question.

---

v Spain), 1970 ICJ 3, 33, identifying categories of human rights whose protection is the interest and obligation of all states: 'Such obligations derive, for example, in contemporary international law, from the outlawing of acts of aggression, and of genocide, as also from the principles and rules concerning the basic rights of the human person, including protection from slavery and racial discrimination. Some of the corresponding rights of protection have entered into the body of international law . . . ; others are conferred by international instruments of a universal or quasi-universal character.'

[89] Article 38 of the ICJ Statute refers specifically to 'general principles of law recognised by civilised nations.'

[90] B Simma and P Alston (1992) at 102.

[91] B Simma and P Alston (1992) at 102.

[92] J Fawcett (1960) at 341–42.

[93] Original credit for the conceptualisation of a multiple obligations structure applicable to all human rights is usually accorded to philosopher Henry Shue's *Basic Rights: Subsistence, Affluence and US Foreign Policy* (1980). See C Scott and P Alston, 'Adjudicating Constitutional Priorities in a Transnational Context: A Comment on *Soobramoney*'s Legacy and *Grootboom*'s Promise' (2000) 16 *South African Journal of Human Rights* 206–68, 215, n 23. Multiple obligations typology manifested in the 'respect, protect and fulfil' structure within the report of Asbjørn Eide, Special Rapporteur of the Sub-Commission for the Prevention of Discrimination and Protection of Minorities, 'Report on the right to adequate food as a human right', UN Doc. E/CN.4/Sub.2/1987/23 (1987), the jurisprudence of the Committee on Economic, Social and Cultural Rights (see eg E/C.12/1999/5, General Comment 12 on the right to adequate food (article 11 ICESCR)), and the Maastricht Guidelines on Violations of Economic, Social and Cultural Rights (1998) 20 *Human Rights Quarterly* 691–705. For a general discussion, relating multiple obligations structure to all human rights in recognition of their universality and unifying normative characteristics, see G Van Hoof, 'The Legal Nature of Economic, Social and Cultural Rights: A Rebuttal of Some Traditional Views' in P Alston and K Tomasevski (eds), *The Right to Food* (1984) 97–110.

As a point of principle the human rights 'baseline' for both Bank and Fund can be taken to be a 'duty of vigilance'[95] to ensure as far as practicable that its actions do not impact negatively upon the abilities of its borrowing members (in particular) to implement their own validly assumed international human rights obligations. In line with relevant jurisprudence of the Committee on Economic, Social and Cultural Rights,[96] a duty of this kind may be argued to arise from the requirement for the IFIs to interpret their Articles of Association in a manner consistent with the human rights provisions of the United Nations Charter, with the International Bill of Rights as an authoritative guide to interpretation. An obligation to 'respect' fundamental human rights also impacts upon the IFIs directly as a matter of general international law.[97] However, defining appropriate practical steps that each of the Bank and Fund should take in order to discharge such duties, and related 'negative' duties such as that of human rights impact analysis,[98] is very much an ongoing enterprise.

Apart from the responsibility to *prevent* adverse human rights impacts (a central aspect of a duty to respect human rights), the other (related) aspects of the imperative for the IFIs to better understand and deal with human rights issues go to the questions of human rights *protection* and *fulfilment*. Obligations to 'protect' against human rights violations might arise in practice in a number of ways including through sub-contractor situations, or cases where stakeholders at country level are victimised for participating in consultations on IFI-supported projects or programmes, or more generally in connection with lending, credit and structural adjustment policies.[99] Duties to 'fulfil' human rights might also conceivably arise, for example, in the context of procedural duties to

---

[94] The interpretation of family rights by the European Court of Human Rights is a case in point. P Alston and G Quinn, 'The Nature and Scope of States Parties' Obligations under the International Covenant of Economic, Social and Cultural Rights' (1987) 9(2) *Human Rights Quarterly* 156, 184.

[95] For an argument in similar terms see P Klein, 'La responsabilité des organisations financiers et les droits de la personne' (1999) *Revue Belge de Droit International* 97, 113.

[96] Committee on Economic, Social and Cultural Rights, 'International Technical Assistance Measures (Art 22),' General Comment No. 2, E/1990/23 (Fourth session, 1990) at paras 6, 8 and 9; and see the country-specific recommendations referred to in Chapter VI, n 122 and accompanying text.

[97] See the discussion of relevant ICJ jurisprudence in B Simma and P Alston, (1992) at 104–6. While not specified in the ICJ cases, the unstated assumption is that 'general principles' rather than customary rules provide the basis for this obligation to 'respect fundamental human rights.' Cf S Skogly (2001) at 151.

[98] See the discussion in chapter VI, nn 209–64 and accompanying text. The 'negative/ positive' distinction is of course not intended to create artificial distinctions between different human rights. All rights—civil, economic, cultural, economic and political—have both positive (costly) and negative (non-interference) dimensions. For an insightful exposé in the context of US constitutional rights theory see S Holmes and C Sunstein, *The Cost of Rights: Why Liberty Depends on Taxes* (1999).

[99] See eg D Bradlow (1996) at 66–75 and 80–89. As considered by Bradlow (taking the case of the IMF), 'protection' refers to the responsibility of the Fund to help protect citizens in member states from human rights abuses. Bradlow limits 'protective' action to cases where human rights abuses cause monetary consequences, for example, in the case of South Africa. The IMF's responses in such cases are defined as 'sanctions,' although there are said to be (at 73) a number of significant limitations on the scope for human rights conditionality in this regard.

cooperate with certain human rights organs,[100] or perhaps in a more promotional context.[101] However, generalising beyond this extent requires more focused analysis than is possible within the scope of this book. The promise of objectivity must in any case not too readily be assumed.

A Critical Review of Unofficial IMF Rebuttals

The question of the IFIs' international human rights obligations has rarely seemed to attract serious scholarly attention within either the Bank or Fund.[102] However this changed quite abrubtly on 7 May 2001 at a consultation in Geneva organised by the Committee on Economic, Social and Cultural Rights and the High Council for International Cooperation, at which the IMF General Counsel François Gianviti presented a 42-page analysis of normative aspects of the relationship between the Fund and the ICESCR.[103] The paper was in essence a rebuttal, although within quite a focused set of inquiries, seeking to argue that the ICESCR (rather than any other relevant instrument) fell beyond the Fund's

---

[100] For a discussion in the context of an inquiry under the ICESCR into the normative implications of the commitment to international cooperation, see P Alston and G Quinn, 'The Nature and Scope of States Parties' Obligations Under the International Covenant on Economic, Social and Cultural Rights' (1987) 9 *Human Rights Quarterly* 156. See also Committee on Economic, Social and Cultural Rights, 'The Nature of States Parties' Obligations (Art 2, par. 1)', General Comment No. 3, E/1990/23 (Fifth session, 1990).

[101] General Comment No. 2 provides (at para 6): 'In positive terms, it [the obligation of UN agencies involved in the promotion of ESCR to ensure that their activities are also fully consistent with CPR] means that, wherever possible, the agencies should act as advocates of projects and approaches, which contribute not only to economic growth or to other broadly defined objectives, but also to enchanced enjoyment of the full range of human rights.' Herbert Morais, former Chief Counsel at the Bank and Assistant General Counsel at the IMF, appears to support this position. After a lengthy discussion of the IFIs' work in human rights-related areas he concludes: 'The [IFIs] . . . are well-positioned, by virtue of their vast resources and influence, to do even more in the years ahead to further promote human rights in their member countries. They can do this both through their own operations and activities and through closer collaboration with other international and national agencies.' H Morais, 'A Festschrift Honoring Professor Louis B Sohn (April 8, 2000): The Globalisation of Human Rights Law and the Role of International Financial Institutions in Promoting Human Rights' (2000) 33 *George Washington International Law Review* 71–96, 95. And indeed the Sub-Commission draft 'Human Rights Principles and Responsibilities for Transnational Corporations and Other Business Enterprises' provide (at para 1) that '[w]ithin their respective spheres of activity and influence, transnational corporations and other business enterprises have the obligation to respect, ensure respect for, prevent abuses of, and promote human rights recognised in international as well as national law.' E/CN.4/Sub.2/2002/WG.2/WP.1, 29 May 2002.

[102] As indicated earlier, the Fund has generally tended to disclaim responsibility under international human rights law on the general grounds of its supposedly limited mandate. The Bank's former General Counsel Shihata wrote extensively on questions concerning width of mandate, to the general effect that 'economic and social' rights (but not civil and political rights) were at least indirectly within the scope of the Bank's concerns, but were most appropriately to be considered residual by-products of the Bank's 'economic' development work, however defined. What has been lacking is a serious appraisal of the extent to which the Bank and Fund as subjects of international law are bound by the various sources of international human rights law, along with a description of the parameters of corresponding obligations.

[103] F Gianviti (2001), see n 3 above.

mandated functions and did not otherwise engage its responsibilities. The paper represents the first public occasion on which a General Counsel of either the Bank or Fund has sought to debate questions relating to mandate width within the international human rights normative framework. As laudable and timely an undertaking as this was, however, the General Counsel's analysis is open to criticism in a number of key respects, and leaves many important questions either unanswered or only half-answered.

Firstly, although perhaps not surprisingly, the General Counsel seems to advocate a rather limited view of the scope of IMF conditionality insofar as economic, social and cultural rights are concerned. It is stated that under Article I(v) 'the Fund has taken the view that its conditionality could include the removal of exchange and trade restrictions, but also the avoidance of measures that may be damaging to the environment or to the welfare of the population. For instance, attention may be given to health and education budgets, safety nets and good governance, including avoidance of corruption. However, this does not mean that the Fund sees itself as trying to substitute itself for the national authorities in determining national priorities. In particular, military expenditures are outside the scope of Fund conditionality pursuant to a [1991] decision of the Executive Board. More recently, there has been a discernible trend toward a reduction in the Fund's involvement in domestic policies through conditionality. The general critieria would be that the Fund should limit its conditionality to macroeconomic variables and to those structural elements that are critical to macro-economic stability.'[104]

The General Counsel's view seems considerably out of kilter with the leverage exercised over client states' domestic policies in practice,[105] and similarly the degree and nature of expansion of the Fund's conditionality menu in recent years, including on issues such as military expenditure.[106] While the 1991 Board decision is no doubt an important reference point on the latter issue, it cannot of itself be considered determinative of the scope of Article I(v) in light of subsequent inconsistent 'practice' within the meaning of Article 31(3)(b) of the Vienna Convention.[107] Even on the General Counsel's own test however, it is difficult to see how an issue like military expenditures could not be regarded as 'damaging to the environment or to the welfare of the population.' The practi-

---

[104] F Gianviti (2001) at 29–30. In the General Counsel's view, 'The World Bank would be expected to strengthen its role in the other areas where structural adjustment is needed.'

[105] See chapter III at 56–63, and 104–11, and contrary appraisal of the IMF's former Assistant General Counsel: H Morais (2000) at 86–95.

[106] See eg D Kapur and R Webb, 'Governance-related Conditionalities of the International Financial Institutions,' *G-24 Discussion Paper Series (UNCTAD)*, No. 6 (August 2000) and the discussions in chapter II at nn 144, 227–30 and accompanying text, chapter IV at 188–93, and chapter V at nn 45–54 and accompanying text. On the question of military expenditure in particular see chapter II, n 144 and accompanying text.

[107] As was discussed earlier in this chapter, 'subsequent practice' within the meaning of Article 31(3)(b) is not confined to the practice of the Executive Board and Board of Governors, notwithstanding express provisions in the Fund's Articles (Article XVIII(a)–(b)) for resolution of disputes concerning interpretation.

cal application of tests framed in such generic terms seems doomed to arbitrariness.

On a more general level it is suggested that the rights reflected in the ICESCR, while representing 'common ground around which members of the United Nations found agreement at a certain point in time,' nowadays 'appear somewhat removed from the realities of today's internally and externally open economy.'[108] The main reasons for this view appear to be that the right to own property as reflected in Article 17 UDHR is not included in the ICESCR, and that in terms of labour protections the ICESCR focuses unduly upon 'the situation of wage-earners who work in their own country and do not have family abroad.'[109] It is suggested that other 'rights', such as the 'right to engage in economic activity,' the 'right to trade,' the 'right to work in other countries (as incomplete as it is)', and the 'right to remit one's earnings to one's family at home,' warrant equal priority with the human rights enumerated in the ICESCR.[110]

This argument reveals the perils of considering the relevance of just one of many potentially applicable human rights instruments in isolation,[111] and of

---

[108] F Gianviti (2001) at 23.

[109] F Gianviti (2001) at 23.

[110] For a similar opinion regarding the limited relevance of human rights to perceived imperatives and rules of the market see E Petersmann, 'Human Rights and International Economic Law in the 21st Century: The Need to Clarify Their Inter-relationships' (2001) *Journal of International Economic Law* 3–39, 38; and E Petersmann, 'Time for a United Nations Action Program for Integrating Human Rights into the Law of Worldwide Organisations: Lessons from European Integration Law for Global Integration Law,' Paper prepared for International Seminar: 'Economic, Social and Cultural Rights in the Actions of the International Development Institutions,' Geneva, 7 May 2001 (on file with author) at 10: 'The [ICESCR] does not protect the economic freedoms, property rights, non-discriminatory conditions of competition and rule of law necessary for a welfare-increasing division of labour satisfying consumer demand through private investments and efficient supply of good, services and job opportunities. The [ICESCR's] social rights are therefore often criticised as a one-sided attempt at redistribution without proper balance among rights and obligations. In the [European Economic Community (EC) and European Economic Area (EA)], by contrast, free movements of goods, services, persons, capital and related payments and non-discriminatory conditions of competition are constitutionally protected as "fundamental rights." Indivisibility of political as well as economic freedom and responsibility, constitutional safeguards of non-discriminatory competition in the economy no less than in the polity, and social rights promoting a "social market economy," have become the hallmarks of postwar European integration law that should serve as models for worldwide integration law.' See also E Petersmann 'Time for a United Nations "Global Compact" for Integrating Human Rights into the Law of Worldwide Organisations: Lessons from European Integration', (2002) 13(3) *European Journal of International Law* 621–50. However on balance it must be considered doubtful how readily transposable these marketised 'fundamental rights' are in the global order, where the origins of human rights spring more clearly from elemental considerations of human dignity and humanity, rather than the dictates of the market. Criticisms of the ICESCR as embodying a 'one-sided attempt at redistribution,' rather than essential preconditions for human dignity and empowerment, seem particularly suspect. For strong criticisms see Howse, R, 'Human Rights in the WTO: Whose Rights? What Humanity? Comment on Petersmann' (2002) 13(3) *European Journal of International Law* 651–60; and Alston, P, 'Resisting the Merger and Acquisition of Human Rights by Trade Law: A Reply to Petersmann' (2002) 13(4) *European Journal of International Law* 815–44, and the discussion on http://www.ejil.org/forum_tradehumanrights/

[111] For example the Convention on the Protection of the Rights of All Migrant Workers and Members of their Families (GA Res 45/158, 18 December 1990; 'Migrant Workers Convention'), while as at July 2002 requiring one further instrument of ratification to enter into force, would be of clear relevance to the questions under review, to the (as yet unproven) extent that this Convention

underestimating the scope of application of established normative standards, properly construed.[112] There is also perhaps a deeper risk at stake, that of confusing legal rights or other kinds of instrumentally compelling claims with 'human rights' inherent to the fundamental worth and dignity of the human being. The General Counsel's position seems to pay insufficient heed to attributes of determinacy and authority embodied in the international human rights regime, safeguarded in no small measure through its resistance to unwarranted diffusion beyond a set of agreed standards—flexible yet determinate in nature—that are capable of being defended as universal. The reinforcement of ICESCR standards in more recent instruments such as the CRC (in addition to 'softer' declarations such as the 1993 World Conference on Human Rights and other such global events), as well as their proliferation in domestic constitutional arrangements, strengthens considerably their claim to contemporary relevance and universality. At a more fundamental level the General Counsel's objection might to some extent also to be based on the false premises that human rights (a) are capable or ought to be capable of providing clear and complete answers to complex macro-policy debates; and (b) are valid points of reference only to the extent of their instrumental—rather than inherent—value.

A number of points must also be made in connection with the General Counsel's interpretation of the relationship between the IMF and the UN under the UN Charter. The General Counsel places considerable reliance on an interpretation of Article 24 of the ICESCR in support of a proposition that the Covenant has no impact upon the Fund's Articles of Agreement. Article 24 (and its equivalent in the ICCPR, Article 46) provide: 'Nothing in the present Covenant shall be interpreted as impairing the provisions of the Charter of the United Nations and of the constitutions of the specialised agencies which define the respective responsibilities of the various organs of the United Nations and of the specialised agencies in regard to the matters dealt with in the present Covenant.' However only the most acontextualised and far-reaching interpretation of Article 24 would support the exculpatory effect claimed. As previously discussed the dominant and most persuasive argument to be advanced regarding the ICESCR's relevance to both the Bank and Fund is not the 'man of straw' that the Covenant is directly binding on them,[113] but that its provisions

---

embodies a contemporary consensus on the expectations and values contained therein. With a considerable degree of elaboration, the Migrant Workers Convention incorporates most of the fundamental rights expressed in the ICESCR, to that extent reinforcing rather than undermining them.

[112] For example, non-discriminatory application of the right to freedom of movement, the right to work, the right to an adequate standard of living, and equality before the law, are among the established human rights essential to the situation of migrant workers. Economic freedom is moreover an element of the right to work as reflected in Article 6 of the ICESCR.

[113] Cf F Gianviti (2001) at 7–9. By analogy, the author cites a number of authorities (at n 7 and accompanying text) for the proposition that 'the European Community is not bound by the provisions of the European Convention on Human Rights, although its members are party to the Convention.' However it also worth mentioning that the European Commission has taken the view that it could adhere to the European Convention on Human Rights, and that this would promote the protection of human rights in Europe. H Schermers and N Blokker (1995) at 1118.

constitute an authoritative interpretation of the fundamental human rights purposes in the UN Charter. This argument is nowhere dealt with, beyond the further straw man that the Fund is an independent body and not an 'agent' of the UN.[114] As far as Article 24 ICESCR is concerned it is difficult to imagine how—on an ordinary reading of material Charter provisions[115] and the generic provisions of the IFIs' Articles outlining their responsibilities vis-à-vis those of the UN—it could reasonably be claimed that the latter provisions could be 'impaired' by explicit recognition of ICESCR responsibilities within appropriate legal and policy parameters. To the contrary, the Committee on Economic, Social and Cultural Rights has made plain its expectations concerning IFI responsibility, unconstrained by an interpretation of Article 24 of the kind suggested by the General Counsel. In any case, it is clearly not a constraint insofar as the scope of application of other instruments such as the CRC is concerned.

Finally in terms of the doors left open, the General Counsel does appear to acknowledge the existence of an indirect and 'negative' obligation on the Fund, deriving from client states' direct obligations under the ICESCR, in line with a 'duty of vigilance' to ensure that the Fund's actions do not frustrate the implementation of the Covenant in the country concerned.[116] The General Counsel also indicates that major violations of economic, social and cultural rights sufficient to trigger 'civil unrest or a lack of foreign financing' would fall within the legitimate scope of 'preconditions' to be considered by the Fund prior to granting access to financial assistance.[117] Finally, the door is left ajar for the direct application to the Fund of obligations under customary international law and obligations *jus cogens* and *erga omnes*.[118] The General Counsel's caveats in this regard go questions of content (as excluding economic, social and cultural rights) and definition, rather than existence of obligations per se under these categories. However notable for its absence was any serious consideration of the scope of application of 'general principles' of international law, all the more

---

[114] F Gianviti (2001) at 9–10. The author concludes, based on an analysis of only one provision in each of the Fund's Articles and Relationship Agreement (Article X and Article I(2) respectively) that the Relationship Agreement 'does not require [the Fund] to give effect to resolutions of the United Nations, such as the resolutions under which the members of the General Assembly adopted the [UDHR] or Covenant, or to international agreements, such as the [ICESCR].' It is not clear why obligations regarding mutual consultation under Articles 3 and 4 of the Relationship Agreement were omitted in the context of a discussion on the Fund's independence, nor Article 63(2) of the Charter which provides that ECOSOC 'may co-ordinate the activities of the specialised agencies through consultation with and recommendations to such agencies and through recommendations to the General Assembly and to the members of the UN'.

[115] Articles 1, 55 and 56 in fact mandate collective responsibility for promotion of the human rights purposes of the Charter. Articles 57 and 63 don't define the parameters for cooperation in the economic and social spheres with any precision, however Article 103 prioritises Charter-based obligations over other agreements operating on the international sphere.

[116] F Gianviti (2001) at 17–18, nn 36–38 and accompanying text. The General Counsel's reservations (at 18) appear to go more to the practicalities of defining the duty, rather than the existence of the duty itself.

[117] F Gianviti (2001) at 30.

[118] F Gianviti (2001) at 11–12, nn 20–28 and accompanying text.

curious an omission in light of the relatively limited coverage of the other sources for relevant purposes.

To conclude, the General Counsel's presentation on 7 May 2001 marks a historic occasion in the legal lives of both the Bank and Fund. Taken in a positive light, the General Counsel's arguments (which one hopes may soon be published, if this has not already occurred prior to this book going to press) constitute a symbolic initial contribution towards staking out common parameters for international human rights legal argumentation, and a useful baseline for further debate. While a fuller critique of the General Counsel's paper is most certainly warranted, perhaps the most significant constraint on its utility for present purposes is that it is confined to a fairly conservative and contestable appraisal[119] of the legal effects on the Fund of just one of numerous relevant human rights instruments—the ICESCR. However in many respects that which was left unsaid was equally important to that which was stated. Whether expressly, impliedly, or perhaps through tacit or studied omission, the General Counsel's paper does help us to identify our common ground, and chart a clearer course towards resolving outstanding disagreements.

Inherent Sources of Authority: The 'Implied Powers' Doctrine

The point of departure for a consideration of the scope of inherent authority within the IFIs' Articles of Agreement is the decision of the ICJ in the *Reparations* case, briefly introduced earlier in the discussion on international legal personality. That case involved inter alia an exploration of the UN's international personality and capacity to operate on the international plane, based on a construction of the organisation's Charter-based functions in the area of international peace and security. The central question before the ICJ was whether the UN by implication from the United Nations Charter has powers to assure its agents limited protection in the performance of international peace and security obligations.[120] The ICJ did not consider it necessary to inquire as to whether the UN would be unable to perform its functions without the capacity to bring a claim on behalf of its agents; rather, it stated that 'to ensure efficient and independent performance of these missions and to afford effective support to its agents, the Organisation must provide them with adequate protection.'[121] In this and in other decisions the ICJ has generally demonstrated a liberal approach towards the finding of implied powers. The Court 'has done so

---

[119] As mentioned previously, the IMF's former Assistant General Counsel Herbert Morais prefers a more expansive interpretation, albeit unsupported to the same degree by detailed argumentation under international human rights law. H Morais (2000).

[120] On the question at issue in the *Reparations* case, reviewing relevant jurisprudence, Brownlie concludes that capacity of an international organisation to espouse claims depends upon: (1) on the existence of legal personality; and (2) on the interpretation of the constituent instrument in light of the purposes and functions of the particular organisation. I Brownlie (5th ed) (1998) at 685.

[121] ICJ Reports (1949), at 183.

where it can be shown that the power claimed relates to and is directed at achieving the purposes and functions given to the organisation by its constituent instrument. The Court has not sought to imply powers only from expressly given powers or from particular stated provisions of the constituent instrument but has implied powers by taking into account the general purposes of the organisation and the conditions of international life.'[122] Action that demonstrably contributes to the fulfilment of an organisation's purposes or that would promote the effectiveness of the institution in carrying out mandated functions has been regarded as being within the competence of the organisation as long as it is not expressly excluded.[123]

However more recently, in a departure from previous jurisprudence, the ICJ has revealed an inclination to interpret implied powers of specialised agencies narrowly. In the *WHO Nuclear Weapons Opinion*,[124] the Court was asked the following question: 'In view of the health and environmental effects, would the use of nuclear weapons by a State in war or other armed conflict be a breach of its obligations under international law including the WHO constitution?' A number of states objected to the admissibility of WHO's request, on the grounds that the question of the legality of nuclear weapons was not within the competence of the Organisation. By an 11:3 majority, the Court upheld those objections, and decided not to render an advisory opinion in respect of the WHO request.

This represents the first time in the ICJ's history that it has refused to render an advisory opinion requested of it.[125] Critical to this unusual result was the Court's finding that the question of the *legality* of nuclear weapons (rather than the *effects* of their use on health) was not one 'arising within the scope of the

---

[122] D Akande (1998) at 445, drawing from *Certain Expenses of the United Nations (Article 17, paragraph 2 of the Charter)*, Advisory Opinion, ICJ Reports (1962), 155 168; and *Effect of Award of Compensation Made by the United Administrative Tribunal Opinion*, ICJ Reports (1954) at 56–57. See also I Brownlie (5th ed) (1998) at 688: 'In practice the reference to implied powers may be linked to a principle of institutional effectiveness. . . . Judicial interpretation may lead to expansion of the competence of an organisation if resort be had to the teleological principle according to which action in accordance with stated purposes of an organisation is *intra vires* or at least is presumed to be. The view has also been expressed that, when the issue of interpretation relates to the constitution of an organisation, a flexible and effective approach is justifiable.' To similar effect see E Lauterpacht, 'The Development of the Law of International Organisations by the Decision of International Tribunals' (1976-IV) 152 *Receuil des Cours* 387, 430–32; B Sloan (1961) at 113–14; and G Fitzmaurice, 'The Law and Procedure of the International Court of Justice: Treaty Interpretation and Certain Other Treaty Points' (1951) 28 *British Yearbook of International Law* 18, 20.

[123] D Akande (1998) at 446.

[124] *Legality of the Use by a State of Nuclear Weapons in Armed Conflict* (Request by the World Health Organisation), *ICJ Reports*, 1996, p 66 [hereafter *WHO Opinion*]. On the same day, 6 July 1996, the ICJ handed down its opinion in *Legality of the Threat of Nuclear Weapons* (Request by the General Assembly), 35 *ILM* 809 and 1345 (1996). For a discussion of the issues on the merits of the General Assembly opinion see eg R Falk, 'Nuclear Weapons, International Law and the World Court: A Historic Encounter'(1997) 91 *American Journal of International Law* 64 ; D Akande, 'Nuclear Weapons—Unclear Law? Deciphering the *Nuclear Weapons Advisory Opinion*' (1997) 68 *British Yearbook of International Law* 165.

[125] D Akande (1998) at 439.

activities' of the WHO.[126] Following the *Reparations* case, the Court observed ⟍ that a grant of power to a specialised agency may either be express or implied from agency's constitution, but that 'such an implication may only be made where such powers are necessary for the fulfilment of duties entrusted to the organisation.'[127] However the Court expressed the view that the competence of international organisations is governed by the 'principle of speciality,' that is to say, 'they are invested by the States which create them with powers, the limits of which are a function of the common interests whose promotion those States entrust to them.'[128] The Court also placed considerable weight on its view of the 'logic of the overall system contemplated by the Charter,' according to which WHO's responsibilities were deemed to be limited to the sphere of public health, and should not be allowed to 'encroach on the responsibilities of other parts of the United Nations system.'[129] Further, the dismissal of the WHO's request in so far as it related to the scope of the obligations under its constitution even seems to go as far as to cast some doubt on the competence of specialised agencies to interpret their own constitutions.[130]

There are a number of criticisms to be made in relation to the reasoning of the majority. Very clearly, the *WHO Opinion* represents a striking departure from the *Reparations* case, *Certain Expenses* advisory opinion, and other ICJ jurisprudence concerning criteria for the implication of implied powers.[131] A less restrictive view, consistent with the preventive purposes of the WHO, would have permitted the WHO to engage in activities dealing with the 'legality' of *any* hazardous activity, including the use of nuclear weapons, where the focus is on prevention of harm to health.[132]

Further, and equally importantly, it is strongly arguable that the Court's 'logic' about the structure of the overall system contemplated by the UN Charter is out of step with the complexity of contemporary realities and problems. The

---

[126] On a construction of its Statute and relevant Charter provisions, the Court in fact held that three conditions must be satisfied before it has jurisdiction to consider a request for an advisory opinion submitted to it by a specialised agency: '(1) the agency requesting the opinion must be duly authorised, under the Charter, to request opinions from the Court; (2) the opinion requested must be on a legal question; and (3) this question must be one arising within the scope of the activities of the requesting agency'—paragraph 10 of the WHO Opinion, *ICJ Reports*, pp 71–72.

[127] D Akande (1998) at 443–44. See also J Alvarez (2001) at 121–23.

[128] Paragraph 25 of the WHO Opinion; ICJ Communiqué No. 96/22, 'Legality of the Use by a State of Nuclear Weapons in Armed Conflict (Request for Advisory Opinion by the World Health Organisation),' 8 July 1996 at 5.

[129] Paragraph 26 of the WHO Opinion. See also D Akande (1998) at 444.

[130] D Akande (1998) at 452–57. To contrary effect, in his dissenting opinion Judge Weeramantry states: 'I find it difficult to accept that an organ of the United Nations, empowered to seek an Advisory Opinion on a question of law, has no competence to seek an interpretation of its own Constitution'—WHO Opinion, *ICJ Reports*, 1996 at 128–29.

[131] D Akande (1998) at 444–46; N White, *The Law of International Organisations* (1996) at 128–31, 133; I Brownlie (1998) at 687–89.

[132] D Akande (1998) at 446–51. And as Akande also observes, the ICJ's ruling seems to have ignored Article 19 of the WHO Constitution, which expressly permits the WHO to promote conventions, and hence, concern itself with activities of a 'legal' nature.

assumption against overlap in the activities of specialised agencies is particularly suspect. As Akande observes:

> Care must . . . be taken in construing the powers of one organisation based on the powers of another organisation. To do this would be a reversal of the principle that an organisation can exercise its function to the full extent as long as its Statute does not impose restrictions on it, and a negation of the principle that the limits of the powers of an international organisation are a function of the common interests entrusted to that organisation. Indeed to suggest that one specialised agency cannot encroach on the responsibilities of others might even discourage co-operation between agencies . . . The underlying point is that it is better to adopt a broad, rather than narrow, construction of the competence of each international organisation. Such an approach would allow for a more complete attack on international problems.[133]

Ideally, the issues confronting the international system ought to define the structure of the responses, not the other way around. Against the institutional legacies of the UN system's functionalist origins,[134] the collective welfare of the global community would best be served by the UN and its specialised agencies being enabled to work together as a team, 'each helping the other with the special expertise that lies within its province,' rather than confining 'their vision within compartmentalised categories of exclusive activity.'[135]

Accordingly it is doubtful that the *WHO Opinion* has definitively displaced the 'principle of effectiveness' in future cases arising for the ICJ's consideration. The strength and consistency of the ICJ's previous jurisprudence is one important factor.[136] The strength of the *WHO Opinion* as a precedent on the question

---

[133] D Akande (1998) at 450–51.

[134] The leading advocates of functionalist theories of international cooperation in the post-World War II period included D Mitrany, *A Working Peace System: An Argument for the Functional Development of International Organisation* (1943); G Niemeyer, *Law Without Force* (1941); and E Haas, *Beyond the Nation State: Functionalism and International Organisation* (1964). The essential premise of functionalism for present purposes is that the role of international institutions should be the provision of services (eg food, health, employment), rather than fundamental unifying principles such as human rights, and moreover that responsibility for delivery of such services can be allocated in a decentralised or even 'polycentralised' fashion. For a critique of some of these assumptions see E Spiro (1979) at 154–57; J Gatthi, 'International Law and Eurocentricity: A Review Essay' (1988) 9 *European Journal of International Law* 184–211; P Alston, 'Making or Breaking Human Rights: The UN's Specialised Agencies and the Implementation of the International Covenant on Economic, Social and Cultural Rights' in *Human Rights and Development Working Papers, No 1, Anti-Slavery Society* (1979) 4–5; and in the particular context of the gradual fusion of human rights with development, J Gatthi, 'Good Governance as a Counter Insurgency Agenda to Oppositional and Transformative Social Projects in International Law' (1999) 5 *Buffalo Human Rights Law Review* 107, 133–41. See further discussion in chapter V below.

[135] Judge Weeramantry (dissenting), WHO Opinion at 170. Indeed Mitrany acknowledged that drawing unduly rigid boundaries around functional organisations posed the danger of stymieing effective cooperation on matters of mutual concern: D Mitrany (1943) at 43–44. For a similar view, critical of the majority decision in the WHO Opinion, see V Leary, 'The WHO Case: Implications for Specialised Agencies' in L Boisson de Chazournes and P Sands (eds), *International Law, the International Court of Justice and Nuclear Weapons* (1999) 112–27; and P Klein, 'Quelques reflections sur le principe de specialité et la 'politicisation' des institutions specialisés' in L Boisson de Chazournes and P Sands (eds) (1999) at 79–91.

[136] See the discussion above nn 120–23 and accompanying text.

at issue is not well served by a 'principle of specialty' that appears to hark back to the long-discredited functionalist origins of the UN system. The 'logic of the system' relied on by the majority ignores the manifold ways in which specialised agencies are in fact being compelled into closer functional relationships, addressing the complex demands of shared and evolving operational responsibilities. Moreover the principle of effectiveness remains very firmly established in municipal and regional legal systems, including the European Court of Justice,[137] with commensurate relevance to the content of 'general principles' of law binding at the international level.[138] With these factors in mind the 'principle of effectiveness' may continue to be regarded, although not without a measure of circumspection, as the material guide both for the implication of powers under the IFI's charters and for the purposes of interpretation under Article 31 of the Vienna Convention.[139]

The Reverse Side of the Coin: The IFIs as Normative Actors

Having regard to the dismissive—or at best restrictive—approach to human rights reflected in the IFIs' official writings and policy statements, one could sometimes be forgiven for imagining that the IFIs policies and activities stand outside the domain of international human rights law altogether. However nothing could be further from the truth.

With particular reference to the Bank, Boisson de Chazournes observes that the Bank's Operational Standards[140] 'create normative and procedural expectations for staff and partners of the Bank and contribute in many ways to forging

---

[137] Case 8/55, Fedechar, ECR 1954–1956, 299, cited in H Schermers and N Blokker (1995) at 160. Jurisprudence of the US Supreme Court is also relevant, eg *United States v Classic*, 313 US 299, 316 (1941), cited in J Alvarez (2001) at 148.

[138] See J Fawcett (1960) at 341–42 on the impacts on the Fund of 'general principles' derived from domestic legal systems.

[139] See J Gold. (1996) at 45, and above nn 6 and 19 and accompanying text.

[140] Operational Standards in this context can be taken to comprise the body of Operational Policies and Operational Directives ostensibly binding upon Bank staff. The 'Morse report', an independent review of the highly criticised 'Narmada' projects (referred to in chapter II), and the 'Wapenhans report', an internal review of Bank operations commissioned in the wake of the Morse report, both highlighted the need to strengthen the quality of the Bank's operations and to enhance transparency and accountability in project implementation. See B Morse and T Berger, *Sardar Sarovar: The Report of the Independent Review* (1992) ('the Morse report (1992)'); and World Bank Memorandum R92–125, 'Effective Implementation: Key to Development Impact,' 3 November 1992 ('Wapenhans report'). Compliance with operational standards was identified as a vital means for achieving these objectives. While discussed further in this chapter and chapter V, examples in terms of social and environmental content include the Environmental Assessment policy, Involuntary Resettlement policy, Indigenous Peoples policy, and policies dealing with the Involvement of Non-Governmental Organisations (NGOs) in Bank-supported Activities, and Disclosure of Operational Information. See L Boisson de Chazournes, 'Policy Guidance and Compliance: The World Bank Operational Standards' in D Shelton (ed), *Commitment and Compliance: The Role of Non-Binding Norms in the International Legal System* (2000) 281–303, 285–88.

and developing accepted practices under international law.'[141] This is said to occur through the incorporation of 'policy requirements'—including relevant Operational Standards—into loan conditions that the borrowing state is contractually bound to fulfil. Accompanied by any number of Bank safeguards against non-compliance, '[t]he policy requirements . . . become enforceable under international law like any other provision of a loan or credit agreement.'[142] The influence of Operational Standards can be leveraged further through co-financing arrangements with private consortia seeking to capitalise on the Bank's relative 'moral authority' and external credibility, thereby minimising their own investment risks.[143] The controversial Chad/Cameroon pipeline project approved by the Bank in the year 2000 is a good example of the Bank's 'moral guarantor' role, enabling it to exercise its policy influence out of all proportion to the volume of its lending.[144] Accordingly to the extent that these Operational Standards reflect or otherwise bear upon the scope of operation of international human rights standards, their enforceability as a matter of international law can have significant human rights normative implications.

The establishment in 1993 of the Inspection Panel[145] strengthens Task Managers' compliance—and indirectly, borrowing country compliance—with binding elements of the Bank's Operational Standards, thereby increasing the normative significance of the policies and the jurisprudence relating to their interpretation.[146] The normative implications are fundamental, as Bradlow states: '[The Panel] is the first forum in which private actors can hold an international organisation directly accountable for the consequences of its failure

---

[141] L Boisson de Chazournes (2000) at 289. See also D Kennedy, 'The Move to Institutions' (1987) 8 *Cardozo Law Review* 841, and J Alvarez (2001) at 138: 'Since 1945, thanks in significant part to the ways [in which] IO charters have been (flexibly) interpreted, most changes in international law have occurred within the framework of international organisations.'

[142] L Boisson de Chazournes (2000) at 289–90.

[143] See eg S Mahony, 'World Bank's Policies and Practice in Environmental Impact Assessment' (1995) 12 *Environmental and Planning Law Journal* 97–115. See also B Kingsbury, 'Operational Policies of International Institutions as Part of the Law-Making Process: The World Bank and Indigenous Peoples' in G Goodwin-Gill and S Talmon (eds), *The Reality of International Law: Essays in Honour of Ian Brownlie* (1999) 323–42, 336.

[144] World Bank, Project Description and Financing, The Chad-Cameroon Petroleum Development and Pipeline Project (Concept Paper) www.worldbank.org/afr/ccproj/concept.htm, visited April 2000. While the merits of the Bank's engagement in Chad continued to be debated throughout the year 2000, it is not without interest from a normative standpoint that the European Parliament, in a Resolution expressing its concern at political persecutions and instability and human rights violations in Chad, called upon the private consortium (consisting of Exxon, Petronas and Chevron) to proceed with the project only if the World Bank assessment was positive and if environmental, social, human rights and revenue management guarantees were taken. European Parliament Resolution on Chad, 44/PE 270.314 (18 June 1998). For a fuller critique see G Hernandez Uriz, 'To Lend or Not to Lend: Oil, Human Rights, and the World Bank's Internal Contradictions' (2001) 14 *Harvard Human Rights Journal* 197.

[145] See above chapter III at n 57 and accompanying text. While as at 2000 the Panel had completed only two investigations under the Resolution establishing it, nonetheless the fact of its establishment had already at that time 'encouraged a Bank-wide process that can help clarify for the staff and management the content of operational policies and procedures and increase their awareness of the need for compliance with them.' L Boisson de Chazournes (2000) at 293.

[146] B Kingsbury (1999) at 332.

to follow its own rules and procedures. The Executive Directors' decision, therefore, constitutes the first formal acknowledgement that international organisations have a legally significant non-contractual relationship with private parties that is independent of either the organisation's or the private actor's relationship with a member state.'[147] With the establishment of similar grievance mechanisms across a range of other international financial institutions,[148] the Panel's normative significance and influence should not be understated.

Certain of the Bank's policy statements and Operational Standards make specific reference to international instruments,[149] thereby promoting respect for them. The Bank's policy of not financing projects which contravene borrowers' international environmental obligations,[150] along with the reinforcement of international principles and rules as 'best practices' to be followed,[151] speak further to the importance of the Bank's international normative role. The Bank has also directly supported certain international environmental treaties with specific projects throughout the world. For example the Bank financed the 'Thailand Forestry Project' in support of the Biodiversity Treaty (which itself was reported to have been ratified by Thailand in exchange for Bank financing to aid in the promotion of biodiversity in Thailand),[152] and initiated the Carbon Investment Fund to invest in projects that result in carbon offsets consistent with the Kyoto Protocol.[153] The Bank also acts as one of the four implementing agencies of the Multilateral Fund for the Implementation of the Montreal Protocol, which

---

[147] D Bradlow (1994) at 554.

[148] For example, the office of the Compliance Advisor Ombudsman at the IFC, although the powers of that office are more focused upon conciliation and arbitration.

[149] Good examples are the Operational Policy 4.20 on Indigenous Peoples, and the Bank's emerging policy on child labour, both of which will be discussed in more detail shortly.

[150] This policy originates in Operational Manual Statement (OMS) 2.36 on Environmental Aspects of the Bank's Work (1984), providing inter alia that the Bank 'will not finance projects that contravene any international environmental agreements to which they are a party.' The principal binding statement is now found in Operational Policy 4.01 on Environmental Assessment: '[Environmental Assessment, or EA] . . . takes into account the obligations of the country, pertaining to project activities, under relevant international environmental treaties and agreements. The Bank does not finance project activities that would contravene such country obligations, as identified during the EA.' See also Opertational Policy 4.36 on Forestry: 'Governments must also commit to adhere to their obligations as set forth in relevant international instruments to which they are a party.'

[151] L Boisson de Chazournes (2000) at 298. The concrete examples given by Boisson de Chazournes are the Bank's reference in its Operational Policy on 'management of cultural property in Bank-financed projects' to borrower obligations under the 1972 Convention Concerning the Protection of the World Cultural and Natural Heritage, and the reference in the Operational Policy on pest management to FAO Guidelines for Packing and Storing Pesticides and the Guidelines on Good Labelling Practice for Pesticides. However there is no reason in principle why international conventions and 'softer' instruments in the human rights sphere or any other area bearing upon sustainable development concerns could not also be invoked or promoted in this fashion.

[152] C Di Leva, 'International Law and Development' (1998) 10 *Georgia International Environmental Law* Review 501, 508.

[153] T Roessler, 'The World Bank's Lending Policy and Environmental Standards' (2000) 26 *The North Carolina Journal of International Law and Environmental Regulation*,' 105–41, 129.

assists developing countries in reducing their consumption of ozone-depleting substances.[154]

Furthermore, while as yet unsupported by the practice and jurisprudence of the Inspection Panel, the influential report of Morse and Berger in 1992 established an important precedent in arguing that Operational Standards should be appreciated and applied in the context of wider public international law standards to which they relate.[155] The Inspection Panel in the highly publicised 'China Western Poverty Alleviation Project' (Qinghai) case appeared to go some way towards interpreting material provisions of OD 4.20 in light of its underlying international human rights law purposes.[156] Moreover international human rights law is arguably relevant to the determination of claims against the Bank and Fund under national or international law,[157] although as at 2002 this potential had not been widely tested.

The Bank as an influential policy actor on the international plane exerts varying degrees of influence on the development of specific international human rights instruments,[158] and its policy influence (principally through Operational Standards) in borrowing countries constitutes a means by which new patterns

---

[154] T Roessler (2000) at 129.

[155] Morse report (1992) at 78, discussed in B Kingsbury (1999) at 330. In the Morse report, with reference to the standards in ILO Convention 107 concerning tribal peoples, it was argued: 'The Bank's principles with respect to tribal peoples arose from a concern for human rights. Failure to design or implement policies that put these principles into effect places these rights at risk.'

[156] Investigation Report of the World Bank Inspection Panel, 'The Qinghai Project: A Component of the China: Western Poverty Reduction Project (Credit No. 3255-CHA and Loan No 4501-CHA),' 28 April 2000, at xxvi–xxvii. In rejecting Management's submission that the 'project as a whole' could constitute an 'Indigenous Peoples Development Plan' under OD 4.20, the Panel adopted a purposive approach to the interpretation of OD 4.20, contruing relevant provisions in light of OD 4.20's purpose which was 'to ensure that the development process fosters full respect for their dignity, human rights and cultural uniqueness,' and to 'ensure that indigenous peoples do not suffer adverse effects during the development process . . . , and that they receive culturally acceptable social and economic benefits.'

[157] As Kingsbury explains in the context of indigenous peoples' rights: 'While the Bank argues that it bears no liability in municipal courts for problems caused by the projects it finances, suits filed against the Bank in Argentina on behalf of persons detrimentally affected by Bank-financed projects have attracted some judicial sympathy, and increasing pressure for such a liability regime may be envisaged in egregious cases, perhaps relying on tort law or breach of a fiduciary duty. International responsibility is also conceivable, possibly in connection with a borrowing state, for example, in a diplomatic protection claim where people in a neighbouring state suffer from a Bank-approved project. Violation of an internationally accepted standard such as ILO Convention 169 may be relevant to the appreciation of such claims under national or international law, certainly where the borrowing or guaranteeing state is a party.' B Kingsbury (1999) at 327. On the general issue of the IFIs' international personality and scope for liability under international human rights law see P Klein, *La responsabilité des organisations internationales dans les ordres juridiques internes et en droit des gens* (1998); F Hand, 'The Legal Mandate of Multilateral Development Banks as Agents for Change Towards Sustainable Development,' 92 *American Journal of International Law* 642; and on general principles of privilege and immunity: C Amerasinghe, *Principles of the International Law of International Organisations* (1996) 370, 375–79, and H Schermers and N Blokker (1995) at 1003–12.

[158] ILO Convention No. 162 (1998) on extreme forms of child labour is said to be a good example, said to reflect the Bank's policy priorities concerning child labour more clearly and succinctly than the more complex and politically challenging CRC. Interviews in Washington DC in February 2000.

of behaviour are shaped, with a bearing on the emergence or consolidation of international practices which may acquire the status of customary norms[159] or general principles of international law. Three examples of this phenomenon are worth mentioning, all on the level of process-oriented standards. Firstly, since its introduction in 1989 the Bank's Environmental Assessment policy has served as a legislative model not only at the national level, but also for multilateral development banks (including the Inter-American Development Bank, Asian Development Bank, and European Bank for Reconstruction and Development), bilateral donor and private sector assistance and investment activities.[160] It reportedly also 'helped pave the way for the inclusion in the [1992] Rio Declaration on Environment and Development of an "Environmental Impact Assessment" requirement as a national instrument.'[161] Secondly, the requirement by both Bank and Fund for public participation or meaningful consultation, however unimpressive the overall track record on implementation might be to date, contributes to emerging expectations and patterns of behaviour with potential normative implications.[162]

Thirdly, in an illustration with strong human rights implications, in May 1997 the Bank distributed a discussion draft of a publication called 'Handbook on Good Practices for Laws Relating to Non-Governmental Organisations.'[163]

---

[159] L Boisson de Chazournes (2000) at 299. See M Shaw, *International Law* (4th ed) (1997) 65 on the potential for international organisations to contribute to the formation of customary international law.

[160] L Boisson de Chazournes (2000) at 299. See also M Bekhechi, 'Some Observations Regarding Environmental Covenants and Conditionalities in World Bank Lending Activities' (1999) 3 *Max Planck United Nations Year Book* 287, 300–1: '[The] practice of inclusion of environmental [assessment] covenants into legal agreements between the World Bank and its borrower countries has greatly assisted in the recognition and the strengthening of a new general principle of international law.'

[161] L Boisson de Chazournes (2000) at 299. Moreover at 299–300: 'Such cross-fertilisation also can be seen in respect of the requirement that riparian countries of an international watercourse be notified in cases of planned measures or projects financed by the Bank. The application of the Bank policy on international waterways [OP 7.50 International Waterways (October 1994)] has contributed significantly to the recognition of this procedural requirement in general international law and to its codification in the UN Convention on the Law of the Non-Navigational Uses of International Watercourses. Such a practice highlights the composite nature of the norm-creating process whereby non-legally binding instruments and policy instruments, such as the Bank Operational Standards, play a role in the formation and development of an international customary norm, enabling *lex ferenda* to become *lex lata*.'

[162] L Boisson de Chazournes (2000) at 300–1: 'The Bank's calls for public participation are numerous, including public consultation of affected people and local NGOs about a project's environmental aspects [OP 4.01 on Environmental Assessment, para 15], community participation and consultations with people affected by a resettlement [OP 4.30 on Involuntary Resettlement, paras 7–10], informed participation of indigenous populations [OP 4.20 on Indigenous Peoples, para 8], and involvement of local groups in the planning, designing, implementing, and monitoring of projects related to the protection of natural habitats [OP 4.04 on Natural Habitats, para 10], or in forestry and conservation management activities [OP 4.36 on Forestry, para 1(c)]. There is no doubt that these policy prescriptions, which are operationalised in the Bank's activities, contribute to a large extent to the development of international rules and standards.'

[163] World Bank, 'Handbook on Good Practices for Laws Relating to Non-Governmental Organisations,' Discussion Draft (May 1997).

With the objective of encouraging governments to facilitate NGO growth and development, the draft Handbook embodied the Bank's attempt to articulate a coherent and principled legal framework for NGO activities at the national level. Interestingly three of its six rationales for this exercise were human rights-related: (1) to implement the freedoms of association and expression; (2) to encourage pluralism and tolerance; and (3) to promote social stability and the rule of law.[164] In this connection the Bank rightly recognised that in order for it to be able to work successfully with NGOs, it is essential that prospective NGO partners be 'freely established and operate without undue constraints; that such NGOs be independent of the government; and be transparent and account-able.'[165] Further, '(o)nly if all segments of society that are or might be involved in projects financed by the Bank can create and operate NGOs freely will the NGO sector reflect the full range of relevant viewpoints and expertise pertinent to a wide variety of development projects.'[166]

The handbook included detailed technical discussions on the content of the right to freedom of association. However numerous criticisms were levelled at the Bank's interpretation, on the grounds that the Bank ignored key elements of the right to freedom of association under international human rights law, pre-scribing an overly-regulatory approach with clear potential for restricting—rather than facilitating—the scope of NGO activity at country level.[167] But interestingly, notwithstanding that the Bank's interpretation of relevant human rights was contestable and that the 1997 consultation draft handbook self-evidently reflected neither official policy nor concluded views on relevant questions of interpretation, there was evidence as at 1999 that a number of borrowing countries had begun to act in reliance upon the content of the con-sultation draft in setting out to draft laws in accordance with its terms.[168]

The general thrust of the preceding survey is *not* that the Bank, having begun to exert its influence on the development of international administrative and

---

[164] World Bank (May 1997) at 9–18.

[165] World Bank (May 1997) at 2.

[166] World Bank (May 1997) at 2. Furthermore at 62–63: 'It is difficult to imagine that NGOs can participate in development as the independent voice of affected groups unless there are sound laws that permit them to be established easily and that protect their right to engage robustly in research, education, and advocacy, even when that means criticizing or opposing government policies or actions. It is also difficult to imagine a legal environment in which NGOs are allowed to participate fully in the selection, design, and implementation of development projects that did not also allow them wide freedom to criticize other policies and actions of government.'

[167] Cf Lawyers Committee for Human Rights, *The Neglected Right: Freedom of Association in International Human Rights Law* (October 1997). Lawyers Committee for Human Rights was a lead critic, and participant, in this context. Interviews in Washington DC and New York in March and April 1999.

[168] Interviews in Washington DC and New York in March and April 1999. On a broader level Kingsbury observers that 'borrowing states, pushed by the World Bank to apply specified standards for resettlement design and compensation, and often supplied with technical assistance from outside to craft the necessary internal measures, frequently adopt World Bank standards as national legal requirements for all projects, even projects in which the Bank is not involved.' Furthermore 'affected groups and NGOs may seize on these standards as defining what is right and minimally fair.' B Kingsbury (1999) at 339.

human rights law in some respects, is thereby bound to wade into a potentially limitless range of related areas as well. Defining the desired limits of engagement is indeed a key challenge, however for the purposes of the present discussion the point is merely to expose the present and potential extent of the Bank's *de facto* law-making role in human rights-related fields, as part of the context in which objections founded on the putative irrelevance of international human rights law to the Bank's work should be criticised.

In principle, if not quite to the same degree, the same argument applies in relation to the Fund.[169] While having nowhere near the Bank's depth and range of engagement with human rights policy issues, and as at 2002 continuing to resist pressures for the adoption of explicit human rights policies, impact statements, and the like, institutional reforms towards enhanced accountability (both internal and external) and transparency—through the considerable policy leverage exerted by the Fund—do have a bearing on the manner in which international norms in those areas might evolve, whether positively or negatively.[170] The formation of an Independent Evaluation Office (IEO),[171] and incremental steps towards transparency of decision-making and public consultation on significant policy matters, are relevant influences in the progressive development of an entitlement in international administrative law that those interested or affected by decisions of the Fund should have an opportunity to be heard.[172] Pressure for the creation of an Ombudsman's Office for the benefit of those adversely affected by a Fund decision or Fund-sponsored program might strengthen the

---

[169] See eg J Alvarez (2001) at 138: 'The many "soft" and hard law obligations of good conduct governing . . . monetary relations . . . can scarcely be understood without an account of the work of . . . the IMF[.] To modern lawyers, the contention that the evolution of custom remains dependent on the initiative and subsequent reaction of individual states seems strikingly out of date, since it ignores the way in which states have had to react to IO activity, and the way in which even their inaction in the face of that activity has affected the relevant rules.'

[170] By analogy with Kingsbury's discussion of the Inspection Panel's policy compliance role: '[i]nternal compliance debates among Bank staff with competing interests . . . increase (or decrease) the normative quality attributed to [operational policies], and thus may come to shape preferences and values.' B Kingsbury (1999) at 338.

[171] This is discussed in more detail in chapter VI.

[172] Such a normative development might be envisaged by analogy with Kingsbury's appraisal of the Bank's consultative practices on policies concerning indigenous peoples: 'Bank staff compiled and distributed reasonably full reports made in [local and regional consultation workshops], and endeavoured to provide reasons for incorporating or not incorporating significant proposals in the revised draft. The process thus bears some resemblance to the "notice and comment" required of certain US government rule-making agencies by the Administrative Procedure Act (USA), and is animated by some of the same principles. Although the process could usefully be further refined and strengthened, its format is an overdue recognition that groups whose interests are seriously affected by a policy ought to be heard in the rule-making process.' Kingsbury, B. (1999) at 325. On the contributions to international administrative law of 'general principles' derived from both municipal and international sources see A Amerasinghe, 'Sources of International Administrative Law' in A Guiffrè (ed), *International law at the Time of its Codification: Essays in Honour of Roberto Ago* (1987) 67–95, 85, 88. And on the contributions of *jus cogens*—or 'foundational' international administrative law—see C Amerasinghe, 'The Future of International Administrative Law' (1996) 45 *International and Comparative Law Quarterly* 773–95, 789, citing the principles of non-retroactivity, non-discrimination, and a (perhaps qualified) prohibition on general reduction of salaries.

development of the law in these areas still, along with further needed reforms in the areas of information disclosure and accountability at Board level, to be discussed more fully in chapter VI.

But however international norms in these areas evolve, and whether they bear directly or indirectly on the development of international human rights norms, the bottom line is that the IFI's (and as at 2002 the Bank in particular) have a very important—if understated and not fully understood—role in their evolution.[173] To this extent the Bank and Fund cannot reasonably 'aprobate and reprobate,' disavowing the relevance of international human rights law to their work, while at the same time—deliberately or otherwise—continuing to shape their progressive development.

THE MEANING OF THE 'POLITICAL PROHIBITION' IN THE BANK'S ARTICLES

Interestingly neither the IBRD's nor the IDA's Articles define the term 'development' for the purposes of their collective development mission, and for the purposes of Article 31 of the Vienna Convention. As independent specialised agencies of the UN, the IBRD and IDA consider their mandates to be limited to 'economic' aspects of the international development process, as will shortly be seen. Given that the Bank formally acknowledges the internationally accepted conception of development as a complex and long-term process with inter-related human rights, economic, political and social dimensions, the implication from this is that all non-'economic' activities fall beyond the scope of their permissible activities.[174]

The principal provision in this regard is Article IV, Section 10, of the IBRD Articles, which provides:

> The Bank and its officers shall not interfere in the political affairs of any member; nor shall they be influenced in their decisions by the political character of the member or members concerned. Only economic considerations shall be relevant to their decisions, and these considerations shall be weighed impartially in order to achieve the purposes stated in Article I.[175]

Further, the IBRD Articles oblige the Bank to ensure that funds loaned will only be used for the purposes for which they were loaned, '. . . with due attention to considerations of economy and efficiency and without regard to political or

---

[173] On a juridical level Kingsbury questions whether the sources of international law embodied in Article 38(1) of the Statute of the International Court of Justice 'sufficiently take account of . . . the notion that international law is not shaped just by the interactions of states, but also by the inter-actions between states . . . and international organisations.' B Kingsbury (1999) at 339.

[174] D Bradlow (1996) at 53–54.

[175] IBRD Articles, Article IV, Section 10. See chapter II, above n 5 for the purposes of the IBRD as stated in Article I. The IDA Articles contain equivalent provisions: see Articles I and V (Section 6) of the IDA Articles.

other non-economic influences or considerations.'[176] The Articles also state that the President, staff and officers of the Bank owe their duty to the Bank and '. . . to no other authority. Each member of the Bank shall respect the international character of his duty and shall refrain from all attempts to influence any of them in the discharge of their duties.'[177]

Hence, it can be seen that the Articles presume a clear delineation between what is 'economic' and within power, and what is 'political' and beyond power. The terms 'economic considerations' (and conversely, 'political or non-economic influences or considerations'), 'political affairs,' and 'political character' (of a member State) are not defined in either the IBRD or IDA Articles.

In the absence of any specific guidance the result is that the Bank itself is left to decide the scope of the term 'economic considerations,' and hence the width of its mandate, and conversely what matters should be excluded as 'political.' Accordingly, consistent with the approach reflected in Article 31(3)(b) of the Vienna Convention, the next step is to consider 'subsequent practice in the application of [the IBRD and IDA Articles of Association] which establishes the agreement of the parties regarding [their] interpretation[.]'[178] Following that discussion, brief consideration is also given to the 'preparatory work of the [IBRD and IDA Articles] and circumstances of [their] conclusion,' in light of the provisions of Article 32 of the Vienna Convention.

The Portuguese and South African Loan Controversies

The Bank's early views concerning the breadth of its mandate were aired in the 1960s during the course of the Portuguese and South African loan controversies. In December 1965 the UN General Assembly adopted two resolutions calling upon 'the specialised agencies of the UN to take necessary steps to deny technical and economic assistance' to the governments of South Africa and Portugal because their respective apartheid and colonial policies were in violation of the UN Charter.[179] The General Assembly's requests were renewed in 1967, at which time the World Bank was in the process of evaluating loan proposals for both countries.[180] While the loans were still pending, the then IBRD President

---

[176] IBRD Articles, Article III, Section 5(b); IDA Articles, Article V, Section 1(g).

[177] IBRD Articles, Article V, Section 5(c); IDA Articles, Article IV, Section 5(c).

[178] Vienna Convention, Article 31(3)(b). See the discussion earlier in this chapter on the criteria regulating the probative value of 'institutional practice' for interpretive purposes.

[179] 'The Policies of the Apartheid Government of the Republic of South Africa,' GA Res 2054 A (XX), 20 UN GAOR, Supp. (No. 14) 16, UN Doc. A/6014 (1966); 'Implementation of the Declaration on th Granting of Independence to Colonial Countries' Peoples,' GA Res. 2105 (XX), 20 UN GAOR, Supp. (No. 14) 16, UN Doc. A/6014 (1966), cited in Lawyers Committee for Human Rights (1995) at 28.

[180] 'The Question of Territories Under Portuguese Administration,' GA Res 2270 (XXII), 22 UN GAOR, Supp. (No 16) 47–48, UN Doc. A/6908 (1967), at para 13; 'The Policies of Apartheid of the Government of the Republic of South Africa,' GA Res. 2307 (XXII), 22 UN GAOR, Supp. (No 16) 19, UN Doc. A/6716 (1967), at para 7, cited in Lawyers Committee for Human Rights (1995) at 28.

circulated the UN Resolutions to the Bank's Executive Directors, with a statement in the following terms:

> [T]he Bank's Articles provide that the Bank and its officers shall not interfere in the
> political affairs of any member and that they shall not be influenced in their decisions
> by the political character of the member or members concerned. Only economic con-
> siderations are to be relevant to their decisions. Therefore, I propose to continue to
> treat requests for loans from these countries in the same manner as applications from
> other countries . . . I am aware that the situation in Africa could affect the economic
> development, foreign trade and finances of Portugal and South Africa. It will therefore
> be necessary in reviewing the economic condition and prospects of these countries to
> take account of the situation as it develops.[181]

When invited by the General Assembly to explain why the Bank could not comply with the Resolutions, the IBRD General Counsel argued that the 'political'
prohibition in the Bank's Articles had two purposes. Firstly, to prevent the
possibility of using Bank financing as leverage against any Bank member in
order to advance the political aims of any other member or group of members.
Secondly, to assure the private capital markets that economic, rather than political, considerations would guide the Bank's financial decisions.[182] The UN legal
counsel rejected the IBRD's contentions, expressing doubt that Article IV of the
IBRD Articles 'was intended to preclude considerations dealt with in the [South
African and Portuguese] resolutions which involved international obligations
under the Charter.'[183] The UN legal counsel expressed the view that the first
sentence of Article IV, Section 10 'would appear to have as its purpose the prohibition of interference in the internal political affairs of a Member State and of
discrimination against a State because of the political character of its
Government. [The counsel] doubted very much that the sentence was intended
to relate to criteria involving international conduct of a State affecting its fundamental Charter obligations.'[184]

While not taking issue with the Bank on the underlying assumption of development as a quintessentially 'economic' activity, the practical implications
flowing from the UN opinion could be quite far reaching, depending upon interpretation. Specifically, to restrict the 'political' prohibition to the degree necessary to permit (or even mandate) the consideration of borrowing State
compliance with its 'fundamental Charter obligations,' including human rights

---

[181] Statement of IBRD President Woods to Executive Directors on 29 March 1966, in statement
of IBRD General Counsel to UN Fourth Committee, 21 UN GAOR, C.4 (1645th mtg.) 317–18
(1966), reprinted in 13 M Whiteman, *Digest of International Law* (1968) at 728, cited in Lawyers
Committee for Human Rights (1995) at 28–29.

[182] See D Bradlow (1996) at 55; Lawyers Committee for Human Rights (1995) at 29.

[183] 21 UN GAOR 4-20, UN Doc. A/C.4 SR 1653 (prov. ed. 1966), reprinted in (1967) 6
International Law Materials 171, 172, cited in Lawyers Committee for Human Rights (1995) at 29.

[184] 21 UN GAOR 4-20, UN Doc. A/C.4 SR 1653 (prov. ed. 1966), reprinted in (1967) 6
International Law Materials 171, 172, cited in Lawyers Committee for Human Rights (1995) at
29–30. The UN legal counsel's interpretation finds support in the drafting history of Article IV,
Section 10. See nn 261–70 below and accompanying text.

obligations under Article 55 of the Charter, would in principle empower the Bank to deny loan applications on the basis of human rights violations.[185]

However the Bank adhered to its own expansive interpretation of the 'political' prohibition during the Portuguese and South African loan controversy, and maintained its refusal to comply with the General Assembly resolutions. This was entirely consistent with the Bank's understanding during the 1960s of 'development' being equated only with economic growth. On this understanding, the term 'economic considerations' in the Bank's Articles were taken to include 'only those issues that were directly relevant to the financial and technical feasibility of the projects [the Bank] was funding and to the project's impact on the economic growth potential of the Member State.'[186] Among the attractions of this restrictive view, at least from the Bank's perspective, were that the sovereignty of the borrowing State remained inviolate, and difficult political judgements in such matters as allocation of project priorities and sharing of costs and benefits could be left entirely to the borrowing State.[187]

The Mandate Expands

The Bank's highly restrictive interpretation of the term 'economic considerations,' and its expansive view of the political prohibition, have ultimately not proved to be sustainable. Lessons of experience have guided the Bank's thinking away from narrow GDP and economic growth-based lending and infrastructure projects, towards a complex multi-faceted vision embracing development in all its political, social, economic and cultural dimensions. The Bank's focus on activities relating to health, education, agriculture and housing grew from the 'basic human needs' dogma of the 1970s, but in an evolved form remains of central relevance to its present development objectives.[188] In line with research and

---

[185] N Moller (1997) at 24–25. For an argument purporting to compel the Bank to incorporate human rights considerations into its lending criteria, see V Mamorstein, 'World Bank Power to Consider Human Rights Factors in Loan Decisions' (1978) 13 *Journal of International Law and Economics* 113.

[186] D Bradlow (1996) at 55.

[187] D Bradlow (1996) at 55.

[188] For a discussion see E Mason and R Asher, *The World Bank Since Bretton Woods* (1973). As at 1997 the Bank defined its 'fundamental objective' as 'help[ing] client countries reduce poverty and improve living standards through a strategy of inclusive development. The first element of this strategy . . . involves policies to promote broad-based, labour-demanding growth and increase the productivity and economic opportunities of the poor. The second element incorporates policies and institutions to improve access to social services, particularly in basic education, primary health care, and nutrition . . . The Third element comprises safety nets and poverty-targeted programs for those who cannot take advantage of income-earning opportunities or who are heavily risk-prone'— World Bank, *Poverty Reduction and the World Bank: Progress in Fiscal 1996 and 1997* (1997) at 1. For a more up-to-date statement of the Bank's anti-poverty philosophy and policy see World Bank, *World Development Report 2000/2001: Attacking Poverty: Opportunity, Empowerment, and Security* (2001).

numerous external impetuses,[189] a number of further dimensions were added to its list of permissible operations, such as policy-based lending, environmental concerns, and gender dimensions.[190] As was seen in chapter II, the Bank's understanding of development problems expanded in the 1990s to embrace governance, participation, economic transformation, and private sector development.[191] Naturally this expansion has been associated with a commensurate increase in complexity of the decisions required to be made, and a ratcheting up of the Bank's involvement and influence in the affairs of some of its member States.[192] The inter-relatedness of these issues has helped to break down the distinction that the international community has sought to maintain between 'domestic' and 'international' issues.[193]

The Bank's Mandate Revisited: The Political Prohibition and the 'Direct and Obvious' Test

Consistent with its growing, albeit selective, appreciation of human rights' relevance, the Bank's legal department has reviewed its position concerning the political prohibition in the Bank's mandate. The mandate has been creatively 'stretched' to include attention to human rights and popular participation, but without 'distorting' its Articles of Agreement, and without conceding that all human rights can be considered.[194] In the former General Counsel's view, '[w]hile the *purposes* of the Bank are exhaustively stated, the *functions* which allow the Bank to serve such purposes may be expanded as deemed necessary or desirable.'[195]

---

[189] The driving forces included environmental and social disasters arising from major infrastructure projects. See eg Morse report (1992).

[190] D Bradlow (1996) at 56.

[191] D Bradlow (1996) at 56.

[192] As former Bank Chief Counsel (and Assistant General Counsel at the IMF) Herbert Morais put it: '[T]he IFIs have have, over the years, significantly expanded the scope of activities that they finance, covering such politically sensitive areas as reform of the civil service, reform of public sector enterprises, legal and judicial reform, reform of local governments, land titling and registration reform, combating corruption, the rights of indigenous peoples and minorities, the rights of people displaced or resettled as a result of projects funded by the international development banks, family planning, and enhancing the rights of women.' H Morais (2000) at 89.

[193] D Bradlow. and C Grossman (1995) at 415. As Bradlow and Grossman observe (at 415): 'It is now almost impossible to find problems that do not have both domestic and international dimensions. In fact, problems have become transnationalised. A proper resolution to each problem, therefore, requires action on both the local and global level.' See also C Grossman and D Bradlow, 'Are We Being Propelled Towards a People-Centred Transnational Legal Order?' (1993) 9 *American University Journal of International Law and Policy* 1.

[194] D Gillies, 'Human Rights, Democracy and Good Governance: Stretching the World Bank's Policy Frontiers' in J Griesgraber and B Gunter (eds), *The World Bank: Lending on a Global Scale* (1996) 101 at 120.

[195] I Shihata, *Issues of 'Governance' in Borrowing Members: The Extent of Their Relevance Under the Bank's Articles of Agreement* (1990) at 13; I Shihata, 'Democracy and Development' (unpublished paper with author) (1996) at 6.

In distinguishing between 'economic' and 'political' factors to date, the legal department has looked at the 'impact the factor has on considerations of efficiency and economy.'[196] On this basis, former General Counsel Shihata defined 'economic factor' within the meaning of the Bank's Articles as any factor which has a 'direct and obvious economic effect relevant to the [Bank's] work.'[197] Further, in order to determine whether the economic effect of a particular factor in a Bank operation is 'direct and obvious,' the economic effect must be: (1) clear and unequivocal; (2) preponderant; and (3) when the issue is associated with political actions or events, the economic effect 'must be of such impact and relevance as to make [it] a Bank concern.'[198]

For the purposes just outlined, the Bank's former General Counsel attempted to define the term 'political' as going to 'the art and practice of running a country or governing.'[199] Political factors would include 'those factors that would require the Bank to take a side in the political system of its Borrower States, such as favouring one political party over another.'[200] The suggested definition would also include 'considerations which might result in Bank decisions being influenced by the principles, opinions, or beliefs of the people or parties holding power in its Member States,' but would not embrace 'such typical economic and technical issues as the "management of money or the finances" or more generally the *efficient* management of the country's resources.'[201] However as the succeeding sections of this chapter will reveal, these suggested limitations have in large measure either been honoured in the breach, or alternatively interpreted in a highly permissive fashion.

Consistency of Human Rights Principles with Instrumental Development Rationales

'Euphemism creep' in development seems to have accelerated over the last several years. 'Participation' and 'empowerment' are core by-words in development policy as preached at the Bank and key development and bilateral donor agencies, justified by lessons of development experience, even if actual programmatic implementation remains uneven at best. Both of those concepts have strong, even if frequently unstated, legal and moral foundations in human rights standards. DFID relies upon Articles 19–21 and 23 of the UDHR as a basis for

---

[196] D Bradlow (1996) at 60.

[197] I Shihata, *The World Bank in a Changing World: Selected Essays* (1995) at 53–97, cited in D Bradlow (1996) at 60.

[198] D Bradlow (1996) at 60; see also I Shihata, 'The World Bank and Non-Governmental Organisations' (1992) 25 *Cornell International Law Journal* 623.

[199] D Bradlow (1996) at 60.

[200] D Bradlow (1996) at 60. Naturally this might give rise to theoretical if not practical tensions, to the extent that—as Amartya Sen counsels—viable political opposition groups form an essential part of an enabling environment for development. See chapter II above, n 85 and accompanying text.

[201] D Bradlow (1996) at 60.

its concerns with participation,[202] and points to links with decentralised governance structures in that regard, providing that 'it takes place within the context of a political framework which promotes the equal rights of all people.'[203] Furthermore one could point to clearly binding equivalent provisions of the ICCPR and ICESCR,[204] and the right of children under Article 12 of the CRC to participate in decisions concerning them, to the extent of their evolving capacities, and similar rights and anti-discrimination guarantees in CEDAW and ICERD.[205]

The concept of 'empowerment' is closely linked to participation both in a normative and functional sense. The Bank's recently published 'Empowerment Sourcebook' reflects possibly the most up-to-date and comprehensive treatments of this subject, and proposes a definition in the following terms: 'the expansion of assets and capabilities of poor people to participate in, negotiate with, influence, control and hold accountable institutions that affect their lives.'[206] Within this conception it can be seen that empowerment and accountability are in fact very much two sides of the same coin, or linked with participation, three sides of a triangle. This broad conception of empowerment can be seen as symbolising people as both subjects of and actors for their own development, entitled to claim and exercise their rights on their own behalves. Experience by other development agencies shows the potential value of international human rights conventions in that context.[207] As with its companion

---

[202] See DFID, 'Strategies for Achieving the International Development Targets: Human Rights for Poor People,' Consultation paper, February 2000 ['*DFID Human Rights Paper* 2000'], at 6. Those articles of the UDHR concern the right to take part in formal political processes; freedom of opinion, expression and association; and the right to form and join trade unions.

[203] *DFID Human Rights Paper* 2000 at 11–12.

[204] Article 8 of the ICESCR provides the right to form and join trade unions. Participation would of course be illusory without basic guarantees concerning the right to education and an adequate standard of living.

[205] A fuller discussion of the normative linkages and programmatic dimensions of participation is given in chapter VI below, nn 170–200 and accompanying text.

[206] D Narayan (ed), *Empowerment and Poverty Reduction: A Sourcebook* (2002) at 13. This definition evidently builds upon Amartya Sen's 'capability approach' to poverty. Under this approach poverty is defined as the absence of capabilities to realize certain freedoms that are themselves fundamentally valuable for minimal human dignity. See A Sen, *Inequality Re-examined* 109 (1992). See also A Sen, *Development as Freedom* (1999). As elaborated in the *Empowerment Sourcebook* (at 13), empowerment is of intrinsic as well as instrumental value. 'In its broadest sense, empowerment is the expansion of freedom of choice and action. It means increasing one's authority and control over the resources and decisions that affect one's life. As people exercise real choice, they gain increased control over their lives. Poor people's choices are extremely limited, both by their lack of assets and by their powerlessness to negotiate better terms for themselves with a range of institutions, both formal and informal. Since powerlessness is embedded in the nature of institutional relations, in the context of poverty reduction an institutional definition of empowerment is appropriate' [as cited in the accompanying text above], strengthening (at 23) 'the demand side of governance.'

[207] An example is provided in the *DFID Human Rights Paper* 2000 at 13: "Poor and powerless people may be excluded from popular human rights movements and focused effort is required to protect and promote their rights. Lessons from Bangladesh show that there are possibilities to do this. Nari Pokkho, a women's human rights organisation, has been working within the framework of the [CEDAW] to support those women most vulnerable to discrimination and abuse. These include women divorced as a result of reproductive health problems, women disfigured from acid

principle of 'participation' however, the prospects for defining objectively grounded programmatic content is a complex and context-specific challenge, requiring recourse to more than just the applicable body of human rights standards.[208]

Human Rights and Social Policy Initiatives

Human rights are recognised as a cross-cutting element of global conferences under UN auspices, including the World Summit on Social Development (Copenhagen) in 1995.[209] Early in 1999 Bank President James Wolfensohn's signalled his intention to 'draw together the Bank's experience of alleviating poverty with the conclusions arrived at during the Copenhagen social summit in 1995 to define a new social code,' which would 'look at controversial issues related to labour rights, human rights, the eradication of poverty, as well as greater equality between men and women.'[210] In a press conference at the 1999 Spring Meetings of the Bank and Fund Wolfensohn described the Copenhagen accords, including the human rights elements, as 'the agenda of the Bank.'[211] Human rights, and economic and social rights in particular, have elsewhere

attacks and sex workers. A three-stage strategy helps women create a voice that counts, then demand answers from state institutions such as the police and health services and, finally, be empowered to demand change.'

[208] For the World Bank, institutional support strategies for strengthening empowerment are considered to fall within four categories: information; inclusion and participation; accountability; and local organisational capacity. *Empowerment Sourcebook* at 31–73.

[209] See UN Doc. A/Conf 166/9, 16 April 1995.

[210] S Kohli, 'World Bank Chief Promotes Proposals for Social Code Binding Nations to Policies,' *South China Morning Post*, p 14. The initiative appears to have originated by request of the Development Committee at a meeting on 5 October 1998. See World Bank, *Principles and Good Practice in Social Policy: Issues and Areas for Public Action. A Draft Note for Discussion by the Development Committee* (April 1999) at 6, citing the following as being among the key objectives for fostering social integration: 'promote respect for diversity; achieve equity between women and men; fotser tolerance and respect human rights; and enhance the participation of all groups of people in their economies, societies and natural environments, including the poor, vulnerable and disadvantaged.'

[211] News Conference by James Wolfensohn, President of the World Bank, IMF Spring Meeting, IMF Headquarters, Washington DC, *Federal Information Systems Corporation, Federal News Service*, 22 April 1999: 'We were asked by the [Bank] board to talk about issues of social policy and the experience of the Bank and what it is that we can do. And we took the—essentially we took our experience and we took the Copenhagen accords, which is the last reflection of the world's commitment to some form of social code, and tried to put down what it was that we're doing in relation to the implementation of the elements of Copenhagen and of our experience in social programs. And essentially what we can do at the Bank is, first of all, try and raise these issues, which we do, in our approaches to our lending; issues that relate to education, to human rights. I got [sic] the Copenhagen thing here, is [sic] really the agenda of the Bank. They want to have an environment to achieve social development, eradicate poverty, [achieve] full employment, sustainable livelihood, social integration, achieving equity between men and women, universal access to education and health, protection of culture and the environment, special focus on Africa and the least-developed countries, [and] ensuring that structural adjustment does not impede social development goals[.] . . . So what we're doing in our daily work is, in fact, trying to implement this.'

been advocated as the 'missing cornerstone' in terms of the Bank's approach to social policy in the wake of the East Asia crisis.[212] However whatever ambition the Bank President may have nurtured to grapple directly with human rights issues, explicit human rights content (and indeed any direct role in formulation of social principles) appeared to diminish markedly as the 'Principles and Good Practices in Social Policy' evolved later in 1999 into a more modest, crisis-focused, set of 'good practices.'[213] The dilution of the President's proposal at Executive Board level undoubtedly diminishes its probative value as a relevant 'practice' for Article 31(3)(b) Vienna Convention purposes.

Comparative Initiatives and Procedures in the Environmental Area

Revised Operational Policy (OP) 4.01 (January 1999), dealing with environmental assessments, makes it clear (at paragraph 3) that the Bank 'does not finance project activities that would contravene' country obligations arising under relevant international environmental treaties and agreements as identified during the environmental assessment. This formally binding directive provides interesting indications of the proper scope of 'relevant rules of international law applicable in the relations between the parties' within the meaning of Article 31(3)(c) of the Vienna Convention. In other words, OP 4.01 makes it clear that international environmental treaty obligations of the Bank's shareholder states *shall* be taken into account, together with the 'context' as defined in Article 31(2) of the Vienna Convention, in interpreting the Bank's Articles of Association.

Strangely however, social and human rights-related international obligations are excluded from OP 4.01, although a rationale for an approach more akin to the Bank's environmental approach emerges from a 1994 Bank review of projects involving involuntary resettlement: 'The potential for violating individual and group rights under domestic and international law makes compulsory resettlement unlike any other project activity.'[214] Yet no audit of international human rights treaties is called for in the OP dealing with involuntary resettlement. Environmental approaches show that a principled position based upon international law is possible, and relevant for the purposes of interpretation of the Articles of Agreement, and that iron clad empirical justifications are no necessary prerequisite.[215] There is no reason in principle why this precedent could

---

[212] B Simma and M Zöckler, 'After the East Asian Crisis: Economic, Social and Cultural Rights as Global Social Standards,' paper presented to ILO/ASEM/World Bank Seminar 'Good Governance of Social Policy in Europe and East Asia,' Bangkok, 26–27 October 2000 at 8.

[213] World Bank, *Managing the Social Dimensions of Crises: Good Practices in Social Policy* (14 September 1999).

[214] LCHR/ELSAM (1995) at 19, n 23 and accompanying text.

[215] Indeed a wide range of factors have been responsible for driving the Bank's agenda on a great many issues. For an indicative list of factors motivating the participation and governance agendas, see M Miller-Adams, *The World Bank: New Agendas in a Changing World* (1999) 71–78 and 104–10.

not be extended to the human rights field, in a manner equally reconcilable with the Bank's mandate.

Human Rights of Indigenous Peoples

In terms of the Bank's operational policies, human rights are addressed specifically only in Operational Directive 4.20 (September 1991) on Indigenous Peoples.[216] The Bank's broad objective towards indigenous people, as stated in paragraph 6 of OD 4.20, 'is to ensure that the development process fosters full respect for their dignity, human rights, and cultural uniqueness.' The Bank's policy is that the strategy for addressing the issues pertaining to indigenous peoples must be based on the *informed participation* of the indigenous people themselves.[217]

The operational centrepiece of OD 4.20 is the requirement for 'Indigenous Peoples Development Plans,' defined as 'a culturally appropriate development plan based on full consideration of the options preferred by the indigenous people affected by the project.'[218] In connection with these Plans, paragraph 15 of OD 4.20 notes that 'In many cases, proper protection of the rights of indigenous people will require the implementation of special project components that may lie outside the primary project's objectives. These components can include activities related to health and nutrition, productive infrastructure, linguistic and cultural preservation, entitlement to natural resources, and education.' The fact that 'special project components' are defined non-exhaustively, and that their express purpose is the 'proper protection of the rights of indigenous people,' leaves considerable scope for the inclusion of project elements drawing explicitly from applicable international human rights instruments.

Moreover under paragraph 15(a) of OD 4.20, 'The plan should contain an assessment of (i) the legal status of the groups covered by this OD, as reflected in the country's constitution, legislation, and subsidiary legislation (regulations, administrative orders, etc.); and (ii) the ability of such groups to obtain access to and effectively use the legal system to defend their rights.'[219] In the absence of

---

[216] For a detailed discussion of drafting history, and strong critique of content and approach, see F MacKay (2002). As at 2002 OD 4.20 was undergoing a conversion process to draft Operational Policy 4.10. MacKay's criticisms of OD 4.20 include failure to meet application human rights standards in terms of participation, indigenous land rights, involuntary resettlement, and process factors such as implementation failure by Bank staff and proceeding with the policy revision to draft OP 4.10 prior to the completion of a relevant OED practice review.

[217] OD 4.20 (September 1991) at para 8. 'Thus, identifying local preferences through direct consultation, incorporation of indigenous knowledge into project approaches, and appropriate early use of experienced specialists are core activities for any project that affects indigenous peoples and their rights to natural and economic resources.'

[218] OD 4.20 (September 1991) at para 14(a).

[219] OD 4.20 (September 1991) at paragraph 15(a). That paragraph goes on to say, 'Particular attention should be given to the rights of indigenous peoples to use and develop the lands that they occupy, to be protected against illegal intruders, and to have access to natural resources (such as forests, wildlife, and water) vital to their subsistence and reproduction.' But on an ordinary reading there is nothing to preclude attention being given to human rights protection in a broader sense.

express indications of a contrary intention, there appears to be no reason why international grievance mechanisms under applicable human rights conventions (eg the ICCPR in connection with the non-discrimination norm and guarantee of equality before the law,[220] or the ICERD or ILO Conventions concerning the human rights of indigenous peoples[221]) ought not be included within the ambit of paragraph 15(a)(ii). Indeed it would be hard to dispute the applicability of relevant international human rights conventions in the context of redress and accountability mechanisms—the cornerstone of any definition of a human rights-based approach—when the Bank has expressly acknowledged the relevance of ILO Conventions 107 and 169 Concerning Indigenous and Tribal Peoples in Independent Countries (where the borrower country has ratified either or both) for the purpose of the identification and definition of 'indigenous peoples.'[222]

Furthermore it is difficult to imagine how access to and effective use of (two separate requirements) mechanisms for legal redress could reliably be assessed without at least a basic level of human rights analysis. 'Access' might be interpreted narrowly to mean the existence of formal avenues of redress, however 'effective use' must necessarily be determined by a much wider range of factors, including an evaluation of cultural compatibility of the mechanisms in question, prevailing levels of education, patterns of representation and exclusion in local political processes, and satisfaction of core minimum economic and social rights guarantees. None of this is to say that Indigenous Peoples Action Plans *must* contain any or all of the above elements; only that in the terms of OD 4.20, the Plans *may* do so, and having regard to OD 4.20's stated purposes, *should* do so.

Human Rights Elements Within HIV/AIDS Strategies

It was seen in chapter II that despite the clear human rights causes and consequences of HIV/AIDS, the Bank's policy and programmatic responses for a long time understated those concerns. Nonetheless as at 2002 a number of HIV/AIDS projects (especially those addressing prevention) had emerged reflecting empowering strategies consistent with the precepts of a human rights approach,[223] occasionally including explicit linkages to legal dimensions of human rights. For example the strategies within the Bank's HIV/AIDS

[220] See ICCPR, Articles 2 and 26.

[221] See eg ILO Conventions No. 107 and 169 Concerning Indigenous and Tribal Peoples in Independent Countries. The practical utility of the complaints procedure under the ICERD (Article 14) is limited, however, by reason of the fact that as at 2001 only 33 of the 157 States parties to the ICERD had made the necessary declaration acknowledging the competence of the Committee on the Elimination of Racial Discrimination (the 18-member body of experts established under Article 8) to receive and consider communications.

[222] S Davis, S Salman and E Bermudez, 'Approach Paper on Revision of OD 4.20 on Indigenous Peoples' at paragraph 7(b) http://www.worldbank.org/essd/.

[223] The distinctive features and comparative advantages of a human rights-based approach to development were canvassed briefly in chapter I above.

Prevention project in Bangladesh include behavioral change communications, promoting condom use, sexually transmitted disease (STD) treatment, empowerment, and creation of an enabling environment. The 'Strengthening of HIV/AIDS Response Capacity' component includes activities specifically directed at 'advocacy, policy refinement and civil rights protection, to create an enabling environment for HIV/AIDS prevention work'. A sub-component of this, in turn, is the review of legislation and policies relevant to the prevention of HIV.[224] The Bank's HIV/AIDS Prevention and Control Project in Jamaica is also of interest, explicitly addressing human rights factors in the diagnostics of the problem. The project includes assistance to the government of Jamaica to reinforce a legal framework/regulations for the protection of human rights of People Living with HIV/AIDS (PLWHA), their families and other vulnerable groups. For PLWHA, this is expressed to include confidentiality, employment, housing, assess to quality and compassionate care, mandatory HIV/AIDS testing for employment insurance and immigration.[225]

Breadth of Mandate on Issues Affecting Children

The Bank's former General Counsel has suggested that legitimate Bank activities in terms of children's rights issues in general could extend to HIV/AIDS and sexually transmitted disease issues, as well as alcohol and drug issues, 'in view, and to the extent, of their effect on economic development.'[226] Early childhood development is another of the Bank's themes; Bank studies have shown that 'promoting the physiological and intellectual development of young children is critical in the formation and development of intelligence, personality and social behaviour.'[227] Further, the Bank 'will, upon the request of borrowing countries, consider financing land mine clearance provided that such clearance is an integral part of a development project or prelude to a future development project or program adopted by the borrower, and is justified on economic grounds.'[228] These activities are justified on the basis that '(i)mproved social indicators and economic growth are now recognised as interrelated. While it is difficult to mea-

---

[224] See http://www4.worldbank.org/sprojects/Project.asp?pid=P069933, HIV/AIDS Prevention project (P069933), Bangladesh (visited May 2002).

[225] See http://www4.worldbank.org/sprojects/Project.asp?pid=P074641, HIV/AIDS Prevention and Control Project (P074641), Jamaica (visited May 2002). To similar effect, but without the human rights-specific legal elements of the Jamaica project, see the HIV/AIDS Prevention and Control Project for Senegal (P074059), http://www4.worldbank.org/sprojects/Project.asp?pid=P074059.

[226] I Shihata, 'The World Bank's protection and promotion of children's rights' (1996) 4 *The International Journal of Children's Rights* 383 at 389.

[227] M Young, 'Investing in Young Children xi,' World Bank Discussion Paper No. 275, 1995, cited in I Shihata, 'The World Bank's protection and promotion of children's rights' (1996) 4 *The International Journal of Children's Rights* 383 at 389.

[228] I Shihata, 'The World Bank's protection and promotion of children's rights' (1996) 4 *The International Journal of Children's Rights* 383 at 390.

sure exactly the direct economic returns of external lending and/or domestic spending on social purposes, the evidence shows that investing in people makes sense not just in human terms, but also in economic terms. Both social indicators, such as life expectancy, infant mortality, and lower population growth rates, and [GDP] improve significantly in countries that invest more in the social sector, ie in education, health, and nutrition.'[229]

The development of the Bank's policy on child labour[230] is an interesting illustration of mandate flexibility. Driven to some degree by embarassing fallout from its unwitting support for bonded child labour in India's silk industry,[231] this relatively new area of concern has been reconciled with the Bank's mandate as follows: 'There are powerful economic arguments for measures to reduce child labour. Premature and extensive engagement in work prevents children from accumulating human capital and having higher earnings in later life, while economic growth is adversely affected by lower rates of productivity growth. In many instances, child work is the result of capital market failures: when households cannot afford education for their children and cannot borrow for this purpose, although the long-term benefits would be high.'[232]

Some human rights implications of child labour can be discerned in the Bank's writings on the subject, but less so its actions. Predictably, human rights discourse itself does not form a significant part of the Bank's own strategies, as far as can be discerned from formal policy papers.[233] However the Bank's child labour policy does recognise relevant provisions of the CRC[234] and various ILO

---

[229] I Shihata, 'The World Bank's protection and promotion of children's rights' (1996) 4 *The International Journal of Children's Rights* 383 at 391.

[230] Child labour was discussed in World Bank, *World Development Report 1995: Workers in an Integrating World* (1995), which noted the limitations of legislation and the significance of poverty as a determinant of child labour. The report called for a multifaceted approach with programs that increase income security, reduce education costs, and improve the quality of schooling. It concluded, 'as the incidence of poverty falls and education improves, child labour will decline. That in turn will make enforcement of legislated bans easier, starting with such universally abhorred forms of child labour as prostitution and hazardous work.' For a general discussion see I Shihata, 'The World Bank's protection and promotion of children's rights' (1996) 4 *The International Journal of Children's Rights* 383.

[231] See Human Rights Watch, *The Small Hands of Slavery: Bonded Child Labour in India* (1996). Embarassed by dislosure of its support for the silk industry, the Bank chose to include NGO monitoring of projects for child labour as a condition of support on future projects.

[232] World Bank, *Child Labour: Issues and Directions for the World Bank* (1998) at 5.

[233] Cf I Shihata, 'The World Bank's protection and promotion of children's rights' (1996) 4 *The International Journal of Children's Rights* 383. Although the Bank's General Counsel discusses children's issues in development in rights terms, to a degree, there is a distinct emphasis (in line with the Bank's general nervousness concerning civil and political rights and conditionality) on economic, social and cultural rights, contrary to the holistic approach advocated in the CRC: 'The Bank's support for children's social, economic, and cultural well-being is based on the conviction that it contributes to a better future for the development of the countries concerned, including the development of more open societies and eventually a better protection of civil and political rights'— I Shihata, 'The World Bank's protection and promotion of children's rights' (1996) 4 *The International Journal of Children's Rights* 383 at 405.

[234] Article 32 of the CRC states: (1) States Parties recognise the right of the child to be protected from economic exploitation and from performing any work that is likely to be hazardous or to interfere with the child's education, or to be harmful to the child's health or physical, mental, spiritual,

Conventions together constituting the relevant international legal framework, and indeed there is anecdotal evidence that the Bank's influence helped shape the content of ILO Convention No. 182 of 1998 (on Extreme Forms of Child Labour), a strictly defined subset of the issues covered by the CRC around which political support is relatively easily rallied. The Bank also recognises the mandates and specialised responsibilities of UNICEF, the ILO, NGOs and other international and national actors, and perhaps most importantly, the need to work in partnership with those actors.[235] To some degree it also recognises the complexity of the underlying causes of child labour, involving cultural, social and economic factors, with important functional linkages to other areas such as educational opportunities, health, family planning and women's rights.[236] Implicitly at least, there seems to be some evidence of the Bank's recognition of the importance of 'empowering' strategies in this context,[237] one of the fundamental cornerstones and comparative advantages of any 'human rights approach' recipe as mentioned earlier.

In the Bank's view, strategies to address child labour should involve: poverty reduction; educating children; improving schooling opportunities so as to increase its value to children and parents; providing support services for working children; raising public awareness; legislating and regulating child labour; and promoting the elimination of 'abusive' child labour through international measures.[238] As to its own role, the Bank has suggested action in the following areas:

moral or social development. (2) States Parties shall take legislative, administrative, social and educational measures to ensure the implementation of the present article. To this end, and having regard to the relevant provisions of other international instruments, States Parties shall in particular: (a) Provide for a minimum age or minimum ages for admission to employment; (b) Provide for appropriate regulation of the hours and conditions of employment; (c) Provide for appropriate penalties or other sanctions to ensure the effective enforcement of the present article.

[235] World Bank, *Child Labour: Issues and Directions for the World Bank* (1998) at 7 and 16.

[236] World Bank, *World Development Report 1995: Workers in an Integrating World* (1995); F Siddiqi and H Patrinos, 'Child Labour: Issues, Causes and Interventions,' Human Capital Development and Operations Policy Working Paper, HCOWP 56 (undated); I Shihata, 'The World Bank's protection and promotion of children's rights' (1996) 4 *The International Journal of Children's Rights* 383 at 403–5; World Bank, *Child Labour: Issues and Directions for the World Bank* (1998) at 8 and 16–17. Further, at the 1995 Women's Conference in Beijing, the World Bank pledged to work towards the goal of universal primary education completions, 60% enrolment rates in secondary education, and parity between boys and girls by the year 2010: C Koch-Weser, 'Children in Development: The Key Challenges Ahead,' Speech at Children First: A Global Forum, The Carter Centre, Atlanta, Georgia, 9 April 1996.

[237] This derives from one particular child labour project, however, the 'Rural Women's Development and Empowerment Project' in India, rather than being reflected in general policy prescriptions—World Bank, *Child Labour: Issues and Directions for the World Bank* (1998) at 15.

[238] World Bank, *World Development Report 1995: Workers in an Integrating World* (1995) at 72–73; World Bank, *Child Labour: Issues and Directions for the World Bank* (1998) at 9–12. By the term 'international measures' (to eliminate abusive child labour) the Bank (at 12) is referring to 'trade-related measures such as trade sanctions, consumer boycotts, social clauses, and certification or labelling schemes.' The Bank has noted numerous practical problems with the implementation of these sorts of measures, however, and in any event considers them to be outside its mandate (at 9 and 12). See also I Shihata, 'The World Bank's protection and promotion of children's rights' (1996) 4 *The International Journal of Children's Rights* 383 at 405.

—Its lending programs in affected countries can be refocused to have more impact on reducing the incidence of harmful child labour. Most Bank-supported projects addressing child labour (indirectly if not directly) have focused on health, nutrition, population and education.[239]

—In terms of its non-lending activities, 'more focus will be given to child labour issues in the Bank's dialogue, helping governments to explore and understand their economic and social implications . . . This is important because the effectiveness of interventions will ultimately depend upon the existence of a social alliance against harmful child labour.'[240] The Bank also proposes to assist through its economic and sector work, research work, increasing partnerships with international organisations and NGOs, and 'raising the awareness and sensitivity of Bank staff.'[241]

—Further, '(w)here agreed with the government, the Bank can help design a [Country Assistance Strategy] that integrates actions to discourage harmful child labour with other complementary interventions, such as initiatives in education, health, family planning, and labour legislation and its enforcement, as well as with other policies designed to reduce poverty, such as employment creation and income generation programs.'[242]

Interestingly, in line with IFC and MIGA policy,[243] the Bank's policy statement on child labour does appear to countenance human rights (child labour) conditionality in certain limited circumstances. The Bank's statement on this issue provides (in part):

> Issues of conditionality must be addressed in the light of the Bank's mandate to promote economic and social development. The Bank cannot assume the role of an enforcement agency for the requirements of national or international law, which have no bearing on its specific operations. Requiring its member countries as a general proposition to enforce certain labour law standards regardless of their relevance to the Bank operations would raise broader issues with respect to the Bank's mandate and cannot be limited only to the subject of child labour. Therefore, *the Bank can only impose conditionalities in this area to the extent that an absence of consistency with*

---

[239] For an account of Bank lending activities with direct benefits for children in the health and education fields see I Shihata, 'The World Bank's protection and promotion of children's rights' (1996) 4 *The International Journal of Children's Rights* 383 at 388–89, and (at 403–5) for child labour impacts.

[240] World Bank, *Child Labour: Issues and Directions for the World Bank* (1998) at 14. Some progress is already evident (at 14): 'The Bank's SAS Region has created an informal consultative group on child labour, bringing together Bank staff, NGOs and others, and has formed a partnership with UNICEF on this issue.'

[241] World Bank, *Child Labour: Issues and Directions for the World Bank* (1998) at 14–16.

[242] World Bank, *Child Labour: Issues and Directions for the World Bank* (1998) at 16.

[243] See MIGA, 'Environmental and Social Review Procedures', para 16, and IFC, 'Harmful Child and Forced Labour Policy Statement' (March 1998) by which the IFC undertook: (a) not to support projects that use 'forced or harmful child labour,' as defined in ILO's Convention No. 29 on Forced and Compulsory Labour (1930) and Article 32(1) of the CRC; and (b) to incorporate the necessary provisions into its contractual documents to implement this policy. See http://www.ifc/org/enviro/Review_Procedure_Main/review_procedure_main.html, visited August 2000.

child labour standards undermines the execution or the developmental objective of its specific programs and projects. This would mean that a provision that the borrower would undertake to enforce its laws would be included in loan agreements *where there are good reasons to believe that exploitative child labour with negative developmental effects may occur*[244] (emphasis added).

Clearly the Bank's 'economic' rationale is providing less and less of a coherent or convincing basis for resisting the incorporation of human rights-based strategies, or programme elements, in its child labour policy to the extent necessary or desirable. As the Bank observes, such activities are undertaken by 'other organisations,'[245] but there is no reason in principle why the Bank could not be doing so as well, in particular respects discussed in chapter VI.

Judicial Reform, Press Freedom, and Other Incremental Human Rights Innovations

The Bank is increasingly getting into the business of including explicit human rights components within broader policy frameworks and project design, although very much on an *ad hoc* basis. For example as at 2000 the 'judicial reform action matrix' in at least one of the dozen or so pilot CDF cases included an extensive section explicitly dealing with human rights.[246] And while the general thrust of the Bank's judicial reform efforts has been on commercial cases, streamlining case management, and improving the legal climate for investment, in particular cases—for example in connection with the Guatemala Judicial Reform Project—the project objectives include accessibility (including access to information, cultural awareness and language training, and establishment of mediation and conciliation centres for the benefit of disadvantaged groups), credibility, and 'equity in the application of the law.'[247] As will be seen shortly, these directions are consistent with recent IADB strategies in the judicial reform area, although the latter more often bring explicit human rights strategies to bear.

---

[244] World Bank, *Child Labour: Issues and Directions for the World Bank* (1998) at 17–18.

[245] World Bank, *Child Labour: Issues and Directions for the World Bank* (1998) at 9.

[246] Interviews at the World Bank in March 2000. The author was not permitted to take a copy of the program document.

[247] D Narayan (ed) (2002) at 289–92. A 'collaborative participatory assessment' in this case was reported to have helped identify the following problems: 'poor performance of the court system, limited citizen access to justice, corruption, poor institutional management, and negative public perception of the judicial branch.' Designed to address these problems, the project has reportedly 'mainstreamed the idea that citizens, as users of judicial services, have a right and obligation to contribute to the design and implementation of reforms. As a result, the reforms that are in place help to bring the law closer to the people.' D Narayan (ed) (2002) at 290. And interestingly (at 290–91) '[i]n addition to process improvements, Guatemala passed a judicial ethics code in April 2001 that has helped generate some unprecedented rulings. For example . . . [t]he Supreme Court denied immunity to a senior Congressman (. . . a former general), stating unequivocally that he must face trial under international human rights law.'

Bank President James Wolfensohn's recent advocacy for freedom of the press, without necessary linkages to the standard instrumental concern for financial transparency,[248] is of further interest as a benchmark of how far express engagement with human rights issues might go, although as at the year 2002 rhetoric of this kind still seemed to bear little relationship to policy or programmatic reality. Of further significance are the emerging empirical linkages between 'civil liberties' and project performance, as was seen in chapter II.[249] While the evidence such as it is to date seems to support direct engagement with only a limited range of civil and political rights for development purposes, a more substantive vision of the prerequisites for political participation and institutional accountability justify the incorporation of mutually supporting economic and social rights linkages.

Finally, it is appropriate to make at least passing mention of the various public stands that the Bank (and occasionally the Fund) have taken in the past on borrowing countries' human rights practices[250]—apart from the case of East

[248] In fact the rationale is strikingly similar to the 'citizens' voice improving government performance' linkage relied on in the Dollar and Pritchett 'Assessing Aid' study. See James Wolfensohn, World Press Freedom Committee, 1999 Harold W Andersen Lecture, 'The Informed Economy: the Role of the Press in Keeping Citizens Aware and Governments Accountable,' 8 November 1999. Referring to findings from the 'Voices of the Poor' consultations, Wolfensohn remarked that: '[T]he first [finding] which differentiates poor people from rich people is lack of voice, the inability to be represented, the inability to convey to the people in authority what it is that they think, the inability to have a search light put on the conditions of inequity. . . . [T]he first thing that [Consultations with the Poor participants] talk about is not money, it's lack of voice, it's lack of the ability to express themselves. [The] [s]econd thing is they don't trust governments, they don't even trust all NGOs. They want to express themselves and be able to express themselves. They want to be able to elect their own people and gain access and representation. A free press is absolutely vital to that objective. If you remove the right to voice and to exposure of issues, you remove the right for equitable development. . . . Freedom of the press is not a gloss, it's not an extra. It is absolutely at the core of equitable development, because . . . if you cannot enfranchise poor people, if they don't have the right to expression, if there is no searchlight on corruption and inequitable practice, you cannot build the public consensus to bring about change.' Amartya Sen's example of a free press as insurance against famines is likewise noteworthy in this context.

[249] See chapter II above, nn 76–81 and accompanying text. For support for the important functional linkages between development and civil and political rights, warranting a narrow interpretation of the Article IV, section 10 'political prohibition,' see A Sfeir-Younis (World Bank Special Representative to the WTO and UN), 'The Linkages Between Economic Development and Human Rights,' at a workshop sponsored by the Bank's Environment and Socially Sustainable Development Network, 2 May 2002, remarking inter alia (per the workshop report) 'that the content of "human rights" should be relegated to the political realm in which the Bank claims it does not get involved is no longer seen as a credible argument.' Sfeir-Younis argued that 'the Bank should deal with issues of civil and political rights, given that many aspects of civil and political rights are not in the realm of politics and that the Bank is already doing a great deal in the area of civil and political rights with its work in anti-corruption, access to justice systems, indigenous peoples and gender equality.' Moreover 'violations of civil and political rights have become a major impediment to the strengthening of democracies and a significant source of disruption of economic activities. . . . [D]emocracy is essential for attaining sustainable development and in defining the content and process of economic and sustainable development.'

[250] The situation in Kenya in 1991 is often cited in this regard, although some insiders have queried the merits of assertions by the Lawyers Committee for Human Rights and others at that time that the Bank was really 'doing human rights' in that case. See below n 355 and accompanying text.

Timor already referred to—and of the fact that international human rights conventions have on occasion been held out by the Bank as benchmarks for social assessment,[251] borrowing country performance, and as a basis for public criticism. One of the most notable instances of this was the Bank's reported allegation in April 2001 that orphanages in Bulgaria 'contravened the CRC.'[252]

Inter-agency Comparison: the Inter-American Development Bank (IADB)

For comparative purposes in exploring development bank mandate flexibility, the IADB presents an important case study. In contrast to the European Bank for Reconstruction and Development (EBRD) whose mandate expressly countenances human rights objectives,[253] the purposes and functions of the IADB as expressed in the Agreement Establishing the Inter-American Development Bank ('IADB Articles') are in many respects identical to the Bank's. The general purpose of the IADB is set out in Article 1, Section 1: '[T]o contribute to the acceleration of the process of economic development of the member countries, individually and collectively.' The functions prescribed to implement that purpose include:

(i)　To promote the investment of public and private capital for development purposes;

(ii)　To utilise its own capital, funds raised by it in the financial markets, and other available resources, for financing the development of the member countries, giving priority to those loans and guarantees that will contribute most effectively to their economic growth;

(iii)　To encourage private investment in projects, enterprises, and activities contributing to economic development and to supplement private invest-

---

[251] See chapter II above, at n. 99 and accompanying text.

[252] See chapter II above, at n 98 and accompanying text. *World Bank Development News* (www.worldbank.org), 2 April 2001: '. . . [T]he World Bank . . . slammed these institutions as "outdated and inefficient" and as contravening the UN convention on the rights of a child.' The extent to which (if at all) the Bank sought to justify its assertion of non-compliance by reference to particular provisions of the CRC or relevant jurisprudence was not disclosed in the media report.

[253] While the EBRD Articles of Agreement require that questions concerning the rule of law, democracy, and human rights shall be considered in the EBRD's work in borrower countries, to the extent that such considerations bear upon the EBRD's economic and financial mandate. However these provisions have generally been interpreted restrictively as declarations of commitment or intent, rather than enforceable legal obligations. See EBRD, *Political Aspects of the Mandate of the European Bank for Reconstruction and Development* (1997); I Shihata, *The European Bank for Reconstruction and Development: A Comparative Analysis of Constituent Agreements* (1990); J Gatthi (1999) at 148–49. Nonetheless former IMF Deputy General Counsel Herbert Morais has argued that the inclusion of such provisions in the EBRD Articles 'reflects an evolution in the thinking of the international donor community that suggests a larger role and responsibility for the international financial institutions generally in promoting good governance, including the rule of law and respect for human rights in their member countries.' H Morais (2000) at 92; H Morais, 'The Bretton Woods Institutions: Coping with Crisis' (1996) 90 *American Journal of International Law* 433.

ment when private capital is not available on reasonable terms and conditions;

(iv) To cooperate with the member countries to orient their development policies toward a better utilisation of their resources, in a manner consistent with the objectives of making their economies more complementary and of fostering the orderly growth of their foreign trade; and

(v) To provide technical assistance for the preparation, financing, and implementation of development plans and projects, including the study of priorities and the formulation of specific project proposals.[254]

The 'political prohibition' is expressed in the provisions of the Articles dealing with 'organisation and management,' in almost identical terms to the Bank's prohibition: 'The Bank, its officers and employees shall not interfere in the political affairs of any member, nor shall they be influenced in their decisions by the political character of the member or members concerned. Only economic considerations shall be relevant to their decisions, and these considerations shall be weighed impartially in order to achieve the purpose and functions stated in Article I.'[255]

The practice of the IADB, which in many respects is consistent with the Bank's own increasing expansiveness, leads one to the conclusion that a relatively narrow 'partisan political' interpretation of the prohibition is warranted. Consistent with the approach of the IDA Deputies during the twelfth IDA replenishment negotiations in 1999,[256] IADB member states have in principle expressly recognised the importance of human rights for development.[257] And while, consistent with the Bank's policies, recognition of the practical relevance of international human rights law lags well behind international environmental law,[258] a sampling of project documents indicates that human rights compo-

---

[254] Article I, Section 2, IADB Articles.

[255] Article VIII, Section 5(f), IADB Articles.

[256] Specifically, it was recognised that 'democracy and respect for human rights have helped create appropriate conditions for development.' There was no equivalent recognition during the 13th replenishment negotiations in 2002, however, although under the heading 'social protection' the Executive Directors did emphasise 'the contributions to poverty reduction that could be made by eliminating harmful child labour, making labour markets more equitable and inclusive, [and] implementing legal reforms to protect poor people's *right to assets* (eg women's property rights) [emphasis added].' IDA, 'Additions to IDA Resources: Thirteenth Replenishment—Supporting Poverty Reduction Strategies,' Report from the Executive Directors of the IDA to the Board of Governors, 25 July 2002 at 31.

[257] See IADB, 'The Bank's Lending Program for the Period of the Eighth General Increase in Resources,' chapter II (1994), para 2.36, http://www.iadb.org/exr/eight/ch2e.htm, visited 15 March 2000.

[258] Quite apart from the lengthier time that environmental issues have been on the international agenda, and the relative strength and consistency of NGO pressure in that area, a putatively rational justification for the environmental v human rights double standard is sometimes offered, to the effect that only environmental issues have distinctly transboundary effects. That this justification is reflected in official IADB records is a matter of some surprise, in view of the obvious and protracted transboundary effects of human rights problems in Latin America in past decades. See eg IADB, 'The Bank's Lending Program for the Period of the Eighth General Increase in Resources,' chapter II (1994), para 2.41: 'Ideally, environmental protection in the countries of the region would reflect a

nents (including specifically the direct relevance of the CRC, CEDAW and other UN instruments) in fact have penetrated into the IADB's program design in particular areas.[259] This emerging recognition at governing body level of human rights' importance to development, and the hesitant and opportunistic expansion of the body of precedent in the work of both the IADB and World Bank,[260] serve to illustrate the incongruousness of traditional interpretations of the breadth of the 'political prohibition.'

Travaux Preparatoires

Subject to the caveats stated at the outset, having regard to the above matters the practice of the Bank in applying its Articles of Association appears to establish agreement on a generous interpretation of the so-called 'political prohibition' in the relevant provisions of the IBRD and IDA Articles of Association, and quite significant scope for the integration of human rights considerations. This conclusion (in the terms of Article 31 of the Vienna Convention) is supported when one has recourse, as provided for in Article 32 of the Vienna Convention, to 'the preparatory work of the [IBRD and IDA Articles] and circumstances of [their] conclusion.'[261]

There is no definitive statement as to what the drafters of the IBRD Articles, Lord Keynes and Harry Dexter White, intended by the use of the term 'political' in Article IV, Section 10.[262] A survey of the Bretton Woods conference proceedings discloses a range of possible explanations. For example a number of statements made at the Bretton Woods Conference by White, Keynes, and by the US Treasury suggest that the purpose of the provision was no more than to ensure that the Bank acted impartially.[263] As Keynes put it: 'If [the World Bank and the IMF] are to win the confidence of the suspicious world, it must not only be, but appear, that their approach to every problem is absolutely objective and ecumenical, without prejudice or favour.'[264] However other possibilities have been

global approach that highlights the universal benefits of proper environmental management to all those who inhabit our planet. . . . [S]olutions to environmental problems, especially global problems, must take imaginative approaches and must envision the availability of financing on concessional terms for environmental projects and components with distinctly global benefits including, for example, projects related to the implementation of the Biodiversity and Climate Change Conventions.'

[259] Internal IADB project documents on justice system reform, on file with author. As at March 2000 the influence of international human rights law seemed strongest in the juvenile justice and judicial education and reform areas.

[260] See above n 246 and accompanying text.

[261] Vienna Convention, Article 32.

[262] J Levinson, 'Repressive Regimes Shouldn't Get a Loan,' *Washington Post*, 15 June 1998 at A23. The circumstances surrounding the conclusion of Article IV, Section 10 of the IBRD Articles bear also on the interpretation of the equivalent provision (Article V, Section 6) of the IDA Articles, for which there is no separate and self-standing justification.

[263] D Bradlow (1996) at 54, n 35.

[264] Speech of Lord Keynes before the Inaugural Meeting of the Board of Governors of the Fund and the Bank, 1946, cited in D Gillies (1996) at 120.

said to include: (a) a strategic concern to accommodate the concerns of the Soviet Union with a view to securing its cooperation in the post-War economic order;[265] (b) a slightly more complex need to take account of the 'tripolar ideological tension between communist Russia, socialist Britain and capitalist America;'[266] and (c) Britain's strategic concern to insulate itself against American economic dominance or anti-Commonwealth bias.[267]

While no single dominant cause can confidently be distilled, nor an exhaustive list of possibilities drawn, it is probable that the basis for the political prohibition lies in a combination of the above factors, all of which were documented concerns of the drafters at Bretton Woods.[268] But, significantly, none of these factors of itself or in combination with the others is sufficient to preclude the consideration of human rights in lending decisions or other matters.

Certainly Keynes' concerns for impartiality, efficiency and effectiveness are no fundamental barrier, as they self-evidently permit the inclusion of any matter (human rights-related or otherwise) which legitimately bears upon the fulfilment of the Bank's purposes, in ways such as those illustrated in the preceding survey of Bank practice.

And as to (a) to (c), a desire of the drafters to avoid biases on grounds of political form or ideology have little or no necessary bearing upon the Bank's capacity to take account of human rights considerations. As Ciorciari observes, '[v]iolations of international human rights law are not inherently tied to any particular form of governance, and intervention taken to protect such rights would not necessarily have a disproportionate impact upon [different regime types].'[269] The more logical and proper objection in this context would spring from degree and manner of exercise of political influence. Even if characterised as an objectionable form through which influence is exercised, this can hardly be an objection that could be regarded as touching universal, objective and validly assumed international legal obligations. Human rights in the sense referred to in this book are matters of international law. While the political sphere undoubtedly overlaps considerably in terms of the development, application and enforcement of international law, to dismiss human rights out of hand as 'political' is to ignore law's essential character and attributes.[270]

---

[265] E Mason and R Asher, *The World Bank Since Bretton Woods* (1973) at 27, and chapter I, n 5 above and accompanying text.

[266] J Ciorciari (2000) at 365–66; J Levinson (1998) at A23.

[267] J Ciorciari (2000) at 366; Gardner, *Sterling-Dollar Diplomacy* (2nd ed) (1969) 18, 26.

[268] J Ciorciari (2000) at 367.

[269] J Ciorciari (2000) at 368.

[270] To this effect see P Alston, 'Environment, Economic Development and Human Rights: A Triangular Relationship?', Remarks, 20–23 April 1988, reprinted in (1988) 82 *American Society of International Law Proceedings* 40, 54.

SCOPE OF INHERENT AUTHORITY WITHIN THE FUND'S MANDATE—AN
'IMPLIED POWERS' ANALYSIS

The problem of maxims for interpretation differs from the problem of the criteria for implying powers. The IMF has been as nimble in escaping debate about maxims as it has been in its treatment of the criteria for implied powers. Maxims as guidelines for interpretation have been the subject of much scholastic disquisition for centuries, and they are still cited approvingly by some courts and authors. The IMF, like others, has relied on them as substitutes for hard thought.[271]

As discussed at the beginning of this chapter, there is no provision within the Fund's Articles analagous to the 'political prohibition' in Article IV, Section 10 of the IBRD Articles, purporting to provide a basis for disclaiming human rights responsibility. Rather, disclaimers of such a kind at the Fund have usually drawn from more foundational assertions of mandate specificity and technical specialisation. Accordingly legal argumentation in the latter case focuses principally on the application of the doctrine of 'implied powers,' focusing on the scope of inherent authority within the Fund's charter rather than a focused application of the Vienna Convention rules of interpretation,[272] However as indicated at the outset, this differentiated application should not be mistaken for mutual exclusivity: the 'implied powers' doctrine bears just as directly on the Bank's mandate as the Vienna Convention principles do in relation to provisions of the Fund's Articles, united to some degree by an underlying principle of institutional effectiveness.

The discussion commences with a brief critical appraisal of some of the more notable objections within the Fund to explicit recognition of human rights responsibilities. The remainder of the discussion deals with how the Fund has applied its mandate in practice, contributing to a more complete and rational framework for case-by-case assessments of the scope of powers necessary for the effective discharge of its purposes.

A Critical Appraisal of Some Standard Disclaimers

The Fund has given a range of reasons for its failure to develop an understanding and capacity to deal with human rights issues, notwithstanding the strong logical and legal imperatives to do so. A number of specific normatively-based objections were discussed earlier in this chapter. Overlapping to some degree with the case advanced in the IMF General Counsel's paper in 2001 on ESCR and the IMF,[273] a range of other legal and policy-based disclaimers are often advanced, reflecting a combination of the following arguments:

[271] J Gold (1996) at 46–47.
[272] See above n 4 and accompanying text.
[273] F Gianviti (2001) above n 3, discussed above at nn 103–19 and accompanying text.

(1) The IMF's mandate under its Articles and subsequent interpretations relates only to macro-economic stabilisation objectives and short-term balance of payments financing. The Fund is not a development institution and has no mandate in the sphere of human rights, and it cannot interfere in the national political affairs of its members.

(2) The Fund would run the risk of losing credibility and the support of its industrialised members and commercial banks, if it entered the business of human rights promotion, especially if this involved an expansion in conditionality.

(3) Likewise, the Fund would not carry the support of developing country members if it began to impose human rights related conditions on financial assistance.

(4) The information available to the Fund, the complexity of human rights interactions and causalities, and the incomplete understanding of all the issues restrict the capacity of any one agency to advise on the relationship between stabilisation, adjustment, and human rights factors. The Fund does not have the requisite resources or technical expertise or experience, and to attempt to get involved in these areas would deflect its energies from its primary overall objectives.

(5) To a significant degree the Fund already does take into account the effects of its programs on social and economic rights, and although its technical judgements are not always correct, its programs overall do enhance the objective of basic needs fulfilment.[274]

To a large degree these arguments have been overtaken by the extent to which the supposed compartmentalisation between orthodox 'economic' and 'other' issues has—through research and often bitter lessons of experience—dissolved, and as an appreciation has dawned of the synergy between social and environmental variables and macro-economic stability. Guided by this and also by baser political considerations, the Fund has already incorporated 'social' and other human rights related issues into its financial assistance policies and other activities, as witnessed in its contemporary anti-poverty drive and advocacy for 'sustainable and equitable growth.' In June 2000 the Fund's Deputy Managing Director Eduardo Aninat commented upon the Fund's evolution in the following way:

> [B]ecause the IMF is the main [macroeconomic] coordinating international decision-making body in the world, it is difficult at this stage of world development for the IMF to simply say 'no, we only deal with the balance of payments problems and monetary and fiscal diagnosis.' The IMF is also a sort of 'biological institution'; it has to evolve with the context from inside and outside.[275]

---

[274] See eg G Helleiner, G Cornia and R Jolly, 'IMF Adjustment Policies and Approaches and the Needs of Children' (1991) 19(12) *World Development* 1823, 1827–29; J van Themaat, 'Some Notes on IMF Conditionality with a Human Face' in P de Waart, P Peters and E Denters (eds), *International Law and Development* (1988) 229–34, 229, and F Gianviti (2001) above n 3.

[275] IMF, 'Interview with Aninat: IMF support focuses on participatory approach, "inclusive growth"' (2000) 29(12) *IMF Survey* 193–96, 194.

Certain other aspects of the above objections have been dealt with already. For instance, it was seen in chapter II that the suggested 'political affairs' prohibition is a contemporary nonsense, having regard both to the circumstances in which the Fund was originally conceived,[276] and to the manner in which it has evolved, to the point where it exercises far-reaching influence in virtually all public policy realms in lower income member states, promoting fundamental structural changes in the name of one particular (contested) brand of economic liberalism. By way of further illustration, there have been numerous occasions where the Fund seems to have acted more as an international political sanctions mechanism, rather than as a regulator and supervisor of the international monetary system. For example, the Executive Board voted to suspend assistance in the case of South Africa in response to apartheid,[277] and in more recent times against Pakistan in response to nuclear testing[278] and the October 1999 military coup. In such cases the 'macro-economic' nexus or 'sustainable growth' rationale, if offered at all, has seemed to constitute a distinctly secondary justification for action.[279]

Further, argument (5) ignores heavily contested assumptions concerning whether the Fund as presently structured ought to be in the business of making influential 'technical decisions' in areas which affect human rights entitlements, and if so, the analytical and procedural framework within which such decisions should be made. That argument also ignores the Fund's negative impacts on human rights in many cases, although as indicated at the outset it is not within the scope of this book to resolve questions of causation in any given case or to speculate as to the overall balance of the human rights ledger.

Further, in relation to argument (2), the positions of the governments of industrialised shareholder states are neither uniform nor stagnant. Governments—as with activists, academics, policy makers and other stakeholders—can be expected to have different views concerning the merits of an active human rights role for the Fund, however that role is proposed to be

---

[276] See eg R Smith, Jr, 'The Politics of IMF Lending' (1984) 4(1) *Cato Journal* 211–41, 217: '[T]he IMF is itself a political institution. It is managed by politically appointed individuals from member nations, and the political interests of its members influence its decisions.' The fear of the Fund becoming a mere 'politician' was voiced by Lord Keynes at the Bretton Woods conference. Speaking as the evil fairy Carabosse, he said: 'You two brats [the Bretton Woods institutions] shall grow up politicians; your every thought and act shall have an *arrière-pensée*; everything you determine shall not be for its own sake or on its own merits but because of something else'—J Horsefield, *The International Monetary Fund 1945–1965* (1969) at 123.

[277] See the discussion in B Rajagopal (1993) at 82, n 4; and D Bradlow, 'Debt, Development and Democracy: Lessons From South Africa' (1991) 12 *Michigan Journal of International Law* 647.

[278] India was spared equivalent action, given that it had not been a recipient of Fund assistance. But India did not escape World Bank sanctions, as the world's largest recipient of Bank assistance.

[279] A macro-economic explanation was offered in the South African case: the 'distortionary effects that apartheid had on the economy and the subsequent impact on the balance of payments deficits.' See B Rajagopal (1993) at 82, n 4; and J Polak, 'The Changing Nature of IMF Conditionality' (1991) 184 *Essays in International Finance* 1, 31. But in the climate of virtually unanimous international condemnation prevailing then, alternative politically-based explanations of the motivation for Fund action are more convincing.

defined. The suggested risks of loss of commercial banks' support should not be overstated, providing that human rights-specific proposals are clearly defined and implemented with objectivity, in view (for example) of the lack of any crippling fallout in response to the Fund's dramatic 'anti-poverty' reorientation,[280] inspired directly by global development conference commitments. And suggestions that the Fund's influence over the donors might be diminished understates the degree of leverage over international resource flows exerted independently by the Fund in practice, and ignores the fact that the policy settings of the Fund are determined overwhelming by a Board dominated by its industrialised G7 members, whose development assistance policies in other forums—bilateral and multilateral—reflect very similar orientations.

Objection (3) however is perhaps more vexing. Developing country objections to the Fund's already wide-ranging conditionality menu continue to be voiced regularly and strongly. While the power dynamics at play between the Fund (through its major industrialised subscribers) and borrowing countries are not as straight-forward as is sometimes made out, the Fund's dominant negotiating position in the ordinary run of cases is clear. Users of the Fund's financial assistance facilities would in the ordinary course naturally be very sensitive to the prospect of intrusive and far-reaching human rights-related conditionalities and to the application of double standards perceived to result in competitive disadvantage to developing countries, notwithstanding the extent to which the Fund's mandate legitimately has broadened. Continuing proposals for an 'Asian Monetary Fund' or less structured regional arrangements for currency stability and crisis aversion can be taken at least in some measure as reflective of this dissatisfaction. But again, the focus of the present discussion should not become

---

[280] This is of course not to say that there has been no adverse reaction altogether, including within Washington DC. See eg Meltzer Commission Report, International Financial Institutions Advisory Commission: Hearing Before the Senate Committee on Foreign Relations, 106th Congress (2000). For a critique of the Meltzer report, including for 'subordinating human development concerns to financial market considerations,' see OXFAM, 'Reforming the IMF,' OXFAM Policy Papers, International Media Briefing, April 2000, http://www.globalpolicy.org/socecon/bwi-wto/imf/oxfam.htm. While the OXFAM critique agrees on the case for slimming the Fund, particular critiques are directed at the Meltzer report recommendations concerning withdrawal of concessional assistance from middle income countries, withdrawal by the Bank from Latin America, (more complete) 'conversion' of IDA loans into grants, and its failure to grapple with core issues of democratic control and accountability within the IFIs. More broadly, OXFAM argues that 'the Meltzer report (and the US Treasury position) suffers from some internal contradictions. The Fund is supposed to act as a lender of last resort, but no new resources are envisaged. Loans will only be made to countries that have achieved "financial soundness," which raises the risk of contagion from those (such as Russia) that have not. Loans [according to Meltzer] should have short maturities and penalty interest rates, which will exacerbate debt problems and add to instability. The more serious criticism is that the G7 have apparently abandoned any attempt at systemic action to tame global capital markets. In reality, no lender of last resort will be able to operate effectively unless this task is addressed, though the Fund will doubtless serve as a convenient scapegoat when the next crisis erupts.' For particular criticisms of Meltzer's recommendation that the PRGF be closed, see J Sewell, N Birdsall and K Morrison (Overseas Development Council), 'The Right Role for the IMF in Development,' *Global Policy Forum*, May 2000, http://www.globalpolicy.org/socecon/bwi-wto/imf/odc.htm.

overly focussed upon the question of conditionality, even if conditionality over the use of resources is in some form is inevitable. Rather, the issues must be viewed in the context of a wider program for institutional reform designed to increase the Fund's accountability and legitimacy.[281]

Finally, in relation to argument (4), it is true that the technical complexities and interactions between human rights factors and economic issues in the context of stabilisation and adjustment are difficult and not yet fully understood. However in principle 'these interactions and causalities are no more difficult to model, investigate empirically, and ultimately understand than are the traditional questions of macro-economics (which are not themselves so fully understood either).'[282] The Fund's own research on distributional issues, equity, and governance, among other issues, is already rapidly expanding the knowledge base, as will be seen in the next section of this chapter. Its co-operative work with the World Bank in the PRSP context and elsewhere may push those boundaries further still. But even more importantly, there is under-utilised (and in many respects, *un*-utilised) potential to tap into and take advantage of a vast body of human rights related expertise and research elsewhere within—and beyond—the United Nations system. The formation and expansion of co-operative relationships would greatly enhance the Fund's capacities to embrace new challenges.

Existing Practice Concerning Human Rights Related Issues

The potential scope of application of human rights principles within the Fund's work arises principally in relation to its surveillance activities under Article IV, and credit decisions under its various financial assistance facilities. While there is no specific reference to human rights anywhere in the Articles, the requirement to interpret the Articles in light of applicable international law rules does inevitably bring international human rights law to bear.

The 1978 second amendment's explicit introduction of 'economic growth' within the ambit of members' obligations under Article IV, Section 1, admits a distinct broadening of the IMF's purposes viz the international monetary system.[283]

---

[281] By way of contrast, some commentators argue for a more limited program of reform, directed not at increasing conditionality, but at extending the Fund's analysis of economic performance beyond its established range of macro-economic variables, with a broadening of the analysis of policy choices, including those relating to human rights issues. See G Helleiner, G Cornia and R Jolly (1991) at 1828. See further the discussion in chapter VI.

[282] G Helleiner, G Cornia and R Jolly (1991) at 1828.

[283] F Gianviti (2001) at 25–27. And as Herbert Morais further elucidates: 'As a matter of practice, the scope of this "consultation" [under Article IV] on "economic and financial policies" has broadened to include such subjects as labour markets, poverty reduction measures, social safety nets, education (eg illiteracy, school enrolment), health, environment, social security reforms, military expenditures, corruption, transparency and accountability in government operations, observance of property rights, enforcement of contract rights, and promotion of the rule of law through legal and judicial reform.' H Morais (2000) at 86.

Furthermore as was discussed in detail in chapter II, the manner in which the Fund's conditionality menu has broadened demonstrates a robust interpretation of Article I(v) insofar as access to the Fund's 'general resources' (which does not include loans under the ESAF or PRGF) is concerned, and a similarly expansive view of the sorts of factors which might be 'destructive of national or international prosperity.'[284] The Interim Committee's Guidelines on Conditionality, and Management's subsequent practice[285] in the application of those guidelines, are likewise of direct relevance under Article 31(3)(a) and (b) of the Vienna Convention in terms of how Article I(v) should be interpreted.[286] Moreover Article 31(3)(c) of the Vienna Convention would appear to admit the application of similar categories of international human rights legal rules as those canvassed in relation to the Bank earlier in this chapter, for reasons analogous to those stated there.

The extent to which the Fund is already actively engaged in issues with clear (but un-stated) human rights dimensions will be shown by reference to its activities in a number of areas including 'good governance' (including corruption), 'equity', and early initiatives promoting the role of women and environmental issues, with a critical examination in each case of the official justification for engagement. It will be shown in each case that the rationales underlying these initiatives could legitimately be extended to embrace related human rights dimensions of the problems with which the Fund is faced, to the extent desirable or legally necessary. Further, the extent to which the Fund is already enmeshed in human rights questions, albeit without addressing them in those terms, diminishes the force of economic rationalalist counter-arguments that issues of a human rights nature are beyond the scope of the Fund's mandate.

(1) Governance

The development of the Fund's role in promoting 'good governance' is said to have been 'evolving pragmatically as more was learned about the contribution that greater attention to governance issues could make to macroeconomic stability and sustainable growth in member countries.'[287] While 'governance' related concerns have been evident in SAP conditionalities for some time,[288]

---

[284] Article 1 of the IMF Articles of Agreement.

[285] See discussion in chapter II above, nn 201–30 and accompanying text.

[286] However it is important to note that many of the Fund's more controversial activities under the HIPC and its concessional lending facilities are not financed through the Fund's 'general resources,' but rather through a combination of resources generated through sales of gold holdings (as authorised by the second amendment in 1978) supplemented by donor country contributions. Therefore a considerable body of relevant practice and material within the terms of Article 31(3)(a) and (b) of the Vienna Convention, bearing upon the proper interpretation of Article I(v), is not strictly germane to an exploration of the proper scope of the Fund's concessional financing conditions.

[287] IMF, *The Role of the IMF in Governance Issues: Guidance Note* (Approved by the Executive Board, 25 July 1997) paragraph 1.

[288] See eg IMF, *Senegal: Enhanced Structural Adjustment Facility Policy Framework Paper, 1998–2000*, 27 February 1998 at 12–17; and in the notable case of the former Yugoslavia, see A Orford (1997).

current initiatives in this area seem to stem from a declaration adopted by the IMF's Interim Committee (as it then was known) on 29 September 1996, which identified 'promoting good governance in all its aspects, including ensuring the rule of law, improving the efficiency and accountability of the public sector, and tackling corruption' as an essential element of a framework within which economies can prosper.[289]

As broad as the Interim Committee's statement appears in its terms, the Fund's approach to operationalisation has for the most part been far less expansive, demarking particular spheres of involvement in accordance within the presumptively firewalled bounds of its macro-economic expertise and periodically reconstructed views as to the limits of its mandate. Hence, the Fund has stated:

> The IMF is primarily concerned with macroeconomic stability, external viability, and orderly economic growth in member countries. Therefore, the IMF's involvement in governance issues should be limited to *economic aspects of governance* . . . [including through]:
>
> —improving the management of public resources through reforms covering public sector institutions (eg the treasury, central bank, public enterprises, civil service, and the official statistics function), including administrative procedures (eg expenditure control, budget management, and revenue collection); and
> —supporting the development and maintenance of a transparent and stable economic and regulatory environment conducive to efficient private sector activities (eg price systems, exchange and trade regimes, and banking systems and their related regulations)' [emphasis added].[290]

The Fund's principal concern has been to focus on 'areas of the IMF's traditional purview and expertise.'[291] The principal criterion governing whether IMF staff should become involved in a governance issue seems to be 'whether poor governance would have *significant* current *or potential* impact on macroeconomic performance in the short and *medium* term and on the *ability of the gov-*

---

[289] IMF, *Partnership for Sustainable Growth* (Interim Declaration, 29 September 1996).

[290] IMF, *The Role of the IMF in Governance Issues: Guidance Note* (Approved by the Executive Board, 25 July 1997) at paragraph 5. See also paragraph 15: '[C]onditionality, in the form of prior actions, performance criteria, benchmarks, and conditions for completion of a review, should be attached to policy measures, including those relating to economic aspects of governance that are required to meet the objectives of a program. This would include policy measures that may have important implications for improving governance but are covered by the IMF's conditionality primarily because of their direct macroeconomic impact (eg the elimination of tax exemptions or recovery of non-performing loans).'

[291] IMF, *The Role of the IMF in Governance Issues: Guidance Note* (Approved by the Executive Board, 25 July 1997) at paragraph 6: 'Thus, the IMF should be concerned with issues such as institutional reforms of the treasury, budget preparation and approval procedures, tax administration, accounting, and audit mechanisms, central bank operations, and the official statistics function. Similarly, reforms of market mechanisms would focus primarily on the exchange, trade, and price systems, and aspects of the financial system. In the regulatory and legal areas, IMF advice would focus on taxation, banking sector laws and regulations, and the establishment of free and fair market entry (eg tax codes and commercial and central bank laws).'

ernment credibly to pursue policies aimed at external viability and *sustainable growth*' [emphasis added].[292]

However this seems to be a reasonably broad statement of eligibility, and one which rests uneasily with official portrayals of the Fund's limited 'balance of payments financing' responsibilities. One can envisage quite a diverse range of factors which might significantly affect medium term macroeconomic performance and a member government's ability (credibly or otherwise) to pursue sustainable growth policies. The effects of apartheid in South Africa, already mentioned, is one example.[293] Given the central place of human beings in sustainable growth strategies, discriminatory election laws, measures which significantly or arbitrarily limit political opposition, and civil or political rights infringements constraining the prospects for meaningful participation, could all conceivably meet the test as stated by the Fund.

As the Interim Committee accepted, subjects falling beyond the Fund's 'economic' areas of comparative advantage can in any event, '*as appropriate*, be part of . . . conditionality for the IMF's financial support where those measures [are] *necessary for the achievement of program objectives*' [emphasis added].[294] Having referred to the Guidelines on conditionality elsewhere in the governance Guidance Note,[295] it is perhaps surprising that the Interim Committee chose to set relatively loose limits for conditionality in areas considered to fall outside the Fund's sphere of comparative advantage, endorsing conditionality in those areas where 'appropriate' and 'necessary for the achievement of program objectives,' in contrast to the more restrictive formulation in paragraph 9 of the Guidelines.[296] Further, in facilitating the pursuit of politically sensitive 'governance' related issues, for the purpose of 'judging the prospects for [successful, in the Fund's terms] policy implementation,' the Interim Committee endorsed an approach that expressly permits the Fund to seek information concerning the 'political situation' in member countries.[297]

Although these interpretations almost certainly extend beyond what was envisaged by the drafters at Bretton Woods, they perhaps are not quite as surprising as they might first appear. In fact they represent little more than tacit

---

[292] IMF, *The Role of the IMF in Governance Issues: Guidance Note* (Approved by the Executive Board, 25 July 1997) at paragraph 9.

[293] See above n 279, although as indicated there, the extent to which the Fund was driven by 'economic' motives there is open to question.

[294] IMF, *The Role of the IMF in Governance Issues: Guidance Note* (Approved by the Executive Board, 25 July 1997) at paragraph 6. Paragraph 15 appears to reflect a slighter higher standard, however, pursuant to which the Fund can recommend conditionality in these other areas 'if it considers that [those] measures are *critical* to the successful implementation of the program' [emphasis added].

[295] IMF, *The Role of the IMF in Governance Issues: Guidance Note* (Approved by the Executive Board, 25 July 1997) at paragraph 7, containing a reference to paragraph 7 of the Guidelines.

[296] See the discussion in chapter II above at n 223 and accompanying text, and J Gold (1979) at 32.

[297] IMF, *The Role of the IMF in Governance Issues: Guidance Note* (Approved by the Executive Board, 25 July 1997) at paragraph 7, regulating 'preconditions,' discussed in chapter II at n 203 and accompanying text, rather than performance criteria.

acknowledgement of the extent to which the Fund—through its adaptation to the circumstances of lower income countries and contemporary focus on sustainable growth and longer-term financial facilities—has already become steeped in the internal political affairs of its members.[298] The Fund's 'governance' prescriptions have in numerous cases extended well beyond areas endorsed by the Interim Committee as being within its ambit of comparative advantage, into areas such as reform of the judicial system,[299] public enterprise reform (privatisation), civil service and central government reform (including fundamentally altering the structure of government through decentralisation),[300] and other matters going to the very heart of members' constitutional arrangements.[301]

(2) Equity

An introduction to the relevance of 'equity' to development was provided in chapter II.[302] In brief, the Fund's examination of this issue seems to have been sparked by an acknowledgement of the distributional consequences of its decisions, and a desire to accept a degree of responsibility for them.[303] As the Fund's former Managing Director Michel Camdessus put it: '[T]he aim of our work at the IMF is to help member countries achieve "high quality growth," meaning growth that is sustainable, that brings lasting full employment and poverty reduction, that promotes greater equity through greater equality of opportunity, that militates against marginalisation, and that respects human freedom,

[298] This is in stark contrast to the Guidance Note's caveat that the Fund should not 'interfere in domestic or foreign politics of any member[,]' and nor should it 'act on behalf of a member country in influencing another country's political orientation or behaviour'—IMF, *The Role of the IMF in Governance Issues: Guidance Note* (Approved by the Executive Board, 25 July 1997) at paragraph 7.

[299] See eg IMF, *Senegal: Enhanced Structural Adjustment Facility Policy Framework Paper, 1998–2000*, 27 February 1998 at 13; IMF, *Indonesia: Supplementary Memorandum of Economic and Financial Policies*, 10 April 1998 at Appendix VII; IMF, *Azerbaijan Republic: Enhanced Structural Adjustment Facility Policy Framework Paper, 1997–2000*, 8 December 1997 at 12.

[300] See eg IMF, *Senegal: Enhanced Structural Adjustment Facility Policy Framework Paper, 1998–2000*, 27 February 1998 at 12–16; IMF, *Indonesia: Supplementary Memorandum of Economic and Financial Policies*, 10 April 1998 at Appendix IV; H Morais (2000) at 89–95; D Kapur and R Webb (1999).

[301] See eg A Orford (1997) at 452–53: 'The direct restructuring of Yugoslav politics occurred through the imposition of conditions requiring constitutional and institutional reforms. During the 1980s, the IMF began to condition access to new credits to Yugoslavia on such reform. The first change required by the IMF related to re-centralisation, or the shifting of political and economic authority from republican governments and banks to the federal government and the National Bank.' See also S Woodward (1995) at 57–74, 82.

[302] Chapter II, nn 49 and 183 and accompanying text.

[303] 'Debate on Equity Invites Diverse Perspectives, Generates Pragmatic Prescriptions,' 27(12) *IMF Survey* (1998) 189; IMF Equity Issues Paper, June 1998 at 9. And at 1: 'Although there are no universally accepted criteria to judge equity, there is a consensus that equity is improved as the incomes of the least fortunate are raised, and especially as families are raised out of poverty . . . [T]here is general agreement that extreme inequality of income, wealth, or other determinants of individual opportunity is socially unacceptable, but little agreement on precisely what constitutes a fair distribution.'

and diversity of cultures, and the environment.'[304] The main justification for the Fund engaging with this issue, in terms of reconciliation with its mandate, is said to arise from a causal connection between 'equity' and economic growth,[305] although not all within the Fund would approve of the legal validity of the 'economic growth' justification (much less the raft of related considerations referred to by the Fund's former Managing Director), nor necessarily support on empirical grounds its claimed causal relationship with 'equity.'

Of particular interest in early Fund-sponsored deliberations on equity is the apparent recognition of the economic and social rights dimensions of the problem, and the fact that both equality of opportunity and 'empowerment' are key elements of any solution. As Amartya Sen has remarked: 'Equity . . . is a multidimensional concept encompassing equality of opportunity and access as well as the distribution of consumption and wealth. *The key to addressing inequality is thus not simply redistribution but empowerment.* Improvements in health, education, nutrition, and land ownership can enable individuals to participate more fully, and more productively, in the economy'[306] [emphasis added]. To the above list could certainly be added a range of civil and political rights necessary for political participation, and the implementation of anti-discrimination norms and minority rights protection mechanisms. As in the case of 'good governance,' this is a potentially broad human rights canvass indeed. While Amartya Sen most certainly does not speak for the IMF, his statements are certainly consistent with the thrust of former IMF Managing Director Camdessus' 'high quality growth' rhetoric. And while as at 2002 distributional issues seemed not yet to have intruded to any significant degree onto the Fund's conditionality menu, the fact that equity is accepted as a relevant matter of discussion at the highest policy levels is nonetheless not without significance both for immediate interpretative purposes and also as a signpost for further possible policy development.

(3) Promoting the Role of Women

Further evidence of the extent to which the Fund is already engaging in human rights-related issues can be gleaned through selective efforts by the Fund to promote the role of women.[307] The conditions attached to Senegal's ESAF loan are illustrative. The relevant provisions of Senegal's Policy Framework Paper are in

---

[304] Extract from an address given by IMF Managing Director, Michel Camdessus, on 7 March 1995 at the UN World Summit for Social Development in Copenhagen, *IMF Survey*, 20 March 1995 at 85.

[305] IMF Equity Issues Paper, June 1998 at 1; 'Debate on Equity Invites Diverse Perspectives, Generates Pragmatic Prescriptions' (1998) 27(12) *IMF Survey* 189, 192.

[306] 'Debate on Equity Invites Diverse Perspectives, Generates Pragmatic Prescriptions' (1998) 27(12) *IMF Survey* 189, and also (at 192–93) for senior IMF officials' endorsement of these remarks.

[307] For a general discussion see IMF, 'Women 2000: IMF support aims to enhance participation by women in social and economic development' (2000) 29(12) *IMF Survey* 202.

fact drawn from the African action platform prepared for the 1995 Beijing World Conference. The five particular areas of focus are: '(i) to strengthen organisational and entrepreneurial capacities; (ii) to develop education and literacy; (iii) to improve women's health, especially reproductive health; (iv) to strengthen the role of women in public affairs; and (v) to implement an effective institutional system for the monitoring and technical and financial execution, of the [Senegalese national action plan for women adopted in November 1996].'[308]

The fact that conditions attaching to the promotion of the role of women through this ESAF facility are related expressly to measures taken by the government of Senegal in satisfaction of its commitments arising from a major international development and human rights conference, might represent to at least some human rights advocates a modest symbolic breakthrough in terms of the Fund's cognisance of human rights' relevance and normative and instrumental importance.[309] The emphasis given to education, health (including reproductive health), and population policy measures as central pillars for longer term 'human resources development' strategies, is particularly noteworthy,[310] as is the Fund's wider and direct embrace of the 'international development goals' (IDGs)—and since September 2000 the Millennium Development Goals (MDGs)[311]—in connection with the discharge of its functions in the PRSP context. However a balanced appraisal of the symbolic importance and practical impacts of these initiatives must acknowledge the aspirational and vague nature of world summit goals, relative to human rights standards under the CEDAW, CRC and other relevant instruments. Without disparaging the high level of political representation evident at the September 2000 Millennium Summit, the goals and targets arising from development summits are most appropriately to be viewed as non-binding and generalised global benchmarks of donor and government commitment—set and monitored against average and aggregate numbers—whereas the latter bring to bear tailored, relatively determinate and binding human rights standards applicable as a matter of international and national law.

---

[308] IMF, 'Senegal: ESAF Policy Framework Paper, 1998–2000,' 27 February 1998, at 20.

[309] IMF, 'Senegal: ESAF Policy Framework Paper, 1998–2000,' 27 February 1998, at 35: the Senegalese government's chief 'objective and target' concerning the role of women is to 'enhance the integration of women into political, economic, and social life.' The chief 'strategies and measures' for achieving this are to implement Senegal's national action plan for women, and 'reduce the rate of female illiteracy by developing functional literacy.'

[310] IMF, 'Senegal: ESAF Policy Framework Paper, 1998–2000,' 27 February 1998, at 19–20 and 34–35.

[311] While the IDGs exclude goals arising from the Vienna World Conference on Human Rights (1993), and while the MDGs are based on averages and aggregates, the latter do include explicit reference to human rights in some respects. See discussion in chapter II, at nn 68–69, 191–92 and accompanying text.

(4) Environmental Issues

The IMF's interest in the environment is said to have arisen in tandem with an emerging appreciation of environmental linkages with macroeconomic policies.[312] However it is clear that NGO and member government pressure added a significant degree of impetus.[313] In particular, the Fund's interest was driven at least in part by the passage of legislation by the US Congress calling upon the United States Executive Director to persuade the Fund to 'carry out a systematic review of the impact of its policies on the environment and sustainable management of natural resources and to encourage the Fund to eliminate or reduce potentially adverse impacts of its programs on the environment.'[314] As the profile of environmental issues has grown, the Fund has modestly expanded its informal interactions with private actors and NGOs, although there is still no guaranteed avenue for public participation or anything like systematic access to relevant Fund information.[315] Environmental issues are now regularly included in Article IV consultations and Fund conditionality on the same basis upon

---

[312] See eg S Fisher, 'Statement to the Meeting of International Parliamentarians, hosted by the Banking Committee of the US House of Representatives and its Subcommittee on International Development,' 21 November 1994 [cited in D Bradlow and C Grossman (1995) at 425], where IMF Deputy Managing Director Stanley Fisher stated that the Fund had begun to expand its work in the environmental area 'to improve understanding of the interactions between macroeconomic policies and the environment.' See also 'IMF Reviews its Approach to Environmental Issues' (1991) 20 *IMF Survey* 124; and 'Seminar Explores Links Between Macro Policy and the Environment' (1993) 22 *IMF Survey* 177.

[313] 'Appendix D: The IMF and the Environment' in International Finance, Annual Report of the Chairman of the National Advisory Council on International Monetary and Financial Policies to the President and to the Congress for Fiscal Year 1990, at 75, cited in W Reinicke (1996) at 297.

[314] W Reinicke (1996) at 297. And further (at 297): 'At the same time there has been an increasing awareness that the [environment] issue cannot be separated from structural adjustment. Take the case of a country that hopes to improve its trade deficit via an increase of timber exports. To do so it proposes a sharp devaluation of its currency. The Fund should consider whether in the long term such a policy, which would result in greatly increased logging activity, is in the interest of sustainable growth. As a result it may actually advise against such a policy or at least require some form of environmental guarantee or safeguard before proceeding with a credit arrangement. In other words, if the Fund "feels strongly about the environmental aspect . . . it might show itself less than forthcoming with a credit arrangement unless the member undertakes to adopt adequate environmental safeguards."' See also J Polak, 'The Changing Nature of Fund Conditionality' (1991) 184 *Essays in International Finance* at 24–29.

[315] See eg R Gerster, 'A New Framework of Accountability for the IMF' in J Cavanagh, D Wysham and M Arruda (eds), *Beyond Bretton Woods: Alternatives to the Global Economic Order* (1994) 94, 99: 'In IMF activities, NGOs have not played a substantial role so far. Of course, it must be conceded that a participatory approach will prove more difficult to realise with regard to macroeconomic issues than with specific projects' . . . [Nevertheless] the IMF should examine ways and means to integrate NGO experience into the policy dialogue, the programme design and the Art[icle] IV consultations. One such example of co-operation occurred in May 1993, when the Fund organised a seminar on macroeconomics and the environment with NGO participation. On rare occasions in earlier years, similar events have taken place at IMF headquarters or in member countries. Although the importance of macroeconomic policy for social and environmental concerns is widely recognised within the Fund, there is no permanent forum for a systematic policy dialogue with NGOs, comparable to the NGO World Bank Committee or the observer status of NGOs in the executive committee of the Montreal Protocol for the Protection of the Ozone Layer.' See also D Bradlow and C Grossman (1995) at 425.

which the 'social' agenda has expanded, namely, for the objective of sustainable long-term economic growth.[316]

An interesting example of the Fund's concern with the environment can be found, again, in the Policy Framework Paper for the Senegalese ESAF. Among the strategies and measures prescribed 'with a view to sustaining long-term economic growth' are the following:

—Have the government adopt the national environmental action plan (PNAE) and prepare an environmental management program to implement its recommendations.

—Improve environmental protection by establishing a framework for environmental impact studies.

—Conduct environmental impact studies for all large investment projects.

—Strengthen local-level capacity to manage the environment and natural resources through the establishment of a national environment foundation and through environmental education.

—Monitor the status of environmental resources through the establishment of an environmental information system.[317]

The fact that the Fund's justification for engaging with environmental issues—the desire to promote sustainable growth—is identical to the reason it is engaging selectively with issues of a human rights character, removes much of the basis for arguments that the issues require separate treatment. Neither does 'political sensitivity' of human rights issues offer a logical basis for distinction, given the intrinsically sensitive issues with which the Fund regularly deals with in its Article IV consultations,[318] credit preconditions and performance criteria, and in other dealings with member states. Accordingly, to the extent that human rights factors serve the purposes of sustainable long-term economic growth, and to the extent that 'economic growth' can now be taken as falling within the Fund's lawful remit, there is no reason in principle why the Fund should be prohibited from addressing them.

(5) Lifting the Veil on the Fund's 'Behind the Scenes' Activities—Labour Rights, Political Prisoners, ILO Conventions, Eenvironmental and Indigenous Peoples' Issues, and East Timor

US Congressional Committee records relating to the IMF's activites in Indonesia reveal a startling proclivity for the Fund to exert policy influence in none-'core' macroeconomic areas where the opportunity arises. In prepared

---

[316] See eg IMF, 'Senegal: ESAF Policy Framework Paper, 1998–2000,' 27 February 1998, at 36; W Reinicke (1996) at 297; and J Polak (1991) at 24–29.

[317] IMF, 'Senegal: ESAF Policy Framework Paper, 1998–2000,' 27 February 1998, at 36. The other prescribed measures relate to the rehabilitation of destroyed habitats, and the preservation of Senegal's biodiversity.

[318] Such as military expenditures, and corruption, to take examples that have already been noted. See H Morais (2000) at 86–95, and D Kapur and R Webb (1999).

testimony at a March 1999 Oversight Hearing on the IMF the Under Secretary for International Finance of the US Treasury Timothy Geithner revealed that the Fund's activities and influence in Indonesia had in fact been exercised across a very broad spectrum of issues:

> Labour rights and environmental concerns have also been addressed in the IMF's discussions and programs within these [Southeast Asian] countries. For example, in response to the urging of the international community, particularly the United States and the IMF, the Indonesian government released a prominent independent union leader, Muchtar Pakpahan, from prison, ratified International Labour Organisation (ILO) conventions on Freedom of Association, and announced its intention to ratify conventions on forced labour, employment discrimination and child labour. In coordination with the World Bank, the IMF program has also included a number of critical environmental policy measures, such as introducing special resource taxes, drafting of a new environmental law, and raising stumpage fees.[319]

Of great interest as well in this context was the pressure exerted by the Fund upon the government of Indonesia later in 1999 to honour its pledges concerning the East Timor referendum outcome,[320] and the measure of responsibility assumed directly by the Fund for social dimensions of its policy prescriptions. None of this need be regarded as especially controversial from the point of view of legal reconciliation with the terms of the Fund's mandate. As discussed earlier, even official interpretations of the mandate within the Fund appear to accept that a very broad range of issues, albeit within apparently arbitrary categories with indistinct limits, need to be considered in the discharge of the Fund's 'core' business of balance of payments financing.[321]

The Year 2000 and Beyond—Increasingly Muddied Waters

The preceding discussion illustrates some of the most interesting policy directions pursued by the Fund in implementing its mandated functions in a manner cognisant of non-'core' macro-economic factors. However the official legal

---

[319] Senate Banking, Housing and Urban Affairs Committee, Subcommittee on International Trade and Finance, Oversight Hearing on the IMF, Prepared Testimony of the Honourable Timothy Geithner, Under Secretary for International Finance, United States Treasury, 10.30 am, Tuesday 9 March 1999. The IMF programs for Brazil were also reported to have reflected concerns over the environment and labour issues: 'With respect to the environment, the US Executive Director emphasised to IMF staff and the Brazilian authorities the importance of protecting environmental expenditures from needed fiscal cuts. When evidence emerged that key pilot programs for environmental protection could suffer deep cuts, the US government and the international financial institutions raised concerns with the Brazilian government and the funds were restored. Similarly, the United States vigorously used its voice to stress the importance of insulating from fiscal cuts programs to enforce labour laws, especially prohibitions against child labour and forced labour, and programs to enforce laws protecting the rights of Brazil's indigenous populations.'

[320] See further discussion in this chapter, above nn 44–45, and below n 350 and accompanying text.

[321] Interviews in Washington DC and New York in February 2000; F Gianviti (2000) at 4–7.

position at the Fund continues to be that—irrespective of the frequently expansive tenor of statements from former Managing Director Michel Camdessus' office and the recent surge into the business of poverty reduction—the IMF *remains* in the 'balance of payments financing business,' nothing more. The correct 'legal view' is said to be that the objectives of economic growth and poverty reduction can *not* strictly be reconciled with the purposes spelled out in Article 1 of the Articles of Agreement.[322] More specifically, the Fund's *purposes* have not changed, however 'its *practice and its mandate* under the Articles of Agreement have evolved to meet the changing needs of its members.'[323]

The Fund's official position regarding its legal competence to take responsibility for human rights issues is well captured in the following remarks, submitted to the High Commissioner for Human Rights in relation to her report on the implementation of the Right to Food at the fifty-sixth session of the Commission on Human Rights, in 2000:

> The International Monetary Fund . . . stated that it was established to promote international monetary cooperation, exchange stability and orderly exchange arrangements, to foster economic growth and high levels of employment, and to provide temporary financial assistance to countries under adequate safeguards to help ease balance of payments adjustments. *In implementing this mandate, the focus is on macro issues and not on the right to food, or any other human right.* However, the Fund is available to work with individual member Governments to establish a stable macroeconomic and financial framework conducive to the implementation of a Government's approach to the right to food, other human rights, or other appropriate policy goals of the authorities.[324] [Emphasis added]

Nonetheless small fissures continue to appear within the overall IMF institutional view, although these are usually of hairline breadth. The statement of the Fund's General Counsel at the 7 May 2001 consultation with the Committee on Economic, Social and Cultural Rights has already been discussed at length. Also noteworthy was an April 2000 consultation in Geneva between human rights experts and UN agencies on the issue of human rights integration, at which the Special Representative of the IMF to the WTO and UN in Geneva remarked

---

[322] Interviews in Washington DC and New York in March and April 1999, and February 2000.

[323] F Gianviti (2000) at 4: 'The Fund is still a monetary agency, not a development agency. It does not fund projects, but still provides only balance of payments support, although the concept of balance of payments support is now more flexible than in the past [in light of the special facilities for developing countries such as the PRGF].' The human rights consequences are correspondingly modest (at 6–7): 'While the Fund remains a monetary institution responsible for maintaining orderly exchange rates and a multilateral system of payments free of restrictions on current payments and whose financial assistance is only for balance of payments purposes, the cumulative effect of changes in its practice and in its Articles of Agreement has introduced new elements to the relationship between the Fund and the [ICESCR].' The General Counsel concludes (at 32–35) that the ICESCR has no direct relevance for the Fund, and that a formal amendment to the Fund's Articles would be required to alter that result.

[324] E/CN.4/2000/48 at para 13. The apparent equating of 'human rights' (such as the right to food) with mere 'policy goals' does not seem to bode well for the inculcation of international human rights law within the IMF's legal and organisational culture.

that: '[I]n the old days, IMF's position towards human rights was to deny any link between its work and human rights, on the basis that there is absolutely no mention of human rights in IMF's articles of agreement.' Nevertheless the IMF Special Representative stated that due its assumption of responsibilities in the poverty reduction (PRSP) context, the IMF had been forced to 'draw upon the UN's expertise' in relation to key social elements such as 'participation.' To this end it was claimed that '[t]he IMF has some experience of information sharing with human rights experts and bodies, which has allowed IMF staff to be sensitised to human rights issues relevant to their work and for the experts to get technical information on IMF areas of expertise.'[325] However the extent of information sharing and details of the channels and procedures—whether formal and systematic or otherwise—were not reported. While *ad hoc* dealings with thematic mechanisms of the Sub-Commission and CHR[326] and limited interaction with the OHCHR have occurred from time to time, there was no evidence as at the year 2002 of any formalised or systematised procedures in that regard, sufficient to indicate a serious acknowledgement of direct human rights responsibility.

Paradoxically, as was seen in chapter II, the Fund is not constrained by a 'political prohibition' in such terms as is found in the Bank's Articles.[327] The lack of such explicit formal constraints seems at one level to make the task of arguing against a further expansion of the Fund's remit considerably more difficult. The contradictions between conservative official interpretations and actual Fund practice seem to bespeak an organisation pushed and pulled in too many directions at once, yearning for the simplicity of a bygone era. The organisation's unconvincing attempts to reconcile its contemporary challenges with traditional interpretations of its mandate risks the very credibility and legitimacy it now so fervently strives for. What purpose is the Fund's 'mandate' intended to serve, if not as a relevant and objective signpost to the functions legitimately to be exercised and institutional capacities legitimately required in order to meet evolving operational challenges?

---

[325] OHCHR, 'Consultation between Right to Development and Economic, Social and Cultural Rights Experts and UN agencies and organisations: "Perspectives for coordination and interaction," ' Note on the Meeting, Palais des Nations, Geneva, 6 April 2000, at 11.

[326] See eg E/CN.4/Sub.2/1999/11, Working paper submitted by J Oloka-Onyango and Deepika Udagama in accordance with Sub-Commission resolution 1998/12.

[327] See eg E/CN.4/Sub.2/1999/11 at para 33: 'Ironically, the Articles of Association of the IMF do not have a bar similar to that invoked by the World Bank whenever the issue of human rights is pursued in a direction found uncomfortable. Paradoxically, the Fund is even more adamant that its operations have nothing to do with human rights, and its methods of work amply demonstrate this. Some observers have nevertheless pointed to a "changed stance" on the part of the IMF which, under pressure from organizations like UNICEF and some States, has begun to discuss the distributional aspects of its policies with a view to the protection of the well-being of vulnerable groups. Nevertheless, even those who have observed such changes come to the conclusion that the "hard core" of IMF programmes has remained largely intact, with a ". . . focus on measures that tighten domestic credit, enhance fiscal revenues, reduce government expenditures, and adjust the exchange rate." '

As suggested above, these questions have obviously been brought to a head since 1999, following the launch of the Fund's joint 'anti-poverty' drive with the Bank. The central contradiction arises from a continuing inability to reconcile fluctuating political imperatives with consistent and objective legal interpretation of the Fund's Articles. The 'political answer' to the Fund's chief dilemmas at the turn of the century is fairly obviously that the Fund should be seen to be 'helping the poor,' responding to the sustained criticisms it has been facing following the East Asian crisis, and the political imperatives relating to HIPC and international debt relief. As one observer put it, helping the poor certainly paints a much more positive public image than 'bailing out the bankers.'[328] But this doesn't appear to change the official 'legal answer' that the Fund was created and remains in business for the specific purpose of 'helping countries with their balance of payments problems.'[329] Against such contradictions, despite the relative importance of the office of legal advisor within the Fund, one cannot help but get the impression that the logical and practical limits of the Fund's mandate as it relates to poverty reduction or indeed any other issue are in fact determined by 'institutional capacity,'[330] budgetary, political and strategic concerns, more than legal ones.

OTHER RELEVANT FACTORS FOR BOTH BANK AND FUND

An Appropriate Policy Environment at the National Level

It is now widely accepted that 'debt relief, like any other form of donor financing, will be as effective as the policy environment into which it is introduced. It is likely to have a lasting impact only in a climate conducive to macro-economic stability and human development.'[331] The Bank's empirical research on the prerequisites for an operationally viable conception of 'governance,' with emphases on anti-corruption and the 'development dividend,' supports these basic findings on the proper policy environment for aid.[332] Accordingly to the

---

[328] Interviews in Washington DC and New York in February 2000.

[329] Interviews in Washington DC and New York in February 2000; F Gianviti (2001).

[330] Nonetheless it is noteworthy that as at March 2000 the personnel situation within the Fund was already beginning to show signs (not without some consternation in certain quarters) of adapting to the anti-poverty challenge, with the recruitment (through DFID funding) of two social development specialists, and with a 'governance' specialist to be added later in 2000. Modest steps, indeed, but their symbolic significance shouldn't be understated.

[331] OXFAM, *From Unsustainable Debt to Poverty Reduction: Reforming the Heavily Indebted Poor Countries Initiative*, prepared by OXFAM GB Policy Department for UNICEF, (August 1999). See also D Dollar and L Pritchett, *Assessing Aid: What Works, What Doesn't, and Why* (1998), although for a cautionary note on that study's methodology and a caveat on the equal importance of donor government policies, see UNCTAD, *Least Developed Countries Report 2002: Escaping the Poverty Trap* (2002) 218–19.

[332] See eg D Kaufman, A Kraay and P Zoido-Lobatón, 'Governance Matters: From Measurement to Action' (2000) 37(2) *Finance and Development* 10–13 at 10. The authors define governance broadly, as 'the traditions and institutions that determine how authority is exercised in a particular

extent that widespread protection and fulfilment of human rights provides a foundation for these goals, it ought to be legitimate for both the Bank and Fund to consider them.

Furthermore as mentioned in chapter II a number of related Bank studies a positive correlation has been found between project performance ('economic rate of return') and observance of 'civil liberties' (measured under the Freedom House and Humana indexes).[333] The chief functional explanation for this positive correlation was said to relate to the 'impact of citizen voice on the performance of government,'[334] rather than mode of electoral democracy. Naturally this explanation is somewhat one-dimensional from a human rights perspective: if the benchmark is in fact 'impact of citizens' voices on government,' then it follows that a core minimum guarantee of economic, social and cultural rights becomes a legitimate threshold consideration in the policy environment in which aid and development activities are being considered, along with essential civil and political rights such as the freedom of expression, freedom of thought, conscience and religion, freedom of association and the press, and so forth.

Congruence of Human Rights with Desirable Elements of Anti-corruption Strategies

One of the Bank's leading researchers on corruption, Daniel Kaufmann, has observed that '[o]ne doesn't fight corruption by fighting corruption[.]' Rather, 'the factors to address are likely to be macroeconomic stability, politics, market-friendly policies, human policies, education, institutional development and accountability.'[335] In other words, confining anti-corruption strategies to a narrow list of traditionally-viewed 'economic' variables is self-defeating.

country.' This includes: '(1) the process by which governments are selected, held accountable, monitored, and replaced; (2) the capacity of governments to manage resources efficiently and formulate, implement, and enforce sound policies and regulations; and (3) the respect of citizens and the state for the institutions that govern economic and social interactions among them.'

[333] See the discussion in chapter II at nn 77–82 and accompanying text, and J Isham, D Kaufman and L Pritchett, 'Civil Liberties, Democracy, and the Performance of Government Projects' (1997) 11(2) *The World Bank Economic Review* 219; and Dollar, D. and Pritchett, L. (1998), at 135–38. And see D Kaufman, A Kraa and P Zoido-Lobatón (2000) at 12, describing (subject to the methodological limitations stated there) the 'development dividend'—in terms of increasing per capita incomes and reduction in infant mortality—correlated with strong 'rule of law index' and high 'voice and accountability.'

[334] D Dollar and L Pritchett, L. (1998) at 136: '[I]ndicators of civil strife (riots, political strikes and demonstrations) are positively related to the [economic rate of return] on Bank projects, but that partial correlation is explained by the fact that there is more of this expression of discontent in countries with more civil liberties. Once one accounts for greater civil liberties, this eliminates any independent impact of civil strife, indicating that when civil liberties allow it there is greater expression of all types of citizen voice and that ultimately this voice is a force for improving government performance.'

[335] *World Bank Development News*, 30 August 1999.

The practical lessons of development experience seem to be driving the research agenda towards broad-based, rights-based and inter-sectoral approaches.[336] Addressing the Bank's governance agenda in Indonesia, the OED has stated that: 'The ingredients missing . . . to combat corruption include: an efficient and effective civil service, an independent judiciary, a transparent and competitive incentive framework, a transparent fiscal framework, and good oversight mechanisms (including a free and open press).'[337] Dangers in compartmentalised approaches were identified by the OED in connection with legal infrastructure reform, discussion of which was said to have been 'confined to the business sector,' with a focus on commercial and bankruptcy law.[338]

As indicated earlier in this chapter, within the overall 'good governance' objective, the International Monetary and Financial Committee has endorsed 'tackling corruption' as an 'essential element of a framework within which economies can prosper.'[339] Corruption is said to be included within the scope of the Fund's Article IV consultations, although the exact extent of this is difficult to determine.[340] The Country Report from Malawi's Article IV consultations in 2002 may signal the outer bounds of progress in this area to date, reflecting quite extensive discussions on issues such as legislative and institutional frameworks against corruption, freedom of the press, freedom of express, and concerns by the Fund as to arbitrary legislative constraints on political opposition.[341] By the late 1990s anti-corruption measures had likewise seemed to become more prominent in conditions attached to ESAF and PRGF arrangements. While enforcement of such conditions has been at best selective in the past,[342] the

[336] See the discussion on 'corruption and the right to information,' and the importance of community empowerment, transparency and accountability, right to participation, and freedom of association in the context of community level 'social audit' anti-corruption initiatives in Rajasthan, India, in Jenkins and Goetz, *Accounts and Accountability: Theoretical Implications of the Right-to-Information Movement in India* (1999), cited in *DFID Human Rights Paper* (2000) at 6. However for a fundamental critique of the illegitimacy and inappropriateness of Western anti-corruption approaches see B Rajagopal, 'Corruption, Legitimacy and Human Rights: The Dialectic of the Relationship' (1999) 14 *Connecticut Journal of International Law* 495.

[337] OED Note (1999) at para 1.15. See also Editorial *Jakarta Post*, 13 October 1999 concerning judicial appointment processes and need for change.

[338] OED Note (1999) at 23, para 3.39. For a more comprehensive discussion of the OED's criticisms see chapter III above, at nn 152–71 and accompanying text.

[339] Interim Committee Declaration: 'Partnership for Sustainable Growth,' 29 September 1996, Washington, DC.

[340] See eg PIN No. 98/46, 'IMF Concludes Article IV Consultations with Mauritius,' 29 June 1998, where the Executive Directors' recommendations to the authorities in Mauritius included improving the 'regulatory, legislative, and other environmental conditions affecting private sector initiatives in the export processing zone, sugar industry, and tourism sector,' and ensuring early passage of anti-money-laundering and economic crime legislation.

[341] IMF Country Report No. 02/181, August 2002, 'Malawi: Article IV Consultation and Economic Program for 2002—Staff Report; Staff Supplement; and Public Information Notice on the Executive Board Discussion. See chapter III above, at n 185 and accompanying text.

[342] There are occasional references to the problem of corruption in publicly available ESAF Policy Framework Papers—see eg 'Georgia: ESAF Policy Framework Paper, 1997–1999,' 24 February 1997, at 7. Further, the Memoranda of Economic and Financial Policies for Indonesia in 1998 contained conditions relating *inter alia* to divestiture of State monopolies (for example in the clove industry), discontinuance of budgetary and extra-budgetary support and privileges to certain

bitter lessons of experience in Indonesia and Kenya and elsewhere have led to a perceptibly stronger albeit still uneven approach.[343]

As further research under the aegis of both the Fund and Bank has revealed, many of the causes of corruption relate to human rights factors, such as the prevalence of poverty, unemployment, absence of labour market risk-spreading mechanisms, and restriction of political competition and 'civil liberties.'[344] Without wishing to go so far as to assert any kind of 'right to a corruption-free society' as a fundamental human right,[345] it nonetheless seems to be the case that in many situations corruption cannot effectively be tackled without addressing the above and other systemic causes.[346] The range of human rights issues required to be addressed in a coherent anti-corruption strategy is potentially very broad, in conjunction with general civil service, legal, judicial and other institutional reforms.

In this regard, World Bank research has specified that '[t]he existence of a free press is of paramount importance. Both the introduction and the continuance of restrictive libel laws protecting politicians and public officials must be opposed to safeguard citizens' freedoms of expression and information.'[347] Beyond the abolition of libel laws, one could envisage a range of reforms that might be

industry and infrastructure projects, transparency in banking, and state enterprise reform, intended to strike at the excesses and nepotism of the former Soeharto regime. The terms of the conditions are somewhat neutral, however, referring to general objectives of privatisation, efficiency, and competition. See generally IMF, 'Indonesia—Memorandum of Economic and Financial Policies,' 15 January 1998; and IMF, 'Indonesia—Supplementary Memorandum of Economic and Financial Policies,' 10 April 1998 at 11–17.

[343] In August 1997 the Fund suspended a loan of $220 million to Kenya after President Moi failed to create a new anti-corruption authority. The Fund was reported to have halted a $120 million loan in 1996 to Cambodia for six months, for similar reasons—*The Times*, 18 August 1997 at 13, discussed in I Senior, 'An Economic View of Corruption' (1998) 9 *The Journal of Interdisciplinary Economics* 145–61, 157. The Fund's assistance to Kenya resumed in 2000, but only upon assumption by Kenya of the strictest and most onerous set of conditions yet attached to any Fund agreement, to safeguard against corruption and to monitor disbursements. See M Holman, 'IMF closes rift with Kenya,' *Financial Times*, 28 July 2000; J Kisero, 'IMF sets tough terms for Kenya,' *Daily Nation*, 31 July 2000; 'IMF Money Threatened by "List of Shame" ', *The East African*, 24 July 2000; and IMF Press Release No. 00/45, 28 July 2000, 'IMF Approves Poverty Reduction and Growth Facility Loan for Kenya.' However several months later the Kenyan program was again imperilled, in part through the government's failure to implement key governance reforms.

[344] C Gray and D Kaufmann, 'Corruption and Development' (1998) 35(1) *Finance and Development* 7, 9–10; P Mauro, 'Corruption: Causes, Consequences, and Agenda for Further Research' (1998) 35(1) *Finance and Development* 11. See also I Senior (1998) at 153–57.

[345] Cf N Kofele-Kale, 'The Right to a Corruption-Fee Society as an Individual and Collective Human Right: Elevating Official Corruption to a Crime under International Law' (2000) 34(1) *The International Lawyer* 149, 163. For a cautionary note on normative dilution through unwarranted expansion see P Alston, 'Conjuring up New Human Rights: A Proposal for Quality Control' (1984) 78 *American Journal of International Law* 607.

[346] C Gray and D Kaufmann (1998) at 10: 'In sum, corruption is a symptom of fundamental economic, political, and institutional causes. Addressing corruption effectively means tackling these underlying causes.'

[347] C Gray and D Kaufmann (1998) at 10. And as to the 'enormous potential of information to identify policy priorities, empower stakeholders, and build political consensus for concerted and informed action to improve governance,' see D Kaufman, A Kraay and P Zoido-Lobatón (2000) at 13.

necessary for securing the freedoms of expression and information, including but not limited to legislative and other measures promoting participation, education, and the introduction of freedom of information legislation.[348] In conjunction with mutually reinforcing 'core minimum' economic and social guarantees,[349] the human rights framework within which the IFIs' anti-corruption strategies could lawfully and legitimately be situated is broad indeed.

Private Oressure Over Human Rights Violations in East Timor

In a fascinating example of active involvement in non-'core' 'economic' matters, in September 1999 the Bank President James Wolfensohn (and former IMF Deputy Managing Director Stanley Fischer) forwarded letters to then-Indonesian President Habibie, expressing concern at human rights abuses then taking place in East Timor, and pressuring the Indonesian government to honour pledges that it had made that it would accept the East Timor referendum outcome.[350] Of course, the IFIs were not alone in the international community in applying such pressure. However according to anecdotal accounts it was the timely and concerted pressure from these two organisations, with their cumulative financial clout leveraged through the international donor community, that most likely tipped the former Indonesian government's hand and forced it to honour the East Timor referendum result and accept an international peace-keeping presence. The fact that the concern for human rights was expressed to reflect the concern of the donor community (Consultative Group for Indonesia) is immaterial; the message in that case from the IFIs was loud and clear.

Other Country-specific Cases

In certain other contexts, the Bank (and Fund) have been demonstrating an increasing willingness, either at G–7 instigation, concerns expressed in Consultative Group meetings, or more or less independently, to take active account of human rights issues, but couching these concerns as 'concerns of the

[348] See eg I Senior (1998) at 158–59, emphasising the importance not only of 'an independent and unthreatened press,' but freedom of information laws and 'a viable system of democratic representation at national and local level.'

[349] For an argument that the liberalisation agenda as promoted by (Western) 'anti-corruptionists' undermines traditional and locally adapted means of ensuring respect for economic, social and cultural rights see B Rajagopal (1999) at 506.

[350] See nn 44–45 above. Correspondence from World Bank President James Wolfensohn and former IMF Deputy Managing Director Stanley Fisher to former Indonesian President Habibie dated September 1999, on file with author. Related accounts obtained during interview program in Washington DC in February 2000. The letter from Bank President Wolfensohn to the Indonesian President is reprinted in H Steiner and P Alston, *International Human Rights in Context: Law, Politics, Morals* (2nd ed) (2000) 1340.

donor community,' to which the IFIs themselves must out of practical and objective necessity be sensitive. Examples include Pakistan (concerns to safe-guard democracy following the October 1999 military coup),[351] Russia (regard-ing human rights abuses in Chechnya),[352] and Myanmar (where the Bank's 1999 analytical report referred to the international community's human rights con-cerns). Together with the East Timor case, this practice of invoking concerns of donors by proxy seems to represent a convenient way of publicly reconciling desired (and often worthy) human rights objectives with positions that prima facie strain conservative interpretations of their mandates. Irrespective of the third party proxy, this growing body of practice makes it difficult to maintain the position that human rights are none of the IFIs' business.

The IFI's reactions in these situations can be compared with their responses to human rights violations and other apparently non-'economic' factors in the past, notably in relation to: (a) India and Pakistan (nuclear testing objec-tions);[353] (b) Nigeria (the November 1995 summary execution by the Abacha government of Ken Saro-Wiwa and eight other Ogoni environmental cam-paigners[354]); and (c) Kenya (widespread human rights abuses, especially in 1999). In the latter case, a Consultative Group meeting in Paris in November 1991 resulted in sanctions on grounds including human rights. The Lawyers' Committee for Human Rights reportedly greeted that case at that time as an example of the Bank assuming an explicit human rights role.[355] However, trans-parency, objectivity and consistency have been lacking in the body of experience

---

[351] As reported in the *World Bank Development News*, 31 March 2000: 'The [Pakistan] loan pro-gram was further complicated by the bloodless military coup in October by General Pervez Musharraf. Even though the IMF's internal rules prohibit it from using political criteria for lending, its discussions on a loan program with Pakistan were put on hold after the coup, with a Fund spokesman saying at the time, "the IMF does not act in a vacuum" when it comes to international relations.'

[352] A serious double standard is apparent as between Russia and Pakistan, however. In latter case the Managing Director issued a blunt warning that Pakistan could lose its IMF aid if democracy was not restored: 'Democracy is in retreat, and when democracy retreats, countries are in danger.' However on the very same day in response to the situation in Chechnya, the Managing Director issued a comparatively technocratic statement that if the Russian 'budget is over-shooting because of an uncontrolled increase of military spending, we shall interrupt our support.' H Steiner and P Alston (2000) at 1448.

[353] See above n 278 and accompanying text.

[354] M Serrill, 'A martyr in vain?', 147(18) *Time International*, 29 April 1996; C Hoff, 'Nigeria exe-cutes 9 activists; world outraged,' *CNN World News*, 20 November 1995, http://www-cgi.cnn.com/WORLD/9511/nigeria/. The IFC immediately cancelled a US\$100 million loan in reaction to the executions, although attributed this to the government's failure to enact certain economic reforms. The US government responded in part by vowing to oppose IMF loans or credits to Nigeria. However the Bank has since maintained active investments in Nigeria, against similar pub-lic dissent that led to Saro-Wiwa's execution. Halifax Initiative, Media Release: 'World Bank pro-vides support for Shell's activities in Nigeria,' 20 June 2001, reporting claims by Owens Wiwa (brother of the late Ken Saro-Wiwa) of human rights abuses associated with Shell's activities. See http://www.halifaxinitiative.org/hi.php/WB/161/.

[355] See Lawyers Committee for Human Rights, *The World Bank: Governance and Human Rights* 56–60 (1993), on the suspension of aid to Kenya (1991) and Malawi (1992). However anecdotal accounts reveal difficulties in distilling a neat and clear characterisation of the Bank's response to Kenyan government's actions in that case.

to date,[356] shortcomings attributable in large measure to structural defects in the IFIs themselves and the mediation of US and G7 strategic interests through their governing bodies.

CONCLUSIONS

While opinion is far from unanimous, the prevailing approach to the interpretation of international organisation charters is in effect to regard them in the same way as national constitutions, however imperfect the analogy, with static or textual approaches giving way to those enabling the effective functioning of the organisation within contemporary expectations and circumstances.[357]

As far as the Bank is concerned, the traditional approach to the interpretation of Article IV, Section 10 was hinged upon the assumption that the Bank's influence was apolitical and technical. The artificiality and falsity of the supposed divisions between 'economic' (as defined from time to time) and 'political' and other factors was laid bare through the course of the Bank's activities throughout the 1980s and 1990s.[358] The corollary is that just about everything that the Bank does is 'political.'

The foregoing analysis of relevant 'practice' within the meaning of Article 31(3)(b) of the Vienna Convention suffices to establish a narrowly circumscribed frame of reference for Article IV, Section 10, and corresponding flexible sphere of operation for the Bank. The correct and preferable interpretation of the 'political' limitation, in light of both principle and practice, ought to be along the lines ventured in 1996 by the UN legal counsel in the *Portuguese and South African loan* case: A prohibition on interference in partisan politics and of discrimination against a State because of the political character of its government, without prejudice to fundamental human rights obligations.[359] An interpretation of this kind duly acknowledges the relevance of rules of international human rights law applicable in the relations between IFI members states,[360] and finds support in the *travaux preparatoires*.[361]

---

[356] See eg Lawyers Committee for Human Rights (1993) at 37–42, noting the Bank's record of support in numerous countries characterised by particularly serious patterns of human rights abuse, such as China, Indonesia, Morocco and Zaire.

[357] 'Lawyers and policy makers assume that when [an international organisation with powers delegated from its members] is created, parties intend to make it effective, and that common sense proposition has led ot the more controversial idea that charter provisions need to be read in light of a "principle of effectiveness." ' J Alvarez (2001) at 136–37.

[358] Former Bank Chief Counsel Herbert Morais is certainly of this view. H Morais (2000) at 89: ''[T]he tests that the IFIs have used to classify particular issues as "political" or "economic" are neither clear nor supported by easily identifiable criteria.'

[359] See above nn 179–84 and accompanying text. The UN legal counsel's opinion in that case was confined to Charter-based human rights obligations, confronting the egregious circumstances of apartheid in South Africa. However in light of the foregoing analysis of the relevance to the IFIs' mandates of human rights obligations under other sources of international law—including 'general principles' of law—no such limitation is necessary here.

[360] Article 31(3)(c) of the Vienna Convention.

[361] Article 32 of the Vienna Convention. See this discussion above at pp 168–69.

As to the scope of inherent authority within the IFIs' charters, the ICJ's marked departure from previous jurisprudence in the *WHO Nuclear Weapons Opinion* might be a source of concern to many human rights activists in the event that the Court were ever called upon to examine questions relating to the IFIs' competences to consider human rights issues.[362] While it is by no means certain that similarly restrictive results would follow, the reliance by the majority on a 'principle of speciality' along with a narrow and strongly contestable conception of the 'logic' of the UN system, might herald a similarly conservative approach in interpreting the IFIs' powers.

On the other hand, the reasoning of the Court does not alter the fundamental requirement flowing from the *Reparations* case that the scope of implied powers must be examined in the circumstances of each particular case. It is unclear how relevant a precedent the *WHO Nuclear Weapons* case would be, in this respect. To a significant degree, the opinion of the majority in that case was the result of an interpretation of specific provisions of the WHO constitution. Not only was Court's reasoning in that regard doubtful on ordinary principles of interpretation, but as has already been seen, both the Bank's and the Fund's Articles prima facie permit a relatively high degree of flexibility in ascertaining the scope of permissible activities.

In any event, it would naïve to imagine that the ICJ operates in a political vacuum. The political and policy considerations arising in an examination of the legality of the use of nuclear weapons—question going to the very heart of international political and security relations—are somewhat different to those affecting an examination of the breadth of the IFIs' mandates.[363] In the latter instance, not only would a purposive interpretation bring the ICJ back in line with its previous jurisprudence, but it would also represent the approach most suited to enabling the Bank and Fund to grapple with the increasingly complex practical challenges with which they are faced, in a manner consistent with the directions in which they have already been compelled to turn. Indeed it is the Fund's emerging co-operative efforts with the World Bank in the PRSP context, and the gradual broadening of their activities into governance, environment and even selective human rights domains, that provide some of the more compelling

---

[362] For a critique of the ICJ's neglect of human rights law see F Tesòn, 'Le peuple, C'est Moi! The World Court and Human Rights' (1987) 81 *American Journal of International Law* 173.

[363] The material differences for present purposes lie not only in the spheres of activity at issue, but in the different constitutions of these international organisations and the relative political influence exerted by major industrialised nations through each. For example, in the former case, the relatively democratically structured WHO governing body would, if given legally-recognised standing in the sphere of international peace and security (although as a practical matter its standing in that arena on issues such as HIV/AIDS and malaria is not in serious dispute), pose a threat to the influence of the five permanent members (P5) of the Security Council whose agendas on health and security related issues will of course not always be consistent with those of WHO's governing body. By contrast those same P5 interests—in particular those of the dominant shareholders in the IFIs who exert greatest control over their policy priorties—would in many respects stand to be promoted, rather than undermined, through a judicially-sanctioned expansion in the IFIs' spheres of operation. This result is of course no more than a reflection of *réalpolitique*, begging an entire raft of questions concerning legitimacy and accountability to be addressed more fully in chapter VI.

evidence (although by no means a completely reliable description) of the sorts of functions that might be necessary for the fulfilment of the duties entrusted to them, and hence, of the allowable nature and scope of their implied powers.

While there is no reason to expect or even necessarily wish for the transmogrification of either the Fund or Bank into a 'human rights organisation,' their respective charters certainly should not be read as limiting the possibilities for constructive engagement with human rights principles, to the extent desirable for the fulfilment of their purposes or necessary as a matter of international law.

V

Practical and Theoretical Impediments to Human Rights Integration

CHAPTER IV concluded that the Articles of Association of both Bank and Fund, having regard to their object and purpose construed in contemporary circumstances, do not impose as significant a constraint on the scope of the IFIs' policy options as is often made out. From the point of view of legal interpretation the Bank and Fund have both duties and a potentially wide field of non-binding policy options under international human rights law.

It may seem paradoxical that the expansion of both the Bank's and Fund's mandates since the 1980s has been driven in particular directions as much by those institutions' critics, as by their supporters. From the perspective of many campaigners, the desire to persuade the IFIs to take on a particular issue or set of issues hitherto considered to fall outside their legitimate domains can be motivated either by reaction to negative externalities arising from their established activities (environmental disasters from major infrastructure projects being a good example, and social impacts of structural adjustment programs another), or on a more strategic and pro-active level, by the hope that the IFIs' collective resources and policy influence will advance 'new' issues in constructive directions.

It is the latter assumption that can be expected to generate most disagreement among both human rights advocates and orthodox development practitioners alike. The central tension from the perspective of the former camp is between the promise of an elevated profile for human rights issues in development, on the one hand, and the risk of normative dilution through inappropriate or insincere operationalisation, on the other, to the possible detriment of the coherence and credibility of human rights in development. This is the core tension that underlies the discussion in the remaining chapters. Resolution of this tension is obviously an inherently subjective undertaking, to which justice cannot be done in the abstract. In lieu of the assuredly futile quest for recipes to resolve this conflict in all situations, the more modest ambition in the succeeding discussion is to identify some of the key factors which need to be taken into account in guiding the nature and extent of IFI engagement with human rights law.

Quite a variety of objections to human rights terminology and operationalisation have been identified in the field of international development at large. The desire to deal in surrogate terms can be explained by a number of factors, including: (1) the desire, through use of malleable and generic formulations, to carve distinctive niches for marketing purposes, in the battle among agencies for limited aid resources; (2) the desire to maintain maximum policy flexibility; (3) adverse reaction to perceived development 'fads;' (4) adverse reactions to the promotion of human rights in excessively abstract and 'legalistic' forms; (5) assumptions concerning the place of confrontational 'violations' based human rights strategies in development; and (6) the functionalist assumption of seeing human rights as 'an essentially political, and thus inherently politicised, concern, to be contrasted with mainstream development activities which, it is thought, can be pursued within a largely neutral, or apolitical framework.'[1] These arguments have been debated at length elsewhere.[2] The emphasis here is on a selection of the most trenchant and frequently voiced obstacles to the introduction of human rights dimensions to the IFIs' work.[3] Drawing from these discussions, chapter VI concludes with a suggestive range of desirable elements of human rights policies, within power of each institution, and appropriate for implementation in the short to medium term.

INSTITUTIONAL AND CULTURAL BARRIERS WITHIN THE BANK

Cultural problems within the Bank, in particular what has become known as Bank staff's 'approval culture,' are inimical to the inculcation of the incentives, skills and approaches required to implement projects with complex environmental and human rights dimensions. The systemic nature of the 'approval culture' problem was first brought to light by an investigation commencing in early 1992 of the Portfolio Management Task Force (PMTF) into the Bank's overall project performance.[4] As Kolk explains, the 'approval culture' appears to relate back, in large part, to the high volume of lending to developing countries during the 1980s. 'In order to demonstrate its crucial and indispensable role as development agency, so the argument goes, [the Bank] had to keep "money

---

[1] P Alston, 'What's in a Name: Does it Really Matter if Development Policies Refer to Goals, Ideals or Human Rights?' in H Helmich in collaboration with E Borghese (eds), *Human Rights in Development Cooperation* (1998) 95–106 at 98–105.

[2] P Alston (1998) at 98–105.

[3] A number of disclaimers specific to the Fund were canvassed in chapter IV, see nn 273–82 and accompanying text. These will not be rehearsed again here.

[4] A Kolk, *Forests in International Environmental Politics: International Organisations, NGOs and the Brazilian Amazon* (1996) at 194. The PMTF report shook the Bank, as it criticised project performance in the Bank's own terms, that is to say, in terms of economic rate of return. See World Bank Memorandum R92–125, 'Effective Implementation: Key to Development Impact,' 3 November 1992 ('Wapenhans report'), referred to in chapter IV above n 140.

moving through the pipeline" or "pushing money out the door,"[5] reflecting a 'pervasive emphasis on loan approval,' to the neglect of project implementation.[6] In this respect the Bank has shown a 'clear preference for large-scale projects which involved large amounts at once, neglected information on possible negative (environmental, social, and even economic) effects of these projects (even when provided by its own staff) and often ignored its own quality requirements. The number of approved proposals and the amounts involved played an important role in the judgement of the career perspectives of the staff, while efficiency was measured by the number of hours spent to get a project through the cycle.'[7] Particular aspects of these cultural problems were elaborated in the Wapenhans report:

(a) As to the project appraisal phase, '[m]any Bank staff perceive appraisals as marketing devices for securing loan approval (and achieving personal recognition),' and 'timely delivery is the dominant institutional value.'[8]

(b) The negotiations phase 'is seen by many Borrowers as a largely *coercive* exercise designed to "impose" the Bank's philosophy and to validate the findings of its promotional approach to Appraisal.'[9]

The problems with project implementation were perceived to encompass 'the pressure to lend, inadequate resources, deficient skills, and distorted incentives.'[10] The 'distorted management and staff incentives' problem was perceived to relate to the Bank's criteria for recruitment and career development, with a focus on Bank staff members' perceptions that 'conceptual and planning activities were valued much higher than implementation and practical management.'[11]

This state of affairs remains has not changed significantly since 1992,[12] and is

---

[5] See B Rich, *Mortgaging the Earth. The World Bank, environmental impoverishment and the crisis of development* (1994) esp at 189; and S George and F Sabelli., *Faith and Credit. The World Bank's secular empire* (1994), cited in A Kolk (1996) at 189.

[6] Wapenhans Report 1992 at 17.

[7] A Kolk (1996) at 189. But as Kolk explains (at 189): 'This is not to say that the "pressure to lend" has necessarily been an explicit policy or been dictated by the higher levels of the Bank. It seems to be perfectly understandable for project staff to want approval for a project, to achieve results, after having worked hard on it for a considerable period of time. This also applies to the inclination to cling to positive aspects of the project and to let them prevail over potentially, but still uncertain, or long-term, negative effects.'

[8] Wapenhans report at 14 and 16.

[9] Wapenhans report at 16.

[10] Wapenhans report at 17, and A Kolk (1996) at 197.

[11] A Kolk (1996) at 197–98. Significantly, Wapenhans report noted that '[s]ignals from senior management are consistently seen by staff to focus on lending targets rather than results on the ground'—Wapenhans report at 23. As for the Bank's response to the Wapenhans report, see World Bank Memorandum R93-62, 'Portfolio Management: Next Steps,' 5 April 1993. For critical comments on its contents, see A Kolk (1996) at 199.

[12] See eg N Bridgeman, 'World Bank Reform in the "Post Policy" Era' (2001) 13 *Georgetown International Environmental Law Review* 1013–46, 1024–37; M Miller-Adams, *The World Bank: New Agendas in a Changing World* (1999) 5. And as Abbasi observes: 'When considering the fine line between buttering up governments and bullying them, employees are acutely aware that their

reflected in a visible weakening of the Bank's social safeguard policies.[13] Most borrowing governments and many within the Bank strongly resist efforts directed towards building a culture of accountability and compliance. For example in the year 2000 in the aftermath of the Inspection Panel's investigation of the Qinghai case,[14] involving findings of large scale non-compliance with social safeguard policies, Bank President Wolfensohn remarked publicly that '[t]here are so many rules and safeguards now that it is becoming very expensive for some borrowers to use us.'[15] Perhaps even more pessimistically the Dutch Executive Director Pieter Stek was reported to have said that 'the [Qinghai] controversy raised the question of whether loan programmes for the Bank were now so constrained by safeguards that it was impossible to make a loan without contravening the rules.'[16]

A former consultant to the World Bank Inspection Panel alleged in 2001 that '[j]ust as [the Bank's] environmental policies were weakened in the 1990s, social

career progression might depend on the way they are perceived by the government that they are lending to, and by subsequent feedback to seniors in Washington. In a climate where greater lending earns bigger plaudits, the danger of pushing rather than holding back on hairline lending decisions is also readily apparent.' K Abbasi, 'The World Bank and World Health: Under Fire,' Vol 318, Issue 7189 *British Medical Journal* (1999) 1003–6, 1006. One can look to Indonesia's case, discussed in chapter III, as a reminder of the potential for compromise of principle in the quest for harmonious business relations with government, especially in circumstances where political space for other potential interlocutors is minimal.

[13] N Bridgeman (2001) at 1024–27; M Civic, 'Prospects for the Respect and Promotion of Internationally Recognised Sustainable Development Practices: A Case Study of the World Bank Environmental Guidelines and Procedures' (1998) 9 *Fordham Environmental Law Review* 231–59; T Roessler, 'The World Bank's Lending Policy and Environmental Standards,' 26 *The North Carolina Journal of International Law and Environmental Regulation*' (2000) 105–41. Operational policies and procedures are codified in the Bank's Operational Manual. A system of Operational Manual Statements and Operational Policy Notes was initiated in the 1970s; after 1987, these began to be consolidated into Operational Directives. The Operational Directives included elements of policy, procedure, and guidance. By the early 1990s, out of an expressed desire to differentiate among these elements, the Operational Directives were converted into a new system that describes Operational Policies (containing the formally binding elements only), Bank Procedures (also formally binding), and Good Practices (discretionary guidance). As at 2002 the conversion process for numerous ODs was still underway.

[14] World Bank, *China Western Poverty Reduction Project Inspection Panel Report* (2000). See the Investigation Report of the World Bank Inspection Panel, 'The Qinghai Project: A Component of the China: Western Poverty Reduction Project (Credit No. 3255-CHA and Loan No. 4501-CHA),' 28 April 2000. For an illuminating critique see N Bridgeman (2001) at 1033–36.

[15] S Sanghera and S Fidler, 'World Bank chief under fire,' *Financial Times*, 14 July 2000.

[16] S Sanghera and S Fidler, 'World Bank chief under fire,' *Financial Times*, 14 July 2000. But during a scathing address to the Executive Board, the US Executive Director Jan Piercy expressed a different perspective: 'It is time for this organisation to see the issue for what it is—delivering on its own commitments to credible internal controls and faithful execution of agreed policies and procedures. It is time to take responsibility.' Piercy's views have subsequently been affirmed unequivocally by the IDA's Executive Board. In their report to the Board of Governors on the 13th replenishment the IDA, the Executive Directors stated their expectation that 'all IDA-financed projects should be in full compliance with the World Bank's environmental and social safeguard policies.' IDA, 'Additions to IDA Resources: Thirteenth Replenishment—Supporting Poverty Reduction Strategies,' Report from the Executive Directors of the IDA to the Board of Governors, 25 July 2002 at 18.

policies are now being weakened.'[17] In March 2001 the UK-based Forest Peoples Program, on behalf of seventy NGOs and individuals from thirty-two countries submitted a letter to the IMF and Bank, alleging that 'in the name of "clarity" and "flexibility", the Bank's policies are, as Bank staff put it, being made [Inspection] "panel-proof." In other words, policies are being made so flexible that staff or borrowers can never be accused of having contravened them and therefore never held to account for problems and failures in implementation. Careful examination of safeguard policies undergoing conversion reveals that binding language is being removed and replaced by statements of "process" and expectation rather than "requirements" and preconditions for loan approval. In this way, compliance with once binding social and environmental provisions is now being left to the discretion and willingness of borrowers.'[18]

The 'approval culture' is but one part of the problem from the perspective of organisational theory. The Bank is above all a technocracy, prizing economists, financial experts and those with other specialised skills, and relying on well-honed and widely applicable lending techniques that can be measured quantitatively.[19] Michael Cernea—the chief advocate for social development concerns at the Bank for twenty years—has remarked that 'the characteristics and biases of an institution's culture tend to put their imprint on the institution's products.'[20] Cernea identified three conceptual biases in the Bank's 'blueprint' approach to development: 'the econocentric model that regards economic and financial variables as the only ones that matter; the technocentric model that addresses the technological variables of development apart from their contextual social fabric; and the commodocentric model that emphasises the "thing" more than the social actors that produce it, highlighting, for example, the Bank's tendency to focus on coffee production but not coffee growers, or water provision but not water users.'[21]

---

[17] N Bridgeman (2001) at 1025.

[18] Letter from the Forest Peoples Program to the World Bank and IMF (2 March 2001), available at http://www.bicusa.org/mdbs/wbg/WbsafeguardssignonMarch20011.pdf, cited in N Bridgeman (2001) at 1025–26. As Kingsbury relates: '[T]he Bank arrangements [vis a vis the Inspection Panel's jurisdiction and lack of explicit policy review role] appear to provide some incentive for management to try to attenuate policies by, for example, incorporating the more demanding provisions in statements of good practice rather than in operational policies, or including phrasing to add wide managerial discretions in obligatory provisions. The long process of conversion to the new format of [(draft) OP's 4.10 on Indigenous Peoples and 4.12 on Involuntary Resettlement] included some internal proposals of this sort, which met with vigorous opposition from other Bank staff and outsiders. As the arduous negotiations in this process among conflicting viewpoints within the Bank, as well as outside consultations and criticism, attest, the Bank system relies on internal staff dynamics, pressure from executive directors, and criticism from bodies ranging from NGOs to the US Congress to maintain and enhance the quality and integrity of policies.' B Kingsbury, 'Operational Policies of International Institutions as Part of the Law-Making Process: The World Bank and Indigenous Peoples' in G Goodwin-Gill and S Talmon (eds), *The Reality of International Law: Essays in Honour of Ian Brownlie* (1999) 323–42, 331–32.

[19] M Miller-Adams (1999) at 6.

[20] M Miller-Adams (1999) at 6.

[21] M Miller-Adams (1999) at 6, and more extensively at 21–32. Miller-Adams summarises (at 6): 'An organisational culture that is technocratic, apolitical, centralised, and biased towards large

As to related institutional barriers, the complaint is sometimes heard that Bank staff 'don't have time to think,' and have no time for training. Existing bureaucratic burdens are said to be significant, with some insiders pointing to the difficulties of convincing middle management of the human rights case. Others complain of the 'endless restructuring' at the Bank, with consequent 'confusion about what the priorities are.'[22] Staff frequently go out on country missions of a few months duration with discrete and concentrated agendas and a relatively 'short term' focus, which are intrinsically difficult to reconcile with rights-based strategies and content. Finally, noting the proliferation of development slogans and philosophies over the last few decades, the resistance within the Bank to perceived 'fads'—into which category human rights are sometimes assumed to fall—is particularly high.

There is not a great deal to be said in response to these additional factors. Cost factors and bureaucratic burdens are an inevitable consequence of any substantial procedural and policy reorientation. In the case of human rights, the necessary personnel, training and institutional adaptation costs could be expected to be quite high. It is ultimately for the Bank itself to take the lead on implementing necessary reforms, and how costs and institutional change are most efficiently and effectively to be carried out. Insofar as safeguard policy compliance is concerned, realistic pre-loan appraisal missions should identify the full costs of safeguard policy compliance for proposed projects, and these costs should be incorporated into the terms of negotiation of the loan agreement.[23]

And as for the characterisation of human rights as a 'fad:' it might seem to some that human rights only entered the international development vernacular in the 1990s. Indeed the most important strides in programmatic terms—in agencies such as UNICEF, UNIFEM, UNAIDS and certain bilateral agencies –undoubtedly took place during that decade. However the relationship between human rights, development and international development cooperation has been the subject of consistent and active debate and scholarship since well prior to the articulation of the Declaration on the Right to Development in 1986. Indeed the inherited body of fundamental human rights standards—reflected in the UN Charter, UDHR and six major international human rights treaties—are at least in part premised upon the close inter-relationship between human rights and economic progress, and the requirement for the progressive realisation of

---

lending programs and a blueprint approach to development will provide a more receptive environment for certain kinds of activities than for others. [For example,] [p]rivate sector development fits readily with key elements of the World Bank's organisational culture, whereas both participation and governance pose greater challenges to it.'

[22] Interviews in Washington DC in February 2000. See also M Miller-Adams (1999) at 5: 'Sweeping plans to revise and streamline [the Bank's] bureaucratic structure have become regular features of Bank life. Usually occurring when a new president assumes control, Bank reorganisations have resulted in a high degree of organisational turmoil and often a loss of staff morale, but do not seem to have achieved either greater simplification or enhanced efficiency.'

[23] N Bridgeman (2001) at 1027.

human rights inter alia within the framework of international cooperation. To dismiss human rights in development as a 'fad' is to ignore the history and normative foundations of the UN system, the progressive strengthening of human rights norms and institutions at national and international levels, and corresponding progress in 'mainstreaming' human rights throughout the UN system's operational activities (development, humanitarian, and peace and security).

INSTITUTIONAL AND CULTURAL BARRIERS WITHIN THE FUND

The institutional barriers at the Fund, foreshadowed in chapter II, are of a somewhat different kind to those emphasised above. Not having any direct involvement in project lending and 'moving money out the door,' IMF staff are relatively free of some of the most trenchant disincentives to human rights integration. And while as at 2002 many might criticise the depth to which the Fund's post-1999 'anti-poverty' orientation has gone, the organisation as a whole does not appear to have been subjected to the same degree to the wide range of development 'fads' that have provoked such resilience and cynicism in many quarters within the Bank. The chief institutional impediments to human rights integration at the Fund, however, are its relative disciplinary homogeneity, coupled with a tight 'command and control' management structure not likely to permit much in the way of innovation 'outside the box', to the extent that this would be necessary or desirable. Financial resources are said to pose another constraint, within an ostensibly 'zero budget growth' environment.[24]

Of course nothing is static in these respects. Much depends upon the shifting sands of G–7 politics and in particular the policy directions at any given time from the US Treasury and Congress, and the extent of organised and sustained public pressure for reform. And indeed in contrast to the Bank, a relatively efficient and coherent management hierarchy and relatively influential General Counsel's office could be viewed as an opportunity rather than a constraint, in the event that an appropriately circumscribed and compelling case for human rights integration could be presented. Social development specialists have permeated the Fund's erstwhile impermeable macro-economic realms, and considerable shifts in rhetoric and policy are evident in terms of the Fund's PRGF re-orientation. The relatively small size of the Fund is itself a comparative advantage. However the changes so far are anything but systematic, and appear to impact only upon limited (albeit important) areas within the Fund's domain. Within the institutional parameters just outlined, and with political winds from Washington driving the Fund's ostensible retreat into narrowly defined spheres of competence,[25] it is difficult to imagine human rights penetrating beyond very

---

[24] Interviews in Washington DC in February 2000.

[25] A Meltzer, *Report of the International Financial Institutions Advisory Commission*. Meltzer Commission Report, International Financial Institutions Advisory Commission: Hearing Before the

superficial levels within the Fund's policies and program activities in the short term.

OTHER INSTITUTIONAL AND DISCIPLINARY BARRIERS

In their wide-ranging survey of governance-related conditionalities Kapur and Webb identify some of the IFIs' chief shortcomings in terms of their track record in reaching beyond their institutional and disciplinary walls: 'The need for tailoring . . . runs into the wall of IFI institutional culture and incentives, which are inimical to the development of country-specific expertise. The Bank's perpetual re-organisations truncate any tendency to acquire such expertise. The issue is moot for IMF, which prides itself on its universal nostrums. In both institutions, personnel incentives encourage rotation rapidly through departments, rather than to develop country- or even region-specific expertise. The traditional predominance of the economics profession in IFI staffing—the social science with the strongest claim to universality—has been another factor in the undervaluation of country-specific knowledge . . . Unlike budget balancing, or road, dam and school construction, IFI contributions to governance problems must build on a close familiarity with country-specific cultural, social and political knowledge. These institutional obstacles to country-specific knowledge are reinforced by the "low brow" valuation that is placed on such knowledge within the academic community from which IFI personnel is drawn, and with which the IFIs carry on a continuous and extensive interaction.'[26]

To these systemic problems were added: (a) in relation to civil service reform initiatives, over-reliance on narrow range of standard interlocutors in 'core ministries' at country level, to design and implement 'one-size-fits-all . . . blueprints in diverse country settings;' and (b) in connection with judicial reform efforts, inherent risk aversion, and a lack of understanding and failure to take account of applicable informal legal and enforcement mechanisms.[27] These difficulties set in sober relief aspirations for the inculcation of the science of human rights within a vast range of local contingencies.

Senate Committee on Foreign Relations, 106th Congress (2000). For a discussion and critique of the Meltzer report see chapter IV above at n 280 and accompanying text. OXFAM has also argued strongly for a smaller, more focused IMF: 'Stabilisation operations should be developed as part of national poverty reduction strategies, not as a set of narrowly-defined macro-economic goals devised in Washington.' OXFAM, 'Reforming the IMF,' OXFAM Policy Papers, International Media Briefing, April 2000, http://www.globalpolicy.org/socecon/bwi-wto/imf/oxfam.htm.

[26] D Kapur and R Webb, 'Governance-Related Conditionalities of the International Financial Institutions' (2000) 6 *G-24 Discussion Paper Series* 10.
[27] D Kapur and R Webb (2000) at 10–11.

It is clear enough that human rights specialists and neo-classical development economists are animated by quite different disciplinary and philosophical traditions.[28] However whether there is anything inherent in human rights and economics *as disciplines* that renders them mutually incompatible is a separate question. It is sometimes suggested, for example, that the human rights framework is absolute, brooking no violation under any circumstances, whereas the interests of economics lie in the maximisation of efficiency, and with trade-offs between competing claims on scare resources.[29] Is there any irreconcileable difference here?

True it is that human rights strategies are not slave to efficiency in the sense understood in economic orthodoxy, and of themselves will not always provide clear answers to policy prioritisation and trade-offs.[30] However there is nothing in the core international human rights standards and associated jurisprudence to suggest that the occurrence of human rights violations through the implementation of structural adjustment programs necessarily impugns or invalidates the entire program on human rights grounds. Certainly in the case of demonstrable violations there should be the possibility of bringing legal or other appropriate forms of action to claim redress.[31] Failing to respect, protect or ful-

[28] See eg A Sfeir-Younis (World Bank Special Representative to the WTO and UN), 'The Linkages Between Economic Development and Human Rights,' at a workshop sponsored by the Bank's Environment and Socially Sustainable Development Network, 2 May 2002, observing that for many human rights specialists there is a 'subtle and profound difference' between traditional economics and human rights, manifest in 'the difference between their deeply rooted values and the value systems they embrace in making their development decisions. The supremacy of the market system and the values that it holds, eg individualism, competitiveness, comparative advantage, and exclusion through purchasing power, seem to be at the core of the debate.'

[29] For one particular dimension of this potential conflict see A Sfeir-Younis, 'The Political Economy of the Right to Development: Is Mainstreaming a New Ethic of Development a Utopia?', Address at the end of the year 2000 open seminar: 'An Exchange on Development,' 19 December 2000, at 8, 10 and 12–13, with the universality of human rights cited as a putative source of inconsistency. See also A Sfeir-Younis, 'Economic, Social and Cultural Rights and Development Strategies: Where Do They Meet?', Statement by the World Bank Special Representative to the United Nations and the World Trade Organisation, International Seminar: 'Economic, Social and Cultural Rights in the Actions of the International Development Institutions,' Geneva, 7 May 2001, arguing, in part, that the human rights debate needs to be 'anchored onto the process of wealth creation.'

[30] See e.g UNDP, *Human Development Report 2000: Human Rights and Human Development* (2000) at 23, suggesting a comparative advantage of 'human development analysis' in this respect.

[31] Article 8 of the UDHR and article 2(3) of the ICCPR provide for the right to a remedy—including but not limited to judicial remedies—in response to violations. Similarly see Committee on Economic, Social and Cultural Rights, General Comment No. 3 (on the nature of States Parties' obligations, Art 2(1)), E/1990/23, at para 5. The 'legal empowerment' initiatives of the Asian Development Bank provide an interesting example of efforts to enliven formal legal channels of redress and promote access to those most in need. See ADB, *Law and Policy Reform at the Asian Development Bank* (2001) available at http://www.adb.org/Documents/Others/Law_ADB/lpr_2001.pdf, including case studies in the Philippines and Bangladesh on how 'legal empowerment' (broadly defined as 'the use of law to increase the control that disadvantaged populations have over

fil the *human right* to adequate housing, food or education is not the same as failing to honour plans, aspirations or non-legally binding entitlements in those areas. However the occurrence of individual human rights violations does not of itself render human rights irreconcilable with economics within the overall development equation.

The proper and relevant nature of inquiry under international human rights law is considerably more nuanced. On the concept of 'progressive implementation' (beyond a core minimum entitlement to any given right), the Committee on Economic, Social and Cultural Rights argues that there is a strong yet rebuttable presumption that retrogressive measures taken in relation to the rights reflected in the ICESCR are not permissible. If any deliberately retrogressive measures are taken, the State party has the burden of proving that they have been introduced 'after the most careful consideration of all alternatives and that they are duly justified by reference to the totality of the rights provided for in the Covenant in the context of the full use of the State party's maximum available resources.'[32]

With this formulation as the relevant and legally valid guide, and the measure one would expect to be applied by domestic courts in adjudicating claims arising under aspects of IFI-sponsored adjustment programs, the premises underlying human rights and economics appear to be more closely reconcilable.[33] In a sense both economics and human rights are directed, within certain defined parameters, towards the optimal resolution of competing claims for scare resources, albeit not on short-run and narrowly constructed 'efficiency'

their lives') can advance good governance and poverty reduction strategies. But one must of course be wary of undue reliance on legal formalism. For a more general discussion of 'micro-development' and law theory and practice, focused on empowering the poor through a mix of legal, political and social mobilisation strategies (law in context), see R Blake, 'The World Bank's Draft Comprehensive Development Framework and the Micro-Paradigm of Law and Development' (2000) 3 *Yale Human Rights and Development Law Journal* 159–89, 169–71. See also C Moser and A Norton, *To Claim our Rights: Livelihood Security, Human Rights and Sustainable Development* (2001) 21–23, reflecting an anthropological understanding of 'legal pluralism,' focusing on law as a 'social process' rather than solely as text or formal legal structures.

[32]   Committee on Economic, Social and Cultural Rights, General Comment No. 3, para. 9; General Comment No. 13 (the right to education, Art 13), E/C.12/1999/10, para. 45, and General Comment No. 14 (the right to the highest attainable standard of health, Art 12), E/C.12/2000/4, para 32.

[33]   See P Hunt, M Nowak and S Osmani, 'Human Rights and Poverty Reduction Strategies: A Discussion Paper' (June 2002) available at http://www.unhchr.ch/development/poverty for a discussion of the synergies between human rights and poverty reduction discourse. On a similar theme but focusing on a 'human rights approach to WTO law,' see E Petersmann, 'Human Rights and International Economic Law in the 21st Century: The Need to Clarify Their Inter-relationships' (2001) *Journal of International Economic Law* 3–39, 23, 38. However for human rights-based critiques of the normative and idealogical assumptions underpinning Petersmann's position see Howse, R, 'Human Rights in the WTO: Whose Rights? What Humanity? Comment on Petersmann' (2002) 13(3) *European Journal of International Law* 651–60, and Alston, P, 'Resisting the Merger and Aquisition of Human Rights by Trade Law: A Reply to Petersmann' (2002) 13(4) *European Journal of International Law* 815–44, and the discussion at http://www.ejil.org/forum_tradehumanrights/

grounds.[34] The recognition of economic and social values as human rights, and human rights more as a science than a theology, could assist considerably in resolving inter-disciplinary confusion and dispelling unduly absolutist conceptions regarding the compatability of human rights with cross-disciplinary assumptions and operational demands.

THE FUNCTIONALIST OBJECTION

The essential premise of functionalism for present purposes is that the role of international institutions should be the provision of services (eg food, health, employment), rather than fundamental unifying principles such as human rights, and moreover that responsibility for delivery of such services can be allocated in a decentralised or even 'polycentralised' fashion.[35] To a significant extent it was this set of assumptions that animated the original design of the UN system, although the seemingly random pattern of its subsequent evolution belies the existence of internal logic or coherent design.

Statements by the Bank's former General Counsel in 1996 appeared to reinforce quite a traditional view of the logic of the UN system, an interpretation consistent with the UN systems original functionalist assumptions and with the majority decision of the ICJ in the *WHO Nuclear Weapons Opinion*. Remarking on the question of the Bank's role in the protection of political rights, the former General Counsel warned:

Drawing the Bank, which is an international institution of a predominantly financial character, directly into politically charged areas, with their typical vagaries and double standards, can only politicise its work and jeopardise its credibility, both in the financial markets where it borrows and in the member countries where it lends. In the final analysis, the purposes of the world community may be better served if *political*

---

[34] For further suggestions as to historical and conceptual synergies see A Sfeir-Younis (World Bank Special Representative to the WTO and UN), 'The Linkages Between Economic Development and Human Rights,' at a workshop sponsored by the Bank's Environment and Socially Sustainable Development Network, 2 May 2002, advocating inter alia an 'inclusive welfare economics' and a conceptual framework for integrating the right to development (interpreted as a 'process through which society allocates rights and entitlements over its productive assets (forms of capital)') with the theory of 'growth, capital accumulation and wealth creation.'

[35] The leading advocates of functionalist theories of international cooperation in the post-World War II period included D Mitrany, *A Working Peace System: An Argument for the Functional Development of International Organisation* (1943); G Niemeyer, *Law Without Force* (1941); and E Haas, *Beyond the Nation State: Functionalism and International Organisation* (1964). For a critique of some of these assumptions see E Spiro (1979) at 154–57; J Gatthi, 'International Law and Eurocentricity: A Review Essay' (1988) 9 *European Journal of International Law* 184–211; P Alston, 'Making or Breaking Human Rights: The UN's Specialised Agencies and the Implementation of the International Covenant on Economic, Social and Cultural Rights' in (1979) *Human Rights and Development Working Papers*, No. 1, Anti-Slavery Society 4–5; and in the particular context of the gradual fusion of human rights with development, J Gatthi, 'Good Governance as a Counter Insurgency Agenda to Oppositional and Transformative Social Projects in International Law' (1999) 5 *Buffalo Human Rights Law Review* 107, 133–41. See further discussion in chapter IV above.

reform is pursued by political organisations, and *political* human rights are monitored by the relevant UN organisations, regional agencies, courts, commissions and the NGOs established for this purpose. These institutions are not only in a better position to weigh political considerations; their representation and voting structure are not tied to financial contributions, as is the case in the Bank. If these institutions are not effective, or are under-resourced, the answer should be to strengthen them, not to ask other organisations with no mandate and no competency in the field to substitute for them. The creation of the office of the UN High Commissioner for Human Rights is a clear recognition of an appropriate allocation of roles in this field. By contrast, further politicisation of international financial institutions, even for a moral purpose, could undermine their standing in financial markets and their ability to play the role for which they have been established.[36]

Possible responses to this line of argument were discussed in chapter IV. In any case, it is doubtful now that the Bank's legal department would seek to rely too slavishly upon such an interpretation, in light of the burgeoning evidence concerning the inter-relationships between civil and political rights and project performance, the instrumental value of accountability in the context of an appropriate environment for aid, the functional imperatives of the PRSP framework, and the Bank's incrementally advancing programmatic engagement with human rights standards and principles in areas previously discussed.

'HUMAN RIGHTS IS BAD FOR BUSINESS'

The claim is sometimes heard that in the increasingly competitive market for international finance, the explicit engagement by the Bank with human rights issues would impose unwarranted and onerous obligations upon its borrowing members, thereby undermining the Bank's competitive position and the commercial value of its bonds. The first limb of this concern—that human rights requirements may import potentially resource-intensive procedural and substantive requirements—is certainly correct, as far as it goes, and hardly surprising, should human rights recognition be intended to operate at any level above window-dressing. However as was seen in chapter IV, in many respects the Bank is already getting into the business of including explicit human rights components within its development policy framework and program design. Moreover there is increasing pressure for private consortia to follow suit, particularly in connection with risky ventures where the Bank's relative external credibility makes it a valuable investment partner.[37] While only incremental and

---

[36] I Shihata (1996) at 9.

[37] G Hernandez Uriz, 'To Lend or Not to Lend: Oil, Human Rights, and the World Bank's Internal Contradictions' (2001) 14 *Harvard Human Rights Journal* 197–231; S Mahony, 'World Bank's Policies and Practice in Environmental Impact Assessment' (1995) 12 *Environmental and Planning Law Journal* 97–115. See also B Kingsbury, 'Operational Policies of International Institutions as Part of the Law-Making Process: The World Bank and Indigenous Peoples' in G Goodwin-Gill and S Talmon (eds), *The Reality of International Law: Essays in Honour of Ian Brownlie* (1999) 323–42, 336.

somewhat opportunistic at the present stage such initiatives, coupled with increasingly open human rights rhetoric, diminish the force of the standard objection that express engagement with human rights would undermine the market value of the Bank's bonds. This conclusion is supported by the explicit recognition of the value of human rights in development by IDA deputies in the IDA 12 replenishment negotiations early in 1999.[38]

DOUBLE STANDARDS

One of the more persistent accusations levelled against the IFIs concerns the double standard in the extent to which the voices and interests of the dominant shareholders and their client States and strategic partners are reflected in deliberations and decisions of the IFIs' governing bodies, as opposed to the interests of States not so aligned. This objection is sometimes suggested to affect the legitimacy of the entire human rights endeavour. The disproportionate influence of both the Bank and Fund on developed and developing countries is one of the most systemic and troubling aspect of this problem. The IMF's advice, for example, can safely be (and frequently is) ignored by major shareholder states, yet carries potentially enormous political, economic and social implications in developing and heavily indebted countries such as Indonesia, Bolivia and Tanzania.[39] One could also look to the example of the World Bank's relations with China, where the Bank's environmental and social safeguard policies appear to be disproportionately flouted.[40] As a politically powerful shareholder

---

[38] See chapter IV above n 256 and accompanying text.

[39] R Borosage 'The IMF, peddling misery,' *International Herald Tribune*, 23–24 September 2000, at 4. Borosage, critical of the Fund's monetary tightening and austerity prescriptions, along with its disproportionate promotion of free trade and anti-inflationary policies, comments that: 'The [F]und's answer to the trade deficit is to slow the US economy, throw Americans out of work and reduce demand for all goods, foreign or domestic. This is like a doctor stemming the bleeding of your arm by stopping your heart. Sensibly US decision-makers have blithely ignored the [F]und's consultation. We [the United States] don't take orders from the IMF; we give them. But for indebted developing countries, the IMF's prescriptions are force-fed.' For the Fund's perspective on some of these claims see T Dawson, 'The IMF's work,' *International Herald Tribune*, 27 September 2000.

[40] See the Investigation Report of the World Bank Inspection Panel, 'The Qinghai Project: A Component of the China: Western Poverty Reduction Project (Credit No. 3255-CHA and Loan No. 4501-CHA),' 28 April 2000, revealing among other things the procedural shortcuts taking in the loan application stage, and multiple failures by Bank Management to follow applicable operational policies, occasionally defended on the grounds that 'in China things are done differently.' For a critique focusing upon the issue of involuntary resettlement in particular, see S Fidler, 'World Bank schemes cost 2.6m their homes,' *Financial Times*, 25 September 2000, commenting upon undisclosed Bank documents claimed to reveal that a majority of the projects creating involuntary displacement are in the East Asia and Pacific (EAP) region, 'and most of them in China.' Furthermore based on Bank data valid as at May 1999, forty percent of all projects involving resettlement were assessed to be 'likely to have significant adverse environmental impacts,' and half of the projects in the EAP region. Strangely the Bank's contemporaneously released 'Annual Review of the Environment: Environment Matters' failed to reflect or address these shortcomings—World Bank News Release No. 2000/077/S, 'World Bank Says Leadership is Critical for Environmental Progress,' 22 September 2000.

as well as the Bank's most significant borrower China, unlike a great many other developing countries, is not prevailed upon to implement measures to ensure freedom of expression, free press, and other items on the expanding good governance menu.

The fact that human rights cannot be promoted and ensured (as appropriate) through the IFIs with equal impact in developed and developing countries is certainly a matter of great concern. The clear need to address the voting structure on the Boards of these institutions and redistribute decision-making power along more democratic and equitable lines having regard to where the impact of decisions is primarily felt, can be expected to defuse bona fide objections of this sort to some degree.[41]

Subject to the progress on the level of institutional reform, among of the chief values of human rights within the normative framework for development are their inherent legitimacy and relative determinacy and objectivity. Ritualistic 'sovereignty' based objections to international 'interference' have lost whatever credence they might once have had.[42] Disclaimers of this kind have always warranted critical scrutiny, in order to distinguish legitimate claims from the disingenuous demands of authoritarian regimes. Moreover as a point of principle it is untenable to suggest that the simple fact that internationally grounded human rights—whether mediated through the IFIs (as appropriate) or otherwise—are subject to more effective and consistent implementation in some countries than others, thereby constitutes good cause to abandon all efforts across the board. Great care needs to be taken not to throw the human rights baby out with the increasingly stale and murky 'state sovereignty' bathwater.

EMPIRICAL JUSTIFICATIONS FOR EVOLVING MANDATES

The comment is frequently made that the Bank relies upon, and is in effect slave to, solidly based empirical justifications for expansion into new areas. Empirical

---

[41] See more detailed discussion in chapter VI.

[42] See chapter IV above, at nn 71–73 and accompanying text. For a powerful contemporary statement on this issue see *Application of the Convention on the Prevention and Punishment of the Crime of Genocide (Bosnia and Herzegovina v. Yugoslavia (Serbia and Montenegro))* (11 July 1996) per Weeramantry J at 2: 'The concept of human rights has long passed the stage when it was a narrow parochial concern between sovereign and subject. We have reached the stage, today, at which the human rights of everyone, anywhere, are the concern of everyone, everywhere. The world's most powerful States are bound to recognise them, equally with the weakest, and there is not even the semblance of a suggestion in contemporary international law that such obligations amount to a derogation of sovereignty.' See also W Reisman, 'Sovereignty and Human Rights in Contemporary International Law' in G Fox and B Roth (eds), *Democratic Governance and International Law* (2000) 239. This is of course not to say that good grounds for *bona fides* objections to human rights-based interventions might not exist in particular cases, or indeed as a question of principle. See eg A Orford, 'Locating the International: Military and Monetary Interventions after the Cold War' (1997) 38 *Harvard International Law Journal* 443. Human rights are still susceptible to misuse as a cloak for disingenuous political motives, although at least at the level of the IFIs, institutional reforms of the sort suggested in chapter VI would be designed to minimise the possible scope for abuse.

studies over the last decade have increasingly borne out the instrumental importance of a wide range of factors euphemistic with human rights, such as participation, freedom of expression and association, 'empowerment,' gender equality, and distributional equity. However still noticeably absent as at the year 2002 were studies apt to confirm the comparative advantages of a 'human rights approach' in the terms in which it is increasingly being advocated—such as *proving* the added value of accountability in legal terms, *proving* human rights' contribution to empowerment, *demonstrating* the benefits from conversion of economic and social 'goods' such as food and education into matters of 'right,' and how that might impact upon macroeconomic design of country programs. The challenges to experimental design are an obvious problem here, as is the regrettable dearth of actual practice upon which empirical studies could be based.

Of course none of this is intended to elevate instrumental considerations above normative ones insofar as rights-based programming is concerned. Human rights are the end in themselves, as well as a means. However from a purely instrumental standpoint it is not reasonable to hold the prospects for human rights integration hostage to the presumed virtues of empiricism in all respects. Environmental analogies are apt in this regard, showing the true extent to which the Bank's agenda has been influenced by external lobbies, pressures and political factors.[43] And as mentioned in chapter III, there is little doubt that particular categories of qualitative work have had just as much influence on the evolution of the Bank's mandate as has work ostensibly based upon empirical justifications.[44]

LIMITATIONS ON CONDITIONALITY AS A LEGITIMATE AND VIABLE HUMAN RIGHTS VEHICLE

The origins, legal basis and contemporary scope of IFI conditionalities were discussed in chapters II and IV. The principal instrumental reasons for the emergence of conditionality have not significantly changed since the 1980s,[45] however conditionality as practiced at the IFIs has more recently been the subject of sustained and quite fundamental attack. For example an extensive review

[43] R Wade, 'Greening the Bank: The Struggle Over the Environment, 1970–1995' in D Kapur, J Lewis and R Webb (eds), *The World Bank: Its First Half Century (Vol. 2)* (1997) 611–734; N Bridgeman (2001) at 1020–21; and the discussion in chapter VI below at nn 305–8 and accompanying text.

[44] As indicated earlier (chapter III, n 5 and accompanying text) it is often claimed that the writings of prominent development economists such as Amartya Sen—whether or not directly empirically-based—significantly influences the Bank's fluctuating priorities.

[45] See eg D Kapur and R Webb (2000) at 1–3, citing the principal rationales as 'protecting the IFIs' financial integrity,' 'overcoming borrower incentives that lead to commitment failure,' conditionalities as 'screening devices which enable a creditor to discriminate between debtor countries willing to use IMF resources to invest and repay and countries which are not,' and more recently as 'bridge to close the credibility gap' in order to facilitate private investment decisions and capital flows.

by Tony Killick in 1995 criticised the Fund's over-reliance on conditionality, as well as a 'proliferation of conditionality in Fund programmes leading to heightened non-compliance.'[46] Stiglitz argued in 1999 that: 'There is increasing evidence that [conditionality] was not [effective]—good policies cannot be bought, at least in a sustainable way. Equally critically, there is a concern that the way the changes were effected undermined democratic processes.'[47] And in a series of fundamental critiques going to both legitimacy and effectiveness Paul Collier has argued: 'The extension of the practice of conditionality from the occasional circumstances of crisis management to the continuous process of economic policy-making has implied a transfer of sovereignty which is not only unprecedented but is often dysfunctional.'[48] Moreover Collier claimed that donor conditionality was 'incredible since its inception,' by reason of the following factors: (a) penalties inflicted by the conditionality regime 'lacked moral legitimacy;' (b) the punishment was excessive relative to the 'crime;' and (c) 'the imposition of penalties was not in the financial interests of the donors.'[49] And in their review of the IFIs' governance-related conditionalities (of particular human rights relevance) in the year 2000, Kapur and Webb criticised the problems of lack of situation-specificity and genuine country ownership, excessive and unequal distribution of the burden of regulatory adjustment, susceptibility to 'faddishness,' persistence of top-down approaches, lack of serious social assessment, exclusive focus on 'internal' rather than external factors such as inequitable terms of trade, and unrealistic time horizons.[50]

These grim findings have potentially significant human rights implications, to the extent that reform proposals need to countenance human rights-based conditionality in some form and in some circumstances. The chorus of critics has provoked considerable reflection as to the alternatives to the promotion of desired policy choices through the vehicle of conditionality, such as the scaling down of lending activities in favour of assistance of a more technical advisory nature, an emphasis on the Bank as a 'knowledge Bank,' and so forth.[51] However there do appear to be some rather fundamental problems with these sorts of alternatives. The first and most obvious is that there are limits to the non-lending services that the IFIs can provide in non-lending areas, partly due to scale, but partly also due to the self-evident fact that in order to exert policy influence it helps to have money on the table. Secondly, in what might seem an absurd extrapolation of the lessons of Dollar and Pritchett's influential 'aid

---

[46] T Killick, IMF Programmes in Development Countries (1995), cited in D Kapur and R Webb (2000) at 7.

[47] J Stiglitz, 'The World Bank at the Millennium' (1999) 109 *The Economic Journal* 591, cited in D Kapur and R Webb (2000) at 7.

[48] P Collier, 'International Financial Institutions in Africa' in A Schedler *et al*, *The Self-Restraining State* (1999), cited in D Kapur and R Webb, (2000) at 7–8.

[49] P Collier (1999) at 319–20, cited in D Kapur and R Webb (2000) at 8.

[50] D Kapur and R Webb (2000).

[51] See eg C Gilbert A Powell and D Vines, 'Positioning the World Bank' (1999) 109 *Economic Journal* 598–633; C Gilbert and D Vines (eds), *The World Bank: Structure and Policies* (2000).

effectiveness' study,[52] to extend lending and other financial assistance only on a 'zero conditionality' basis would be tantamount in practice to limiting access to those who least need it.[53]

Finally and perhaps most fundamentally, an unduly superficial focus upon conditionality as an instrument diverts the spotlight from the political interests pulling the strings behind the scenes. It is simply not realistic to expect the dominant industrialised members—whose interests have been so well served by the IFIs' energetic promotion of the neo-liberal paradigm—to abandon conditionality altogether in the wider sense discussed earlier in chapter III. The IFIs are but two vehicles, albeit especially influential ones, through which such interests have been and to some extent will continue to be ventilated. As vital as it is to moderate these excesses, expose underlying political interests and reform these institutions for the sake of their legitimacy and effectiveness, the central strategic challenge is to do so in ways that minimise the risk of dominant powers' disengagement from multilateral cooperation.[54]

On the fairly safe assumption that fundamental institutional reform is a long-term undertaking, one can expect that conditionality in some form will be here to stay for some time to come. But while to some degree inevitable, it does not necessarily follow that conditionality should be the main vehicle upon which human rights reforms at the IFIs should be based. Far-reaching structural reforms of the sort canvassed in chapter VI are a prerequisite to principled, consistent and even-handed application of conditionality in all its forms. Recommendations concerning human rights-based conditionality need to be viewed in this cautionary light, and against the lessons of experience distilled by Killick, Stiglitz, Collier, Kapur, Webb and others.

STIFLING OF PROGRESSIVE LOCAL INITIATIVES?

Without question, the institutional prerequisites for effective accountability in human rights terms pose serious challenges for most countries in the medium to long term. The concern is sometimes expressed that attempts to formalise or systematise human rights strategies or inverventions at the national level might backfire, in terms of crowding out the scope for progressive local level and community initiatives. Given the great diversity within and between societies, progressive national legislation consistent with international human rights standards may often be difficult to achieve in other than a lowest common

---

[52] D Dollar and L Pritchett, *Aid Effectiveness: What Works, What Doesn't and Why* (1998).

[53] The situation is of course not as straight-forward as this, as low income countries do not all, by definition, have poor institutions and policies such as to disqualify themselves from unconditional assistance. C Burnside and D Dollar, 'Aid, Growth, The Incentive Regime and Poverty Reduction' in C Gilbert and D Vines (eds.) (2000), 210–27 at 224. See also nn 88–91 below and accompanying text, on how the 'fungibility' phenomenon impacts on this equation.

[54] For echoes of this kind of concern see J Weidner, 'World Bank Study' (2001) 7 *Buffalo Human Rights Law Review* 193–226, 226.

denominator way. Alternatively, relieved of the technocratic and onerous burden of formalistic human rights-based initiatives, a good deal of creativity could be unleashed at community and local levels 'under the radar'.[55]

This suggested scope for creativity is obviously enhanced considerably by the operational flexibility exercised by country directors within a highly decentralised organisation. In formal terms country offices' discretions appear to be limited only to the extent that binding Operational Directives (ODs) (or converted Operational Policies or Bank Procedures) dictate. However as was seen earlier in this chapter even these relatively loose parameters seemed to be facing something of a watering down in the overall OD review process.[56] Regulatory weakening obviously presents serious potential pitfalls. Even if, for argument's sake, a lowering of the bar were to create more space at national level for individual initiative and creative approaches in some cases, it self-evidently also permits departure from 'best practices' on social issues virtually across the board. Even more seriously, the absence of consistent minimum standards within ODs, OPs and BPs and (enforced) national laws increases the possibilities for human rights *violations* 'under the radar.'

On the whole it is difficult to find the 'let a hundred flowers bloom' argument against standardised human rights approaches convincing. For one thing, it appears to ascribe to the human rights analytical and procedural framework a higher degree of rigidity, prescription and remoteness than need necessarily be the case,[57] and fails adequately to explain how an overt human rights regulatory role would necessarily galvanise opposition to subtle behind-the-scenes creativity. To the contrary, history in certain parts of East Africa, Asia and elsewhere has shown how even quite 'formal' human rights institutions and standards can be activated to good effect to aid those seeking to improve official responsiveness to human rights demands.[58] But perhaps an even more basic point is that, as far as can be discerned, those advocating incremental progress by stealth would not appear to have a particularly impressive repository of experience upon which to rely. There appears to be considerably more to be said for the promotion of standardised approaches, with human rights as a central element, as part of a more general strategy to lift performance across the board, even if (for argument's sake) this were to come at the expense of the stifling of a relatively small number of ad hoc initiatives.

---

[55] Interviews in Washington DC in February 2000. In the same vein another commentator, referring to the Bank's 'disparate, incoherent' and indirect human rights approach, regarded this as being better than trying to introduce a formal human rights policy, because under the present situation (with Wolfensohn having given a 'yellow to green light') there is room for creativity and to have 'interested people leading out in front.'

[56] See above nn 17–18 and accompanying text.

[57] See above n 31 and accompanying text.

[58] See eg Y Ghai, 'The Kenyan Bill of Rights: Theory and Practice' in P Alston (ed), *Promoting Human Rights Through Bills of Rights: Comparative Perspectives* (1999) 187–240, and the discussion above n 31 and accompanying text.

CULTURAL RELATIVISM IN CONTEXT

One often hears the claim—within the IFIs and elsewhere—that human rights based approaches are 'individualistic' or 'western' and not easily reconcilable with, for example, obligations and duties to community and family. Human rights are often perceived to bring in or prioritise the values of particular (politically dominant) groups, at the expense of localised culture and adaptation. International documents and associated human rights standards, it is said, have limited impact and relevance to indigenous culture and local value systems and forms of social organisation.

It is difficult to address these kinds of concerns in the abstract.[59] On a purely positivistic plane the starting point is clear enough: all states have voluntarily ratified or acceded to and are bound in good faith to implement at least one (in most cases, several) of the six core UN human rights treaties.[60] However on a deeper level of analysis, cultural relativist objections frequently understate or ignore the significant degree of flexibility within the international human rights normative framework—properly understood—for accommodating cultural diversity, and the practical possibilities and imperatives to tailor human rights implementation strategies to local level realities.[61] In answer to those positing an accessively absolutist or 'hyperindividualistic' conception of human rights,[62] it must be understood that the global human rights framework is in fact premised upon the existence of 'rights in society,' as evidenced for example within standard limitations clauses.[63] Furthermore there are explicit provisions, for example in the nearly-universally ratified CRC, supporting rights in the

---

[59] For general discussions see P Alston (1998); H Steiner and P Alston, *International Human Rights in Context: Law, Politics, Morals* (1996) at 166–255; J Bauer and D Bell (eds), *The East Asian Challenge for Human Rights* (1999); Y Ghai (1998); M Freeman, 'Fifty Years of Development of the Concept and Contents of Human Rights' in P Baehr, C Flinterman and M Senders (eds) (1999) at 38–39.

[60] As mentioned in chapter I, as at 2002, 80% of UN member states had adhered to four or more of the six core treaties. All but two states (the USA and Somalia) had adhered to the CRC. See also the discussion in chapter IV on non-treaty sources of international human rights law, including rights and obligations as a matter of customary international law, general principles of law, and *jus cogens*. And as noted by Shashi Tharoor, developing countries—notably India, China, Chile, Cuba, Lebanon and Panama—played an active and influential part in drafting the UDHR. See S Tharoor, 'Are Human Rights Universal?', *Commentary: Project Syndicate*, June 2002, available at http://www.project-syndicate.cz/series/series_text.php4?id=890.

[61] For a useful discussion of these parameters in the African context see B Ibhawoh, 'Between Culture and Constitution: Evaluating the Cultural Legitimacy of Human Rights in the African State' (2000) 22 *Human Rights Quarterly* 838–60.

[62] For a critique of US rights-talk on such grounds see M Glendon, *Rights Talk: The Impoverishment of Political Discourse* (1991), x: 'Our current American rights talk . . . is set apart from rights discourse in other liberal democracies by its starkness and simplicity, its prodigality in bestowing the rights label, its legalistic character, its exaggerated absoluteness, its hyperindividualism, its insularity, and its silence with respect to persona, civic and collective responsibilities.'

[63] See eg Article 29 of the UDHR, reflected in numerous provisions within the Covenants and core conventions.

context of the family environment, and the importance of the idea of individuals as duty-bearers.[64]

At another level still, one must be careful of who it is that is voicing the cultural relativist objection. Citizens and government frequently have different perspectives on the extent to which internationally-grounded human rights traditions actually are 'foreign.'[65] And in some cases it is quite plain that lack of infiltration of so-called 'western' human rights into mainstream policy making is due simply to lack of awareness,[66] rather than deep-seated or intrinsic incompatibility.

A number of these points are well brought out in connection with the 'Asian values' variant of the cultural relativist objection. As Yash Ghai notes, the strongest proponents of the 'Asian values' challenge are 'a few leaders in Southeast Asia.'[67] These and other advocates claim that the values of Asian, in particular Confucian, culture have helped to ensure economic stability and development, in a manner conducive to social harmony, unlike the individualistic and confrontational manifestations of so-called Western human rights traditions. Ghai identifies a number of key elements of 'Asian values' claims:

[64] For an excellent overview of these issues see International Council on Human Rights Policy, *Taking Duties Seriously: Individual Duties in International Human Rights Law—A commentary* (1999).

[65] Indeed as the Sri Lankan expert at the special session of the UN Sub-Commission on Prevention of Discrimination and Protection of Minorities in the summer of 1998 remarked: 'It is my observation, Mr Chairman, that almost always those [cultural relativist] arguments are raised not by the ordinary people, but by governments or groups in society which have much to lose by recognising the universality and indivisibility of human rights. No ordinary human being would deny the need to be treaty equally and with dignity, to speak freely, not to be arrested and detained arbitrarily, to be free from torture, to have an adequate standard of living, to be entitled to just conditions of labour and so on. To say these norms are nothing but a western development is to deny to non-western societies the humane and democratic legacies of their own religions and cultures.' Statement by RKW Goonsekera, 26 August 1998, cited in R Higgins, 'The Continuing Universality of the Universal Declaration' in P Baehr, C Flinterman and M Senders (eds) (1999) 17–26 at 26.

[66] Consensus was recently reached among the United Nations Economic Commission for Africa (UNECA) and the Bank and UNICEF on 15 principles concerning education and health, called the 'Addis Ababa Consensus on Principles of Cost Sharing in Education and Health.' See See *Implementing the 20/20 Initiative: Achieving Universal Access to Basic Social Services*, A joint publication of UNDP, UNESCO, UNFPA, UNICEF, WHO and the World Bank (September 1998) at 22–25. According to one participant in that process interviewed in February 2000, the 'fact of ratification of the CRC was persuasive with the African Finance Ministers,' facilitating the consensus reached. However those Ministers had had no prior knowledge of the Convention's existence for the countries concerned. Nonetheless the CRC appeared to be of considerable instrumental importance, adding 'a powerful additional argument,' putting over the point that the issues in question were 'not optional.'

[67] Y Ghai, 'Human Rights and Social Development: Towards Democratisation and Social Justice,' paper prepared for UNRISD as part of its review of Copenhagen (World Social Summit, 1995) +5 (2000) at 13. See also S Tharoor (June 2002): 'Objections to the applicability of human rights standards are all too frequently voiced by authoritarian rulers and power elites to rationalise violations that sustain them in power. Just as the Devil can quote the scripture for his purpose, Third World communitarianism can be the slogan of a deracinated tyrant trained, as in the case of Pol Pot, at the Sorbonne. The authentic voices of the South know how to cry out in pain. Those are the voices that must be heeded.' See also A Sen, 'Human Rights and Asian Values: What Lee Kuan Yew and Li Peng Don't Understand About Asia,' *The New Republic* (14 and 21 July 1997) at pp 33–40.

1. the rights of States, in particular the 'principles of respect for national sovereignty, territorial integrity and non-interference in the internal affairs of states,' and the importance of a particular conception of the right to development premised upon the sovereignty of states;
2. condemnation of practices associated with the West and the imbalance in the international system, including selective condemnation of legacies of colonial practices,[68] the use of human rights conditionalities in international development assistance, and other factors contributing to an unjust international economic order;
3. a focus upon states as the appropriate framework for the definition and enforcement of rights;
4. criticism of the 'imposition of incompatible standards,' and the need to understand rights in the context of 'national and regional peculiarities' and various historical, cultural and religious backgrounds; and
5. the prioritisation of economic development as a putative precondition for the enjoyment of human rights.[69]

There are many reasons to view such claims with suspicion. As Ghai remarks:

> There is little evidence that Asian economic success (such as it is) owes itself to family or community structures or to any other aspect of Asian values. Instead it is the role of the state (and their misappropriation) which have played a decisive role in private accumulation and production. Those of us who live in the more economically successful parts of Asia are not struck by the cohesion of the community, or the care that the community or family provides, or benevolent governments, or a public disdain for democracy. Instead we notice the displacement of the community by the pretensions and practices of the state. Far from promoting reconciliation and consensus, the state punishes its critics, suppresses the freedom of expression without which no dialogue is possible, and relies on armed forces rather than persuasion (and some leaders are rather 'unconfucianly' litigious!)[70]

The doctrine of Asian values was strongly disavowed by the 1993 statement by Asian NGOs on the 'Asian values' claim in the lead up to the World Conference on Human Rights in Vienna, and also by the Asian Charter of Human Rights (1997), and is generally invoked to serve only 'those who are perched on the higher reaches of the state and the market.'[71]

Other more particular assertions regarding the relative priority of economic and social rights—often couched in terms of a 'right to development' in the statist and self-serving sense referred to earlier by Ghai—over civil and political

---

[68] 'Asian states such as Indonesia, China or Burma with colonies or other forms of foreign occupation are fully absolved of any wrong doing.' Y Ghai (2000) at 14.

[69] Y Ghai (2000) at 14.

[70] Y Ghai (2000) at 14.

[71] Y Ghai (2000) at 14–15. For a Singaporean critique of 'Asian values' see N Englehart, 'Rights and Culture in the Asian Values Argument: The Rise and Fall of Confucian Ethics in Singapore' (2000) 22 *Human Rights Quarterly* 548–68.

rights likewise have been shown to be suspect, both on empirical grounds,[72] and in light of the presumed instrumental basis upon which they were often said to rest.[73] As Amartya Sen has noted, and as the East Asian crisis partly demonstrates, civil and political rights in fact help to safeguard economic security, in the sense that such rights draw attention to major social disasters and induce an appropriate response.[74] As mentioned earlier, this seems to be very closely related to the rationale ostensibly driving the Bank's emerging advocacy on issues such as a free press, and freedom of expression.

PROBLEM OF APPLICABILITY OF HUMAN RIGHTS TO NON-STATE ACTORS

It is sometimes claimed that focusing upon the IFIs' human rights responsibilities is of little utility, when one considers the relative magnitude of private capital flows and the impacts of non-governmental actors' (including TNCs, import/export banks and export credit agencies and so forth) upon people's lives. It is beyond the scope of this book to canvass issues of the private reach of international law in any depth. However a number of contextual remarks are warranted, along with a few substantive legal observations.

The problem of the limited formal reach of international human rights law is certainly one of the more serious limitations on its capacity to contribute to sustainable development at country level. An increasing range and number of non-state actors are indeed shaping the opportunities and lives of people in developing countries, consistent with the phenomenon of the 'shrinking state.' Business, both foreign investors and local enterprises, now plays a fundamental role in promoting the prospects for economic development.

However it is inappropriate to point to the burgeoning influence of private capital and actors as a basis for disclaiming or minimising the importance of the IFIs' human rights responsibilities. Firstly, the policies promoted by the IFIs themselves are responsible in no small measure for the privatisation of governance and acceleration of the 'shrinking state' phenomenon. Presiding over the divestiture of power without a corresponding concern for responsibility ranks among the IFIs' most critical shortcomings to date. Secondly, as was argued in chapter III the appropriate measure of the IFIs' influence is not determined by the relative size of official and private capital flows alone. The catalyzing impacts of the Bank's and Fund's 'seal of approval' and continuing practice of cross-conditionality render the true equation far more complex than is sometimes portrayed. And finally, in the Bank's case, recent experience in connection

---

[72] A Sen, 'Human Rights and Economic Achievements' in J Bauer and D Bell (eds), *The East Asian Challenge for Human Rights* (1999) 88–99 at 91. On the relationship between authoritarianism and economic performance, Sen concludes that '[t]he selective anecdotal evidence goes in contrary directions, and the general statistical picture does not yield any clear relationship at all.'

[73] A Sen (1999) at 90–94. And see Y Ghai (1998) at 129.

[74] A Sen (1999) at 95–96.

with the controversial Chad/Cameroon pipeline project has demonstrated quite compellingly how valuable an ally the Bank can be for TNCs and private consortia for risk mitigation and public relations purposes.[75] As risk-averse as the Bank is itself, and as problematic as the Chad/Cameroon project might be,[76] the leveraging of the Bank's social safeguard policies through relatively modest contributions (in financial terms) to joint ventures with private actors represents an important and emerging area of Bank influence.

A great range of initiatives are underway to attempt to fill the lacuna of private sector responsibility, exemplified by the ongoing normative work under the auspices of the Sub-Commission on the Promotion and Protection of Human Rights.[77] Much of this work is focused upon direct human rights responsibilities of private actors themselves, witnessed in the proliferation of various codes of conduct,[78] the most prominent of which to date has been the UN Secretary-General's 'Global Compact' of shared values and principles at the World Economic Forum at Davos, Switzerland.[79] As further explained in connection with the Forum in 2000, the Global Compact has nine core principles that are divided into categories dealing with general human rights obligations, standards of labour, and standards of environmental protection.[80] And not least of all, perhaps in acknowledgement of its joint responsibilities with private consortia, the Bank has published an overview of 'Governance and Human Rights' principles applicable to corporations operating in the energy resources sector,[81] an

---

[75] See above n 37 and accompanying text.

[76] G Hernandez Uriz (2001) at 230: '[I]n the opinion of NGOs opposing the project, there is high probability of failure on every front: the environmental risks are too high, oil revenues are susceptible to embezzlement, and the oil flow may exacerbate social and political instability in an already fragile environment.' For similar concerns see US Congress, House Committee on International Relations, Subcommittee on Africa, 'The Chad-Cameroon Pipeline: A New Model for Natural Resource Development,' Testimony by Peter Rosenblum, Director, Human Rights Program, Harvard Law School, 18 April 2002, http://www.house.gov/international_relations/rose0418.htm. For the Bank's position see World Bank, 'The Chad-Cameroon Petroleum Development and Pipeline Project: Questions and Answers,' http://www.worldbank.org/afr/ccproj/questions/.

[77] See E/CN.4/Sub.2/1999/9, by which the sessional working group on the working methods and activities of transnational corporations of the Sub-Commission decided to consider developing a code of conduct for companies based on human rights standards, and E/CN.4/Sub.2/2000/WG.2/WP.1, 25 May 2000, 'Principles relating to the human rights conduct of companies: Working paper prepared by Mr David Weissbrodt,' and E/CN.4/Sub.2/2002/WG.2/WP.1, 29 May 2002, containing the Sub-Commission's draft 'Human Rights Principles and Responsibilities for Transnational Corporations and Other Business Enterprises.'

[78] For a brief survey of these see E/CN.4/Sub.2/2000/WG.2/WP.1 at 4–5.

[79] See http://www.unglobalcompact.org.

[80] Businesses are asked to support and adopt those principles, the first two of which are to support and respect the protection of internationally proclaimed rights within their sphere of influence and make sure they are not complicit in human rights abuses. See E/CN.4/Sub.2/2000/WG.2/WP.1 at 4–5.

[81] 'Governance and Human Rights: Overview,' http://www.worldbank.org/ogsimpact/ghrover view.pdf. Perhaps unsurprisingly, a weaker normative approach is evident here than in comparable work in the Sub-Commission (cf n 80 below): 'It is increasingly accepted that companies have a responsibility to ensure that their operations do not contribute to human rights violations, to avoid complicity in human rights violations, and to ensure that company activities reinforce good governance and respect for human rights. . . . Unlike governments, there is no corresponding international

especially controversial area of development in Chad, Nigeria, Angola and elsewhere.[82]

As DFID has noted there is a strong need to maximise the 'positive impact' of commercial activity, and ensure that commercial enterprises do not violate applicable human rights standards.[83] However as a point of principle this cannot be permitted to detract from the primary responsibilities of states parties to implement their validly assumed and binding obligations under international human rights treaties. The Maastricht Guidelines on Violations of Economic, Social and Cultural Rights[84] indicate that it is the responsibility of states to ensure that transnational corporations [TNCs] do not deprive people of their human rights, and in particular that 'states are responsible for violations of economic, social and cultural rights that result from their failure to exercise due diligence in controlling the behaviour of such non-state actors.'[85] As DFID has noted, '[s]ome international authorities, such as the Inter-American Court of Human Rights, have incorporated this guidance into their rulings but, to date, there have been few successful cases of states being held legally responsible for human rights violations perpetrated by enterprises operating within their national borders.'[86]

As indicated in chapter IV the IFIs themselves as subjects of international law may in certain circumstances have obligations to 'protect' against human rights violations in programme countries, including perhaps in relation to private sector partners or sub-contractors.[87] While further development of the law relating

law that obliges corporations to respect human rights. However, in the energy industry, best human rights practices are evolving in the absence of law.'

[82] See above n 76, and: Human Rights Watch, 'The International Monetary Fund's Staff Monitoring Program for Angola: The Human Rights Implications,' Backgrounder by Human Rights Watch (2000), http://www.hrw.org/press/2000/06/ango-0623-back.htm; Human Rights Watch, *The Enron Corporation: Corporate Complicity in Human Rights Violations* (1999); Human Rights Watch, *The Price of Oil: Corporate Responsibility and Human Rights Violations in Nigeria's Oil Producing Communities*; Human Rights Watch, *Angola Unravels: The Rise and Fall of the Lusaka Peace Process* (1999); T Karl, *The Paradox of Plenty: Oil Booms and Petrol States* (1997); and Gelb, A., *Oil Windfalls: Blessing or Curse?* (1986).

[83] DFID, 'Strategies for Achieving the International Development Targets: Human Rights for Poor People,' Consultation paper, February 2000 ['*DFID Human Rights Paper* 2000'] at 14. Interestingly the Sub-Commission draft 'Human Rights Principles and Responsibilities for Transnational Corporations and Other Business Enterprises' provide (at para 1) that '[w]ithin their respective spheres of activity and influence, transnational corporations and other business enterprises have the obligation to respect, ensure respect for, prevent abuses of, and promote human rights recognised in international as well as national law.' E/CN.4/Sub.2/2002/WG.2/WP.1, 29 May 2002.

[84] See Maastricht Guidelines on Violations of Economic, Social and Cultural Rights (1998) 20 *Human Rights Quarterly* 691–705, at 698. The Guidelines were agreed at a meeting of experts, at the invitation of the International Commission of Jurists, in Maastricht, 22–26 January 1997.

[85] Maastricht Guidelines on Violations of Economic, Social and Cultural Rights (1998) 20 *Human Rights Quarterly* 691–705, at 698. In terms of the three-tiered 'respect, protect and fulfil' typology of obligation, this would fall within the requirement on states to 'protect' human rights.

[86] *DFID Human Rights Paper* (2000) at 14.

[87] See the discussion in chapter IV at nn 93–101 and accompanying text, suggesting scope for international legal obligations in certain circumstances to 'protect' in addition to 'respect' (and to a more limited extent, promote or fulfil) human rights standards.

to human rights responsibilities of private actors is clearly warranted, especially in relation to the challenging sphere of cross-border activities, the more readily identifiable obligations of other important duty-bearers—namely states and the IFIs—must not be permitted to fade from view. Privatisation of governance is indeed a challenge to human rights implementation, and the IFIs' as agents of that transition owe a particular responsibility—on international legal as much as moral grounds—to ensure that human rights protection does not vanish into the corporate ether as a consequence.

FUNGIBILITY OF AID FOR DEVELOPMENT

The issue of 'fungibility'[88] of financial assistance or development aid is a more fundamental issue than mere targeting desired goals and tracking expenditures. 'Fungibility' means that even if funds provided by the IFIs are directed towards the desired ends, in practice this means that other funds at the government's disposal that might have been earmarked for those same purposes are thereby freed up to go to completely different ends, including possibly regressive purposes such as military expenditures.[89] Perhaps the most likely solution to the 'fungibility' issue—which itself is only a critical problem to the extent that funds are freed up for wasteful or destructive purposes[90]—is for the IFIs and national level stakeholders to be able to have a seat at the table at the outset when the national budget is prepared,[91] with discussions carried out in a transparent and partici-

---

[88] The definition of 'fungible' in the Concise Oxford Dictionary is: '*adj. Law* (of goods etc. contracted for, when an individual specimen is not meant) that can serve for, or be replaced by, another answering to the same description. *Fungibility n*. . . . 'serve (in place of).'

[89] As others have expressed it, '[e]ven the most rigorous project selection or loan conditions cannot guarantee effective aid in a distorted environment. This is because of problems with fungibility: aid pays not for the items against which it is earmarked, but for the marginal expenditure it makes possible.' OXFAM, *From Unsustainable Debt to Poverty Reduction: Reforming the Heavily Indebted Poor Countries Initiative*, prepared by OXFAM GB Policy Department for UNICEF, (August 1999). For a more detailed of aid fungibility and its consequences see S Devarajan and V Swaroop, 'The Implications of Foreign Aid Fungibility for Development Assistance' in C Gilbert and D Vines (eds) (2000), 196–209.

[90] 'In granting aid, donors often require that proceeds be used for the purposes for which they were granted. The recipient could fulfil that conditionality by spending aid money for the purposes for which it was given. Yet, the earmarked funds may be releasing resources—that are already available to the recipient—for some other purpose. Is this a bad outcome? Not necessarily. Proponents of foreign aid argue that notwithstanding the diversion of local spending, aid money is intrinsically more effective than local spending as it comes packaged with technical assistance and superior management skills of donor agencies. Indeed, it is quite likely that donor involvement may increase the rate of return on the project. It may also lead to changes in policy, institutions and project design. Yet, if aid funds crowd-out domestic resources from that activity, they may end up financing, at the margin, very different and perhaps undesirable activities. In such a case, the developmental impact of external assistance may be quite different from that perceived from traditional measures of project success including the economic rate of return.' S Devarajan and V Swaroop (2000) at 199.

[91] S Devarajan and V Swaroop (2000) conclude (at 207) that '[w]hile increasing restrictions on donor assistance to reduce fungibility may have some impact, a better approach could be to tie aid resources to an overall public expenditure programme [Public Expenditure Reform Loan (PERL)]

patory fashion. Utopia? This is of course something very close to the PRSP's rationale and intended modus operandi. To the extent that this kind of process can be carried out effectively, then the issue reverts later to a slightly more straight-forward one of targeting, and attempting as far as possible to track any 'leakages' from budgeted purposes.

CONCLUDING COMMENTS

There should be no doubt about the magnitude of the challenges confronting those seeking to provoke more active concern by the IFIs with relevant obligations under international human rights law, and the programmatic integration of human rights to the extent necessary or desirable. The seriousness of the barriers to integration will obviously vary to a large degree in accordance with the ambitiousness and scope of the reform programme contemplated. Some barriers—for example the entrenched problem of retrograde bureaucratic incentives—will be more difficult to resolve than those stemming from clashes of disciplinary perspectives, or misunderstandings as to what human rights actually entails in normative and operational senses.

But the critical point is that objections, as with rationales for human rights integration, must be able to withstand critical scrutiny. The examples from the foregoing discussion demonstrate that broadly drawn disclaimers must be analysed with particular rigour, in order to expose underlying doctrinal, political or bureaucratic premises and biases. The residual kernel of cogent objections, constituting an important part of the frame of reference for human rights integration, may eventually be revealed to be but a fraction of that which was initially apparent.

that provides adequate resources to crucial sectors. The implications of this new mode of assistance for the World Bank are both minimal and significant. They are minimal because, in a sense, the Bank has been transferring assistance in this way all along. If—as the evidence shows—project assistance is fungible, the Bank has been financing the government's budget anyway. Furthermore, much of the Bank's project assistance involves providing advice to governments about policy and institutional reform—precisely the kind of dialogue that would continue under a PERL. But the implications are significant because moving to a PERL would make all these activities explicit. In addition, it would change the Bank's relationship with its client countries. Instead of imposing conditions on quick-disbursing loans, such as [SALs], or financing projects that are essentially enclaves in a country, the Bank would be supporting the client country's development programme through budgetary support, and assisting the country in managing all of its public resources.'

VI

An Agenda for Reform

INTRODUCTORY REMARKS

THE legal analysis in chapter IV permits the IFIs considerable scope to factor human rights directly into their work.[1] That chapter showed that international human rights law may impact at a potentially significant number of levels upon how the Articles of Association of each of the Fund and Bank ought to be interpreted in a given case. The levels of obligation range from those incumbent upon member states *erga omnes* or as a matter of *jus cogens*, custom and general principles of law, to the potential relevance of quasi-universal instruments such as the CRC under Article 31(3)(c) of the Vienna Convention, through to Charter-based obligations with the UDHR and core treaty standards as an authoritative guide to interpretation. A potentially broad range of human rights-related policy options also exists, beyond the range of measures readily identifiable with sources of international legal obligation.

The ensuing discussion deals with issues of more or less equal relevance to both the Bank and Fund. The recommendations are chiefly suited for short to medium-term implementation, and accordingly presuppose the continued existence of the Bank and Fund in more or less their present form, without prejudice to the validity of more fundamental and longer-term proposals.[2] Moreover, although human rights should, based upon chapters III–V, be considered and to a significant extent operationalised by the IFIs,[3] the question of 'how' that is to

---

[1] See eg D Bradlow, 'The World Bank, the IMF and Human Rights' (1996) 6(1) *Transnational Law and Contemporary Problems* 47.

[2] These would include either bringing the IFIs more closely into the relationship with the Economic and Social Council (ECOSOC) envisaged in the UN Charter, or perhaps more realistically in the medium to long term, establishing an 'Economic Security Council' in line with proposals in the mid-1990s from the Human Development Report office (Human Development Report 1994), the Commission on Global Governance in 1995, and echoed most recently in UNDP (Human Development Report Office), *Human Development Report 2002: Deepening Democracy in a Fragmented World* (2002) (herafter HDR 2002) at 117–18. See also S Daws and F Stewart, 'Global Challenges: An Economic and Social Security Council at the United Nations,' Report Sponsored by Christian Aid, June 2000, http://www.christian-aid-org.uk/indepth/0006unec/unecon2.htm.

[3] For arguments that donor governments should give the Bank a 'clear mandate to shift to a rights-based approach' as a means of empowering local and national level actors and challenging the 'conventional development juggernaut,' see K Horta, 'Boundaries in the Field of Human Rights: Rhetoric and Reality: Human Rights and the World Bank' (2002) 15 *Harvard Human Rights Journal* 227–43.

occur is one which needs to be addressed in the context of ongoing institutional reform debates and arguments regarding appropriate division of labour between the Bank and Fund and other relevant actors, in the PRSP context[4] and more broadly.

DECKCHAIRS ON THE TITANIC: STRUCTURAL PREREQUISITES TO POLICY REFORMS

> We threw out that system in 1832—votes tied to property and money and what we called 'rotten boroughs' representation. I'm surprised that a European individual can be so complacent about the lack of democracy in representation.[5]

It is pointless to consider policy reforms (human rights-based or otherwise) without addressing the underlying structural issues upon which policy implementation depends.[6] A number of these—such as the 'approval culture' problem and related incentive problems—were canvassed in chapter V, and to a large extent boil down to deficiencies in accountability.

Dollar and Pritchett's 'Aid Effectiveness' study[7] showed, among other things, that a lack of transparency and accountability in policy-making will result in bad policies. While intended to refer to the situation in borrowing countries, there is no reason in principle why this principle can not be extrapolated to the institutions of governance of the Bank and Fund themselves.

Beyond its instrumental value in governance and development, 'accountability' may appropriately be seen as the *leitmotif* of the international human rights regime.[8] The true salience of the concept emerged through the 'standard setting' to 'implementation' phases of international human rights law, grounded in the requirement for a remedy for human rights violations under international law,[9] the relatively detailed provisions of the 1998 Declaration on Human Rights

---

[4] For an internal assessment of progress to date see IMF, PIN No. 02/30, 15 March 2002, 'IMF Executive Board Reviews the Poverty Reduction and Growth Facility (PRGF),' http://www.imf.org/external/np/sec/pn/2002/pn0230.htm.

[5] Remarks by George Mudie MP to IMF Managing Director Horst Köhler, giving evidence to the Treasury Select Committee of the UK Parliament on 4 July 2002. Köhler was fielding questions concerning the quality of the IMF's democratic credentials and representativeness. Bretton Woods Project, *Bretton Woods Update* (July/August 2002) at 5.

[6] For strong arguments to this effect see N Bridgeman, 'World Bank Reform in the "Post Policy" Era' (2001) 13 *Georgetown International Environmental Law Review* 1013–46, 1045–46: 'Reform in the 'post-policy' era will require a clear message from an organised NGO movement. The new structural reform agenda must take priority over further policy reforms, requiring leadership from donor governments as well. Without these components, the Bank will be unable to prevent harm to the environment and those it aims to help.'

[7] D Dollar, and L Pritchett, *Assessing Aid: What Works, What Doesn't, and Why* (1998). However for a cautionary note on the econometric robustness of these authors' findings see UNCTAD, *The Least Developed Countries Report 2002: Escaping the Poverty Trap* 218–19 (2002), arguing that aid effectiveness depends on both aid recipients' policies and aid donors' policies.

[8] P Alston, 'Towards a Human Rights Accountability Index' (2000) 1(2) *Journal of Human Development* 249, 259.

[9] See eg Article 2(3) ICCPR, article 8 of the UDHR, and the discussion in chapter V above at n 31 and accompanying text.

Defenders,[10] and a long series of General Assembly and Commission on Human Rights resolutions condemning impunity and calling for cooperation with the full range of UN human rights mechanisms.[11] Human rights are a vital reference point for initiatives to enhance accountability not only at the level of the Fund and Bank, but at country level.[12]

Lines of accountability both internally (or vertically) and externally (or horizontally) need strengthening at both the Bank and Fund.[13] The need for effective external accountability mechanisms has become acute, in line with the IFIs' significant intrusion into national policy realms, weilding political power without commensurate representation or responsibility. Lines of accountability at the national level are obfuscated and undermined when the IFIs' dominant interlocutors—the central banks and finance ministries—effectively determine or crowd out policy making and Ministerial responsibility in portfolios such as health, education and social security.[14] Accountability mechanisms at the national level are further undermined as a consequence of large-scale privatisations, as Orford and

[10] The full name is the Declaration on the Right and Responsibility of Individuals, Groups and Organs of Society to Promote and Protect Universally Recognised Human Rights and Fundamental Freedoms (GA Res 53/144 (1998), Annex). Adopted by the GA without a vote, the Declaration 'affirms many dimensions of the concept of accountability including the right to submit criticisms and proposals to government bodies, the right to benefit from an effective remedy and to be protected in the event of human rights violations, the right to complain, the right to unhindered access to and communication with international bodies with competence to consider complaints ("communications") alleging human rights violations, and the obligation of states to take measures to promote full and equal access to international documents in the field of human rights, including documents relating to reporting by the state in question.' P Alston (2000) at 261.

[11] P Alston (2000) at 260.

[12] As Katherine Marshall has noted: '[G]overnment accountability depends upon effective institutions, clear rules and respect for individual rights. . . . No matter in what system of government, the availability of information aids accountability, particularly from an active press and community groups.' K Marshall, 'Operational Lessons and Challenges for Social Development after the East Asian Crisis,' paper prepared for Manila Social Forum: New Social Agenda for East and South-east Asia, 8–12 November 1999 at 4.

[13] For an excellent overview of the accountability deficit see N Woods, 'Making the IMF and World Bank More Accountable' (2001) 77(1) *International Affairs* 83–100, focusing on: (a) deficiencies in developing country membership on the Executive Boards; (b) the remoteness of Board representatives from their own national level constituencies and the interests of those most deeply impacted by IFI programmes and prescriptions; and (c) the failure of the Executive Boards to hold staff and management to account.

[14] Stiglitz observes that the IMF's governance structure is particularly suspect to the extent that it includes a 'large role for Central Bank governors, who typically are neither representative of the population as a whole nor, increasingly, directly accountable to the electorate.' J Stiglitz, 'Introduction' in C Gilbert and D Vines (eds), *The World Bank: Structure and Policies* (2000) 1–9, 5. And as Woods observes: '[T]he work of both the IMF and the World Bank has broadened and deepened far beyond the purviews of the finance ministries or central banks with which they are negotiating. This means that, through conditionality and loan agreements, the Fund and Bank are making finance ministries or central banks formally accountable for policies which should properly lie within the scope of other agencies, and for which those other agencies are domestically accountable. A policy affecting the distribution of health care, for example, we would expect to be the responsibility of a minister of health, whom we would expect to be answerable for it to voters and his or her society at large. Yet as the Fund and Bank intrude further into these kinds of decisions, the risk is that the line of accountability they establish with the Finance Ministry or Central Bank will override other agencies and local or democratic accountability.' M Woods (2001) at 89.

Beard observe: '[w]hile privatised agencies may be accountable in a limited sense to new shareholders, the formerly broad requirement that such agencies be accountable to the polity is destroyed by privatisation.'[15]

As far as internal accountability at the Bank is concerned, as was seen in chapter V, the OD 'conversion' process has been strongly criticised as diminishing the non-discretionary content of OPs and BPs, diluting their inherent value and weakening the already inadequate incentives for compliance. The reaffirmation by the IDA Executive Directors in 2002 of the need for Bank staff to comply with safeguard policies is certainly both timely and welcome.[16] However pressures on task managers for hasty completion of social safeguard reports, the omission of policy compliance costs from the project approval process, staff and senior management incentives to overlook deficient environmental assessments, and failure to link task managers' performance appraisals to their record of policy compliance, pose fundamental barriers to any policy reform agenda.

Moreover the Operations Evaluation Department's policy review and quality control mandate has not made as significant an impact upon the quality of the Bank's work as one might've hoped, nor provided any serious counterweight to the retrograde institutional incentives that are at the heart of so many ills.[17] Nor are that Department's evaluations yet made systematically available to the public. The Inspection Panel—with relevance for both internal and external lines of accountability—has most certainly performed a very useful role in its first several years of operation, although with a few notable exceptions[18] the terms of

---

[15] A Orford and J Beard, 'Making the State Safe for the Market: The World Bank's *World Development Report 1997*' (1998) 22 *Melbourne University Law Review* 195, 208. And also (at 210): 'The broader meaning of accountability [the duty owed by the state to investors] used with respect to private actors is demonstrated clearly by the addition of the opinions of foreign investors—the only outside voices introduced directly into [the World Bank's 1997 World Development Report] to disturb the flow of expert advice.' On a more general level see I Duncanson, 'Unchartered Lands in an Age of "Accountability"' (1997) 3(1) *Res Publica* 3.

[16] IDA, 'Additions to IDA Resources: Thirteenth Replenishment—Supporting Poverty Reduction Strategies,' Report from the Executive Directors of the IDA to the Board of Governors, 25 July 2002 at 18, discussed in chapter V above at n 16 and accompanying text.

[17] For misgivings relating to the operation of the Operations Evaluation Division, see A Kolk, *Forests in International Environmental Politics: International Organisations, NGOs and the Brazilian Amazon* (1996) 211, and B Kingsbury, 'Operational Policies of International Institutions as Part of the Law-Making Process: The World Bank and Indigenous Peoples' in G Goodwin-Gill and S Talmon (eds), *The Reality of International Law: Essays in Honour of Ian Brownlie* (1999) 323–42, 329, asserting that '[s]ome internal review is provided by the [OED], but this body is oriented toward lessons to be drawn from experience, rather than strict accountability.' Selective perceptions of the OED as being removed from reality, or even a burial ground for less dynamic Bank staff, do nothing to enhance that Department's standing and policy impacts.

[18] The exceptions (cases where the Panel's investigations were not curtailed through unwarranted intervention by Bank Management) include: (a) Inspection Panel, Investigation Report, Nepal: Arun III Proposed Hydroelectric Project and Restructuring of IDA Credit—2029—NEP, Doc. INSP/SecM95–3 of 21 June 1995; (b) World Bank, *China Western Poverty Reduction Project Inspection Panel Report* (2000). See the Investigation Report of the World Bank Inspection Panel, 'The Qinghai Project: A Component of the China: Western Poverty Reduction Project (Credit No. 3255–CHA and Loan No. 4501–CHA),' 28 April 2000; and (c) Investigation Report of the World

the Resolution establishing it have rarely been implemented rigorously and faithfully.[19] While the situation has improved since 1999, in a number of cases prior to that time Management was permitted a significant degree of discretion in pre-empting Panel investigations through submitting to the Board hastily assembled 'remedial action plans,' effectively curtailing the proper discharge of the Panel's compliance review functions.[20]

However as important as safeguarding the Panel's independent investigation functions is, this will only assist substantively insofar as the Bank's operational policies themselves are worthy of upholding. While the Qinghai case perhaps suggests some scope for the Panel to interpret operational policies in light of their underlying human rights purposes (as appropriate),[21] the Panel mechanism itself is a relatively remote, costly and time-consuming one,[22] and should not

Bank Inspection Panel, Report No. 23998, 'Uganda: Third Power Project—Credit 2268–UG; Fourth Power Project—Credit 3345–UG and the Bujagali Hydropower Project—PRG No. B 003–UG, IPN Request RQ01/3 of 7 August 2001,' 23 May 2002.

[19] For a recent assessment of the Panel's record to date see Roos, 'The World Bank Inspection Panel' (2001) 5 *Max Planck Yearbook of United Nations Law* 475–521. However the Panel has produced positive outcomes even in cases falling short of full investigation, as Roos (at 514–15) notes: 'Roughly half of all complaints filed with the Inspection Panel to date resulted in some favourable outcome not only for the Requesters, but also for other project-affected people, and often the environment, too.' The benefits from the mere filing of a Request have been claimed to include remedial action plans (although the potential of these plans to circumvent the Panel's investigation function and contravene the Bank's own policies on participation has attracted controversy), the appointment of independent inspectors other than the Panel inspectors, the creation of a local monitoring panel, and additional financing to address social and environmental issues.

[20] For a discussion of this problem see B Kingsbury (1999) at 333. The second of two 'Clarifications' of the Resolution establishing the Inspection Panel was carried out between 1997–1999, the result of which was to diminish the scope for circumvention of the Panel by Management 'remedial action plans.' IBRD Resolution 93/10, and IDA Resolution 93/6, 22 September 1993. See http://wbln0018.worldbank.org/ipn/ipnweb.nsf/WRelease/9203E5F9E8E33 EA5852568D9004B25B6 for the text of the Clarification, the discussion below n 175 and accompanying text, and D Bradlow, 'Precedent-Setting NGO Campaign Saves the World Bank's Inspection Panel' (1999) 6 *Human Rights Brief* 7–27. This does not necessarily mean that the Panel since 1999 has enjoyed complete independence, however: see N Bridgeman (2001) at 1039–40. Critics continue to call for the establishment of a more rigorously independent appeals and review Commission with 'power to investigate complaints against the Bank, full access to internal files, power to review and investigate violations of international law in World Bank-funded projects, and with findings and recommendations that are binding unless reversed by a significant majority of the Bank's directors.' See A Orford, 'Globalisation and the Right to Development' in P Alston (ed), *People's Rights* (2001) 127–84, 153, and n 63 below and accompanying text.

[21] See chapter IV above, at n 156 and accompanying text.

[22] See eg R Wade, 'A defeat for development and multilateralism: the World Bank has been unfairly criticised over the Qinghai resettlement project,' *Financial Times*, 4 July 2000; N Woods (2001) at 93–94. Wade reports that the Bank's East Asia Region spent approximately US$3 million on work responding to the Panel's investigation, and that the cost of the extra work called for by the Panel was estimated at around US$4 million, or 10% of the total loan. Naturally this is a somewhat artificial assessment, on the assumption that Management and the national authorities ought to have carried out much if not all of the 'extra work' without the need for Panel proceedings. However, in light of the costs involved (said to undermine the Bank's competitive advantage) and fear of an inquisitorial process, Wade reports that Bank staff have become loath to contemplate projects involving either resettlement or indigenous peoples. Woods suggests (at 94) the IFC's and MIGA's 'Compliance Advisor Ombudsman' model as one possible alternative horizontal accountability mechanism.

deflect attention from the issue of accountability for the quality of the operational policies themselves.[23]

A further defect in internal accountability, with equal relevance to the Bank and Fund, is that the Executive Board exercises no real effective oversight over staff and Management.[24] The reasons for this relate not just to Management's broad operational discretion and the lack (to varying degrees as between Bank and Fund) of binding operational policy guidance, but to such factors as: (a) the limited practical possibilities for Executive Directors to assimilate and comprehend in a timely fashion the often weighty and complex issues before them; (b) the Board's proclivity for decision-making outside of formal meetings where Management's influence can more readily be exercised; (c) the tendency of Management to present unified positions to the Board, and (d) the preponderance of 'peer protection' rather than 'peer pressure' at Board level, reflecting Executive Directors' divided institutional and national loyalties.[25]

As for external accountability and legitimacy, again with equal relevance to the Bank and Fund, the chief and seemingly most intractable weakness relates to the significant under-representation of developing country interests at Executive Board level.[26] For example as at December 2000 there was just one Executive Director on the IMF Board with a voting share of 3.26 per cent to represent the interests of 21 anglophone African countries, and a similar situation for those same countries on the Bank Board. Furthermore the assumptions of the 'universal' and 'public' character of the IFIs—reflected in the initial allocation of a fixed number (250) of 'basic votes' to all members—have been undermined by the proportional increased apportionment over time of 'weighted votes,' determined according to members' quotas. The result is that the proportion of basic votes to total votes has diminished from its high point of 12.4 per cent of all votes in 1955, to 2.1 per cent in the year 2002 for both the Bank and Fund.[27]

Measures to increase the IFIs' accountability and transparency are minimum prerequisites their legitimacy and continued carriage of an active global

---

[23] To similar effect see HDR 2002 at 115.

[24] OXFAM was prompted to remark that '[IMF] staff are able to operate much as they please.'OXFAM (1999) at 14.

[25] World Bank, *Report of AD Hoc Committee on Board Procedures*, 26 May 1992; and IMF, 'External *Evaluation of IMF Surveillance: Report by a Group of Independent Experts* (1999) 34.

[26] See eg testimony of Ngaire Woods and Kevin Watkins to United Kingdom House of Commons, Select Committee on Treasury, Third Report, 18 February 2000. A reform of this kind will be difficult to achieve in view of the fact that an amendment to the IFIs' Articles of Agreement requires the approval of a 60% majority of the membership having a total of 85% of the voting power. The United States, for one, is hardly likely to vote in favour of the abolition of its effective veto on each Executive Board. Yet, this does not detract from the need to seek improvements acceptable to all that would improve the system as a whole. See eg D Türk, 'Participation of Developing Countries in Decision-Making Processes' in P de Waart, P Peters. and E Denters (eds), *International Law and Development* (1988) 341–57, 349.

[27] HDR 2002 at 114; N Woods, 'The Challenge of Good Governance for the IMF and the World Bank Themselves' (2000) 28(5) *World Development* 823.

role.[28] By the turn of the century certain advances had undoubtedly taken place. The World Bank adopted an information disclosure policy in 1993, expanding its scope by 2001 to include the release of HIPC and PRSP documents including summaries of Board discussion in relation thereto, and papers by IDA deputies on replenishment negotiations.[29] The disclosure policy was expanded in September 2001 to include a greater number of project-related documents and chairman's summaries of Board discussions of CAS's and Sector Strategy Papers. A more systematic approach to accessing Bank archives has reportedly also been developed.[30]

In the Fund's case, as at 2001 summaries of Board discussions on Article IV consultations and Letters of Intent were being released in approximately 80 per cent of cases,[31] along with publication of key policy papers, relatively detailed Country Reports, and quite comprehensive information on its own financial position on a monthly and quarterly basis.[32] The Fund's *ad hoc* external evaluation experiment resulted in the publication of independent expert reports on ESAF (referred to earlier), and the Fund's surveillance and research activities.

Furthermore, at least partially through external pressure,[33] the Board resolved in April 2000 to establish an 'Independent Evaluation Office'[34] (IEO; initially abbreviated EVO) to 'complement the IMF's ongoing internal and external evaluation activities,'[35] conducting objective and independent

---

[28] For a grim assessment see the IMF Oversight Hearing testimony of Gerald O'Driscoll in March 1999: 'International agencies, by their design, are insulated from democratic accountability. Yet they are amply funded, to the tune of may billions of dollars. Human beings, shielded from accountability or realistic financial constraints, will even with the best of intentions begin to behave irresponsibly. Nothing short of fundamental institutional reform will alter behaviour.' Senate Banking, Housing and Urban Affairs Committee, Subcommittee on International Trade and Finance, Oversight Hearing on the IMF, Prepared Testimony of Mr Gerald O'Driscoll, Senior Fellow, The Heritage Foundation, 10.30 am, Tuesday 9 March 1999.

[29] HDR 2002 at 115.

[30] HDR 2002 at 115.

[31] N Woods (2001) at 91.

[32] Senate Banking, Housing and Urban Affairs Committee, Subcommittee on International Trade and Finance, Oversight Hearing on the IMF, Prepared Testimony of the Honourable Timothy Geithner, Under Secretary for International Finance, United States Treasury, 10.30 am, Tuesday 9 March 1999.

[33] J Polack, *IMF Study Group Report: Transparency and Evaluation; Report and Recommendations by a Special Study Group convened by the Centre of Concern*, April 1998; A Wood and C Welch, *Policing the Policemen—The Case for an Independent Evaluation Mechanism for the IMF*, Bretton Woods Project and Friends of the Earth US, April 1998.

[34] 'Semi-independent', rather than independent, would be a better description. HRD 2002 at 116.

[35] IMF Press Release No. 00/27, 10 April 2000. The principal internal evaluation mechanisms are self-evaluation by the operational departments, and evaluations by the Office of Internal Audit and Inspection (OIA). In recent years the former have included a focus on Fund-supported programs in the East Asian crisis, the ESAF and surveillance, while the OIA has reviewed the resident representative program and Fund technical assistance. IMF, 'IMF Executive Board Report to the IMFC on the Establishment of the Independent Evaluation Office (EVO) and its Terms of Reference,' 12 September 2000. See also IMF, 'Making the IMF's Independent Evaluation Office (EVO) Operational: A Background Paper,' 7 August 2000.

evaluations on issues relevant to the Fund's mandate.[36] The IEO is claimed to be 'fully independent' from the IMF's Management and staff, and to operate 'at arm's length' from the Executive Board.[37] While the budget of the IEO is subject to the Executive Board's approval, its preparation occurs independently of the budetary process over which IMF Management has authority. Moreover the Office's work programme is established by the Director 'in light of consultations with interested stakeholders, from both inside and outside the IMF.'[38] The work programme is required to be presented for review by the Executive Board, but is not subject to the Board's approval.[39] Within relatively permissive terms of reference, IEO evaluations are intended to be able to cover the full range of IMF activities, extending 'in principle, to issues relevant to the IMF's mandate but not now part of its activities.'[40]

With an eye towards transparency, issues papers and draft terms of reference for particular studies are required to be posted on the IEO's website for public comment. Publication of evaluations will be accompanied by comments from IMF Management and staff and from country authorities where appropriate, along with the Board's conclusions on considering the evaluation reports. Once an evaluation report is made public, formal comments (within a given notice period) will be invited from 'external stakeholders,' and an 'outreach conference' convened to discuss it. The work of the IEO will itself be subject to external evaluation after a three-year period.[41]

As at 2002 the IEO had been fully established and had formulated its work programme for 2002–2003.[42] Two issues papers for proposed IEO evaluations

[36] IMF, 'Independent Evaluation Office (IEO) of the IMF: Goals and Instruments,' 19 October 2001, http://www.imf.org/external/np/ieo/gai.htm. The categories of 'issues relevant to the IMF's mandate' are: (a) systematic evaluations of the IMF's general policies; (b) comparative cross-country analyses of the IMF's economic policy advice, both in the context of surveillance and in the context of IMF-supported programs; and (c) evaluations of completed country operations.

[37] IMF, 'Independent Evaluation Office (IEO) of the IMF: Staffing,' 19 October 2001, http://www.imf.org/external/np/ieo/ind.htm. The Director of the Office is appointed by the Executive Board for a term of four years, renewable for a further three years. The Director is ineligible for appointment to a staff position at the IMF following his or her term. While the terms and conditions governing appointment to the IEO are set by the Executive Board (to ensure that the IEO is staffed with 'independent and qualified personnel'), the Director of the Office is solely responsible for personnel recruitment, including engagement of consultants on particular projects as required.

[38] In terms of external consultations there was some suggestion that the scope of the IEO's consultations (at least as at October 2001) was skewed towards the North, with meetings (apart from a mid-September 2001 poverty reduction strategy forum in Senegal) being held with NGOs, government authorities, academics and policy analysts in Boston, Washington, London, Paris and Berlin. IMF, 'Independent Evaluation Office (IEO) of the IMF: Work Program,' 19 October 2001, http://www.imf.org/external/np/ieo/def101901.htm. However any definitive assessment of this question was at that time premature.

[39] IMF, 'Independent Evaluation Office (IEO) of the IMF: Staffing,' 19 October 2001, http://www.imf.org/external/np/ieo/ind.htm.

[40] IMF, 'Independent Evaluation Office (IEO) of the IMF: Work Program,' 19 October 2001, http://www.imf.org/external/np/ieo/def101901.htm.

[41] IMF, 'Independent Evaluation Office (IEO) of the IMF: Transparency,' 19 October 2001, http://www.imf.org/external/np/ieo/tra.htm.

[42] IMF, 'Status Report for the IMFC on the Independent Evaluation Office (IEO)', http://www.imf.org/external/NP/ieo/2002/imfc/index.htm.

had been made public by August 2002: one concerning fiscal adjustment in IMF-supported programmes, and the other on the role of the Fund in recent capital account crises. A third investigation on the topic of prolonged use of Fund financial resources was planned to commence thereafter.[43] As timely as the chosen subjects for evaluation are, as at 2002 it was premature to assess the rigour and independence with which the IEO could be expected to carry out its substantive functions. Certain structural limitations might well arise to frustrate ambitions for independence and policy impact. Perhaps mosts notable among these, the Director (appointed by the Board) can be dismissed at any time by the Board, and a significant portion of the staff of the IEO (although not a majority) are recruited from inside the Fund.[44] The Board naturally exercises control over the Office's budget, and notwithstanding the 'strong presumption' of prompt publication of the Office's findings, the Board retains a discretion to refrain from publication in 'exceptional circumstances,'[45] without any guiding criteria for 'exceptional' having yet been defined.[46]

The Fund proclaims with pride the 'unique institutional leverage' enjoyed by the IEO through the closeness of its affiliation with the Board and (through its 'ability to hire part of its staff from the IMF') Management, with its proximity facilitating the Board's monitoring of the implementation of the IEO's recommendations.[47] Whether such a relationship and associated structural shortcomings are inimical to the demands of independence and rigour will presumably be high on the agenda for the external review in 2005 of the IEO's first three years of operations.

[43] IMF, 'Fiscal Adjustment in IMF-Supported Programs,' Issues Paper for an Evaluation by the Independent Evalution Office (IEO), 18 June 2002; IMF, 'The Role of the IMF in Recent Capital Account Crises,' Issues Paper for an Evaluation by the Independent Evaluation Office (IEO), June 2002, the latter focusing on the Fund's experiences in Indonesia, Brazil, and Korea. The remaining (7–9, subject largely to the budgetary situation) topics for 2003–2005 will be selected from the following: (1) PRGF/PRSP (proposed joint evaluation with the Bank's OED); (2) the IMF's advice on financial sector restructuring after a crisis; (3) structural conditionality in IMF-supported programmes; (4) the role of IMF surveillance in crisis prevention; (5) the IMF's advice on exchange rate policy; (6) IMF technical assistance; (7) private sector involvement; (8) the IMF's approach to capital account liberalisation; (9) the role of multilateral surveillance; (10) 'additional country case (possibly Argentina or Turkey);' and (11) 'low-income country case.' IMF, 'Status Report for the IMFC on the Independent Evaluation Office (IEO)', http://www.imf.org/external/NP/ieo/2002/imfc/index.htm.

[44] IMF, 'IMF Executive Board Report to the IMFC on the Establishment of the Independent Evaluation Office (EVO) and its Terms of Reference,' 12 September 2000; IMF, 'Independent Evaluation Office (IEO) of the IMF: Staffing,' 19 October 2001, http://www.imf.org/external/np/ieo/sta.htm.

[45] IMF, 'IMF Executive Board Report to the IMFC on the Establishment of the Independent Evaluation Office (EVO) and its Terms of Reference,' 12 September 2000; IMF, 'Independent Evaluation Office (IEO) of the IMF: Transparency,' 19 October 2001, http://www.imf.org/external/np/ieo/tra.htm.

[46] The official position is that the 'final decision on publication will be made by the Executive Board, in accordance with such procedures as the Board may wish to specify.' IEO/IMF, 'Standard Rules for Review and Publication of Evalution Reports and Other IEO Documents,' 19 August 2002, at p 2.

[47] IMF, 'Independent Evaluation Office (IEO) of the IMF: Goals and Instruments,' 19 October 2001, http://www.imf.org/external/np/ieo/gai.htm.

For all the significant improvements in transparency and accountability carried out by the Fund in recent years, there are still further areas where improvements are necessary. As OXFAM has observed: 'much of the country programme information now posted on the IMF's website is made available too late to facilitate genuine public debate; and huge gaps in public disclosure remain.'[48] As at 2002 the results of internal reviews—including the work of the Office of Internal Audit and Inspection, and internal staff evaluations—were still not being made publicly available.[49] This is no small omission, critically limiting the prospects for informed external evaluation of how well or poorly the Fund is discharging its tasks, and for outsiders to offer support to change agents inside the organisation.[50] The sweetheart deal between the USA and Europe governing appointment to the office of Managing Director and Deputy Managing Director points to another important area of need for enhanced transparency and procedural reform.[51]

One of the most striking deficiencies in the IFIs' legitimacy and effectiveness, the minutes of Board meetings are still not published by either the Bank or Fund, which in conjunction with the consensus voting practice, continues to mask the relations of power underpinning the IFIs' decision-making.[52] Continued secrecy in this regard is defended out of a professed desire for collegiality and frank discussions. Interestingly, the Monetary Policy Committee of the Bank of England once defended its own opaque practices on the same grounds, 'debunked by the subsequent experience of that agency, whose minutes and votes have been recorded and published shortly after meetings since 1998.'[53] While one should perhaps not be naïve about how fully such reforms will lay bare pernicious and extraneous political machinations in Board decision-making, greater trans-

---

[48] OXFAM (1999) at 14.

[49] HDR 2002 at 116; N Woods (2001) at 91.

[50] 'By publishing critical reports, institutions can catalyse public attention and external pressure for change, helping to overcome inertia or vested interests within the organisation.' HDR 2002 at 116.

[51] See eg R Dale, 'Lessons of the IMF Succession Debacle,' *International Herald Tribune*, 7 March 2000. Formally, all members of the Bank and Fund Executive Boards are supposed to appoint the institutons' President and Executive Director, respectively.

[52] For a specific instance where transparency of Board proceedings may have had a direct bearing on the realisation of the right to health (in Tanzania) see R Naiman, 'Why We Must Open the Meertings of the IMF and World Bank Boards: The Case of User Feeds on Primary Health in Tanzania,' *Attac News*, 20 June 2001, http://www.globalpolicy.org/socecon/bwi-wto/wbank/2001/openmeeting.htm. In this particular instance a leaked summary of the Boards' consideration of the draft PRSP for Tanzania, including on the issue of user fees for health. The summary of the Bank Board discussion suggests that the Board accepted the inclusion of user fees, on the basis that 'the poor were exempt from these charges.' This decision is reported to run contrary evidence that exemption schemes do not work, and contrary also to US legislation in October 2000 requiring the US representative on the IFIs' Boards to oppose any loan or credit agreement which included user fees in connection with access to health or primary education. Naturally, assuring more rigorous compliance by the US Executive Directors with their own 'voice and vote' legislation is very much a double-edged sword. But whatever the practical challenges involved, the underlying rationale to expose policy preferences and ideological biases on the IFIs' Board is undoubtedly a sound one.

[53] HDR 2002 at 115.

parency in the Boardroom is most certainly a vital and necessary step in the right direction.

In summary the chief institutional reforms that are required in the short to medium term include:

1. a changed voting structure at both Bank and Fund Board level to enhance developing members' voices, thereby enhancing both legitimacy and effectiveness;[54]
2. arrangements to allow representatives from countries directly affected by IFIs' programs standing to participate in Board discussions concerning that country, perhaps along with other key stakeholders on a rotating basis;[55]
3. measures to assist in enhancing the accountability of Executive Directors to their own governments and voters;[56]
4. taking necessary measures to ensure more effective control by the Board over Management and staff;
5. improving the gender balance in high level decision-making at both the Bank and Fund;[57]
6. urgent attention to the 'approval culture' problem and associated retrograde incentives, ensuring that policy compliance costs are factored into loan approval arrangements, and that staff and supervisors' own performance appraisals are linked to policy compliance and (as far as possible) development effectiveness;
7. modifying the consensus voting requirement and ensuring that the Bank and Fund make public both the agenda and minutes of Executive Board meetings,[58] as a means of exposing political interests and policy preferences in the Executive Boards' decision-making;
8. transparent and equitable procedures for appointment to senior posts in the institutions, eliminating the 'cosy' deal between Europe and the US regarding appointment to the top position in the Bank and Fund, and making the selection process more substantive in terms of the candidates' objective qualifications and views on policy;
9. continued progress towards full publication by the Fund of Article IV consultation reports, Country Reports and other country-specific

---

[54] For suggested alternatives to a one-member one-vote system, hedging against risk of dominant members withdrawal, see J Weidner, 'World Bank Study' (2001) 7 *Buffalo Human Rights Law Review* 193–226, 226.

[55] See eg N Woods (2000) at 836 and N Bridgeman (2001) at 1041–42, arguing for a more equitable system of voting rights, with broader representation including a group of rotating seats made up of Northern and Southern NGOs.

[56] N Woods (2001) at 100.

[57] Incredibly, as at 2002 there were no women at all on the IMF's Board of Directors, and only 8% on the Bank's Board: HDR 2002 at 115, quoting figures from the Women's Environment and Development Organisation.

[58] United Kingdom House of Commons, Select Committee on Treasury, Third Report, 18 February 2000.

information,[59] with limited case-by-case exceptions justified publicly by reference to clear and objectively grounded 'commercial in confidence' criteria;

10. full publication by the Bank of all OED reports, and by the Fund of its internal evaluations, and timely public disclosure by the Bank of project appraisal documents;[60]

11. a requirement that conditionality by the IFIs be imposed only to the extent: (a) necessary under their mandates,[61] and (b) that appropriate mechanisms exist to ensure that the IFIs themselves can be held accountable to people affected by their actions,[62] consistent with these reform suggestions;

12. the formalisation of mandatory public consultations by IFI country missions, or at least formalisation of a right to make submissions and that appropriate avenues exist for genuine participation in policy-making by those likely to be affected;

13. measures to ensure that the IMF's IEO has the requisite degree of resources, expertise, and independence, in order to strengthen both internal and external lines of accountability, with particular regard to reforms: (a) militating against arbitrary dismissal of the IEO's Director; (b) safeguarding against the arbitrary exercise by the Board of its budgetary powers, (c) permitting the IEO Director a wider measure of discretion than currently exists concerning the IEO's staffing profile; and (d) mandating the publication of all IEO reports within a given time limit following their submission to the Board for comment;

14. measures to ensure the effective and independent functioning of the Inspection Panel in accordance with the terms of the Resolution by which it was established;[63]

---

[59] United Kingdom House of Commons, Select Committee on Treasury, Third Report, 18 February 2000.

[60] The Bank does release short summaries of projects that it is considering funding, and often provides more extensive detail in informal consultations with NGOs, however a more transparent approach needs to be systematised, prior to decisions being taken at Board level. See eg P Blustein, 'Critics Get World Bank to Ease Disclosure Policy,' *Washington Post*, 6 September 2001, p A02.

[61] See eg M Feldstein (1998) at 27: '[The IMF] should not use the opportunity to impose . . . economic changes that, however helpful they may be, are not necessary to deal with the balance-of-payments problem and are the proper responsibility of the country's own political system. In deciding whether to insist on any particular reform, the IMF should ask three questions: Is this reform really needed to restore the country's access to international capital markets? Is this a technical matter that does not interfere unnecessarily with the proper jurisdiction of a sovereign government? If the policies to be changed are also practised in the major industrial economies of Europe, would the IMF think it appropriate to force similar changes in those countries if they were subject to a Fund program?' On Feldstein's test, conditionality is justified only if the answer to all three questions is 'yes.'

[62] For a similar recommendation see United Kingdom House of Commons, Select Committee on Treasury, Third Report, 18 February 2000.

[63] See A Orford (2001) at 153, discussed above n 20 and accompanying text, for a more far-reaching proposal of establishing an appeals and review Commission with compulsory powers and investigative functions, including investigating breaches of international law. See also D Clark, 'The

15. by analogy with to the Inspection Panel, the establishment by the Fund of an independent Ombudsman's office as a means for promoting external accountability, with compulsive powers of investigation and publication of reports,[64] ensuring that those affected by the Fund's actions have an avenue of redress, and perhaps more directly, that the Fund adheres to such operational policies and procedures as might be conceived in future.

It is almost certain that no set of institutional reforms seeking to promote transparency, democratisation of decision-making and accountability will of itself succeed in removing the basis for the 'double standards' objection discussed in chapter V, which to a large extent takes root in more fundamental ideological divisions and 'New International Economic Order' debates of the 1970s. The polarisation of North v. South positions has if anything intensified in the post-Cold War era, and ever more so it would seem in the fragmented and insecure world post-'September 11.' Realistically, there is every likelihood that the field of human rights will continue to find itself as one of the many battlegrounds upon which terms of trade within the globalised order are to be fought. Rather than grope for a utopian ideal, it is better simply to acknowledge, although not capitulate to, the diversity of national interests animating international law-making and policy-making, and the certainty that they will continue to be ventilated among other places in the governing bodies of the IFIs. Institutional reforms, even if not sufficient of themselves, must be pursued as far as possible, as a prerequisite to the legitimacy and sustainability of the human rights-specific reforms discussed in this chapter.[65]

World Bank and Human Rights: The Need for Greater Accountability' (2002) 15 *Harvard Human Rights Journal* 205–26, 224–26, recommending the establishment of a 'Development Effectiveness Remedial Team' to help provide effective remedial assistance to local communities where the Inspection Panel has identified violations of Bank policies resulting in harm. As important an idea as this is in principle, the institutional embodiment of the principle that the requirement to 'respect' human rights necessarily implies provision for redress in the case of violations, the suggested limitation of recourse to the sphere of the Inspection Panel's jurisdiction and the Bank's social safeguard policies is certainly a significant constraint.

[64] Compulsive powers might be drawn at the outer bounds of a proposed Ombudsman's mandate, having regard to the non-project orientation of the Fund's work at country level, in contrast to mediation and conciliation role of the kind played by the IFC's (and MIGA's) Compliance Advisor Ombudsman. See www.ifc.og.

[65] To similar—but perhaps even more cautionary—effect see N Woods (2001) at 100: '[U]ltimately there are limits to how accountable the IMF and World Bank can be to the governments and peoples most affected by their lending and policies. This raises a more profound issue as to how far-reaching the activities of relatively unaccountable agencies should be. In his essay on whether international institutions can be democratic, political theorist Robert Dahl warns that we should be "wary of ceding the legitimacy of democracy to non-democratic systems." His point is that domestic political systems have a potential to be democratically accountable in a way that international organisations cannot. The implication is that the IMF and the World Bank should be reined in from far-reaching policy conditionality. Their activities should be limited to those for which they can claim to be effectively accountable.' See also R Dahl, 'Can International Organisations be Democratic?' in I Shapiro and C Hacker-Cordon (eds), *Democracy's Edges* (1999) 19–36, 33.

THE DEMAND FOR HUMAN RIGHTS POLICIES

Subject to the foregoing, there is a need for a human rights policy that is grounded in the IFIs' respective international legal obligations, and the legal obligations of their Board member states. There were interesting moves afoot in this regard in the Bank as at August 2002, with the Bank President having directed his staff to prepare a 'human rights strategy.'[66] But such developments aside, having regard to the matters discussed in chapter IV it seems clear enough that the IFIs in fact already have de facto human rights policies. To a significant degree the debate at the Bank (although to a far lesser extent, the Fund) has moved on from acknowledging a limited discretion to consider human rights issues, to postulating their legal duty to—at a minimum—respect human rights,[67] and to promote or operationalise certain limited human freedoms of a civil and political nature.[68]

To this extent, consistent with both principle and the general direction of ongoing reforms to enhance transparency and accountability, it would make strategic sense from the IFIs' perspectives to bring these disparate human rights strands together within formal policies. Beyond the objective of coherence and effectiveness,[69] formalisation in this manner would have the effect of communicating clearly what can and cannot legitimately be expected from the Bank and

[66] Bretton Woods Project, *Bretton Woods Update* (July/August 2002) at 1: 'Bank Declaration of Human Rights.' The aim as stated by the Bank's General Counsel Ko-Yung Tung was to prepare a strategy which 'without overstepping our mandate or compromising our advantage of political neutrality in the eyes of our members, fully realises our mission's tie to the advancement of human rights.' Relatively few details beyond this were available as at August 2002, however some brief clarifications by the General Counsel gave cause to wonder whether this initiative was countenanced on acknowledgement of the Bank's direct responsibilities under international human rights law, or alternatively was intended to do little more than reiterate the basic assumptions of the Bank's 1998 publication 'Development and Human Rights: the Role of the World Bank:' '[H]uman rights [to the General Counsel] fundamentally means respecting the dignity of each individual. Poverty being an abject indignity, our mission of fighting poverty directly involves the advancement of human rights. Human rights is also tied closely to our efforts in promoting the rule of law through our legal and judicial reform activities. We are not, however, a "world government" or "world policeman"—we do not legislate human rights, nor do we enforce them. We are a development bank, and as such we assist our member states and their citizens to realise their rights by helping them address crucial issues of health, environment, education and other basic needs.'

[67] See D Clark (2002), discussed above n 63 and accompanying text. The legal requirement to 'respect' human rights should imply provision of avenues for recourse in the event of violations in which the IFIs are complicit.

[68] To similar effect see G Brodnig, 'The World Bank and Human Rights: Mission Impossible?', *Carr Centre for Human Rights Policy Working Paper* T-01-05 (2001) at 20.

[69] The case is well stated by Hernandez Uriz in connection with the Bank's forays in Chad/Cameroon pipeline project: 'Chad's human rights situation will determine the success of the project. The World Bank is, however, ill-equipped to tackle the country's problems, particularly with respect to corruption and revenue mismanagement, due to its lack of a coherent human rights policy. New policies relating to human rights have been adopted as a result of criticism or past project failures rather than as the result of a well thought-out plan.' G Hernandez Uriz, 'To Lend or Not to Lend: Oil, Human Rights, and the World Bank's Internal Contradictions' (2001) 14 *Harvard Human Rights Journal* 197–231, 230.

Fund on human rights issues, and thereby minimise the scope for inconsistencies and public criticism.[70]

A further problem with de facto human rights policies is that their disparate and disconnected threads are spun behind closed doors, uninformed by external perspectives of relevance and value from both instrumental and principled (including legal) standpoints. This is of course consistent with the atmosphere of secrecy that continues to shroud a large proportion of the Fund's internal deliberations on matters of potentially profound human rights impact, notwithstanding recent cautious reforms towards increased transparency and accountability.

In a like manner to the Bank's public consultation process on Operational Policy development, for the sake of credibility and legitimacy the IFIs' human rights policies need to be formulated in a manner which recognised the entitlement of those likely to be affected by IFI policies to participate.[71] Regularisation and transparency of process promotes objectivity, and consequently legitimacy, objectives ever more important to both the Bank and Fund in the sobering aftermath of the East Asian crisis. As will be seen shortly below, such is its importance in public policy making, transparency is increasingly being mandated as a matter of constitutional right in certain national legal systems.[72]

Transparently conceived human rights policies would promote coherence not only in terms of the IFIs' internal policies, but coherence overall in terms of the messages being sent from the international system to the national level.[73] Equally importantly, a process of open consultation would ensure that the IFIs' human rights policies take proper account of all relevant instrumental and legal perspectives, strengthening the conceptual foundations for the collective pursuit—within the scope of agencies' various mandates and comparative advantages—of shared human rights objectives. The specific suggestions canvassed in the remainder of this chapter might be considered as possible starting points in the IFIs' deliberations and consultations on the content of formalised human rights policies.

Finally human rights, to the extent that they can or must be included within the IFIs' work, should be entrenched as far as possible within non-discretionary

---

[70] As Bradlow remarks: 'The IMF's policy on human rights is even harder to detect [than the World Bank's]. The primary evidence of an IMF position on human rights is found in the writings and statements of its representatives. Like the Bank, the IMF sends contradictory signals in these statements'—D Bradlow (1996) at 79.

[71] Secrecy, by contrast, benefits those shareholders with the greatest ability to pursue national strategic and sectoral interests through the IFIs, as the various testimonies to the US Congress' March 1999 Oversight Hearings on the IMF (discussed earlier) reveal.

[72] See below nn 150–52 and accompanying text, focusing on constitutional human rights jurisprudence in South Africa and India.

[73] For example in late 1999 a trade Union representative in Bulgaria was reported to have complained that the IMF, among other things, refused to allow an increase in the minimum wage, at the same time that the Committee on Economic, Social and Cultural Rights declared its concern about the growing poverty in Bulgaria and about the 'disintegration of the social networks.' The complaint was that 'the two world institutions must communicate to each other. It should not be that one of them orders and the other criticises.' *World Bank Development News*, 8 December 1999.

policy directives. Human rights-relevant elements within the Bank's ODs and OPs were canvassed in chapter IV. Pressures to dilute the non-discretionary content of relevant ODs (or OPs or BPs) through the ongoing 'conversion' process must be resisted. Subject to that, policies of similar kinds need to be introduced in the Fund, in recognition of that institution's equally significant human rights impacts. As far as the Bank is concerned in particular, the rationales for this recommendation relate principally to the following factors: (a) the 'approval culture' problem and retrograde institutional and cultural incentives discussed in chapter V; (b) the decentralised structure[74] and the diversity of opinion within the Bank, and consequent difficulties in ensuring coherent and consistent policy approaches across all Regions and Networks; (c) the increasing measure of discretion vested in country directors; (d) the increasing degree of competition for scare resources, set against an expanding range of corporate policy priorities; (e) the proliferation of guidance materials and weighty 'tool kits' by the Networks which anecdotal accounts suggest are rarely accorded due attention in the Regions; and (f) the need to 'constitutionalise' human rights within the legal framework of the Bank's policy-making and operational activities.[75]

ACCOUNTABILITY AND EVALUATION IN HUMAN RIGHTS TERMS: THE QUEST FOR RELEVANT INDICATORS AND BENCHMARKS

Accountability and evaluation are in a functional sense two facets of the same question: 'Accountability by whom, to whom, and in terms of what criteria?' The different layers or directions of accountability—internal and external (or vertical and horizontal)—were canvassed in the preceding section. Evaluation is ordinarily broken down to two analytical levels: (1) individual program or portfolio evaluations in terms of development effectiveness or other specific program criteria; and (2) evaluation of overall institutional performance and effectiveness, which corresponds more directly to the question of institutional accountability. This breakdown is not watertight however, as no relevant assessment of (2) can logically occur in isolation from an aggregate assessment of (1). However the emphasis in the present discussion will be on (1), exploring in particular the scope for the infiltration of human rights-based accountability precepts into orthodox programme evaluation frameworks. There is an important practical premise as well: human rights policy re-orientations will simply not be taken seriously if they are undertaken in a notional or half-hearted fashion, without attention to monitoring and evaluation. In order to have any

---

[74] The Bank is more decentralised than it used to be, with (as at 1999) approximately 2,500 local staff members, however decision-making power still rests to a significant extent with headquarters staff visiting the country on project missions. C Gilbert, A Powell, and D Vines, 'Positioning the World Bank' (1999) 109 *Economic Journal* 598–633.

[75] 'Constitutional' analogies only take us so far in this context, however the safeguarding of the Inspection Panel's independent policy compliance role might be expected to help ensure an interpretation of operational standards consistent with both normative and evolving practical demands.

credibility, the process needs to be driven—and be seen to be driven—by method rather than mantra.

Whether as a consequence of the Secretary-General's 1997 reform proposals[76]—which stress the cross-cutting nature of human rights across every programme of the United Nations—or otherwise, many organisations and specialised agencies are embarking upon the process of exploring what a rights-based approach might mean for their work.[77] While as at 2002 the Bank had only just embarked on this task (and the Fund not at all), the human rights community nonetheless has an important role to play in helping to communicate the content of these rights, and in concert with development agencies and financial institutions, exploring ways in which human rights might be operationalised. The development of appropriate means and methodology for capturing and communicating the 'valued added' of human rights in development activities is a necessary part of the broader human rights mainstreaming challenge.

A good deal of reflection on human rights-related indicators was carried out within the UN system in the late 1990s, including within the World Bank,[78] UNDP (principally although not exclusively through its HDRs), follow-up processes to major international development conferences, analytical work of thematic mechanisms of the Commission on Human Rights (such as the Special Rapporteur on the Right to Education[79]), the work of the Committee on Economic, Social and Cultural Rights in areas such as education,[80] CCA/UNDAF, and in other areas.[81] In a recommendation directed principally at the Commission on Human Rights, the Secretary-General said:

> [W]ith respect to the issue of identifying indicators and benchmarks, and in light of the integration of human rights in the development process, the Commission may wish to envisage possible ways of sharpening practical approaches for the realization of eco-

[76] See GA Res. A/51/950 (1997).

[77] E/CN.4/2000/47, Economic, Social and Cultural Rights, Report of the Secretary-General submitted pursuant to Commission on Human Rights resolution 1999/25, at para 10.

[78] See eg F Kaufmann, A Kray P and Zoido-Lobatón, *Aggregating Governance Indicators* (1999); and P Alston (2000) at 257–59.

[79] E/CN.4/2000/6.

[80] E/CN.4/2000/47 at para 42, and see the Committee's general comments concerning articles 13 and 14 of the Covenant.

[81] For a relatively up to date overview of international initiatives see S Fukuda-Parr, 'In search of indicators of culture and development: review of progress and proposals for next steps,' Paper given at UNDP Second Global Forum on Human Development, Rio de Janeiro, 9–10 October 2000; A Chapman, 'Indicators and Standards for Monitoring Economic, Social and Cultural Rights,' Paper given at UNDP Second Global Forum on Human Development, Rio de Janeiro, 9–10 October 2000; and UNDP Human Development Report 2000. For conceptual developments at a UNICEF meeting on indicators in Geneva, 9–12 February 1998, and subsequent adaptation to sub-Saharan Africa, see Y Nwe (Regional Monitoring and Evaluation Officer, UNICEF/WCARO), 'Monitoring and Evaluation Issues in the Context of the CRC,' Discussion paper prepared for the WCAR Meeting of Programme Coordinators and Child Rights focal points, Abidjan, March 1998, Annex 1: 'Annotated list of Global Child Rights indicators relevant to Sub-Saharan Africa developed at the Regional Workshop for Programme Coordinators and Child Rights focal points, Abidjan, 15–20 March 1998, with suggestive list of 70 mainly quantitative (but some qualitative) indicators grouped in thematic clusters based upon the CRC's provisions.

nomic, social and cultural rights, including the right to education. One possibility would be for the identification of indicators and benchmarks to create a positive impact on treaty recommendations. Equally, the mainstreaming of human rights within the work of the United Nations would support the future integration of human rights treaty recommendations, including support for data collection, indicator disaggregation and benchmark-setting, into country programmes that are being developed with Governments. Existing frameworks for country programmes include the United Nations Development Assistance Framework (UNDAF), the Comprehensive Development Framework (CDF) of the World Bank (the country programme developed after the preparation of a Poverty Reduction Strategy Paper). See the Executive Summary in a recent Oxfam publication entitled 'The IMF: wrong diagnosis: wrong medicine.' On its page 3, the IMF is being requested to follow the approach taken by the World Bank by redesigning its programmes and placing human development considerations at the centre of its operations.[82]

On the specific example of the right to education, the Secretary-General has suggested that:

> The complementarity of these ongoing activities [of the Committee on Economic, Social and Cultural Rights and the Special Rapporteur on the Right to Education] and their shared goals would seem to provide a sound basis for an ongoing discussion with statisticians of the development of indicators to reflect the various aspects of the right to education. In view of this, the Commission may wish to consider options for providing opportunities for human rights experts to participate in meetings of statisticians discussing education matters and for statisticians to follow relevant discussions on indicators, benchmarks and the content of human rights norms.[83]

As timely and pertinent as the Secretary-General's recommendations undoubtedly are, however, there may be limitations on the progress that an intergovernmental body such as the Commission might be expected to achieve on as controversial a question as human rights indicators.[84] Serious caveats are likewise warranted on the short-term prospects for constructive collaboration between human rights practitioners and statisticians. The slow process towards

---

[82] E/CN.4/2000/47 at para 40. The recommendation in the OXFAM publication referred to there very much reflects the rationales said by the Bank and Fund to underpin the PRSP reform process, although the suggestion to enshrine 'human development considerations at the centre of its operations' would almost certainly be resisted by the Fund's legal department.

[83] E/CN.4/2000/47 at para 43.

[84] P Alston (2000) at 252–53: '[Composite] indices have not even been discussed by the Commission on Human Rights, although some governmental delegations did choose to air in that forum their strong objections to the [Human Freedom Index] put forward in the HDR in 1991. In general, the political constraints that apply to an inter-governmental body such as the Commission, and especially to one in which there are strong pressures to proceed in relation to such matters on the basis of a consensus, are far from being conducive to any openness to the possibility of adopting or even implicitly endorsing any type of composite index. Indeed, in many respects, it may be argued that such an exercise should not be considered by, let alone undertaken under the auspices of, a body such as the Commission.' While this assessment is expressed to apply to composite indexes, there is no reason why it should not apply to the quest for human rights indicators more generally.

the elaboration of human rights indicators in the CCA/UNDF context,[85] in particular, warns that immediate expectations in this regard should not be set too high.

Nonetheless, a number of generally accepted quality criteria can be identified, to help chart the course ahead. In order to constitute valid and useful tools (especially in situations involving conflicting interpretations, interests or human rights claims) human rights indicators need to be: (a) verifiable and based on reliable information; (b) highly significant in terms of the right in question; (c) replaceable (ie when data on indicators are being collected by another source, would they yield the same information?); (d) valid (ie does it measure what it should be measuring?); (e) based on reliable and available information; and (f) developed and agreed upon at the outset of the policy process in question.[86]

The voyage of discovery en route to relevant and reliable human rights evaluation methodologies is likely to be a long one, in light of the persistent conflict between disciplinary perspectives and systemic deficiencies in data availability and quality.[87] This quest must nonetheless be informed by—and seek to redress—shortcomings in orthodox methodologies from a human rights perspective, including:

(a) excessive reliance upon global summit goals rather than more specific and targeted measures calibrated against the normative content of human rights;[88]

---

[85] For the May 2002 consolidated version of the CCA/UNDAF guidelines see http://www.dgo. org/documents/2222-CCA___UNDAF_Guidelines___English.doc. While work on CCA indicator development has been underway within the UN Development Group since at least 1999, by 2002 only a relatively modest set of civil and political rights indicators had resulted (dealing mainly with the form of the law in the areas of 'democracy and participation, administration of justice, and security of the person'). Moreover economic, social and cultural rights indicators were all but absent, in deference to numerical averages and aggregates derived from global conference commitments. Anecdotal accounts suggest that clashes of inter-agency and inter-disciplinary perspectives—including between human rights and development professionals and statisticians—are part of the reason for the relatively slow progress.

[86] Humanist Committee on Human Rights (HOM), 'Conference Report: Human Rights Impact Assessment for Policy Measures with an External Effect,' 19–20 November 2001, Brussels (on file with author), at 8–9.

[87] See the discussion on this issue in chapter III, and also T Hammarberg, 'Searching the truth: the need to monitor human rights with relevant and reliable means,' Conference paper, 'Statistics, Development and Human Rights,' Conference organised by the International Association for Official Statistics in Montreux, Switzerland, 4–8 September 2000 at 1–5.

[88] T Hammarberg (2000) at 8: 'The problem with such global goals is of course that they tend to be based upon an approach of averages and therefore not necessarily relevant as planning tools for a number of countries.' Hammarberg puts their usefulness no higher than as 'starting points in the discussions between governments and international agencies.' The Bank's OED has been critical of the IDA's record to date with performance evaluation. IDA Executive Directors—underscoring the need to develop indicators to evaluate progress of IDA programmes at both country and global levels—have laid considerable importance to achieving coherence with the MDGs in this respect. IDA, 'Additions to IDA Resources: Thirteenth Replenishment—Supporting Poverty Reduction Strategies,' Report from the Executive Directors of the IDA to the Board of Governors, 25 July 2002 at 31.

(b) a bias towards quantitative rather than qualitative and process-oriented evaluation methodologies;

(c) inability to capture: (i) behaviour change; (ii) patterns of disparity and discrimination in a manner permitting in-depth analysis of systemic causes and cross-sectoral linkages; (iii) quality of participation and degree of empowerment of local actors; (iv) other longer-term political, social and cultural variables, towards which human rights-based approaches are principally directed; (v) procedural and substantive consequences of treating economic and social values, goods or services, in particular, as human rights; (vi) the nature and content of obligations for delivery of development outcomes, including obligations of conduct as well as result,[89] and (vii) the requirement for mechanisms for redress in the event of violations.[90]

One of the most significant challenges is to explore further synergy between national benchmark-setting and the monitoring of the rights enunciated in human rights treaties.[91] Research and policy development at UNICEF and UNDP have signalled some interesting directions in this regard. For example among the 'possible indicators for Legislative Assistance Programs' identified by the UNDP Evaluation Office are:

—Increased laws drafted/enacted by legislatures (number of bills, hearings, etc) regarding civil and political rights and socio-economic and cultural rights;

—increased ratification and implementation of international human rights treaties;

—regular government assessments (in collaboration with NGOs) of country's human rights situation and submissions to UN human rights treaty bodies [including the] Commission on Human Rights, Committee on Economic, Social and Cultural Rights, etc.; and

—greater parliamentary/legislative consultation with citizens[, including] parliamentary commissions, number of citizens being consulted, survey of citizen/NGO opinion on draft laws, and per cent of citizens/NGOs who believe they are being represented by/have access to Members of Parliament/Members of Legislative Assemblies.[92]

---

[89] Obligations of conduct would include such things as the immediate obligation to 'take steps' and formulate policies and plans for the realisation of human rights (see eg Committee on Economic, Social and Cultural Rights, General Comment No. 3 (1990)). In the context of the goal of reducing infant mortality, one of the obligations of conduct may include 'the number of child-births attended by health professionals,' or provision of related infrastructure and health education, while the obligation of result would relate more specifically to percentage of children dying at birth. On a more general level Thomas Hammarberg argues that 'it has to be accepted in a number of cases that we measure effort rather than final results, hoping that such input would eventually lead to results.' T Hammarberg (2000) at 8.

[90] Again, it is important to keep in mind the range of non-legal—as well as judicial—avenues that might be explored within a given context, as well as the need to focus specifically on improving access to justice and related accountability mechanisms within the overall framework for rights-based programming. See the discussion in chapter V above at n 31 and accompanying text.

[91] E/CN.4/2000/47 at para 42.

[92] See UNDP Evaluation Office, 'Legislative Assistance Programs' (1999) (working paper on file with author).

Furthermore in a 1998 study within UNICEF's South Asian Regional Office on the meaning and purposes of evaluation, a range of possible methodological consequences of a human rights-based approach were identified, with particular reference to UNICEF's operationalisation of the CRC:[93]

—Using the Maastricht guidelines on violations of ESCR as the benchmark, recognition of the three-tiered typology of states' obligations (respect, protect and fulfil), with description of the various types of implementation measures required, along with express recognition of an obligation of *conduct* requiring 'demonstrable action reasonably calculated to realise the enjoyment of rights.'[94]

—The requirement under Article 4 CRC to 'do the maximum with maximum available resources,' requiring that the state must be able to 'demonstrate good faith by showing that actions have been taken or are being taken to give children the priority they deserve[,]' and where national resources are insufficient, 'the international community should make every effort to support well-conceived programmes aimed at realising rights.'[95]

—The importance of duty-bearers, in contradistinction to the idea of 'stakeholders' in evaluation practice. The challenge of a rights-based evaluation was said to be 'to proactively search for, involve, and retain the interest of key duty-bearers in the evaluation process,' and help them understand what it is that they need to do better to fulfil their obligations.

—The requirement for 'broad participation in evaluation of national programs involving individuals from different levels of government and civil society.'

—The role of evaluation, itself, in helping to build awareness and understanding about economic and social human rights and concomitant duties.[96]

—The relevance of treaty-body Concluding Observations to the programming process, and the limitations of traditional household survey methodology in capturing many key facets, comparative advantages and outcomes of rights-based programming.

—Technical implications for evaluation methodology arising from the CRC's non-discrimination principle, and the requirement to involve children in evaluations in line with their evolving capacities.[97]

---

[93] R Pearson (SARO regional monitoring and evaluation officer), 'State programmes realising social rights of children—propositions for structuring evaluations contrasted with three years of experience in Nepal and Pakistan' (internal analytical paper, undated circa 1998).

[94] See above n 89 and accompanying text.

[95] This is similar to the structure of the 'progressive realisation' obligation reflected in General Comment No. 3 of the Committee on Economic, Social and Cultural Rights, although (while article 4 of the CRC lacks any reference to 'progressive realisation') it may have been appropriate to include an obligation of conduct on the State in question to actively seek international assistance where existing resources are inadequate.

[96] The same should also have been said for civil and political rights, of course.

[97] Article 12 of the CRC establishes the child's right to participate in decisions affecting him or her, in line with his or her evolving capacities. For other useful initiatives see Y Nwe (Regional

The IFIs' work, and that of the Bank in particular, has been expanding rapidly into 'quality of process' areas and challenging issues of governance, participation, gender equality and empowerment and so forth, leaving evaluation methodology lagging.[98] The lessons from other agencies' early experience in evaluation may be of relevance for the IFIs' purposes, with a focus not only upon the shortcomings and initiatives just identified,[99] but upon the need to bring accountability into the evaluation picture, modifying indicators, benchmarks, and methodologies accordingly. Engaging with human rights specialists, bodies or agencies on identification of appropriate indicators and national level benchmarks for accountability would be good starting point.[100] Consistent with proposals for a process-based 'human rights accountability index,'[101] the framework for evaluation of programme implementation would be strengthened considerably with elements designed to capture: (a) the legal foundations of accountability, such as the extent to which the programme country has ratified or acceded to the six core human rights treaties and accepted optional complaints procedures; (b) procedural dimensions of accountability, such as the submission or non-submission of reports under the six core conventions, and attitude towards requests for information or consent to country missions from special procedures and thematic mechanisms of the Commission on Human Rights, and (c) responsiveness-related factors, going to the quality of compli-

Monitoring and Evaluation Officer, UNICEF/WCARO), 'Monitoring and Evaluation Issues in the Context of the CRC,' Discussion paper prepared for the WCAR Meeting of Programme Coordinators and Child Rights focal points, Abidjan, March 1998; and M Patel, 'Rights Based Evaluation of Programme Priorities,' internal discussion draft, Abidjan, March 1997.

[98] This is certainly not to say that methodology development is stagnant, however. The Bank's 'Governance Indicators Dataset' provides suggests a reasonably broad range of indicators—subjective as much as objective—for evaluating 'governance,' not only in the narrow sense of economic management but overlapping to some degree with wider prerequisites for an enabling environment for development. See HDR 2002 at 36–37, mentioning 'voice and accountability' (measuring free and fair elections, press freedom, civil and political rights, transparency, involvement of military in politics, and others, using a variety of sources including Freedom House), 'political stability and lack of violence' (measuring perceptions of likelihood of destabilisation through ethnic tension, social unrest, armed conflict, constitutional changes and other factors, measured through a variety of sources including the Economist Intelligence Unit), 'government effectiveness' (measuring such things as 'bureaucratic quality', transactions costs, quality of public health care, and 'government stability), and rule of law and corruption, albeit with a more limited focus on the commercial sphere.

[99] For a range of other useful suggestions see HDR (2000) at 89–111, and C Mokhiber, 'Toward a Measure of Dignity: Indicators for Rights-Based Development,' Conference paper, 'Statistics, Development and Human Rights,' Conference organised by the International Association for Official Statistics in Montreux, Switzerland, 4–8 September 2000.

[100] From the beginning the Committee on Economic, Social and Cultural Rights has attached considerable importance to the concept of nationally-specific 'benchmarks' for monitoring progressive realisation. General Comment No. 1 (1989), para 6; P Alston, 'International Governance in the Normative Areas' in *Background Papers: Human Development Report 1999* (1999) 1–35, 15–18. Attention to the development of human rights *indicators* by the UN human rights bodies, however, has been neglected. P Alston (2000) at 252.

[101] P Alston (2000).

ance with relevant requests and obligations.[102] Emphasis must be placed on subjective as much as objective indicators.

TAILORING AND LOCAL OWNERSHIP

The tortoise knows how to make love to his wife.[103]

The recent history of development is littered with foreign template failures, transplanted with arrogance and missionary zeal by external experts. In a functional sense the imperatives of tailoring and local ownership are closely related, each vital prerequisites for accurate situation analysis and sustained implementation.[104] As seen in the previous chapter, some of the most trenchant barriers to the implementation of locally-relevant and tailored approaches are those inherent in the IFIs as institutions: the Bank's 'perpetual re-organisations' and disincentives to country-specific expertise, the Fund's adherence to 'universal nostrums,' the perpetuation of top-down approaches and inappropriate time horizons, and the persistence of disciplinary blinkers, valuing economics without sufficient regard to vital cross-disciplinary perspectives and interactions.

These objections relate to the point that human rights on a functional and institutional level *are local*. International obligations in the human rights area are in a real sense owned by the programme countries concerned, with governments assuming chief responsibility as both executor and trustee for their implementation. While the content of human rights standards as expressed in relevant international instruments is to varying degrees imprecise, and while dedicated efforts will frequently be necessary to establish organic linkages between local perceptions and values and international formulations of rights, human rights norms—as elaborated by human rights treaty-bodies, courts and other relevant institutions—are eminently adaptable to social, political and legal realities at national and local levels.

On a formal legal level in particular, the rapid rate of subscription to the core UN human rights conventions has ensured the proliferation of broad-based

---

[102] P Alston (2000) at 264–67. In similar vein Thomas Hammarberg invokes the approach of the CRC Committee of 'monitoring the monitors,' a process-based approach depending for its validity upon assumptions drawn from the responsive and effective functioning of processes and institutions. T Hammarberg (2000) at 4.

[103] Ghanaian proverb. See T Friedman, 'It takes a village: Africans forge new weapons against AIDS,' *International Herald Tribune*, 28–29 April 2001, p 8.

[104] See eg T Killick, 'Adjustment and Economic Growth' in J Broughton and K Lateef (eds) (1995) at 152. Killick remarks (at 152): '[i]n general, . . . to be effective, measures to promote adaptation must emanate from an understanding by responsible ministers of the actions necessary, with policies emerging organically, as it were, through local decision and implementation processes, and tailor-made to domestic conditions in a way that is only feasible when designed locally. The success of home-grown programs is far from guaranteed, of course, because the possibility of misdesign is still present and shocks can supervene. However, they stand a better chance of success than the opposite case of Washington-designed programs that are to a substantial degree wished on more or less reluctant governments desperate for money.'

human rights laws at the national level. Also noteworthy is the proliferation of National Human Rights Institutions (NHRIs) and human rights ombudsmen and similar institutions in developed and developing countries alike, promoting awareness of applicable human rights standards and ensuring that government legislative, executive and administrative activities are consistent with them. And at the macro level, waves of constitutionalism over the last century have transformed national legal orders at an unprecedented rate, giving constitutionally entrenched status to internationally valid human rights norms.[105]

Constitutional courts have increasingly been giving substance to these norms, adjudicating on development-related claims in connection with housing, education, industrial relations, employment, and a great range of related human rights.[106] The independent and effective functioning of courts and NHRIs of course varies across a wide spectrum, and as with development programmes themselves, are threatened in the circumstances where they are needed most, in climates of crisis and political oppression. However some of these institutions have shown remarkable degrees of robustness and independence within the most challenging of economic and political circumstances.[107] Development and structural adjustment programs have stumbled time and again for failure to take these laws and institutions into account, or alternatively assuming them to be infinitely malleable. However local actors and institutions must themselves be allowed to stumble, en route to genuine ownership of their development agendas. The prospects for sustainable implementation would be improved immensely with a more wide-ranging and strategic assessment of national and local level legal mechanisms, with due attention to legal empowerment strategies.[108] The IFIs' conditionalities—as necessary and appropriate[109]—should be

---

[105] For a discussion see M Darrow and P Alston, 'Bills of Rights in Comparative Perspective' in P Alston (ed) *Promoting Human Rights Through Bills of Rights: Comparative Perspectives* (1999) 465–524.

[106] See eg M Darrow and P Alston (1999); and see below nn 132–52 and accompanying text.

[107] One could point for example to the surprising degree of willingness shown by the Indonesian NHRI established by the former Soeharto government—KOMNASHAM—to investigate large scale human rights violations by the Indonesian military in the mid to late 1990s, and also to the Supreme Court of Zimbabwe's willingness in the year 2000 to strike down as illegal the Mugabe government's controversial 'fast track' program of land 'reform,' a thorn in the side of that regime's relationship with the IFIs and the international community at large. See 'Mugabe threatens to expel Whites fighting land reform,' *The Times of India On-line*, 3 December 2000: 'Zimbabwe's highest court, the Supreme Court, has declared the government land resettlement program illegal because the [land] seizures are not performed in accordance with legislation passed by Mugabe's ruling party in April.' See also UNOCHA, 'Zimbabwe: Government "ignores" Supreme Court,' *Integrated Regional Information Networks (IRIN)*, 13 November 2000; D Musanda, 'Zimbabwe: Bid for land funding stillborn,' *Africa News*, 21 September 2000; D Muleya, 'Zimbabwe: Pressure mounts on Mugabe,' *Africa News*, 1 December 2000; and D Muleya and V Kahiya, 'UN abandons Zimbabwe,' *Africa News*, 11 August 2000.

[108] See chapter V at n 31 and accompanying text.

[109] 'Necessary' refers to the need to minimise the overall burden of conditionality for the purposes of program implementation. 'Appropriateness' calls into question a range of other variables, such as minimum standards of courts' and NHRIs' independence and the consistency of national and local laws with applicable international human rights standards. For more detailed discussion see chapter V, nn 45–54 and accompanying text.

linked to these locally relevant laws and processes,[110] tapping into and strengthening existing structures rather than risking their erosion by foreign transplants.

PROGRAMMATIC RELEVANCE OF ECONOMIC,
SOCIAL AND CULTURAL RIGHTS AS HUMAN RIGHTS

It is quite an irony that in the face of traditionalist interpretations Article IV, section 10 of the Bank's Articles and wider paranoia concerning the infiltration of 'political' issues into the IFIs' domains, civil and political rights (or at least civil liberties and a limited number of related freedoms) have come to be embraced ahead of economic and social rights within the IFIs' policy and progammatic concerns, particularly so in the case of the Bank.[111] As was seen in chapter IV the Bank, and to a lesser extent the Fund, have been perfectly willing in recent times to proclaim the relevance of their work to the realisation of 'economic, social and cultural rights,' albeit understood in a residual and reductionist sense as a 'good' or 'value' or positive externality or perhaps even discretionary entitlement or some kind.

However as at 2002 there has been not the slightest hint of recognition within the orthodox development community that economic, social and cultural human rights are actually 'human rights' in the sense that the term 'rights' is normally taken to mean, involving real, immediate and binding consequences, with avenues for judicial or administrative review and remedies in the event of demonstrable violations. Rather, in contrast to the more limited civil and political freedoms held dear within the neo-liberal framework, it is assumed that economic and social rights are merely aspirational and programmatic in nature, presumptively consonant with the ends of economic development, but importing no substantive legal, policy or programmatic implications.

Any balanced and workable human rights policy of the Bank and Fund would need to 'transcend the stale and unhelpful ideological point-scoring'[112] that has

---

[110] See eg D Kapur and R Webb, 'Governance-related Conditionalities of the International Financial Institutions,' 6 *G-24 Discussion Paper Series* 18 (2000): '[Governance-related conditionalities] have focused on drafting new rules instead of trying to enhance the convergence between formal rules and practice by pressing borrower governments to act in accordance with their *own* laws. The sovereign must have the right to legislate; but the sovereign cannot argue that it has the freedom to legislate while at the same time selectively enforcing its own laws. The IFIs' efforts are likely to carry greater legitimacy and be more helpful if they use [governance-related conditionalities] to hold governments' feet to fire if they violate their own constitutions, laws and legislation rather than pressing for new laws and legislation drafted from the outside.' As sound a lesson of experience as this is, however, it is worth recalling that local and national laws are not always consistent with applicable international human rights standards, and should be critically reviewed in this light as a prequisite to the scheme of operation advocated by Kapur and Webb.

[111] See chapter IV above, with particular regard to the Bank's empirical research on civil liberties and project performance, the instrumental values of freedom of expression and free press, and the civil and political rights aspects of the good governance and anti-corruption agenda and related prerequisites to an enabling environment for development and sustained, equitable economic growth.

[112] M Darrow and P Alston, 'Bills of Rights in Comparative Perspective' in P Alston (ed), *Promoting Human Rights Through Bills of Rights: Comparative Perspectives* (1999) 465–524, 509.

stifled human rights debate so far, and recognise the indivisibility and equal claim to legitimacy of all kinds of human rights. This is not the place to re-till the vast terrain of scholarship on the historical and philosophical underpinnings of the international human rights framework, and in particular the normative foundations of the 'indivisibility' principle.[113] However it will be useful to expose a select few of the more pernicious and trenchant fallacies impeding recognition of economic and social rights as such, with an eye towards the policy implications for the IFIs.

Economic, social and cultural human rights are, of course, just as concrete and relevant as civil and political human rights in development policy and programming terms. According to the ICESCR economic, social and cultural rights are to a large extent to be implemented progressively, subject to the maximum extent of available resources.[114] Article 4 of the CRC avoids as far as possible arbitrary distinctions between different kinds of rights, and in particular omits any explicit reference to 'progressive implementation' of rights, affirming instead 'the minimum degree of protection owed,'[115] that is to say, that ESCR are to be implemented 'to the maximum extent of available resources' and 'where needed, within the framework of international cooperation.'[116] While the jurisprudence of the Committee on the Rights of the Child (a relatively new Committee) was somewhat under-developed as at 2002, the Committee on Economic, Social and Cultural Rights confirmed in a series of General Comments between 1990 and 2000 that States parties have a 'core obligation to ensure the satisfaction of, at the very least, minimum essential levels of each of the rights' set forth in the ICESCR.[117] Were it otherwise, economic and social rights 'would largely be deprived of [their] raison d'être.'[118]

Where resources are limited, states parties have a clear obligation to explore the avenues for international cooperation and assistance.[119] While Article 2(1)

---

[113] For an extensive inquiry into the normative and rational underpinnings of the 'indivisibility' principle in the context of the relative neglect of socio-economic rights in Africa, see S Agbakwa, 'Reclaiming Humanity: Economic, Social and Cultural Rights as the Cornerstone of African Human Rights' (2002) 5 *Yale Human Rights and Development Law Journal* 177, 180–86.

[114] See Article 2(1) of the ICESCR and Article 4 of the CRC.

[115] C Scott, and P Alston, 'Adjudicating Constitutional Priorities in a Transnational Context: A Comment on *Soobramoney*'s Legacy and Grootboom's Promise, (2000) 16 *South African Journal of Human Rights* 206–68, 228.

[116] Article 2(1) of the ICESCR obliges states parties to 'take steps, individually and through international assistance and cooperation,' with a view to the progressive realisation of the rights enumerated in the Covenant by all appropriate means. Article 4 of the CRC provides that ESCR should be implemented within the maximum extent of available resources and 'as needed, within the framework of international cooperation.' While Article 4 is silent on which particular rights fall within this category, the requirement to pursue 'full implementation' is included in substantive provisions in the CRC concerning the right to education (Article 28), health (Article 24) and social security (Article 26).

[117] See General Comment No. 3 (1990) at para 10; and General Comment No. 14 (2000). The Committee has begun to identify 'core' obligations in connection with the rights to food, education and health: see General Comments No. 11, 13 and 14 respectively.

[118] General Comment No. 3 (1990) at para 10.

[119] P Alston and G Quinn, 'The Nature and Scope of States Parties' Obligations Under the International Covenant on Economic, Social and Cultural Rights' (1987) 9 *Human Rights Quarterly*

of the ICESCR puts this obligation in open-textured terms,[120] the Committee on Economic, Social and Cultural Rights has found that the 'core obligation' to fulfil the 'minimum essential levels' of economic, social and cultural rights gives rise to international responsibilities for developed states and others 'in a position to assist.'[121] The Committee's country-specific recommendations are increasingly reflecting this principle, with clear implications for donor country members on the IFIs' Executive Boards.[122] Concluding observations for borrower countries likewise routinely situate obligations under the ICESCR within the framework of the IFIs' activities, whether in connection with 'positive aspects,'[123] or (more commonly) 'factors and difficulties impeding the implementation of the Covenant'[124] or 'principal subjects of concern,'[125] in many cases leading to recommendations that the State party take its ICESCR obligations into account in all aspects of its negotiations with the IFIs.[126] While expressly applying to the rights contained in the ICESCR, the reasoning

156; M Craven, *The International Covenant on Economic, Social and Cultural Rights: A Perspective on its Development* (1995) 149; General Comment 3 (1990); General Comment 2 (1990).

[120] More specific formulations can be found in various substantive provisions of the CRC, including Article 23(4) concerning information exchange in the field of preventive health care, Article 24(4) concerning the right to highest attainable standard of health, and Article 28(3) concerning the right to education.

[121] General Comment No. 14, para 45.

[122] See for example E/C.12/1/Add.54, 1 December 2000 at para 31 (Concluding observations for Belgium), and E/C.12/1/Add.43, 23 May 2000, para 20 (Concluding observations for Italy). In the former case the Committee encouraged the government of Belgium 'as a member of international organisations, in particular IMF and World Bank, to do all it can to ensure that the policies and decisions of those organisations are in conformity with the obligations of States parties to the [ICESCR], in particular the obligations contained in Article 2.1 concerning international assistance and cooperation.'

[123] eg in the case of the Republic of the Congo: 'The Committee notes with appreciation that at the request of the Government, specialised agencies such as [the IMF and World Bank] are assisting the Republic of the Congo in addressing its innumerable problems, as follows: (a) In 1998, the IMF decided to provide the Republic of the Congo with a special post-conflict recovery credit of 10 million [US] dollars; the IMF also indicated that health, education and social spending were at the top of the expenditure priority list[.]' E/C.12/2000/21 at para 200.

[124] E/C.12/2000/21 at para 152 (Egypt): 'The Committee is of the view . . . that some aspects of structural adjustment programmes and economic liberalisation policies introduced by the Government of Egypt, in concert with [IFIs], have impeded the implementation of the Covenant's provisions, particularly with regard to the most vulnerable groups of Egyptian society[.]'

[125] E/C.12/2000/21 at para 526 (Morocco): 'The Committee regrets that the State party does not take its obligations under the Covenant into consideration in its negotiations with [IFIs].'

[126] In the case of Morocco: 'The Committee strongly recommends that Morocco's obligations under the [ICESCR] be taken into account in all aspects of its negotiations with international financial institutions, like the [IMF, World Bank] and the World Trade Organisation, to ensure that economic, social and cultural rights, particularly of the most vulnerable groups of society, are not undermined.' E/C.12/2000/21 at para 549. In very similar terms see the concluding observations for Egypt reproduced in E/C.12/2000/21 at para 170. Sometimes, as in the case of Mongolia, the recommendation is put more generally: 'The Committee recommends that the State party continue to seek international cooperation and assistance, as provided for in articles 2, paragraph 1, and 23 of the Covenant, to enhance its efforts to improve the implementation of economic, social and cultural rights in Mongolia. The Committee would appreciate information, in the fourth [next] periodic report of Mongolia, on the status of the "Poverty Partnership Agreement" signed with the Asian Development Bank.' See E/C.12/2000/21 at para 279.

underlying this emerging body of jurisprudence is relevant to the proper interpretation of the economic, social and cultural rights guarantees in the CRC.

Putative distinctions between 'generations' of human rights tied to characterisations of correlative obligations as either 'positive' or 'negative'[127]—with the
latter sitting most comfortably within the neo-liberal paradigm—have become
very tired and discredited.[128] It is clear that human rights of all kinds carry
different blends of positive and negative obligations and that in any event, as
Amartya Sen has observed, the existence and validity of human rights do not
rely upon proof of perfectly correlative duties whether positive or negative in
character.[129] The existence of human rights must be distinguished from the
question of their implementation. As with civil and political rights, economic
and social rights do import obligations of an immediate character, to 'take steps'
to implement the rights by all appropriate means, to the maximum extent of
available resources.[130] Moreover as with certain categories of civil and political
rights, 'core' obligations are non-derogable,[131] equally—if not more—applicable in times of emergency.

Finally on the question of justiciability, recent landmark decisions of the
South African Constitutional Court concerning the right to adequate housing
and the right to the highest attainable standard of health have demonstrated
clearly the relevance of international human rights jurisprudence in terms of
how human rights standards connect with national and local level realities, and
the extent to which economic and social rights can legitimately be subject to
judicial review with the programmatic implications that that entails.[132] In the
Grootboom case[133] the Constitutional Court declared that the government of
South Africa had breached its obligations in failing to include within the state's
housing policies any provision at all for basic shelter for the most disadvantaged
in a particular region. This finding, based upon the rights to shelter and to
adequate housing as reflected in the South African constitution (in terms similar
with but not identical to parent provisions of the ICESCR and CRC),[134] pro-

---

[127] For a proposed 'neutral' (in addition to negative) obligation, see S Skogly, *The Human Rights Obligations of the World Bank and the International Monetary Fund* (2000) 45, 135–36, although cf M Darrow, 'Human Rights Accountability of the World Bank and IMF: Possibilities and Limits of Legal Analysis' (2003 forthcoming) 12(1) *Social and Legal Studies* 133–44, 134–36.

[128] For one of the more influential critiques see S Holmes and C Sunstein, *The Cost of Rights: Why Liberty Depends on Taxes* (1999).

[129] UNDP, *Human Development Report 2000: Human Rights and Human Development* 25 (2000).

[130] Article 14 of the ICESCR is a particular example of a time-bound obligation, requiring States parties to 'work out and adopt' within two years an action plan for the progressive implementation of the principle of compulsory education free of charge for all.'

[131] General Comment No. 14, para 47; P Alston and G Quinn (1987).

[132] C Scott and P Alston, (2000).

[133] *Government of RSA and others v Grootboom and others*—Case No. CCT11/00 (4 October 2000).

[134] Section 26(1) of the South African Constitution guarantees the right to have access to adequate housing. Section 26(2), dealing with the State's obligation in that regard, requires the State to
take '*reasonable legislative and other measures, within its available resources, to achieve the progressive realisation of this right.*' This is not identical to the content and typology of State party

vided welcome vindication at the national level of the justiciability (within certain limits) of economic and social rights, in a manner foreclosing unreasonable fears of judicial interference in policy-making. The Court did not—nor could it—delve into the micro-management of the state budget and decide that certain types of housing were due to certain groups of people within a particular time, with funding to be made available from (say) the defence budget. Rather, based upon all available evidence applied against a core criterion of 'reasonableness,'[135] the Court was able to reach a more direct and limited conclusion in negative terms that—within all resources available to the state—the failure to make any provision at all for the minimal shelter needs of its people in certain areas was not 'reasonable' in the context of the requirement to progressively implement the right in question.[136]

Moreover in July 2002 the South African Constitutional Court in *Minister for Health v Treatment Action Campaign (TAC)*[137] illustrated clearly and convincingly how a constitutionally guaranteed right to health, within the appropriate limits of its justiciability, could impact constructively on development policy debates and help save potentially large numbers of lives.[138] The background

---

obligation reflected in Article 2(1) of the ICESCR, as interpreted in General Comment No. 3 (1990). One of the key points of departure concerns the interpretation by the Constitutional Court (at para 33 of Yacoob J's judgement) of the concept of the 'core content' of the right of access to adequate housing, regarded by the Court as having a bearing on the question of 'reasonableness' under section 26(2) of the Constitution, but not constituting a self-standing right in and of itself (although it is possible that the Court misinterpreted the 'core content' criterion reflected in General Comment No. 3 as being congruent to the content and extent of immediately realisable rights in a given situation). Moreover the precise typology of obligation under section 7(2) of the South African Constitution is to 'respect, protect, promote and fulfil' human rights guarantees, rather than CESCR's 'respect, protect, and fulfil' (fulfilment in turn being sub-divided into 'facilitate and provide'). But such minor differences aside, General Comment 3 and parent provisions of the ICESCR and CRC were considered at length by the Court in *Grootboom*'s case, and were relied upon to a significant degree in support of the Court's reasoning and ultimate findings.

[135]   See Article 26(2) of the South African Constitution.

[136]   These rights must of course be implemented within the prevailing social and historical context, as Yacoob J found (at paras 93–94): '[93] This case shows the desperation of hundreds of thousands of people living in deplorable conditions throughout the country. The Constitution obliges the State to act positively to ameliorate these conditions. The obligation is to provide access to housing, health-care, sufficient food and water, and social security to those unable to support themselves and their dependants. The State must also foster conditions to enable citizens to gain access to land on an equitable basis. Those in need have a corresponding right to demand that this be done. [94] I am conscious that it is an extremely difficult task for the State to meet these obligations in the conditions that prevail in our country. This is recognised by the Constitution which expressly provides that the State is not obliged to go beyond available resources or to realise these right immediately. I stress however, that despite all these qualifications, these are rights, and the Constitution obliges the State to give effect to them. This is an obligation that Courts can, and in appropriate circumstances, must enforce.'

[137]   *Minister for Health and Others v Treatment Action Campaign and Others*, Case CCT 8/02 (5 July 2002).

[138]   On the right to the highest attainable standard of health in international law see eg Articles 12 and 24 of the ICESCR and CRC respectively, along with General Comment No. 14 (2000) of the Committee on Economic, Social and Cultural Rights which elaborates on the normative requirements of accessibility, affordability and acceptability. Section 27(1) of the South African Constitution guarantees everyone the right of *access* to health care services (including reproductive

circumstances to this case were quite notorious, arising from the RSA government's refusal over a number of years to make a certain anti-retroviral drug—nevirapine—widely available to the population (within resources available to the government) in order to reduce the incidence of intrapartum mother-to-child transmission of HIV/AIDs. As with *Grootboom*'s case the task before the Court under relevant constitutional human rights provisions was one of judging the 'reasonableness' of the government's actions in the present case, rather than purporting to assume executive or legislative prerogatives.

Following *Grootboom*'s case, the Court found that any national programme for the realisation of socio-economic rights must 'be *balanced and flexible and make appropriate provision for attention to . . . crises, and to short, medium and long-term needs. A programme that excludes a significant segment of society cannot be said to be reasonable.*'[139] With the cost of nepiravine being admitted to be within the resources available to the State, and the administration of the drug being a relatively simple procedure (and one that on available evidence could of itself significantly reduce—even if not eliminate entirely—perinatal mother-to-child HIV transmission), the Court readily found that the government's policy on restricting access to nepiravine could not be defended as 'reasonable.'[140] Accordingly, the Court directed a review of that policy in accordance with a range of basic parameters, including that the government:

(a) remove existing restrictions on access to nepiravine;

(b) permit and facilitate the use of nepiravine for the purpose of reducing the risk of mother-to-child transmission of HIV;

(c) within its available resources, devise and implement a 'comprehensive and coordinated programme to realise progressively the rights of pregnant women and their newborn children to have access to health services to combat mother-to-child transmission of HIV;'

(d) include within the above programme (within available resources) reasonable measures for counselling and testing pregnant women for HIV, counselling HIV-positive pregnant women on the options open to them to reduce the risk of mother-to-child transmission of HIV, and making appropriate treatment available to them for such purposes.[141]

---

health care, sufficient food and water, and social security, including, if persons are unable to support themselves and their dependants, appropriate social assistance). Section 27(2) obliges the State to take 'reasonable legislative and other measures, within its available resources, to achieve the progressive realisation of each of these rights.'

[139] *Minister of Health and Others v Treatment Action Campaign and Others*, para 68 (p 41), citing Yacoob J in *Grootboom*'s case at para 34.

[140] See pp 54–73 of the Court's judgement.

[141] See pp 73–77 of the Court's judgement for the full text of the orders. Significantly, recognising the constitutional prerogatives of the legislature and executive, the Court also held (at Order No 4, page 76) that the substantive orders given by the Court 'do not preclude government from adapting its policy in a manner consistent with the Constitution if equally appropriate or better methods become available to it for the prevention of mother-to-child transmission of HIV.'

One could look further to relevant jurisprudence of the Supreme Court of India, interpreting a constitutionally guaranteed right to life as embracing ostensibly non-binding 'directive principles' in the area of education,[142] and necessary components of the 'right to live with dignity.'[143] Much of this jurisprudence vindicates only the 'negative' (non-interference) aspects of ESCR, for example in the sense of ruling forced evictions unlawful or that the right to education cannot arbitrarily be denied, rather than 'positive' requirements of the kind seen in the *TAC* case. However one should not under-estimate the potentially positive and empowering externalities leveraged through outwardly 'negative' obligations to respect human rights. Security of tenure (an aspect of the right to adequate housing)[144] is an excellent example. As observed in the Bank's World Development Report for 2003,[145] '[r]emoving the threat of summary eviction makes possible economic and social transformation of informal slum settlements, giving residents entitlements and responsibilities that change their relationships with formal institutions and with each other.'[146] Witnessed through official programmes to regularize *favelas* (slums) in Brazil, for example, security of tenure has been observed to trigger 'a virtuous circle of equitable access to urban assets, as well as political and economic inclusion, giving residents rights and responsibilities as citizens with a stake in the city's future.'[147] In this sense safeguarding the 'non-interference' (negative) aspects of a human right can serve to empower claim-holders to take up their own rights and responsibilities as actors for sustainable development.

Moreover there are signs of Indian constitutional human rights jurisprudence moving in even more progressive directions. In a landmark preliminary ruling in

---

[142] M Darrow and P Alston (1999). See also *Olga Tellis v Bombay Municipal Corporation* (1985, 3 SCC 545), in which the Indian Supreme Court held that forced eviction would result in a deprivation of the ability to earn a livelihood. The Court further noted that the ability to earn a livelihood was essential to life and thus the forced evictions would result in a violation of the right to life as embodied in Article 21 of the Indian Constitution.

[143] *Maneka Gandi v Union of India* (1978, 1SCC 248). See also *Francis Coralie v Union Territory of Delhi* (AIR 1981, SC 746) in which, building upon *Maneka Gandi*, the Indian Supreme Court stated that the right to life includes the right to live with human dignity and all that goes along with it, namely the bear necessities of life such as adequate nutrition, clothing, and shelter.

[144] The right to housing under international law is an aspect of the right to an adequate standard of living in Article 11(1) of the ICESCR. Legal security of tenure is one aspect of the content of this right, as the Committee on Economic, Social and Cultural Rights elaborates (General Comment No. 4 (Sixth Session, 1991) at paragraph 8(a)): 'Tenure takes a variety of forms, including rental (public and private) accommodation, cooperative housing, lease, owner-occupation, emergency housing and informal settlements, including occupation of land or property. Notwithstanding the type of tenure, all persons should possess a degree of security of tenure which guarantees legal protection against forced eviction, harassment and other threats. States parties should consequently take immediate measures aimed at conferring legal security of tenure upon those persons and households currently lacking such protection, in genuine consultation with affected persons and groups.'

[145] World Bank, *World Development Report 2003: Sustainable Development in a Dynamic World* (2002) (hereafter WDR 2003).

[146] WDR 2003 at 9.

[147] WDR 2003 at 16.

2001[148] the Supreme Court of India appeared to break new ground in upholding numerous substantive or 'positive' aspects of the right to food (an implied incident of the constitutionally protected right to life). Challenging what Jean Drèze labelled 'the scandalous persistence of endemic hunger in India,'[149] in 2001 citizens' organisations in Rajasthan brought a petition demanding that surplus food stocks of the Food Corporation of India—offically earmarked for famines but rotting in large silos while people nearby starved—be distributed to those in need. The Court duly ordered the government authorities to implement the nutrition programme, and to adopt specific measures to ensure public awareness and transparency of these programmes. Moreover state governments were directed to introduce cooked mid-day meals in primary schools within six months.[150]

The Court's order concerning the need for transparency in public policy, supported by the reasoning of the Constitutional Court of South Africa in the *TAC* decision,[151] is of particular significance, grounding an instrumentally valuable 'governance' principle as a matter of legal right. Transparency and freedom of information are vital prerequisites to effective participation, enlivening the processes of political and social mobilisation that these cases reveal as so vital for linking legal standards and redress mechanisms with local level action and realities.[152]

Cases of the above kind demonstrate clearly the importance and comparative advantages to development of appreciating economic and social entitlements as 'human rights.' Understood as such, economic and social rights are not fanciful claims or discretionary entitlements, but legally enforceable claims within defined parameters with potentially significant impacts upon development issues of concern to the Bank and Fund. The *TAC* circumstances are of partic-

---

[148] *People's Union for Civil Liberties v Union of India and others* (Supreme Court of India, Writ Petition (Civil) No. 196 of 2001). For a more detailed analysis see C Gonslaves, 'The Spectre of Starving India' (August/September 2002) 1(3) *Combat Law: The Human Rights Magazine* 4.

[149] L Drèze, 'From the Courts to the Streets' (August/September 2002) 1(3) *Combat Law: The Human Rights Magazine* 14.

[150] C Gonsalves (2002) at 12.

[151] See chapter III above at n 120 and accompanying text.

[152] As Drèze argues: 'The Supreme Court orders are extremely useful in strengthening the bargaining power of all those who are working for the realization of the right to food in India. But it would clearly be naïve to expect these orders to be implemented without further public pressure. And even if they are implemented, the realization of the right to food requires much more than legal provisions and sanctions.' The author proceeds to illustrate how elements of a broad-based popular movement for the realization of the right to food was underway in India, through such initiatives as a 'national day of action on mid-day meals' on 9 April 2002, and a public hearing on hunger and the right to food in Manatu on 9 July 2002. As to the latter, Drèze remarked that '[a] public hearing may not sound like an effective response to the problem of hunger, but in fact it is a major step towards breaking the vicious circle of poverty and disempowerment in which the people of Manatu are trapped. The hearing was an opportunity for people to learn about their entitlements (most of them were in the dark in that respect) and to voice their demands. It gave them a glimpse of the possibility of change, a sense of their collective power, and an opportunity to discuss what could be done. The public hearing in Manatu was also a wake-up call for the bureaucrats, contractors, dealers and money-lenders who have been mercilessly exploiting the local people for so long.' J Drèze (2002) at 15.

ular interest in this regard, with the human rights case (as vindicated through an activist legal profession and functioning court system, admittedly not a set of ingredients one finds everywhere) carrying the day when political and economic arguments alone had failed. In this and similar contexts economic and social human rights—understood as such—provide important means of strengthening and supporting development policy and programming, within certain basic institutional prerequisites and mutually supportive social and political mobilisation strategies.

EDUCATION FOR ALL—A ROLE FOR THE CRC AND ICESCR

One of the highest priority development policy issues in the year 2000—on the 10 year review of the Jomtien conference commitments—was the issue of universal access to free of charge primary education. Apart from being an end in itself, research is definitively bearing out the critical importance of basic education, particularly girls' education, for long term development ends. As Oxfam senior policy adviser Kevin Watkins has commented, 'the right to education is as much about economic sense as it is about morality and social justice.'[153] On the 10-year review of Jomtien, James Wolfensohn has declared that '[e]ducation must be at the core of every nation's development and poverty reduction strategy.'[154] Wolfensohn added that '[s]uccess will depend on strong partnerships among developing and developed countries, international agencies like those of the UN and the World Bank, and civil society.' In similar vein to his HIV/AIDS appeal for Africa, he added that '[w]e should pledge that no country with a sound plan to achieve education for all its children will fail for lack of help and money.'[155]

Yet this debate appeared to take place completely outside the human rights framework, notwithstanding the near universal commitments by governments under the CRC to the implementation of free primary education compulsory for all, along with secondary and tertiary education accessible to all,[156] and various other ends related to purposes and quality of education.[157] Important and widely applicable rights and obligations in the ICESCR, along with relevant jurisprudence from the Committee on Economic, Social and Cultural Rights,[158]

---

[153] K Watkins, *International Herald Tribune*, 25 April 2000, at 6; cited in *World Bank Development News*, 25 April 2000.

[154] F van Leeuwen and J Wolfensohn, *International Herald Tribune*, 25 April 2000, at 6; cited in *World Bank Development News*, 25 April 2000.

[155] F van Leeuwen and J Wolfensohn, *International Herald Tribune*, 25 April 2000, at 6; cited in *World Bank Development News*, 25 April 2000.

[156] See Article 28 of the CRC.

[157] Article 29 of the CRC.

[158] The CESCR's General Comments 11 (concerning Plans of Action for Primary Education under Article 14) and 13 (concerning the Right to Education under Article 13) are of central importance. See E/C.12/1999/4 and E/C.12/1999/10, respectively. Provisions of numerous other international instruments including the CEDAW should also serve as basic normative and programmatic references.

were likewise ignored. A failure to concentrate upon these and like legal sources increases the risks of missing important conceptual and functional perspectives, and deprives policy makers of valuable tools through which universal education objectives could be grounded in binding legal obligation and monitored accordingly.

General Comment No. 13 goes to great lengths in recalling relevant provisions of the ICESCR and CRC and other international instruments, as a basis for describing the desired ends of education, and the nature of states parties and other organisations' (including the IFIs') obligations progressively to fulfil those rights.[159] General Comment No. 13 explains what, as a matter of international law under the Covenant, 'free of charge' means, including a discussion on the potentially regressive effects of various kinds of direct and indirect costs of education.[160] The introduction of school fees accompanying structural adjustment programs will often be incompatible both with Article 28 of the CRC[161] and Article 13 of the ICESCR. States parties have an obligation to ensure that their actions as members of international organisations, including the IFIs, take due account of the right to education.[162] Having regard to the detrimental effects that fees of various kinds have had on the implementation of the right to education in crisis-affected countries in Africa, East Asia and elsewhere in the 1990s, attention to those issues within the framework of Plans of Action for Primary Education, and within the framework of the IFIs' programming and advocacy activities at country level, would constitute an as yet unexplored and potentially valuable contribution to the realisation of common human rights imperatives and development goals.

The IFIs need to be aware of relevant provisions of the CRC and ICESCR and CEDAW concerning the nature of states parties' obligations (including those incumbent upon states parties as voting members on the Executive Board of the IFIs) both immediately and progressively to implement the right to education, and need to be in a position to assist states parties as required to prepare and implement Plans of Action for Primary Education under Article 14 ICESCR.[163] The immediacy of the obligation to provide primary education free of charge for all must be brought to the forefront of development planning, along with certain other immediate obligations 'to take steps' toward the realisation of secondary, higher and fundamental education,[164] and to

---

[159] E/C.12/1999/10 at paras 43–60.

[160] E/C.12/1999/4 at para 7.

[161] To this effect see eg S de Vylder, *Development Strategies, Macro-economic Policies and the Rights of the Child*, Discussion Paper for Radda Barnen (1996) at 38.

[162] E/C.12/1999/10 at para 56. See also the Maastricht Guidelines on Violations of Economic, Social and Cultural Rights (1998) 20 *Human Rights Quarterly* 691–705, 698–99.

[163] E/C.12/1999/4 at para 11.

[164] E/C.12/1999/10 at paras 51–52. See General Comment No. 3, para 2, of the Committee on Economic, Social and Cultural Rights: 'While full realisation of the relevant rights may be achieved progressively, steps towards that goal must be taken within a reasonably short time after the Covenant's entry into force for the States concerned. Such steps should be deliberate, concrete and targeted as clearly as possible towards meeting the obligations recognised in the Covenant.'

implement obligations without discrimination on the grounds set forth in the relevant instruments.[165]

Guided by these international instruments, the nature of the right to education as an economic, social, cultural and civil and political right, needs to be fully understood, epitomising the indivisibility and interdependence of all human rights.[166] States parties and the IFIs need to take account of the strong presumption of the impermissibility of any retrogressive measures taken in relation to the right to education,[167] and the central importance of the non-discrimination norm. The ways in which violations of the right to education might occur,[168] and could be circumvented, need to be understood by the IFIs as well as states parties to the CRC, ICESCR and CEDAW. A coordinated approach to the implementation of the right to education among all development actors at the national and international levels is required, based upon this legal framework. The Bank and Fund need to pay greater attention to the right to education in all their policies and activities, including lending policies, credit agreements, structural adjustment programs, the development of national poverty reduction strategies, and other measures taken in response to the debt crisis.[169]

PARTICIPATION IN HUMAN RIGHTS TERMS

The Bank's record in terms of operationalising a principled and effective conception of 'participation'[170] provides sobering lessons for the inculcation of human rights criteria within its policies and activities more generally. The former head of the Bank's NGO Unit put the matter quite bluntly: '[W]hile participation ideally [means] "efficiency, equity and empowerment," wide consensus inside the Bank has so far only reached as far as the efficiency argument. . . . While there was agreement that NGO participation is desirable where it improved World Bank operations, the idea of participation as having an intrinsic value met some resistance.'[171]

---

[165] See Articles 2(2) ICESCR and 2(1) of the CRC.

[166] E/C.12/1999/4 at para 2. For comments on the normative content of the right to education, see E/C.12/1999/10 at paras 4–42.

[167] E/C.12/1999/10 at para 45: 'If any deliberately retrogressive measures are taken, the State party has the burden of proving that they have been introduced after the most careful consideration of all alternatives and that they are fully justified by reference to the totality of the rights provided for in the Covenant and in the context of the full use of the State party's maximum available resources.'

[168] E/C.12/1999/10 at para 59.

[169] E/C.12/1999/10 at para 60.

[170] See discussion in chapter III. On the importance of participation in the structural adjustment context, see eg S Skogly, 'Structural Adjustment and Development: Human Rights—An Agenda for Change' (1993) 15 *Human Rights Quarterly* 751–78, 764–66.

[171] Summary of the Fourth Meeting of the World Bank/NGO Asia Pacific Committee, Bangkok, 1–2 July 1998. The barriers to the mainstreaming of participation can be traced to some of the organisational cultural problems canvassed in chapter V, as Miller-Adams explains: 'While the

The overall record to date on 'participation' within the IFIs is unenviable. Deficiencies within the iPRSP and PRSP contexts were discussed at some length in chapter III.[172] The overall evidence available as at 2002 suggested that most IFI programs and operations were at best 'consultative', rather than strongly participatory. Empowerment and participation are officially regarded as important within the Bank,[173] however official guidance appears to be very widely overlooked, with some insiders confessing that the Bank simply 'does not know how to do it.'[174] Experience elsewhere is not encouraging either. For example under the Second 'Clarification' (or Review) of the Resolution Establishing the Inspection Panel, 'remedial action plans' are permitted in limited circumstances, in relation to which the Panel is required to assess the 'adequacy of consultation with affected parties.'[175] However in light of practice so far, and in view of the technical and methodological challenges in assessing participation, the requirement seems likely to be a 'dead letter' in practice.

Participation needs to be iterative, informed by poor peoples' experiences and perspectives at all stages. To be considered effective, participation must ultimately be characterised by a genuine capacity to control the economic and political agendas. It must mean more than merely participating as an economic unit, or 'consumer of public services.'[176] Collective participation in this very real sense must logically involve the capacity of people to determine the political and

value of participatory approaches has been accepted at the Bank's most senior levels, commitment to practicing them has not permeated the Bank's operations. . . . Beyond their poor fit with the Bank's dominant paradigm and its standard approach to lending, participatory projects challenge other aspects of the Bank's organisational culture. They take more time and involve smaller amounts of money than infrastructure or adjustment loans, thereby undermining the Bank's ability to move large amounts of money quickly. They require a greater field presence, challenging the Bank's centralised organisational model in which the overwhelming proportion of Bank staff is located in Washington, not in the borrowing country. They require that the Bank work closely with leaders of grassroots organisations and other NGOs, challenging the Bank's usual practice of interacting primarily with governments. And they require knowledge of the culture and society of local populations, calling into question the Bank's reliance on quantitative indicators and the influence of economists on its staff. M Miller-Adams, *The World Bank: New Agendas in a Changing World* (1999) 70–71.

[172] See chapter III above at nn 132–51 and accompanying text.

[173] See eg World Bank, *Participation Sourcebook* (1996); and D Narayan (ed), *Empowerment and Poverty Reduction: A Sourcebook* (2002).

[174] Interviews in Washington DC and New York, February 2000.

[175] (1) See paras 15 and 16 of the Second Clarification conclusions. These action plans—agreed between borrower and Bank and 'in consultation' with the requesters or 'affected parties'—are not allowed to pre-empt the Panel's investigation, and will 'normally be considered by the Board in conjunction with the Management's report' following the Panel's investigation and submission of findings to the Board. Communications between Management and the Board until that time are prohibited (para 2 of the clarification). (2) In relation to these types of 'action plans', however, as at 2002 it was unclear how the Panel would assess the 'adequacy of consultation with affected parties.' The sole criterion in para 16 is that the Panel's assessment is to be 'based on the information available to it by all available means,' but it is hard to see how definitive an assessment would be possible, given similar barriers in assessing participation in other contexts, eg the PRSP. (3) There is no express provision in paras 15 or 16 that the Board will be bound in any way by the Panel's findings on the adequacy of the Bank's 'consultation with affected parties.'

[176] A Orford and J Beard (1998) at 209–10.

economic systems under which they live, and whether economic and social models imposed by the Fund (in consultation with local elites or otherwise) are desirable or appropriate for the country concerned.[177]

There is a need for the IFIs to consider operationalising 'participation' within a human rights framework. A move in this direction would be consistent with the spirit and rationale of Bank's highly publicised 'Voices of the Poor'[178] participatory poverty research, and is otherwise not entirely unsupported by precedent in the Bank's past lending practices. According to one commentator, the Bank has imposed conditions upon borrowing countries relating to participation of (or more accurately consultation with) NGOs on project related concerns 'on at least a couple of occasions in the past.'[179]

The core UN human rights treaties do not purport to establish a complete operational template for 'participation' for development policy or programming, however their provisions do at least constitute a thumbnail sketch of essential normative underpinnings for development purposes. Firstly both the UDHR and the ICCPR guarantee the right to take part in government or in the conduct of public affairs, and to have access, on general terms of equality, to public services.[180] As to Article 25 of the ICCPR, the Human Rights Committee has stated that 'conduct of public affairs . . . is a broad concept which relates to the exercise of political power, in particular the exercise of legislative, executive and administrative powers . . . [covering] all aspects of public administration, and the formulation and implementation of policy at international, national, regional and local levels.'[181] However the Committee has been careful not to construe Article 25 as providing an 'unconditional right' of any directly affected group, large or small, to choose the precise modalities of participation.[182] As

---

[177] A Orford and J Beard (1998) at 209.

[178] D Narayan and P Petesch (eds.), *Voices of the Poor: From Many Lands* (2002); D Narayan, R Chambers, M Shah and P Petesch (eds.) *Voices of the Poor: Crying Out for Change* (2002); and R Patel, K Schafft, A Rademacher and S Koch-Schulte (eds), *Voices of the Poor: Can Anyone Hear Us?* (2002).

[179] Interviews in Washington DC in February 2000. However the way that these conditions were worded in the respective loan agreements reportedly made the consultation requirements relatively easy to satisfy.

[180] Article 21 UDHR and Article 25 of the ICCPR. The treatment of the concept of 'active, free and meaningful' participation in Article 4 of the 1986 Declaration on the Right to Development is of course directly relevant as evidence of the manner in which normative developments might crystallise in future. However in view of the uncertain status of the 1986 Declaration in international law, set against the comparative advantages of well established and binding international human rights law as described in chapter I, detailed discussion of the former is beyond the scope of this book.

[181] General Comment No. 25 (1996).

[182] *Marshall et al v Canada* (Communication no. 205/1986), at para 5.5: 'It must be beyond dispute that the conduct of public affairs in a democratic State is the task of representatives of the people, elected for that purpose, and public officials appointed in accordance with the law. Invariably, the conduct of public affairs affects the interest of large segments of the population or even the population as a whole, while in other instances it affects more directly the interest of more specific groups of society. Although prior consultations, such as public hearings or consultations with the most interested groups may often be envisaged by law or have evolved as public policy in the conduct of public affairs, article 25(a) of the Covenant cannot be understood as meaning that

with other relevant normative provisions, Article 25 should be regarded as setting some of the essential parameters for participation (in countries that have ratified the ICCPR)—and ruling out certain things from the range of permissible policy options[183]—rather than furnishing detailed answers to programmatic content.

Of further normative significance are: (a) Article 12 of the CRC, ensuring the right of a child to express views 'freely in all matters affecting the child,' with weight being given in accordance with the child's evolving capacities; (b) numerous Articles in the CEDAW guaranteeing women equal participation rights in political, public and cultural life, and specifically for rural women in connection with participation in development planning;[184] (c) provisions of the ICESCR guaranteeing participation in connection with the right to form and join trade unions and the enjoyment of cultural rights;[185] (d) Article 5 of the ICERD prohibiting inter alia racial discrimination in connection with participation in political and public life and the enjoyment of economic, social and cultural rights;[186] and (e) the collective right of self-determination as proclaimed in the UN Charter, the ICCPR and ICESCR.[187] The rights to freedom of expression, association and conscience guaranteed by the ICCPR are essential prerequisites to the fulfilment of political participation rights, as are core minimum economic, social and cultural rights guarantees. Moreover Article 1(4) of the ICERD and Article 4 of the CEDAW make it clear that temporary special measures may be required to achieve equality for disadvantaged groups, and to that extent are not unlawful under each Convention.

Similarly, DFID has identified 'participation' as one of three 'underlying principles, integral to the realisation of all human rights' and the achievement of the

any directly affected group, large or small, has the unconditional right to choose the modalities of participation in the conduct of public affairs. That, in fact, would be an extrapolation of the right to direct participation by the citizens, far beyond the scope of article 25(a).' See the discussion of this issue in M Scheinin, 'The Right to Enjoy a Distinct Culture: Indigenous and Competing Uses of Land' in T Orlin, A Rosas and M Scheinin (eds), *The Jurisprudence of Human Rights Law: A Comparative Interpretive Approach* (2000) 163–64. For a critique of the Committee's decision in that case see M Turpel, 'Indigenous People's Rights of Participation and Self-Determination: Recent International Legal Developments and the Continuing Struggle for Recognition' (1992) 25(3) *Cornell International Law Journal* 579–602, 596.

[183] An obvious example would be the 'negative' requirement that certain groups of people (dalits pursuant to article 1 of the ICERD, women under the CEDAW, children under article 12 of the CRC, minorities or others) not be arbitrarily excluded.

[184] Articles 7, 13 and 14(2) of the CEDAW. According to the latter provision: 'States parties shall take all appropriate measures to eliminate discrimination against women in rural areas in order to ensure, on a basis of equality of men and women, that they participate in and benefit from rural development and, in particular, shall ensure to such women the right: (a) To participate in the elaboration and implementation of development planning at all levels.'

[185] Articles 6 and 15 of the ICESCR.

[186] Participation rights of minorities in particular are addressed in a wide range of international human rights instruments, such as Article 27 of the ICCPR, Article 2(2) of the UN Declaration on the Rights of Persons Belonging to National or Ethnic, Religious and Linguistic Minorities (1992), and at a regional level, Article 15 of the Council of Europe Framework Convention for the Protection of National Minorities (1995).

[187] See common Article 1 of the ICCPR and ICESCR.

Copenhagen and OECD international development targets.[188] It has elsewhere been described as 'in many ways the key to release the power of fusion between development and human rights[,]' representing 'an opportunity for a holistic fusion of the operational and normative aspects of development and human rights approaches.'[189]

According to DFID's analysis '[e]ffective participation requires that the voices and interests of the poor are taken into account when decisions are made and that poor people are empowered to hold policy makers accountable. Accountability is therefore essential to participation.'[190] DFID therefore place emphasis upon essential civil and political rights and guarantees as the appropriate legal underpinning for the instrumental value of participation, relying in particular upon the freedom of expression, free press and access to information, and freedom of association.[191] In a wide-ranging survey of relevant international human rights instruments, including the CRC (Article 12), UDHR, ICCPR, ICESCR, CEDAW and various regional instruments, Clarence Dias likewise attaches significance to fundamental civil and political rights guarantees, although warns that 'considerable work lies ahead in elaborating the political, economic, social and cultural aspects of the content of the right to participation.'[192]

It is difficult to imagine in the abstract how the adequacy of participation in the PRSP context[193] or otherwise can accurately be evaluated, and according to what types of criteria, standing in the shoes of national level authorities and civil society. Without wanting to overstate their policy impacts or predictive value, baseline human rights criteria may help signpost answers to some of these questions,[194] as well as reinforce the normative imperative. While the difficulties of distilling an agreed set of civil and political rights indicators are well known,[195]

---

[188] *DFID Human Rights Paper* (2000) at 3. The other two principles are 'inclusion' and 'obligation.' Participation is said to involve 'enabling people to claim their human rights through the promotion of the rights of all citizens to participation in, and information relating to, the decision-making processes which affect their lives.'

[189] T Jones, 'The Right to Participation' in UNDP (ed), *Human Development and Human Rights: Report of the Oslo Symposium* (2–3 October 1998) ('*Oslo Symposium Report 1998*') at 213–21, emphasising the instrumental links to the concept of empowerment.

[190] *DFID Human Rights Paper* (2000) at 19. The synergy between empowerment and accountability is also reflected strongly in the World Bank's 'Empowerment Sourcebook.' D Narayan (2002).

[191] *DFID Human Rights Paper* (2000) at 19–22.

[192] C Dias, 'The Human Right to Participation' in *Oslo Symposium Report 1998* 208–12.

[193] Interestingly, the staff of the Bank and Fund are only required to 'describe' rather than evaluate consultative and participatory processes under the PRSP. The Boards, however, must surely retain some discretion to reject processes that in all the circumstances are patently inadequate and subversive of the PRSP's entire rationale, as indeed the Bank has done in isolated instances in the past.

[194] According to Bradlow a finding by the IFIs that adequate participation has occurred should be based on 'ability [of stakeholders] to organise, the level of freedom of speech in the country, and the ability of citizens to obtain information on the proposed policies.' D Bradlow (1996) at 83. To this list could be added freedom of the press, along with the range of mutually supportive rights under the UN Charter, UDHR, and the six core human rights treaties, discussed above.

[195] P Streeten, 'Human Rights and Their Indicators' in *Oslo Symposium Report 1998* at 88–96.

consistent with early research by the Bank[196] and with approaches taken within certain of the UNDP's Human Development Reports, reliance could at least partly be placed upon Freedom House or Humana indicators, supplemented by a 'human rights accountability index' of the sort discussed earlier.[197] But further to the work of DFID and Dias and others on civil and political rights, 'participation' in development context naturally must extend to embrace mutually reinforcing core economic, social and cultural rights guarantees, along with the non-discrimination norm and a focus on the excluded, especially in countries where women are systematically marginalised or where racial, caste[198] or ethnic divisions are rife.

The chief advantages of an approach of the above kind lie in its objectivity and specificity, planted firmly in the bulwark of international legal principle, yet allowing a necessary measure of discretion to authorities, actors and stakeholders at country level as to the design of socially and culturally appropriate models of participation. Naturally the danger in setting too high a bar in this respect is that countries will be driven away, and in setting too low a bar the process will be subverted entirely. As challenging a course as this is to chart, especially posited against the urgent demands for debt relief in the case of HIPC countries, as a matter of both principle and practice the need is compelling.

In moot if not all IDA countries 'participation' will be meaningless without serious and sustained capacity-building efforts and principled perseverance for the long term. The Bank's patchy record on long-term implementation of projects (as opposed to the approval phase),[199] coupled with the Fund's conservatism and the inherent difficulty in weighing the urgency of debt relief against process-oriented imperatives,[200] are cause for sobriety in this regard. As at 2002 the jury was still well and truly 'out' on the extent to which participation and 'ownership' could be translated into something meaningful and genuine under the PRSP framework, and whether human rights could be expected to occupy anything beyond a tokenistic role.

INSTITUTIONAL IMPLICATIONS OF THE PRSP PROCESS

As discussed earlier, the assumptions underpinning the PRSP initiative are intended by the IFIs to constitute the standard way of doing business under all

---

[196] P Landell-Mills and P Serageldin, *Governance and the External Factor* (1991). And as mentioned elsewhere, the Aid Effectiveness study in 1998 relies on these types of measures in drawing conclusions on the national level institutional preconditions for effective aid. See D Dollar and L Pritchett (1998).

[197] See P Alston (2000).

[198] The Committee on the Elimination of Racial Discrimination interprets 'descent' in the definition of racial discrimination (article 1 of the ICERD) as including caste-based discrimination.

[199] See the discussion in chapter V concerning the problem of retrograde institutional incentives.

[200] However it is important to emphasise that participation is not just a question of 'process' in this context. Human rights are of course values in their own right, as well as instruments for sustainable implementation and 'national ownership' ends.

concessional lending and assistance policies. The core assumptions concerning participation and local ownership—while driven substantially by external pressures—are consistent with the directions of the IFIs' research and programme evaluations, and clearly necessitate a greater measure of policy flexibility than each institution (and especially the Fund) has been willing to display in the past. If carried out properly, within an appropriate time frame, the human rights gains overall from planning approaches modelled upon the PRSP could be significant, in terms of empowering people to make claims on their own behalves, contributing to a general awareness and culture of human rights, along with instrumental gains from the higher priority accorded to human rights in development planning. And to the extent that the core assumptions of transparent decision-making and accountability could be applied in reciprocal fashion to the IFIs themselves, the legitimacy dividend might well have direct and positive implications for the effectiveness of the entire enterprise, at the level of local perception and ownership, and also in terms of international agency and bilateral donor 'buy-in.'

However, working out an appropriate and effective division of labour between Bank and Fund in the PRSP context remains one of the chief challenges.[201] As at the year 2002 it was by no means certain that the Fund's relative dominance over the Bank would be significantly altered by the practical demands of the PRSP process. To the extent that the Fund's policy influence and muscle is exercised out of proportion to the Bank's, it is no adequate solution in the institutional reform context simply to delineate human rights, along with social issues in general, as exclusively within the Bank's preserve. Whether initiatied by the IFIs or not, human rights are beginning to filter through to PRSP's in particular countries, in some cases with quite profound implications for prospects for sustainable development (for example in Rwanda's case).[202] In such situations it can be dangerous and self-defeating for Bank and Fund staff not to bring an informed position to the table.[203]

[201] This concern is implicit even within official documents. See eg IMF, 'Review of the Poverty Reduction and Growth Facility: Issues and Options', Prepared by the Policy Development and Review Department and Fiscal Affairs Department, 14 February 2002, at para 39: 'The benefits of the [July 2001 Bank/Fund strategy for collaboration within the PRSP context] are beginning to be seen on a country-by-country basis, while Fund and Bank staff work on specific procedures and modalities to implement these decisions routinely in joint country work. The framework [takes into account] the different cultures and structures of the two institutions. Collaboration has already proved fruitful in specific PRGF cases with more focused programs, but benefits should become more evident in future with the routine implementation of the strengthened collaboration framework.' See also IMF, PIN No. 02/30, 15 March 2002, 'IMF Executive Board Reviews the Poverty Reduction and Growth Facility (PRGF),' http://www.imf.org/external/np/sec/pn/2002/pn0230.htm. For a broader discussion of the history and difficulties of Bank/Fund interaction, with suggestions as to how their competencies and responsibilities might be defined more clearly, see C Gilbert, A Powell and D Vines, 'Positioning the World Bank' in C Gilbert and D Vines (2000) 39–86 at 70–72.

[202] See chapter III above, nn 145–46 and accompanying text.

[203] In neither case mentioned above—Nicaragua or Rwanda—did the staffs of the Bank or Fund express a view on the human rights institutional dimensions of those countries' PRSPs, a striking omission in Rwanda's case in particular, in view of the high priority attached by the Rwandan government to human rights in the context of reconciliation, poverty reduction and sustainable

Civil society participation and poverty/macro-economic inter-linkages are so fundamental to the PRSP process that the Fund must find ways to more effectively inter-relate with other relevant actors and normative and conceptual frameworks, and independently develop informed positions on intersection issues.[204] There are isolated signs that the Fund has begun to 'encourage member governments and development partners to consider human rights in the design of poverty reduction strategies.'[205] But what does does this mean in a practical sense? Where are the values-added of human rights in this context, and what are the limits of legal obligation? Are all human rights to be included, or only a narrow set of 'good governance' or civil and political liberties surrogates? How should the client government go about more effectively integrating human rights in PRSPs? What resources and partnerships could be required in a given case? The reasonable limits of the Fund's direct responsibilities in this area still remain to be drawn.

Subject to the implementation of a potentially far-reaching set of internal and external accountability reforms, it is almost certainly desirable in the short term

---

development. IDA/IMF, 'Rwanda: Poverty Reduction Strategy Paper—Joint Staff Assessment,' Prepared by the Staffs of the World Bank and the International Monetary Fund, 18 July 2002; IDA/IMF, 'Nicaragua: Poverty Reduction Strategy Paper—Joint Staff Assessment,' Prepared by the Staffs of the World Bank and the International Monetary Fund, 27 August 2001. By contrast, a modest exception proving the rule, in Malawi's case the staffs commented that the 'discussion of the links between human rights, democracy, and development' in Malawi's PRSP were 'well cast.' IMF/IDA, 'Joint Staff Assessment: Malawi,' 23 August 2002, at paragraph 28. But deeper substantive probing of the human rights/democracy/development linkages was not ventured.

[204] See chapter II above, at nn 232–33 and accompanying text. Indeed in the history of the ESAF, and currently under the PRGF, Fund staff have often brought independent positions on social issues to the table, for example in connection with the issue of HIV/AIDS and access to food in Malawi, and in connection with recommendations that governments 'improve the process of participation and consultation with civil society,' as well as their 'poverty and social impact analysis and monitoring.' See chapter III below at n 185 and accompanying text; IMF Country Report No. 02/181, August 2002, 'Malawi: Article IV Consultation and Economic Program for 2002—Staff Report; Staff Supplement; and Public Information Notice on the Executive Board Discussion;' IMF/IDA, 'Joint Staff Assessment: Malawi,' 23 August 2002; and IMF Country Report No. 190, 'Republic of Moldova: 2002 Article IV Consultations, First Review Under the Three-Year Arrangement Under the Poverty Reduction and Growth Facility and Request for Waiver of Performance Criteria—Staff Report; Public Information Notice and News Brief on the Executive Board Discussion,' at para 41. See also IMF, PIN No. 02/30, 15 March 2002, 'IMF Executive Board Reviews the Poverty Reduction and Growth Facility (PRGF),' http://www.imf.org/external/np/sec/pn/2002/pn0230.htm, in which the Fund's Executive Board welcomed the progress to date in incorporating poverty and social impact analyses (PSIA) into PRGF-supported programmes and staff documents, and urged continued improvements in coordination and definition of roles with the Bank. The Executive Directors also observed that there was 'scope for more extensive and effective communications with the authorities, development aid partners, and civil society in PRGF countries, and in reporting on these communications in staff reports.' The Directors 'agreed that Fund staff need to more actively explain to a broad audience their views and analysis regarding the links between the macro-economic framework and growth and poverty reduction outcomes in the context of work on PRGF-supported programs.'

[205] S Pereira Leite, 'Human Rights and the IMF,' 38(4) *Finance and Development*, http://www.imf.org/external/pubs/ft/fandd/2001/12/leite.htm. Sérgio Pereira Leite is an Assistant Director in the IMF's Office in Europe.

to draw the Fund's responsibilities relatively narrowly.[206] However the mere fact of the Fund's involvement within the PRSP context—with the responsibilities it bears (at a minimum) to respect human rights under international law—mean that it is no longer acceptable to wash its hands of these issues entirely.

A logical consequence of the foregoing is that the Fund will need to widen its staffing profile, recruiting beyond its usual cadre of macro-economists, in order properly to implement the PRSP. Voluntary contributions facilitated the recruitment of the Fund's first two Social Development Specialists in the organisation's Africa division, and as at March 2000 a Governance specialist was said to be in the offing. Such modest beginnings need to be expanded, if division of labour with the Bank on 'social' issues is to be rendered efficient and meaningful. The incentives for the improvement and broadening of the Fund's capacities within the PRSP context would undoubtedly be increased by implementing the Executive Board's recommendation concerning the need for more opening up more extensive channels of communication within PRGF countries, and critically, reporting on these communications systematically within staff reports.[207]

Of course, not all would agree that the engagement by the Fund with a wider range of issues, in circumstances where the record of inter-agency cooperation is poor, is necessarily a good thing. Indeed the external political pressures driving the Fund's ostensible retreat in mid-2000 into narrowly defined macro-economic bounds,[208] with the division of labour with the Bank modified accordingly, are considerable. Many within the Fund would presumably support such a move, welcoming the organisation's detachment from messy structural and social responsibilities and the unenviable record of inter-agency cooperation, paving the return to a nostalgic age when macro-economic problems were accepted as being within the exclusive realms of the technicians, and nobody was calling for accountability.

The PRSP initiative has undoubtedly made the IFIs' lives harder, and the Fund's life in particular, in terms of encouraging policy flexibility and forcing a

---

[206] Indeed subject to needed improvements to the Fund's transparency and accountability mechanisms, there is a strong case that its proper role in relation to 'social issues' in general should be along the limited lines envisaged by OXFAM prior to the promulgation of the PRSP initiative itself, and reflected within it as a basic premise: 'to identify, through dialogue with others, financing strategies for achieving human development goals set in national poverty reduction plans.' OXFAM International Policy Paper, *Outcome of the IMF/World Bank September 1999 Annual Meetings: Implications for Poverty Reduction and Debt Relief* (October 1999) at 24. The ODI has likewise favoured a more limited focus for the Fund on 'advising on and monitoring macroeconomic policy and restoring stability in crisis-hit countries.' J Sewell, N Birdsall and K Morrison (Overseas Development Council), 'The Right Role for the IMF in Development,' *Global Policy Forum*, May 2000, http://www.globalpolicy.org/socecon/bwi-wto/imf/odc.htm. However the idea of a smaller and more focused IMF is by no means inconsistent with the requirement that the organisation builds basic capacities for carrying out its minimum obligations to 'respect' human rights entitlements in force as a matter of international law.

[207] IMF, PIN No. 02/30, 15 March 2002, 'IMF Executive Board Reviews the Poverty Reduction and Growth Facility (PRGF),' http://www.imf.org/external/np/sec/pn/2002/pn0230.htm, discussed n 204 above.

[208] See eg *World Bank Development News*, 16 July 2000; S Pereira Leite (2001).

re-think on alternative development models. Properly implemented, the IFIs' lives will be made harder still. In practical terms the Fund has been challenged to situate its work within a broader development and socio-political context, thereby calling for a re-examination of its institutional capacities, questioning its insularity and disciplinary homogeneity, and mandating interactions and programme cooperation with a hitherto unheard-of range of potential actors. A lapse into 'head in the sand' denial, or giving in to nostalgia, are not viable alternatives, in circumstances where there is still a needed—albeit carefully circumscribed—role for the Fund to play.

INTEGRATING HUMAN RIGHTS WITHIN SOCIAL IMPACT ANALYSIS
AND SOCIAL ASSESSMENT

Two facets of social assessment need to be distinguished at the outset here: (a) social assessment within the IFIs' overall 'social analysis' diagnostic framework, in which the Bank (rather than the Fund) has assumed the lead role, for the general objectives of informing project and program design, implementation and evaluation; and (b) 'social impact analysis,' designed to calibrate the social impacts at country level of IFI supported policies and programs. As the following discussion reveals, these two processes—while distinct—are strongly inter-related. While sourced for the most part to the Bank's operational policies[209] and comparative advantages, (a) and (b) each have very clear relevance to the functions and responsibilities of the Fund as well. It is appropriate to focus first on the more particular and operationally specific framework of 'social impact analysis,' proceeding thereafter to the overarching theme of social assessment.

Social Impact Analysis

There is nothing especially new about analysis of poverty and social impacts of public action. Many of the methods now considered to be a standard part of project analysis can reportedly be attributed to early economic analytical work of the Bank in the 1960s and 1970s.[210] Beyond the 'project' level of analysis, the international fallout from the structural adjustment controversies of the 1980s

---

[209] See Operational Manual Statement (OMS) 2.20 'Project Appraisal;' OD 4.01 (Environmental Assessment); OD 4.15 (Poverty Reduction); OD 8.60 (Adjustment Lending Policy); OP 4.20 (The Gender Dimension of Development); GP 14.70 (Involving Nongovernmental Organisations in Bank-Supported Actions).

[210] L Squire and H van der Tak, *Economic Analysis of Projects* (1975); C Timmer, W Falcon and S Pearson, *Food Policy Analysis* (1983); World Bank, 'A User's Guide to Poverty and Social Impact Analysis' (draft prepared by the Poverty Reduction Group and Social Development Department), 19 April 2002, at 2–3.

and 1990s subsequently ushered the distributional impacts of 'policies' to centre stage.[211]

As far as Bank's own experience is concerned, the genesis of the 'social impact analysis' (SIA; sometimes referred to as 'social impact assessment') procedures of the Bank is the 'do no harm' thesis, arising originally (for the most part) in the 'involuntary resettlement' context.[212] Negative impacts of the Bank's activities are to a large extent socially constructed. The 'triggers' for SIA in the Bank have traditionally related to issues of land acquisition, and land use changes, which the Bank has for a long time recognised as having clear winners are losers.[213] The Bank has reportedly in the past sought to expand the scope of its SIAs beyond these kinds of issues, however this was generally viewed as 'opening a can of worms,' given that virtually all of the Bank's structural and sector work, for example in relation to such core policy areas as privatisation, has social impacts.[214]

However in a promising development a joint Bank/IMF working group was established early in 2001 to develop a methodological approach to SIA and a work programme to operationalise SIA in Bank and Fund programmes supporting PRSP processes.[215] Moreover as at 2002 the Bank's Poverty Reduction Group and Social Development Department had embarked on the production of a 'User's Guide' to poverty and social impact analysis (PSIA), purporting to reflect key lessons of experience to date and equip practitioners carrying out such analyses at country level.[216] The term 'PSIA' in the Bank's draft User's Guide refers generally to the 'analysis of the distributional impact of policy reforms on the well-being or welfare of different stakeholder groups, with particular focus on the poor and vulnerable.'[217] In so doing, PSIAs are intended to address issues of sustainability and risks to policy reform arising from the social

[211] G Cornia, R Jolly F and Stewart (eds.), *Adjustment with a Human Face* (1988); World Bank, 'A User's Guide to Poverty and Social Impact Analysis' (draft prepared by the Poverty Reduction Group and Social Development Department), 19 April 2002, at 3.

[212] For the requirement for to analyse, and consider the benefits from, 'pro-poor' development strategies (into which category one might place human rights strategies) in the *long* term, see L Whitehead and G Gray-Molina, 'The Long Term Politics of Pro-Poor Policies,' paper prepared for the World Development Report 2000/1: 'The Responsiveness of Political Systems to Poverty Reduction,' Donnington Castle, 16–17 August 1999. For brief comments on the normative foundations of 'negative' obligations such as the requirement to conceive and carry out human rights impact analyses see chapter IV above.

[213] Interviews in Washington DC in March and April 1999 and February 2000.

[214] Interviews in Washington DC in March and April 1999 and February 2000. On the failure of social assessment in connection with the implementation of the Bank's OD 4.20 on indigenous peoples, see B Kingsbury, 'Operational Policies of International Institutions as Part of the Law-Making Process: The World Bank and Indigenous Peoples' in G Goodwin-Gill and S Talmon (eds), *The Reality of International Law: Essays in Honour of Ian Brownlie* (1999) 323–42, 328–29.

[215] IMF, 'Social Impact Analysis of Economic Policies: A Factsheet,' August 2001, http://www.imf.org/external/np/exr/facts/sia.htm.

[216] World Bank, 'A User's Guide to Poverty and Social Impact Analysis' (draft prepared by the Poverty Reduction Group and Social Development Department), 19 April 2002, at 2.

[217] World Bank, 'A User's Guide to Poverty and Social Impact Analysis' (draft prepared by the Poverty Reduction Group and Social Development Department), 19 April 2002, at 2.

impacts of policy changes. A number of principles for operationalising PSIA's are presented in the draft User's Guide, along with a range of potential analytical tools geared to particular purposes and circumstances.[218]

As important as the above developments are, there are serious deficiencies in the record of implementation. As at 2002 only one half of all PRGF-supported programmes refered to some kind of PSIA, with a 'rigorous analysis' having taking place in only one-third of cases.[219] Policies were modified in some of these cases (reflecting a concern for the poor), and about two-thirds of PRGF-supported programmes included counterveiling measures to take account of adverse impacts on the poor. However these counterveiling measures were not always accompanied by a PSIA, the depth and quality of which in any event was found to vary considerably across programmes.[220] Data limitations, weak national capacity, time constraints, analytical constraints, and a lack of donor coordination have been identified as the key obstacles to more widespread and systemic PSIAs.[221] Moreover, while national authorities are expected to take the lead in this area and incorporate this analysis into their PRSPs, the Fund reports that 'PSIA has been largely absent in countries' PRSPs.' Further guidance to Fund and Bank staff has reportedly been issued on this problem, 'and PRGF documents are expected to include a description of PSIA being carried out in each PRGF country and also discussions with the authorities on the social impact of key reforms.'[222]

There are obvious shortcomings, in human terms, of PSIA within the scheme indicated so far. A 'human rights' impact assessment alternative may offer significant potential for improvement, on the levels of process as much as

---

[218] World Bank, 'A User's Guide to Poverty and Social Impact Analysis' (draft prepared by the Poverty Reduction Group and Social Development Department), 19 April 2002, at 4–45.

[219] IMF, 'Review of the Poverty Reduction and Growth Facility: Issues and Options', Prepared by the Policy Development and Review Department and Fiscal Affairs Department, 14 February 2002, at paragraph 21.

[220] IMF, 'Review of the Poverty Reduction and Growth Facility: Issues and Options', Prepared by the Policy Development and Review Department and Fiscal Affairs Department, 14 February 2002, at paragraph 21. Executive Directors reacted quite strongly to this state of affairs, requesting 'that documents for PRGF-supported programmes routinely provide a description of PSIA being carried out in the country, including a quantitative description of the likely impact of major macroeconomic and structural measures on the poor and a summary of countervailing measures being implemented to offset any adverse effects.' IMF, PIN No. 02/30, 15 March 2002, 'IMF Executive Board Reviews the Poverty Reduction and Growth Facility (PRGF),' http://www.imf.org/external/np/sec/pn/2002/pn0230.htm.

[221] IMF, 'Review of the Poverty Reduction and Growth Facility: Issues and Options', Prepared by the Policy Development and Review Department and Fiscal Affairs Department, 14 February 2002, at paragraph 22; World Bank, 'A User's Guide to Poverty and Social Impact Analysis' (draft prepared by the Poverty Reduction Group and Social Development Department), 19 April 2002, at 3.

[222] IMF, 'Review of the Poverty Reduction and Growth Facility: Issues and Options', Prepared by the Policy Development and Review Department and Fiscal Affairs Department, 14 February 2002, at paragraph 22. Moreover IMF staff are expected to 'summarise the relevant PSIA in program documentation, drawing on the work of the World Bank and other development partners, and integrate it into program design. Additional follow up efforts in research, training, and the compilation of best practices is needed.'

substance, consistent with the IFIs' responsibilities not to impair member states' abilities to honour their validly assumed obligations under international human rights law. It is worth recalling that recommendations for impact statements of this sort have been made on numerous occasions in the past by the Committee on Economic, Social and Cultural Rights,[223] the Commission on Human Rights,[224] the 1993 World Conference on Human Rights,[225] the 1995 World Summit for Social Development,[226] and numerous international development symposiums and independent experts.[227]

The IFIs clearly need to consider both the short term and the long term impact of their operations on different social groups, and on the relations between these groups.[228] This is of course an inherently challenging undertaking, however the integration of human rights standards and principles may lend an additional degree of methodological rigour to this process, militating no doubt against over-hasty or ideologically driven presumptions of 'short-term (human rights) trade-off for long term overall gain.'[229] Based on applicable normative standards, human rights impact analyses would need to be sensitive as far as possible to a wider range of factors than have characterised most SIA or PSIA initiatives to date. The factoring in of 'discrimination', rather than merely instrumental concerns for 'vulnerability', means that gender, disability, patterns of racially-based exclusion and age, national or ethnic or social origin, descent

---

[223] General Comment No. 2 of the Committee on Economic, Social and Cultural Rights, paras 6, 8 and 9.

[224] E/CN.4/1999/95 (3 February 1999) at para 23.

[225] World Conference on Human Rights, Vienna, 14–25 June 1993, UN Doc. A/Conf 157/24, Part I at 28, para 4, and Part II, para 2.349.

[226] World Summit for Social Development, Copenhagen, 6–12 March 1995, UN Doc. A/Conf 166/9, 16 April 1995, para 27.

[227] For example human rights impacts assessments were advocated by the UNDP Oslo Symposium on development and human rights in 1998. See also K Tomesevski, 'Monitoring Human Rights Aspects of Sustainable Development' (1992) 8 *American Journal of International Law* 77. And Ernst-Ulrich Petersmann has even urged the UN (through expansion of the Secretary-General's 'Global Compact' initiative) to call upon all international organisations to submit ' "annual human rights impact statements" examining and explaining the contribution of their respective laws and practices to the promotion of human rights.'

[228] As Bradlow remarks in connection with the IMF: 'While this human rights impact analysis may be qualitative and not very accurate, it should enable the IMF and other stakeholders in the operation to assess the likely effects of the proposed policies. In this sense, the indicator will contribute to IMF operations that promote human rights in that they are sensitive to the needs of all stakeholders in the operation, enhance transparency in IMF operations, and enhance IMF accountability.' D Bradlow (1996) at 84. See also S Skogly (1993) at 774–76.

[229] The IMF warns that '[s]ome macro-economic and structural policies with adverse social impacts in the short-term may be indispensible for medium- and long-term growth and poverty reduction. In addition, while certain policies may entail social costs, these may be less than what would have been the case without the intervention.' IMF, 'Social Impact Analysis of Economic Policies: A Factsheet,' August 2001, http://www.imf.org/external/np/exr/facts/sia.htm.

(including caste), political affiliation, sexual orientation, religious belief and geographic location,[230] may all demand examination in a given situation.

As with PSIAs, a human rights impact assessment methodology must proceed from the recognition that 'not all sustainable and equitable operations produce only positive human rights results.'[231] Consistent with the Bank's PSIA policy developments, Bradlow has argued that human rights-based analyses must include a procedural framework for assessing and balancing likely human rights consequences, and determining when an operation can proceed. In this respect regard might be had to criteria such as: 'the existence of less harmful alternatives, the duration of the negative human rights impacts, the adequacy of the opportunity for the stakeholders who will suffer the negative human rights impacts to participate in the design and implementation of the project, the availability of a means for the stakeholders to petition the operation's decision-makers for redress of the grievances which arise during the course of the operation, and the nature and quantity of compensation available to those who suffer losses as a result of the operation.'[232] The requirement for such assessments could in due course be included in the express terms attaching to IFI assistance, reminiscent of the way environmental issues have on occasion been treated.[233] With national authorities bearing principal responsibility for undertaking such analyses within the PRSP context, it is vital that these processes

---

[230] These criteria are drawn from the anti-discrimination provisions in the core UN human rights treaties.

[231] D Bradlow (1996) at 84.

[232] D Bradlow (1996) at 84. Bradlow describes the advantages in the following way: 'The [human rights] analysis, which necessarily will require public participation, should stimulate public debate and promote public knowledge about the proposed operation. Thus, while this analysis may complicate the design phase of the operation, it should facilitate implementation of the operation. It should also help ensure that [Fund] operations are responsive to the needs of the stakeholders and the constraints of the context within which they will take place'—D Bradlow (1996) at 84–85. He goes on to remark (at 85) that 'a modified version of this approach may be required in situations of crisis, where time is of the essence and decision-makers need to act with discretion to avoid market actions that would undermine their [Fund]-supported stabilisation strategies. In these cases more emphasis will need to be placed on post hoc mechanisms, such as appeals processes, to ensure that all stakeholders are treated fairly. In addition, a more human rights-sensitive proposal can be applied once the acute phase of the crisis is over.'

[233] See eg IMF, 'Senegal—ESAF Policy Framework Paper 1998–2000,' 27 February 1998, at 36. This requires the collection of information on the international legal commitments of member states, and on their compliance with those commitments. International co-operation would greatly facilitate this task. Bradlow and Grossman suggest a role for conditionality in this respect: '[T]he IMF could make it a term of its [SBA] that the borrower state provide [it] with information on all pertinent international agreements to which it is party, on its interpretation of its obligations arising out of these agreements, and on the measures it has taken or intends to take to comply with these agreements . . . The [Fund] should then use this information to ensure that [it only funds] projects, policies, and stabilisation and adjustment programs that promote compliance with validly assumed international obligations'—D Bradlow and C Grossman, 'Limited Mandates and Intertwined Problems: A New Challenge for the World Bank and the IMF' (1995) 17 *Human Rights Quarterly* 411–42, 439. And for a comparative analysis of the World Bank's environmental assessment procedure, and of a proposed 'ethno-national assessment' procedure, see W Reinicke, 'Can International Financial Institutions Prevent Internal Violence? The Sources of Ethno-National Conflict in Transitional Societies' in A Chayes and A Chayes (eds), *Preventing Conflict in the Post-Communist World: Mobilising International and Regional Organisations* (1996) 281–338, 320–23.

(including local capacity-building requirements) be properly costed and factored into the overall financing of the programme, subject to public participation and rigorous monitoring.

Serious efforts are needed to build on existing PSIA methodology development initiatives, and ensure that they are incorporated within the Bank's operational policies. Consistent with the directions of Bank Management's current endeavours, the scope of officially sanctioned operational policies in this area must be considerably broader than the traditional categories of involuntary resettlement and other 'land use changes.' Macro-economic policies subject to human rights impact assessment would include exchange rate adjustments, anti-inflationary reforms and fiscal tightening measures.[234] As to structural and sector reforms the list of priorities would include major infrastructure projects, privatisation, user fees for education and health, policies concerning fuel or agricultural subsidies and international trade, domestic prices, civil service reform and legal reform.[235] In the broader context of structural adjustment this would mean looking at the content of an adjustment programme[236]—including timing and sequencing—and for each element asking: 'what does this mean for the poor and disadvantaged, by reference to applicable human rights standards?'[237] The Bank and Fund should do this at each stage, be prepared to change direction if necessary, and implement counterveiling measures as appropriate to compensate for identified human rights violations.

---

[234] For criticisms of the Fund's anti-inflationary and fiscal tightening focus in the context of the Argentina crisis see J Stiglitz, 'Argentina's Lessons', *Project Syndicate* (January 2002), http://www.project-syndicate.cz/series/series_text.php4?id=760, and J Sachs, 'The IMF is Bleeding Argentina to Death,' *Project Syndicate* (April 2002), available at http://www.project-syndicate.cz/series/series_text.php4?id=850, discussed in chapter III above at nn 126–27 and accompanying text. See also IMF, 'Fiscal Adjustment in IMF-Supported Programs,' Issues Paper for an Evaluation by the Independent Evaluation Office (IEO), 18 June 2002, discussed above n 43 and accompanying text.

[235] Most of these issues are indeed already contemplated: IMF, 'Social Impact Analysis of Economic Policies: A Factsheet,' August 2001, http://www.imf.org/external/np/exr/facts/sia.htm.

[236] 'The shift from broad-based "stabilisation and adjustment" suggests that PSIA be undertaken on a reform-specific basis. Such an approach also makes the task of analysing the impact of several reforms more tractable. While conceptually preferable, few tools are able to assess the combined effect of a series of policy changes in a single analytical framework—and these tend to be complex and data intensive. Therefore, it is often more practical to disaggregate expected overall impacts to individual reforms, and consider sequencing on a reform-specific basis. Consideration of the impacts of a "package" of reforms is still pertinent, however. Where they cannot be analyzed in a single analytical framework, their combined effects on various groups such as the poor may be most practically considered by independently assessing the impact of each reform set on each group. However, such an approach will tend to lose interaction effects.' World Bank, 'A User's Guide to Poverty and Social Impact Analysis' (draft prepared by the Poverty Reduction Group and Social Development Department), 19 April 2002, at 6.

[237] In human rights terms the relevant questions would need to be quite specific, such as: 'What does a proposed policy or measure mean for women of particular racial background in a given area? What does it mean for single women-headed households? What does it mean for children outside the formal education system? What are the most appropriate mechanisms and processes for redress of human rights violations? How is the borrowing country's ability to implement its obligations under relevant human rights conventions—as reflected in applicable treaty body recommendations—affected thereby?'

The right to a remedy under international human rights law, applied flexibly with due regard to local context and capacities,[238] offers much to reinforce this aspect of PSIAs. Human rights considerations strengthen the case for stakeholder participation, emphatically rule out violations of the non-derogable 'core content' of all human rights, and demand that deliberately retrogressive measures be considered only after all other options have been exhausted, justified by reference to an overall assessment of the human rights situation. The impact assessments themselves should be open to public scrutiny and comment, in order to ensure transparency and strengthen accountability.

Some degree of prioritisation of human rights standards may be essential as a matter of practicality, given that they may well be in excess of one hundred or so human rights or environmental treaties in force for the country concerned. Reliance on the six core treaties might represent an appropriate starting point, along with relevant national laws and constitutional standards. The effectiveness of this approach would depend in some measure on the relative clarity of the normative content of standards in force in a given situation. Recourse should be had in this regard to the country-specific recommendations of the human rights treaty bodies, which—along with relevant General Comments—should be taken as authoritative guides to interpretation, subject to a transparent and critical appraisal in each case of the cogency of the reporting process.[239] For countries that comply regularly with their reporting obligations under the treaties, the priorities identified by the treaty bodies—'reality-checked' against the views of national level constituencies—could contribute towards a more objectively grounded, focused and manageable human rights impact assessment procedure.

Admittedly however the IFIs' resources and procedures at present are not suited to case-by-case determinations of the precise nature of shareholder states' human rights obligations in particular circumstances. Such evaluations can be difficult to achieve even for human rights experts, and attempts to define clear boundaries of lawful limitations—such as the requirement to implement economic and social rights within the 'maximum extent of available resources'—are necessarily context-specific and complex even in relation to one human right taken alone. Some degree of outsourcing might be necessary to the extent of limitations on the IFIs' institutional elasticity, a factor of particular relevance to the IMF. But even with the assistance of external experts or human rights expert bodies, it will not necessarily be easy in practice for Management and the

---

[238] See chapter V above at n 31 and accompanying text.

[239] Relevant factors to be considered in this context would include the completeness of the report including adequacy and currency of data and frankness in disclosure of shortcomings in implementation of the treaty in question, timeliness of its submission to the treaty body in question, delay in consideration of the report by the treaty body, thoroughness of the treaty body's dialogue with the State party and extent of compliance with requests for additional information (as evidenced by the treaty body's own assessment in its Concluding Observations), and extent to which information from non-government sources was factored into the report itself and the treaty body's review processes.

Executive Boards (much less national authorities) to predict the impacts of proposed projects, loans and credit decisions, and whether those impacts would be likely to result in a breach of a member's international human rights obligations. As was seen earlier, the science of human rights-based indicator development is an ongoing one, insofar as human rights of all kinds (civil, economic, social, cultural and political) are concerned.[240]

By reason of the factors just stated, ambitions for agreed methodology should not be set at unrealistic levels of certainty insofar as the prospects for identification of actual or imminent human rights violations is concerned. Human rights are not 'trumps' in all situations, and should not be expected of themselves to resolve policy trade-offs and identify optimal policy choices for development goals. Furthermore proof of violations in particular cases cannot, under ordinary human rights principles, be dispositive of the question of the overall compatibility of a project or programme with international human rights law. A more nuanced approach taking into account (among other things) the essential normative characteristics of economic and social entitlements as human rights is required, directed towards the evaluation and fulfilment of the 'core content' of human rights in the given situation, and states parties' obligations (a) to take immediate and concrete steps towards progressive realisation of rights; (b) not to derogate from the fulfilment of essential minimum human rights guarantees; and (c) to justify any deliberately retrogressive measure by reference to the totality of the rights to which people likely to be affected by a Bank or Fund-sponsored initiative are entitled.[241]

Finally, akin to the Bank's Environmental Impact Assessment procedure, a graduated response linked to an assessment of 'high' to 'low' human rights impact would be appropriate. Under such a system certain types of intervention (drawn from lessons of experience so far) might warrant automatic human rights impact assessment as a matter of course, in accordance with transparent guidelines, with threshold specifications included as to timeframe, consultation requirements and costing.[242] Examples of interventions within this category might include privatisation, trade liberalisation, fiscal contraction and public sector reform measures, and major infrastructure projects. Consultations on

---

[240] For a useful synthesis of current methodological challenges in 'human rights impact assessment' methodology development, see Humanist Committee on Human Rights (HOM), 'Conference Report: Human Rights Impact Assessment for Policy Measures with an External Effect,' 19–20 November 2001, Brussels (on file with author).

[241] See the discussion earlier in this chapter on the operational implications of economic, social and cultural rights. While many of the relevant principles are drawn from the jurisprudence of the Committee on Economic, Social and Cultural Rights and the provisions of the ICESCR, the Committee's reasoning on the nature of the obligations relating to economic and social rights is of potentially systemic relevance. See C Scott, 'Reaching Beyond (Without Abandoning) the Category of "Economic, Social and Cultural Rights" ' (1999) 21(3) *Human Rights Quarterly* 633.

[242] On the comparative costs of World Bank and ADB social assessment processes, indicative only, see below n 256 and accompanying text, suggesting that costs could be expected to rise where detailed 'social safeguard' analyses are required. However the incorporation of the latter analyses within overall social assessment costs reportedly does achieve significant efficiencies.

methodology and identification of appropriate pilot program areas for such impact assessments are essential first steps in what one can assume will be a lengthy process, if undertaken seriously.

Social Assessment

'Social analysis' was first introduced into Bank operations as the 'sociological' aspect of project appraisal in Operational Manual Statement (OMS) 2.20 (1984),[243] although the use of 'social assessments' to inform this appraisal process began only in the 1990s. 'Social assessment'—officially regarded as one of three approaches to social analysis[244]—is undertaken by the borrower at the Bank's request in order to incorporate stakeholders' views into project design and to establish a more participatory process for implementation and monitoring. Initially, Bank staff undertook the social assessments personally. However by financial year 2001, scientists from the project country carried out over 80 per cent of social assessments, 'allowing more direct application of country knowledge and local language skills.'[245]

Like the social analysis conducted by the Bank, social assessment is claimed to be 'both a process, and a set of products.' The ideal social assessment is said to be built on the following five pillars: '(1) a process through which the borrower better understands how the socio-cultural, institutional, historical and political contexts influence the social development outcomes of specific investment projects and sector policies; (2) a means to enhance equity, strengthen social inclusion and cohesion, promote transparent governance and empower the poor and vulnerable in the design and/or implementation of the project; (3) a mechanism to identify the opportunities, constraints, impacts and social risks associated with policy and project design; (4) a framework for dialogue on development priorities among social groups, civil society, grassroots organisations, different levels of government and other stakeholders; and (5) an approach to identify and mitigate the potential social risks, including adverse social impacts, of investment projects.'[246]

Social assessment is regarded by the Bank as advisable for project approval under the following circumstances: '(a) the project is likely to have adverse social impacts, particularly on the vulnerable and the poor; (b) influential stake-

---

[243] World Bank, *Social Analysis Sourcebook* (working draft, 6 August 2002), http://www.world bank.org/socialanalysissourcebook/ (hereafter 'Social Analysis Sourcebook'). See also M Cernea (ed), *Putting People First: Sociological Variables in Rural Development* (2nd ed) (1991).

[244] The other two variants are 'upstream macro-social analysis,' undertaken by the Bank as inputs into the Country Assistance Strategy (CAS), and project-level social analysis (or 'social appraisal'), the 'due diligence' process undertaken by the Bank for sociological appraisal of the opportunities, constraints and likely impacts as an integral part of project appraisal, to examine whether the project's likely social development outcomes justify Bank support.

[245] Social Analysis Sourcebook: 'Social assessment—Responsibility for Social Assessment.'

[246] Social Analysis Sourcebook.

holders contest the project's objectives or design; (c) social development outcomes are at risk; or (d) a knowledge gap about social development in a project
area or sector makes it impossible for the Bank to endorse the project without
further examination.'[247]

Subject to the nature of the identified need, the terms of reference for social
assessments could be expected to require the exploration of a wide range of
subjects including: (i) the objectives of the social assessment and links to
intended social development outcomes and impacts of the project; (ii) the
project's socio-cultural, institutional, historical and political context; (iii) legislative and regulatory considerations pertinent to the project; (iv) the opportunities, constraints and likely social impacts of the proposed operation; (v) what
the Bank terms the 'five entry points of social analysis' (ie participation; stakeholders; social risks; social diversity and gender; and rules, institutions and
behaviour);[248] (vi) the social assessment's implications for the consideration of
alternative implementation arrangements; (vii) operational recommendations
for project design, implementation, monitoring and evaluation, and (viii) identification of adequate monitoring and evaluation procedures and indicators.[249]

However the implementation of social assessment procedures at the Bank[250]
appears to be anything but standardised. Approaches vary quite widely across
the various Regions, perhaps seeming to be better defined in the Southeast Asian
area. Moreover independent evaluations and anecdotal evidence raise serious
questions as to how effectively or systematically 'participatory poverty assessments' and gender analysis have been integrated to date.[251] And as the OED

[247] Social Analysis Sourcebook: 'Social Assessment—Deciding whether to do a social assessment.'

[248] Social Analysis Sourcebook: 'The Scope of Social Analysis—the Five Entry Points.' There are
obvious links between agency and structure. Among the questions to be asked are: 'What is the normative framework? What are the applicable customs, and how will these be impacted by the project?' The institutional analysis is critical for sustainability, in purely instrumental terms. As the
Sourcebook provides, '[t]he institutional analysis should include a detailed assessment of formal and
informal organisations likely to affect the project and the informal rules and behaviours among
them.' The stakeholder analysis must identify all those affected by the project, as well as the actors
who can deliver on outcomes. Likewise actors who have 'veto power' must be identified, at the local
and national levels, and strategies devised as to how they can be engaged. The analysis should disaggregate data by gender and identify the underlying causes of vulnerability.

[249] Social Analysis Sourcebook: 'Social Assessment—The facets and phases of social assessment.'

[250] Although primary responsibility for implementation of social assessment rests officially with
the borrowing country, the Bank's retains an important role in numerous respects including in relation to the development of the terms of reference for such assessments, advising on content and coverage, supporting the borrower through stakeholder seminars or other participatory efforts,
assisting with the mobilisation of resources, and even carrying out the assessments directly in a
small proportion of cases. Social Analysis Sourcebook: 'Social Assessment—Responsibility for
social assessment.'

[251] In the case of gender see eg A Whitehead and M Lockwood, *Gender in the World Bank's
Poverty Assessments, Six Case Studies from Sub-Saharan Africa,* United Nations Research Institute
for Social Development (2000) http://www.unrisd.org. The study assesses the extent to which gender has been incorporated within six Bank poverty assessments. The conclusions disclose considerable variation in the manner in which gender was considered: 'In none of [the six case studies was]
there an adequate, let alone strong, analysis of gender that could form a basis for policies to assist
poor women in Africa.' Furthermore 'perhaps the most disappointing aspect of the review of the six

observed in connection with the Bank's performance in Indonesia, there is a strong need for the Bank to institute 'subjective' poverty lines based upon people's own assessments of the adequacy of their consumption, rather than adhering solely to 'traditional survey methods.'[252] The Bank's 'Voices of the Poor'[253] survey in the late 1990s was a good example of this, however value of subjective and qualitative assessments such as this needs to be recognised, on equal footing with quantitative survey methods.[254]

In light of these shortcomings social assessment procedures at the Bank need to be standardised, formalised and made a central part of the Bank's work, through a transparent and consultative process.[255] This is not intended to impose a straightjacket on creative and culturally sensitive approaches, nor to downplay the potentially significant costs involved.[256] But mandating comprehensive consideration of social aspects of project and program design and implementation, standardised as far as feasible across all Regions, would help to ensure that social issues are brought to the fore and considered in an integrated fashion and on equal footing with macro-economic factors, and that such assessments are carried out automatically, rigorously and consistently.

---

case studies is that the accumulation of evidence that men and women experience poverty differently has had little influence in practice.' For the sobering record with both gender and the environment, see Operations Evaluation Department, *IDA's Partnership for Poverty Reduction: An Independent Evaluation of Fiscal Years 1994–2000* (2002).

[252] OED Note (1999) at paras 3.30, 3.32 and 3.35.

[253] Above n 178.

[254] As the Sourcebook notes, the right 'mix' of qualitative and quantitative research methods will vary from project to project. 'Numerical information can be more easily aggregated, but it can miss out on nuance and texture. General coverage aids representativeness, but it can lose context. Statistical inference can help in the discussion on causality, but misses out on the power of inductive approaches. And so on.' R Kanbur, 'Qualitative and Quantitative Poverty Appraisal: The State of Play and Some Questions.' Paper presented at 'Qual/Quant' Conference, Cornell University, USA, 15–16 March 2001.

[255] Interviews in Washington DC in March and April 1999 and February 2000. An external expert study concerning the proposed Nam Theun 2 hydroelectric dam in Lao PDR likewise recommended in 1998 that the Bank formulate a comprehensive 'social' policy, in view of the inadequacies and gaps within the existing social safeguard policy arrangements. See chapter III above at nn 84–88 and accompanying text for more detailed discussion of the Nam Theun 2 case.

[256] As pointed out in the Sourcebook, costs vary greatly 'by country, project type and scope, research tools and methods and local skills and capacity.' In the FY 2001 the mean cost was US$36,000, and the median was US$25,000, excluding the Bank staff costs. Costs are greater if a more detailed analysis is necessary to consider social safeguard policies in the social assessment. By way of comparison the Asia Development Bank's (ADB's) Project Preparatory Technical Assistance ('feasibility study') stage can reportedly cost up to $600–800,000, where a 4–6 month full time team study is necessary. Social assessments are reportedly necessary for every project supported by the ADB, the only exceptions being for 'fast-disbursing crisis loans,' or loans less than $150,000, which can be approved quickly by the ADB President without the feasibility study phase. In practical terms the social assessment usually requires workshops with stakeholders, including with the participation of social science specialists. This is said to be a standard part of the project cycle, and the objective of flexibility is met through the promulgation of guidelines for each sector, reflecting different requirements for each.

An interesting model for comparative purposes is that presented in the report of the World Commission on Dams in 2000 on large dam projects.[257] As the Commission observed: 'Considerable support exists for rights, particularly basic human rights [including the UDHR, ICCPR and ICESCR], to be considered as a fundamental reference point in any debate on dams[.] . . . Clarifying the rights context in a proposed project is an essential step in identifying those legitimate claims and entitlements that might be affected by the proposed project—or indeed, its alternatives. It is also the basis for effective identification of stakeholder groups that are entitled to a role in the consultative process, and eventually in negotiating project-specific agreements relating, for example, to benefit sharing, resettlement or compensation.'[258]

On this basis, and having regard to the 'risks' involuntarily assumed by people in project-affected areas, the Commission advocated a 'rights and risks approach' to options assessment and planning and project cycles, to determine who participates and what issues must be on the agenda.[259] According to the Commission, the 'rights and risks' approach 'empowers decision-making processes based on the pursuit of negotiated outcomes, conducted in a open and transparent manner and inclusive of all legitimate actors involved in the issue, thereby helping to resolve the many and complex issues surrounding water, dams and development. While presenting greater demands at early stages of options assessment and project design, it leads to greater clarity and legitimacy for subsequent steps in decision-making and implementation.'[260]

---

[257] World Commission on Dams, *Dams and Development: A New Framework for Decision-Making (An Overview)* www.dams.org (16 November 2000) at 21–22. It is important to note however that 'senior Bank water sector staff are strongly resisting efforts to implement WCD into existing Bank operational policies and are working with the report's strongest critics to argue that these recommendations are unrealistic and unworkable. However, the Bank has stated that it will use the report "as a valuable reference to inform its decision-making process when considering projects that involve dams."' A Imhof, 'An Analysis of Nam Theun 2 Compliance with World Commission on Dams Guidelines,' (May 2001) at 1–2. Perhaps some measure of reassurance can be taken from the report of the IDA Executive Directors to the Board of Governors on the 13th replenishment the IDA, affirming the importance of IDA staff complying with all social safeguard policies. The IDA deputies moreover 'noted the Bank's early support for the World Commission on Dams (WCD) and asked that IDA take into account the core values and strategic priorities suggested by the WCD for preparing and evaluating dam projects.' IDA, 'Additions to IDA Resources: Thirteenth Replenishment—Supporting Poverty Reduction Strategies,' Report from the Executive Directors of the IDA to the Board of Governors, 25 July 2002 at 18.

[258] The Commission also advocated the inclusion of the 'notion of risk' as an 'important dimension to understanding how, and to what extent, a project may have an impact on such rights.' Risk in this context refers not only to risks voluntarily assumed and managed by the project developers, but those affected by the project upon whom the externally managed risks are involuntarily thrust.

[259] World Commission on Dams (16 November 2000) at 22. In the Commission's view, '[d]ealing with risks cannot be reduced to consulting actuarial tables or applying a mathematical formula. In the end, as in the case of rights and entitlements, they must be identified, articulated and addressed explicitly. This will require the acknowledgement of risk to be extended to a wider group than governments or developers in order to include both those affected by a project and the environment as a public good.'

[260] World Commission on Dams (16 November 2000) at 22.

To summarise, human rights has a relevant but substantially unexplored role in terms of providing a (compulsorily) inter-sectoral framework for analysis, and a basis in legal obligation for the empowerment and participation of those whose voices need to be heard in project and program design, implementation and evaluation. Human rights can aid significantly as an analytical tool, exposing prevailing disparities and discrimination issues along ethnic, economic, political or other lines,[261] and helping to understand the inter-relationships between legal frameworks and issues such as women's economic participation.[262] The rights framework can help also to identify and balance competing claims, for example to property rights on the one hand, and land users' (for example subsistence farmers or herders) on the other, with the different sets of capacities and vulnerabilities underlying each.[263]

While the predictive value of human rights should in most situations not be over-estimated, human rights can at a minimum serve the valuable function of contributing to the ordering of priorities, and identifying issues that as a matter of legal entitlement and corresponding obligation cannot be bartered away. Human rights can also make valuable contributions to the 'process' dimensions of social assessment. In this respect the role of human rights is strongly linked to the instrumental goals of participation, empowerment, and sustainability, opening up space for civic engagement and local ownership, and mandating space at the table for the voiceless, vulnerable and excluded. With quality of process grounded in legal foundations, substantive benefits from social assessment might be expected more readily to follow.[264]

---

[261] For similar recommendations see *DFID Human Rights Paper* (2000) at 22. For an illustration of how ILO Convention 169 and related international instruments concerning indigenous peoples could usefully be factored into social assessment, along with an indication of certain limitations in their reach insofar as the 'unique rights of semi-contacted and uncontacted peoples' are concerned, see P Caffrey, 'An Independent Environmental and Social Assessment of the Camisea Gas Project,' Commissioned by the Peruvian indigenous organisations: The Machiguenga Council of the Urubamba River (COMARU) and the Inter-Ethnic Association of the Peruvian Amazon (AIDESEP), April 2002, at pp 17, 23–24, 35 and 39–40. For a brief overview see Amazon Watch, News Release, 'Independent Evaluation of Peru's Camisea Gas Project Reveals Violations of World Bank Environmental Standards,' 6 May 2002, http://www.amazonwatch.org/megaprojects/camisea_report_020506.html.

[262] See the example of the work in progress in the Bank's Middle East and North Africa Region in this respect, subject to the caveats mentioned, in chapter II above, at n 100 and accompanying text.

[263] However as emphasised at the outset, one must not over-estimate the potential for rights analysis of itself to resolve competing claims or complex policy debates in all situations.

[264] The connection between human rights-sensitive assessment and strategy development cannot be too readily assumed however. The Bank's development framework for Afghanistan, for example, identifies human rights as part of the problem (including violations of children's and women's rights and protecting child combatants), but not as part of the 'guiding principles for recovery and reconstruction:' http://lnweb18.worldbank.org/SAR/sa.nsf/Attachments/df/$file/n-df.pdf.

CAVEATS ON PRIVATISATION

Privatisation of public services and utilities warrants especially close critical scrutiny, on instrumental as much as principled grounds. Firstly, as has been witnessed in both Russia and Indonesia (to name a couple of the most notorious examples), the scope for corruption in newly privatised enterprises is notorious. Moreover as Joseph Stiglitz reveals, there has been an 'element of ideology' in the Bank's push to privatise pension funds in developing countries.[265] Ideological bias does nothing to promote the legitimacy and sustainability of IFI-sponsored reform programs. As an alternative and ideologically neutral framework of inquiry, as suggested by Stiglitz, the IFIs might consider looking to 'improve the quality of bureaucracies operating public programs.'[266] Stiglitz's criticisms link to perhaps the most fundamental objection to the privatisation mission from a human rights perspective, namely, that the unbridled and often de-contextualised promotion of privatised forms of governance severely undermines governments' capacities to honour their obligations under applicable human rights conventions.

The IFIs need to treat seriously people's entitlements under international and national human rights laws. Dialogue with members governments and all other relevant stakeholders must be initiated by the IFIs themselves on ways in which proposed redistribution of power to the private sector can be achieved in a manner respectful of these inherent and inalienable rights and corresponding duties.[267] This is not to say that a human rights-based approach is necessarily antithetical to privatisation in principle. However a critical review is required of the extent to which the IFIs' zest for privatisation is driven by ideological or alternatively instrumental goals. At the very least an *ex ante* appraisal of likely human rights impacts should be undertaken in each situation,[268] along with a

---

[265] *World Bank Development News*, 6 April 2000. See also S Grusky, 'Privatisation Tidal Wave: IMF/World Bank Water Policies and the Price Paid by the Poor,' 22(9) *International Monitor*, available at http://multinationalmonitor.org/mm2001/01september/sep01corp2.html.

[266] *World Bank Development News*, 6 April 2000. For a similar cautionary note, focusing on the need for an appropraite 'ownership structure' prior to contemplating privatisation reforms, see R Kanbur and D Vines, 'The World Bank and Poverty Reduction: Past, Present and Future' in C Gilbert and D Vines (eds.) (2000) 87–107, at 102.

[267] For an indication of some of the principles relevant to achieving a balance between private service provision and government accountability for economic and social rights, focusing upon article 24 of the CRC and the state's obligation to fulfil core minimum entitlement of the enjoyment of the right in question, see A Nigam and S Rasheed, 'Financing of Fresh Water for All: A Rights Based Approach,' *UNICEF Staff Working Papers, Evaluation, Policy and Planning Series* No. EPP-EVL-98-003 (1998).

[268] See the discussion on the integration of human rights within social impact analysis and social assessment, earlier in this chapter. The Bank's Inspection Panel also plays a potentially useful role in this regard, as its investigation into the Bujagali Hydropower Project in Uganda (involving the privatisation of Uganda's power distribution sector) reveals. See World Bank Inspection Panel, Report No. 23998, 'Uganda: Third Power Project—Credit 2268–UG; Fourth Power Project—Credit 3345–UG and the Bujagali Hydropower Project—PRG No. B 003–UG, IPN Request RQ01/3 of 7 August 2001,' 23 May 2002. The Panel's report raised concerns relating to the costs of privatised

guarantee to implement countervailing measures to the extent of anticipated human rights violations.

The CRC has been ratified by, and is legally binding in, all countries in the world except for Somalia and the US. Its holistic framework provides an ideal conceptual basis for the implementation of rights which the Bank has appropriately identified as being central to the campaign to eliminate abusive forms of child labour,[269] including the rights to: education (including quality of education); adequate standard of living; protection from exploitation; health and health services; leisure, reaction and culture; and survival and development.[270] These rights are guaranteed within the framework of non-discrimination norms and family responsibilities, and include unique provisions promoting the empowerment of children as actors for development in their own right, strategies the value of which the Bank has already recognised.[271] 'Participation' of children themselves is one particularly important innovation in the Convention, a central component of the Bank's efforts to achieve sustainable development.

As indicated in chapter IV, Article 32 of the CRC specifically embraces other relevant conventions concerning child labour. The Committee on the Rights of the Child considers ILO Convention No. 138 of 1973 (the Minimum Age Convention) to be one such relevant standard,[272] and ILO Convention No. 162 is another. The implementation of the CRC is supported on a world-wide basis by international agencies—in particular UNICEF—and NGOs, and includes legislative, administrative, and other appropriate measures.[273] These activities

services for consumers, among a range of other deficiencies in compliance with social safeguard policies (including OP 4.01 on Environmental Assessment and OD 4.30 on Involuntary Resettlement). Other observers have warned of dangers of repeated strikes relating to privatisation that have marred Uganda's power sector in mid-2002, and unresolved political conflict relating thereto. See International Rivers Network, 'Management Response to Bujagali Inspection Panel Report: Some notes and recommendations,' 20 June 2002, http://www.irn.org/programs/bujagali/index/ASP?id=020603.wbmisleads.html.

[269] See discussion in chapter IV, nn 226–45 and accompanying text.

[270] CRC Articles 29, 27, 36, 24, 31 and 6, respectively.

[271] CRC Articles 2, 5, and 12–18.

[272] R Hodgkin and P Newell, *Convention on the Rights of the Child: Implementation Handbook* (1998) at 430. Other relevant standards are mentioned in World Bank, *Child Labour: Issues and Directions for the World Bank* (1998) at 5–6, and R Hodgkin and P Newell (1998) at 429–33. By 1996, 49 States had ratified the Minimum Age Convention. However, according to the ILO, only 21 of these are developing countries, and did not include any countries in Asia, where over half of all working children are found. The Minimum Age Recommendation (ILO No. 146), adopted in 1973, provides detailed guidance on the implementation of the Minimum Age Convention.

[273] CRC Articles 4, 32 and 44–45. But in order to be able to assume a relevant role in the implementation of the CRC, the Bank might need to reconsider its view that 'legislation and regulation are the concerns of governments,' although it does concede that it 'can discuss this in the country dialogue'—World Bank, *Child Labour: Issues and Directions for the World Bank* (1998) at 9. The above statement is inconsistent, for example, with the expansion of the Bank's mandate to include

complement those of the ILO, to a significant degree, and are consistent with the kinds of activities that the Bank indicates that it already undertakes in this area.

Working more closely with the standards in the CRC and other relevant international instruments offers prospects for increased clarity in the application of child labour standards in particular country circumstances, with the benefit of State Party reports, NGO and specialised agency information, and the expert views of both the Committee on the Rights of the Child[274] and the ILO Committee of Experts. Beyond the potential sphere of cooperation with relevant human rights treaty bodies and use of their output, the views of human rights expert bodies on consideration of country reports may be of considerable value to Bank staff in assisting to determine the occurrence of 'exploitative child labour with [possible] negative developmental effects,'[275] for the purpose of warranting suspension of lending activities or other remedial responses.

Naturally, applicable human rights standards and relevant treaty body recommendations number among a great many relevant resources for the Bank for these purposes. From a purely instrumental standpoint one should not underestimate the potential for standards-based resources to facilitate objective decision-making on such difficult issues as child labour. However from a normative standpoint, flowing from the discussion in chapter IV, the case for increased understanding is compelling: the IFIs (including the Bank) must at the very least discharge an obligation to 'respect' CRC-based standards, ensuring that their activities do not contribute to violations of States' own obligations thereunder. 'Positive' programmatic obligations are harder to define with precision, however the scope of CRC-based policy options within the scope of its lawful mandate seem potentially broad, signposted to some extent by the IFC's and MIGA's relatively robust policy approaches on child labour conditionality.[276]

RECOGNITION OF RELEVANT UNITED NATIONS DECISION-MAKING BODIES

The IFIs constitutive documents require that they 'consider' the UN's decisions and recommendations.[277] The IFIs have interpreted these provisions as not

---

assistance for legal reform '(t)o review and modify legal and regulatory frameworks to improve women's access to assets and services, and take institutional measures to ensure that legal changes are implemented . . . with due regard to cultural sensitivity': World Bank, 'Operational policy on the gender dimension of development,' OP 4.20, April 1994, para 2(b). Legal reform efforts of this nature have in fact become part of the Bank's work in *inter alia* Mauritania, Pakistan and Uganda (see K Tomasevski, 'Integration of a Gender Perspective into UN Technical Co-operation on Human Rights,' Working Paper, February 1998 at 13), and also as discussed earlier in connection with the Bank's emerging responses to HIV/AIDs and in the judicial reform sector.

[274] CRC Articles 44–45. For examples of the Committee's child labour recommendations in particular country situations, see R Hodgkin and P Newell (1998) at 434–41.

[275] World Bank, *Child Labour: Issues and Directions for the World Bank* (1998) at 17–18.

[276] See above chapter IV, at nn 226–45 and accompanying text.

[277] See Article IV of the IMF/UN Relationship Agreement, and Article V, Section 8(b) of the IBRD Articles of Association.

requiring them to comply with UN decisions and recommendations, although this interpretation is not universally accepted.[278] The IMF Relationship Agreement also requires the IMF to give 'due consideration' to UN requests for the introduction of agenda items at the Board of Governors' meetings.[279] Further, subject to the need to safeguard confidential information, the Fund is obliged 'to the fullest extent possible' to arrange to exchange information, special reports and publications with the World Bank.[280] However overall Fund in particular has 'jealously guarded' the independence bestowed by its constitutive documents, interpreting it 'as precluding the United Nations from requiring [it] to undertake specific action and as granting [it], in effect, completely independent decision-making power on all issues.'[281]

As a consequence, the Fund has 'felt free to reject the recommendations and decisions of not only the United Nations, but also of other specialised agencies.'[282] It has continued to develop and apply policy in a predominantly independent fashion, within artificially circumscribed disciplinary and analytical bounds, out of step with the rapid expansion of its activities into complex political, economic, social, environmental and human rights domains.[283] The challenges arising in these overlapping domains are not the sole province of any one international body or agency, and their complexity demands co-operative and coherent responses. Accordingly, the Fund's practices in this regard are ultimately unsustainable. While the Bank has evolved into a far broader church by comparison, the overall record of inter-institutional collaboration remains in serious need of reform.

The IFIs undoubtedly need to increase the nature and level of their co-operation with other agencies, including UN agencies.[284] It has been argued

---

[278] D Bradlow and C Grossman (1995) at 434–45.

[279] Article III of the IMF/UN Relationship Agreement.

[280] Articles I(3) and V of the IMF/UN Relationship Agreement.

[281] D Bradlow and C Grossman (1995) at 435. For a fuller discussion on the IFIs' relationship agreements see chapter IV above, pp 50–57.

[282] D Bradlow and C Grossman (1995) at 435. See also F Gianviti, 'Economic, Social and Cultural Rights and the International Monetary Fund (30 May 2001; unpublished paper on file with author), discussed in chapter IV above at nn 103–19 and accompanying text.

[283] Although inter-agency interaction is minimal, it is by no means non-existent. The Fund's relations with the Bank, in particular, expanded rapidly within the PFP and ESAF framework—see generally J Polak (1994). And it would also not be correct to say that Fund policy has evolved completely within a vacuum. The Fund has occasionally changed its policy in response to dialogue with other agencies, for example, to aspects of its conditionality policies, in light of a UNICEF study on adjustment [G Cornia, R Jolly and F Stewart (eds), *Adjustment with a Human Face* (1987)]—see D Bradlow and C Grossman (1995) at 436. However the Fund's organisational culture or 'personality' is still characterised by a high degree of inflexibility, discipline and doctrinal purity (even compared with that of the World Bank), having regard to which the prospects for short-term improvement in inter-agency co-operation should not too readily be over-estimated: see eg J Polak, *The World Bank and the IMF: A Changing Relationship* (1994) at 21.

[284] For an argument for closer and more formalised co-operation between the ILO and the IMF, see L Beutler, 'The ILO and IMF: Permissibility and Desirability of a Proposal to Meet the Contemporary Realities of the International Protection of Labour Rights' (1988) 14 *Syracuse Journal of International Law and Commerce* 455–77.

elsewhere—on a construction of UN Charter-based sources of law and relevant provisions of the IFIs' Relationship Agreements with the UN—that cooperation with UN bodies and working groups established by mandate of Charter-based organs is, with certain minor qualifications, a matter of legal obligation.[285] Whether such a selective and highly qualified duty can be justified on such grounds,[286] the principal difficulty no doubt lies in determining the limits of its application.

However the normatively-based argument unfolds, the first necessary step for the IFIs on instrumental rationales alone is to improve inter-agency communication, in order to begin to discuss appropriate analytical and procedural frameworks for resolving overlapping issues, thereby promoting the prospects for consistent and coherent approaches.[287] This imperative is especially strong in the IMF's case, as Helleiner, Cornia and Jolly have observed: 'Neither efficiency nor the necessary co-operative spirit are served by their involvement only after the IMF has developed its own positions on the basis of unnecessarily limited and incomplete information.'[288] There is also a case for the IFIs to re-examine relevant provisions of their Articles and Relationship Agreements with the United Nations in light of 'relevant rules of international law'[289] (such as Article

---

[285] S Skogly (2001) at 167–72. Looking at relevant provisions of the IBRD/UN Relationship Agreement (as cited above) in particular, Skogly argues (at 168) that 'the Relationship Agreement should be interpreted as having some practical implications in terms of a duty to favourably cooperate, without which the whole rationale of the agreement would be absent, and the status of specialised agency would be undifferentiated from other international organisations. With a view to the obligation to respect human rights, this agreement . . . may be interpreted to imply a duty (if the information requested does not constitute a violation of the confidence of any of its members) on the part of the Bank to make information available and in other ways assist the United Nations in its human rights work. It would at least be possible to assert an obligation to respond to specific requests from the UN and its subsidiary bodies on information concerning human rights aspects of the Bank's policy.' Moreover an argument for a binding legal duty to 'provide information and cooperation' in response to requests from the Working Group on the Right to Development (CHR Res. 1998/72) is proposed (at 171)—subject to considerations of confidentiality and proportionality (or 'common sense' on the part of the Working Group itself)—on the basis of the 'structural relationship between the [CHR], its subsidiary organs and the specialised agencies.'

[286] For a critique see M Darrow, 'Human Rights Accountability of the World Bank and IMF: Possibilities and Limits of Legal Analysis (2003 forthcoming) 12(1) *Social and Legal Studies* 133, 136–39.

[287] D Bradlow and C Grossman (1995) at 437: 'This should involve extensive and formalised exchanges of information, ideas and expertise among the staffs of all relevant organisations. These inter-organisation communications should include training programs for the staffs, as well as a structured program of continual discussion on issues of mutual concern. Joint training programs could be supplemented by staff exchanges [with the Global Environment Facility serving as a possible model]. Inter-staff discussions should be supplemented by the incorporation of mutually useful information in their country and thematic reports. These reports should also include discussions of the relevant findings and recommendations of other international organisations. For these exchange programs to be effective, [the Fund] should effectively involve non-governmental actors in all discussions, and training and staff exchange programs.' For a similar recommendation see G Helleiner, G Cornia and R Jolly, 'IMF Adjustment Policies and Approaches and the Needs of Children' (1991) 19(12) *World Development* 1823–34, 1832.

[288] G Helleiner, G Cornia and R Jolly (1991) at 1832.

[289] Article 31(3)(c) of the Vienna Convention.

103 of the UN Charter[290]), and within the increasingly flexible bounds of their mandates, publicly acknowledge the importance of complying with relevant decisions of the UN.[291]

INTERACTIONS WITH THE HUMAN RIGHTS TREATY BODIES

The Bank's and Fund's small Geneva and New York offices as at 2002 permitted little in the way of focused and sustained interaction with the six human rights treaty bodies (discussed in more detail below),[292] which as at 2002 collectively met for approximately forty-eight weeks a year. At a minimum both the Bank and Fund need to make themselves aware of the six core international human rights treaties as part of the overarching legal framework in which they operate at the international and national levels, as part of the basis for an informed assessment of their own—as much as their members'—legal obligations. A programme of increased interaction with the human rights treaty bodies, even if on a selective basis, would in principle form an important part of a human rights mainstreaming strategy. As indicated earlier[293] some commentators argue that increased interaction of this kind is in some circumstances, and perhaps only in relation to some of the treaty bodies, a matter of binding obligation.[294] However as was the case in connection with possible obligations of cooperation with UN Charter-based bodies, irrespective of whether a legal grounds for a limited duty can be identified and defended, the principal difficulty lies in determining the limits of its application. Substantive dimensions of necessary interaction probably fall to be determined as much by policy considerations as legal analysis in this context.

Dealings between the IFIs and the treaty-body committees to date have been sporadic and not always especially constructive. This has only partly been the

---

[290] Article 103 of the UN Charter elevates UN members States' Charter-based obligations over other treaty-based obligations in international law. See the discussion in chapter IV, nn 64–80 and accompanying text.

[291] D Bradlow and C Grossman (1995) at 439. As those authors state (at 438): 'The increasing encroachment of [the IMF] into the work of other international organisations requires [it] to rethink [its] obligations under general principles of international law. In addition to acknowledging that the Security Council Resolutions adopted pursuant to chapter VII of the UN Charter are binding, the [IMF] need[s] to recognise evolving trends in international law and to make explicit [its] interpretations of international law's applicability to [its] field of operation. For example, in light of current international concern with democratisation and good governance, the [IMF] should explicitly state what [it views as its] obligation in promoting such aspects of democratisation and good governance as freedom of speech and association.'

[292] Five of the human rights treaty bodies are based in Geneva, and the other—CEDAW—in New York. As at December 2000 the IMF and Bank had only token presences in each.

[293] See above nn 285–86 and accompanying text.

[294] S Skogly (2001) at 167–72. This assertion appears to be limited to a duty to respond to recommendations from the Committee on Economic, Social and Cultural Rights under Article 22 of the ICESCR, as elaborated by the Committee in its General Comment No. 2 (1990), justified (at 170–71) on the grounds that 'consistent refusal' on the part of the IFIs to the Committee's proposals and recommendations 'would render this whole section of the Covenant useless.'

fault of the IFIs themselves, however. Certain treaty bodies—the ICESCR[295] and CRC Committees in particular—have taken more deliberate and strategic steps than others in terms of visualising human rights implementation within a wider context, fostering inter-agency collaboration and exchanges. In consultation with external experts, UN insiders and of course the Committees themselves, the IFIs need to calibrate their strategies of engagement accordingly, setting goals at realistic levels in light of the scope of the various treaty bodies mandates,[296] and a level-headed appraisal of existing strengths and weaknesses.[297]

Options for interaction in the shorter term include: (a) participation at working methods discussions at the annual meetings of the Chairpersons of Treaty Bodies (which presently occurs to some degree), in order to contribute to discussions on cooperation; (b) contribution of country-specific economic and social data to improve the factual and statistical basis for Committees' human rights recommendations, especially insofar as evaluations of budget allocations and structural and institutional prerequisites for human rights fulfilment are concerned;[298] (c) participation at relevant 'theme days' held by the respective Committees; (d) as appropriate and on invitation of the Committees concerned, contribution to the development of 'General Comments', assisting to clarify the application of human rights treaty standards in fields of concern to the IFIs; and perhaps in the longer run (e) facilitate technical assistance for the implementation of treaty body recommendations of direct relevance to the Bank's mandated concerns.[299] Recommendations of these kinds might go some way towards

---

[295] The 7 May 2001 discussion day of the CESCR is a good example. See chapter IV above at nn 103–19 and accompanying text.

[296] There is a need to ensure that the integrity of each treaty body's functions under their respective conventions is not unwittingly sacrificed to well-intended but overly-ambitious efforts to 'mainstream' treaty body outputs.

[297] One particularly needs to keep in mind constraints on the Committee's (and UN Secretariat's) capacities, disciplinary expertise and profiles in this regard, with particular regard to the difficulties in effectively processing significant quantities of economic data within the framework of the consideration of a particular State Party report. Against such factors, and having regard to the legitimate differentiation in mandate width under the six core treaties, it would be counterproductive for expectations concerning the immediate impacts of enhanced cooperation to be set an unrealistically high levels.

[298] For evidence of the relevance of Bank-produced information to the ICESCR Committee, see eg E/C.12/2000/21 at para 269 (concluding observations for Mongolia), concerning the incidence of poverty and limited effectiveness of social safety nets. Moreover the IFIs have reportedly furnished the Committee with information in connection with the latter's procedure on non-reporting states. For the example of the Solomon Islands see S Skogly (2001) at 133–34.

[299] For example, recommendations from the CEDAW Committee might in many situations support the Bank's project work in 'engendering development' (see chapter II above, nn 83 and 100 and accompanying text), including but not limited to bolstering the case and shaping the contours for the legal framework for development and women's empowerment. CRC recommendations could be of particular value in connection with the Bank's projects and policies in the education and child labour areas. ICCPR standards and corresponding treaty body recommendations bear directly on the Bank's judicial reform and rule of law activities (and indeed to the overarching enabling environment for development), and the ICESCR standards have obvious relevance in the education, labour market reform, and agricultural policy reform areas, among others.

promoting jurisprudence and Concluding Observations of greater value both from the IFIs' perspectives, and in terms of the integration of human rights in development at the country level, with the further promise of fostering dialogue and functional linkages at the national level between human rights and social development constituencies and those traditionally linked exclusively to Finance and Development Ministries.[300]

EXPANDED COMMUNICATION AND MODES OF COOPERATION WITH HUMAN RIGHTS NGOS

Democratically elected governments, with varying degrees of objective justification, almost inevitably regard themselves as legitimate representatives of their people and therefore as dominant interlocutors with the IFIs in all dealings with them. By the same token, whatever the relative strength of their democratic credentials, governments have time and again failed to uphold their responsibilities to their constituencies insofar as their dealings with the IFIs are concerned. Freedom of expression, freedom of association, a free press and effective political and legal checks and balances are widely accepted as vital ingredients for an enabling environment for development, yet all too often the voices of minorities, the victimised and the disenfranchised are silent in national development policy debates.

Human rights NGOs are among the more important constituencies in this context, and a vital channel through which the voices of the victims can be heard and human rights concerns registered. Moreover, it is frequently argued, issues-based NGOs legitimately raise a broader set of moral and ethical concerns that the IFIs—operating within a relatively limited set of values—should be forced to consider.[301] The functions now performed by human rights NGOs go well beyond advocacy, extending into participation in international dispute settlement (including playing a vital role in enlivening the Inspection Panel mechanism to those in need), judicial and quasi-judicial proceedings, and participating more generally in global policy debates and the operations of international organisations.[302]

Yet objections as to NGOs' legitimacy, representiveness and accountability are often levelled by governments, as a basis for attempts to regulate or other-

---

[300] For similar recommendations see S de Vylder (1996) at 72: 'The main findings from the national [reports to the Committee under the CRC] should be used as a key input in strategic decision-making in connection with, for example, Public Expenditure Reviews and in design of structural adjustment programs. This would require increased participation by professional economists in the elaboration of national reports and the inclusion of economists on the UN Committee on the Rights of the Child. It would also, and primarily, require a thorough rethinking in domestic and international institutions which are responsible for the design and implementation of, say, monetary policies, labour market policies and trade and exchange rate policies.'

[301] N Woods, 'The Challenges of Multilateralism and Governance' in C Gilbert and D Vines (eds), *The World Bank: Structure and Policies* (2000) 132–56, 149.

[302] For illustrations of this expansion in roles and responsibilities see Roos (2001) at 491.

wise limit NGOs' activities on broadly drawn 'public interest' grounds or other criteria inimical with fundamental civil and political rights. Ensuring an appropriate degree of freedom and political space within which human rights (and other) NGOs can function, energising local capacities and assisting to keep government (along with national and international elites) honest, is one of the most critical development challenges in any given situation. The World Bank's efforts in 1997 to develop a 'handbook of good practices on laws relating to NGOs' reveals the deep political and philosophical tensions underlying this debate.[303]

This does not diminish the case for critical scrutiny of NGO influence and lines of accountability at both international and national levels.[304] As Woods observes, 'NGOs have played a vital role in prising the Bank open, increasing its transparency and introducing a new kind of accountability. However, as NGOs come to play an increasing role—under the banner of democratisation—the question arises as to whether they are a constituency to whom the Bank ought to be accountable, and if so, why.'[305] A serious danger at the international level is that the strengthening of channels for NGO influence might indirectly enhance the influence of the United States, thereby further jeopardising the IFIs' legitimacy and effectiveness.[306] The record of US-based NGOs' influence—in 'unholy alliance' with certain US Congressmen—in lobbying the Bank for the Inspection Panel[307] and for stronger environmental safeguards is perhaps as much cause for concern as celebration from this point of view. The inclusion of NGOs must aim to enhance the legitimacy of the IFIs, 'and not simply [their] popularity on Capitol Hill.'[308]

---

[303] See chapter IV above at nn 163–68 and accompanying text.

[304] N Woods (2001) at 97; C Abugre and N Alexander, 'Non-governmental Organisations and the International Monetary and Financial System' (1998) 9 *International Monetary and Financial Issues for the 1990s* 107–25, suggesting that more systematic consideration be given to criteria such as the effectiveness, internal decision-making structure, membership and accountability of NGO groups being consulted.

[305] N Woods (2000) at 149.

[306] N Woods (2000) at 149.

[307] 'Importantly, the relationship between NGOs and the World Bank has been a triangular one including the US Congress. . . . Politically, the victory of the environmental NGOs in pushing for the Inspection Panel was possible only because of the unholy alliance they formed with US Senator Kasten (Rep., Wisconsin), Chair of the Senate Appropriations Subcommittee on Foreign Operations, otherwise known for his strong anti-foreign aid stance. In grouping with [anti-World Bank] forces in the US Congress, NGOs not only increased their own influence, but also that of the US Congress itself. The danger here is that the US Congress will continue, and perhaps augment, its demands for particular conditions to be imposed by the World Bank on borrowing countries: whether it be concerning the environment or birth control. Such unilateralism can only erode the mulilateral character and accountability of the World Bank, undermining the legitimacy of the advice and conditions it sets for its borrowers.' N Woods (2000) at 149–50. Woods also observes (at 150) the related problem of the comparatively loud voices of the US-based NGOs effectively resulting in a 'double counting' of US policy preferences as expressed on the Bank's Executive Board, citing the example of active lobbying for 'Sierra Club' values (eg the protection of endangered species) in the 1980s, rather than for developing country environmental priorities such as tropical agriculture or water. See also C Abugre and N Alexander (1998) at 116; N Woods (2001) at 99.

[308] N Woods (2000) at 151.

This history of this particular web of influence serves a useful warning of the need to scrutinise underlying political interests and lines of accountability within any framework for policy influence, including those involving NGOs. Equally importantly one must not lose sight of the dangers in focusing too high a degree of attention on NGO interactions, to the possible exclusion of representative democratic institutions at the national level which have all too often been sidelined from the macro- development debates. However none of this detracts from the critical need for free and robust civil society movements at both national and international levels, and for expansion of political space and strengthening of national and local level NGOs in many of the IFIs' poorer client states in particular.[309] Human rights NGOs are potentially key players at both the national and international levels in this regard, working for stronger accountability through the integration of human rights at all levels of development policy and planning. Southern (developing country) NGOs—'stakeholders' in a very direct sense of the term—must in particular be brought more actively into the fold.[310]

Without prejudice to the need for representative balance and critical rigour, initiatives to formally regulate NGO activity should be resisted, with the risks of over-regulatory approaches outweighing by far the potential benefits. Rather, the Bank and Fund should focus on developing frameworks for cooperation and formalised information exchange, and as appropriate, programmatic interaction, with human rights NGOs. In an interesting sign of early beginnings, as at April 2000 the Bank's East Timor website contained a link to the website of Human Rights Watch and its campaigns (among other things) for protection of refugees, and prosecution of those responsible for gross human rights violations.[311] By 2002 a 'human rights' word search on the Bank's website could be expected to reveal scores if not hundreds of 'hits,' many of them linking to the mutually supporting activities of human rights NGOs.[312] Publicity of this kind,

---

[309] P Nelson, *The World Bank and Non-Governmental Organisation: The Limits of Apolitical Development* (1995); J Fox and L Brown, *The Struggle for Accountability: The World Bank, NGOs and Grassroots Movements* (1998).

[310] N Woods (2001) at 96–98.

[311] See http://wbln0018.worldbank.org/eap/eap.nsf?OpenDatabase, visited 15 April 2000.

[312] A 'human rights' word search on www.worldbank.org on 20 August 2002 disclosed the following highlights: (a) Amnesty International publications on human rights principles for companies; (b) Human Rights Watch reports on corporate complicity (especially that of transnational oil companies) in human rights violations, and correspondingly, management primers and other publications by the oil companies themselves concerning their human rights responsibilities; (c) annual reports of major human rights NGOs; (d) the US State Department's annual Country Report on Human Rights Practices; (e) workshop reports by various Networks within the Bank on human rights in the context of environmental protection (April 2001) and the gender dimension of human rights (June 2000); (f) ratification charts of major international human rights instruments (ICCPR, ICESCR, CEDAW, the CRC, and ILO Conventions) bearing on gender discrimination issues in the labour market in the Middle East and Northern Africa Region; (f) a wide range of institutional links (including to the Lawyers Committee for Human Rights) and thematic discussions of human rights instruments and access to justice issues in the context of judicial reform; (g) a landmark workshop sponsored by the Environment and Socially Sustainable Development Network in May 2002 on 'Human Rights and Sustainable Development: What Role for the World Bank?'; and (h) reports of

implying an important recognition of functional connectedness, represents an important beginning. Exploring avenues for constructive collaboration—as appropriate—is the next step.

The practical hurdles to more systematic constructive engagement should not be underestimated, however, especially from the perspective of the Fund, a historically compartmentalised and rarefied repository of specialist knowledge. However certain development NGOs, most notably OXFAM, by means of engaging on the same terms have already begun to make impressive strides in this regard at headquarters level, playing a constructive, active and influential role in international policy debates on (for example) debt relief and HIPC, the PRSP, and the 'Education for All' (Jomtien follow-up) campaigns. OXFAM's experience might well provide useful lessons for particular human rights NGOs, although naturally not all are suited or inclined towards an 'insider' role. The post-Seattle radicalisation of the anti-globalisation protest movement might present further strategic openings, encouraging Management at the Bank and Fund to welcome to the table the 'new moderates,' hitherto branded as extremists or loony leftists.

INTERACTIONS WITH THE OHCHR

The question of inter-agency interaction within the human rights mainstreaming context is too vast a subject to do justice to here. As indicated earlier, contemporary understandings of development issues challenge the inherited set of institutions at the international community's disposal. The question of the IFIs' cooperation with the OHCHR is but one small aspect of this overall picture, albeit an aspect rendered somewhat more compelling by reason of the OHCHR's human rights 'mainstreaming' mandate.[313] However the focus of the present inquiry should not be taken to imply any lesser need for the IFIs to explore more effective cooperation with other international agencies with shared developmental concerns, and generally more explicit operational expression of the UN system's human rights purposes, with particular regard to the imperatives of country level cooperation within the CCA/UNDAF framework.[314]

The High Commissioner for Human Rights is the principal UN official with responsibility for human rights and is accountable to the Secretary-General. The post of High Commissioner was created in 1993, as mandated by the the Vienna

the High Commissioner for Human Rights' 'Presidential Fellow's Lecture' to the Bank in December 2001, and joint OHCHR/World Bank learning seminar on human rights and development in June 2002.

[313] 'Renewing the United Nations: A Program for Reform,' Report of the Secretary-General, UN Doc. A/51/950 (1997), especially at para 78, clarifying that human rights should be a cross-cutting concern of the UN system.

[314] For the May 2002 consolidated version of the CCA/UNDAF guidelines see http://www.dgo. org/documents/2222-CCA___UNDAF_Guidelines___English.doc.

World Conference on Human Rights. The OHCHR is based in Geneva, Switzerland, with a very small office at United Nations Headquarters in New York, and staff and field presences in all regions of the world. The number of staff as at 2001 was slightly in excess of 400 world-wide. The mandate of the High Commissioner focuses on the promotion and protection of internationally agreed human rights. Examples of key objectives in pursuance of that mandate are human rights advocacy at national and international levels, human rights education and promoting access to human rights information, NHRI strengthening, supporting international human rights bodies (such as annual meetings in Geneva of the Commission on Human Rights—a 53-member political body—and the Sub-Commission on Promotion and Protection of Human Rights, an expert body), providing secretariat support for meetings of the human rights treaty bodies, encouraging regional dialogue and cooperation on human rights, human rights technical cooperation and in-country field work, and as mentioned above, leading efforts to more effectively 'mainstream' human rights within the UN system's four main programmes: development cooperation, peace and security, economic and social affairs, and humanitarian affairs.[315]

In early 2000 the Independent Expert on structural adjustment policies and the Special Rapporteur on the effects of foreign debt on the full enjoyment of economic, social and cultural rights submitted their joint report to CHR 56.[316] That report, while focused exclusively upon economic and social rights, contained recommendations of relevance to broader efforts to promote the integration of human rights into the work of the IFIs. A number of the recommendations focused upon perceived shortcomings within the OHCHR in that regard:

> In the course of conducting country visits and the Washington seminars, it became clear to both of us that, with respect to our two economic mandates which the Commission on Human Rights established two years ago, the current programme of the Office of the High Commissioner for Human Rights has limited impact on the ongoing debate and discussions taking place in many quarters, particularly concerning the need to insert a human rights perspective into global economic governance.
>
> . . . As it is currently constituted, OHCHR may have the minimal intellectual capacity and the required qualified personnel with substantive skills in international political economy to handle these mandates competently. However, it does not have the necessary resources required for mainstreaming these economic mandates into the activities of all United Nations agencies, let alone provide support to national Governments eager to develop a counter-project to the policies of the Bretton Woods institutions. We feel strongly that the current staffing and management structures are out of touch with the most dynamic debates and activities taking place outside of the United Nations system and existing internal expertise is not being utilized properly.
> . . .

---

[315] OHCHR, *Annual Appeal 2002: Overview of Activities and Financial Requirements* (2002).
[316] E/CN.4/2000/51, Annex.

Secondly, we believe that the Office of the High Commissioner is missing an excellent opportunity to make an impact on economic, social and cultural rights because of the inability of top management and the current professional staff to identify strategic entry points in the global policy discourse where the human rights agenda can be placed centre stage. We feel particularly strongly that with the exception of the High Commissioner herself, who has been an effective advocate of economic rights, top management at OHCHR are either unfamiliar with the substantive discourse on the links between human rights, economic globalization and the struggle to reform global economic governance, or they simply do not care at all. Talking about economic and cultural rights in the abstract is not enough. The Office of the High Commissioner must be proactive at the technical level and ensure that economic, social and cultural rights are strongly integrated in the activities and programmes of the multilateral financial institutions and the regional development banks.

As a result of the above-mentioned institutional problems, the Office of the High Commissioner for Human Rights is completely absent from key economic forums that require human rights integration. Key among these are the Consultative Group meetings, multilateral trade negotiating forums, regional and subregional economic blocs, HIPC reviews for debt cancellation, and national consultative forums on developing national poverty strategy frameworks. OHCHR's relations with the World Bank, IMF, WTO and the regional development banks are non-existent, or at best superficial. Failure to include human rights in the programs and activities of these key global institutions at the inception stage will ultimately result in the denial of economic, social and cultural rights of millions of people worldwide. For it is at this level that OHCHR should have its greatest influence, and not at the annual Commission 'jamboree'.

We therefore make a special appeal to Member States, the Secretary-General of the United Nations, and the High Commissioner for Human Rights to take urgent action to strengthen the responsiveness of OHCHR in the area of economic, social and cultural rights (economic mandates) by strengthening OHCHR's internal research and analytical capacity, and its technical assistance support to countries in macroeconomic policy and trade and investment-related topics that have a direct bearing on the promotion and protection of human rights. While we recognize the financial problems confronting the entire United Nations system, refocusing the work of the Office of the High Commissioner for Human Rights can easily be done from existing resources although more money would help to move the process faster and deepen the quality of intervention both at the global and local levels.[317]

The Special Rapporteur and Independent Expert appear to set rather a high bar for the OHCHR, whose foreseeable capacity to influence global economic debates is constrained severely (just as are those of the IFIs in different respects) by its very small size and limited institutional elasticity.[318] Among the more significant constraints upon the operational and programmatic capacity of the OHCHR, taking as a given its relatively recent and modest institutional origins, are probably attributable to the requirements of UN regulations on

---

[317] E/CN.4/2000/51, Annex, paras 94–99.
[318] On the idea of institutional elasticity see W Reisman, 'Through or Despite Governments: Differentiated Responsibilities in Human Rights Programs' (1987) 72 *Iowa Law Review* 395.

administrative, recruitment and financial procedures, and the limited capacity of existing administrative systems to spend and account for extra-budgetary funds beyond relatively modest limits.

The financial constraints under which the UN as a whole is forced to labour have a disproportionate impact on the OHCHR's share of the UN's regular budget. In 2001, OHCHR's total income was US$52.8 million, of which US$21.4 million came from the United Nations regular budget and US$31.2 million from voluntary contributions.[319] The General Assembly's Budget Committee (the so-called 'Fifth Committee')[320] has evinced little inclination over the years to equip the OHCHR to function effectively beyond 'core' non-discretionary functions such as servicing the CHR and its numerous mandates, working groups and thematic mechanisms, the servicing of the Sub-Commission on the Promotion and Protection of Human Rights, the servicing of human rights treaty bodies, and carrying out research and reporting activities concerning the right to development. And while extra-budgetary funds for the Office have increased significantly since the year 2000,[321] there are limits—politically and practically—to which the Office can go in relying disproportionately upon such contributions. To this extent, the appeal by the Special Rapporteur and Independent Expert to Member States could not have been more timely.

This is of course not to say that nothing is being done in these areas, nor that nothing further can be done. The rather bleak assessment by the Special Rapporteur and Independent Expert of the level of commitment and initiative within the OHCHR's modest capacities belies to some degree the OHCHR's clear 'catalytic' strategic orientation since the UN Secretary-General's reform programme of 1997.[322] If senior management in fact were disinterested in human rights mainstreaming issues at the date of the experts' report, it has certainly not been the case since. The period 2000–2002 has spawned an increasing range of projects and initiatives in recent years directed towards the operationalisation of human rights in development (including human rights integration within poverty reduction strategies),[323] along with a gradual

---

[319] OHCHR, *Annual Appeal 2002: Overview of Activities and Financial Requirements* (2002).

[320] The member State-appointed 'experts' on the Advisory Committee on Administrative and Budgetary Questions (ACABQ)—whose function it is to make recommendations to the Fifh Committee—reflect a similar schism.

[321] Activities for 2002 were envisaged to require US$78.2 million, of which only US$22.5 million was expected from the UN regular budget. OHCHR, *Annual Appeal 2002: Overview of Activities and Financial Requirements* (2002).

[322] See above n 313.

[323] See P Hunt, M Nowak and S Osmani, 'Discussion Paper and Draft Guidelines: Human Rights and Poverty Reduction Strategies' (June 2002). The 'Integration of Human Rights within Poverty Reduction Strategies' project of the OHCHR was initiated in 2001 at the request of the Committee on Economic, Social and Cultural Rights. Three experts (listed above) drafted a discussion paper on the subject of the integration of human rights in poverty reduction strategies, which formed the basis for a lengthy series of consultations including at the World Bank and IMF. A workshop involving numerous stakeholders including several representatives of the Bank and Fund was convened at the OHCHR in June 2002 to consider the consultants' draft guidelines, intended for completion as a completed first draft in September 2002. A country level piloting phase was envisaged to follow thereafter.

increase in the frequency and deepening of quality of interaction with the IFIs (the Bank in particular) at both senior management and working level.[324]

As to some of the earlier evidence of the OHCHR's cooperative relations with the IFIs, the High Commissioner's report to fifty-sixth session of the Commission on Human Rights identified the following initiatives concerning the implementation of the right to development: (1) the elaboration by the OHCHR of a 'strategy for its participation in the CDF process;' and (2) in light of a joint meeting in 1999 of the independent expert on structural adjustment policies and Special Rapporteur on foreign debt with the Bank and Fund, 'intensifying its working relations with the Bank . . . with a view to providing support, when requested, to country programmes.' The report also indicated, albeit in a non-specific fashion, that 'contacts between the OHCHR and the IMF [were] continuing.'[325]

As opposed to a pattern of incremental advancement, it might behove the longer term prospects for inter-agency cooperation if an explicit framework, perhaps initially pitched at the level of an informal understanding, could be developed in consultation with the IFIs as a guide to further interaction. The point of departure for such a policy should be the shared fundamental human

---

[324] See n 312 above, with reference to the High Commissioner's 'Presidential Fellow's Lecture' to the Bank on 3 December 2001, and joint OHCHR/World Bank learning seminar on human rights and development on 10–11 June 2002. The text of the High Commissioner's lecture, entitled 'Bridging the Gap Between Human Rights and Development: From Normative Principles to Operational Relevance,' is available at http://www.worldbank.org/wbi/B-SPAN/sub_mary_robin son.htm. The 'learning seminar' report is likewise available, through http://www.worldbank.org/WBSITE/EXTERNAL/. On the broader range of activities see OHCHR, *Annual Appeal 2002: Overview of Activities and Financial Requirements* (2002). The designation of regional advisers ('regional representatives') to promote human rights mainstreaming at regional level, formalisation of cooperation with UNDP through a Memorandum of Understanding (MOU) and a joint global programme programme piloting methodology development in rights-based development programming, formalisation of cooperation through an MOU with the Department of Peacekeeping Operations, and pursuit of a range of other joint agency agreements and initiative with UNAIDS, Habitat, among others.

[325] See E/CN.4/2000/20 at paras 15 and 19. Some of the more regular exchanges in the past have revolved around the High Commissioner's mandate for reporting on the implementation of the 'right to development,' pursuant to GA Res. 48/141. See E/CN.4/2000/20 for an outline of some of the activities being carried out under this mandate, including (at para 15): a joint meeting of the independent expert on structural adjustment policies and Special Rapporteur on Foreign Debt with (among others) the Bank and Fund; and (at para 19) modes of cooperation or at least some form of basic communication with the Bank and Fund. As indicated earlier the political pressure from the General Assembly's Fifth Committee for the High Commissioner to focus resources on activities promoting the 'right to development' (within unclear parameters raising questions concerning the place of civil and political rights, and who—people(s) or states—are the parties in whom the right is vested) are considerable, notwithstanding the unclear status of the 1986 Declaration on the Right to Development under international law. To the extent that the right to development is itself premised upon the realisation of all economic, social, political, cultural and civil human rights, an alternative approach (albeit not specifically mandated by the Commission on Human Rights, and certainly overlooking some of the more important normative innovations embodied in the 1986 Declaration itself) would be for the High Commissioner to request information on the extent to which relevant and binding international human rights standards have or have not been factored in to the IFIs' policies and activities, and whether any specific measures have been taken to promote their objectives or at least militate against the likelihood of facilitating breaches.

rights values underpinning all UN system actors and activities. However any workable framework for cooperation must equally reflect—without capitulating to—inherited institutional realities, taking into account not only the IFIs' institutional complexities (and to some extent, inertia) and the sobering lessons of experience as far as gender and environmental mainstreaming are concerned, but also the corresponding constraints on the OHCHR's own capacities and institutional elasticity.

The task of identifying entry points seems to be easier in the case of the Bank than for the Fund, however efforts need to be applied to both. Agreement on a modest number of targeted areas for interaction is the most critical step at an early stage, ideally on a small number of thematic or programmatic areas where each agency (notwithstanding their mismatch in capacities and disciplinary profiles) could bring distinctive and worth while perspectives to the table, such as gender, HIV/AIDs, and perhaps broader issues concerning the operationalisation and relevance of human rights standards, principles and legal frameworks in development policy and programming, including within the framework of PRSPs and national level MDG reporting processes.[326] Consideration could also be given to the expansion of the Bank's internal informal 'learning groups' on values, ethics and participatory development,[327] and encouragement of linkages between such groups and external advocates and stakeholders.[328] Expansion of training would presumably be a prerequisite to ambitions for setting in place a sustainable process of interaction.[329]

Subject to early progress in these areas and to how institutional capacities evolve, medium term initiatives might include such matters as staff exchanges, and formalisation of relations at agency head level through a memorandum of understanding, with expansion at every stage framed against a hard-headed and objective appraisal of the purpose to be served—and value-added as against feasible alternatives—by the initiative in question. Subject to this, longer term possibilities might include:

---

[326] A potentially useful example of this concerns the OHCHR's 'Human Rights and Poverty Reduction Strategy' project (above n 323 and accompanying text). Bank and Fund staff were included in consultations on early drafts of the poverty reduction and human rights guidelines, and also in the June 2002 consultation in Geneva.

[327] For a brief history of these see M Miller-Adams (1999) at 74–75.

[328] Interactions between Bank and Fund representatives at the 7 May 2001 consultation with the Committee on Economic, Social and Cultural Rights were already mentioned. Informal in-house 'human rights' workshops have been conducted at the Bank for a long time, although largely at the initiative of interested and motivated staff, without senior management imprimatur. But an in-house Legal Department seminar on human rights issues was convened early in 1999, with the blessing of the Bank President, at which several NGOs and invited academics were invited to share their perspectives. This has been followed up with similar exchanges, and ad hoc meetings with the High Commissioner for Human Rights and officials from her Office. 'On-line' discussion groups moderated by the Bank and or Fund offer additional possibilities in this regard.

[329] One must bear in mind the inadequacy of training programs in and of themselves, and likely staff resistance on grounds of competing work demands, preference for orthodox approaches, and general 'fad resistance.'

1. an evaluation of the relationship between the PRSP process and human rights,[330] and in light of the lessons from that evaluation, sponsorship of initiatives at both headquarters and national levels to integrate human rights more explicitly and effectively within that context;

2. support at the international level for the strengthening of the reporting and monitoring mechanisms serviced by the OHCHR;

3. support at the national level for the establishment of independent and effective NHRIs[331] and creation of conditions for the free and active operation of human rights and development NGOs, and promoting the participation of these actors in PRSP or other relevant development planning processes at the national level;

4. promotion at the national level, in the course of dialogues with national level interlocutors, of the goal of universal ratification of the six core UN human rights treaties and removal of reservations in relation thereto;

5. support for the OHCHR's and partner agencies' technical assistance activities at country level, including those directed at human rights reporting and implementation of the six core treaties;

6. interaction with the OHCHR on a small number of strategically selected sectoral issues of mutual concern, subject to case-by-case assessment of strategic potential, with possible areas including access to justice, democratic institution-building, gender in development, HIV/AIDS, and cooperating towards the implementation of particular economic, social and cultural rights 'as human rights' (rather than discretionary entitlements, luxuries, or charitable development goals); and

7. support for the integration of human rights within national development planning frameworks, budget processes, and macro-economic policy debates.[332]

---

[330] This could build upon the initial experience with the OHCHR's 'Human Rights and Poverty Reduction Strategies' project, having particular regard to lessons from experience as the draft guidelines emanating from the first phase of this project are piloted at country level.

[331] There are isolated instances—notably those of Nicaragua and Rwanda—of NHRI strengthening being included within PRSPs to date. See chapter III above, at nn 145–46 and accompanying text.

[332] For recommendations along some of these lines see *DFID Human Rights Paper* (2000) at 22–23. That paper also recommended support for the development of National Plans of Action for human rights (NHRAPs), ideally to be framed and considered alongside national poverty reduction plans. Without detracting from NHRAPs' importance in many circumstances, the imperative of 'mainstreaming' human rights may in some circumstances be better served by efforts to integrate human rights standards and principles as far as possible directly within existing national level poverty reduction and development planning frameworks, rather than establishing separate 'human rights-specific' planning processes with attendant risks of marginalisation from mainstream policy debates. However generalisations on this difficult question only go so far. Much depends on the national context, pre-existing extent of human rights awareness and planning, and the seriousness with which human rights reforms of whatever kind are undertaken. For suggestions as to conditions likely to make NHRAP's effective see OHCHR, *Handbook on National Human Rights Plans of Action* (2002), available at www.unhchr.ch. Subject to the conditions therein being satisfied, IFIs' support for NHRAPs and their associated 'human rights basline study' planning processes (with the longer term view of merging that process with 'participatory poverty assessments' under PRSP and national development planning auspices) may well be warranted.

VII

Concluding Remarks

———⊰•⊱———

THE MATTERS discussed in chapters III–V lead to the conclusion that there is both need and scope for the IFIs to take better and more explicit account of human rights concerns in their work. This is of course not to suggest that the IFIs should be the lead promoters of human rights in the international system, however it can safely be said that human rights demand a much higher place than they presently occupy.

Set against the controversies and challenges faced by the IFIs, and having regard to their mandates and comparative advantages, chapter VI suggested a range of areas where the integration of human rights is either necessary as a matter of international law, or desirable on instrumental rationales. The core minimum obligation incumbent directly upon both the Bank and Fund as specialised agencies of the UN system and subjects of international law is a duty of vigilance to ensure that their policies and programs do not facilitate breaches of their member states' human rights treaty obligations. The legal and moral rationales for this 'do no harm' obligation are consistent with those underpinning the Bank's social safeguard policies, and OD 4.01 on Environmental Assessment particular. The effective implementation of this basic obligation will call for serious attention and resources to be devoted to the development of methodology and capacity for human rights impact assessments. Clearly neither the Bank nor Fund presently possess the expertise to carry out this kind of inquiry on their own. The development of constructive and sustainable linkages with human rights experts, NGOs and specialist institutions is an essential prerequisite to the implementation of workable procedures in this and virtually all other subjects canvassed in chapter VI.

The essential purpose of human rights policies for the Bank and Fund should be to acknowledge that each has responsibilities under international human rights law. Construing the mandates of the Bank and Fund in light of applicable sources of international human rights law, one can conclude that these duties start from a 'negative' requirement to 'respect' applicable human rights principles. The requirement not to facilitate breaches is the most obvious example of this kind of duty, although one might equally argue that the institutions' collective zeal for privatisation of essential services might warrant review in this light.[1]

---

[1] In particular, by respecting the presumption against unwarranted retrogression, ensuring that any deliberate diminution in enjoyment of economic and social rights is justified by reference to the

As observed by the Committee on Economic, Social and Cultural Rights, finance and investment issues are in no way exempt from the requirement that international organisations take whatever measures they can to assist governments to act in ways which are compatible with their human rights obligations and to seek to devise policies and programmes which promote respect for those rights.[2]

The extent to which it might also be argued that the IFIs have legally binding duties to 'protect' and 'fulfil' human rights standards has not been addressed in depth in this book. Nonetheless it was seen that the obligation to 'respect' human rights standards has in certain contexts been held to convey duties of a positive kind,[3] and moreover that a range of reasonably clearly grounded obligations to 'protect', and arguably 'promote' human rights standards could be identified.[4] Further research on these normative questions is clearly required, particularly insofar as the identification of obligations of a positive kind are concerned. However the uneven record of mainstreaming gender and the environment at the Bank—despite years of public clamour, operational policy promulgation, rhetoric and recruitment[5]—sounds a cautionary note for the prospects for serious human rights integration.

It was also shown that the IFIs enjoy a potentially broad range of policy options for human rights operationalisation, even to the extent that direct linkages to binding sources of human rights seem less readily demonstrable. The extent to which such discretionary engagement is desirable as a matter of policy within each institution is a matter of debate, especially insofar as the Fund is concerned. Pushed and pulled in a variety of directions throughout the 1990s, as at the turn of the century the Fund's appetite for adventurism appeared to have lessened, with political pressures urging it away from development-related issues and large bailouts, towards a quieter preventive role and a more circumscribed focus upon macro-economic fundamentals. In such circumstances, the likelihood of the Fund seeking to extend its activities more directly into development realms, with attendant prospects for increased human rights integration, must be considered minimal.

This does not necessarily mean that the staff of the Fund—as much as the Bank—ought to be obviated from understanding human rights normative and instrumental linkages with macro-economic and development issues, and bringing informed positions on such matters to the table in PRSP negotiations and

---

totality of such rights, implementing a human rights impact assessment (within applicable methodological constraints), and guaranteeing the implementation of countervailing measures to the extent of foreseeable violations.

[2] 'Globalisation and Economic, Social and Cultural Rights,' statement of the Committee on Economic, Social and Cultural Rights, May 1998, at paragraph 5.

[3] See chapter IV above, at n 94 and accompanying text.

[4] See chapter IV above, at nn 95–101 and accompanying text.

[5] This is especially so in the case of the environmental agenda. See R Wade, 'Greening the Bank: The Struggle Over the Environment, 1970–1995' in D Kapur, J Lewis and R Webb (eds), *The World Bank: Its First Half Century* (Vol. 2) (1997) 611–734, and for the sobering record with both gender and the environment, Operations Evaluation Department, *IDA's Partnership for Poverty Reduction: An Independent Evaluation of Fiscal Years 1994–2000* (2002).

like forums. These linkages are already surfacing in isolated cases,[6] and can be expected to increase to the extent that participation at the national level is carried out in a free and meaningful fashion. However, for both the Bank and Fund, assumption of human rights responsibilities beyond the extent necessary under international law should be subject at a minimum to the implementation of the structural reforms discussed in chapter VI, directed towards strengthening each institution's internal and external accountability incentives and mechanisms, for the sake of both legitimacy and effectiveness.[7] Balancing these demands with counterveiling political pressures from Washington DC, ensuring the continued commitment (however wavering or selective) to multilateralism of the world's sole superpower, remains among the IFIs' most significant challenges.[8]

Subject to the above, and to further clarification of normative linkages, priority areas for reform implementable in the short to medium term within the scope of the IFIs' mandates, appropriately construed, would include:

—integration of human rights within social impact analysis and social assessment procedures;
—recognition and operationalisation of economic and social rights including assisting in the development of appropriate indicators and national level benchmarks to that end;
—expanding and deepening professional interaction with UN system actors and relevant human rights bodies in particular;
—factoring human rights more effectively and consistently into the PRSP process;
—operationalisation of participation in human rights terms; and
—in the Bank's case, more widespread and substantive incorporation of international human rights standards within operational policies in such areas as child labour, indigenous peoples, HIV/AIDS and gender.

These are precisely the matters on which the IFIs need to engage in dialogue with specialist bodies and others affected by their activities, in the course of consultations on human rights policy development. Each institution needs to undertake a serious review of the scope of their respective mandates, construed in light of practical contemporary demands and applicable international law rules,

---

[6] See eg chapter VI at n 203 and accompanying text.
[7] See chapter VI above, at nn 5–65 and accompanying text.
[8] As Ngaire Woods observes, 'the World Bank's close relationship with the United States creates tensions for the institution, which both must please its most powerful political master and at the same time maintain its independence and credibility both as a technical agency (with technical expertise as opposed to political/ idological solutions), and a multilateral organisation. In order to be effective, the Bank needs to be perceived by all its member countries as a legitimate multilateral organisation, pursuing predominantly developmental objectives in a rule-based way. It needs recognised credibility and expertise in economic policy based on the scope and depth or its research. In order to enjoy this legitimacy, the Bank also needs a visible degree of political independence from interference by its most powerful members.' N Woods, 'The Challenges of Multilateralism and Governance,' in C Gilbert and D Vines (eds), *The World Bank: Structure and Policies* (2000) 132–156, 136–37.

as a basis for moving the consultative process forward. Consistent with the Bank's (and to a lesser degree the Fund's) policy development procedures in other areas, transparent and participatory processes will not only enhance the perceived objectivity and legitimacy of the policies themselves and ensure the inclusion of all relevant perspectives, but will strengthen the legitimate expectation as an emerging principle of international administrative law that those whose interests are affected by a proposed policy or action have the right to be heard prior to its promulgation.

As explained at the outset, this book to a great extent has deliberately avoided some of the most vexing questions of principle and practice in this field, notably: How precise can we be about the legal and policy implications of the human rights mainstreaming imperative for the Bank and Fund, having regard to relevant sources of obligation under international law, and where lie the limitations? The approach in the book has been deliberately suggestive or indicative on the policy and practical dimensions, with the foundational normative arguments likewise warranting further focused research.[9] However in addressing specifically the core exercise of legal interpretation in chapter IV, it is hoped that a contribution will be made to the central task that ought to lie before the legal departments of both Bank and Fund: revisiting the inherited doctrine of conservative legal establishments, and adopting an objective and contextualised interpretation of their charters sufficient to meet the demands of principle and the central operational challenges of the time.

This book has also been unabashedly grounded in some measure of *realpolitique*, taking the institutional inheritances of the post-WWII economic and political order to some extent as a given, as a basis for conceptualising the IFIs' normative and functional relationships with international human rights law. This should not be mistaken for implicit endorsement of the status quo, nor as undermining the basis for more foundational critiques seeking to contest the dominant neo-liberal paradigm that the IFIs so effectively embody. To the contrary, the discussion in chapter VI identified a potentially wide spectrum of reform possibilities, the viability of most of which was premised upon a set of basic institutional reforms designed to enhance the institutions' accountability, legitimacy, and strengthen lines of democratic responsiveness. In the absence of serious reforms of such kinds, vesting the IFIs with further responsibilities of whatever kind only adds urgency and weight to the case for more far-reaching political change.

While not a dominant focus within this book, it was also stressed that any serious reform programme in the human rights or indeed any other 'new issue'

---

[9] The most comprehensive scholarly effort to date to calibrate policy reforms for the IFIs by reference to categories of human rights obligation under international law is S Skogly, *The Human Rights Obligations of the World Bank and the International Monetary Fund* (2001), subject to qualifications expressed in chapter IV. For a critique see M Darrow, 'Human Rights Accountability of the World Bank and IMF: Possibilities and Limits of Legal Analysis' (2003 forthcoming) 12(1) *Social and Legal Studies* 133–44.

area must take account of organisational theoretical perspectives on the prospects for transformation. The evolutionary paths of the Bank and Fund have been characterised by fitting the task to the organisation, rather than the organisation to the task.[10] In contrast to the 'Christmas tree' model of development or finance 'add-ons,' human rights are not likely to impact at any kind of systemic or fundamental level in the longer term in the absence of strong alliances of both internal and external advocates, congruence with broader substantive trends in the development and finance fields, reconciliation with the IFIs' respective organisational cultures, and resolution of retrograde incentives (such as the 'approval culture' in the Bank's case) and related structural problems.[11]

Above all, reform discussions in this area must be guided by at least some measure of modesty.[12] While the theory of human rights in development is not new, practical questions governing operationalisation most certainly are. Reform debates are too readily polarised through uncompromising positions and blinkered assumptions of both development economists and human rights advocates alike. The escalation of the anti-globalisation movement has undoubtedly brought more attention and pressure to these and related issues at the dawn of the new millennium, with the result that an increasing range of actors including development and human rights NGOs are finding common vocabulary and more secure standing with the Bank and Fund. There is a pressing need to expand this common ground, and set the course for sustainable change through strategically targeted steps in the short to medium term. The science in this is new and evolving, as are the working relationships. These uncertainties coupled with the human rights values at stake demand the abandonment of hollow promises and empty rhetoric, in favour of sober yet principled reflection on what—with the pieces we find on the table—may realistically be achievable.

---

[10] In the case of the Bank see eg B Crane and J Finkle, 'Organisational Impediments to Development Assistance: The World Bank's Population Program' (1981) 36(4) *World Politics* 518.

[11] M Miller-Adams, *The World Bank: New Agendas in a Changing World* (1999) 146–47.

[12] To this general effect see H Bergesen and L Lunde, *Dinosaurs or Dynamos? The United Nations and the World Bank at the Turn of the Century* (1999) 194–95: 'The uncertainty surrounding development as social learning, if taken seriously, implies that all actors should be careful about promising quick and tangible results. . . . It is by recognising that they will not and should not be the dynamos of development that [the UN and World Bank] can avoid the fate of the dinosaurs.'

Annex

Explanatory note: In most cases interviewees—particularly within the Bank and Fund—expressed the wish not to have statements or views attributed to them. Accordingly, within the body of this book, references to interview-based material to which such a caveat applies are sourced generically, in a manner calculated not to identify the interviewee.

WASHINGTON DC, MARCH 1999

1. Mike Stevens, Governance, World Bank
2. Professor Jerome Levinson, American University
3. Professor Daniel D Bradlow, American University
4. Philip O'Keefe, Central Asia Region, World Bank
5. Lee Irish, NGO Unit, World Bank
6. Myles Wickstead, Alternative UK Executive Director, Executive Board, World Bank
7. William Holder, Deputy General Counsel, IMF
8. Mark Blackden, Gender Specialist, Africa Region, World Bank
9. John Clark, NGO Unit, World Bank
10. Louis Forget, Legal Department, World Bank
11. Jenni Klugman, PREM, World Bank
12. David Freestone, Environment Department, World Bank
13. Alfredo Sfeir-Younis, External Relations Department, World Bank

NEW YORK, MARCH/APRIL 1999

1. Bert Theuermann, Counsellor, Permanent Mission of Austria to the United Nations
2. Tish Armstrong, Lawyers Committee for Human Rights
3. Stefanie Grant, Lawyers Committee for Human Rights
4. Elsa Stamatopoulou, OHCHR (NY)
5. Christian Privat, Consultant, Programme Division, UNICEF
6. Rebeca Rios-Kohn, UNDP Human Rights Advisor
7. Guillamette Meunier, Programme Officer, Child Rights, Division of Evaluation, Policy and Planning, UNICEF
8. Jane Connors, Women's Rights Unit, Division for the Advancement of Women, Department of Economic and Social Affairs
9. Thord Palmlund, Special Adviser, Management Development and Governance Division, Bureau for Development Policy, UNDP
10. Hervé Lecoq, Programme Specialist, UN Development Group Office

11. Ian Hopwood, Chief, Evaluation, Office of Evaluation, Policy and Planning, UNICEF
12. Marjorie Newman-Williams, Deputy Director, Programme Division, UNICEF
13. Bruce Jones, Humanitarian Affairs Officer, Policy Development Unit, Office for the Coordination of Humanitarian Affairs
14. Nora Galer, Senior UN Affairs Officer; Office of UN Affairs and External Relations, UNICEF
15. Christopher Coleman, Chief, Policy and Analysis Unit, Office of the Under-Secretary General, Department of Peace-Keeping Operations
16. Shashi Tharoor, Director of Communications and Special Projects; Office of the Secretary-General
17. Richard Morgan, Deputy Director, Programme Division, UNICEF
18. John Hendra, Director, Division for Resources Mobilisation, Bureau for Resources and External Affairs, UNDP
19. Teresa Whitfield, Special Assistant to the Assistant Secretary-General for Political Affairs, Department of Political Affairs
20. Iain Levine, Representative, Amnesty International
21. Karin Landgren, Chief, Child Protection Section, Programme Division
22. Michael Møller, Special Assistant to the Under-Secretary-General, Department of Political Affairs
23. Shepard Forman, Director, Centre on International Cooperation, New York University
24. Cesare Romano, Associate, Centre on International Cooperation, New York University
25. Alvarro de Soto, Assistant Secretary-General, Department of Political Affairs
26. David Malone, Director, International Peace Academy
27. Elizabeth Cousens, Director of Research, International Peace Academy
28. Danilo Türk, Ambassador Extraordinary and Plenipotentiary, Permanent Representative of Slovenia to the United Nations
29. Edward Mortimer, Principal Officer, Executive Office of the Secretary-General
30. Goro Onojima, Human Rights Officer, OHCHR NY

INDONESIA, 12–16 OCTOBER 1999

1. Stephen Woodhouse, UNICEF Representative to Indonesia and Malaysia.
2. Yoshi-teru Uramoto, Senior Programme Officer, Planning and Advocacy, UNICEF.
3. Anne-Marie Fonseka, Project Officer, Child Protection, UNICEF.
4. Jiyono, Education Officer, UNICEF.
5. Emmy Jansen, Project Officer, CEDC/AIDS, UNICEF.
6. Soedjati Djiwandono, Socio-political analyst and newspaper columnist.
7. Sandy (Samuel) Lieberman, Country Sector Coordinator for Human Development, World Bank country office in Indonesia.
8. Sri Mulyani Indrawati, Director, Institute for Economic and Social Research, Faculty of Economics, University of Indonesia.
9. Adnan Buyong Nasution, Adnan Buyong Nasution and Partners, Advocates and Counsellors at Law.
10. Anwar Nasution, Senior Deputy Governor, Bank Indonesia.

11. Dr Suharto, Director, Centre for Physical Fitness and Education, Ministry of Education and Culture.
12. Dr Yulfita Raharjo, Director, Centre for Population and Manpower Studies, Indonesian Institute of Sciences (LIPI).
13. Dr Mochtar Pabottingi, political analyst in LIPI.
14. Dr Hermawan 'Kikiek' Sulistiyo, Southeast Asian Area Specialist, LIPI.
15. Frans Winarta, Managing Partner, Frans Winarta and Partners, Attorneys and Counsellors at Law.
16. Irwanto, Senior Researcher, Centre for Societal Development Studies, Catholic University of Indonesia Atma Jaya.
17. Ms Purnianti, Department of Criminology, Faculty of Social and Political Sciences, University of Indonesia.
18. Sri Hariningsih, Directorate of Legislation, Ministry of Justice.
19. Satish Mishra, Head/Chief Economist, UN Support Facility for Indonesian Recovery (UNSFIR).
20. Iyanatul Islam, Senior Economist, Regional Policy, UNSFIR.
21. Prof Dr Yaumil Chairiah Agoes Achir, Coordinating Ministry for People's Welfare.
22. Indra Djati Sidi, Chairman of Research and Development, Department of Education and Culture.
23. Cecile Gregory, Senior Project Implementation Officer (Education and Health), Asian Development Bank.
24. Dr Fasli Jalal, BAPPENAS.
25. Binny Buchori, Executive Secretary, International NGO Forum on Indonesian Development (INFID).
26. Sugeng Bahagijo, Information Manager, INFID.
27. Suyono Yahya, UNICEF consultant.
28. Nono Sumarsono, Plan International Indonesia.
29. Muhammed Joni, Program Officer with Indonesian Institute for Children's Advocacy (LAAI), and member of Child Protection Body (LPA) in Northern Sumatra.
30. Rostymaline Munthe, Executive Director, Ecuation Committee for Indonesian Creative Labour Foundation (KOMPAK).
31. Mohammed Farid, Yogyakarta-based children's rights NGO 'Samin', and UNICEF consultant.
32. Dr Heddy Shri Ahimsa Putra, Senior Researcher, Puspar-UGM, Centre for Tourism Research and Development, Gadjah Mada University.
33. Jennifer McAvoy, Disaster Relief Coordinator, OXFAM GB Indonesia, Yogyakarta.
34. Adidananta, Executive Director, HUMANA/GIRLI (a street children NGO in Yogyakarta).
35. Prof Dr Moeljarto Tjokrowinoto, Researcher, Puspar-UGM, Centre for Tourism Research and Development, Gadjah Mada University.
36. Dr Sutaryo, Paediatrician, Consultant Haematologist, School of Medicine, Gadjah Mada University.
37. Prof Sello Sumardjan, Social Science Foundation.
38. Nora de Guzman, Communications Officer, UNICEF.
39. Marja Toivola, Assistant Project Officer, Training, UNICEF.
40. Pandji Putranto, National Programme Coordinator, ILO.
41. Joshua Felman, Senior Resident Representative, IMF.

WASHINGTON DC, 7–17 FEBRUARY 1999

1. Mark Blackden, Gender Specialist, Africa Region, World Bank.
2. Hans Juergen Gruss, Chief Counsel, Middle East and North Africa Division, Legal Department, World Bank.
3. Sabine Schlemmer-Schulte, Legal Department, World Bank.
4. Alan Ruby, Manager, Education Sector, East Asia and Pacific Region, World Bank.
5. Tony Gaeta, External Affairs, World Bank.
6. Steve Commins, Office of the Vice-President for Human Development, World Bank.
7. Keith Hansen, HIV/AIDS Thematic Team, World Bank.
8. Daniel Bradlow, Professor of Law and Director, International Legal Studies Program, Washington College of Law, American University.
9. Anthony R Boote, Assistant Director, Official Financing Operations Division, Policy Development and Review Department, IMF.
10. Mike Jendrzejczyk, Washington Director, Asia Division, Human Rights Watch.
11. Eduardo G Abbott, Executive Secretary, Inspection Panel, World Bank.
12. James MacNeill, Member, Inspection Panel, World Bank.
13. Antonia Macedo, Assistant Executive Secretary, Inspection Panel, World Bank.
14. Caroline M Robb, Social Development Officer, Africa Department, IMF.
15. Kazuhide Kuroda, Consultant, Post Conflict Unit, Social Development Department, World Bank.
16. John Clark, Principal Social Development Specialist, East Asia and Pacific Region, World Bank.
17. Colin Scott, Post Conflict Unit, Social Development Department, World Bank.
18. Koen Davidse, Advisor to the Executive Director for Armenia, Bosnia-Herzegovina, Bulgaria, Croatia, Cyprus, Georgia, Israel, FYR Macedonia, Moldova, the Netherlands, Romania and Ukraine, World Bank.
19. Daniel PM Owen, Social Development Specialist, Technical and Environment Department, Environmental and Social Review Unit, International Finance Corporation (IFC).
20. Ciprian Fisiy, Social Development Team Leader, Poverty Reduction and Social Development, Africa Region, World Bank.
21. Jessica Poppele, Country Officer, Indonesia Country Program, World Bank.
22. Richard E Messick, Senior Public Sector Specialist, Public Sector Group, Poverty Reduction and Economic Management, World Bank.
23. Aline Coudouel, Poverty Group, Poverty Reduction and Economic Management, World Bank.
24. Jacob Gammelbaard, Public Sector Management Specialist, Poverty Reduction and Economic Management—Public Sector Unit, World Bank.
25. Harold H Alderman, Food and Nutrition Policy Advisor, Rural Development, World Bank.
26. William E Holder, Deputy General Counsel, IMF.
27. Bona Kim, Child Labour Specialist, World Bank.
28. John Mitchell, Comprehensive Development Framework (CDF) Secretariat, World Bank.
29. Greg Toulmin, CDF Secretariat, World Bank.
30. François Gianviti, General Counsel, IMF.

31. Gita Gopal, Operations Evaluation Department (OED), World Bank.

NEW YORK, 21–25 FEBRUARY 2000

1. Jan Vandemoortele, Chief Economist, Division of Evaluation, Policy and Planning, UNICEF.
2. Eva Jespersen, Policy Advisor, Division of Evaluation, Policy and Planning, UNICEF.
3. Rebeca Rios-Kohn, Principal Human Rights Advisor, Management Development and Governance Division, Bureau for Development Policy, UNDP.
4. Marta Santos Pais, Director, Division of Evaluation, Policy and Planning, UNICEF, and former Member and Rapporteur of the Committee on the Rights of the Child.
5. Dorothy Rozga, Senior Project Officer, Programme Division, UNICEF.
6. Lois Whitman, Executive Director, Children's Rights Division, Human Rights Watch.
7. Drew McVey, Human Rights Officer, Office of the High Commissioner for Human Rights (OHCHR).
8. Engelbert Theuermann, Counsellor, Permanent Mission of Austria.
9. Elizabeth Cousens, Director of Research, International Peace Academy.
10. Hervé Lecoq, Programme Specialist, United Nations Development Group Office.
11. Marjorie Newman-Williams, Deputy Director, Programme Division, UNICEF.
12. Patricia Armstrong, Lawyers Committee for Human Rights.
13. Iain Levine, Amnesty International.
14. Ilene Cohn, Office of the Special Representative of the Secretary-General for Children in Armed Conflict.
15. Benedict Kingsbury, Professor of Law, New York University.

Bibliography

Explanatory note: This bibliography contains a number of references of general relevance to the subjects under consideration in this thesis, in addition to those specifically cited therein.

1. 'Adjustment with a Human Face: Record and Relevance' (1991) 19(12) *World Development* 1801–64.
2. 'Maastricht Guidelines on Violations of Economic, Social and Cultural Rights' (1998) 20 *Human Rights Quarterly* 691–705.
3. 'Symposium Issue on the Analysis of Poverty and Adjustment' (1991) 5 (May) *World Bank Economic Review* 177–393.
4. 'Symposium: The Implementation of the International Covenant on Economic, Social and Cultural Rights (the Limburg Principles on the Implementation of the International Covenant on Economic, Social and Cultural Rights)' (1987) 9 *Human Rights Quarterly* 121–35.
5. Abbasi, K, 'The World Bank and World Health: Under Fire' (1999) 318 *British Medical Journal* 1003.
6. Abugre, C and Alexander, N, 'Non-governmental Organisations and the International Monetary and Financial System,' *International Monetary and Financial Issues for the 1990s* Vol. 9 (Geneva, UNCTAD, 1998), 107–25.
7. Afshar, H (ed), *Women and empowerment: illustrations from the Third World* (New York, St Martin's Press, 1998).
8. Akande, D, 'The Competence of International Organisations and the Advisory Jurisdiction of the International Court of Justice' (1998) 9(3) *European Journal of International Law* 437–67.
9. Aké, C, 'The Democratisation of Disempowerment in Africa' in J Hippler (ed), *The Democratisation of Disempowerment: The Problem of Democracy in the Third World* (London, Pluto Press, 1995), 70–89.
10. Alderman, H, 'Food Subsidies and the Poor' in D Lal and H Myint (eds), *Essays on Poverty, Equity and Growth* (Washington, DC, World Bank, 1990).
11. Alston, P, 'The Fortieth Anniversary of the Universal Declaration of Human Rights: A Time More for Reflection than for Celebration' in J Berting, P Baehr, J Burgers and C Flinterman (eds), *Human Rights in a Pluralist World* (Westport, CT, Meckler, 1990), 1–14.
12. —— 'Human Rights and the Basic Needs Strategy for Development', Anti-Slavery Society. *Human Rights and Development Working Papers* 2 (1979), 1.
13. —— 'International Governance in the Normative Areas', *Globalisation with a Human Face: Background Papers to Human Development Report 1999* (New York, UNDP, 1999), 1–36.
14. —— 'International Trade as an Instrument of Positive Human Rights Policy (1982) 4 *Human Rights Quarterly* 155.
15. ——, 'Making or Breaking Human Rights: The UN's Specialised Agencies and the Implementation of the International Covenant on Economic, Social and Cultural

Rights', Anti-Slavery Society. *Human Rights and Development Working Papers* 1 (1979), 4–5.

16. ——'Resisting the Merger and Aquisition of Human Rights by Trade Law: A Reply to Petersmann' (2002) 13(4) *European Journal of International Law* 815–44.

17. ——'Towards a Human Rights Accountability Index', *Background Papers: Human Development Report 2000* (2000).

18. ——'The United Nations' Specialised Agencies and Implementation of the International Covenant on Economic, Social and Cultural Rights' (1979) 18 *Columbia Journal of Transnational Law* 79–118.

19.——'What's in a Name: Does it Really Matter if Development Policies Refer to Goals, Ideals or Human Rights?' in H Helmich, H (ed) in collab with E Borghese, *Human Rights in Development Cooperation (SIM Special No. 22)* (Utrecht, SIM (Netherlands Institute for Human Rights), 1998), 95–106.

20. Alston, P and Quinn, G, 'The Nature and Scope of States Parties' Obligations under the International Covenant on Economic, Social and Cultural Rights' (1987) 9 *Human Rights Quarterly* 156–229.

21. Alston, P, and Simma, B, 'The Sources of Human Rights Law: Custom, *Jus Cogens*, and General Principles' (1992) 12 *Australian Year Book of International Law* 82–108.

22. Altvater, E (ed), *The Poverty of Nations: A Guide to the Debt Crisis From Argentina to Zaire* (London, Zed Books, 1991).

23. Alvarez, J, 'Constitutional Interpretation in International Organisations' in I-M Coicaud and V Heiskanen (eds), *The Legitimacy of International Organisations* (New York, United Nations University Press, 2001), 104–54.

24. Amerasinghe, C, 'Interpretation of Texts in Open International Organisations' (1995) *British Yearbook of International Law* 175–209.

25. ——'Sources of International Administrative Law' in A Guiffrè (ed), *International law at the Time of its Codification: Essays in Honour of Roberto Ago* (Milan, Multa Paucis AG, 1987), 67–95.

26. ——'The Future of International Administrative Law' (1996) 45 *International and Comparative Law Quarterly* 773–95.

27. Anand, S and Kanbur, S, 'Inequality and Development: A Critique' (1993) 41(1) *Journal of Development Economics* 19.

28. Anand, S, and Sen, A, *Sustainable Human Development: Concepts and Priorities* (New York, United Nations Development Programme, Office of Development Studies, 1996).

29. Andersen, R, 'How Multilateral Development Assistance Triggered the Conflict in Rwanda' (2000) 21(3) *Third World Quarterly* 441–56.

30. Andreassen, B, and Eide, A (eds), *Human Rights in Developing Countries, 1987/88.* (Copenhagen, Akademisk Forlag, 1988).

31. Andreassen, B, and Swinehart, T (eds), *Human Rights in Developing Countries: 1990 Yearbook* (Kehl am Rhein, NP Engel Verlag, 1991).

32. ——(eds), *Human Rights in Developing Countries: Yearbook 1991* (Oslo, Scandinavian University Press, 1992).

33. ——(eds), *Human Rights in Developing Countries: Yearbook 1993* (Copenhagen, Nordic Human Rights Publication, 1993).

34. Andrews, D, Boote, A, Rizavi, S and Singh, S, *Debt Relief for Low-Income Countries: The Enhanced HIPC Initiative* (Washington, DC, International Monetary Fund, 1999).

35. Annan, K, 'Essay: Strengthening United Nations Action in the Field of Human Rights: Prospects and Priorities' (1997) 10 *Harvard Human Rights Journal* 1–10.
36. Annas, G, 'Human Rights and Health: The Universal Declaration of Human Rights at 50' (1998) 339(24) *The New England Journal of Medicine* 1778.
37. Antic, T and Walton, M, *Social Consequences of the East Asia Financial Crisis*. (Washington, DC, World Bank, 1998).
38. Apodaca, C, 'Measuring Women's Economic and Social Rights Achievement' (1998) 20(1) *Human Rights Quarterly* 139.
39. Ascher, W, ' New Development Approaches and the Adaptability of International Agencies: The Case of the World Bank' (1983) 37(3) *International Organization* 415–39.
40. Baehr, P, Hey, H, Smith, J and Swinehart, T (eds), *Human Rights in Developing Countries: Yearbook 1994* (Deventer, Kluwer Law and Taxation Publishers, 1994).
41. —— (eds), *Human Rights in Developing Countries: Yearbook 1995* (The Hague, Kluwer Law International, 1995).
42. Baily, M, 'Defining the Decent Minimum' in A Chapman (ed), *Health Care Reform: A Human Rights Approach* (Washington, DC, Georgetown University Press, 1994), 167–85.
43. —— 'Our irrelevant right to health care' (1998) 16(2) *Yale Law and Policy Review* 407.
44. Ball, N, Friedman, J and Rossiter, C, 'The Role of International Financial Institutions in Preventing and Resolving Conflict' in D Cortright (ed), *The Price of Peace: Incentives and International Conflict Prevention* (1997), 243–64.
45. Bandow, D, 'The IMF: A Record of Addiction and Failure' in D Bandow and I Vasquez (eds), *Perpetuating Poverty: The World Bank, the IMF, and the Developing World* (Washington, DC, CATO Institute, 1994), 15–36.
46. Bandow D. and I. Vásquez eds., *Perpetuating Poverty: The World Bank, the IMF and the Developing World* (Washington, DC, CATO Institute, 1994).
47. Bardhan, P, 'The Political Economy of Development Policy: An Asian Perspective' in L Emmerij (ed), *Economic and Social Development into the XXI Century* (Washington, DC, Inter-American Development Bank/The Johns Hopkins University Press, 1997), 273–87.
48. Bekhechi, M, 'Some Observations Regarding Environmental Covenants and Conditionalities in World Bank Lending Activities' *Max Planck United Nations Year Book* 3 (1999): 287.
49. Belot, I, 'The Role of the IMF and the World Bank in Rebuilding the CIS' (1995) 9 *Temple International and Comparative Law Journal* 83–113.
50. Benerji, A and Ghanem, H, 'Does the Type of Political Regime Matter for Trade and Labour Market Policies?' (1997) 11(1) *World Bank Economic Review* 171.
51. Berg, W and Thole, G, 'IMF Policies and Their Adverse Consequences for Human Rights' (1986) 3 *GDR Committee for Human Rights Bulletin* 164–74.
52. Berger, M and Beeson, M, 'Lineages of Liberalism and Miracles of Modernisation: The World Bank, the East Asian Trajectory and the International Development Debate' (1998) 19(3) *Third World Quarterly* 487–504.
53. Berger, S, 'Introduction' in S Berger and R Dore (eds), *National Diversity and Global Capitalism* (Ithaca, NY, Cornell University Press, 1996), 1–28.
54. Bergesen, H and Lunde, L, *Dinosaurs or Dynamos? The United Nations and the World Bank at the Turn of the Century* (1999).

55. Berry, A, and Stewart, F, 'Market Liberalization and Income Distribution: The Experience of the 1980s' in R Culpeper, A Berry and F Stewart (eds), *Global Development Fifty Years after Bretton Woods: Essays in Honour of Gerald K Helleiner* (New York, St Martin's Press, 1997), 211–51.

56. Beutler, L, 'The ILO and IMF: Permissibility and Desirability of a Proposal to Meet the Contemporary Realities of the International Protection of Labor Rights' (1988) 14 *Syracuse Journal of International Law and Commerce* 455–77.

57. Biersteker, T, 'Reducing the Role of the State in the Economy: A Conceptual Exploration of IMF and World Bank Prescriptions' (1990) 34 *International Studies Quarterly* 477–92.

58. Bird, G, 'Borrowing from the IMF: The Policy Implications of Recent Empirical Research' (1996) 24(11) *World Development* 1753–60.

59. —— 'Crisis Averter, Crisis Lender, Crisis Manager: The IMF in Search of a Systemic Role' (1999) 22(7) *The World Economy* 955.

60. Blake, R, 'The World Bank's Draft Comprehensive Development Framework and the Micro-Paradigm of Law and Development' (2000) 3 *Yale Human Rights and Development Law Journal* 159–89.

61. Bleicher, S, 'UN v IBRD: A Dilemma of Functionalism' (1970) 24 *International Organization* 31–47.

62. Boeninger, E, 'Governability and Equity: Key Conditions for Sustained Development' in L Emmerij (ed), *Economic and Social Development into the XXI Century* (Washington, DC, Inter-American Development Bank/The Johns Hopkins University Press, 1997).

63. —— 'Governance and Development: Issues and Constraints' in L Summers and S Shah (eds), *Proceedings of the World Bank Annual Conference on Development Economics 1991* (Washington, DC, The World Bank, 1992), 267–302.

64. Boisson de Chazournes, L, 'Policy Guidance and Compliance: The World Bank Operational Standards' in D Shelton (ed), *Commitment and Compliance: The Role of Non-Binding Norms in the International Legal System* (2000), 281–303.

65. Boisson de Chazournes L and Sands, P (eds), *International Law, the International Court of Justice and Nuclear Weapons* (Cambridge, Cambridge University Press, 1999).

66. Bollen, K, 'Political Rights and Political Liberties in Nations: An Evaluation of Human Rights Measures, 1950 to 1984' in T Jabine and R Claude (eds), *Human Rights and Statistics: Getting the Record Straight* (Philadelphia, University of Pennsylvania Press, 1992), 188–215.

67. Bradlow, D, 'Debt, Development, and Human Rights: Lessons from South Africa' (1991) 12 *Michigan Journal of International Law* 647–89.

68. —— 'Human Rights, Public Finance and the Development Process: A Critical Introduction' (1992) 8 *American University Journal of International Law and Policy* 1–18.

69. —— 'International Organizations and Private Complaints: The Case of the World Bank Inspection Panel' (1994) 34(3) *Virginia Journal of International Law* 553–613.

70. —— 'A Test Case for the World Bank' (1996) 11(2) *American University Journal of International Law and Policy* 247–94.

71. —— 'Precedent-Setting NGO Campaign Saves the World Bank's Inspection Panel' (1999) 6 *Human Rights Brief* 7–27.

72. —— 'The World Bank, the IMF, and Human Rights' (1996) 6 *Transnational Law and Contemporary Problems* 47–90.

73. Bradlow, D and Grossman, C, 'Limited Mandates and Intertwined Problems: A New Challenge for the World Bank and the IMF' (1995) 17(3) *Human Rights Quarterly* 411–42.

74. Bradlow, D and Schlemmer-Schulte, S, 'The World Bank's New Inspection Panel: A Constructive Step in the Transformation of the International Legal Order' (1994) 54(2) *Heidelberg Journal of International Law* 392–415.

75. Breman, J, 'Politics of Poverty and a Leaking Safety Net' (1999) 34(20) *Economic and Political Weekly* 1177–78.

76. Bretton Woods Project, *Policing the Policemen: The Case for an Independent Evaluation Mechanism for the IMF* (London, Bretton Woods Project, 1998).

77. Bridgeman, N, 'World Bank Reform in the "Post Policy" Era' (2001) 13 *Georgetown International Environmental Law Review* 1013–46.

78. Broches, A, 'International Legal Aspects of the Operations of the World Bank' (1959) 98 *Receuil des Cours* 304.

79. —— *Selected Essays : World Bank, ICSID and Other Subjects of Public and Private International Law* (Dordrecht, Martinus Nijhoff, 1995).

80. Brodnig, G, 'The World Bank and Human Rights: Mission Impossible?', *Carr Centre for Human Rights Policy Working Paper* T-01-05 (2001).

81. Broughton, J, 'From Suez to Tequila: The IMF as Crisis Manager' (2000) 110 *The Economic Journal* 273–91.

82. Brown, B, *The United States and the Politicization of the World Bank. Issues of International Law and Policy* (London, Kegan Paul International, 1992).

83. Browne, R, 'Alternatives to the International Monetary Fund' in J Cavanagh, D Wysham and M Arrunda (eds), *Beyond Bretton Woods: Alternatives to the Global Economic Order* (London, Pluto Press, 1994), 57–73.

84. Buergenthal, T, 'International Human Rights Law and Institutions: Accomplishments and Prospects' (1988) 63 *Washington Law Review* 1.

85. Buhl, C, *A Citizen's Guide to the Multilateral Development Banks and Indigenous Peoples* (Washington, DC, Bank Information Center, 1995).

86. Cahn, J, 'Challenging the New Imperial Authority: The World Bank and the Democratisation of Development' (1993) 6 *Harvard Human Rights Journal* 160.

87. Carley, M and Bustelo, E, *Social Impact Assessment and Monitoring: A Guide to the Literature* (Boulder, CO, Westview Press, 1984).

88. Carment, D and James, P, 'Escalation of Ethnic Conflict' (1998) 35(1) *International Politics* 65–82.

89. Carrasco, E and Ayhan Kose, M, 'Income Distribution and the Bretton Woods Institutions: Promoting an Enabling Environment for Social Development' (1996) 6 *Transnational Law and Contemporary Problems* 1–46.

90. Carreau, D, 'Le moyens de pression économique au regard du FMI, du GATT et de l'OCDE' (1984–1985) 18(1) *Belgian Review of International Law* 20–33.

91. —— 'Why Not Merge the International Monetary Fund (IMF) with the International Bank for Reconstruction and Development (World Bank)?' (1990) 62 *Fordham Law Review* 1989.

92. Caufield, C, 'Masters of Illusion: The World Bank and the Poverty of Nations' (London, Macmillan, 1996).

93. Cavanagh J, Wysham, D and Arruda, M (eds), *Beyond Bretton Woods: Alternatives to the Global Economic Order* (London, Pluto Press, 1994).

94. Cernea, M, *Involuntary Resettlement in Development Projects: Policy Guidelines in World Bank Financed Projects* (1988).

95. —— (ed), *Putting People First: Sociological Variables in Rural Development* (2nd ed) (Oxford, Oxford University Press, 1991).

96. Chandrasekhar, C, 'An Alternative to Structural Adjustment' in J Griesgraber and B Gunter (eds), *The World Bank: Lending on a Global Scale* (London, Pluto Press with Center of Concern, 1996), 38–64.

97. Chapman, A, 'Conceptualizing the right to health: a violations approach' (1998) 65(2) *Tennessee Law Review* 389.

98. —— (ed), *Health Care Reform: A Human Rights Approach* (Washington, DC, Georgetown University Press, 1994).

99. Chayes, A and Chayes, A, *The New Sovereignty: Compliance with International Regulatory Agreements* (1995).

100. —— (eds), *Preventing Conflict in the Post-Communist World: Mobilising International and Regional Organisations* (1996).

101. Chenery, H, Ahluwalia, M, Bell, C, Duloy, J and Jolly, R, *Redistribution with Growth* (New York, Oxford University Press, 1974).

102. Chossudovsky, M, *The Globalization of Poverty: Impacts of IMF and World Bank Reforms Place* (London, Zed, 1998).

103. Chua, A, 'The Paradox of Free Market Democracy: Rethinking Development Policy' (2000) 41(2) *Harvard International Law Journal* 287–379.

104. Ciorcari, J, 'The Lawful Scope of Human Rights Criteria in World Bank Credit Decisions: An Interpretive Analysis of the IBRD and IDA Articles of Agreement' (2000) 33 *Cornell International Law Journal* 331.

105. Civic, M, 'Prospects for the Respect and Promotion of Internationally Recognised Sustainable Development Practices: A Case Study of the World Bank Environmental Guidelines and Procedures' (1998) 9 *Fordham Environmental Law Review* 231–59.

106. Clark, D, 'The World Bank and Human Rights: The Need for Greater Accountability' (2002) 15 *Harvard Human Rights Journal* 205–26.

107. Claude, R, and Jabine, T, 'Exploring Human Rights Issues with Statistics' in T Jabine and R Claude (eds), *Human Rights and Statistics: Getting the Record Straight* (Philadelphia, University of Pennsylvania Press, 1992), 5–34.

108. Cleary, S, 'The World Bank and NGOs' in P Willetts (ed), *'The Conscience of the World': The Influence of Non-Governmental Organisations in the UN System* (London, Hurst & Company, 1996), 63–97.

109. Cline, W, *International Debt Re-examined* (1995).

110. Cock, J and Webster E, 'Environmental and Social Impact Assessments' in J Griesgraber and B Gunter (eds), *The World Bank: Lending on a Global Scale* (London, Pluto Press, 1996), 81–100.

111. Cogen, M, ' Human rights, prohibition of political activities and the lending-policies of World Bank and International Monetary Fund' in S Chowdbury, E Denters and P de Waart (eds), *The Right to Development in International Law* (The Netherlands, Kluwer Academic Publishers, 1992), 379.

112. Collier, P, *Aid Allocation And Poverty Reduction* (Washington, DC, World Bank, 1999).

113. ——*Consensus-Building, Knowledge and Conditionality* (Washington, DC, World Bank, 2000).
114. Collier, P and Gunning, P, 'The IMF's Role in Structural Adjustment' (1999) 109 *Economic Journal* 634–51.
115. Congressional Research Service, *Debt Reduction: Initiatives for the Most Heavily Indebted Poor Countries* (Washington, DC, US Congressional Research Service, 1999).
116. Conklin, M and Davidson, D, 'The IMF and Economic and Social Human Rights: A Case Study of Argentina, 1958–1985' (1986) 8 *Human Rights Quarterly* 227–69.
117. Coraggio, J, 'Human Capital: The World Bank's Approach to Education in Latin America' in J Cavanagh, D Wysham and M Arrunda (eds), *Beyond Bretton Woods: Alternatives to the Global Economic Order* (London, Pluto Press, 1994), 166–74.
118. Corbett J and Vines, D, 'Asian Currency and Financial Crises: Lessons from Vulnerability, Crisis and Collapse' (1999) 22(2) *The World Economy* 155–77.
119. Cornia, G, Jolly, R and Stewart, F (eds), *Adjustment with a Human Face* (Oxford, Clarendon Press, 1988).
120. Creencia, F, 'The Accountability of NGOs' (1994) 38(3) *Philippine Journal of Public Administration* 224–36.
121. Culpeper, R, *Titans or Behemoths?* (Boulder, Lynne Rienner Publishers, 1997).
122. Culpeper R, Berry A and Stewart, F (eds), *Global Development Fifty Years after Bretton Woods* (New York, St Martins Press, 1997).
123. Curran, W, 'The Constitutional Right to Health Care' (1989) 320 *New England Journal of Medicine* 789.
124. Curtis, E, 'Child Health and the International Monetary Fund' (1998) 352(9140) *Lancet* 1622–24.
125. Dahl, R, 'Can International Organisations be Democratic?' in I Shapiro and C Hacker-Cordon (eds), *Democracy's Edges* (Cambridge, Cambridge University Press, 1999), 19–36.
126. Danaher, K (ed), *50 Years is Enough: The Case against the World Bank and the International Monetary Fund* (Boston, South End Press, 1994).
127. Dankwa, E and Flinterman, C, 'Commentary by the Rapporteurs on the Nature and Scope of States Parties' Obligations' (1987) 9 *Human Rights Quarterly* 136–46.
128. Dankwa, V, Flinterman, C and Leckie, S, 'Commentary to the Maastricht Guidelines on Violations of Economic, Social and Cultural Rights' (1998) 20 *Human Rights Quarterly* 705–30.
129. Darrow, M, 'Human Rights Accountability of the World Bank and IMF: Possibilities and Limits of Logical Analysis' (forthcoming 2003) 12(1) *Social and Legal Studies* 133–44.
130. Dayton, J, *World Bank HIV/AIDS Interventions: Ex Ante and Ex Post Evaluation* (Washington, DC, World Bank, 1998).
131. de Boer, S, 'Culture and Governance in Reflections on "Good Governance"' in A de Ruijter and L van Vucht Tijssen (eds), *Cultural Dynamics in Development Processes* (The Hague, UNESCO Publishing/Netherlands Commission for UNESCO, 1995), 69–87.
132. de Kadt, F, 'How Well do Economists Serve Development Theory and Practice?' in L Emmerij (ed), *Economic and Social Development into the XXI Century* (Washington, DC, Inter-American Development Bank/Johns Hopkins University Press, 1997).

133. ——'Of Markets, Might and Mullahs: A Case for Equity, Pluralism and Tolerance in Development' (1985) 13(4) *World Development* 549–56.

134. de Vries, B, and Chandrasekhar, C, 'The World Bank's Focus on Poverty' in J Griesgraber and B Gunter (eds), *The World Bank: Lending on a Global Scale* (London, Pluto Press, 1996), 65–80.

135. de Vries, M, *The IMF in a Changing World 1945–85* (1986).

136. de Vylder, S, *Development Strategies, Macro-economic Policies and the Rights of the Child, Discussion Paper for Radda Barnen* (Sweden, Radda Barnen, 1996).

137. ——*Sustainable Human Development and Macroeconomics: Strategic Links and Implications. A UNDP Discussion Paper* (New York, UNDP, 1996).

138. ——'Macroeconomics and the Rights of the Child' in Rädda Barnen (ed), *Making the Link: A Report from the International Seminar on Macroeconomics and Childrens Rights (focusing on developing countries), Midrand, South Africa, 2–6 November 1998* (Stockholm, Rädda Barnen, 1999), 13–19.

139. Dell, S, 'The History of the IMF' (1986) 14(9) *World Development* 1203–12.

140. ——'On Being Grandmotherly: The Evolution of IMF Conditionality' (1981) 144 *Essays in International Finance* 1–38.

141. ——'The Question of Cross-Conditionality' (1988) 16(5) *World Development* 557–68.

142. ——'Stabilisation: The Political Economy of Overkill' in J Williamson (ed), *IMF Conditionality* (1983), 17–45.

143. Dell, S and Lawrence, R, 'Towards an Equitable International Adjustment Process' (1979) 1 *Trade and Development* 53–66.

144. Demetrios, J, 'Human Rights, Democracy and Development: The European Community Model' (1994) 7 *Harvard Human Rights Journal* 1.

145. Demetrius, F, Tregurtha, E and MacDonald, S, 'A Brave New World: Debt, Default and Democracy in Latin America' (1986) 28(2) *Journal of Interamerican Studies and World Affairs* 17–38.

146. Denters, E, 'IMF Conditionality: Economic, Social and Cultural Rights, and the Evolving Principle of Solidarity' in P de Waart, P Peters and E Denters (eds), *International Law and Development* (Dordrecht, Kluwer Academic Publishers, 1998).

147. ——*Law and Policy of IMF Conditionality* (The Hague, Kluwer Law International, 1996).

148. Department for International Development (UK), *Strategies for Achieving the International Development Targets: Human Rights for Poor People, Consultation paper, February 2000* (UK, DFID, 2000).

149. Department of the Treasury. *United States Participation in the Multilateral Development Banks in the 1980s* (Washington, DC, US Government Printing Office, 1982).

150. Dias, C, 'The Human Right to Participation' in UNDP (ed), *Human Development and Human Rights: Report of the Oslo Symposium (2–3 October 1998)* (New York, UNDP, 1998), 208–12.

151. Dollar, D and Kraay, A, 'Growth Is Good for the Poor', *Working Paper Series*, no 2587 (Washington, DC, World Bank, 2000).

152. Dollar, D and Pritchett, L, *Assessing Aid: What Works, What Doesn't, and Why,* (Washington, DC, World Bank, 1998).

153. Donnelly, J, 'Development Rights Trade-offs: Needs and Equality' in J Donnelly, *Universal Human Rights in Theory and Practice* (Ithaca, NY: Cornell University Press, 1989), 163–83.

154. —— 'Human Rights and Development: Complementary or Competing Concerns?' (1984) 36(2) *World Politics* 255–83.

155. —— 'Human Rights and Human Dignity: An Analytic Critique of Non-Western Conceptions of Human Rights' (1982) 76(2) *American Political Science Review* 303–16.

156. —— 'Human rights, Democracy, and Development' (1999) 21(3) *Human Rights Quarterly* 608.

157. —— 'International Human Rights and Health Care Reform' in A Chapman (ed), *Health Care Reform: A Human Rights Approach* (Washington, DC, Georgetown University Press, 1994), 124–39.

158. —— 'Non-Western Conceptions of Human Rights' in J Donnelly (ed), *Universal Human Rights in Theory and Practice* (Ithaca, NY, Cornell University Press, 1989), 49–65.

159. Dore, R, 'Convergence in Whose Interest?' in S Berger, and R Dore (eds), *National Diversity and Global Capitalism* (Ithaca, NY, Cornell University Press, 1996), 366–74.

160. Dreze, J and Sen, A, *Hunger and Public Action* (1989).

161. Dunkerton, K, 'The World Bank Inspection Panel and Its Effect on Lending Accountability to Citizens of Borrowing Nations' (1995) 5 *Journal of Environmental Law* 226–61.

162. Easton, S and Rockerbie, D, 'Does IMF Conditionality Benefit Lenders?' (1999) 135(2) *Weltwirtschaftliches Archiv* 347–57.

163. Eckaus, R, 'How the IMF Lives with Its Conditionality' (1986) 19 *Policy Sciences* 237.

164. Edwards, R, *International Monetary Collaboration* (1985).

165. —— 'The World Bank and the International Monetary Fund' (1986) 80 *Proceedings of the Annual Meetings of the American Society of International Law* 21.

166. Edwards, S, 'Structural Adjustment in Highly Indebted Countries' in J Sachs (ed), *Developing Country Debt and Economic Performance (Volume 1, The International Financial System* (1989), 159–207.

167. Eichengreen, B, *Toward a New International Financial Architecture: A Practical Post-Asia Agenda* (Washington, DC, Institute for International Economics, 1999).

168. —— 'Managing the World Economy Under the Bretton Woods System: An Overview' in P Kenen (ed), *Managing the World Economy: Fifty Years After Bretton Woods* (1994), 46–47.

169. Eichengreen, B, Tobin, J and Wyplosz, C, 'Two Cases for Sand in the Wheels of International Finance' (1995) 105 *Economic Journal* 162–72.

170. Eide, A, 'Choosing the Path to Development: National Options and International Regulations, the Impact for Human Rights' (1980) 11 *Bulletin of Peace Proposals* 349–60.

171. —— 'Realization of Social and Economic Rights and the Minimum Threshold Approach' (1989) 19(1–2) *Human Rights Law Journal* 35–51.

172. —— *The Right to Adequate Food*, E/CN.4/Sub.2/1987/23 (1987).

173. —— *Right to Adequate Food as a Human Right*, E.89.XIV.2 (Geneva, United Nations, 1989).

174. —— *Report updating the study on the right to food* (Geneva, United Nations, 1998).

175. Eide, A, Eide, W, Goonatilake, S *et al* (eds), *Food As a Human Right* (Tokyo, United Nations University, 1984).
176. Einhorn, J, 'The World Bank's Mission Creep' (2001) 80(5) *Foreign Affairs* 22–35.
177. Elahi, M, ' The Impact of Financial Institutions on the Realization of Human Rights: Case Study of the International Monetary Fund in Chile' (1986) 6 *Boston College Third World Law Journal* 143–60.
178. Elson, D, 'Economic Paradigms Old and New: The Case of Human Development' in R Culpeper, A Berry and F Stewart (eds), *Global Development Fifty Years after Bretton Woods: Essays in Honour of Gerald K. Helleiner* (New York, St Martin's Press, 1997), 50–71.
179. Ely Yamin, A, 'Defining Questions: Situating Issues of Power in the Formation of a Right to Health under International Law' (1996) 18(2) *Human Rights Quarterly* 398–438.
180. —— 'Reflections on Defining, Understanding and Measuring Poverty in Terms of Violations of Economic and Social Rights under International Law' (1997) 4(2) *Georgetown Journal on Fighting Poverty* 273–307.
181. Emmerij, L, 'A Critical Review of the World Bank's Approach to Social-Sector Lending and Poverty Alleviation' in UNCTAD, *International Monetary and Financial Issues for the 1990s* (New York, United Nations, 1995).
182. —— 'Development Thinking and Practice: Introductory Essay and Policy Conclusions' in L Emmerij (ed), *Economic and Social Development into the XXI Century* (1997).
183. —— (ed), *Economic and Social Development into the XXI Century* (1997).
184. —— 'The Social Question and the Inter-American Development Bank' in O Stokke (ed), *Foreign Aid towards the Year 2000: Experiences and Challenges* (London, Frank Cass & Co. Ltd., 1996), 309–32.
185. Engel, S, ' "Living" International Constitutions and the World Court (The Subsequent Practice of International Organs Under Their Constituent Instruments)' (1967) 16 *International and Comparative Law Quarterly* 865.
186. Escuder, C, *Involuntary Resettlement in Bank-Assisted Projects: An Introduction to Legal Issues* (Washington, DC, Legal Department, World Bank, 1988).
187. Eshag, E, 'Some Suggestions for Improving the Operation of IMF Stabilisation Programmes' (1989) 128(3) *International Labour Review* 297–320.
188. Espiell, H, 'Universality of Human Rights and Cultural Diversity' (1998) 50(4) *International Social Science Journal* 525.
189. Evans, H, ' Debt Relief for the Poorest Countries: Why Did It Take So Long?' (1999) 17(3) *Development Policy Review* 267–79.
190. Falk, R, 'Cultural Foundations for the International Protection of Human Rights' in A An-Na'im (ed), *Human Rights in Cross-Cultural Perspectives: A Quest for Consensus* (Philadelphia, University of Pennsylvania Press, 1992), 44–64.
191. FAO, *The Right To Food: in Theory And Practice* (Rome, FAO, 1998).
192. Fassbender, B, 'The United Nations Charter As Constitution of the International Community' (1998) 36 *Columbia Journal of Transnational Law* 529–619.
193. Fatouros, A, 'Comments on International Law and Economic Development' in *Sixtieth Annual Meeting of the American Society of International Law, First Session*, 18–28 (Washington, DC, American Society of International Law, 1966).
194. —— 'The World Bank's Impact on International Law: A Case Study in the International Law of Cooperation' in G Wilner (ed), *Jus et Societas: Essays in*

Tribute to Wolfgang Friedmann (The Hague, Martinus Nijhoff Publishers, 1979), 62–95.

195. Fawcett, J, 'Détournement de Pouvoir by International Organisations' (1957) 33 *British Yearbook of International Law* 311.

196. —— 'The Place of Law in an International Organisation' (1960) 36 *British Yearbook of International Law* 321.

197. Feeney, P, *Accountable Aid: Local Participation in Major Projects* (Oxford, Oxfam GB, 1998).

198. Feldstein, M, 'Refocusing the IMF' (1998) 77(2) *Foreign Affairs* 20.

199. —— 'A Self-Help Guide for Emerging Markets' (1999) 78(2) *Foreign Affairs* 93–109.

200. Felice, W, 'Militarism and Human Rights' (1998) 74(1) *International Affairs* 25–40.

201. Felice, W, 'The Viability Of The United Nations Approach To Economic And Social Human Rights in a Globalized Economy' (1999) 75(3) *International Affairs* 563.

202. Ferrer, A, 'Development and Underdevelopment in a Globalized World: Latin American Dilemmas' in L Emmerij (ed), *Economic and Social Development into the XXI Century* (Washington, DC, Inter-American Development Bank/The Johns Hopkins University Press, 1997), 178–88.

203. Fine, B, 'The Developmental State is Dead—Long Live Social Capital?' (1999) 30 *Development and Change* 1–19.

204. Fischer, S, 'Response—In Defense of the IMF: Specialised Tools for a Specialised Task' (1998) 77(4) *Foreign Affairs* 103–6.

205. —— 'The IMF and the Asian Crisis,' Forum Funds Lecture at the University of California Los Angeles, 20 March 1998, http://www.imf.org/external/np/speeches/1998/032098.HTM.

206. Foreign Affairs, 'Report: The Future of the International Financial Architecture. A Council on Foreign Relations Task Force' (1999) 78(6) *Foreign Affairs* 169–84.

207. Forsythe, D (ed), *Human Rights and Development: International Views* (New York, St Martin's Press, 1989).

208. Franck, T and Hawkins, S, 'Juctice in the International System' (1989) 10 *Michigan Journal of International Law* 127–62.

209. Frenkel, R and O'Donnell, G, 'The "Stabilisation Programs" of the IMF and Their International Impacts' in R Fagan (ed), *Capitalism and the State in US-Latin American Relations* (1979), 171.

210. Frick Curry, W and Royce, J, 'Enforcing Human Rights: Congress and the Multilateral Banks', *International Policy Report* (February) (1985), 1–22.

211. Friends of the Earth, *The IMF: Selling the Environment Short* (Washington, DC, Friends of the Earth, 1999).

212. Garten, J, 'Lessons for the Next Financial Crisis' (1999) 78(2) *Foreign Affairs* 76–92.

213. Gatthi, J, 'Good Governance as a Counter Insurgency Agenda to Oppositional and Transformative Social Projects in International Law' (1999) 5 *Buffalo Human Rights Law Review* 107–74.

214. —— 'Human Rights, the World Bank and the Washington Consensus: 1949–1999' (2000) 94 *American Society of International Law Proceedings* 144.

215. Gavin, M and Rodrik, D, 'The World Bank in Historical Perspective' (1995) 85(2) *American Economic Review, Papers and Proceedings* 329–34.

216. Gellner, E, *Relativism and the Social Sciences* (Cambridge, Cambridge University Press, 1985).

217. George, S, 'The World Bank and its Concept of Good Governance' in J Hippler (ed), *The Democratisation of Disempowerment: The Problem of Democracy in the Third World* (London, Pluto Press, 1995), 205–9.

218. George, S, and Sabelli, F, *Faith and Credit: The World Bank's Secular Empire* (Boulder, CO, Westview Press, 1994).

219. Gerster, R, 'A New Framework of Accountability for the IMF' in J Cavanagh, D Wysham and M Arrunda (eds), *Beyond Bretton Woods: Alternatives to the Global Economic Order* (London, Pluto Press, 1994), 94–108.

220. Gewirth, A, 'The Right to Economic Democracy' in A Gewirth, *The Community of Rights* (Chicago, University of Chicago Press, 1996), 257–310.

221. Ghai, D, *Social Development and Public Policy: Some Lessons from Successful Experiences* (United Nations Research Institute for Social Development, 1997).

222. Ghai, D and Hewitt de Alcantara, C, *Globalization and Social Integration: Patterns and Processes* (1994).

223. Ghai, D (ed), *The IMF and the South: The Social Impact of Crisis and Adjustment* (1991).

224. Ghai, Y, *Human Rights and Social Development: Towards Democratisation and Social Justice. Paper prepared for UNRISD as part of its review of Copenhagen (World Social Summit, 1995) +5* (2000).

225. Gianviti, F, 'Economic, Social and Cultural Rights and the International Monetary Fund (30 May 2001, unpublished paper on file with author).

226. Gibbon, P, 'The World Bank and African Poverty, 1973–91' (1992) 30(2) *Journal of Modern African Studies* 193–220.

227. —— 'The World Bank and the New Politics of Aid' (1993) 5(1) *European Journal of Development Research* 35–62.

228. Gilbert, C and Vines, D (eds), *The World Bank: Structure and Policies* (Cambridge, UK, Cambridge University Press, 2000).

229. Gilbert, C, Powell, A and Vines, D, 'Positioning the World Bank' (1999) 109 *Economic Journal* 598–633.

230. Gillies, D, 'Human Rights, Democracy and Good Governance' in J Griesgraber and B Gunter (eds), *The World Bank: Lending on a Global Scale* (London, Pluto Press, 1996), 101–41.

231. —— *Human Rights, Democracy, and 'Good Governance': Stretching the World Bank's Policy Frontiers* (Ottawa, International Centre for Human Rights and Democratic Development, 1994).

232. —— 'Human Rights, Governance, and Democracy: The World Bank's Problem Frontiers' (1993) 1 *Netherlands Quarterly of Human Rights* 3–24.

233. Gilles, D and Dias, C, *Human Rights, Democracy and Development* (Geneva, United Nations Centre for Human Rights, 1992).

234. Gold, J, 'Certain Aspects of the Law and Practice of the International Monetary Fund' in S Schwebel (ed), *The Effectiveness of International Decisions* (Leyden, AW Sijthoff, 1971), 71–99.

235. —— 'Conditionality' (1979) 31 *IMF Pamphlet Series*.

236. —— *Interpretation: The IMF and International Law* (The Hague, Kluwer, 1996).

237. —— *Legal and Institutional Aspects of the International Monetary System: Selected Essays* (Washington, DC, IMF, 1979).

238. ——*Legal and Institutional Aspects of the International Monetary System. Selected Essays: Volume II* (Washington, DC, IMF, 1984).

239. —— 'Natural Disasters and Other Emergencies Beyond Control: Assistance by the IMF' (1990) 24(3) *The International Lawyer* 621.

240. —— 'Political Considerations are Prohibited by IMF When the Fund Considers Requests for Use of Resources' (1983) *IMF Survey* 146.

241. ——*The Rule of Law in the International Monetary Fund* (Washington, DC, IMF, 1980).

242. —— 'Symmetry as a Legal Objective of the International Monetary System' (1980) 12 *New York University Journal of International Law and Politics* 423–77.

243. —— ' "[T]o Contribute Thereby to Development": Aspects of the Relations of the International Monetary Fund with its Developing Members' (1991) 10 *Columbia Journal of Transnational Law* 267.

244. —— 'Use of the International Monetary Fund's Resources: "Conditionality" and "Unconditionality" as Legal Categories' (1971) 6 *Journal of International Law and Economics* 1.

245. —— 'Weighted Voting Power: Some Limits and Some Problems' (1974) 68 *American Journal of International Law* 687–89.

246. Goldsmith, A, 'Democracy, Property Rights and Economic Growth' (1995) 32(2) *Journal of Development Studies* 157–74.

247. Goldstein, M and Montiel, P, 'Evaluating Fund Stabilisation Programs with Multicountry Data: Some Methodological Pitfalls' (1986) 44 *IMF Staff Papers* 2.

248. Goldstein, R, 'The Limitations of Using Quantitative Data in Studying Human Rights Abuses' in T Jabine and R Claude (eds), *Human Rights and Statistics: Getting the Record Straight* (Philadelphia, University of Pennsylvania Press, 1992), 35–61.

249. Gómez, A and Meacham, D (eds), *A Human Rights Perspective: Women, Vulnerability and HIV/AIDS* (Santiago, Latin American and Caribbean Women's Health Network, 1998).

250. Goodin, R, 'The Development-Rights Trade-off: Some Unwarranted Economic and Political Assumptions' (1979) 1(2) *Universal Human Rights* 31–42.

251. Gostin, L, 'Tribute to Jonathan Mann: Health and Human Rights in the AIDS Pandemic' (1998) 26(3) *The Journal of Law, Medicine & Ethics* 256.

252. Gostin, L and Mann, J, 'Towards the Development of Human Rights Impact Assessment for the Formulation and Evaluation of Health Policies' (1994) 1(1) *Health and Human Rights*.

253. Gould-Davies, N and Woods, N, 'Russia and the IMF' (1999) 75(1) *International Affairs* 1–22.

254. Greenwood, C, 'Customary Law Status of the 1977 Additional Protocols' in A Delissen and G Tanja (eds), *Humanitarian Law of Armed Conflict: Challenges Ahead* (Dordrecht, Martinus Nijhoff Publishers, 1991), 93–114.

255. Griesgraber, J (ed), *Rethinking Bretton Woods: Towards Equitable, Sustainable and Participatory Development, Conference Report and Recommendations* (London/ Easthaven, Conn., Pluto Press, with Center of Concern, Washington, DC, 1996).

256. Griesgraber, J and Gunter, B (eds), *Development: New Paradigms and Principles for the Twenty-first Century* (London, Pluto Press, 1996).

257. —— (eds), *Promoting Development Effective Global Institutions for the Twenty-first Century: Rethinking Bretton Woods* (London, Pluto Press, 1995).

258. —— (eds), *The World Bank: Lending on a Global Scale* (London, Pluto Press, 1996).

259. Griffin, K, *Culture, Human Development and Economic Growth* (Geneva, United Nations Research Institute for Social Development and UNESCO, 1997), 17.

260. ——'Globalization and Development Cooperation: A Reformer's Agenda' in R Culpeper, A Berry and F Stewart (eds), *Global Development Fifty Years after Bretton Woods: Essays in Honour of Gerald K Helleiner* (New York, St Martin's Press, 1997).

261. Griffin, K and McKinley, T, *New Approaches to Development Cooperation* (New York, Office of Development Studies, United Nations Development Programme, 1996).

262. Grossman, C and Bradlow, D, 'Are We Being Propelled Towards a People-Centred Transnational Legal Order?' (1993) 9 *American University Journal of International Law and Policy* 1.

263. Ground, R, 'A Survey and Critique of IMF Adjustment Programs in Latin America' in UN Economic Commission for Latin America and the Caribbean, *Debt, Adjustment and Renegotiation in Latin America: Orthodox and Alternative Approaches* (Boulder, CO, Lynne Rienner Publishers, 1986), 101–58.

264. Guitián, M, 'Fund Conditionality: Evolution of Principles and Practices' (1981) 38 *IMF Pamphlet Series*.

265. ——'The Unique Nature of the Responsibilities of the International Monetary Fund' (1992) 46 *IMF Pamphlet Series*.

266. Gunning, J, *Rethinking Aid. Paper presented at the 12th Annual Bank Conference on Development Economics (ABCDE), World Bank, Washington, DC, 18–20 April 2000* (Washington, DC, World Bank, 2000).

267. Guyett, S, 'Environment and Lending: Lessons of the World Bank, Hope for the European Bank for Reconstruction and Development' (1992) 24 *International Law and Politics* 889–955.

268. Gwin, C, *US Relations With the World Bank, 1945–92* (Washington, DC, The Brookings Institution, 1994).

269. Haas, E, *Beyond the Nation State: Functionalism and International Organisation* (1964).

270. Hadda, W, Carnoy, M, Rinaldi, R and Regel, O, *Education and Development: Evidence for New Priorites* (1990).

271. Haeuber, R, 'The World Bank and Environmental Assessment: The Role of NonGovernmental Organizations' (1992) 12 *Environmental Impact Assessment Review* 331–47.

272. Haggard, S, 'The Politics of Adjustment: Lessons from the IMF's Extended Fund Facility' (1985) 39(3) *International Organization* 505–34.

273. Haggard, S and Kaufman, R, 'Economic Adjustment and the Prospects for Democracy' in S Haggard and R Kaufman (eds), *The Politics of Economic Adjustment: International Constraints, Distributive Conflicts, and the State* (Princeton, NJ, Princeton University Press, 1992), 319–250.

274. ——'The Politics of Stabilization and Structural Adjustment' in J Sachs (ed), *Developing Country Debt and Economic Performance* (Chicago, University of Chicago Press, 1989), 209–54.

275. Haggard, S and Mo, J, 'The Political Economy of the Korean Financial Crisis' (2000) 7(2) *Review of International Political Economy* 197–218.

276. Halverson, K, 'Privatisation in the Yugoslav Republics' (1991) 25(6) *Journal of World Trade* 65–66.

277. Hammarberg, T, 'Searching the truth: the need to monitor human rights with relevant and reliable means', *Statistics, Development and Human Rights,' Conference organised by the International Association for Official Statistics, Montreux, Switzerland, September 2000.*

278. Hancock, G, *The Lords of Poverty* (New York, Atlantic Monthly Press, 1989).

279. Handl, G, 'The Legal Mandate of Multilateral Development Banks As Agents for Change Towards Sustainable Development' 92 *American Journal of International Law* 642.

280. Harper, C, *Globalisation and Children's Well-being: Frameworks for Understanding (Background Paper 1: 'Globalisation, Social Development and Child Rights'—A Project for UNICEF* (London, Overseas Development Institute, 1999).

281. —— 'The Social Impacts of Economic Policies: The Experience of Transitional Countries' in Rädda Barnen (ed), *Making the Link: A Report from the International Seminar on Macroeconomics and Childrens Rights (focusing on developing countries), Midrand, South Africa, 2–6 November 1998* (Stockholm, Rädda Barnen, 1999), 35–54.

282. Head, J, 'Lessons from the Asian Financial Crisis: The Role of the IMF and the United States' (1998) 7(2) *Kansas Journal of Law and Public Policy* 70–99.

283. Helleiner, G, Cornia, G and Jolly, R, 'IMF Adjustment Policies and Approaches and the Needs of Children' (1991) 19(12) *World Development* 1823–34.

284. Heller, P, Bovenberg, A, Catsambas, T, Chu, K and Shome, P, *The Implications of Fund-Supported Adjustment Programs for Poverty: Experiences in Selected Countries* (1988).

285. Hernandez Uriz, G, 'To Lend or Not to Lend: Oil, Human Rights, and the World Bank's Internal Contradictions' (2001) 14 *Harvard Human Rights Journal* 197–231.

286. Hewlett, S, 'Human Rights and Economic Realities in Developing Nations' in T Farer (ed), *The Future of the Inter-American System* (New York, Praeger Publishers, 1979), 83–118.

287. Hexner, E, 'Interpretation by Public International Organisations of their Basic Documents' (1959) *American Journal of International Law* 341.

288. —— 'Human Rights and Economic Realities: Tradeoffs in Historical Perspectives' (1979) 94(3) *Political Science Quarterly* 453–73.

289. Hippler, J (ed), *The Democratisation of Disempowerment: The Problem of Democracy in the Third World* (1995).

290. Horsefield, J, *The International Monetary Fund 1945–1965* (1969).

291. Horta, K, 'Rhetoric and Reality: Human Rights and the World Bank' (2002) 15 *Harvard Human Rights Journal* 227–43.

292. House of Commons (United Kingdom) Select Committee on Treasury, *Third Report: The International Monetary Fund* (London, House of Commons (United Kingdom), 2000).

293. Howard, R, 'The Full-Belly Thesis: Should Economic, Social and Cultural Rights Take Priority over Civil and Political Rights?, Evidence from Sub-Saharan Africa' (1983) 4 *Human Rights Quarterly* 467.

294. Howard, R and Donnelly, J, 'Introduction' in J Donnelly and R Howard (eds), *International Handbook of Human Rights* (Westport, CT, Greenwood Press, 1987), 1–28.

295. Howse, R, 'Human Rights in the WTO: Whose Rights? What Humanity? Comment on Petersmann (2002) 13(3) *European Journal of International Law* 651–60.

296. Human Rights Council of Australia, *The Rights Way to Development: A Human Rights Approach to Development Assistance* (1995).

297. Human Rights Watch, *The International Monetary Fund's Staff Monitoring Program for Angola: The Human Rights Implications. A Backgrounder by Human Rights Watch* (New York, Human Rights Watch, 2000).

298. —— *The Need for Human Rights Benchmarks: A Human Rights Watch and Afronet Memorandum* (New York, Human Rights Watch, 2000).

299. —— 'The Relationship of Political and Civil Rights to Survival, Subsistence and Poverty', *Human Rights Watch* (September) (1992).

300. Hunt, P, 'State Obligations, Indicators, Benchmarks, and the Right to Education' (1998) 4 *Human Rights Law and Practice* 109.

301. Hurrell, A, 'International Relations and the Promotion of Democracy and Human Rights' in *The Third World after the Cold War, Ideology, Economic Development and Politics: Queen Elizabeth House Conference* (Oxford, Queen Elizabeth House, University of Oxford, 1995).

302. Hurrell, A and Woods, N (eds), *Inequality, Globalization, and World Politics* (New York, Oxford University Press, 1999).

303. Imbert, P, 'Rights of the Poor, Poor Rights?: Reflections on Economic, Social and Cultural Rights' (1995) 55 *Review of the International Commission of Jurists* 85–98.

304. IMF, *Concluding Remarks by the Chairman of the IMF's Executive Board—Poverty Reduction Strategy Papers—Operational Issues and Poverty Reduction and Growth Facility—Operational Issues (Executive Board Meeting 99/136, 21 December 1999), 27 December 1999* (Washington, DC, IMF, 1999).

305. —— 'Debate on Equity Invites Diverse Perspectives, Generates Pragmatic Prescriptions' (1998) 27(12) *IMF Survey* 189.

306. —— *External Evaluation of Surveillance: Report* (Washington, DC, IMF, 1999).

307. —— *External Evaluation of the ESAF: Report by a Group of Independent Experts* (Washington, DC, IMF, 1998).

308. —— *HIPC Initiative Strengthening the Link Between Debt Relief and Poverty Reduction* (Washington, DC, IMF, 1999).

309. —— *The IMF and the Poor* (Washington, DC, IMF, 1998).

310. —— *The IMF's Poverty Reduction and Growth Facility* (Washington, DC, IMF, 2000).

311. —— *Issues Paper: IMF Conference on 'Economic Policy and Equity,' Prepared by the Expenditure Policy Division of the IMF for the Conference on Economic Policy and Equity, 8–9 June 1998, Washington, DC* (Washington, DC, IMF, 1998).

312. —— *The Poverty Reduction and Growth Facility (PRGF)—Operational Issues* (Washington, DC, IMF, 1999).

313. —— *Press Release No. 00/27, 10 April 2000: 'IMF Established Independent Evaluation Office'* (Washington, DC, IMF, 2000).

314. —— *Press Release No. 00/48, 16 August 2000: 'IMF Executive Board Establishes Code of Conduct'* (Washington, DC, IMF, 2000).

315. —— 'Remarks by Aninat: International community collaborates on design of policies to promote poverty reduction' (2000) 29(13) *IMF Survey* 211–12.

316. —— *Report of the Acting Managing Director of the International Monetary and Financial Committee on Progress in Reforming the IMF and Strengthening the Architecture of the International Financial System* (Washington, DC, IMF, 2000).

317. —— *The Role of the IMF in Governance Issues: Guidance Note (Approved by the Executive Board, 25 July 1997)* (Washington, DC, IMF, 1997).
318. ——'Social Dimensions of the IMF's Policy Dialogue' (1995) 47 *IMF Pamphlet Series*.
319. —— *Social Policy Issues in IMF-Supported Programs: Follow-up on the 1995 World Summit for Social Development* (Washington, DC, IMF, 2000).
320. —— 'Vienna address: Sugisaki reviews issues and reforms that have absorbed the IMF over past 15 years' (2000) 29(13) *IMF Survey* 215–16.
321. —— 'Women 2000: IMF support aims to enhance participation by women in social and economic development' (2000) 29(12) *IMF Survey* 202.
322. IMF and International Development Association, *Poverty Reduction Strategy Papers—Status and Next Steps (Prepared by the Staffs of the IMF and World Bank, approved by Jack Boorman and Masood Ahmed, 19 November 1999)* (Washington, DC, IMF and International Development Association, 1999).
323. Institute for Development Studies, *Poverty Reduction Strategies: A Part for the Poor?* (UK, Institute for Development Studies, 2000).
324. Isham J, Kaufmann, D and Pritchett, L, *Governance and Returns on Investment: An Empirical Investigation* (Washington, DC, World Bank, 1995).
325. ——'Civil Liberties, Democracy, and the Performance of Government Projects' (1997) 11(2) *World Bank Economic Review* 219.
326. Jabine, T, 'Indicators for Monitoring Access to Basic Health Care as a Human Right' in A Chapman (ed), *Health Care Reform: A Human Rights Approach* (Washington, DC, Georgetown University Press, 1994), 233–60.
327. Jackson, J, 'Measuring Human Rights and Development by One Yardstick' (1985) 15 *California Western International Law Journal* 453.
328. Jardine, M, 'East Timor, the United Nations, and the International Community: Force Feeding Human Rights into the Institutionalised Jaws of Failure' (2000) 12(1) *Pacifica Review: Peace, Security and Global Change* 47–62.
329. Jayasuriya, D (ed), *HIV Law, Ethics and Human Rights: Text and Materials* (New Delhi, UNDP, 1995).
330. Jenkins, R and Goetz, A, 'Accounts and Accountability: Theoretical Implications of the Right-to-Information Movement in India' (1999) 20(3) *Third World Quarterly* 603–22.
331. Jha, R and Saggar, M, 'Towards a More Rational IMF Quota Structure: Suggestions for the Creation of a New International Financial Architecture' (2000) 31 *Development and Change* 579–604.
332. Johnson, B and Schaefer, B, *The International Monetary Fund: Outdated, Ineffective, and Unnecessary* (Washington, DC, The Heritage Foundation, 1997).
333. Johnson, O and Salop, J, *Distributional Aspects of Stabilization Programs in Developing Countries* (1980).
334. Johnston, T and Melcher, N, *A New Agenda for Social Development: Recommendations for the 1995 World Summit on Social Development* (1994).
335. Johnstone, I, 'Treaty Interpretation: The Authority of Interpretative Communities' (1991) 12 *Michegan Journal of International Law* 418.
336. Jolly, R, 'Adjustment with a Human Face: A UNICEF Record and Perspective on the 1980s' (1991) 19(12) *World Development* 1807–21.
337. ——'The Myth of Declining Aid' in R Culpeper, A Berry and F Stewart (eds), *Global Development Fifty Years after Bretton Woods: Essays in Honour of Gerald K. Helleiner* (New York, St Martin's Press, 1997), 121–36.

338. Jones, P, *World Bank Financing of Education: Lending, Learning and Development* (London, Routledge, 1992).

339. Jones, R, 'The Consequences of International Interdependence and Globalisation' in R Jones (ed), *Globalisation and Interdependence in the International Political Economy: Rhetoric and Reality* (London, Pinter Publishers, 1995), 199–216.

340. —— 'The Future of International Interdependence and Globalisation' in R Jones (ed), *Globalisation and Interdependence in the International Political Economy: Rhetoric and Reality* (London, Pinter Publishers, 1995), 219–28.

341. Jones, T, 'The Right to Participation' in UNDP (ed), *Human Development and Human Rights: Report of the Oslo Symposium (2–3 October 1998)* (New York, UNDP, 1998), 213–21.

342. Joshi, A and Moore, M, *The Mobilising Potential of Anti-Poverty Programmes* (UK, Institute for Development Studies, 2000).

343. Kahler, M, 'External Influence, Conditionality, and the Politics of Adjustment' in S Haggard and R Kaufman (eds), *The Politics of Economic Adjustment: International Constraints, Distributive Conflicts, and the State* (Princeton, NJ, Princeton University Press, 1992), 89–138.

344. Kanbur, R and Vines, D, 'The World Bank and Poverty Reduction: Past, Present and Future' in C Gilbert and D Vines (eds), *The World Bank: Structure and Policies* (Cambridge, UK, Cambridge University Press, 2000), 87–107.

345. Kapur, D, 'The IMF: A Cure or a Curse?' (1998) *Foreign Policy* 111.

346. Kapurn D, Lewis, J and Webb, R (eds), *The World Bank: Its First Half Century* (Washington, DC, Brookings Institution Press, 1997).

347. Kapur, D and Webb, R, 'Governance-Related Conditionalities of the International Financial Institutions' (2000) 6 *G-24 Discussion Paper Series (UNCTAD)*.

348. Kaufman, D, Kraay, A and Zoido–Lobatón, P, 'Governance Matters: From Measurement to Action' (2000) 37(2) *Finance and Development* 10–13.

349. Kenny, K, *When Needs are Rights: An Overview of UN Efforts to Integrate Human Rights in Humanitarian Action* (Providence, RI, Thomas J Watson Jr Institute for International Studies, 2000).

350. Keohane, R, 'International Institutions: Can Interdependence Work?' (1998) Spring *Foreign Policy* 82–96.

351. Killick, T, 'Adjustment and Economic Growth' in J Broughton and K Lateef (eds), *Fifty Years After Bretton Woods: The Future of the IMF and the World Bank* (1995), 139–59.

352. —— 'Can the IMF Help Low-Income Countries? Experiences with its Structural Adjustment Facilities' (1995) 18(4) *World Economy* 603–16.

353. —— *IMF Programmes in Developing Countries: Design and Impact* (London, Routledge, 1995).

354. —— 'Kenya, the IMF, and the Unsuccessful Quest for Stabilisation' in J Williamson (ed), *IMF Conditionality* (1983), 381–413.

355. —— 'Low-Income Countries and the IMF: A Case of Structural Incompatibility?' in R Culpeper, A Berry and F Stewart (eds), *Global Development Fifty Years After Bretton Woods: Essays in Honour of Gerald K. Helleiner* (New York, St Martin's Press, 1997), 90–120.

356. Killick, T, Moazzam, M and Manuel, M, 'What Can We Know About the Effects of IMF Programmes?' (1992) 15 *World Economy* 575–97.

357. Killick, T with Malik, M, 'Country Experiences with IMF Programmes in the 1980s' (1992) 5 *World Economy* 599–632.

358. Kim, JY *et al* (eds), *Dying for Growth: Global Inequality and the Health of the Poor* 87 (2000).

359. Kindt, J, 'Providing for Environmental Safeguards in the Development Loans Given by the World Bank Group to the Developing Countries' (1975) 5 *Georgia Journal of International and Comparative Law* 540–57.

360. Kingsbury, B, 'Operational Policies of International Institutions as Part of the Law-Making Process: The World Bank and Indigenous Peoples' in G Goodwin-Gill and S Talmon (eds), *The Reality of International Law: Essays in Honour of Ian Brownlie* (Oxford,: Clarendon Press, 1999), 323–42.

361. ——'Sovereignty and Inequality' in A Hurrell and N Woods (eds), *Inequality, Globalization and World Politics* (New York, Oxford University Press, 1999), 66–94.

362. Kirkland, A, 'Female Genital Mutilation and the United States Vote at International Financial Institutions' (1999) 20 *Womens Rights Law Reporter* 147–58.

363. Klein, P, 'La Responsabilité Des Organisations Financiers Et Les Droits De La Personne' (1999) *Revue Belge De Droit International* 97.

364. ——*La responsabilité des organisations internationales dans les ordres juridiques internes et en droit des gens* (1998).

365. Kneller, R, 'Human Rights, Politics, and the Multilateral Development Banks' (1980) 6 *Yale Studies in World Public Order* 361–426.

366. Köchler, H (ed), *Economic sanctions and development* (Vienna, International Progress Organization, 1999).

367. Kolk, A, *Forests in International Environmental Politics: International Organisations, NGOs and the Brazilian Amazon* (1996).

368. Konadu Agyemang, K, 'Structural Adjustment Programs And The Perpetuating Of Poverty And Undevelepment in Africa : Ghana's Experience Revisited' (1998) 17(2/3) *Scandinavian Journal Of Development Alternatives* 127.

369. Körner, P, Maass, G, Siebold, T and Rainer, T, *The IMF and the Debt Crisis: A Guide to the Third World's Dilemmas* (1986).

370. Krasner, S, *Structural Conflict: The Third World Against Global Liberalism* (Berkeley, CA, University of California Press, 1985).

371. Krueger, A, 'The Role of Multilateral Lending Institutions in the Development Process' (1989) 7(1) *Asian Development Review* 1–20.

372. ——'Whither the World Bank and the IMF' (1996) XXXVI(4) *Journal of Economic Literature* 1983.

373. Krueger, A and Rajapatirana, S, 'The World Bank Policies Towards Trade and Trade Policy Reform' (1999) 22(6) *The World Economy* 717–40.

374. Krugman, P, 'The Return of Depression Economics' (1999) 78(1) *Foreign Affairs* 56–74.

375. Krugmann, H, 'Overcoming Africa's Crisis: Adjusting Structural Adjustment Towards Sustainable Development in Africa' in K Mengisteab and B Loban (eds), *Beyond Economic Liberalisation in Africa: Structural Adjustment and the Alternatives* (1995) 129.

376. Kumado, K, 'Conditionality: An Analysis of the Policy of Linking Development Aid to the Implementation of Human Rights Standards' (1993) 50 *Review of the International Commission of Jurists* 23–30.

377. Künnemann R, 'Violations of the Right to Food' in T van Boven, C Flinterman and I Westendorp (eds), *The Maastricht Guidelines on Vilations of Economic, Social and cultural Rights* (Utrecht, SIM, 1998).

378. Landell-Mills, P and Serageldin, I, 'Governance and External Factor' (Washington, DC, World Bank, 1992).

379. ——'Governance and the Development Process' (1991) September *Finance and Development* 14–17.

380. Lane, T, Ghosh, A, Hamann, J, Phillips, S, Schulze-Ghattas,M and Tsikata, T, *IMF-Supported Programs in Indonesia, Korea and Thailand: A Preliminary Assessment* (Washington, DC, IMF, 1999).

381. Lawyers Committee for Human Rights, *An Update to 'The World Bank: Governance and Human Rights* (New York, Lawyers Committee for Human Rights, 1995).

382. ——*The World Bank: Governance and Human Rights.* (New York, Lawyers Committee for Human Rights, 1993).

383. ——*The World Bank, NGOs and Freedom of Association: A Critique of the World Bank's Draft 'Handbook on Good Practices for Laws Relating to Non-Governmental Organisations'* (New York, Lawyers Committee for Human Rights, 1997).

384. Lawyers Committee for Human Rights, and Institute for Policy Research and Advocacy, *Human Rights and the World Bank in Indonesia: In the Name of Development* (New York, LCHR, 1995).

385. Lawyers Committee for Human Rights, and Venezuelan Program for Human Rights Education, *Halfway to Reform: The World Bank and the Venezuelan Justice System* (New York, Lawyers Committee for Human Rights, 1996).

386. Leckie, S, 'Another Step Towards Indivisibility: Identifying the Key Features of Violations of Economic, Social and Cultural Rights' (1998) 20 *Human Rights Quarterly* 81–124.

387. Leckow, R, 'The International Monetary Fund and Strengthening the Architecture of the International Monetary System' (1999) 30 *Law and Policy in International Business* 117–30.

388. Lensink, R and White, H, 'Assessing Aid: A Manifesto for Aid in the 21st Century?' (2000) 28(1) *Oxford Development Studies* 5–18.

389. Levinson, J, 'The International Financial System: A Flawed Architecture' (1999) 23(1) *The Fletcher Forum of World Affairs* 1–56.

390. Lichtenstein, C, 'Aiding the Transformation of Economies: Is the Fund's Conditionality Appropriate to the Task?' (1994) 62 *Fordham Law Review* 1943.

391. ——'Does International Human Rights Law have Something to Teach Monetary Law?' (1989) 10 *Michigan Journal of International Law* 225–30.

392. Loescher, G, 'US Human Rights Policy and International Financial Institutions' (1977) *The World Today* 453–63.

393. Lowenfeld, A, *The International Monetary System* (1984).

394. Lucas, M, 'The International Monetary Fund's Conditionality and the International Covenant on Economic, Social and Cultural Rights: An Attempt to Define the Relation' (1992) 25 *Revue Belge de Droit International* 104–35.

395. Lundy, P, 'Limitations of Quantative Research in the Study of Structural Adjustment' (1996) 42 *Soc Sci Med* 313.

396. MacDonald, E, 'Playing by the Rules: The World Bank's Failure to Adhere to

Policy in the Funding of Large-Scale Hydropower Projects' (2001) 31 *Environmental Law* 1011–49.

397. MacKay, F, 'Universal Rights or a Universe Unto Itself? Indigenous Peoples' Human Rights and the World Bank's Draft Operational Policy 4.10 on Indigenous Peoples,' (2002) 17 *American University International Law Review* 527–624.

398. Mahony, S, 'World Bank's Policies and Practice in Environmental Impact Assessment' (1995) 12 *Environmental and Planning Law Journal* 97–115.

399. Malloy, M, 'Shifting Paradigms: Institutional Roles in a Changing World' (1994) 62 *Fordham Law Review* 1911.

400. Mamorstein V., 'World Bank Power to Consider Human Rights Factors in Loan Decisions ', *Journal of International Law and Economics* Vol. 13 (1978), 113.

401. Mann, F., 'The "Interpretation" of the Constitutions of International Financial Institutions' (1968/9) 43 *British Yearbook of International Law* 1.

402. Mann, J, Gostin, L, Gruskin, S, Brennan, T, Lazzarini, Z and Fineberg, H, 'Health and Human Rights' (1994) 1 *International Journal of Health and Human Rights* 7–23.

403. Mann, J, Gruskin, S, Grodin, M and Annas, G (eds), *Health and Human Rights: A Reader* (New York, Routledge, 1999).

404. Marmorstein, V, 'World Bank Power to Consider Human Rights Factors in Loan Decisions' (1978) 13(1) *Journal of International Law and Economics* 113–36.

405. Marshall, K, *Social Dimensions of the East Asia Crisis: Some Reflections Based on Experience from the Adjustment Eras in Africa and Latin America. Paper for IDS East Asia Crisis Meeting, 13–14 July, 1998* (Washington, DC, World Bank, 1998).

406. Mason, E, and Asher, R, *The World Bank Since Bretton Woods.* Washington, DC, Brookings Institution, 1973.

407. Matheson, M, 'The Opinions of the International Court of Justice on the Threat or Use of Nuclear Weapons' (1997) 91 *American Journal of International Law* 417–35.

408. Maxwell, S, *Solutions Outside the Box: Can We Finally Implement the Human Right to Food? (Paper presented to the UNDP/UNHCHR/Government of Norway Symposium on Human Development and Human Rights, Oslo, 2–3 October 1998* (1999).

409. Mayobre, E (ed), *G-24: The Developing Countries in the International Financial System* (Boulder, Lynne Rienner, 1999).

410. McCorquodale, R and Fairbrother, R, 'Globalization and Human Rights' (1999) 21(3) *Human Rights Quarterly* 735.

411. McGee, R with Norton, A, *Participation in Poverty Reduction Strategies: A Synthesis of Experience with Participatory Approaches to Policy Design, Implementation and Monitoring* (UK, Institute for Development Studies, 2000).

412. McGillivray, M, 'The Human Development Index: Yet Another Redundant Composite Development Indicator?' (1991) 19 *World Development* 1461–68.

413. McGoldrick, D, 'Sustinable Development and Human Rights: An Integrated Conception' (1996) 45 *International and Comparative Law Quarterly* 796–818.

414. Meltzer, A, *Report of the International Financial Institutions Advisory Commission.* Meltzer Commission Report, International Financial Institutions Advisory Commission: Hearing Before the Senate Committee on Foreign Relations, 106th Congress (2000).

415. Mengisteab, K and Loban, B (eds), *Beyond Economic Liberalisation in Africa: Structural Adjustment and the Alternatives* (1995).

416. Miller-Adams, M, *The World Bank: New Agendas in a Changing World* (London, Routledge, 1999).
417. Minton-Beddoes, Z, 'Why the IMF Needs Reform' (1995) 74(3) *Foreign Affairs* 123–33.
418. Mitrany, D, *A Working Peace System: An Argument for the Functional Development of International Organisation* (1943).
419. Mokhiber, C, 'Toward a Measure of Dignity: Indicators for Rights-Based Development', *Statistics, Development and Human Rights,' Conference organised by the International Association for Official Statistics, Montreux, Switzerland, September 2000.*
420. Moller, N, 'The World Bank, Human Rights, Democracy, and Governance' (1997) 15(1) *Netherlands Quarterly of Human Rights* 21–45.
421. Monshipouri, M, *Democratisation, Liberalisation and Human Rights in the Third World* (1995).
422. —— 'Promoting Universal Human Rights: Dilemmas of Integrating Developing Countries' (2001) 4 *Yale Human Rights and Development Law Journal* 25–61.
423. —— 'State Prerogatives, Civil Society, and Liberalisation: The Paradoxes of the Late Twentieth Century in the Third World' (1997) 11 *Ethics and International Affairs* 240.
424. Morais, H, 'A Festschrift Honoring Professor Louis B Sohn (April 8, 2000): The Globalisation of Human Rights Law and the Role of International Financial Institutions in Promoting Human Rights' (2000) 33 *George Washington International Law Review* 71–96.
425. —— 'The Bretton Woods Institutions: Coping With Crisis' (1996) 90 *American Society of International Law Proceedings* 433.
426. Moris, H, 'The World Bank and Human Rights: Indispensable Partnership Or Mismatched Alliance?' (1997) 4(1) *Ilsa Journal of International and Comparative Law* 173.
427. Morley, S, 'Structural Adjustment and the Determinants of Poverty in Latin America' in N Lustig (ed), *Coping with Austerity: Poverty and Inequality in Latin America* (Washington, DC, The Brookings Institution, 1995), 42–70.
428. Morse, B, and Berger, T, *Sardar Sarovar: The Report of the Independent Review.* (Ottawa, Resources Futures International, 1992).
429. Morton, J, *The Poverty of Nations: The Aid Dilemma at the Heart of Africa* (London, IB Taurus Publishers, 1994).
430. Moser, C and Norton, A, *To Claim our Rights: Livelihood Security, Human Rights and Sustainable Development* (London, Overseas Development Institute, 2001).
431. Mosley, P, 'The World Bank's Changing Views' in P Mosley, J Harrigan and J Toye (eds), *Aid and Power: The World Bank and Policy-Based Lending* (London, Routledge, 1991).
432. Mosley, P, Harrigan, J and Toye, J (eds), *Aid and Power: The World Bank and Policy-Based Lending* (London, Routledge, 1991).
433. Mukhopadhyay, S (ed), *Women's Health, Public Policy, and Community Action* (New Delhi, Manohar Publishers, 1998).
434. Mussa, M, 'Argentina and the Fund: From Triumph to Tragedy' (2002) 67 *Policy Analyses in International Economics* (Institute for International Economics.
435. Myers, R (ed), *The Political Morality of the International Monetary Fund* (New York, Transaction Books, 1987).

436. Myrdal, G, *Against the Stream: Critical Essays on Economics* (1975).

437. Naim, M, 'Fads and Fashion in Economic Reforms: Washington Consensus or Washington Confusion?' (2000) 21(3) *Third World Quarterly* 505–28.

438. Nanda, V, 'Human Rights and Environmental Considerations in the Lending Policies of International Development Agencies: An Introduction' (1988) 17(1) *Denver Journal of International Law and Policy* 29–37.

439. Nanda, V, Shepherd, G and McCarthy-Arnold, E, *World Debt and the Human Condition: Structural Adjustment and the Right to Development* (Westport, CT, Greenwood Press, 1993).

440. Narayan, D (ed), *Empowerment and Poverty Reduction: A Sourcebook* (Washington, DC, World Bank, 2002).

441. Narayan, D, Chambers, R, Shah, M and Petesch, P (eds), *Voices of the Poor: Crying Out for Change* (Washington, DC, World Bank, 2002).

442. Narayan, D and Petesch, P (eds), *Voices of the Poor: From Many Lands* (Washington, DC, World Bank, 2002).

443. Narveson, J, 'Democracy and Economic Rights' in P Frankel, E Frankel, F Miller and J Paul (eds), *Economic Rights* (Cambridge, Cambridge University Press, 1992), 29–61.

444. Ndulu, B, 'International Governance and Implications for Development Policy in Sub-Saharan Africa: A Review of Experience and Perspectives for the Future' in R Culpeper, A Berry and F Stewart (eds), *Global Development Fifty Years after Bretton Woods: Essays in Honour of Gerald K Helleiner* (New York, St Martin's Press, 1997), 330–55.

445. Nelson, J, 'Poverty, Equity, and the Politics of Adjustment' in S Haggard and R Kaufman (eds), *The Politics of Economic Adjustment: International Constraints, Distributive Conflicts, and the State* (Princeton, NJ, Princeton University Press, 1992), 221–69.

446. —— 'Promoting Policy Reforms: The Twilight of Conditionality?' (1996) 24(9) *World Development* 1551–59.

447. Nelson, P, *The World Bank and Non-Governmental Organizations: The Limits of Apolitical Development* (London and New York, Macmillan Press and St Martin's, 1995).

448. Netherlands Institute of Human Rights, *The Right to Food: From Soft to Hard Law: Report of the International Conference organized by the Netherlands Institute of Human Rights (SIM) in cooperation with the Norwegian Human Rights Project and the Christian Michelsen Institute, Norway, from 6–9 June 1984* (Utrecht, Netherlands Institute of Human Rights, 1984).

449. NGO Working Group on the World Bank, *The Implications of Loan/ Aid Resumption for Poverty Eradication and Citizens Participation in Kenya: Analysis and Recommendations* (Kenya, NGO Working Group on the World Bank, 2000).

450. Nigam, A and Raheed, S, 'Financing of Fresh Water for All: A Rights Based Approach', *UNICEF Staff Working Papers, Evaluation, Policy and Planning Series*, No. EPP-EVL-98-003 (1998).

451. Nixson, F and Walters, B, 'The Asian Crisis: Causes and Consequences' (1999) 67(5) *The Manchester School* 496–523.

452. Norton, A, *Globalisation: Linkages to the Rights and Well-being on Children and Challenges to Social Policy (Background Paper 3: 'Globalisation, Social*

Development and Child Rights'—A Project for UNICEF) (London, Overseas Development Institute, 1999).

453. Nowak, M and Swinehart, T (eds), *Human Rights in Developing Countries: 1989 Yearbook* (Kehl am Rhein, NP Engel Verlag, 1989).

454. Nurick, L, 'Certain Aspects of the Law and Practice of the International Bank for Reconstruction and Development' in S Schwebel (ed), *The Effectiveness of International Decisions* (Leyden, AW Sijthoff, 1971), 100–28.

455. Nyamu, C, 'How Should Human Rights and Development Respond to Cultural Legitimisation of Gender Hierarchy in Developing Countries?' (2000) 41(2) *Harvard International Law Journal* 381–418.

456. O'Malley, B, *Justice, Human Rights and the World Bank: An Examination of the Allocation of Health Resources in Developing Countries* (1998).

457. OECD, *DAC Scoping Study of Donor Poverty Reduction Policies and Practices* (Paris, Organisation for Economic Co-operation and Development, 1999).

458. ——*Measuring Social Well-Being: A Progress Report on the Development of Social Indicators* (Paris, Organisation for Economic Co-operation and Development, 1976).

459. ——'Sustainable Development: Policy Statement' (1992) 22(1) *Environmental Policy and Law* 56–57.

460. Oloka-Onyango, J, 'Poverty, Human Rights, and the Quest for Sustainable Human Development in Structurally-Adjusted Uganda' (2000) 18(1) *Netherlands Quarterly of Human Rights* 23–44.

461. Orentlicher, D, 'Separation Anxiety: International Responses to Ethno-Separatist Claims' (1998) 23(1) *Yale Journal of International Law* 1–78.

462. Orford, A, 'Contesting Globalization: A Feminist Perspective on the Future of Human Rights' (1998) 8 *Transnational Law and Contemporary Problems* 171.

463. ——'Globalisation and the Right to Development' in P Alston (ed), *People's Rights* (Oxford, Oxford University Press, 2001), 127–84.

464. ——'Locating the International: Military and Monetary Interventions after the Cold War' (1997) 38 *Harvard International Law Journal* 443.

465. Orford, A and Beard, J, 'Making the State Safe for the Market: The World Bank's World Development Report 1997' (1998) 22 *Melbourne University Law Review* 195.

466. Overseas Development Council, *ODC Task Force Report: The Future Role of the IMF in Development* (Washington, DC, Overseas Development Council, 2000).

467. Owen H, 'The World Bank: Is 50 Years enough?' (1994) 73 *Foreign Affairs* 97–108.

468. Oxfam, *Development and Rights: Selected Essays from Development in Practice* (Oxford, Oxfam, 1998).

469. ——*East Asian 'Recovery' Leaves the Poor Sinking* (UK, Oxfam, 1998).

470. ——*Education Now: Break the Cycle of Poverty* (UK, Oxfam, 1999).

471. ——*From Unsustainable Debt to Poverty Reduction: Reforming the Heavily Indebted Poor Countries Initiative, prepared by OXFAM GB Policy Department for UNICEF* (New York, UNICEF, 1999).

472. ——*Growth with Equity is Good for the Poor* (Oxford, Oxfam, 2000).

473. ——*Halfway There? G–7 Must Now Make Debt Agreement Work for the Poorest* (UK, Oxfam, 1999).

474. ——*The IMF: Wrong Diagnosis, Wrong Medicine* (UK, Oxfam, 1999).

475. ——*Outcome of the IMF/World Bank September 1999 Annual Meetings: Implications for Poverty Reduction and Debt Relief* (UK, Oxfam, 1999).

476. ——*Rigged Rules and Double Standards: Trade, Globalisation and the Fight Against Poverty* (UK, Oxfam, 2002).

477. Oxfam and UNICEF, *Debt Relief and Poverty Reduction: Meeting the Challenge* (UK, Oxfam, 1999).

478. Palley, T, 'Towards a New International Economic Order' (1999) *Dissent* 48–52.

479. Panic, M, 'The Bretton Woods System: Concept and Practice' in J Michie and J Smith (eds), *Managing the Global Economy* (Oxford, Oxford University Press, 1995), 37–54.

480. Parikh, K and Srinivasanm T, 'Poverty Alleviation Policies in India: Food Consumption Subsidy, Food Production Subsidy and Employment Generation' in M Lipton and J van der Gaag (eds), *Including the Poor* (Washington, DC, World Bank, 1993).

481. Patel, R, Schafft, K, Rademacher, A and Koch-Schulte, S (eds), *Voices of the Poor: Can Anyone Hear Us?* (Washington, DC, World Bank, 2002).

482. Pattanaik, P, *Cultural Indicators of Well-being: Some Conceptual Issues* (Geneva, United Nations Research Institute for Social Development and UNESCO, 1997).

483. Paul, J, 'International Development Agencies, Human Rights, and Humane Development Projects' in I Brecher (ed), *Human Rights, Development and Foreign Policy: Canadian Perspectives* (Washington, DC, Institute for Research on Public Policy, 1993), 275–327.

484. ——'The United Nations and the Creation of an International Law of Development' (1995) 36(2) *Harvard International Law Journal* 307–28.

485. Paul, J, and Dias, C, *Promoting and Protecting Human Rights in and through Sustainable Human Development* (1996).

486. Pauly, L, 'Good Governance and Bad Policy: The Perils of International Organisational Overextension' (1999) 6(4) *Review of International Political Economy* 401–24.

487. Payer, C, *The Debt Trap: The IMF and the Third World.* (New York, Monthly Review Press, 1974).

488. ——*The World Bank: A Critical Analysis* (London, Monthly Review Press, 1982).

489. Peabody, J, 'Economic Reform and Health Sector Policy: Lessons from Structural Adjustment Programs' (1996) 43 *Soc Sci Med* 823.

490. Perry, M, 'Are Human Rights Universal? The Relativist Challenge and Related Matters' (1997) 19(3) *Human Rights Quarterly* 461.

491. Petersmann, E, 'Human Rights and International Economic Law in the 21st Century: The Need to Clarify Their Inter-relationships' (2001) *Journal of International Economic Law* 3–39.

492. ——'Time for a United Nations "Global Compact" for Integrating Human Rights into the Law of Worldwide Organisations; Lessons from European Integration (2002) 13(3) *European Journal of International Law* 621–50.

493. Petersmann, H, 'The Right to Development in the United Nations, an Opportunity for Strengthening Popular Participation in Development: Programs and Prospect' in J Jekewitz, K Klein, J Kuhne and H Petersmann (eds), *Das Menschenrecht zwischen Freiheit und Verantwortung: Festschrift für Karl Josef Partsche* (Berlin, Duncker und Humbolt, 1989), 125–40.

494. Picciotto, S and Haines, J, 'Regulating Global Financial Markets' (1999) 26(3) *Journal of Law and Society* 351–68.

495. Piddington, K, 'The Role of the World Bank' in A Hurrell and B Kingsbury (eds), *The International Politics of the Environment: Actors, Interests, and Institutions* (Oxford, Clarendon Press, 1992), 212–27.

496. Plater, Z, 'Damming the Third World: Multilateral Development Banks, Environmental Diseconomies, and International Reform Pressures on the Lending Process' (1988) 17(1) *Denver Journal of International Law and Policy* 121–53.

497. Please, S, *The Hobbled Giant: Essays on the World Bank.* (Boulder, CO, Westview Press, 1984).

498. Polak, J, 'The Changing Nature of IMF Conditionality' (1991) 184 *Essays in International Finance* 1.

499. ——*IMF Study Group Report: Transparency and Evaluation. Report and Recommendations by a Special Study Group Convened by the Center of Concern* (Washington, DC, Center of Concern, 1998).

500. —— *The World Bank and the IMF: A Changing Relationship* (1994).

501. Pollis, A, 'Cultural Relativism Revisited: Through a State Prism' (1996) 18(2) *Human Rights Quarterly* 316–44.

502. Pradhan, M, *Measuring Poverty Using Qualitative Perceptions Of Welfare* (Washington, DC, World Bank, 1998).

503. Pyatt, G, 'Measuring Welfare, Poverty and Inequality' (1987) 97 *Economic Journal* 459–67.

504. Quibria, M, 'Understanding Poverty: An Introduction to Conceptual and Measurement Issues' (1991) 9(2) *Asian Development Review* 90–112.

505. Rädda Barnen (Save the Children, Sweden), *Making the Link: A Report from the International Seminar on Macroeconomics and Childrens Rights (focusing on developing countries), Midrand, South Africa, 2–6 November 1998* (Stockholm, Rädda Barnen, 1999).

506. Rajagopal, B, 'Crossing the Rubicon: Synthesizing the Soft International Law of the IMF and Human Rights' (1993) 11 *Boston University International Law Journal* 81–107.

507. ——'Human Rights and Development', Contributing Paper Prepared for Thematic Review No. 4, World Commission on Dams (Regulation, Compliance and Implementation Options) (1999).

508. —— 'From Resistance to Renewal: The Third World, Social Movements, and the Expansion of International Institutions' (2000) 41(2) *Harvard International Law Journal* 529–78.

509. Ramcharan, B, 'The Role of the Development Concept in the UN Declaration on the Right to Development and in the UN Covenant' in P de Waart, P Peters and E Denters (eds), *International Law and Development* (Dordrecht, Martinus Nijhoff, 1988).

510. Ranis, G, 'Successes and Failures of Development Experience since the 1980s' in L Emmerij (ed), *Economic and Social Development into the XXI Century* (Washington, DC, Inter-American Development Bank and Johns Hopkins University Press, 1997), 81–98.

511. Ravallion, M, *Poverty Comparisons: A Guide to Concepts and Methods* (1992).

512. Ravallion, M and Bidani, B, 'How Robust is a Poverty Profile?' (1994) 8(1) *World Bank Economic Review* 75–102.

513. Ravallion, M and Huppi, M, 'Measuring Changes in Poverty: A Methodological Case Study of Indonesia During an Adjustment Period' (1991) 5(1) *World Bank Economic Review* 57–82.

514. Ravallion, M and Lokshin, M, *Subjective Economic Welfare* (Washington, DC, World Bank, 1999).

515. Reinicke, W, 'Can International Financial Institutions Prevent Internal Violence?: The Sources of Ethno-National Conflict in Transitional Societies' in A Chayes and A Chayes (eds), *Preventing Conflict in the Post-Communist World: Mobilizing International and Regional Organizations* (Washington, DC, The Brookings Institution, 1996), 281–338.

516. Reisman, W, 'Sovereignty and Human Rights in Contemporary International Law' in G Fox and B Roth (eds), *Democratic Governance and International Law* (Cambridge, UK, Cambridge University Press, 2000), 239.

517. —— 'Through or Despite Governments: Differentiated Responsibilities in Human Rights Programs' (1987) 72 *Iowa Law Review* 395.

518. Rich, B, *Mortgaging the Earth: The World Bank, Environmental Impoverishment, and the Crisis of Development* (Boston, Beacon Press, 1994).

519. —— 'The Multilateral Development Banks, Environmental Policy, and the United States' (1985) 12 *Ecology Law Quarterly* 681–745.

520. Ringen, S, 'Direct and Indirect Measures of Poverty' (1988) 17(3) *Journal of Social Policy* 351–65.

521. Rlik, R and van Praag, B, *Subjective Poverty Line Definitions* (Rotterdam, Erasmus University, 1989).

522. Robb, C, *Can the Poor Influence Policy? Participatory Poverty Assessments in the Developing World* (Washington, DC, World Bank, 1999).

523. Robertson, E, 'Measuring State Compliance with the Obligation to Devote the 'Maximum Available Resources' to Realizing Economic, Social and Cultural Rights' (1994) 16(4) *Human Rights Quarterly*.

524. Robicheck, E, 'The International Monetary Fund: An Arbiter in the Debt Restructuring Process' (1984) 23 *Columbia Journal of Transnational Law* 143–54.

525. Robinson, M, *Development and Human Rights: the Undeniable Nexus. Speech of Mary Robinson, United Nations High Commissioner for Human Rights (UNHCHR), Geneva, 26 June 2000.* (Geneva, United Nations, 2000).

526. —— *Constructing an International Financial, Trade and Development Architecture: the Human Rights Dimension (Swiss Federal Institute of Technology: 17th Presidential Lecture, by Mary Robinson, United Nations High Commissioner for Human Rights, Zurich, 1 July 1999)* (Geneva, United Nations, 1999).

527. —— *Human Rights: Challenges for the 21st Century. First Annual Dag Hammarskjöld Lecture by Mary Robinson, UN High Commissioner for Human Rights, Uppsala, Sweden, 1 October 1998* (1998).

528. Rodgers, G, *Overcoming Exclusion: Livelihood and Rights in Economic and Social Development* (1994).

529. Rodrik, D, 'Globalisation, Social Conflict and Economic Growth' (1998) 21(2) *The World Economy* 143–58.

530. —— 'Where Did All the Growth Go? External Shocks, Social Conflict, and Growth Collapses' (1999) 4 *Journal of Economic Growth* 385–412.

531. Roessler, T, 'The World Bank's Lending Policy and Environmental Standards' (2000) 26(1) *The North Carolina Journal of International Law and Environmental Regulation* 105–41.
532. Roos, 'The World Bank Inspection Panel' (2001) 5 *Max Planck Yearbook of United Nations Law* 475–521.
533. Ryan, C, 'Peace, Bread and Riots: Jordan and the International Monetary Fund' (1998) VI(2) *Middle East Policy* 54–66.
534. Sachs, J, 'Conditionality, Debt Relief, and the Developing Country Debt Crisis' in J Sachs (ed), *Developing Country Debt and Economic Performance, 1: The International Financial System* (Chicago, University of Chicago Press, 1989), 255–95.
535. ——'International Economics: Unlocking the Mysteries of Globalisation' (1998) *Foreign Policy* 97–111.
536. ——'Managing Global Capitalism' (1999) 32(1) *The Australian Economic Review* 3–16.
537. Sachs, J and Larrain, F, *Macroeconomics in the Global Economy* (1993).
538. Sadasivam, B, 'The Impact of Structural Adjustment on Women: A Governance and Human Rights Agenda' (1997) 19(3) *Human Rights Quarterly* 630–65.
539. Sadik, N, *The State of the World Population, 1997: The Right to Choose, Reproductive Rights and Reproductive Health* (New York, United Nations Population Fund Association, 1997).
540. Sadoulet, E and de Janvry, A, 'Poverty Alleviation, Income Distribution, and Growth during Adjustment' in N Lustig (ed), *Coping with Austerity: Poverty and Inequality in Latin America* (Washington, DC, The Brookings Institution, 1995), 101–45.
541. Salda, A, *The International Monetary Fund: A Selected Biography* (New Brunswick, NJ, Transaction Books, 1992).
542. Salvatore, D, 'The International Monetary System: Past, Present, and Future' (1994) 62 *Fordham Law Review* 1975–88.
543. Samuels, H, 'Hong Kong on Women, Asian Values, and the Law' (1999) 21(3) *Human Rights Quarterly* 707.
544. Sanford, J, 'The World Bank and Poverty: A Review of the Evidence on whether the Agency has Diminished Emphasis on Aid to the Poor' (1989) 48 *American Journal of Economics and Sociology* 151–64.
545. Sano, H, 'Development and Human Rights: The Necessary, but Partial Integration of Human Rights and Development' (2000) 22 *Human Rights Quarterly* 734–52.
546. Santos-Pais, M, *Guidelines for the Formulation of the United Nations Development Assistance Framework (UNDAF)—Which Role for the Convention on the Rights of the Child? (UNICEF policy document)* (New York, UNICEF, 1997).
547. ——'A Human Rights Approach in Development Activities and the Requirements for its Operationalisation' in UNDP ed., *Human Development and Human Rights: Report of the Oslo Symposium (2–3 October 1998)* (New York, UNDP, 1999).
548. —— *A Human Rights Conceptual Framework for UNICEF, Innocenti Essays (No. 9) (1999)* (Florence, UNICEF Innocenti Research Center, 1999).
549. Saunders, P and Whiteford, P, *Measuring Poverty, a Review of the Issues: Report Prepared for the Economic Planning Advisory Council* (1989).
550. Saxena, R and Bakshi, H, 'IMF Conditionality: A Third World Perspective' (1988) *Journal of World Trade* 67–79.

551. Schmitz, G and Gillies, D, *The Challenge of Democratic Development: Sustaining Democratization in Developing Societies* (Ottawa, North-South Institute, 1992).

552. Scott, C, 'Reaching Beyond (Without Abandoning) the Category of "Economic, Social and Cultural Rights"' (1999) 21(3) *Human Rights Quarterly* 633.

553. Scott, C and Alston, P, 'Adjudicating Constitutional Priorities in a Transnational Context: A Comment on *Soobramoney*'s Legacy and Grootboom's Promise' (2000) 16 *South African Journal of Human Rights* 206–28.

554. Selowsky, M, *Protecting Nutrition Status in Adjustment Programs: Recent World Bank Activities and Projects in Latin America* (Washington, DC, World Bank, 1991).

555. Sen, A, 'The Concept of Development' in H Chenery and T Srinivasan (eds), *Handbook of Development Economics* (Amsterdam, North-Holland, 1988).

556. ——*Development as Freedom* (New York, Alfred A Knopf, 1999).

557. ——'Development Thinking at the Beginning of the 21st Century' in L Emmerij (ed), *Economic and Social Development into the XXI Century* (Washington, DC, Inter-American Development Bank and the Johns Hopkins University Press, 1997).

558. ——'Development: Which Way Now? (1983) 93(372) *Economic Journal* 742–62.

559. ——'Human Rights and Economic Achievements' in J Baur and D Bell (eds), *The East Asian Challenge for Human Rights* (1999).

560. ——'Women's Survival as a Development Problem' (1989) 43 *Bulletin of the American Academy of Arts and Sciences*.

561. Sengupta, A, 'The Functioning of the International Monetary System: A Critique of the Perspective of the Industrial Countries' (1986) 14(9) *World Development* 1213–31.

562. ——'Realising the Right to Development' (2000) 31 *Development and Change* 553–78.

563. Senior, I, 'An Economic View of Corruption' (1998) 9(2) *The Journal of Interdisciplinary Economics* 145–62.

564. Serageldin, I, *Poverty, Adjustment and Growth in Africa* (Washington, DC, World Bank, 1989).

565. Shah, S, 'Illuminating the Possible in the Developing World: Guaranteeing the Human Right to Health in India' (1999) 32(2) *Vanderbilt Journal of Transnational Law* 435.

566. Sharma, M, 'What Role can Rights Play in the Work of International Agencies?' (1995) 44(4) *American University Law Review* 1097–104.

567. Sharma, S, 'Constructing the New International Financial Architecture: What Role for the IMF?' (2000) 34(3) *Journal of World Trade* 47–70.

568. Shepherd, G and Nanda, V, *Human Rights and Third World Development* (Westport, CT, Greenwood Press, 1985).

569. Shihata, I, 'Conference on Human Rights, Public Finance, and the Development Process' (1992) 8 *American University Journal of International Law and Policy*.

570. ——'Democracy and Development' (1997) 46 *International and Comparative Law Quarterly* 635.

571. ——*The European Bank for Reconstruction and Development: a Comparative Analysis of the Constituent Agreement* (London, Dordrecht, Boston, Graham & Trotman, M Nijhoff, 1990).

572. ——'Human Rights, Development and International Financial Institutions' (1992) 8 *American University Journal of International Law and Policy* 27.

573. —— 'Involuntary Resettlement in World Bank Financed Projects' in I Shihata, *The World Bank in a Changing World: Selected Essays* (Dordrecht, Martinus Nijhoff, 1991), 181–99.

574. ——*Issues of 'Governance' in Borrowing Members, the Extent of their Relevance under the Bank's Articles of Agreement: Memorandum of the Vice-President and General Counsel* (1990).

575. —— 'The World Bank and Human Rights: An Analysis of the Legal Issues and the Record of Achievements' (1988) 17 *Denver Journal of International Law and Policy* 39–66.

576. —— 'The World Bank and Non-Governmental Organizations' (1992) 25 *Cornell International Law Journal* 623–41.

577. —— *The World Bank in a Changing World: Selected Essays* (Dordrecht, Martinus Nijhoff Publishers, 1991).

578. —— *The World Bank Inspection Panel* (New York, Oxford University Press, 1995).

579. —— *The World Bank Inspection Panel in Practice* (Oxford, New York, Oxford University Press, 2000).

580. —— 'The World Bank's Protection and Promotion of Children's Rights' (1996) 4 *International Journal of Children's Rights* 383.

581. Shin, E, 'The International Monetary Fund: Is it the Right or Wrong Prescription for Korea?' (1999) 22(3) *Hastings International and Comparative Law Review* 597–615.

582. Skogly, S, 'Human Rights and Economic Efficiency: The Relationship between the Social Cost of Adjustment and Human Rights Protection' in P Baehr, H Hey, J Smith and T Swinehart (eds), *Human Rights in Developing Countries Yearbook, 1994* (Deventer, Kluwer Law and Taxation Publishers, 1994), 43–66.

583. —— 'The Position of the World Bank and the International Monetary Fund in the Human Rights Field' in R Hanski and M Suksi (eds), *An Introduction to the International Protection of Human Rights: A Textbook* (Turku/Åbo, Finland, Institute for Human Rights, Åbo Akademi University, 1997), 193–208.

584. —— 'Structural Adjustment and Development: Human Rights, an Agenda for Change' (1993) 15 *Human Rights Quarterly* 751.

585. —— *The Human Rights Obligations of the World Bank and International Monetary Fund* (London, Cavendish Press, 2001).

586. Sloan, B, 'The United Nations Charter as a Constitution' (1961) 1 *Pace Year Book of International Law* 61.

587. Smith F Jr, 'The Politics of IMF Lending' (1984) 4(1) *Cato Journal* 211–41.

588. Snyder, F and Slinn, P (eds) *International Law of Development* (Abingdon, Professional Books, 1987).

589. Sohn, L, 'The Human Rights Law of the Charter' (1977) 12 *Texas International Law Journal* 129.

590. —— *The Human Rights Movement: From Roosevelt's Four Freedoms to the Interdependence of Peace, Development and Human Rights* (Cambridge, MA, Human Rights Program, Harvard Law School, 1995).

591. Solan, M, Jones, S, Dicker, R and Waller, S, 'Indonesia: Intersection of Human Rights, Financial Markets and Competition Policy (Panel Discussion)' (1999) 25(1) *Brooklyn Journal of International Law* 161–82.

592. Sorel, J, 'Sur quelques aspects juridiques de la conditionnalité du FMI et leurs conséquences' (1996) 7(1) *European Journal of International Law* 42–66.

593. Soros, G, 'Capitalism's Last Chance?' (1998) (Winter) *Foreign Policy* 55–66.
594. Spiro, E, 'Front Door or Back Stairs: US Human Rights Policy in the International Financial Institutions' in B Rubin and E Sprio (eds), *Human Rights and US Foreign Policy* (Boulder, CO, Westview, 1979), 133–61.
595. Squire, L and van der Tak, H, *Economic Analysis of Projects* (Baltimore, Johns Hopkins University Press, 1975).
596. Stallings, B, 'International Influence on Economic Policy: Debt, Stabilization, and Structural Reform' in S Haggard and R Kaufman (eds), *The Politics of Economic Adjustment: International Constraints, Distributive Conflicts, and the State* (Princeton, NJ, Princeton University Press, 1992), 41–88.
597. Standing, G, 'Global Trajectories: Ideas, Transnational Policy Transfer and "Models" of Welfare Reform', *European University Institute, Conference arranged by the European Forum, Florence, 25–26 March 1999, paper entitled 'New Development Paradigm or Third Wayism? A Critique of the World Bank Rethink'* (1999).
598. ——'Social Protection in Central and Eastern Europe: A Tale of Slipping Anchors and Torn Safety Nets' in G Esping-Andersen (ed), *Welfare States in Transition: National Adaptations in Global Economies* (London, Sage Publications, 1996), 225–55.
599. Stecher, H with Bailey, M, *Time for a Tobin Tax? Some Practical and Political Arguments* (UK, Oxfam GB, 1999).
600. Stein, M, 'Conflict Prevention in Transition Economies: A Role for the European Bank for Reconstruction and Development?' in A Chayes and AH Chayes (eds), *Preventing Conflict in the Post-Communist World: Mobilizing International and Regional Organizations* (Washington, DC, The Brookings Institution, 1996), 339–80.
601. Steiner, H, 'Cultural Relativism and the Attitude of Certain Asian Countries towards the Universality of Human Rights' in Senate Department Research Section, *Constitutions, Rights and Democracy: Past, Present and Future* (Canberra, Department of the Senate, 1995), 17–32.
602. Stern, NwF, 'The World Bank as an "Intellectual Actor" ' in D Kapur, J Lewis and R Webb (eds), *The World Bank: Its First Half Century* (Washington, DC, Brookings Institution Press, 1997), 523–609.
603. Stewart, F, *Basic Needs Strategies, Human Rights and the Right to Development* (1988).
604. ——'The Many Faces of Adjustment' (1991) 19(12) *World Development* 1847–64.
605. Stiglitz, J, *An Agenda for Development in the Twentieth Century: Keynote Address to the Ninth Annual Bank Conference on Development Economics,' Washington, DC, 30 April 1997* (Washington, DC, World Bank, 1997).
606. ——'Introduction' in C Gilbert and D Vines (eds), *The World Bank: Structure and Policies* (Cambridge, UK, Cambridge University Press, 2000), 1–9.
607. ——'The Insider: What I Learned at the World Economic Crisis', *The New Republic Online* (2000).
608. ——*Participation and Development: Perspectives from the Comprehensive Development Paradigm. Remarks at the International Conference on Democracy, Market Economy and Development, Seoul, Korea, 27 February 1999* (Washington, DC, World Bank, 1999).
609. ——'Redefining the Role of the State: What should it do? How should it do it? And how should these decisions be made?' *Speech Presented on the Tenth Anniversary of MITI Research Institute, Tokyo, 17 March 1998* (Washington, DC, World Bank, 1998).

610. ——*The Role of Government in Economic Development: Paper Delivered at the Annual Bank Conference on Development Economics, World Bank, Washington, DC, April 25–26, 1996* (Washington, DC, World Bank, 1996).

611. ——'The World Bank at the Millennium' (1999) 109 *Economic Journal* 577–97.

612. Storey, A, 'Economics and Ethnic Conflict: Structural Adjustment in Rwanda' (1999) 17 *Development Policy Review* 43–63.

613. Strauss, J and Duncan, T, *Health, Nutrition and Economic Development* (1995).

614. Streeten, P, 'Human Rights and their Indicators' in UNDP (ed), *Human Development and Human Rights: Report of the Oslo Symposium (2–3 October 1998)* (New York, UNDP, 1998), 88–96.

615. Stremlau, J and Sagasti, F, *Preventing Deadly Conflict: Does the World Bank Have a Role?* (Washington, DC, Carnegie Corporation of New York, 1998).

616. Subbarao, K, Bonnerjee, A, Braithwaite, J, Carvalho, S, Ezemenari, K, Graham, C and Thompson, A, *Safety Net Programs and Poverty Reduction: Lessons from Cross-Country Experience* (Washington, DC, World Bank, 1997).

617. Sullivan, D, 'The Nature and Scope of Human Rights Obligations Concerning Women's Right to Health' (1995) 1(4) *Health and Human Rights* 368–69.

618. Sullivan, K, 'ICPD+5: Reaffirming Women's Right To Health' (1999) 47 *Development Bulletin* 9.

619. Swaminathan, R, 'Regulating Development: Structural Adjustment and The Case for National Enforcement of Economic and Social Rights' (1998) 37(1) *Columbia Journal of Transnational Law* 161.

620. Takahashi, K (ed), *Globalization and the challenges of poverty alleviation* (Tokyo, Foundation for Advanced Studies on International Development, 1998).

621. Tarantola, D and Gruskin, S, 'Children Confronting HIV/AIDS: Charting the Confluence of Rights and Health' (1997) 3(1) *Health and Human Rights* 60–86.

622. Tarullo, D, 'Logic, Myth, and the International Order' (1985) 26(2) *Harvard International Law Journal* 533–52.

623. Taylor, L, 'Editorial: The Revival of the Liberal Creed—The IMF and the World Bank in a Globalised Economy' (1997) 25(2) *World Development* 145–52.

624. Taylor, L and Pieper, U, *Reconciling Economic Reform and Sustainable Human Development: Social Consequences of Neo-Liberalism* (New York, Office of Development Studies, UN Development Programme, 1996).

625. Tesòn, F, 'Le peuple, C'est Moi! The World Court and Human Rights' (1987) 81 *American Journal of International Law* 173–85.

626. Themaat, Jv, 'Some Notes on IMF Conditionality with a Human Face' in P Peters, E Denters and P de Waart (eds), *International Law and Development* (1988), 229–34.

627. Timmer, C, Falcon, W and Pearson, S, *Food Policy Analysis* (Baltimore, Johns Hopkins University Press, 1983).

628. Tinbergen, J, 'The Right to Health: An Economist's View' in R Dupuy (ed), *Le droit à la santé en tant que droit de l'homme* (Alphen aan den Rijn, Sijthoff & Noordhoff, 1979).

629. Tjønneland, E, *The World Bank and Poverty in Africa: A Critical Assessment of the Bank's Operational Strategies for Poverty Reduction* (Oslo, Norwegian Royal Ministry of Foreign Affairs, 1998).

630. Tobin, J, 'A Proposal for International Monetary Reform' (1978) 4 *Eastern Economic Journal* 153–59.
631. Tobin, J and Ranis, G, 'Flawed Fund', *The New Republic Online* (1998).
632. Todaro, M, 'Ethics, Values, and Economic Development' in K Thompson (ed), *Ethics and International Relations: Ethics in Foreign Policy* (New Brunswick, NJ, Transaction Books, 1985), 75–97.
633. Tomasevski, K, *Between Sanctions and Elections: Aid Donors and their Human Rights Performance* (London, Pinter, 1997).
634. ——'Conceptual Confusion: Access to Food, Food Entitlements, Freedom From Hunger, Right to (Adequate) Food' in Netherlands Institute of Human Rights, *The Right to Food: From Soft to Hard Law: Report of the International Conference organized by the Netherlands Institute of Human Rights (SIM) in cooperation with the Norwegian Human Rights Project and the Christian Michelsen Institute, Norway, from 6–9 June 1984* (Utrecht, Netherlands Institute of Human Rights, 1984).
635. ——'Defining Violations of the Right to Food' in F Coomans and GJH van Hoof (eds), *The Right to Complain about Economic and Cultural Rights: Proceedings of the Expert Meeting on the Adoption of an Optional Protocol to the International Covenant on Economic, Social and Cultural Rights, held from 25–28 January 1995 in Utrecht* (Utrecht, SIM, 1995), 115–26.
636. ——*Development Aid and Human Rights* (New York, St Martin's Press, 1989), 234.
637. ——*Development Aid and Human Rights Revisited* (London, Pinter Publishers, 1993).
638. ——'Health Rights' in A Eide, C Krause and A Rosas (eds), *Economic, Social and Cultural Rights: A Textbook* (Dordrecht, Martinus Nijhoff Publishers, 1995), 125–42.
639. ——'Indicators' in A Eide, C Krause and A Rosas (eds), *Economic, Social and Cultural Rights: A Textbook* (Dordrecht, Martinus Nijhoff Publishers, 1995), 389–402.
640. ——'International Development Finance Agencies' in A Eide, C Krause and A Rosas (eds), *Economic, Social and Cultural Rights: A Textbook* (Dordrecht, Martinus Nijhoff Publishers, 1995), 403–14.
641. ——'Economic Costs of Human Rights' in C Flinterman, M Senders and P Baehr (eds), *Innovation and Inspiration: Fifty Years of the Universal Declaration of Human Rights* (Amsterdam, Royal Netherlands Academy of Arts and Sciences, 1999), 49–60.
642. ——'Monitoring Human Rights Aspects of Sustainable Development' (1992) 8 *American Journal of International Law* 77.
643. Tomuschat, C, 'Obligations Arising for States Without or Against Their Will' (1993) *Hague Recueil Des Cours (1993-IV)* 241.
644. Townsend, P, 'The Need for a New International Poverty Line' in K Funken and P Cooper (eds), *Old and New Poverty: The Challenge for Reform* (London, Rivers Oram Press, 1995), 29–54.
645. ——'A Sociological Approach to the Measurement of Poverty: A Rejoinder to Professor Amartya Sen' (1985) 37 *Oxford Economic Papers* 659–68.
646. Trubitt, B, 'International Monetary Fund Conditionality and Options for Aggrieved Fund Members' (1987) 20 *Vanderbilt Journal of Transnational Law* 665–97.

647. Tshuma, L, 'The Political Economy of the World Bank's Legal Framework for Economic Development' (1999) 8(1) *Social and Legal Studies* 75–96.

648. Türk, D, 'Development and Human Rights' in L Henkin and J Hargrove (eds), *Human Rights: An Agenda for the Next Century* (Washington, DC, American Society of International Law, 1994), 167–82.

649. —— 'How World Bank-IMF Policies Adversely Affect Human Rights' (1992) 33 *Third World Resurgence* 16.

650. —— 'The Human Right to Development' in P Van Dijk, GJH Van Hoof, A Koers and K Mortelmans (eds), *Restructuring the International Economic Order: The Role of Law and Lawyers* (Deventer, Kluwer Law, 1986), 85.

651. —— 'Participation of Developing Countries in Decision-Making Processes' in P Peters, E Denters and P de Waart (eds), *International Law and Development* (1998), 341–57.

652. Tuwayjiri, 'A, *Identity and globalization in the perspective of the right to cultural diversity* (Rabat, Islamic Educational, Scientific and Cultural Organization, 1997).

653. Tvedt, T, *Angels of mercy or development diplomats?: NGOs & foreign aid* (Trenton, NJ, Africa World Press, 1998).

654. Udall, L, *A Citizens' Guide to the World Bank's Information Policy* (Washington, DC Bank Information Centre, 1994).

655. —— 'The World Bank's Revised Information Policy and New Inspection Panel: Public Accountability or Public Relations?' in J Cavanagh, D Wysham and M Arruda (eds), *Beyond Bretton Woods: Alternatives to the Global Economic Order* (London, Pluto Press, 1994), 145–54.

656. Udombana, N, 'The Third World and the Right to Development: Agenda for the Next Millennium' (2000) 22 *Human Rights Quarterly* 753–87.

657. ul Haq, M, Kaul, I and Grunenberg, I (eds), *The Tobin Tax. Coping with Financial Volatility* (New York and Oxford, Oxford University Press, 1996).

658. Umozurike, U, 'Human Rights and Development' (1998) 50(4) *International Social Science Journal* 535.

659. UN Secretary General, *Report of the Seminar on Appropriate Indicators to Measure Achievements in the Progressive Realization of Economic, Social and Cultural Rights: Report by the Secretary-General*, E/CN.4/Sub.2/1989/19 (1993).

660. UNCTAD, *The Least Developed Countries Report 2002: Escaping the Poverty Trap* (2002).

661. *Final Report: The UNDP Regional Training Workshop and Seminar on Human Rights and Sustainable Human Development (Colombo, Sri Lanka, 21–24 June 1999) and a Preliminary Programme Note Implementing a Rights-Based Approach* (1999).

662. UNDP (ed), *Globalisation with a Human Face: Background Papers to the Human Development Report 1999* (New York, UNDP, 1999).

663. —— *Governance for Sustainable Human Development: A UNDP Policy Document* (New York, UNDP, 1997).

664. —— (ed), *Human Development and Human Rights: Report of the Oslo Symposium (2–3 October 1998)* (New York, UNDP, 1999).

665. —— *Human Development Report 2000: Human Rights and Development* (New York, Oxford University Press, 2000).

666. —— *Human Development Report 2002: Deepening Democracy in a Fragmented World* (New York, Oxford University Press, 2002).

667. ——*Integrating Human Rights With Sustainable Human Development : A UNDP Policy Document* (New York, UNDP, 1998).

668. ——*UNDP Poverty Report* (New York, UNDP, 1999).

669. ——Regional Bureau for Africa, *Progress against poverty in Africa* (New York, UNDP, 1998).

670. UNDP, UNESCO UNFPA UNICEF WHO and the World Bank, *Implementing the 20/20 Initiative: Achieving Universal Access to Basic Social Services* (New York, UNICEF, 1998).

671. Unger, B and van Waarden, F, 'Introduction: An Interdisciplinary Approach to Convergence' in B Unger and F van Waarden (eds), *Convergence or Diversity?: Internationalization and Economic Policy Response* (Aldershot, Avebury, 1995), 1–36.

672. UNICEF, *Development Cooperation within a Rights Framework: Conceptual and Programmatic Issues (UNICEF policy document)* (New York, UNICEF, 1997).

673. ——*A Human Rights Approach to UNICEF Programming for Children and Women: What It Is, And Some Changes It Will Bring* (New York, UNICEF, 1998).

674. ——*Programme Policy and Procedure Manual: Programme Operations* (New York, UNICEF, 1999).

675. ——*Programming for Children's and Women's Rights: UNICEF Mali's Experience (UNICEF policy document)* (New York, UNICEF, 1997).

676. United Nations, *The 20/20 Initiative: Achieving Universal Access to Basic Social Services for Sustainable Human Development* (New York, United Nations, 1995).

677. ——*Effects of structural adjustment policies and foreign debt on the full enjoyment of all human rights, particularly economic, social and cultural rights*, E/CN.4/RES/2000/82 (2000).

678. ——*ACC Guidance Note for the Resident Coordinator System on Field Level Follow-up to Global Conferences* (1998).

679. ——*ACC Sub-Committee on Nutrition Symposium on the Substance and Politics of a Human Rights Approach to Food and Nutrition Policies and Programmes (12 April 1999, Geneva). 'The Human Right to Food and Nutrition': Mary Robinson, High Commissioner for Human Rights* (1999).

680. ——*Consultation between Right to Development and Economic, Social and Cultural Rights Experts and UN agencies and organisations: 'Perspectives for coordination and interaction.' Note on the Meeting, Palias des Nations, Geneva, 6 April 2000* (Geneva: United Nations (OHCHR), 2000).

681. ——*Copenhagen Declaration on Social Development in Report of the UN World Summit for Social Development (1995)*, A/CONF.166/9 (1995).

682. ——*Crisis or Reform: Breaking the Barriers to Development*, E.84.II.C.4 (1984).

683. ——*Development under Siege*, E.87.II.A.18 (1987).

684. ——*Economic, Social and Cultural Rights. Report of the Secretary-General submitted pursuant to Commission on Human Rights resolution 1999/25*, E/CN.4/2000/47 (2000).

685. ——*Effects of structural adjustment policies on the full enjoyment of human rights: Report by the Independent Expert, Mr Fantu Cheru, submitted in accordance with Commission decisions 1998/102 and 1997/103*, E/CN.4/1999/50 (1999).

686. ——*General Comment No. 11 (Committee on Economic, Social and Cultural Rights, Twentieth Session, 1999): Plans of action for primary education (Art. 14 CESCR)*, E/C.12/1999/4 (1999).

687. ——*General Comment No. 12 (Committee on Economic, Social and Cultural Rights, Twentieth Session, 1999): The right to adequate food (art. 11)*, E/C.12/1999/5 (1999).

688. ——*General Comment No. 13 (Committee on Economic, Social and Cultural Rights, Twenty-first Session, 1999): The right to education (Art. 13 CESCR)*, E/C.12/1999/10 (1999).

689. ——*General Comment No. 14 (Committee on Economic, Social and Cultural Rights, Twenty-Second Session, 2000): The right to the highest attainable standard of health (Art. 12 CESCR)*, E/C.12/2000/4 (2000).

690. ——*General Comment No. 2 (Committee on Economic, Social and Cultural Rights, Fourth Session, 1990): International technical assistance measures (Art. 22 CESCR)* 02/02/90, E/1990/23 (1990).

691. ——*General Comment No. 3 (Committee on Economic, Social and Cultural Rights, Fifth Session, 1990): The nature of states parties' obligations (Art. 2 para. 1 of the CESCR)*, E/1990/23 (1990).

692. ——*The Hidden Crisis in Development: Development Bureaucracies*, E.88.III.A.9 (1988).

693. ——*Housing and Economic Adjustment* (New York. Department of International Economic and Social Affairs, United Nations, 1988).

694. ——*Human Development in the 1980s and beyond* (New York. United Nations, 1989).

695. ——*Human rights and extreme poverty. Report submitted by Ms A-M Lizin, independent expert, pursuant to Commission resolution 1999/26*, E/CN.4/2000/52 (2000).

696. ——*Human rights and extreme poverty. Report submitted by Ms A-M Lizin, independent expert, pursuant to Commission resolution 1998/25*, E/CN.4/1999/48 (1999).

697. ——*Human rights as the primary objective of international trade, investment and finance policy and practice: Working paper submitted by J Oloka-Oyango and Deepika Udagama, in accordance with Sub-Commission resolution 1998/12*, E/CN.4/Sub-2/1999/11 (1999).

698. ——*Report of the Seminar on Appropriate Indicators to Measure Achievements in the Progressive Realization of Economic, Cultural and Social Rights*, A/CONF.157/PC/73 (1993).

699. ——*Joint report by the Special Rapporteur on the Effects of Foreign Debt on the Full Enjoyment of Economic, Social and Cultural Rights, Mr Reinaldo Figueredo, and the Independent Expert on Structural Adjustment Policies, Mr Fantu Cheru. Debt relief and social investment: Linking the Heavily Indebted Poor Countries (HIPC) initiative to the HIV/AIDS epidemic in Africa, post-hurricane Mitch reconstruction in Honduras and Nicaragua, and the Worst Forms of Child Labour Convention 1999 (Convention No. 182) of the International Labour Organisation*, E/CN.4/2000/51 (2000).

700. ——*Managing Human Development* (New York, United Nations, 1988).

701. ——*Programme of Action Adopted at the International Conference on Population and Development, Cairo, 5–13 September 1994* (New York, Department for Economic and Social Information and Policy Analysis, United Nations, 1995).

702. ——*Progress report of the Special Rapporteur on the right to education, Katarina Tomasevski, submitted in accordance with Commission on Human Rights resolution 1999/25*, E/CN.4/2000/6 (2000).

703. ——*The Realisation of Economic, Social and Cultural Rights. Final Report submitted by Danilo Türk, Special Rapporteur, Subcommission for the Prevention of Discrimination and Protection of Minorities, 49th Session*, E/CN.4/Sub.2/1992/16 (1992).

704. ——*The Realization of the Right to Development: Global Consultation on the Right to Development as a Human Right* (New York, United Nations, 1991).

705. ——*Renewing the United Nations: A Programme for Reform*, A/51/950 (1997).

706. ——*Report of the High Commissioner for Human Rights and follow-up to the World Conference on Human Rights, submitted pursuant to Commission resolution 1999/54*, E/CN.4/2000/12 (2000).

707. ——*Report of the open-ended working group on structural adjustment programmes and economic, social and cultural rights on its second session, 1–3 March 1999*, E/CN.4/1999/51 (1999).

708. ——*The right to adequate food and to be free from hunger: Updated study on the right to food, submitted by Asbjørn Eide in accordance with Sub-Commission decision 1998/106*, E/CN.4/Sub.2/1999/12 (1999).

709. ——*The Right to Development: Report of the High Commissioner for Human Rights submitted in accordance with Commission on Human Rights resolution 1999/79*, E/CN.4/2000/20 (1999).

710. ——*The Right to Education*, A/37/521 (1982).

711. ——*The right to food: Report of the High Commissioner for Human Rights*, E/CN.4/1999/45 (1999).

712. ——*The right to food: Report of the High Commissioner for Human Rights submitted in accordance with Commission resolution 1999/24*, E/CN.4/2000/48 (2000).

713. ——*Strengthening International Financial Arrangements and Addressing Poverty: Note by the Secretary-General*, E/2000/8 (2000).

714. ——*Working paper submitted by J Oloka-Onyango and Deepika Udagama in accordance with Sub-Commission resolution 1998/12*, E/CN.4/Sub.2/1999/11 (1999).

715. United States Department of the Treasury, *Report on IMF Reforms: Report to Congress in accordance with Sections 610(a) and 613(a) of the Foreign Operations, Export Financing and Related Programs Appropriations Act, 1999* (Washington, DC, United States Department of the Treasury, 2000).

716. United States Government Audit Office, *Developing Countries: Debt Relief Initiative for Poor Countries Faces Challenges*, GAO/NSIAD-00-161 (2000).

717. Uvin, P, *Aiding Violence: The Development Enterprise in Rwanda* (West Harford, CT, Kumarian, 1998).

718. Valverde, G, 'Democracy, Human Rights, and Development Assistance for Education : the USAID and World Bank in Latin America and the Caribbean' (1999) 47(2) *Economic Development and Cultural Change* 401–19.

719. van Boven, T, 'The Right to Development and Human Rights' (1982) 28 *International Commission of Jurists Review* 49–56.

720. ——'The Right to Health' in R Dupuy (ed), *Academy of International Law* (Alphen ann den Rijn, Sijthoff & Noordhoff, 1987).

721. van de Laar, A, *The World Bank and the Poor* (Boston, Martinus Nijhoff Publishing, 1980).

722. van de Walle, D and Nead K, *Public Expenditures and the Poor: Incidence and Targeting* (Washington, DC, World Bank, 1993).

723. van der Hoeven, R, 'Adjustment with a Human Face: Still Relevant or Overtaken by Events?' (1991) 19(12) *World Development* 1835–45.

724. van der Hoeven, R and Anker, R (eds), *Poverty Monitoring: An International Concern* (New York, St Martin's Press, 1994).

725. van Dijk, M, 'Socio-economic Development Funds to Mitigate the Social Costs of Adjustment: Experiences in Three Countries' (1992) 4(1) *European Journal of Development Research*.

726. van Hoof, GJH, 'Asian Challenges to the Concept of Universality' in P Baehr, GJH van Hoof and J Smith (eds), *Human Rights: Dutch and Chinese Perspectives* (The Hague, Martinus Nijhoff Publishing, 1996), 1–15.

727. —— 'The Legal Nature of Economic, Social and Cultural Rights: A Rebuttal of Some Traditional Views' in P Alston and K Tomasevski (eds), *The Right to Food* (1984), 97–110.

728. —— 'Problems and Prospects with Respect to the Right to Food' in P Van Dijk, GJH Van Hoof, A Koers and K Mortelmans (eds), *Restructuring the International Economic Order: The Role of Law and Lawyers* (Deventer, Kluwer Law, 1987), 107.

729. van Hoof GJH and Tahzib, B, 'Supervision with Respect to the Right to Food and the Role of the World Bank' in P de Waart, P Peters and E Denters (eds), *International Law and Development* (Dordrecht, Nijhoff, 1988), 317.

730. Vashee, B, 'Democracy and Development in the 1990s' in J Hippler (ed), *The Democratisation of Disempowerment: The Problem of Democracy in the Third World* (London, Pluto Press, 1995), 195–204.

731. von Benda-Beckmann, K, 'Western Law and Legal Perceptions in the Third World' in J Berting, P Baehr, J Burgers and C Flinterman (eds), *Human Rights in a Pluralist World* (Westport, CT, Meckler, 1990), 225–36.

732. Wachtel, H, 'Tobin and other Global Taxes' (2000) 7(2) *Review of International Political Economy* 335–52.

733. Wade, R, 'Globalization and its Limits: Reports of the Death of the National Economy are Greatly Exaggerated' in S Berger, and R Dore (eds), *National Diversity and Global Capitalism* (Ithaca, NY, Cornell University Press, 1996), 60–88.

734. —— 'Greening the Bank: The Struggle Over the Environment, 1970–1995' in D Kapur, J Lewis and R Webb (eds), *The World Bank: Its First Half Century, Vol. II* (Washington, DC, Brookings Institution Press, 1997), 611–734.

735. Warner, M, 'Which Way Now? Choices for Mainstreaming "Public Involvement" in Economic Infrastructure Projects in Developing Countries' (1999) 17 *Development Policy Review* 115–39.

736. Webb, D, 'Legal and Institutional Reform Strategy and Implementation: A World Bank Perspective' (1999) 30 *Law and Policy in International Business* 161–70.

737. Weidner, J, 'World Bank Study' (2001) 7 *Buffalo Human Rights Law Review* 193–226.

738. Weiss, E. Sureda, A and Boisson de Chazournes, L (eds), *The World Bank, International Financial Institutions, and the Development of International Law* (Washington, DC, American Society of International Law, 2000).

739. Werner, DD with Weston, D, Sanders, J, Babb, S and Rodriguez, B, *Questioning the Solution: The Politics of Primary Health Care and Child Survival* (Palo Alto, CA, Healthwrights, 1997).
740. White, N, *The Law of International Organisations* (1996).
741. Whitehead, A and Lockwood, M, *Gender in the World Bank's Poverty Assessments, Six Case Studies from Sub-Saharan Africa* (United Nations Research Institute for Social Development, 2000).
742. Williams, L, 'Eradicating Female Circumcision—Human Rights and Cultural Values' (1998) 6(1) *Health Care Analysis* 33.
743. Williamson, J, 'The Lending Policies of the International Monetary Fund' in J Williamson (ed), *IMF Conditionality* (1983), 605–60.
744. —— 'On Judging the Success of IMF Policy Advice' in J Williamson (ed), *IMF Conditionality* (1983), 129–43.
745. Wolfensohn, J, *'The Challenge of Inclusion,' World Bank Annual Meetings Address, Hong Kong SAR, China, 23 September 1997* (Washington, DC, World Bank, 1997).
746. —— *Speech, World Press Freedom Committee, 1999 Harold W Andersen Lecture, 'The Informed Economy: the Role of the Press in Keeping Citizens Aware and Governments Accountable,' 8 November 1999* (1999).
747. —— *The World Bank and the Evolving Challenges of Development. Speech at the Overseas Development Council Congressional Staff Forum, Washington, DC, 16 May 1997.* (Washington, DC, World Bank, 1997).
748. Wood, A, *The International Monetary Fund's Enhanced Structural Adjustment Facility: What Role for Development?* (London, Bretton Woods Project, 1997).
749. Woods, N, 'Making the IMF and World Bank More Accountable' (2001) 77(1) *International Affairs* 83–100.
750. —— 'The Challenges of Multilateralism and Governance,' in C Gilbert and D Vines (eds), *The World Bank: Structure and Policies* 132–56 (Cambridge, Cambridge University Press, 2000).
751. —— 'The Challenge of Good Governance for the IMF and the World Bank Themselves' (2000) 28(5) *World Development* 823.
752. Woodward, D, *Globalization, Uneven Development And Poverty: Recent Trends And Policy Implications* (New York, UNDP, 1998).
753. —— *The IMF, the World Bank and Economic Policy in Rwanda: Economic, Social and Political Implications (Report for Oxfam)* (Oxford, Oxfam, 1996).
754. Woodward, S, *Balkan Tragedy: Chaos and Dissolution After the Cold War* (1995).
755. World Bank, *Adjustment Lending: An Evaluation of Ten Years of Experience* (Washington, DC, Country Economics Department, World Bank, 1988).
756. —— *'Ah yes: Governance!'* (Washington, DC, World Bank, 1994).
757. —— *Assessing Development Effectiveness: Evaluation in the World Bank and the International Finance Corporation* (Washington, DC, World Bank, 1998).
758. —— 'A User's Guide to Poverty and Social Impact Analysis' (draft prepared by the Poverty Reduction Group and Social Development Department), 19 April 2002.
759. —— *The Bank's Relations with NGOs: Issues and Directions* (Washington, DC, NGO Unit, Social Development, World Bank, 1998).
760. —— *Child Labour: Issues and Directions for the World Bank* (Washington, DC, World Bank, 1998).
761. —— *Global Synthesis: Voices of the Poor* (Washington, DC, World Bank, 1999).

762. —— *Governance and Development* (Washington, DC, World Bank, 1992).
763. —— *Governance: The World Bank's Experience* (Washington, DC, World Bank, 1994.
764. ——*Grassroots Organizations: Their Contribution to the Fight Against Poverty* (Washington, DC, World Bank, 1992).
765. —— *Handbook on Good Practices for Laws Relating to Non-Governmental Organisations, discussion draft May 1997* (Washington, DC, World Bank, 1997).
766. —— *Helping Countries Combat Corruption: The Role of the World Bank* (Washington, DC, World Bank, 1997).
767. —— *How Adjustment Programs Can Help the Poor: The Experience of the World Bank* (Washington, DC, World Bank, 1989).
768. ——*IDA's Partnership for Poverty Reduction: An Independent Evaluation of Fiscal Years 1994–2000* (Washington, DC, World Bank, 2002)
769. ——*Implementing the World Bank's Strategy to Reduce Poverty: Progress and Challenges* (Washington, DC, World Bank, 1993).
770. ——*Intensifying Action Against HIV/AIDS in Africa: Responding to a Development Crisis* (Washington, DC, World Bank, 2000).
771. —— *Making Adjustment Work for the Poor: A Framework for Policy Reform in Africa* (Washington, DC, World Bank, 1990).
772. —— *Management Development, the Governance Dimension: A Discussion Paper* (Washington, DC, World Bank, 1991).
773. —— *Management Report and Recommendation in Response to the Inspection Panel Investigation Report, China: Western Poverty Reduction Project, Qinghai Component (Credit No. 3255-CHA; Loan No. 4501-CHA)* (2000).
774. —— *Managing the Social Dimensions of Crises: Good Practices in Social Policy (14 September 1999)*. (1999).
775. —— *Memorandum from James D Wolfensohn to the Board, Management and Staff of the World Bank Group: A Proposal for a Comprehensive Development Framework (A Discussion Draft), 21 January 1999* (Washington, DC, World Bank, 1999).
776. ——*Memorandum from Vice President and Secretary: Comprehensive Development Framework (CDF) Progress Report (SecM99-642, 14 September 1999)* (Washington, DC, World Bank, 1999).
777. —— *Poverty Reduction and the World Bank : Progress in Fiscal 1998* (Washington, DC, World Bank, 1999).
778. —— *Poverty Reduction Handbook* (Washington, DC, World Bank, 1993).
779. —— *Poverty Reduction Strategy Papers: Internal Guidance Note (The World Bank Group, Operations Policy and Strategy, 21 January 2000)* (Washington, DC, World Bank, 2000).
780. ——*Principles and Good Practice in Social Policy: Issues and Areas for Public Action. Paper prepared by the World Bank for the World Bank/IMF Development Committee (April 1999)* (1999).
781. ——*Priorities and Strategies for Education: A World Bank Review* (Washington, DC, World Bank, 1995).
782. —— *Resettlement and Development: The Bankwide Review of Projects Involving Involuntary Resettlement, 1986–1993* (Washington, DC, Social Policy and Resettlement Division, Environment Department, World Bank, 1996).
783. —— *Sector Strategy: Health, Nutrition, and Population* (Washington, DC, Human Development Network, World Bank, 1997).

784. ———*Social Analysis Sourcebook* (Washington, DC, World Bank, working draft, 6 August 2002).
785. ———*Social Assessment: Incorporating Participation and Social Analysis into the Bank's Operational Work* (Washington, DC, World Bank, 1994).
786. ———*Structural Adjustment and Poverty: A Conceptual, Empirical, and Policy Framework* (Washington, DC, World Bank, 1989).
787. ———*Sub-Saharan Africa: From Crisis to Sustainable Growth* (Washington, DC, World Bank, 1989).
788. ———*Taking Action to Reduce Poverty in Sub-Saharan Africa* (Washington, DC, World Bank, 1997).
789. ——— *Targeted Programs for the Poor During Structural Adjustment* (Washington, DC, World Bank, 1988).
790. ——— *Trends in Poverty* (Washington, DC, World Bank, 1999).
791. ——— *Operational Directive 4.30 on Involuntary Resettlement, 29 June 1990* (1990).
792. ——— *The World Bank Participation Sourcebook* (Washington, DC, World Bank, 1996).
793. ———*World Development Report 1982: International Development Trends, Agriculture and Economic Development, World Development Indicators* (New York, Oxford University Press, 1982).
794. ——— *World Development Report 1988: Opportunities and Risks in Managing the World Economy, Public Finance in Development, World Development Indicators* (New York, Oxford University Press, 1988).
795. ——— *World Development Report 1989: Financial Systems and Development* (New York, Oxford University Press, 1989).
796. ———*World Development Report 1990: Povert* (New York, Oxford University Press, 1990).
797. ———*World Development Report 1991: The Challenge of Development* (New York, Oxford University Press, 1991).
798. ———*World Development Report 1995: Workers in an Integrating World* (New York, Oxford University Press, 1995).
799. ———*World Development Report 1996: From Plan to Market* (Washington, DC, World Bank, 1996).
800. ———*World Development Report 2000/2001: Attacking Poverty: Opportunity, Empowerment, and Security* (Washington, DC, World Bank, 2000).
801. World Bank Operations Evaluation Department, *1998 Annual Review of Development Effectiveness* (Washington, DC, World Bank, 1999).
802. ———*1999 Annual Review of Development Effectiveness* (Washington, DC, World Bank, 2000).
803. ———*Country Assistance Note: Indonesia, Report of the Operations Evaluation Department, 4 February 1999.* (Washington, DC, World Bank, 1999).
804. ———*The Drive to Partnership: Aid Coordination and the World Bank* (Washington, DC, World Bank, 1999).
805. ———*Investing in Health: Development Effectiveness in the Health, Nutrition and Population Sector* (Washington, DC, World Bank, 1999).
806. ———*Nongovernmental Organisations in World Bank-Supported Projects* (Washington, DC, World Bank, 1999).
807. World Bank and IMF Development Committee, *Background Paper: Building Poverty Reduction Strategies in Developing Countries (DC/99-29, 22 September*

1999) (Washington, DC, World Bank and IMF Development Committee, 1999).

808. ——*Progress Reports on Heavily Indebted Poor Countries (HIPC) and Poverty Reduction Strategy Papers (PRSPs), DC/2000-10, 15 April 2000* (Washington, DC, World Bank and IMF Development Committee, 2000).

809. World Commission on Dams, *Dams and Development: A New Framework for Decision-Making* (2000).

810. Yokota, Y, 'Non-Political Character of the World Bank' (1976) 20 *Japanese Annual of International Law* 39–64.

811. Youssef, N, 'Women's Access to Productive Resources: The Need for Legal Instruments to Protect Women's Developmental Rights' in J Peters and A Wolper (eds), *Women's Rights, Human Rights: International Feminist Perspectives* (New York, Routledge, 1995), 279.

812. Zaidi, S, *The New Development Paradigm: Papers on Institutions, NGOs, Gender and Local Government* (Oxford, Oxford University Press, 1999).

813. Zamora, S, 'Sir Joseph Gold and the Development of International Monetary Law' (1989) 23(4) *The International Lawyer* 1009–26.

814. Zuckerman, E, *Poverty and Adjustment: Issues and Practices* (Washington, DC, World Bank, 1988).

Index